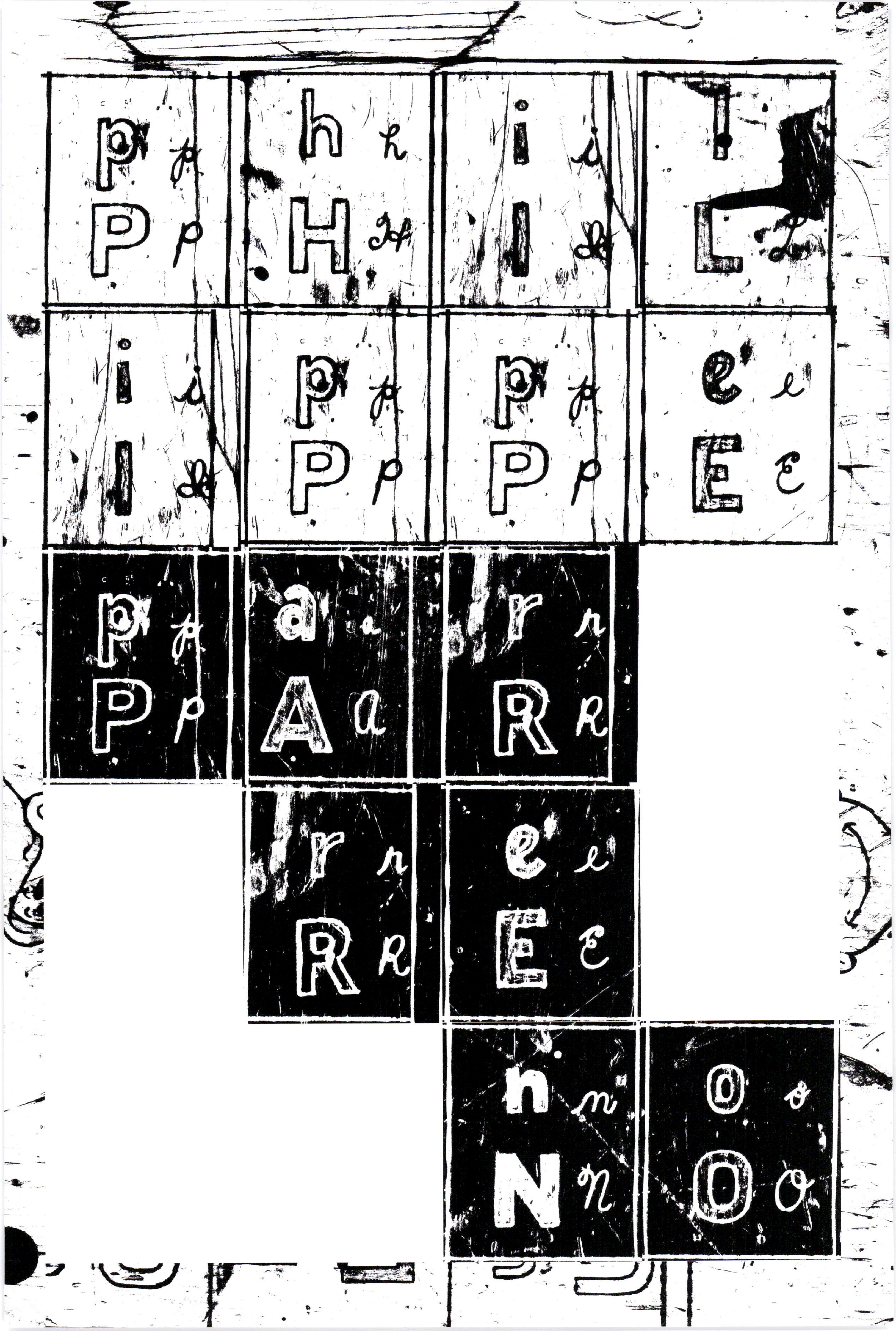
PHIL
IPPE
PAR
RE
NO

The organization of the exhibition "Philippe Parreno" was greatly assisted by Maja Hoffmann and the following galleries: Air de Paris (Paris), Pilar Corrias Inc. (London), Friedrich Petzel Gallery (New York) and Esther Schipper (Berlin).

Published by
JRP|Ringier
Letzigraben 134
CH-8047 Zurich
www.jrp-ringier.com

ISBN: 978-3-03764-033-3

in co-edition with Éditions du Centre Pompidou, Paris

ISBN: 978-2-84426-411-4

French Edition available by Éditions du Centre Pompidou

Cover: *Portes de l'île de Porquerolles* [Doors of Porquerolles Island] © M/M (Paris), 2009

Title Pages: *Even Dopey Was Insured*, combined typography © M/M (Paris), 2009

Centre national d'art et de culture Georges Pompidou

The Centre national d'art et de culture Georges Pompidou is a national public establishment under the supervision of the Ministry of Culture (law n° 75-1 of January 3, 1975).

Alain Seban
President

Agnès Saal
Managing Director

Alfred Pacquement
Director of the Musée national d'art moderne – Centre de création industrielle

Bernard Blistène
Director of the Cultural Development Department

Françoise Pams
Director of the Communications Department, Representative for Partnerships and International Development

François Trèves
Chairman of the Society of Friends of the Musée national d'art moderne

Exhibition

Chief Curator
Christine Macel

Research Supervisor
Mélanie Mermod

Coordinator
Anna Hiddleston

Trainees
Raphaële Coutant
Carola Annoni
Hermann Wendler

Production
Dominique Rault-Kalabane
assisted by
Ludivine Rousseaux

Production Trainee
Marianne Saïe

Architect
Laurence Le Bris

Registrar
Lora Houssaye

Lighting/Interface Programing
Benoît Lalloz

Workshops and Technical Units

Management of Exhibition Space
Veronica Ortega-Lo-Cascio

Electrical Workshop
Jonathan
Faustin Girault
Rémi Navarro

Lighting
Jacques Rodrigues

Carpentry
Philippe Delapierre
Patrice Richard
Pascal Dumont
Ludovic Heissler

Painting
Mokhlos Farhat
Emmanuel Gentilhomme
Dominique Gentilhomme
Lamri Bouaoune
Sofiane Saal

Installation and Hanging
Michel Nait
David Rouge
Jean-Marc Mertz

Audiovisual Department

Artistic and Technical Manager
Gérard Chiron

Handling
Vahid Hamidi

Manager
Christophe Bechter
Emmanuel Rodoreda

Musée national d'art moderne – Centre de création industrielle

Director
Alfred Pacquement

Deputy Directors
Brigitte Leal
(Collections)
Frédéric Migayrou
(Industrial Creation)
Didier Ottinger
(Cultural Programing)

Administrator
Sylvie Perras

Bibliothèque Kandinsky
Didier Schulmann

Head of the Collections Unit
Catherine Duruel

Production Department

Director
Catherine Sentis-Maillac

Head of the Administration and Financial Unit
Laure Rolland,
Assistant Director

Head of the Events and Programs Unit
Martine Silie

Head of the Artworks Management Unit
Annie Boucher

Head of the Architectural and Museum Production Unit
Katia Lafitte

Head of the Audiovisual Unit
Laurie Szulc

Educational and Public Programs Department

Director
Vincent Poussou

Assistant Director
Cléa Richon

Head of the Educational Department
Marie Rouhète

Head of the Youth Programs Department
Patrice Chazottes

Project Supervisors
Odile Fayet
Nadine Combet

Communications Department

Director
Françoise Pams

Press Department
Isabelle Danto

Press Attachée
Dorothée Mireux

Graphic Department
Christian Beneyton

Internal Communications
Marie-Annick Hamon

Administrative and Financial Management
Yann Bréheret

Information and Telecommunications Systems Management

Director
Olivier Trouvé

Micro-Computer Technician
Raffaele Docimo

Other exhibitions

Kunsthalle Zürich

Director and Curator
Beatrix Ruf

Board Verein Kunsthalle Zürich
Maja Hoffmann (President), Cristina Bechtler, Jacqueline Burckhardt, Matthias Fatzer, Jean-Pierre Hoby, Thomas Koerfer, Sabine Parenti, Mark A. Reutter, Uli Sigg

Kunsthalle Zürich would like to thank the following for their continuous support: Präsidialdepartement der Stadt Zürich, Luma Stiftung, and for special support: Swiss Re

Limmatstrasse 270,
CH-8005 Zürich
T +41 (0)44 272 15 15
F +41 (0)44 272 18 88
info@kunsthallezurich.ch
www.kunsthallezurich.ch

Irish Museum of Modern Art

Director
Enrique Juncosa

Head of Exhibitions
Rachael Thomas

Curator
Sean Kissane

Projects Curator
Caroline Hancock

Assistant Curator
Lucia Pietroiuski

Board Members
Eoin Mc Gonigal (Chairperson), Rosemary Ashe, Conor Bowman, Frank X. Buckley, Valerie Connor, Eamon Delaney, Brendan Flynn, Chris Flynn, Kevin Kelly, Anne O'Donoghue, Áine O'Driscoll, Emer O'Kelly, Brian Ranalow, Patricia Tsouros

Royal Hospital, Military Road, Kilmainham, Dublin 8, Ireland
T +353-1-6129900
F +353-1-612 9999
info@imma.ie
www.imma.ie

Center for Curatorial Studies and Art in Contemporary Culture

Executive Director
Tom Eccles

Director of the Graduate Program
Maria Lind

Director of Library and Archives
Ann E. Butler

CCS *Board of Governors*
Marc Lipschultz (Chairman), Leon Botstein (ex officio), Lori Chemla, Kathryn Chenault, Martin Eisenberg, Carla Emil, Marieluise Hessel (Founding Chairman), Marguerite Hoffman, Maja Hoffmann, Audrey Irmas, Adam Lindemann, Eugenio Lopez, Melissa Schiff Soros, Richard W. Wortham III

Bard College, Annandale-on-Hudson, NY 12504-5000, USA
T 845-758-7598
F 845-758-2442
ccs@bard.edu
www.bard.edu

Catalogue

Editor
Christine Macel

English Text Editor
Karen Marta

Research Supervisor
Mélanie Mermod

Copy Editing and Coordination
Geneviève Munier
assisted by
Jeanne Alechinsky
Xavier de Beauchaine
Marion Diez and Amarante Szidon

Graphic Design
M/M (Paris)

Layout
Laure Cérini

Translations from the French
Anna Hiddleston
Simon Pleasance & Fronza Woods
Zoe Stillpass
Caroline Taylor-Bouché

Translation from the Spanish
Jonathan Brennan

Assistant Managers
Isabelle Charles-Planchet
Xavier Delamare
Danielle Malemanche

Production
Audrey Chenu

Photo Laboratory
Valérie Leconte
Bruno Descout

Video Laboratory
Didier Coudray

Photographs of the works
Jean-Claude Planchet

Publishing Department

Acting Director
Jean-Christophe Claude

Editorial Unit
Françoise Marquet

Commercial Unit
Benoît Collier

Rights and Contracts Management
Claudine Guillon
Matthias Battestini

Publications Administration
Nicole Parmentier

Sales Administration
Josiane Peperty

Multimedia Department
Guy Morvan
Frédéric Nassar

Communications
Évelyne Poret

Philippe Parreno
Edited by Christine Macel
with the collaboration of Karen Marta

**Exhibition held at the Centre Pompidou, Galerie Sud,
from June 3 to September 7, 2009**

Three other distinct exhibitions are presented:
at the Kunsthalle Zürich, Zurich, from May 9 to August 16, 2009
at the Irish Museum of Modern Art, Dublin,
from November 4, 2009 to January 24, 2010
at the CCS, Bard College, Annandale-on-Hudson, New York,
spring 2010

Centre Pompidou
jrp|ringier

Acknowledgements

First and foremost we wish to thank the artist and his entire studio team, Marie Auvity, Zoe Stillpass and Virginie Oudjane, for their work and for their enthusiasm; as well as Karen Marta for her precious contribution to the editing of the texts.

We would also like to express our gratitude to Maja Hoffmann for her involvement in Philippe Parreno's work and her support for this exhibition.

We are also grateful to the artist's galleries which have been especially supportive of this project: Florence Bonnefous and Hélène Retailleau for their availability and their research, and the whole team from the Air de Paris gallery; Esther Schipper, Christophe Wiesner and Barbara-Brigitte Mak from the Esther Schipper gallery (Berlin); Pilar Corrias, Lucy Bestwick, Isabella Maidment and Annabelle von Girsewald from Pilar Corrias Inc. (London); and Friedrich Petzel and Andrea Teschke from the Friedrich Petzel Gallery (New York).

For their support and valuable help, our thanks also go to:

Charles Arsène-Henry, Nicolas Becker, Marc Blondeau, Alexandre Bohn, Lionel Bovier, Kevin Conroy Scott, Simon Critchley, Marie-Stéphane de Sercey, Xavier Douroux, Bernard Joisten, Pierre Joseph, Enrique Juncosa, Caroline Hancock, Darius Khondji, Erin Knutson, Lionel Kopp, Richard Lagrange, Benoît Lalloz, Maria Lind, Édouard Merino, Hans Ulrich Obrist, Johan Olander, Suzanne Pagé, Roberto Prual-Reavis, Beatrix Ruf, Luc Saucier, Jörn Schafaff, Hervé Schneid, Nancy Spector, Karen Tanguy, Rachael Thomas, François Trèves, Éric Troncy, Anna-Léna Vaney, Victorien Vaney, Mark Vanmoerkerke, Suzanne Widmer.

as well as all those who have contributed to the exhibition, but have preferred to remain anonymous.

This catalogue of the artist's works could not have been produced without the support of the following people and institutions:

Burt Aaron, Hervé Acker, Henry Allsopp, Sandra Antelo-Suarez, Agnès b., Joe Barron, Rüdi Bechtler, Elaine Berger, Judith and Ron Berk, Martin Bethenod, Charles Betlach, Carole Billy, Collection Rey-Nouvion, Gisela Blanc, Marc Blondeau, Nicolas Bourriaud, David Brognon, Cees and Inge de Bruinlieu, M. Brunet, Doris Bucher, Daniel Buchholz, Brian D. Butler, Philippe Cohen, Patrick Charpenel, Martine de la Châtre, Pierre Cornette-de-Saint-Cyr, Rosa and Carlos de la Cruz, Amalia Dayan and Roy Brand, Éric Decelle, Mr. and Mrs. Demirdjian, Fabio Desideri, Michèle Didier and Pierre Iserbyt, Denyse Durand-Ruel, Gilles Dusein, Marcia Eitelberg, Isabel Ernst, Franca Fabbri, Charles Firmin-Didot, Anoushka Fisz, Nadia Forloni, Anna Friebe-Reininghaus, Nunzia and Vittorio Gaddi, Laurent Gardien, Marc and Josée Gensollen, Douglas Gordon, Martin Guesnet, Jean-Paul Guy, Swetlana Heger and Plamen Dejanov, Dana Hirt, Carsten Höller, Axel Huber, Philippe Jaffré, Leo Katz, Sunjung Kim, Walter Klosterfelde, Thomas and Janine Koerfer, Clémence and Didier Krzentowski, David Laurie, Fabienne Leclerc, Noël Le Gall, Olivier Letang, Hervé Loevenbruck, Gregorio Magnani, Gió Marconi, Sandra Marinopoulos, Édouard Merino, Ghislain Mollet-Viéville, Prince Albert of Monaco, Tommaso Corvi Mora, Tim Nye, Roger and Marie-Christine Pailhas, Gregory Papadimitriou, Konstantinos Papageorghiou, Claudine Papillon, France Paringaux, Christine Park, Delphine Pastor, Emmanuel Perrotin, S. and J.-M. Phéline, François Pinault, Colette and Michel Poitevin, René Praz and Bruno Delavallade, Cesar and Mima Reyes, Jean Rosen, Yves Rouart, Myriam and Jacques Salomon, Martine and Michel Samuel-Weis, Stephan Schmidt-Wulffen, Harvey S. Shipley Miller, Natalie Seroussi and Daniel Wust, Karen and Andy Stillpass, Fabrice Stroun, Micheline Szwajcer, Michael Trier, Léo Van Tuyckom, Juan Manuel Varez Benegas, Ben Vautier, Christiane Vielhaber, Emilio Rui Vilar, Jack and Nell Wendler, Christophe Wiesner; 21st Century Museum of Contemporary Art, Kanazawa, Japan; Anna Sanders Films, Paris, France; Banca Svizzera Internationale (BSI) Art Collection, Lugano, Switzerland; Bunbury Management Corp., Geneva, Switzerland; CCA Kitakyushu, Kitakyushu, Japan; Centre international de recherche sur le verre et les arts plastiques (Cirva), Marseilles, France; Collector's Circle, New York, United States; Communauté de communes de l'Auxois Sud et le Syndicat d'initiative de Pouilly-en-Auxois, France; Daimler Art Collection, Stuttgart and Berlin, Germany; Foundation 20.21, New York, United States; Fondation Louis Vuitton pour la Création, Paris, France; Fonds national d'art contemporain (Fnac), Puteaux, France; Fonds régional d'art contemporain (Frac) Bourgogne, Dijon, France; Fonds régional d'art contemporain (Frac) Corse, Corte, France; Fonds régional d'art contemporain (Frac) Languedoc-Roussillon, Montpellier, France; Fonds régional d'art contemporain (Frac) Lorraine, Metz, France; Fonds régional d'art contemporain (Frac) Nord-Pas-de-Calais, Dunkirk, France; Fonds régional d'art contemporain (Frac) Poitou-Charentes, Angoulême, France; Fonds régional d'art contemporain (Frac) Provence-Alpes-Côte d'Azur, Marseilles, France; Fonds régional d'art contemporain (Frac) Rhône-Alpes, Villeurbanne, France; Fondazione Sandretto Re Rebaudengo, Turin, Italy; Gabinetto G.P. Vieusseux, Florence, Italy; Gió Marconi gallery, Milan, Italy; Haunch of Venison gallery, London, United Kingdom; Massimo di Carlo gallery, Milan, Italy; Neugerriemschneider gallery, Berlin, Germany; Solomon R. Guggenheim Museum, New York, United States; Irish Museum of Modern Art, Dublin, Ireland; Jones Day, Reavis & Pogue, New York, United States; The Judith Rothschild Foundation, New York, United States; Landesbank Baden-Württemberg, Stuttgart, Germany; Le Magasin, Grenoble, France; musée d'Art moderne Grand-Duc Jean (Mudam), Luxembourg; musée d'Art moderne de la Ville de Paris, Paris, France; musée d'Art contemporain, Lyons, France; Museum of Contemporary Art North Miami, Miami, United States; Museum of Modern Art (MoMA), New York, United States; Peconic Fine Arts LLC, New York, United States; Pinchuk Art Centre, Kiev, Ukraine; Sammlung Energieversorgung Niederösterreich (EVN AG), Vienna, Austria; Sommer Contemporary Art, Tel Aviv, Israel; Sudwest LB, Stuttgart, Germany; Tate Modern, London, United Kingdom; Thyssen-Bornemisza Contemporary Art, Vienna, Austria; Van Abbemuseum, Eindhoven, Netherlands; Walker Art Center, Minneapolis, United States; Watari-UM, The Watari Museum of Contemporary Art, Tokyo, Japan.

We also extend our heartfelt thanks to the various teams at the Centre Pompidou who, in their respective ways, have offered us their assistance.

Index of graphic symbols:
◊ line break
⧫ line skip
◁ introduces description of the work
¬ introduces caption of the work
• separator in caption of the work
‡ first exhibition of the work
|| editions of the work
| separator in edition of the work
§ courtesy
∫ collection

Philippe Parreno is part of a generation of artists who, since the 1990s, have striven to rethink the standards of the art object, within a logic that is at once collaborative and does not seek definitive solutions, by adding to the production of forms a line of thinking about the conditions of their appearance and their presentation.

It fell to the Centre Pompidou, a laboratory whose project is to clear new ground, to usher in new excursions into space and time, and show the œuvre of this major figure in the French and international art scene.

From objectless exhibition to exhibition as object, Philippe Parreno conceives the work as a sign around which a community is established to invent a new way of being together, involving a collective development of meaning. By creating unexpected social rituals, and initiating new kinds of encounters likely to produce sharing and bonding, Philippe Parreno challenges the foundations of our social contract.

Devised as an area for dialogue and boundless discussion between beholder and work, the exhibition at the Centre Pompidou offers ambitious reflection about the role of art in the production of a new sociability. As is invariably the case with Philippe Parreno, this show introduces a novel kind of output.

The Centre Pompidou is pleased to invite visitors to discover, or rediscover, the work of an artist who has managed to cast his eye forward, in order to draw the figures of truth of his day and age, and open up future workshops from a swathe of narratives and stories.

Alain Seban
President of the Centre Pompidou

This exhibition is in keeping with a sequence of shows with an anthological spin, similar to others held at the Centre Pompidou over the last few years, featuring artists in the French scene. And each show has, in its turn, helped us to pinpoint the state of each artist's work. By inviting Philippe Parreno, we were keen to offer one of the most innovative artists of the moment a chance to avail himself of nothing less than a set, in which to bring together some of the quintessential features of his approach—something this artist likes doing. Our expectations have been amply fulfilled, with Parreno taking over the South Gallery space, with all its transparency and breadth, transforming it in novel ways, and treating it like a screening room, alternating light and dark.

Philippe Parreno capsizes the idea of categories, breaking with that traditional distinction between the moment of creation (the studio) and the moment of public dissemination (the exhibition). With him, as for others of his generation—like those he has known since the Grenoble School of Fine Arts—the exhibition's time-frame alone activates the work, which is otherwise inert and meaningless. Here, the work of art is revealed solely in its programming, often linked with the memory of an event. Parreno demolishes both the idea of style, and usual aesthetic criteria; he challenges the notion of artist/*auteur*, likes exchange and collaboration, and alters the TV and film models which are his main sources of inspiration. The way a work is shown can take on unexpected forms: a mock-advertisement in a cinema, a book, a performance delegated to an actor, a ventriloquist or an impersonator. His thinking about exhibitions as a medium prompts him to envisage new distribution networks. The film *Zidane*, made with Douglas Gordon, is a striking example of this, because it was distributed in cinemas just like Hollywood productions.

So exhibiting Philippe Parreno means, perforce, expecting a fresh look at picture-making, both in its operational method and through the way the spectator grasps it. As visitors to the Centre Pompidou will be able to discover, the artist has opted for a spectacular arrangement whereby, on an extraordinary scale, they can pass through a kind of space-time where reality, imagery and commentary all dovetail.

My thanks to Philippe Parreno both for having accepted our invitation—and those from other institutions: the Kunsthalle Zürich, the Irish Museum of Modern Art in Dublin, and the Bard College in New York—and for having devised a novel and ambitious project for this major Paris show. I am also extremely grateful to all those who have worked on this undertaking, in particular the artist's galleries: Air de Paris (Paris), Esther Schipper (Berlin), Pilar Corrias (London), and Friedrich Petzel (New York). My warmest thanks also go to Maja Hoffmann, responsible for the existence and loan of major works. Last but not least, this exhibition would not have been possible without the Centre Pompidou team which has presided over every stage of this complex project, with a special mention for Christine Macel, chief curator at the Musée national d'art moderne, who, with her habitual energy, was at the artist's side in all the different production stages, as well as editing the impressive catalogue marking this occasion.

Alfred Pacquement
Director of the Musée national d'art moderne –
Centre de création industrielle

In a lush and verdant mountainscape, a spray of yellow flowers swiftly opens to the accompaniment of a dramatic piece of music by Edgar Varèse. The images in this short 35 mm film have been randomly edited in such a way that they differ with each viewing, thanks to a computer program that upsets the linearity of an action that is at once innocuous and magical. In its initial version, *El sueño de una cosa* or "Dream of One Thing", a work forever in post-production, was shown in movie theaters in Sweden as the advertisement for some dream thing, rather than any consumer item.

Dream of one thing: this title of Philippe Parreno's work recently acquired by the Centre Pompidou could just as well go with the project devised by the artist in answer to the invitation made to him to occupy the South gallery today. What we have here is threefold: a daydream about absent and ghostlike objects; being caught by surprise by a curtain being lowered and a 70 mm film with a hyper-real presence; and the looming up, at certain moments in the exhibition, of shadow theatre enacted by children with puppets in the form of monsters, or made with posters of masterpieces.

Throughout this most exciting past year, spent with one of the most beguiling artists of his generation, a succession of projects has come into being, each informing the next. The allusion to Merlin the wizard tallies with a body of work that has recently taken short cuts, as is the artist's wont, towards novel figures, like those of the ventriloquist, the magician, and the director. The show, which is still in the production stage as this introduction is being penned, results more from the scoring of works than their hanging. A score played in time and space, with their constants and their variations, the way Parreno likes to see them, in order to re-invent the very notion of the exhibition in accordance with a time code—a concept which has infused his work since its earliest days.

The actual notion of an artwork is no longer part of the terminology adopted by the artist who prefers talking about "projects" and "practices", terms which convey his ongoing questioning of the very definition of art. But the moment seemed apt to recap his career by way of a rich and complex catalogue, where some of the illustrative material is hitherto unpublished. This work owes a great deal to the unflagging support of the artist's galleries, Air de Paris (Paris)—and of Florence Bonnefous in particular—and Esther Schipper (Berlin).

Parreno has created this book as well as its corollary: a same-sized publication, but aimed at children, with his own writings. *Parade?* was produced in cooperation with Johan Olander, who drew the illustrations, creating characters from the artist's actual work, in a collaborative approach and an aesthetics of partnership dear to Parreno. The M/M (Paris) twosome devised these two linked volumes for the occasion.

The various institutions inviting the artist in conjunction with the Centre Pompidou all played their part in this work, via contributions from Enrique Juncosa and Maria Lind, while Hans Ulrich Obrist readily agreed, as ever, to handle the dialogic aspect. Karen Marta was our vital editor throughout the preparation of these two books, and we thank her for the ideas and the care that she brought to the project.

Philippe Parreno has the gift of polyphony, more than any other. We are grateful to him for his generosity and his creativity, both fuelling our thinking and our imagination.

Christine Macel
Chief Curator, Centre Pompidou, Paris

Radically rethinking the practices of art, exhibition and book making, Philippe Parreno constantly explores unknown territories and incites renewed interrogations and playfulness. Reality and non-reality become extraordinary spectacles, ongoing peripheral dialogues and boundary crossings. Parreno is a multi-faceted artist that we have all enjoyed working and dreaming with over the years.

At IMMA, Parreno co-curated the anagrammatically titled exhibition *.all hawaii eNtrées / luNar reGGae* in 2006. This was developed as an event, accompanied by a blurred catalogue, documenting one moment in a continuum of cultural production and international dialogue resulting in a vibrating temporality.

At Kunsthalle Zürich in 2002, Philippe Parreno co-curated the collaborative project *No Ghost Just a Shell.* To mark the closing of the project or rather mark the freeing of the project for new scenarios to develop, a contract enabled its protagonist, the 'empty shell' manga character AnnLee, to be in charge of the future use of her identity. The exhibition was developed as a chapter of the project, integrating all the works in a site-specific narrative. It then traveled to different venues, adding further scenarios, in parallel with a catalogue as art work.

The exhibition at the Center for Curatorial Studies, Bard College will play on the characteristics of the institution located on the campus of a liberal arts college. A number of graduate students will work with Parreno and Maria Lind, director of the graduate program, in the CCS Galleries as well as in the Hessel Museum of Art and on campus. This follows from several projects which Parreno and Lind have worked on together, for example Moderna Museet Projekt in 2001 for which the artist made a short film, *El Sueño de Una Cosa*. For one month the film was shown unannounced as part of the commercials played in movie theaters across Sweden.

The Kunsthalle, Zürich, the Irish Museum of Modern Art, Dublin, the Centre Pompidou, Paris and the Center for Curatorial Studies, Bard College, New York, present very distinct and site-specific exhibitions in each institution in 2009 and 2010. As a consequence, we are delighted to collaborate with the Editions du Centre Pompidou on two publications to coincide with these events: this present catalogue of Philippe Parreno's work to date and its companion children's book of monsters written by the artist and illustrated by Johan Olander.

We are thankful to all involved.

Enrique Juncosa, Director, Irish Museum of Modern Art, Dublin
Maria Lind, Director, Graduate Program, Center for Curatorial Studies, Bard College, New York
Beatrix Ruf, Director, Kunsthalle Zürich

Voice-Over. Prologue and Corpus of Works

Christine Macel

It is indeed difficult to write a catalogue of an artist who rearranges notions of intellectual property and copyright, does not archive the past, plays with the relationship between objects and language, creates performances and ephemeral events and seeks out collaborations—"preferring the symphony to the concerto."[1] Perhaps no system can pin him down, but this catalogue, based on archives and memories, offers a new look at Philippe Parreno, as well as, in the end, a lot of work and more objects than expected.

Parreno's artistic practice comes out of the somewhat rebellious attitude of the generation growing up in the 1970s, a generation who rejected the ideology of utopia. Opposed to Jean Baudrillard's thesis of a reality in agony[2] replaced by simulacra, Parreno is rather part of a generation of "the return of the real."[3] He attempts to take on the real, without hierarchy, from everyday objects to popular culture in an aesthetic of recycling. He followed the model of cyberpunks and hackers, recognizing himself in their appropriation strategies "to find a subject contemporary to these techniques."[4] Parreno would rather create real virtuality than virtual reality, in particular with the *images gelées* [frozen images] which materialize film sequences. Blurring the limits between the real and its representation and relying on an aesthetic of plurality, Parreno wants to show that there is no difference between an event, its image and its perception. "The computer image is not a tool for exploring reality ... It modifies the real."[5]

The notions of *exhibitions in real time,* of *spaces of freedom* and of *alliance*[6] are inherent to Parreno's practice which works around new technologies of the image, television, film and pop music, characterized by the remix and sampling. His artwork was seen by a public audience for the first time in 1988 when *Fleurs* (1987) appeared on French television as the background for a weather forecast. His approach concerns a universe of particular references, where television culture and good jokes hold an important place. With a certain ease and a sharp sense of dark humor,[7] Parreno played the role of the idiot in the guise of an art critic in *No More Reality* (1991–1993) and avoided the issue. Several works illustrate the jokes and memories of retirement home residents. Television and film, both as modes of production and exhibition models, inspired the artist to take on the role of actor, producer, film director and artistic director. Parreno asserts his interest in the space-time of production which allows for meaning to arise.[8] The artist's commitment to time as an inseparable and manipulable component of the exhibition was influenced by Daniel Buren's[9] dedication to the artwork's interdependency on its spatial context. Organizing events, Parreno plays with a work's visibility time. His interest in the medium of the exhibition leads him to conceive of the latter as a work in itself, as a time loop, and resulted in *Snow Dancing* a major piece from the 1990s.

1. Interview with Kate van den Boogert, "Studio Parreno, Alien, Philippe Parreno", *Tate International Arts and Culture Magazine*, no.3, January–February 2003, p.53.

2. Jean Baudrillard, *Agonie des Realen*, Berlin, Merve Verlag, 1978. Baudrillard comes back to the notion in *Simulacres et Simulation* [Simulacra and Simulation], Paris: Galilée, "Débats" collection, 1981, p.70.

3. Hal Foster, *The Return of the Real: The Avant-garde at the End of the Century*, Cambridge: MIT Press, 1996.

4. Philippe Parreno quoted by Nicolas Bourriaud, "Primeurs", *Beaux-Arts Magazine*, no.78, April 1990, p.109.

5. Philippe Parreno, "La Peur des anges/ Fear of Angels", *Documents sur l'art* [Documents on Art], no.1, October 1992, p.56.

6. This term is taken from Michel Maffesoli.

7. Nicolas Bourriaud, "Philippe Parreno", *Galerie Magazine*, February-March 1992, p.68-69.

8.See Nicolas Bourriaud, *Postproduction*, Berlin/New York: Sternberg Press, 2002.

9. Parreno's teacher at the Institut des hautes études en arts plastiques (directed at the end of the 1980s by Pontus Hulten), Daniel Buren, remarked that "if art has been interested in space, curiously it has never been interested in time."

Since *No More Reality,* speech, language and time are more important than the object and space. The object's materiality is grounded in the circumstances of its production and the object cannot be separated from its exhibition context. Influenced by Jean-François Lyotard's[10] and Serge Daney's critique of "language games" and analysis of the role of the visual artist and filmmaker as semiologist,[11] Parreno takes the cultural signs of the early 1990s as his subject and medium. Through rigorous experimentation, Parreno intuitively built up a body of work which, little by little, becomes aware of its own questions.

Siberia (1988), marked the first of a series of collaborations,[12] a production model which would become an integral part of Parreno's ongoing practice. His commitment to *an art of collaboration,* not of a formal group but of conversations between friends as well as a commitment to a practice of writing enriches his own projects and creates scenarios for other artists. Sharing intellectual property[13] is a means of politicizing his practice. Parreno's desire to work within the social field and various communities corresponds to an aesthetic of reception, already important for the students of Foucault and Barthes, and articulated by Nicolas Bourriaud in 1998.[14] The artist endeavours to build exhibition *situations* or circuits, places to move across where everyone can create his or her own story. More interested in procedures than in resolutions, Parreno defines art as a process rather than an object, an extract of normalized museum time.

Film no longer just tells a story but is the means to explore questions such as those related to production. The project *No Ghost Just a Shell* (1999–2002) conceived with Pierre Huyghe, gave relational reality to the manga character AnnLee. The film *Zidane* (2006) questions the possibility of presenting a subject's image in the present. This *portrait of the 21st century* marks a return to the image, to the moment, to real time, as if they were the last sanctuary in the face of a present gone schizophrenic. Un-mediated media, spectacle and theatre also allow Parreno to pursue his interest in polyphony. Whereas in the 1990s he focused on the actor, the child, the impersonator,[15] the television presenter, the clairvoyant and the hypnotist, from the years 2000, he explored the manga character, the publisher, the conjurer, the ventriloquist and the stage director.

Through these ghosts, these virtual shadows, these masks and these ventriloquists, an empty shell haunts us. Parreno shows events, memories, words, absences. Curious about everything, always working on several projects at once, extending his studio to many different places, scared of boredom more than anything else, this artist works to make real that which is doomed to disappear.

Visual documentation is more problematic than textual documentation, especially for the 1990s. The artist refused to document his exhibitions for a long time so as not to produce "images of images," transforming experience into simulacra. Many photographs have

10. Jean-François Lyotard, *La Condition postmoderne. Rapport sur le savoir* [The Post-modern Condition. A Report on Knowledge], Paris: Les éditions de Minuit, "Critique" collection, 1979.

11. Serge Daney, *Devant la recrudescence des vols de sacs à mains. Cinéma, télévision, information (1988-1991)* [Owing to an Increase in Handbag Thefts. Cinema, Television, Information (1988-1991)] Lyons: Aléas, 1991; second edition reworked and corrected, 1997, p.116.

12. In particular with Pierre Joseph, Bernard Joisten and Dominique Gonzalez-Foerster who are all from Grenoble and studied at the same experimental school Emmanuel-Mounier where Gilles Lipovetsky taught, and the École supérieure d'art in Grenoble (where Philippe Parreno went from 1983 to 1988).

13. Against the notion of authorship, signature and intellectual property, Parreno works with an aesthetics of "alliance."

14. Nicolas Bourriaud, *Esthétique relationnelle* [Relational Aesthetics], Dijon: Les presses du réel, 1998.

15. Philippe Parreno impersonates Jean-Luc Godard in several works and the television presenter Yves Lecoq impersonates numerous media personalities.

however been taken by others, such as those by Éric Troncy for *Snow Dancing,* which are the only ones that exist of this work today.

The list of works was drawn up in close collaboration with the artist, with Florence Bonnefous who supplied us with Parreno's archives and her memory, and with Hélène Retailleau at Air de Paris gallery in Paris. Esther Schipper in Berlin and Jörn Schafaff[16] also greatly contributed to this venture which would not have been possible without the committed and meticulous work of Mélanie Mermod, head of research, for the list of works and their descriptions and the help of Marie Auvity and Zoe Stillpass at Philippe Parreno's studio.

16. Jörn Schafaff, *How We Gonna Behave, Philippe Parrenos Angewandtes Kino*, PhD thesis, Freien Universität Berlin, 2008, unpublished.

As for the collections, only the first edition acquired by a public collection is mentioned. In the absence of such an acquisition of a work or of one of its editions, the first or only private collection is mentioned. When certain pieces were made only for the time of the exhibition, no courtesy is mentioned. The artist has chosen not to mention some works that were intended, in their conception and execution, to be ephemeral.

The projects not realized or materialized by preparatory work do not appear on this list.

All the works' titles were reviewed by the artist who has occasionally chosen to discard or change them. As requested by the artist, some projects (printed objects, design, installations made for certain exhibitions) do not figure on this list as they cannot be considered as works.

The images, limited in number, have been chosen by the artist according to the available material, image quality and personal choice.

The choice of works with in depth commentaries was made by the artist. *(See page 28)*

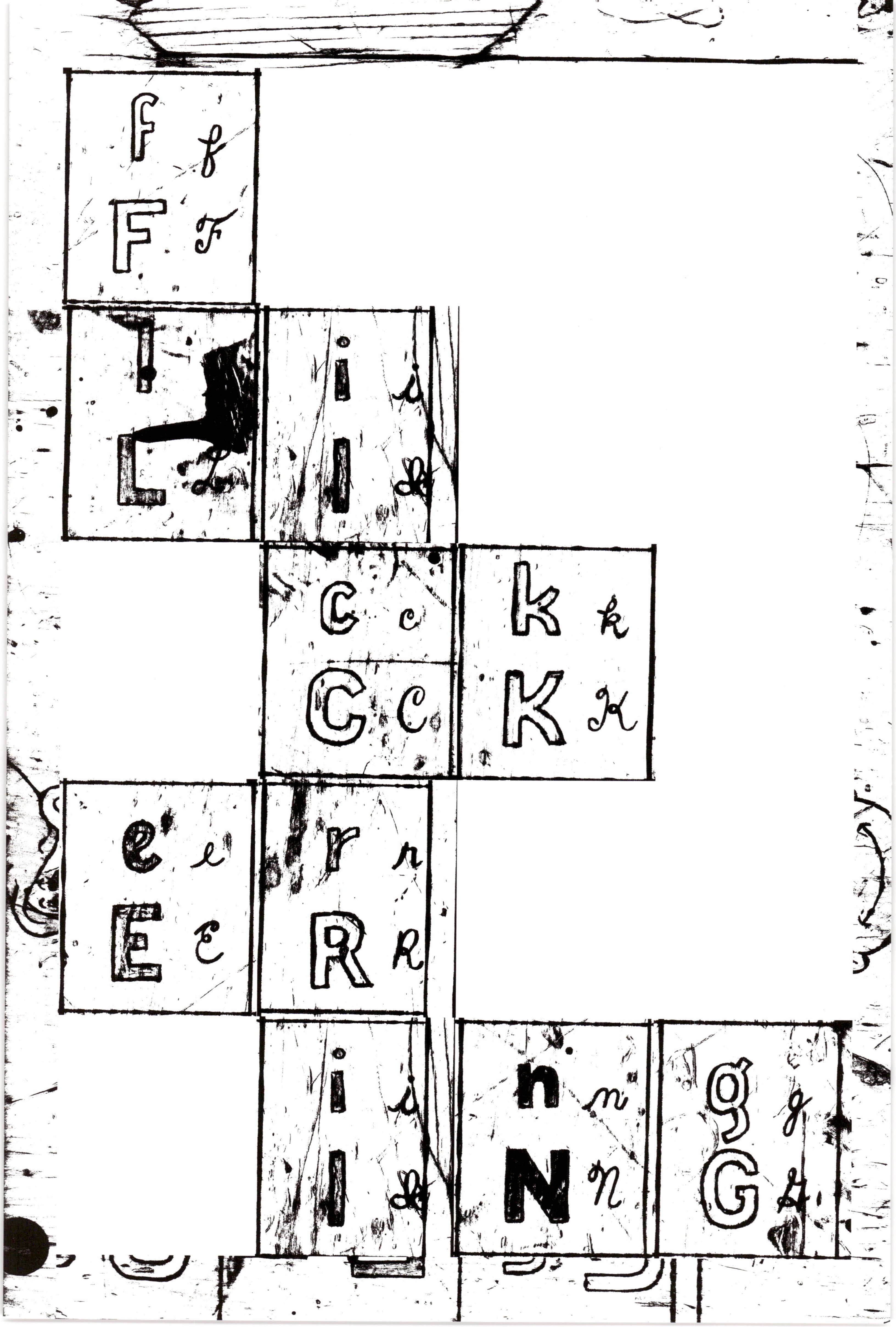
f f F F
l L
i i I I
c c C C
k k K K
e e E E
r r R R
i i I I
n n N N
g g G G

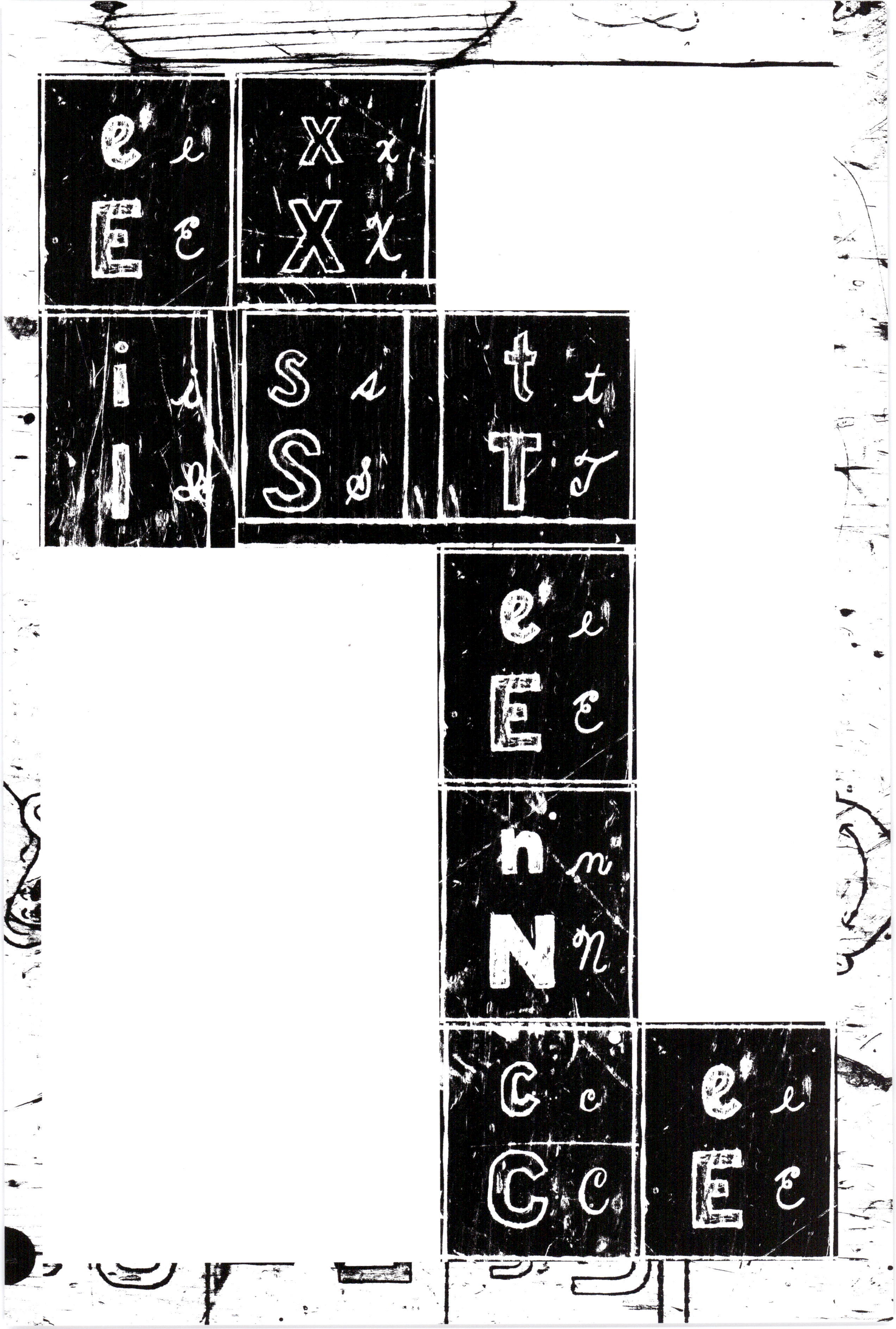
e e E E
x x X X
i i I I
s s S S
t t T T
e e E E
n n N N
c c C C
e e E E

Time Travel: A Flickering Existence ◊ *A series of interviews conducted by Hans Ulrich Obrist with Philippe Parreno between 2001 to 2008. Edited by Karen Marta*

Hans Ulrich Obrist: There is, I think, a sentence that really sums up your relationship with your work: you say, "Today, there are no longer images that are beautiful, there are chains of images." I think this phrase could also be a departure point for this conversation.

Philippe Parreno: Yes, what I meant by chain, I think, is a dynamic structure: pre-production, production, post-production, these narrative instances depend upon each other. In the course of the chaining of these sequences, a narrative unfolds. An image, a building, or a film comes from a more vast narrative structure, to which they belong and which they are elements of. In robotics, people use a very precise term, but I don't remember it anymore. But we can talk about a threshold of tolerance or linear adjustment to describe this time frame, this delta in which a number of events can occur, it's a semiotic chain. I like meta-stories, stories of stories. Is an object always the end of something? Does everything really always start with a scenario and end with an object? Should there always be a happy ending to everything? Why shouldn't there be many endings given to stories?

So you want to escape that fate?

The degree of resolution of an idea depends on an economic choice, which either you make, or is imposed on you. I am often more interested in procedures than in resolutions. In *The Shining* [1980], by Stanley Kubrick, there's a scene in which the cook explains to the little boy—"You know Doc, when something happens it can leave traces of itself behind, it's like when you burn toast."

Precisely. It seems to me that most collaborations between artists and architects are motivated by this research about the difference between conceiving and realizing a project. Where do you locate the beginning of this common interest of architects and artists for different modes of exhibiting and experimenting, and for ephemeral, undetermined forms?

There was of course the collaboration between Yves Klein and Claude Parent on immaterial architecture. There were also other forms of collaboration like Rauschenberg's *White Paintings* [1951] on which Merce Cunningham projected a film, and John Cage wrote his silent piece for the event. But radical architecture disappeared after the Venice Biennale in 1972. The history of architecture is a history of the object, there are some exceptions, for example Parent/Klein. But it's the same for visual art. There are no art books that retrace the history of the exhibition.

Yes, the history of art is one of objects, and to a lesser extent one of exhibitions. Exhibitions aren't collectible, and in this case they aren't archived. As soon as time passes, they tend to be forgotten. This amnesia that affects exhibition history has pernicious and very deep effects.

If the amnesia is the symptom I wonder what the disease is?

And it's striking to see to what extent the questioning of the object by artists is a recurrent question that disappears and reappears. The early 1990s made a very explicit return to forms of questioning the object. How do you envision the way in which you treat this question in relation to the ways artists did in the 1960s and 1970s?

From the 1980s on, Sony and Thompson have been after the issue of resolution. The point is not to produce images, but to produce images with a good resolution. This idea was really like a virus. The issue was widely discussed in the 1960s and 1970s when some artists sold emptiness. In the 1960s and 1970s, the question of the object was debated around very spectacular political and aesthetic questions. If today I wanted to approach these questions with Lawrence Weiner or Daniel Buren, I would quickly sound like an illiterate brainless neo-liberal.

Jean-François Lyotard asked these questions in 1985, in the exhibition *Les Immatériaux* [Centre Pompidou, Paris]. Was that exhibition important for you?

It was a superb exhibition. It provided a reading experience. The catalogue of *Les Immatériaux* was printed on slips of paper. It was made up of a series of exchanges between different people during a period of time. A sort of intranet had been set up. That was the first time the internet was used as a tool, not as an icon, but as a tool. The show in itself was surprising in the curatorial choices, in the manner in which objects and experiences were arranged.

Was it a philosophical exhibition, like some complained at the time?

***Les Immatériaux* was an exhibition producing ideas through a display of objects in a space. It was very different from writing a book or developing a philosophical concept. And that's precisely what I loved about that exhibition, that it wasn't a conceptual exhibition. I learned later that Lyotard wanted to do another exhibition, *Resistance*. "Resistance" isn't a good title. You immediately think about a series of moral issues. But when I met him, I understood that he meant in fact resistance in another way. In school when you study physics you are told that frictional forces are not important—the forces of two surfaces in contact let certain axioms become uncertain. I think that's what *Resistance* was supposed to be about.**

Why not try to realize Lyotard's second exhibition? That could really work against the widespread amnesia of the history of exhibitions.

Someone should try to find his notes. Posthumous books are published, why not a posthumous show?

It would also be an occasion to reintroduce some slowness in the world of exhibitions, which has been hectic as far as the number of exhibitions is concerned. It would be another form of resistance.

I think that this is a responsibility artists have or you have. But I like to move around, in a way I like to be distracted. Hard to defragment myself.

When you talk with other artists about this kind of alternative, what kind of project do you imagine: are you thinking not only of exhibitions but works, and publications as well?

Books are great exhibition displays... maybe the experience of reading will become fundamental again. Reading is also a physical state; it demands a particular attention, a floating attention. The moments where you disconnect from reading, when you start dreaming, are very pleasant. You are at once inside your head imagining things while you're being spoken to. I have lots of stupid ideas for books. I would love to make a book of images on the history of medical representation. From Leonardo da Vinci to virtual reality and synthetic images, all the techniques of representation have been invented by medicine. It would be fascinating to trace such a history. Modeling the liver happened in 3-D before making *Terminator 2*. Another book would be on the manner in which men have rationalized their relation to their waste. There are ethnologists today studying the manner in which the question of the greenhouse effect is managed by nations. They study how nations can negotiate between themselves. New extra-national bodies are created. In the same way that plumbing redesigned cities, the treatment of the greenhouse effect will modify our landscape. The Palace of Versailles had been designed to evacuate odors... The Tokyo accords are a part of the history of the treatment of human secretions. That would make a beautiful book, a book of landscapes and of very spectacular spaces. I would also love to make a book on zoos. Zoos are very accurate mirrors of the way we see ourselves in cities. I like the idea that zoos are the unconscious of cities.

Maybe the next thing we should talk about is Grenoble, and the question of utopia and experimentation that you experienced living in Grenoble in the 1970s, when the city was a "laboratory" of a new city. Maybe you can tell me about how Grenoble played the role of a toolbox during these years. Dominique Gonzalez-Foerster already told me a lot about her years in Grenoble. I'd like to hear about your experiences at the time.

You see, everything depended on the teachers who had a lot of courage and political conviction, and it all stopped when these people left. It was a very specific moment. We benefited from both this enthusiasm and this bankruptcy.

Were there real teachers, and very few conventionalists, in these schools?

Yes, very convincing militants. Belatedly, at high school, there was Gilles Lipovetsky who taught French and philosophy, and also at high school there was a drawing professor. There was also this cultural center where we went with the school to see Carolyn Carlson or Pina Bausch. You could really fall flat on your face from time to time, but it was all fraught with an educational dynamic.

And when, and in particular, how did this all end?

With the increase of Decaux signs...

You mean the outdoor advertising company?

Yes, Decaux, postmodernism, the end of political engagement, the disappearance of lightning bugs and red poppies, the morals of baby boomers, the arrival of Michel Platini at the Juventus Turin.

That's also what your film *Credits* [1999] deals with in some ways?

Yes, it also comes from the fact that when you spend your childhood in a ZUP [Zones Urbaines Prioritaires/Urban Priority Zones] you see some houses being born and some dying. There weren't any images of those ZUPs. A text served as a model for *Credits*; it's at the end of Pier Paolo Pasolini's text derived from *Heretical Empiricism*, where he speaks of the multiplicity of necessary viewpoints for observing an event. In fact it's the figure of the hologram. For Pasolini, only a harmonization of subjective points of view can offer a precise image of a given situation. To have an image of the Kennedy assassination, according to Pasolini, one must show all the films that were shot around the procession. While showing all these films, time would be lengthened and suspended like a hologram. I applied this idea, and I went to see kids that I grew up with, but also Michel Poniatowski who was the Home Secretary under de Gaulle and many other key personalities of that period, like Angus Young [guitar player of AC/DC], that I loved. I then went to see the people who had been directly involved with the ZUP and the ZAC [Zones d'aménagement concerté/Zones of adjusted development] questions. The ZUP, contrary to the "Grands Ensembles," were much less spectacular programs.

Jean-Luc Godard also shot La Villeneuve, Grenoble's experimental housing and social project. That's were he established his production and distribution company Sonimage.

Yes, and he participated with Anne-Marie Miéville on Villeneuve's cable channel. They also worked on the film, *France tour détour deux enfants* [1977-1978] there, recording interviews with kids. *Credits* was a collection of intersecting viewpoints, designed to form or reform an image. It's a bit like all these interviews you do. In your case, you are the point of intersection between people, whereas there it was an absent image.

Did you record or archive these conversations in one way or another?

No. I recorded nothing. I started to have an idea of an image while talking with everyone. The recording of these discussions is this scene with trees with plastic bags tied to the branches. Kids would hook the plastic bags in the trees that the mayor planted in the vacant lots in the city. They did this to recuperate their playground, which the mayor had destroyed through green design. The ZUP were never completed.

Melancholy seems to be at the heart of your reflection in those days.

Yes, it's a dark sentiment, it's [Jean-Pierre] Melville... I love these stories. Melancholy can maybe offer a political alternative.
Why did I think that melancholy was somehow an appropriate feeling? I mean appropriate in a way that some tools are more appropriate than others when you have to find a solution to a problem. *Film noir* is somehow relevant. You know the typical *film noir* that opens with a long scene, no dialogue, where the villain played by Alain Delon lies on his bed endlessly smoking a cigarette. The characters develop a unique relationship towards time and history, but that's another issue. The melancholic is a peculiar person who has an object of desire but lost the desire itself. That is to say, he lost that which makes him desire the desired object: the object-cause-of-your-desire which is never the desired object.

There is the whole question of time. You conceived a show that dealt with this.

It was quite a reduced idea of all that. But the title was good, *Facteur Temps* [1994]—"Postman Time" in English but in French "facteur" is the postman and also the factor.

Talking about time, I would like to speak about Cedric Price with you who was the architect of time. When you read his book[1] recently you said that his writings and drawings were butterflies.

1. Hans Ulrich Obrist (Ed.), *Re: CP* (Basel: Birkhäuser, 2002).
Postman Time, 1995, Vienna, photograph of the performance.

Oh yes, I was very inspired! I even made up a few sentences that I thought I had read; but I think I made them up.

What were they about?

It dealt with the idea that a normal way to produce new institutions would be to make them so personal and so ephemeral that they would last for the time of the will of the person who started it. So when you decide to change your ideas, the institution would close down. But he never said that; I made it up: institutions with an expiry date.

This idea that it could have a limited lifespan, he basically said it when he stated that the book could only be sold until 2006 because by then the author might have changed his mind. It's like institutions having an expiry date.

That's like the idea of Jacques Guillot who created the Magasin [a center for contemporary art in Grenoble, France].

Did you know him?

Yes. Structurally, the Magasin was not supposed to last more than 15 years. It could be built with a low budget; the walls would not be thick enough and the roof would leak. Because it was an art center and not a museum, it was planned not to last forever. But then he died and they tried to make the space survive the author—and then all the problems started. They spent the entire budget trying to fix the building.

That's the great thing about Cedric Price. He wanted the "Interaction Centre" [a cultural center in London] to exist for 10 or 15 years. It was taken down a few years before Cedric died. When the press called and said, "Mr. Price, your masterpiece is being dismantled." He said, "I am enchanted, I am very, very happy."

A flickering existence.

"Flickering Existence" is a great title for this conversation.

Institutions are not necessarily meant to be permanent. They have to be reassessed. But for that I guess you need to have people who are willing to create, to negotiate. People who are willing to play.

Cedric Price went very far. He would tell people who wanted to buy a house and commission him to design it, "you better buy a car or get divorced."

The *Snow Dancing* project was inspired by those public art spaces I really discovered art in. Art centers, not museums, you know, those contemporary art centers built generally in factories or industrial warehouses. The book *Snow Dancing* was structured like a theater play describing a party that lasted for an hour and 30 minutes. It takes about an hour and 30 minutes to read the book. We played the party for about the same time. The show

opened when the party was over. The party produced an exhibition. But to go back to the flickering labels, it's a great idea by Cedric Price.

In Montreal, in his show at the Canadian Centre for Architecture, which was his last big show, Price used umbrellas and when there was an umbrella on the label it meant anticipation because he anticipated that it was going to rain. Boulez spoke about the density of polyphony. He said that he discovered in Elliott Carter [American composer] this idea of superposing structures.

I like the idea that he played the music of his friend.

In the same way you could imagine that Dominique [Gonzalez-Foerster] could play a show of yours, you could imagine a cast that plays a show of Rirkrit [Tiravanija]; it could be a good group show.

Yes, why not ask artists to edit other artists' works?

It could be a sequence of events in a space. That is something we should start. I would like to return once more to the issue of your unrealized projects. You wanted to create something like Christmas.

I want to create a new party, a new festival, something pagan, something that people will celebrate, something inscribed in the calendar, like Christmas. That's another project. And then what else?

There's this idea for an exhibition like the one in the 19th century that introduced swimming pools.

Yes, that's funny, isn't it? Some people invented the swimming pool in England for an exhibition. The theme was the experience of swimming, the experience of water—so people would visit an exhibition of swimming. That's how the swimming pool was introduced, then people really liked to go to swim in cities and nowadays we have competitions in them. It would be fantastic to conceive an exhibition that would produce a new "something." I give you that as my "unrealized" project. I made a project for your "unrealized project" questions. I guess it's a realized one now.

Continued from page 17.

Fleurs [Flowers], 1987 ◁ Hi8 video, color, mute, 52' ‡ First presentation: Canal +, 1988 || Unedited § Courtesy of the artist **In this first video by Philippe Parreno, the filmed sequence already functions as a formal intervention. Made while he was a student at the École supérieure d'art in Grenoble, the video is a continuous shot of a bouquet of flowers. The camera was tripoded and the only motion within the sequence is generated by controlling the zoom and focus of the lens. Parreno sent the video to television stations across France, allowing them to broadcast it in whatever form they wished, free of copyright restrictions. In 1988, a few seconds of *Fleurs* [Flowers] were used as a background for a weather forecast on the French television channel Canal +. Intervening in the backdrop of a television program, opposed to the ubiquitous white space of the gallery was a strategy previously utilized by General Idea, a model artists group of the time[1] and by Gerry Schum's projects *Fernseh Galerie* and *Videogalerie* in the late 1960s and 1970s. In these two works, Schum attempted to convince German television channels to broadcast artist videos so that art could be made accessible to everyone. Parreno expanded upon these strategies by blurring the boundaries between the artwork and its exhibition space having released his imagery to the networks free of copyright. ◊ Parreno was influenced by Jean-Luc Godard who, from 1974 to 1978 was more interested in making video and television programs than films. During this time Godard made *Numéro deux* (1975), two television series including *France tour détour deux enfants* (1977–1978).[2] In addition to these projects, Godard also made a number of television tests with Anne-Marie Miéville at the Sonimage studio in Grenoble. ◊ During this same time, Parreno was acutely aware of *Vidéogazette* (1972–1976), the first public access channel in Villeneuve, a suburb of Grenoble. Moreover, during the 1970s, he is a fervent reader of *Cahiers du cinéma* and of Serge Daney,[3] who later wrote in the newspaper *Libération* about films shown on television for those who had discovered " ... cinema at the time of its ruin."[4] By the 1980s, television ads and music videos, which had already begun to saturate the audio-visual landscape, were undoubtedly a pop cultural influence on *Fleurs*. In Parreno's earliest work his use of the language of commercial television is indicative of his fascination with media as a manifestation of leisure in Postmodern society.[5]**

Siberia, 1988 With Bernard Joisten and Pierre Joseph ◁ Installation in an isothermal maritime container (approx. 300 × 250 × 600 cm): ¬ *Robocop, Top Model, Paysage antarctique,* Acrylic paintings on PVC (Bernard Joisten) • *Prototype Mitsubishi, Mouse Apple, Cellule nerveuse sur microprocesseur, CD, Supraconductivité,* photographs printed on Duratrans and mounted on backlit Plexiglas light box (Pierre Joseph) • *Untitled,* digital animation on monitor, 30 × 15", on a loop (Philippe Parreno) ‡ "19&&," February 28–April 10, 1998, Le Magasin – Centre national d'art contemporain, Grenoble, France § Courtesy of the artists ***Siberia,* a "container" of images, challenges**

1. Philippe Parreno, "General Idea," *Documents sur l'art*, no.4, October 1993, p.22-26.

2. Tom McDonough, "City of Cineastes: Cinéma," a recent exhibition in Grenoble, brought together three generations of artists who have explored video and film-based imagery," *Art in America*, September 2006, p.60-65.

3. Philippe Parreno and Hans Ulrich Obrist, *The Conversation Series*, Cologne: Walter König, 2008, p.45.

4. Serge Daney, *Devant la recrudescence des vols de sacs à mains. op. cit.*, p.11. Daney also writes "Television is not made to be seen, but to be viewed" (*op. cit.*, p.61).

5. Parreno, who often uses this term, is more influenced by Jean-François Lyotard's thoughts on the end of "meta-narratives" —*La Condition postmoderne* [The Postmodern Condition], 1979— than by the Marxist analysis of Frédric Jameson whose text *Postmodernism, or, the Cultural Logic of Late Capitalism*, was only published in 1991 (Duke University Press) and in French in 2007 (*Le Postmodernisme ou la Logique culturelle du capitalisme tardif*, Ensba, "D'art en questions.")

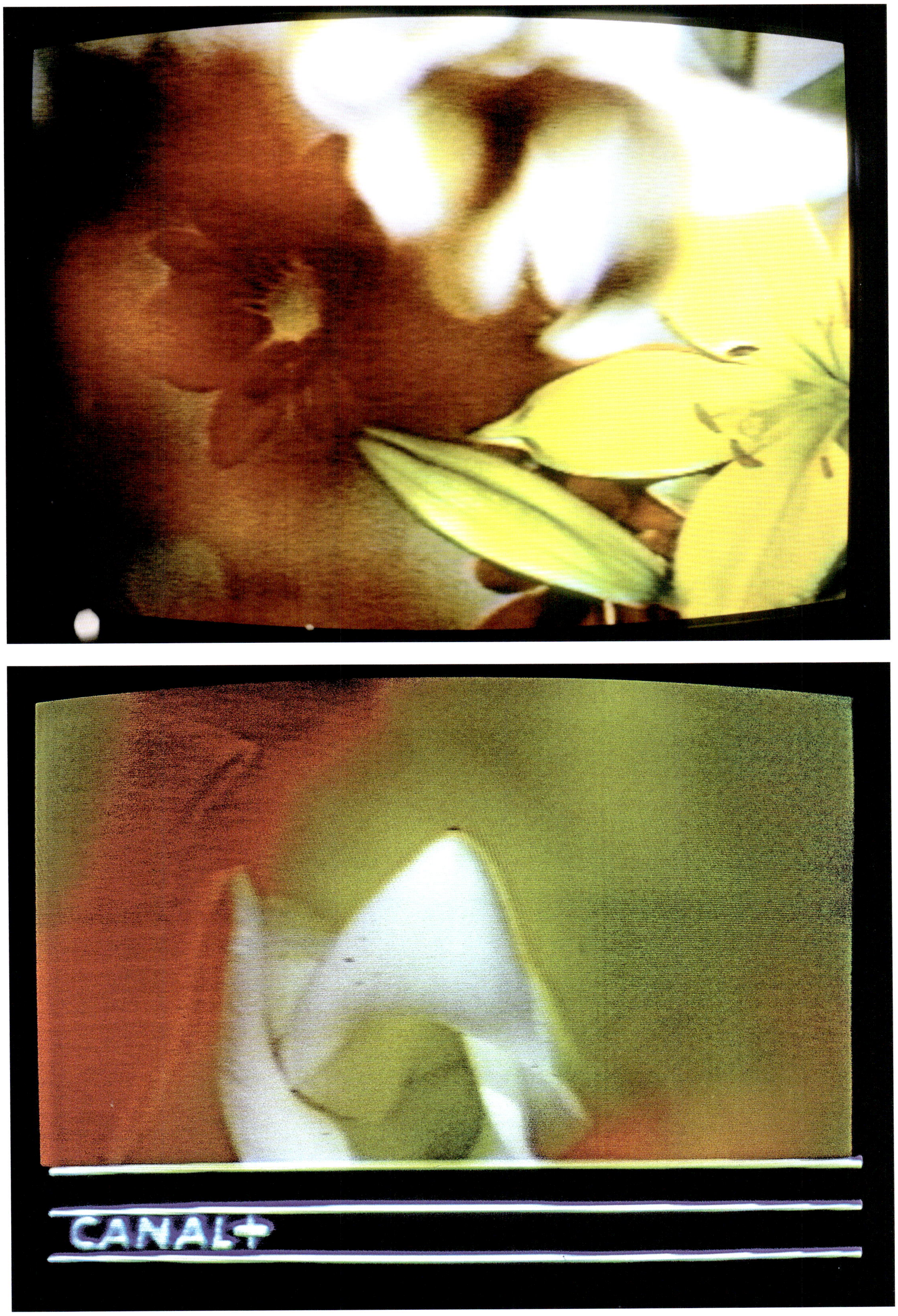

Fleurs, 1987, video (presentation on Canal + channel, 1988)

the logic of both the collaborative process and group exhibition. Each artist is both curator and producer participating in a shared work. Referencing a satellite or a "white room" (an industrial research laboratory whose function is to minimize the concentration of particles), lit images made by the three artists in a sort of imaginary *frozen moment* are placed in an isothermal white lacquered marine container and installed in front of the doors of the Magasin in Grenoble. Each artist chose a particular medium thereby eliminating the hierarchy among mediums: Bernard Joisten used acrylic paint on PVC; Pierre Joseph used a back lit photo mounted on Plexiglas, printed on Duratrans film; and Parreno used a digital animation on a loop of an Arctic ice floe. The found image, from a book by Jacques Cousteau, colored with the computer program Paintbox (which was the equivalent of today's Photoshop), continuously changes color, creating the illusion of an animated image. The exhibition's title, *Siberia* refers to "cold" technology at a period when Monaco's *Imagina Salon* dedicated to new image technology was at its height.

Hyper Hyper, 1988

Hyper Hyper, 1988 With Dominique Gonzalez-Foerster, Bernard Joisten and Pierre Joseph ⊲ ¬ 5 laminated color photocopies, 42 × 60 cm • graffiti "Hyper Hyper" written on the wall in magenta spray-paint ‡ "Salon de la jeune sculpture," May 19–June 26, 1988, quai d'Austerlitz, Paris, France || edition of 1 and 1 artist's proof ʃ Private collection, Paris, France ♦ **Malette Hyper Hyper, 1988** With Dominique Gonzalez-Foerster, Bernard Joisten and Pierre Joseph ⊲ ¬ Mecanorma briefcase with the adhesive label "Hyper Hyper," 42 × 43 × 9 cm • 5 laminated color photocopies, 29.2 × 40.8 cm || 5 editions (= editions of 5) ʃ First private collection: private collection, Paris, France § Courtesy Air de Paris, Paris ***Malette Hyper Hyper*** **is indeed "the first *smart* exhibition," which isviewable through the intermediary of a screen and consists of five A1 laminated color photocopies. At the center of this project is *Malette Hyper Hyper*, a briefcase printed with the logo *Hyper Hyper* (the color chosen by the buyer) which contains five miniature laminated color photocopies of the *Salon de la jeune sculpture*—thus rendering it portable through reproduction. The artwork functions as group project and potentiality, rather than a realized totality. Through this project, Dominique Gonzalez-Foerster, Bernard Joisten, Pierre Joseph and Parreno reject the concept of personalization and instead celebrate the multiplicity of choice by creating an interactive virtual exhibition.[6]**

6. Arielle Pélenc, "Espèces d'espaces [Kinds of Spaces]: Dominique Gonzalez-Foerster, Bernard Joisten, Véronique Joumard, Pierre Joseph, Ange Leccia, Philippe Parreno, Jean-Luc Vilmouth," *Grenoble in Innsbruck* (exhib. cat.), Galerie de l'Institut français in Innsbruck, 1990, np.

Composit, 1988 With Bernard Joisten and Pierre Joseph ⊲ Installation: ¬ *Gabrielle Lazure-Gore, Microrobot,* Acrylic paintings on PVC and Plexiglas (Bernard Joisten) • *Marithé & François Girbaud, J.-P. Gaultier, Hérouville Saint-Clair Project Tour, Cheb Kader, Dirk Bikkembergs,* Laminated C-prints (Pierre Joseph) • *Kyle MacLachlan in Blue Velvet by David Lynch,* superposition of screen printed black and white images (Philippe Parreno)

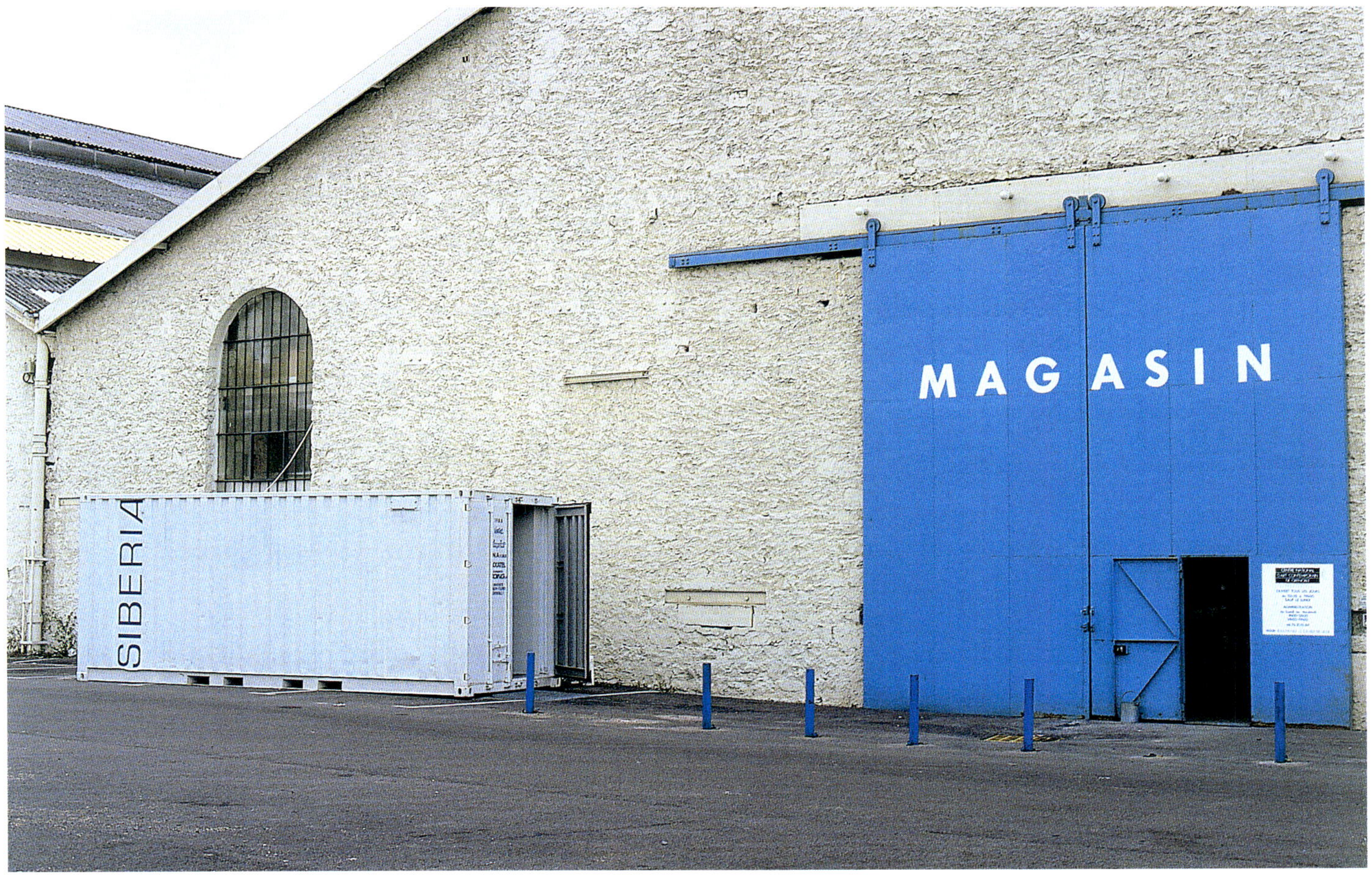

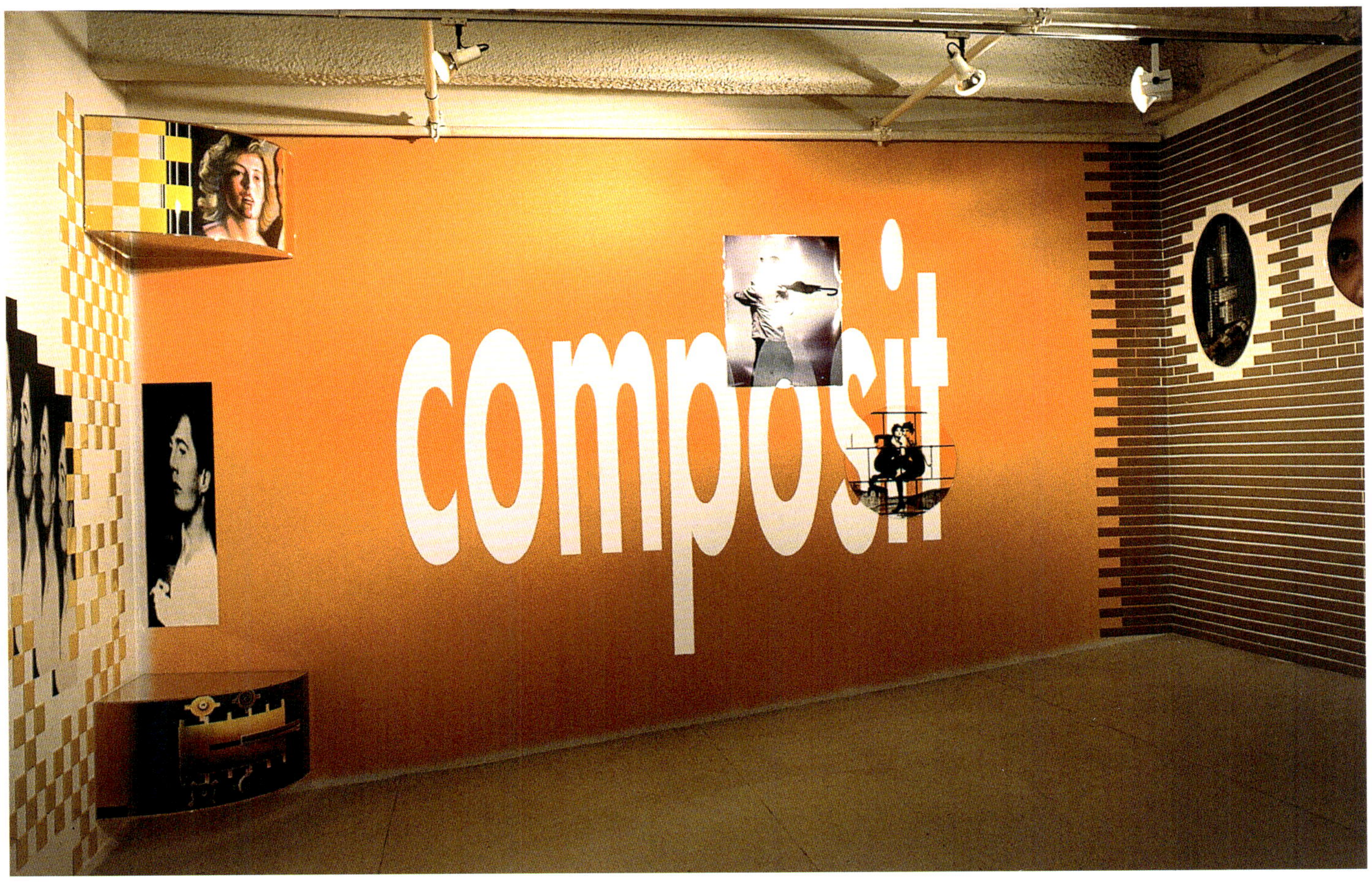

Siberia, 1988, with Bernard Joisten and Pierre Joseph, exhibition view "19&&", Le Magasin, Grenoble
Composit, 1988, with Bernard Joisten and Pierre Joseph, exhibition view "Situation", Crédac, Ivry-sur-Seine

• orange wall with large white inscription "composit"; variable dimensions ‡ "Situation," September 7–October 16, 1988, Crédac, Ivry-sur-Seine, France || 1 edition § Courtesy of the artists **This collaborative project brings together paintings by Bernard Joisten, photographs by Pierre Joseph and screen prints by Parreno. Printed vertically, the portrait of the actor Kyle MacLachlan consists of many silk screen prints, layered one print on top of the other and slightly overlapping—leaving the collage's tears and gaps visible as if each part forms a pixel belonging to a larger image. It is a commentary on new technologies of the image, which we continually integrate in both public and private spheres, often unaware of their limitations and distortions.**

Histoire de tableaux-fantômes [History of Phantom Paintings], 1988 With Dominique Gonzalez-Foerster, Bernard Joisten and Pierre Joseph ◊ Brown leather hard back book, 209 pages, title and authors inscribed in gold on the back; 20.5 × 17.2 × 2.2 cm § Courtesy of the artists **This book contains a collection of twenty tales written by P'ou Song-Ling (1640–1715), entitled *Contes étranges du cabinet Leao* (Strange Tales from Leao's Collection), as well as an inset made for a project for the Musée d'Art moderne de la Ville de Paris.**

Ozone

Sac Ozone [Ozone Bag], 1988/1989/1990 With Dominique Gonzalez-Foerster, Bernard Joisten and Pierre Joseph ◊ Contents of sport bag personalized according to the answers given by whoever acquires the "Ozone Questionnaire." ‡ *"Les Ateliers du Paradise: un film en temps réel"* [Studios of Paradise: a film in real time] by Pierre Joseph, Philippe Parreno and Philippe Perrin, August 6–September 8, 1990, Air de Paris, Nice, France || Edition of 4 ∫ First public collection: Frac Corse, Corte, France (edition 1/4, destroyed by a fire) ∫ First private collection: private collection, Paris, France (edition 2/4) ♦ **Ozone, 1989** With Dominique Gonzalez-Foerster, Bernard Joisten and Pierre Joseph ◊ Installation: ¬ fifteen trash cans filled with various documents (Dominique Gonzalez-Foerster) • *Dinosaures* [Dinosaurs], 2 Acrylic paintings on a projection screen, 120 × 90 cm each (Bernard Joisten) • *8 Diapositives géantes* [8 Giant Slides] (Pierre Joseph) • *Objets fun* [Fun Objects]: windsurf sail, hand gliding sail, diving suit (Philippe Parreno) • exhibition poster • 10 blue folding stools; variable dimensions ‡ "Ozone," October 14–December 16, 1989, Apac, Nevers, France; exhibition curator: Éric Troncy || 1 edition (work destroyed in a fire) ∫ Past collection Frac Corse, Corte, France ♦ **Stand Ozone, 1989** With Dominique Gonzalez-Foerster, Bernard Joisten and Pierre Joseph ◊ Installation: ¬ 12 trash cans filled with various documents (Dominique Gonzalez-Foerster) • *Dinosaures,* 2 Acrylic paintings on projection screen, 120 × 90 cm each (Bernard Joisten) • *3 Diapositives géantes* [3 Giant Slides] (Pierre Joseph) • *Objets fun* [Fun Objects]: red inflatable sleigh, diving suit (Philippe Parreno) • exhibition poster • 3 blue folding stools; variable dimensions ‡ November 15–November 22, 1989, Esther

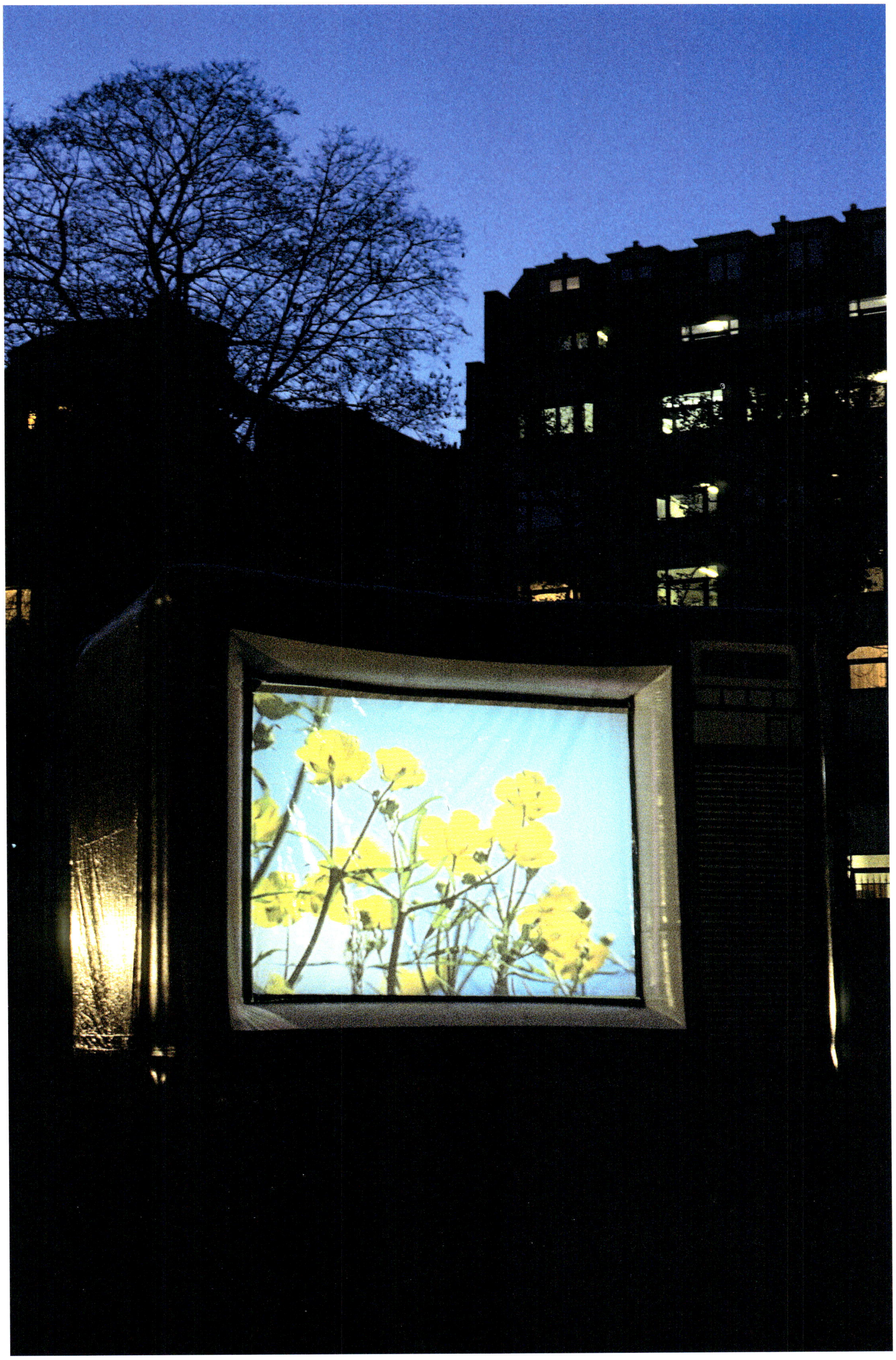

Vidéo Ozone, 1989, with Bernard Joisten, Dominique Gonzalez-Foerster and Pierre Joseph, exhibition view "De l'instabilité", CNAP, Paris

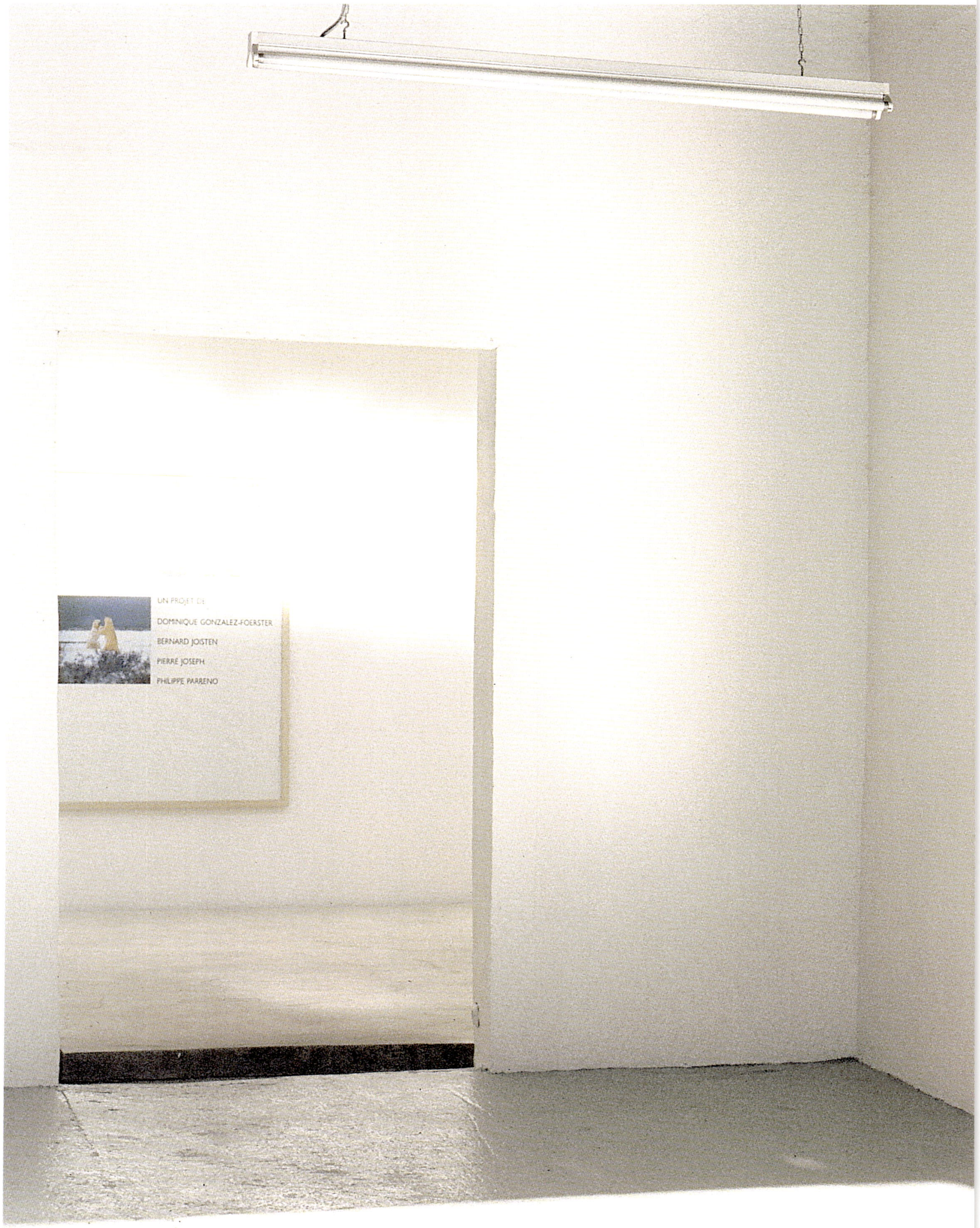

Posters **Ozone, 1989,** exhibition view "Ozone", Apac, Nevers

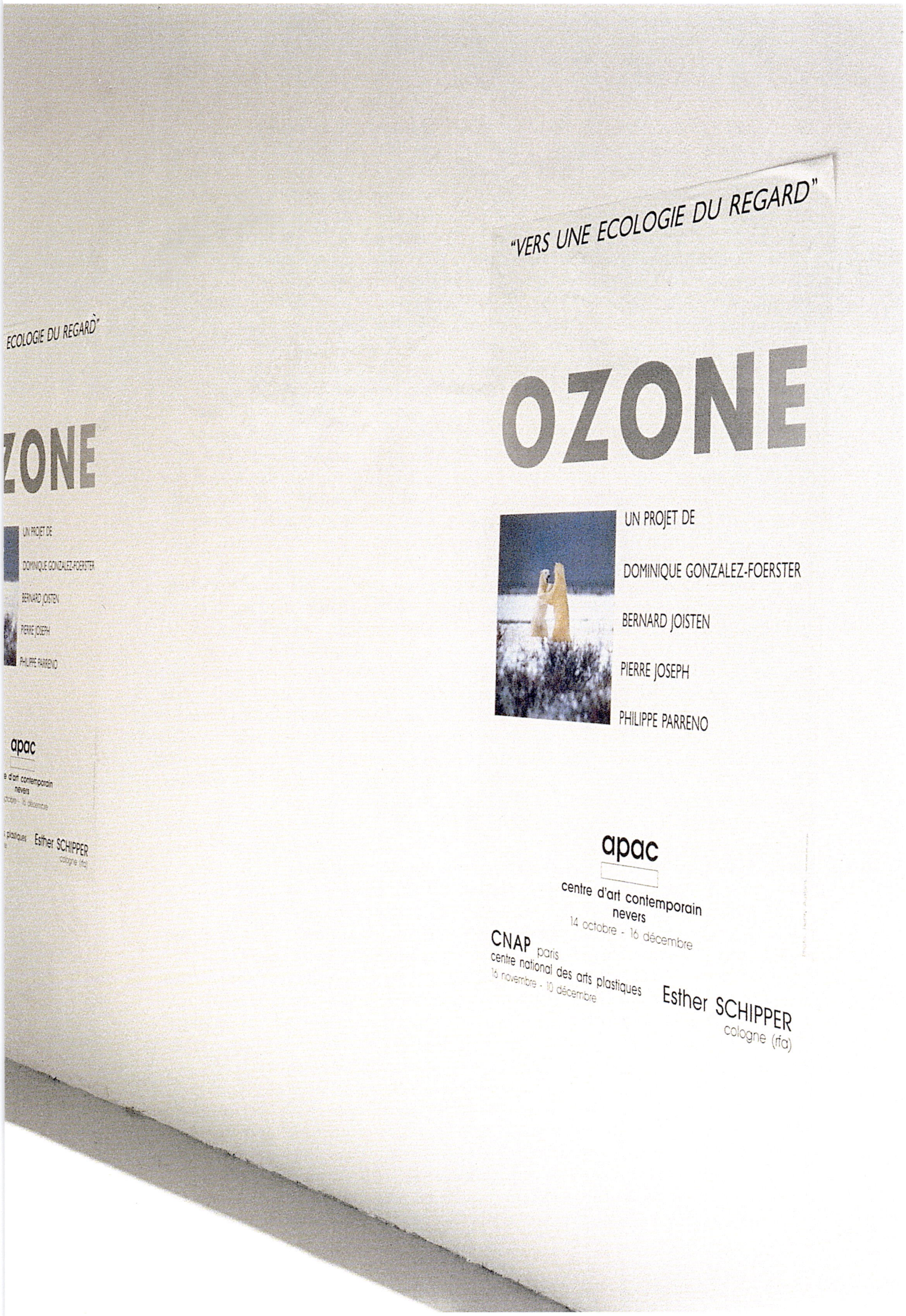
"VERS UNE ECOLOGIE DU REGARD"
OZONE
UN PROJET DE
DOMINIQUE GONZALEZ-FOERSTER
BERNARD JOISTEN
PIERRE JOSEPH
PHILIPPE PARRENO
apac
centre d'art contemporain
nevers
14 octobre - 16 décembre
CNAP paris
centre national des arts plastiques
16 novembre - 10 décembre
Esther SCHIPPER
cologne (rfa)

Schipper Gallery booth, Art Cologne, Cologne, Germany || Elements sold separately ʃ Several private collections ⧫ **Bombe Ozone [Ozone Spray], 1989** With Dominique Gonzalez-Foerster, Bernard Joisten and Pierre Joseph ⊲ Evian spray covered with a black and white adhesive sticker with the inscription "ozone" and a pixilated drawing, pink or blue lid ‡ November 15–November 22, 1989, Esther Schipper Gallery booth, Art Cologne, Cologne, Germany || 100 editions ʃ First collection: private collection, Paris, France ⧫ **Video Ozone, 1989** With Bernard Joisten, Dominique Gonzalez-Foerster and Pierre Joseph ⊲ Installation: ¬ giant inflatable television (500 × 700 × 400 cm) • projector, Dub Master Beta cam, silent, 4'55" • Video direction: François Reymond • music: *Coma II* by S'Express (Mark Moore and Philip Glass), with the authorization of Rhythm King label. ‡ "De l'instabilité" [Of Instability], November 16–December 10, 1989, Cnap/Centre national des arts plastiques, Paris (exhib. cat.); exhibition curators: Martine Baur and Jean-Michel Foray || 1 edition ʃ Collection Fnac, Puteaux, France **Neither a brand nor product, *Ozone* is a program with multiple modes of access created and managed by the four artists; an exhibition envisioned "as a laboratory of data that can generate different forms."[7] The project *Ozone* consists of three distinct components: a sports bag, an exhibition and a video installation. It refers to a new "ecology" of the image through a process of formal interventions, such as remixing, recycling and sampling. For the first time, the artists group themselves under the common name *Ozone* while still keeping their own signatures to assume a partially unified position, which demonstrates a collective concern for the future of the planet. By retaining their individual signatures, they differentiate their proto-group from standard leftist organizations, such as the Green party in Germany or international Greenpeace initiatives. The project was completed over the course of two years which is exactly the time it takes to make a film, Parreno remarked. The ambition of Parreno's artistic model rivals the density of narrative contained within a film, and perhaps even the prodigious output twenty-four images per second. ◊ The *Sac Ozone,* is a mutable commodity. The future owner fills out the "Ozone Questionnaire" which indicates for example his/her astrological sign, his/her favorite animal, his/her recurring dream and his/her taste in music. The contents of the sports bag then are meant to reflect the myriad tastes of the consumer. Dominique Gonzalez-Foerster states, "the modalities for the redistribution of the artist's and spectator's roles" are sketched, the latter being invited "to make 50% of the work."[8] Similar to *Malette Hyper Hyper, Sac Ozone* is an object-exhibition with numerous versions. ◊ In *Ozone,* 1989, a group installation-exhibition mounted at the Apac in Nevers, Parreno showed his *Fun Objects* which can be thought of as metaphors for consumption and leisure—included are: a windsurf sail, a hand-gliding sail and a diving suit. The selection of these specific objects for the exhibition was influenced by Gilles Lipovetsky's analysis of consumer culture and happiness.[9] Also included in the exhibition, were photographs mounted on cardboard**

7. Éric Troncy, *Surface de réparations* [Surface of repairs] (exhib. cat.), Dijon, Frac Bourgogne, 1995, p.46.

8. *Ibid.*

9. Arielle Pélenc, "Espèces d'espaces: Dominique Gonzalez-Foerster, Bernard Joisten, Véronique Joumard, Pierre Joseph, Ange Leccia, Philippe Parreno, Jean-Luc Vilmouth," *op.cit.*

of Bruno Gouvy sky surfing. This work disappeared in a recent fire at the Frac in Corsica. A smaller version of *Ozone, Stand Ozone* was exhibited in the form of an art fair booth in 1989 with a new version of *Fun Objects* (still existing) and an edition of *Bombe Ozone*, a spray can with a special "Ozone" label. ◊ Finally *Video Ozone* mixes frozen frames with extracts from Super 8, 3D and 16mm films, all relating to the perception of nature and the environment. 3D animation sequences, the filmed exploits of Bruno Gouvy and Patrick Edlinger, the presentation of current ecological issues, extracts from Manga cartoons and family films are shown in succession to the music of Mark Moore and Philip Glass ("S'Express") in a remix style similar to the House Music of the era. The video is projected within a huge inflatable television bought at a trade show. The piece can be shown in an exhibition space, a park or even a video art festival. During a period of increasing awareness about the greenhouse effect and holes within our ozone layer, *Vidéo Ozone* proposes a kind of giant, calm, nuanced documentation."[10] The work marks a new era of television, advertising and video clips characterized by mixing and sampling.

10. *De l'instabilité* [From Instability] (exhib.cat.), Paris, Centre national des arts plastiques, 1989, p.24-25.

Galerie intelligente [Intelligent Gallery], 1989 With Pierre Joseph ‡ Collaborative project for the opening of the Galerie des Archives, Paris, France, November 30, 1989–January 13, 1990 All the works from the *Image intelligente* series consist of a photograph to which a loudspeaker and motion detector are fixed, thus triggering the audio when approached by the viewer.

Image intelligente (Trial, Cascade) [Intelligent Image (Trial, Waterfall)], 1989 With Pierre Joseph ⊲ ¬ C-print on foam board (60 × 90 cm) • loudspeaker (approx. 17 × 8 × 3 cm) stuck onto the photograph • motion detector (2 × ø 1.7 cm) under the loudspeaker • tape • photograph by Hélène Guermonprez || 1 edition ʃ Private collection, Monaco In *Image intelligente (Trial, Cascade)*, a photograph of a motocross cyclist driving through a water fall while the loudspeaker plays a recording of the bike and driver passing under the cascading water.

Image intelligente (Mer, Cloche) [Intelligent Image (Sea, Bell)], 1989 With Pierre Joseph ⊲ ¬ C-print on foam board (60 × 90 cm) • loudspeaker (approx. 17 × 8 × 3 cm) stuck onto the photograph • motion detector (2 × ø 1.7 cm) under the loudspeaker • tape • photograph by Hélène Guermonprez || 1 edition ʃ Private collection, Monaco *Image intelligente (Mer, Cloche)*, a seaside photograph. The loudspeaker plays the sound of a bell ringing.

Image intelligente (Jardin, Centrale nucléaire) [Intelligent Image (Garden, Nuclear Power Station)], 1989 With Pierre Joseph ⊲ ¬ C-print on foam board (60 × 90 cm) • loudspeaker (approx. 17 × 8 ×3 cm) stuck onto the photograph • motion detector (2 × ø 1.7 cm) under the loudspeaker • tape || 1 edition *Image intelligente (Jardin, Centrale nucléaire)*, a photograph of a wild and flourishing garden next to *La Hague*. The loudspeaker plays the ambient noises of a nuclear power station.

Image intelligente (Pinson, Science-fiction) [Intelligent Image (Finch, Science-Fiction)], 1989 With Pierre Joseph ◊ ¬ C-print on foam board (60 × 90 cm) • loudspeaker (approx. 17 × 8 × 3 cm) stuck onto the photograph • motion detector (2 × ø 1.7 cm) under the loudspeaker, tape; photograph by the Jacana Agency || 1 edition ∫ Private collection, Monaco ***Image intelligente (Pinson, Science-fiction)*****, a photograph of a finch on a branch. The loudspeaker plays an unknown science-fiction film sound track.**

Image intelligente (Oiseaux, Piano) [Intelligent Image (Birds, Piano)], 1989 With Pierre Joseph ◊ ¬ C-print on foam board (60 × 90 cm) • loudspeaker (approx. 17 × 8 × 3 cm) stuck onto the photograph • motion detector (2 × ø 1.7 cm) under the loudspeaker • tape • photograph by Christophe Durand-Ruel || 1 edition ∫ Private collection, Monaco ***Image intelligente (Oiseaux, Piano),*** **a photograph of birds. The loudspeaker plays the sound of a piano.**

Image intelligente (Éléphants, Bruitage cinéma) [Intelligent Image (Elephants, film sound effects)], 1989 With Pierre Joseph ◊ ¬ C-print on foam board (60 × 90 cm) • loudspeaker (approx. 17 × 8 × 3 cm) stuck onto the photograph • motion detector (2 × ø 1.7 cm) under the loudspeaker, • tape • photograph by Christophe Durand-Ruel || 1 edition ∫ Private collection, Monaco ***Image intelligente (Éléphants, Bruitage cinéma),*** **a photograph of elephants. The loudspeaker plays sound effects from an unknown film.**

P.I.P. Fleurs [P.I.P. Flowers], 1989 With Pierre Joseph ◊ Installation: ¬ television • videotape recorder *Picture in Picture* • videotape *Fleurs*, [Flowers] 52', on a loop ‡ "Galerie intelligente" (Intelligent Gallery), November 30, 1989–January 13, 1990, Galerie des Archives, Paris, France § Courtesy of the artists ***P.I.P. Fleurs*** **[P.I.P. Flowers] is a video installation using the first** ***Picture in Picture*** **system. Parreno's video** ***Fleurs*** **appears continually in the upper right-hand corner of the screen while the rest of the screen shows the television's usual channels.**

How We Gonna Behave, 1990 With Bernard Joisten and Pierre Joseph, ‡ "The Köln Show," April 24–May 26, 1990, Max Hetzler Gallery, Cologne, Germany
How We Gonna Behave, 1990 With Bernard Joisten and Pierre Joseph ◊ Installation: ¬ *They live* Polarizing linear glasses and glass suspension (Bernard Joisten) • 10 pairs of *Reebok Pump* sneakers available for visitors (Pierre Joseph) • *Create Your Own Program*, video, 2'35" (Philippe Parreno) • *A Do It Yourself Catalogue* (Bernard Joisten, Pierre Joseph and Philippe Parreno) § Courtesy of the artists ♦ **A Do It Yourself Catalogue, 1990** With Bernard Joisten and Pierre Joseph ◊ ¬ Disposable camera (approx. 11 × 6 × 3 cm) • printed band || 50 editions ∫ First private collection: private collection, Paris, France **As part of the group installation-exhibition** ***How We Gonna Behave*****, at the Max Hetzler Gallery in Cologne,**

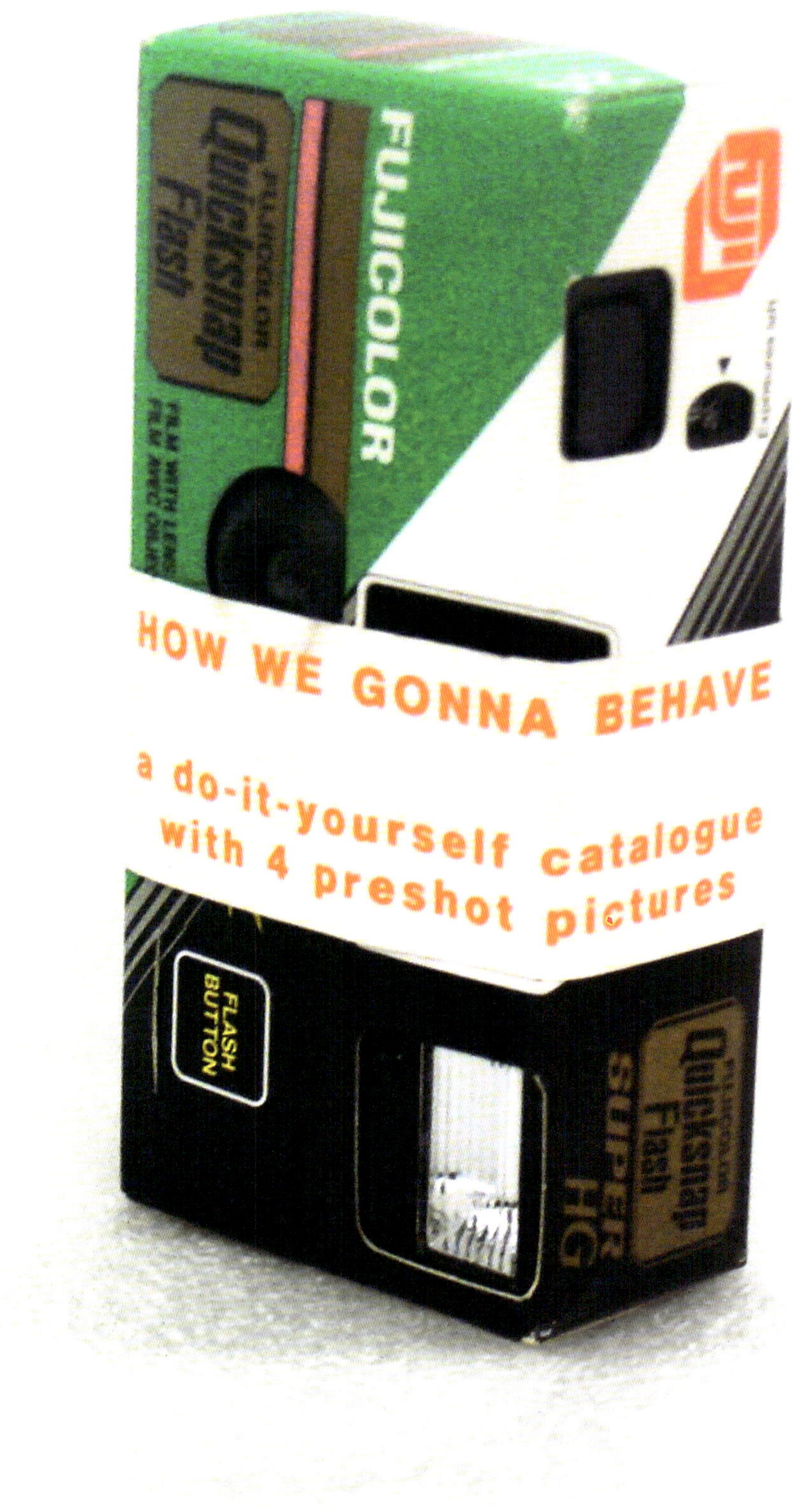

A Do It Yourself Catalogue, 1990, with Bernard Joisten and Pierre Joseph

Parreno presents *Create Your Own Program,* a short video of a narrator reading the exhibition text. In addition to Parreno's video, Joseph presents 10 pairs of Reebok Pumps available for the visitor to wear on a walk around Cologne, and Joisten offers a pair of polarizing linear glasses to look at a stereoscopic poster. The three artists also publish a *Do It Yourself* catalogue presented in the form of a disposable camera wrapped in a printed band. The camera includes four photographs already taken by the artists—the rest of the roll must be shot and developed by the buyer. "Contemporary art has become an art of real time," they write in the exhibition brochure: "We take our work very seriously, but we also have a lot of fun." This work is the art of young people who sometimes have the feeling that their "future is already written in advance" and thus offers the spectator the chance to create his or her reality.

Untitled, 1990 ◁ My First Sony walkmen hung on the wall with infrared headphones, sound track ‡ "French Kiss," May 3–June 17, 1990, Halle Sud, Geneva, Switzerland (exhib. cat.); exhibition curator: Éric Troncy **Parreno places a pair of acoustic infrared headphones for the viewer to wear, which receive broadcasts from local radio stations.**

Composit II, 1990 With Bernard Joisten and Pierre Joseph ◁ Installation: ¬ *Immune System*, adhesive reflectors (Bernard Joisten) • *Hérouville Saint-Clair Project tour, Tchernobyl, feuille irradiée, Data Glove VPL, Vanessa Paradis, Ninja Turtle,* C-prints and ceramic (Pierre Joseph) • *Vues de la Chine* [Views of China], giant color photocopies, variable dimensions (Philippe Parreno) • Halogen flashlights, color filters, variable dimensions ‡ "Court-métrages immobiles" (still short films), May 27–September 30, 1990, Prigioni, Italy, for the XLIV Venice Biennial (exhib. cat.); exhibition curator: Nicolas Bourriaud § Courtesy of the artists **Flashlights are placed on the floor of an unlit exhibition for viewers to explore the works in dim directional light.**

Les Ateliers du Paradise: un film en temps réel [Studios of Paradise: a film in real time], 1990 With Pierre Joseph and Philippe Perrin ‡ August 6–September 8, Air de Paris, Nice, France

Les Ateliers du Paradise: un film en temps réel [Studios of Paradise: a film in real time], 1990 With Pierre Joseph and Philippe Perrin ◁ *Trampoline* (Pierre Joseph) • *Mur Ozone* and *La Bibliothèque du Paradise* (Philippe Parreno) • *P.I.P Fleurs* (Pierre Joseph and Philippe Parreno) • *Panoplie* (Philippe Perrin) • *Love Fame Hate,* 3 molds of Marcel Cerdan's fist, gold, silver, bronze, engraved (Philippe Perrin) • *Philippe Perrin Ultra light,* PLV color photo on cut wood (Philippe Perrin) • *719-223-UB,* cardboard box, revolver, press clippings, stamped registration form, (Philippe Perrin) • *Strictly Business in Aqua blue: Le regard du requin* (Philippe Perrin) • 50 *T-shirts des Ateliers du Paradise,* edition GDL (Pierre Joseph, Philippe Parreno and Philippe Perrin) • one unpacked *Sac Ozone* (Dominique Gonzalez-Foerster,

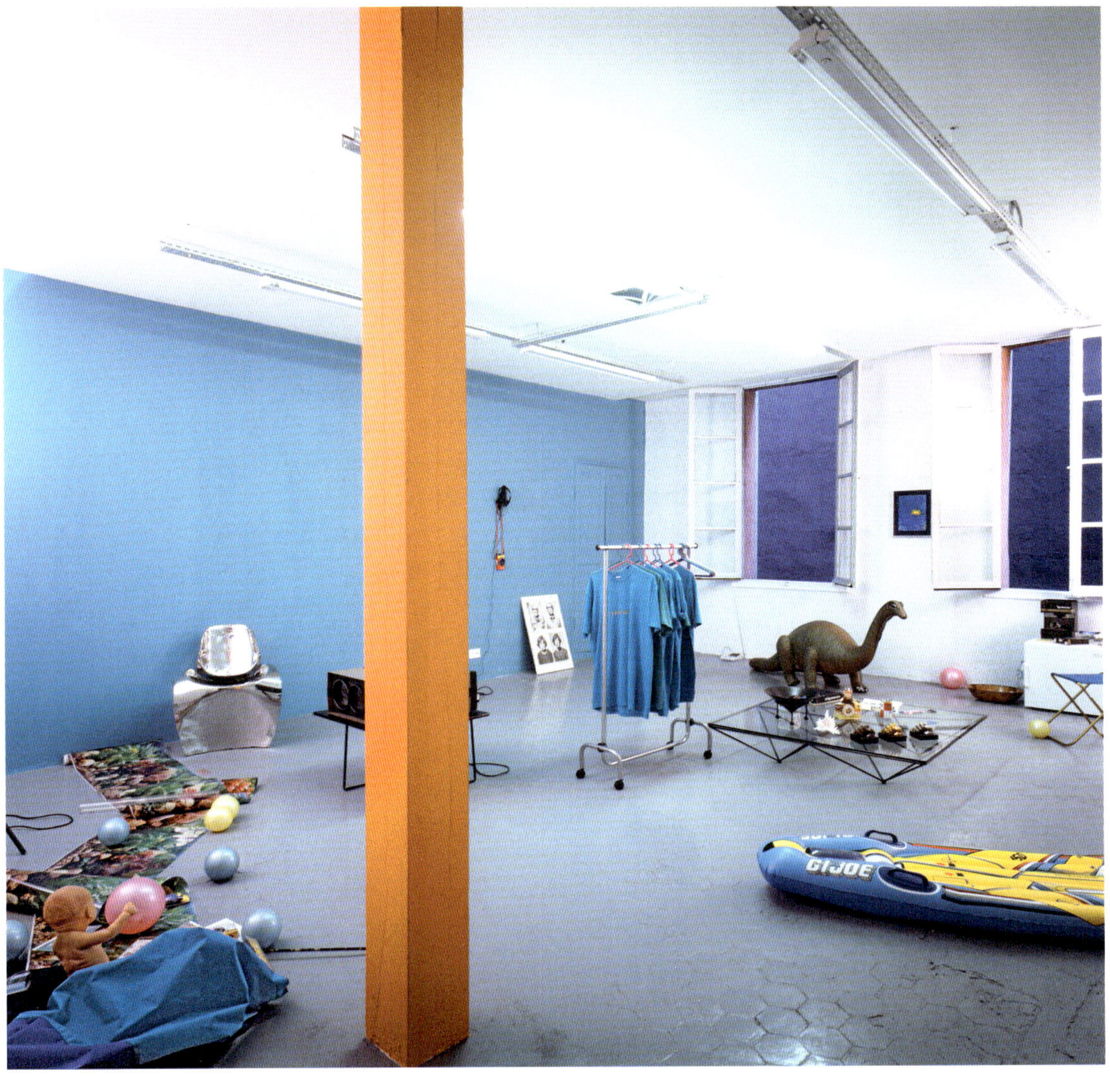

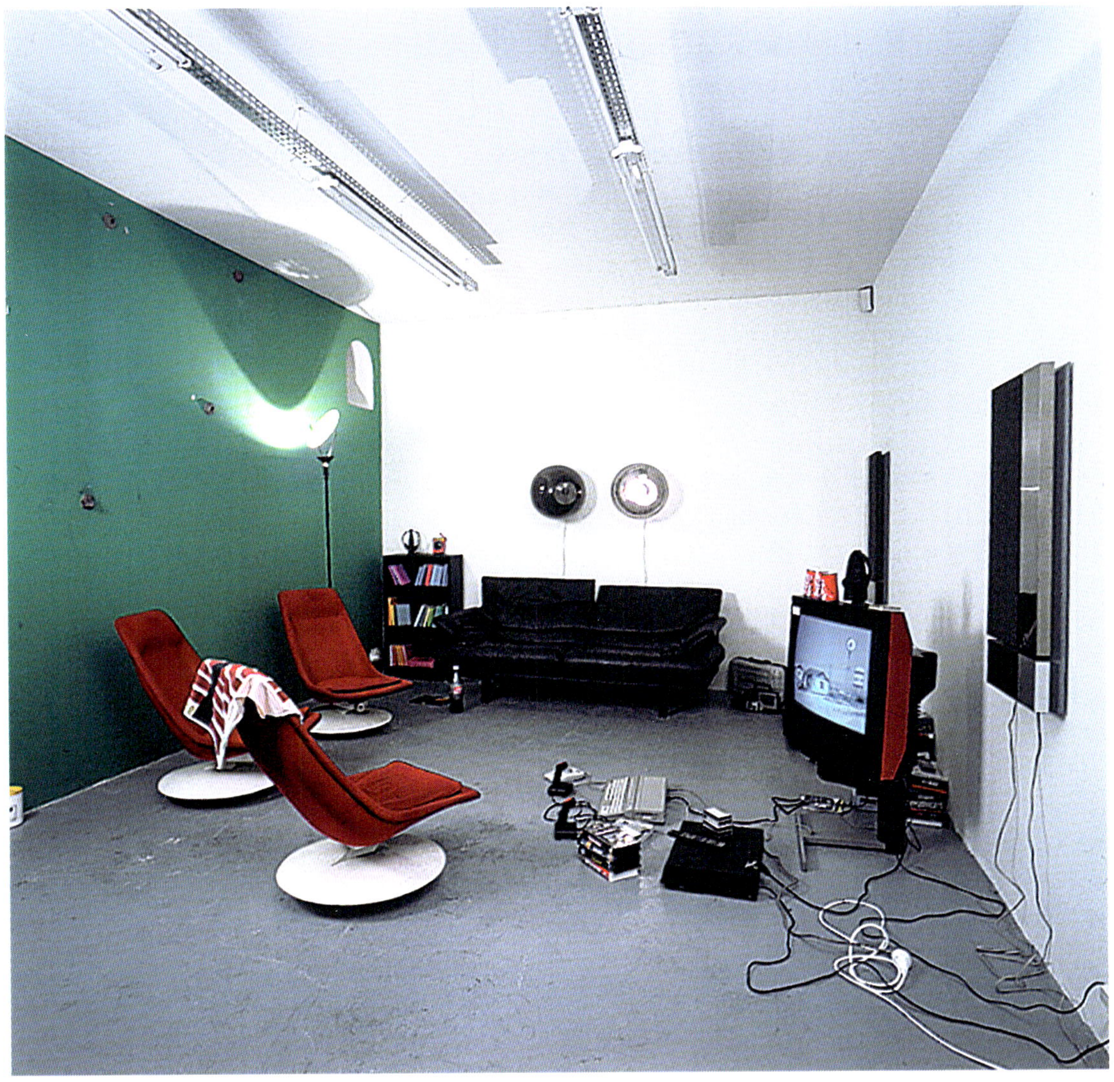

Les Ateliers du Paradise : un film en temps réel, 1990, with Pierre Joseph and Philippe Perrin, exhibition views, Air de Paris, Nice

Bernard Joisten, Pierre Joseph and Philippe Parreno) • Works by other artists: *Double Switch Piece* (Angela Bulloch) • 3 *Peluche* (3 stuffed animals), one red, one brown, one purple (Laurent Faulon) • 1 *Save* trash can (Dominique Gonzalez-Foerster) • 1 poster (Bernard Joisten) • *Hommage à Freud (*Michel Journiac) • 1 pink *Air de Paris* poster (Louise Lawler) • child's drawing (Édouard Merino) • *Big Nude # 3*, 1980, silver print, 200 × 100 cm (Helmut Newton) • *Maison no 8* (Andreas Schulze) ◁ Installation: ¬ 1 wall painted orange • 1 wall painted apple-green • 1 wall painted blue • 1 bay window • 1 black leather sofa • 3 red swivel chairs • 1 Ron Arad chair • 1 Decathlon work-out bench • 1 fitness bicycle • 1 shelf with archives • 1 work table • 1 fan on turning pedestal • 1 metal ladder • 1 Minitel 12 • 1 Royal typewriter • 1 Macintosh SE computer • 1 LaserWriter printer • 1 Atari play station • 1 Bang & Olufsen Hi-Fi system • 1 Bang & Olufsen television • 1 JVC videotape recorder • 1 video projector • 1 Minolta camera • 1 Combo tape recorder • 1 Panasonic wireless telephone answering machine • 1 alarm clock in the form of an Indian playing a tom-tom • 1 stocked refrigerator • 1 Nespresso coffee machine • 1 pack of Marlboro Gold cigarettes • scissors • pens • cutting knives • Spanish white out and yellow pigment • 1 bouquet of tuberoses • 1 V8 video • 1 advertising poster of the video game magazine *Génération 4* • 1 poster of the film *Baxter* • 1 excerpt from the screenplay of *Baxter* • 1 photo of K9 • post cards • mail • 1 jar of magnesia for rock climbing • 3 battery powered dancing bottles of Coca-Cola • 1 stoïaque • blouses, Jean-Paul Gaultier pants and T-shirts • 1 metal and glass coffee table • 1 fruit bowl with fruit and vegetables • playing cards • dice • 1 pearl shell emitting the sound of the sea • 1 Halogen lamp • 1 pair of flippers • 1 inflatable mattress • 1 Castel Plage mattress • audio tapes, (*Le Grand Bleu*, Vanessa Paradis, Cheb Kader, Prince, Patrick Juvet, Michel Polnareff, Soul II Soul, Serge Gainsbourg, Sex Pistols, UB40, The Clash, etc.) • videotapes (*Le Grand Bleu*, *Excalibur*, *Highlander*, *New York 1997*, *Raging Bull*, *Mad Max I*, *II* and *III*, *L'Aventure intérieure*, *Le Nom de la rose*, all the *James Bond* films, *La Belle et la Bête*, etc.) • video games ("Ferrari," "Falcon," "Batman," "Raiders of the Lost Arc," "Future Dreams," "Chase H.Q.," etc.) § Courtesy of the artists and the Air de Paris Gallery, Paris **♦ T-shirts des Ateliers du Paradise [T-shirts from the Studios of Paradise], 1990** With Pierre Joseph and Philippe Perrin ◁ || Edition of 50 T-shirts in three colors: blue, green and pink. Each T-shirt is embroidered on the front with a word in gold thread ("l'espion" (the spy), "la gifle" (the slap), "le pourquoi" (the why), etc.) and, on the back, the exhibition's credits. || Production: GDL Edition, Nice ʃ Several private collections § Courtesy of the artists and the Air de Paris Gallery, Paris **♦ La Bibliothèque du Paradise [The Library of Paradise], 1990** ◁ Installation: ¬ Ikea shelf (106 × 60 × 28 cm) • 34 books and 34 covers, each of a different color ‡ "Les Ateliers du Paradise: un film en temps réel," August 6–September 8, 1990, Air de Paris Gallery, Nice, France || First edition of an un-numbered series § Courtesy Air de Paris Gallery, Paris

♦ **Mur Ozone [Ozone Wall], 1990** ◁ 20 rock climbing grips, variable dimensions and arrangements || First edition of an un-numbered series § Courtesy Air de Paris Gallery, Paris **Parreno, Joseph and Philippe Perrin asked their new gallery, Air de Paris (formed by Édouard Merino and Florence Bonnefous) to aid in acquiring an informal summer studio.[11] Located at 18 rue de la Barillerie, Nice, the artists transformed the gallery for one month into a living space —a place offering new models of habitation based on the most up to date technology. Around a sofa and armchairs was a television, an Atari video game station, a video library of popular films, a record collection of the generation's hits—from Vanessa Paradis to the music of the Luc Besson film *Le Grand Bleu* (1988)—, a Minitel, a computer, a typewriter, an exercise bicycle, a well stocked refrigerator and a coffee machine, etc. Displayed against brightly painted walls are several works by Helmut Newton, Louise Lawler, Joisten and Angela Bulloch mixed with works by the show's artists including *Mur Ozone, La Bibliothèque du Paradise* and displayed on a shelf was a new sound piece by Parreno that could be played on a *My First Sony Walkman*. *Mur Ozone,* having been previously exhibited among other works at the *Ozone* booth at Art Cologne in 1989, was incorporated into this exhibition. Molded dolphin and griffin heads which function as grips allow the viewer to traverse the walls. During the opening on August 6, 1990, a rock climber used the grips as a stylized climbing wall to navigate the gallery without ever touching the ground. ◊ The *Bibliothèque du Paradise* presented thirty or so books, each wrapped in a different color paper on a low Ikea shelf. The books were chosen by Parreno for their informational value, but then transformed into aesthetic objects, based upon a non-relational taste-based system of coding. ◊ The blue *T-shirts* from the *Ateliers du Paradise* (an edition of fifty, although five-hundred were originally planned) were printed with the exhibition title and credits on the back. In addition, on the front of each shirt a different word was sewn in gold thread, eg.: "pomme" [apple], "diable" [devil], "requin" [shark], "ex-boyfriend" etc. and were worn by the public at the opening. The shirts, by designating different characters, animals and objects, schematize a role-playing game where the viewers become actors in an improvisational narrative, which the film director Marion Vernoux wrote a screenplay on the gallery's computer as she observed the random interactions between gallery-goers.[12] ◊ This event in "real time," a fundamental notion in Parreno's work, merges a conceptual narrative (screenplay) with the event (opening) that it describes in order to create a subjective, and cultural model of time. "Confinement, real time, games and the exhibition of everyday life are then at the heart of this project … in a 'particular resemblance' to the future TV reality show *Big Brother*." This "seminal project" in the conception of the artwork as a means of producing "relations"[13] is especially active on the day of the opening, a great moment of conviviality, which is progressively transformed into a "meeting place."[14]**

11. We should note here the influence of Gilles Lipovetsky's thought, prevalent at that time, on the aesthetic of self-service, à la carte service and of the informal —*L'Ère du vide* [The Era of Void], *op.cit.*

12. Reproduced in *Documents sur l'art*, no.8, 1996, p.112-113.

13. Éric Troncy, "Comment l'art contemporain a inventé la TV-realité" [How Contemporary Art invented TV reality], *Beaux-Arts Magazine*, no.242, July 2004, p.44-48.

14. Olivier Antoine, director of the Art:Concept Gallery in Nice, remembers that "the exhibition was more of a set than a living studio" except for the opening when "the visitors found themselves in the most entertaining room: in front of the television with video games or watching videos available in the gallery," *Documents sur l'art*, no.8, 1996, p.109.

Once Upon a Time… in City Bild, 1990 With Pierre Joseph ‡ "Once Upon a Time… in City Bild," October 13–November 10, 1990, Esther Schipper Gallery, Cologne, Germany

Once Upon a Time… in City Bild, 1990 With Pierre Joseph ⊲ Installation: set up of previous exhibition ("City Bild" by Peter Fend, September 14–October 5, 1990) ¬ 1 video installation *La Fée* [The Fairy] (Brandt model color television monitor 1970) • *La Fée*, VHS videotape, color, sound, 32' • golden aluminum paper crown • Afghan rug with design of Kalashnikovs and tanks 1988 • mattress, 250 × 150 × 10 cm • cushions) • 1 sound installation *The Never Ending Story* • 1 sound installation *Once Upon a Time… in City Bild* • 4 posters of exotic landscape photos (2 of tropical forests and 2 of Pacific beaches), stuck behind the windows of the exhibition space (Dominique Gonzalez-Foerster) • turquoise carpet • anamorphous color copy • giant alarm clock (H.: 24 cm; diam.: 42 cm) frozen at 11 o'clock • lamp projecting a rainbow on the wall, variable dimensions § Courtesy of the artists and Esther Schipper, Berlin ♦ **The Never Ending Story, 1990** With Pierre Joseph ⊲ Installation: ¬ 4 infrared headphones • 4 walkmen • 1 radio tape player • 5 audio tapes *The Never Ending Story* (several radio shows play on a loop: the news, an educational speech, a weather forecast and an advertisement) || 1 edition § Courtesy Esther Schipper, Berlin and Air de Paris, Paris ♦ **Once Upon a Time… in City Bild, 1990** With Pierre Joseph ⊲ VHS video, color, sound, 60'; box with green and gold cover designed by the artists || 10 editions § Courtesy Esther Schipper, Berlin and Air de Paris, Paris **At the Esther Schipper Gallery in Cologne, Joseph and Parreno decided to mount an exhibition within an exhibition. By extending the previous show, Peter Fend's *City Bild,* a continuously moving utopian city whose energy is provided by the decomposition of seaweed, they subverted the normative time of an exhibition, as well as created a larger context for *City Bild* by producing a science-fiction tale through different media: videos (*Once Upon a Time… in City Bild* and a VHS tape with a green and golden cover); audio tapes (*The Never Ending Story* of radio news, an educational talk, a weather forecast and an advertisement); a giant clock shows the time (frozen at eleven o'clock at night). A monitor, placed next to an Afghan woven rug incorporating imagery of war, plays a video entitled *La Fée* [The Fairy], an advertisement for chocolate. Although chocolate has disappeared from this universe, a fairy explains that eating chocolate makes one happy. Dominique Gonzalez-Foerster is commissioned to make four posters of a tropical landscape which were placed in front of each window of the exhibition space.**

No More Reality

No More Reality, une vidéoconférence, 1991 Other title: *No More Reality I* ⊲ U-matic video transferred onto VHS, color, sound, 38'; direction: Georges Rey || Edition Videodrome Collection [Air de Paris, France] ‡ May 23–27, 1991, Air de Paris / Esther Schipper / Art Forum booth, Art Jonction, Nice, France || 50 editions

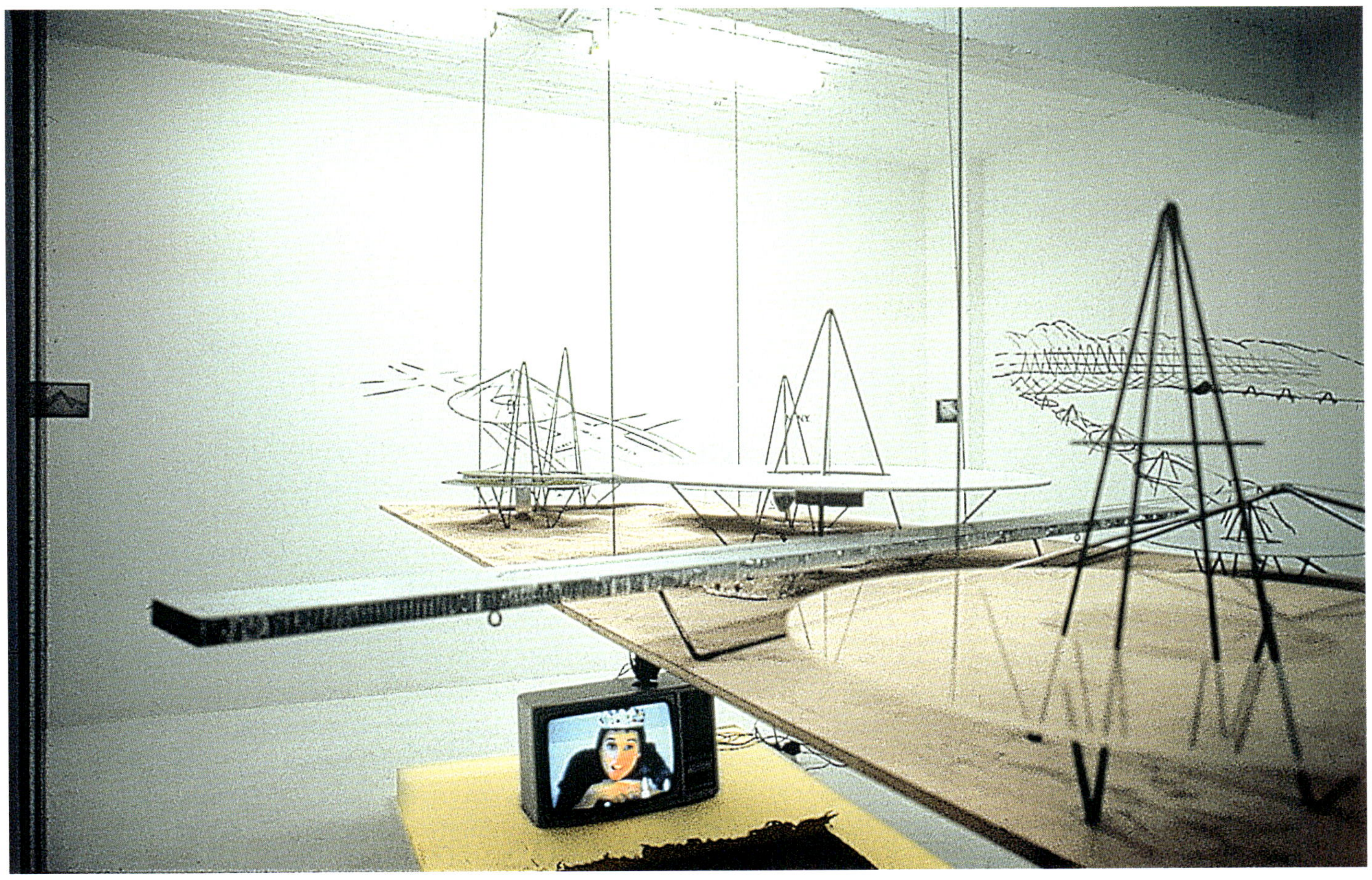

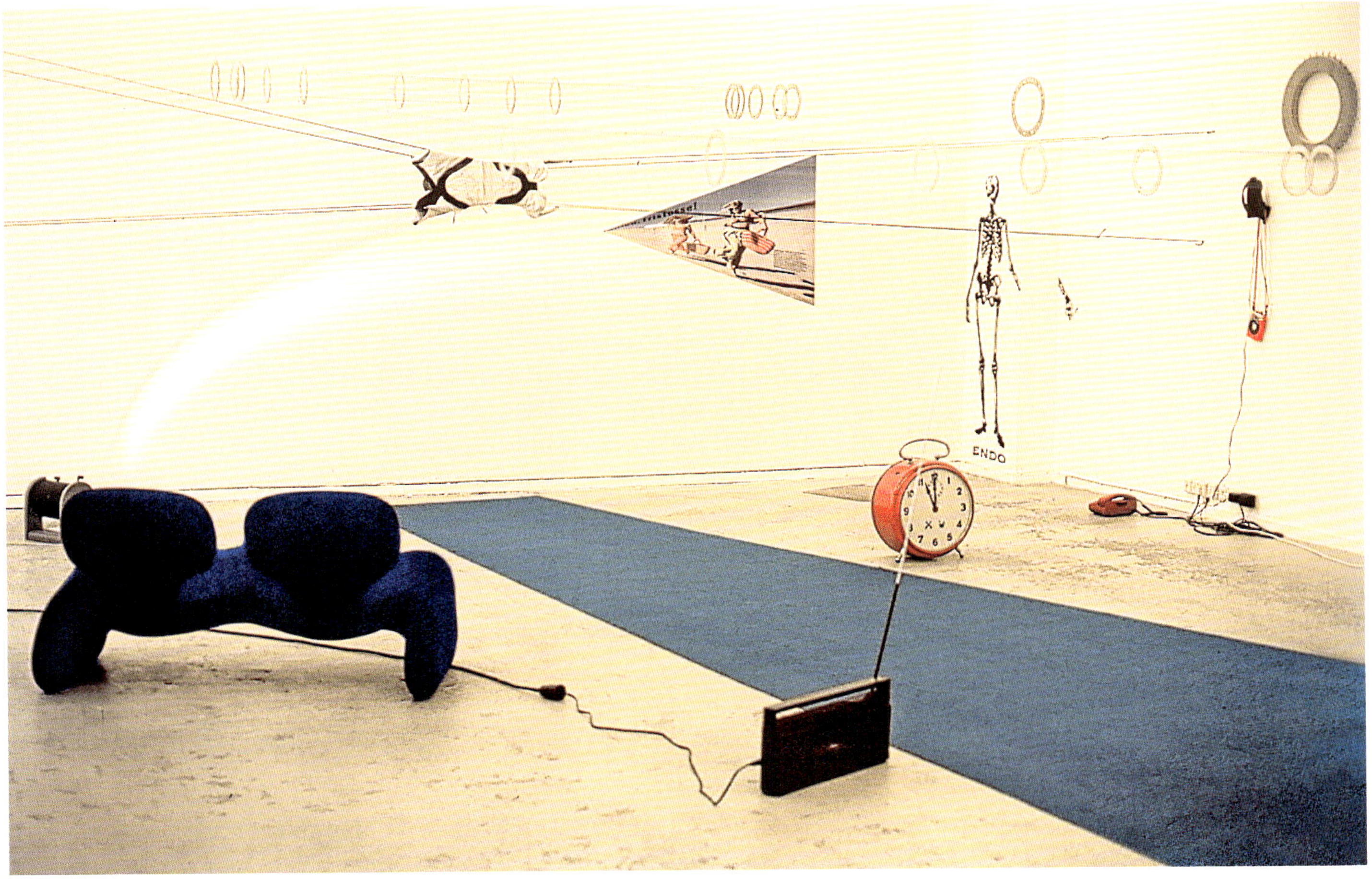

Once Upon a Time... in City Bild, 1990, with Pierre Joseph, exhibition views, Esther Schipper, Berlin

in VHS copyleft || Un-numbered U-matic edition with projection rights for institutions ʃ First public collection: Frac Lorraine, Metz, France § Courtesy Air de Paris Paris **Presented for the first time in May 1991 at Art Jonction in Nice, the video, *No More Reality, une vidéoconférence* is a caricature of an art critic played by Parreno who speaks in incomprehensible verbiage in five different languages. A close up shot shows the artist repeating the slogan "No more reality" while hitting his head and grimacing. The stuttering character is inspired by Ron Pearlman's portrayal of Salvatore in the film *The Name of the Rose,* and gives a lecture about the relationship between art and power, from Filippo Lippi to Daniel Buren, that is both comical and pathetic. Through imitation, this video satirizes the hierarchical-cultural implications of specialized language. ◊ The video was also presented in 1992 as an installation projected onto the back of a transparent PVC curtain. The curtain blocks the exhibition entrance so that the visitor has to walk through an enlarged image of the artist's talking head in order to pass through the exhibition. ◊ Taking an anthropological stance, Parreno observes the disjointed relationship between language and behavior as a means to question the nature of the "real," playfully utilizing impersonations of Jean-Luc Godard or Jacques Toubon by Yves Lecoq, a sensibility which informed works such as *Vous la connaissez ?* [Do you know this one?].**
No More Reality, 1991 ◁ C-print mounted on aluminum and framed, 78 × 66 cm || 1 edition ʃ Private collection, Monaco || **First C-print of the photograph used for the cover of the VHS tape *No More Reality, une vidéoconférence.*** ♦ **No More Reality, 1991** ◁ C-print mounted on aluminum and framed, 75 × 62 cm || 1 edition ʃ Private collection, Lille, France || **Second C-print, with different frames and dimensions, of the photograph used for the cover of the VHS tape *No More Reality, une vidéoconférence.*** ♦ **No More Reality, la manifestation [No More Reality, the demonstration], 1991** Other title: *No More Reality II* ◁ Installation: ¬ collection of banners • black and white photocopied flyers on colored paper distributed at the entrance of the Villa Arson in Nice • video *No More Reality, la manifestation* presented on a television monitor; variable dimensions ‡ "No Man's Time," June 6–September 30, 1991, Villa Arson, Nice, France (exhib. cat.); exhibition curator: Éric Troncy § Courtesy Air de Paris, Paris ♦ **No More Reality, la manifestation, 1991** Other title: *No More Reality II* ◁ U-matic video transferred onto Beta cam SP, color, sound, 4'; direction: Bertrand Corre || Edition Videodrome Collection [Air de Paris] ‡ "No Man's Time," June 6–September 30, 1991, Villa Arson, Nice (exhib. cat.); exhibition curator: Éric Troncy || 50 VHS editions under copyleft; U-matic un-numbered edition with projection rights for institutions ʃ First public collection: Frac Lorraine, Metz, France § Courtesy Air de Paris, Paris ♦ **No More Reality, 1991** Other title: *475 Frames From Gremlins 2* ◁ Installation: ¬ photocopier • Mogwai stuffed animal • a hundred black and white photocopies, variable dimensions ‡ "No Man's Time," June 6–September 30, 1991, Villa Arson, Nice (exhib. cat.); exhibition curator: Éric Troncy || 1 edition

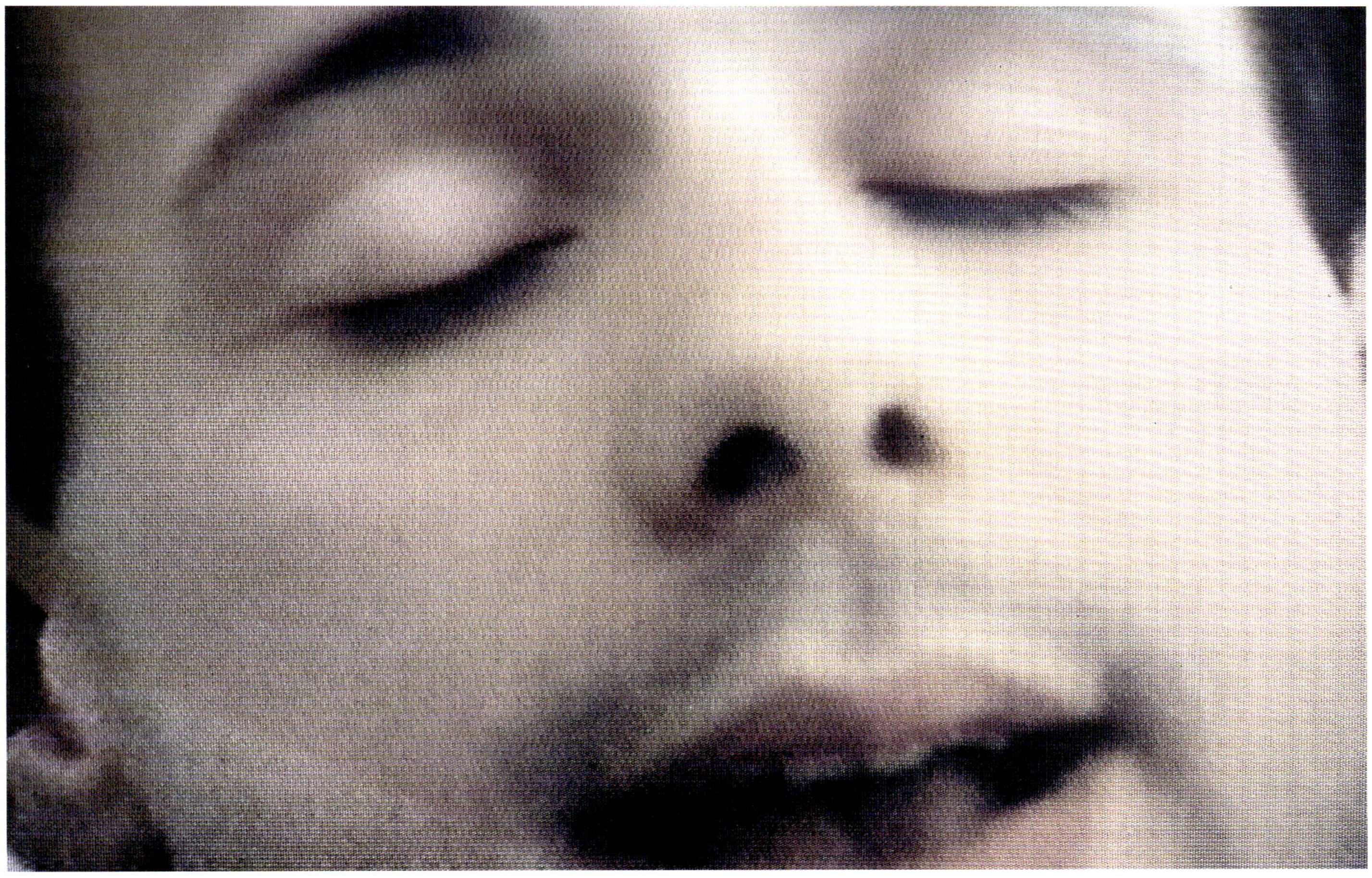

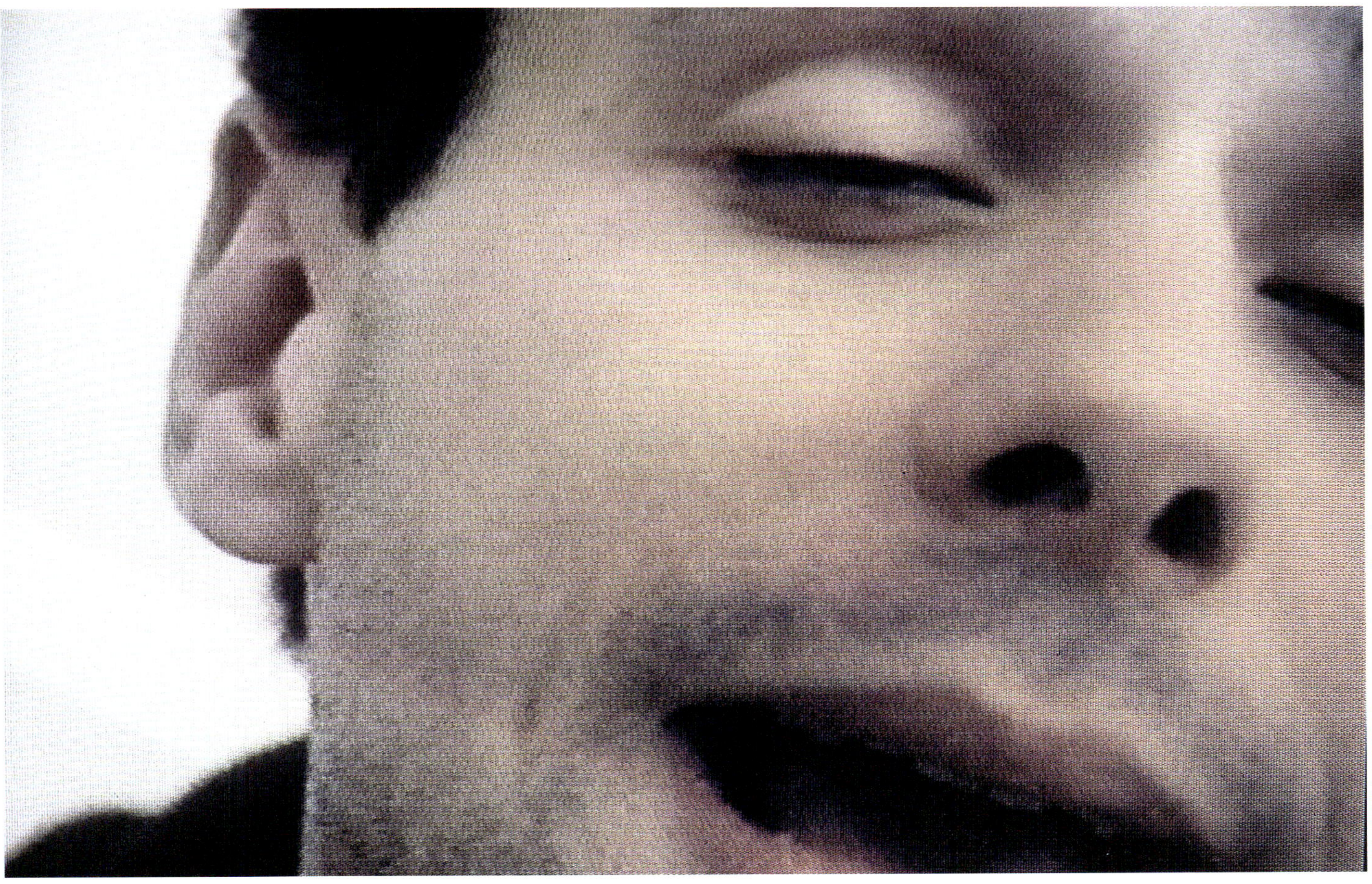

No More Reality, une vidéoconférence, No More Reality I, 1991, video

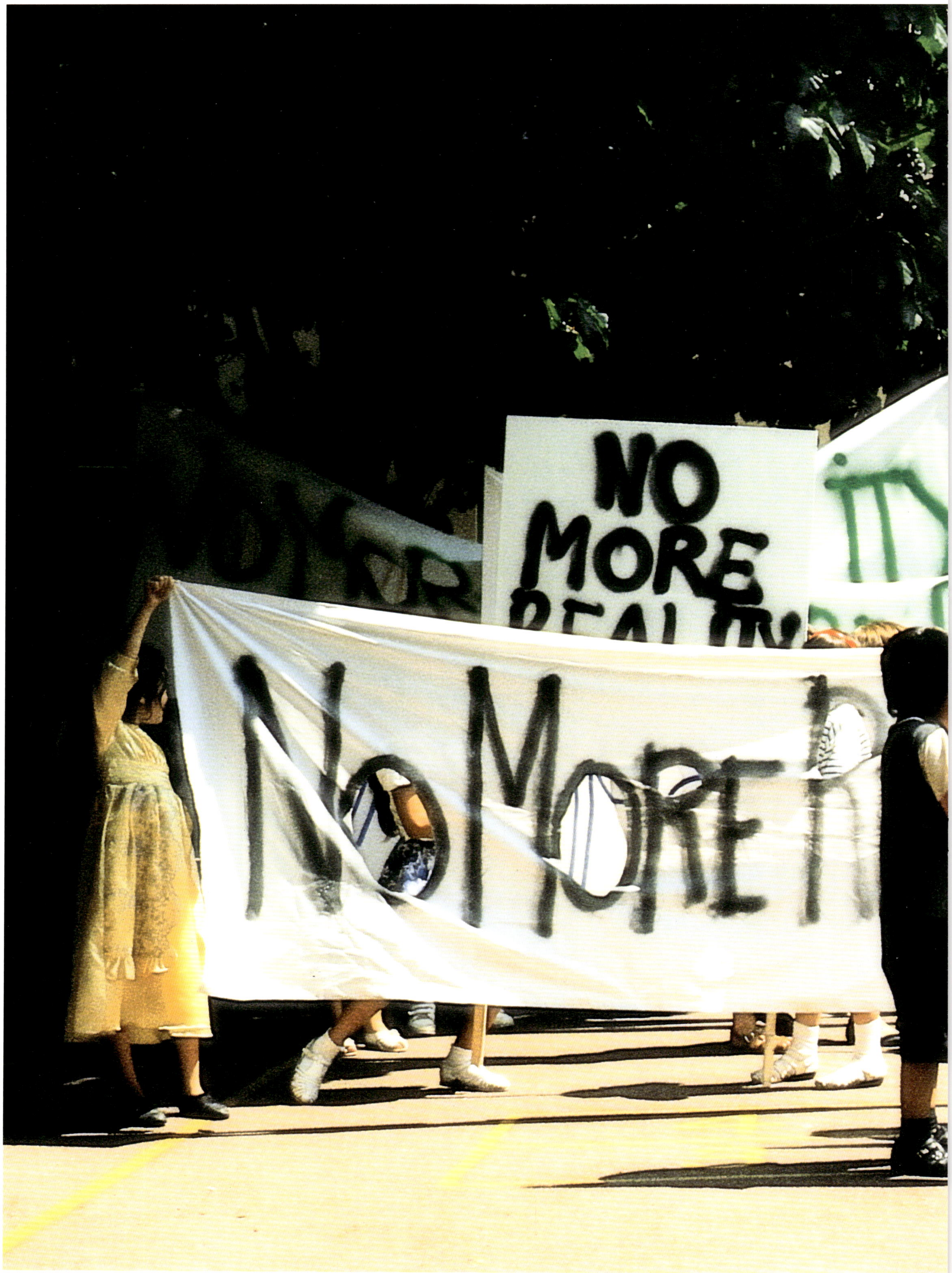

No More Reality, la manifestation, No More Reality II, 1991

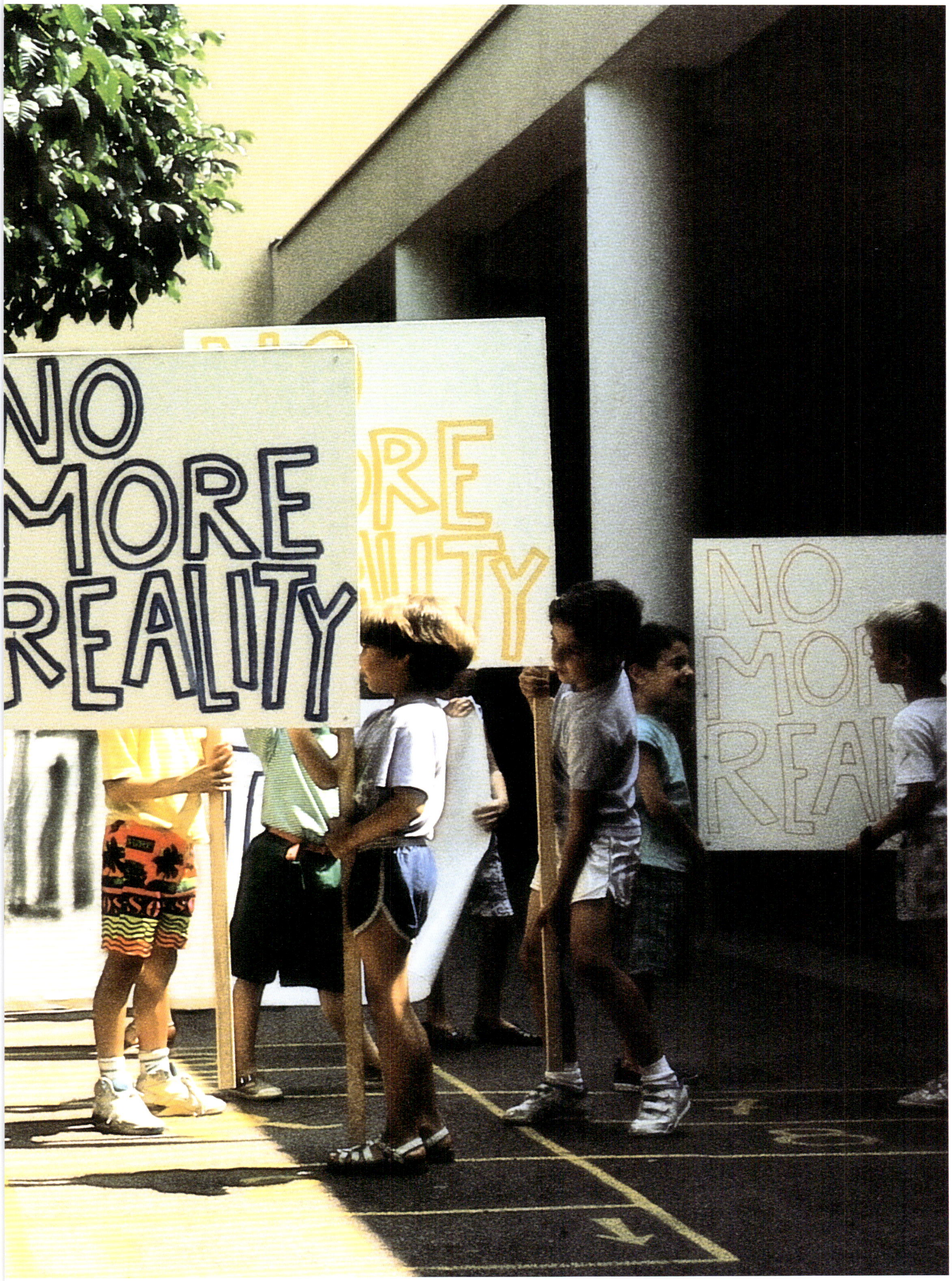
NO
MORE
REALITY

15. Philippe Parreno in *No Man's Time*, exhibition catalogue directed by Christian Bernard, Nice, Villa Arson, 1991, p.124-193.

ʃ Private collection, Paris, France ♦ **No More Reality, 1991** Other title: *150 Frames From Alf* ◁ Installation: ¬ toaster • around one hundred pieces of toast; variable dimensions ‡ "No Man's Time," June 6–September 30, 1991, Villa Arson, Nice (exhib. cat.); exhibition curator: Éric Troncy || 1 edition ʃ Private collection, Lille, France ♦ **No More Reality, 1991** Other title: *180 Frames From Twin Peaks* ◁ Installation: ¬ Acrylic paint on wooden panel • two sticks; 245 × 200 × 95 cm ‡ "No Man's Time," June 6–September 30, 1991, Villa Arson, Nice (exhib. cat.); exhibition curator: Éric Troncy || 1 edition ʃ Private collection, Venice, Italy

Between 1991 and 1993, the slogan "No more reality" refered to a number of different works. Both the first incarnation, *No More Reality, une vidéoconférence* and the exhibition "No Man's Time," curated by Éric Troncy in addition to the last *75 Frames From Batman Returns* and *125 Frames From Hook* in the exhibition "Le Principe de réalité" [The Principle of Reality] were organized at the Villa Arson in Nice. "No more reality" was the jingle recorded on a continious loop intented for a pirate radio station, Radio Réalité, which would only be heard at the Villa Arson in Nice. However, the project was not realized until 1995, for *Snow Dancing*. ◊ *No More Reality, la manifestation* [No More Reality, the demonstration], a short video (50 copies under copyright and shown under copyleft) along with four photographs document a performance that was the end result of a workshop organized by Parreno in a primary school in Nice. Seven and eight year old children march around a playground shouting "No more reality" waving banners printed with the same slogan. This work gives voice to a disenchanted era where the television image is a "game" or "construction" designed to create "a real effect." Parreno recalls a time at the beginning of the decade when "students went out into the streets shouting 'money, we want money to study better'" and at the same time stole Burberry scarves.[15] Substituting children for adults reinforced the feeling of a depoliticized demonstration, of the *derealization* of the protest's social context. ◊ In the exhibition "No Man's Time," Parreno sets up situations rather than simple objects. With the exception of the video playing on a monitor along with related pamphlets and banners, all of the objects are *frozen images*, i.e. frames from television or films. A wooden panel inscribed "Welcome to Twin Peaks" is installed at the entrance of the Villa Arson garden alluding to the opening credits of David Lynch's television series, *Twin Peaks*. A toaster and approximately one hundred pieces of toast in the gallery bar reference a scene from the television series *Alf* (directed by Tom Patchett). Among these tableaus, the protagonist-creature Gizmo from the films *Gremlins* and *Gremlins 2* (directed by Joe Dante) is portrayed as a stuffed toy flattened on a copier and reproduced in black and white photocopies. ◊ No longer concerned with the individual nuances of reproduction, as in Richard Prince's re-photographs which critique and denounce illusion, Parreno embraces a positive-feedback aesthetic which blurs the lines between fiction and reality by embracing images from popular memory. The questioning of authorship leads to the appropriation of a new genre that contextualizes reality as a

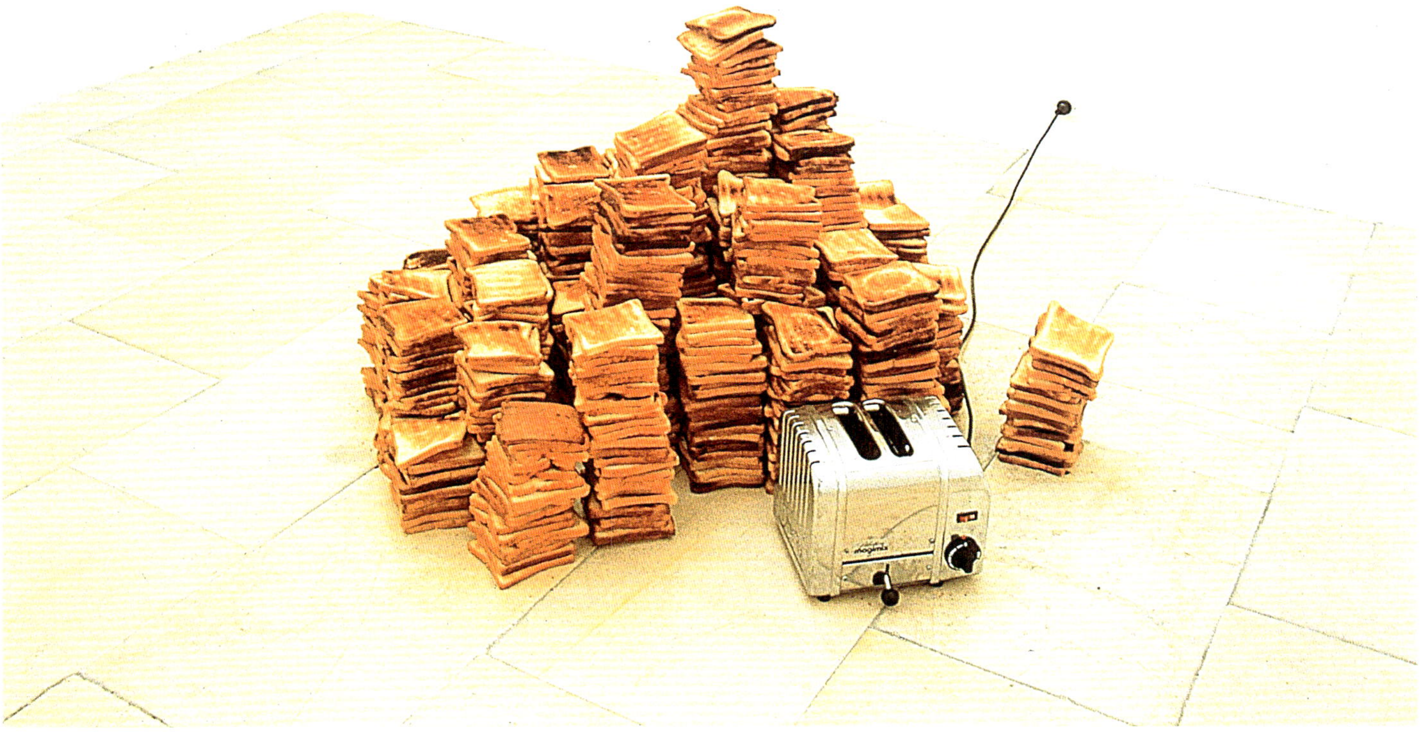

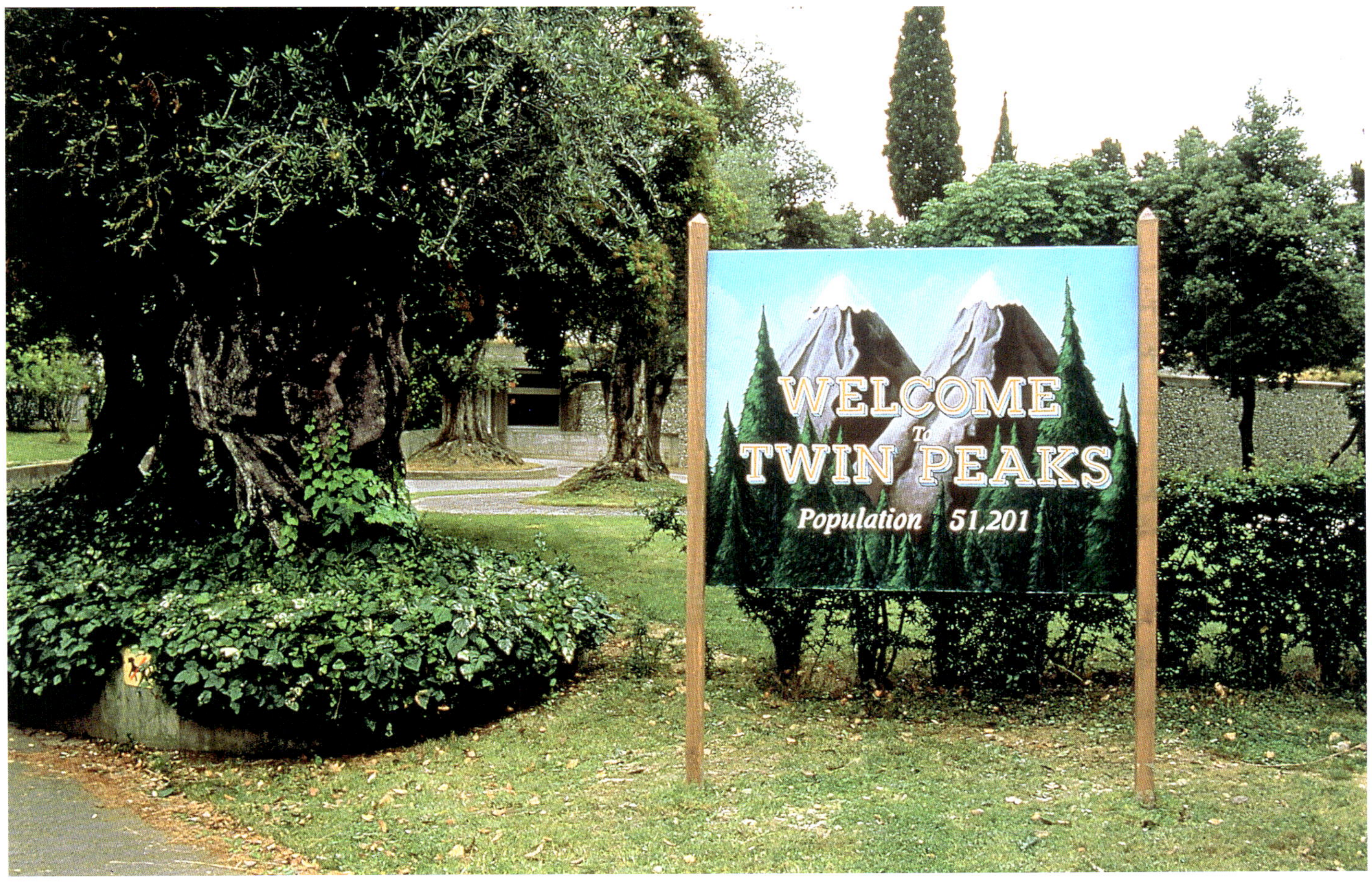

No More Reality, 150 Frames From Alf, **1991,** exhibition view "No Man's Time", Villa Arson, Nice
No More Reality, 180 Frames From Twin Peaks, **1991,** exhibition view "No Man's Time", Villa Arson, Nice

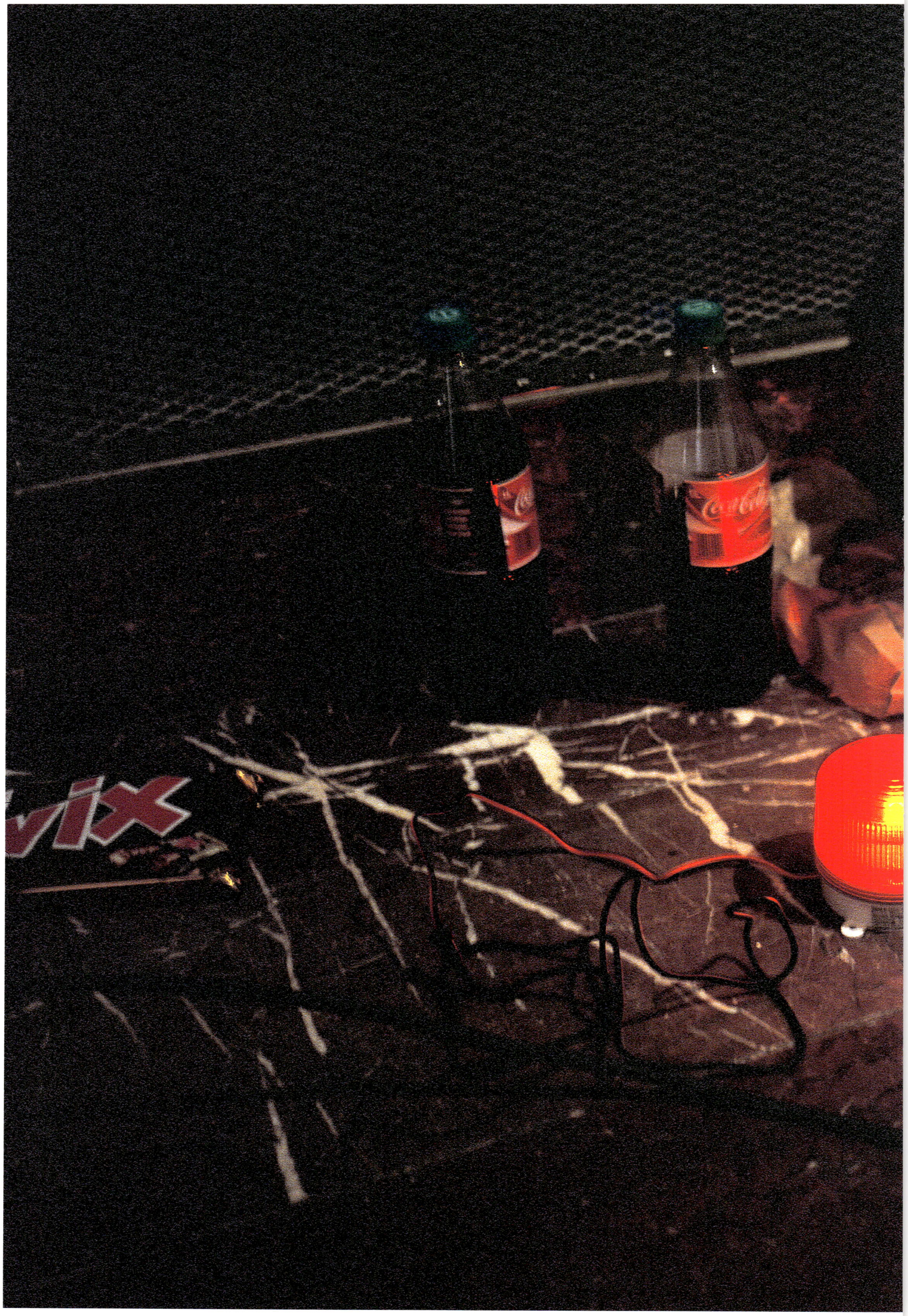

Radio Réalité, 2004, exhibition view "Utopia Station", Haus der Kunst, Munich

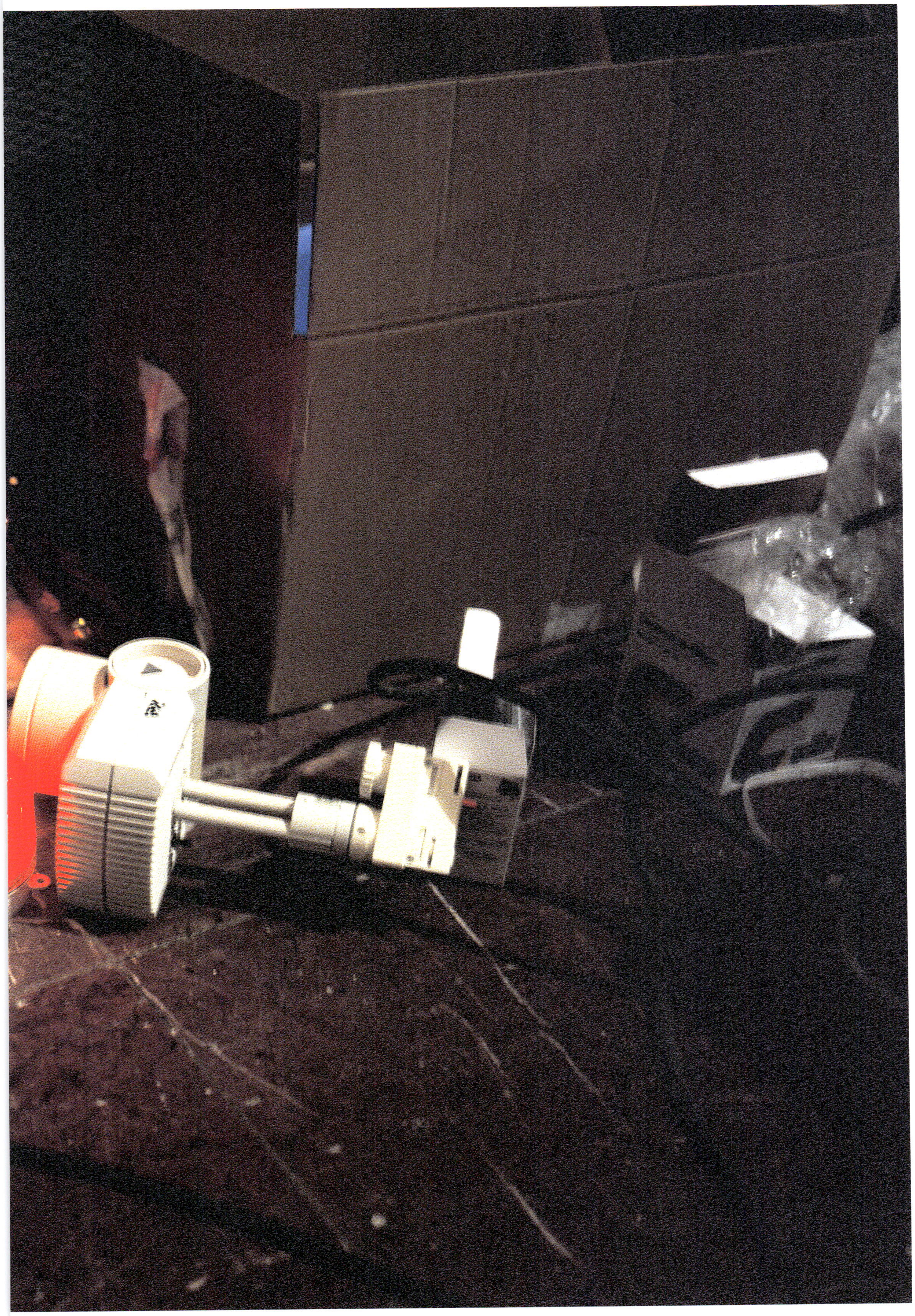

response to "no-more-reality." ◊ Parreno's aesthetic time is a construction predicated upon the understanding that reality can be manipulated, and is indeed protean, and transposed. The word "frame" in the subtitle of *150 Frames From Alf*, for example, is the 150 still-frames from the film. These works are like freeze frames viewed on a television—invoking the now ubiquitous "pause" button, whereby the viewer physically manipulates cinematic time. As Parreno said to the art critic Nicolas Bourriaud:[16] "There is no fundamental difference between the real, the image and the commentary. I am looking for time spaces where these three elements can be approached simultaneously."[17] ◊ At the beginning of the 1990s, Parreno became fascinated with "virtual reality," an expression coined by Jaron Lanier, a self-made man whose company VPL Research[18] developed stereoscopic vision helmets and data gloves that made it possible to "touch" virtual objects, thus immersing the video game player into an entirely synthetic environment.[19] For Parreno, the work only really exists if it is activated by an exhibition or a collector—this is why he did not systematize this body of work or others by titles, but rather emphasizes the syntax of an exhibition and the relationship of the ideas as the linguistic bridge.

16. At the end of the 1980s Philippe Parreno meets Nicolas Bourriaud who exhibits his works for the first time with the group work *Composit II* in "Courts-métrages immobiles" [Immobile short films] at the Venice Biennial 1990.

17. *Art press*, in no.208, December 1995, p.42.

18. See catalogue *No Man's Time*, fax reproduced p.125.

19. *Ibid.*

No More Reality, 1991 ◁ Graffiti made with ketchup ‡ "French Kiss II," July 14–September 30, 1991, Apac, Nevers, France; exhibition curator: Eric Troncy § Courtesy of the artist The slogan "No more reality" is graffitied in ketchup on one of the exhibition walls.

Snaking, 1991 With Pierre Joseph ◁ Installation: ¬ 1 neoprene suit prototype (L.: 200 cm) • 10 color C-prints (60 × 80 cm) • stencil drawings of the silhouette of a snaker (black spray paint, approx. 20 × 20 cm) • various objects on the ground (origami, pebbles, baseball ball, plastic ear, pine cone, bone for dog to gnaw, etc.) • waterproof container named *Snaking Spot*, bearing the inscription "snaking" and can contain the objects on the ground; variable dimensions ‡ "Try Snaking," July 5–September 15, 1991, Air de Paris Gallery, Nice, France || 1 edition ʃ Collection Frac Poitou-Charentes, Angoulême, France Pierre Joseph and Philippe Parreno invent a new sport called *snaking*. The different elements related to this sport are presented during the exhibition "Try Snaking."

Try Snaking, 1991 With Pierre Joseph ◁ ¬ Portfolio of 10 C-prints (13 × 18 cm) and stencil || 8 editions § Courtesy Air de Paris, Paris, France

Try Snaking, 1991/1992 With Pierre Joseph ◁ Neoprene suit, L.: approx. 200 cm || 3 editions made to measure ʃ First collection: private collection, Monaco

Composit III, 1991 With Bernard Joisten and Pierre Joseph ◁ Group of two installations: ¬ Installation in the bedroom: a wall with false bricks made of brown tape and cute into fives (approx. 550 × 300 cm)

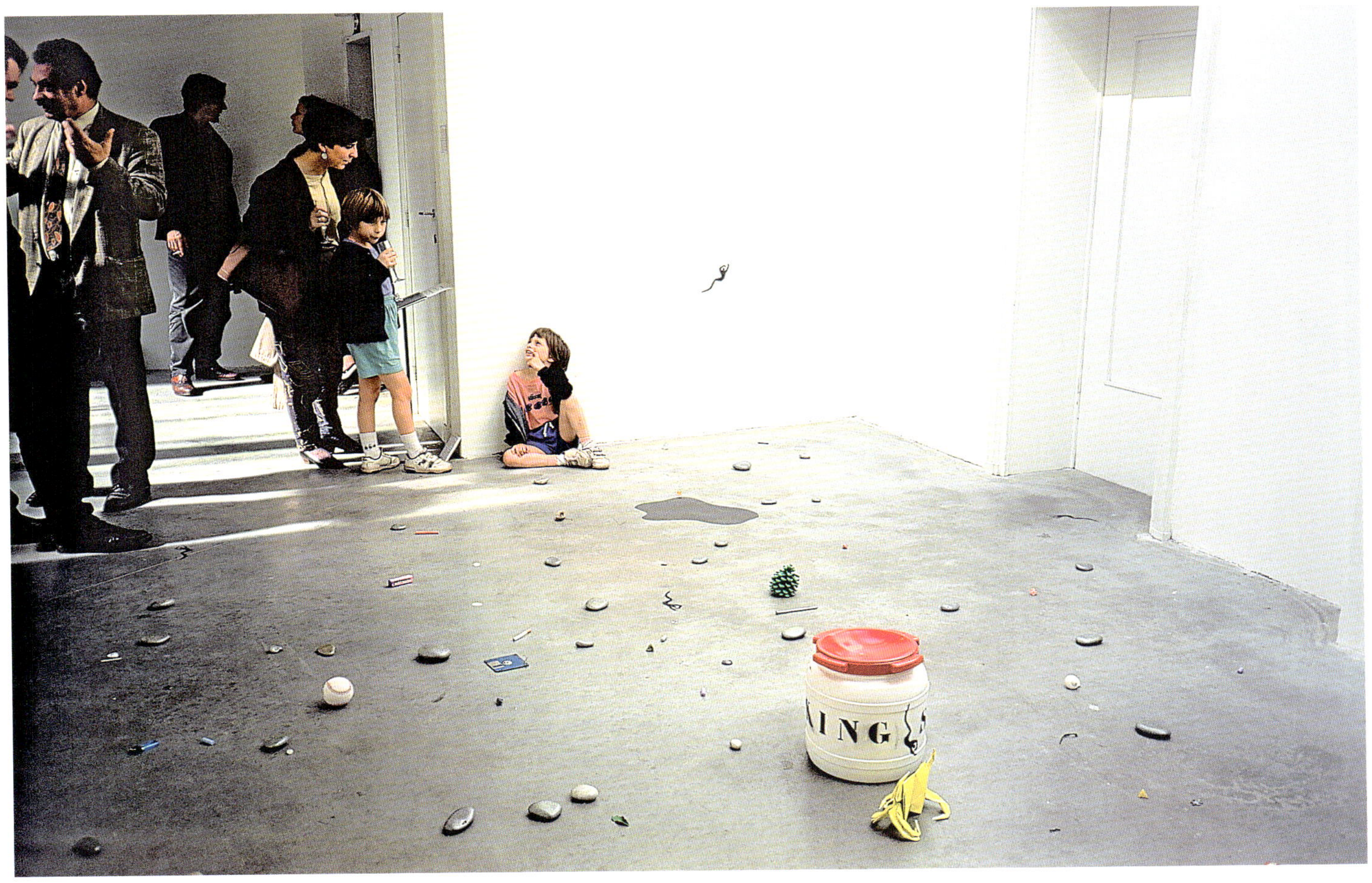

Try Snaking, 1991, exhibition view, Air de Paris, Nice

• 1 graffiti "composit" made with red, black and silver spray paint (approx. 400 × 200 cm) • *Meuble de synthèse (Lampe)* [Synthetic furniture (Lamp)], polished brown wood, (approx. H: 65 cm, diam.: 45 cm) • *Meuble de synthèse (Table basse)* [Synthetic furniture (Coffee table)], polished blue and yellow wood, (approx. 90 × 160 × 90 cm) • six drawers let from the inside and fixed to a varnished wall; various images on the walls (variable techniques and dimensions) • ¬ Installation in the garden: natural rock • engraved gold and silver metal sword, approx. 65 × 30 × 3 cm, ‡ summer 1991, private property, Roquebrune-Cap-Martin, France || 1 edition ʃ Private collection, Roquebrune-Cap-Martin, France

La Vérité* [The Truth*], 1991 With Dominique Gonzalez-Foerster, Bernard Joisten and Pierre Joseph ◁ Installation: ¬ large books in colored carpet (Dominique Gonzalez-Foerster) • knotted rope hanging from the ceiling (Pierre Joseph) • mound of earth with glass trinkets (Bernard Joisten) and street sign (Philippe Parreno) ‡ "L'Amour de l'art" [The Love of Art], September 3–October 13, 1991, Ist Lyons Biennial, Lyons, France (exhib. cat.) § Courtesy of the artists **The title's asterisk refers to the work's subtitle "When everything is hidden, we no longer want to play..."**

La Vérité [The Truth], 1991 ◁ Blue enamel paint on aluminum (approx. 60 × 20 cm) ‡ "L'Amour de l'art" [The Love of Art], September 3–October 13, 1991, Ist Lyons Biennial, Lyons, France (exhib. cat.) || edition of 1 and 1 artist's proof ʃ Private collection, Nice, France **The street sign indicates "the truth" as a place.**

U-Vision, 1991 With Dominique Gonzalez-Foerster, Bernard Joisten and Pierre Joseph ◁ Installation: ¬ 2 × 5 monitors placed not far from the information stands in 2 metro stations, in Vienna • 2 × 5 tape recorders • 2 videotapes *U1-rotes Program,* color, silent, 3' (Philippe Parreno) • 2 videotapes *U2-violettes Programm,* color, silent, 3' (Pierre Joseph) • 2 videotapes *U3-oranges Programm,* color, silent, 3' (Bernard Joisten) • 2 videotapes *U4-grünes Programm,* color, silent, 3' (Dominique Gonzalez-Foerster) • 2 videotapes *U5-blaues Programm,* color, silent, 3' (Dominique Gonzalez-Foerster, Bernard Joisten, Pierre Joseph and Philippe Parreno); dimensions 2 × approx. 50 × 150 cm ‡ "Topographie II: Untergrund," September 27–November 3, 1991, Wiener Festwochen, Vienna, Austria (exhib. cat.) § Courtesy of the artists **Two identical set ups, installed in two metro stations in Vienna during the Wiener Festwochen 1991, are each composed of five monitors placed behind a glass case, presenting five different 3 minutes "programs" on a loop.**

No More Reality, 1991 ◁ Framed color C-print, 80 × 64 cm ‡ "Xmas Show," December 14, 1991–February 14, 1992, Air de Paris Gallery, Nice, France || 1 edition ʃ Private collection, Hossegor, France **Unique print of a photograph of the demonstration "No More Reality."**

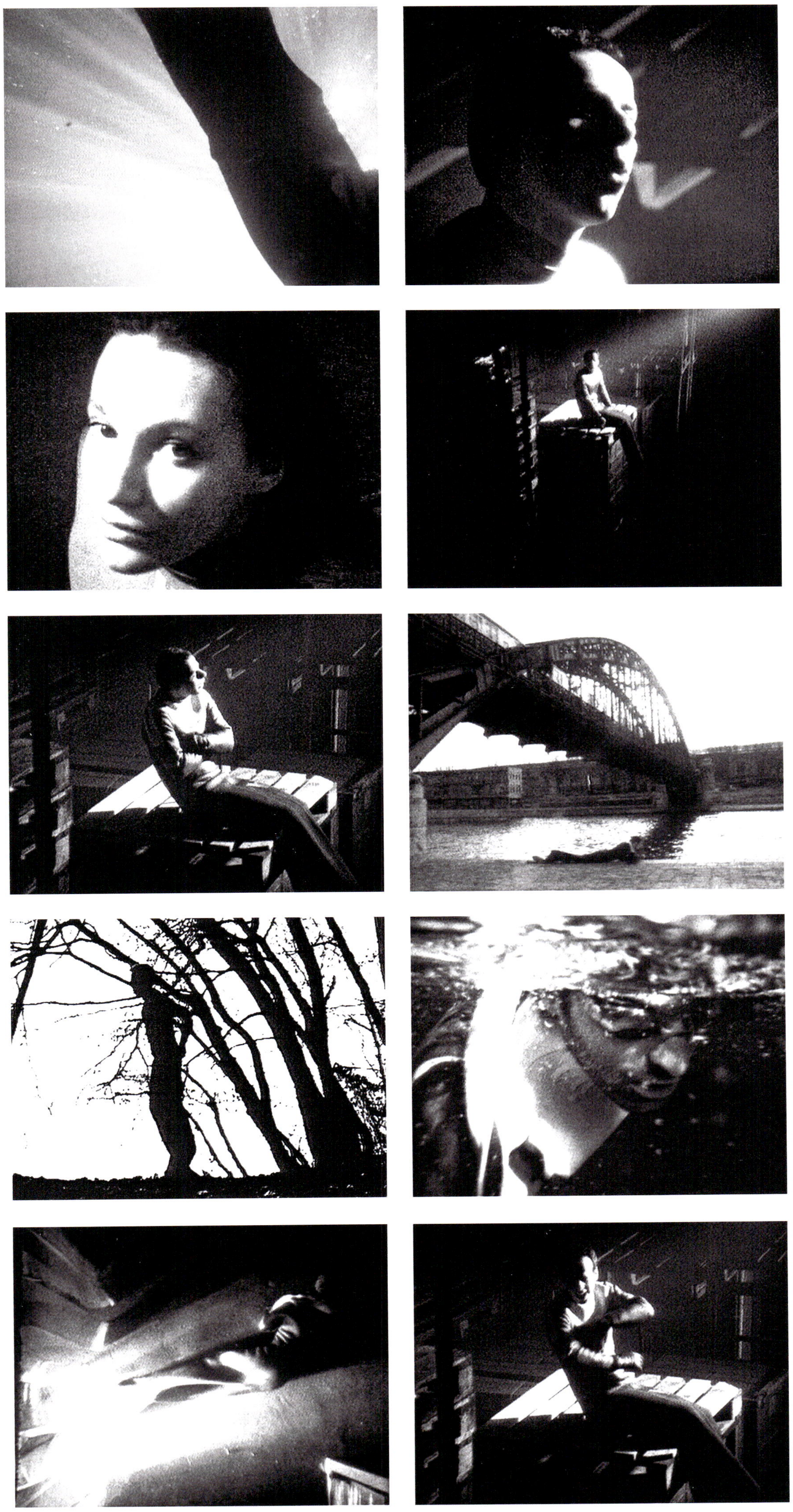

Snaking, 1992, with Pierre Joseph, film

No More Reality, 1991 ⊲ Color C-print, 64 × 80 cm ‡ "Xmas Show," December 14, 1991–February 14, 1992, Air de Paris Gallery, Nice, France || 1 edition ʃ Private collection, Samuso, South Korea **Unique print of a photograph of the demonstration "No More Reality."**

No More Reality, 1991 ⊲ Color C-print, 80 × 64 cm ‡ "Xmas Show," December 14, 1991–February 14, 1992, Air de Paris Gallery, Nice, France || 1 edition ʃ Private collection, Paris, France **Unique print of a photograph of the demonstration "No More Reality."**

No More Reality, 1991 ⊲ Color C-print, 62 × 93.5 cm ‡ "Xmas Show," December 14, 1991–February 14, 1992, Air de Paris Gallery, Nice, France || 1 edition ʃ Private collection, South Korea **Unique print of a photograph of the demonstration "No More Reality."**

No More Reality, 1991 ⊲ Color C-print, 60 × 90.5 cm ‡ "Xmas Show," December 14, 1991–February 14, 1992, Air de Paris Gallery, Nice, France || 1 edition ʃ Private collection, Paris, France **Unique print of a photograph of the demonstration "No More Reality."**

No More Reality, 1991–1992 ⊲ Installation: back projection on transparent PVC screen (approx. 220 × 90 cm) of the video *No More Reality (une vidéoconférence),* copy of the Betacam SP master, color, sound, 38' ‡ "Philippe Parreno," February 1–March 7, 1992, Claudine Papillon Gallery, Paris, France || edition of 1 and 1 artist's proof ʃ Private collection, Paris, France **Here the *No More Reality* video is presented in an installation where it is projected onto the back of a transparent PVC curtain. This curtain blocks the exhibition entrance so that the visitor has to walk through an enlarged image of the artist's face in order to enter the other rooms.**

L'Expérience interdite [The Forbidden Experience], 1992 ⊲ Installation: ¬ *La Bibliothèque du Paradise* • stool • hanging rope • white saturated Rosco paint; variable dimensions ‡ "Il faut construire l'hacienda" [The Hacienda must be built], January 8–March 8, 1992, CCC, Tours (exhib. cat.); exhibition curator: Nicolas Bourriaud and Éric Troncy § Courtesy of the artist

Radio revenants: la radio de l'au-delà [Radio Shade: the radio of the next world], 1992 ⊲ Installation: ¬ 10 posters (photocopies on fluorescent orange paper) • computer screen displaying the year 1991 • 6 loudspeakers • sound track made of ten songs whose writers or performers died in 1991. ‡ "Philippe Parreno," February 1–March 7, 1992, Claudine Papillon Gallery, Paris, France || 3 editions ʃ First private collection: private collection, Paris, France

Untitled, 1992 ⊲ Film fog machine ‡ "Philippe Parreno," February 1–March 7, 1992, Claudine Papillon Gallery, Paris, France ʃ Collection of the artist

Mémoire vivante [Living Memory]

The series *Mémoire vivante* is based on interviews by Parreno with elderly people in retirement homes. The recurring memories of images or situations experienced by these people are represented by various objects. Due to a lack of labels or titles the gallery or museum staff tells the visitor the story linked to the object. This story must only be told orally.

Mémoire vivante, 1992 ◁ Installation: square of felt material with yellow hem, 250 × 350 cm ‡ "Philippe Parreno,"February 1–March 7, 1992, Claudine Papillon Gallery, Paris, France || 1 edition ʃ Private collection, Paris, France ♦ **Mémoire vivante, 1992** ◁ Small sailing jacket in navy blue wool, jersey with a sailor collar, white pants ‡ "Philippe Parreno," February 1–March 7, 1992, Claudine Papillon Gallery, Paris, France || 1 edition § Courtesy of the artist ♦ **Mémoire vivante, 1992** ◁ Installation: ¬ scarf (pink, orange and green flower pattern on white background) • folding chair (wood and beige fabric), approx. 90 × 60 × 60 cm ‡ "Philippe Parreno," February 1–March 7, 1992, Claudine Papillon Gallery, Paris, France || 1 edition ʃ Private collection, Paris, France ♦ **Mémoire vivante, 1992** ◁ Installation: ¬ ticket collector's uniform and cap • red cloak; approx. 200 × 200 cm ‡ "Philippe Parreno," February 1–March 7, 1992, Claudine Papillon Gallery, Paris, France || 1 edition ʃ Private collection, Bourbon-Lancy, France

Vous la connaissez ?

The *Vous la connaissez ?* series is based on funny stories. The gallery staff approaches the visitor and asks "Do you know this one?" before telling him/her the story to which the objects refer. These jokes can only be told orally.

Vous la connaissez ? [Do You Know This One?], 1992 ◁ Installation: ¬ stuffed donkey • white handkerchief • a joke told to the visitor; approx. 50 × 40 × 100 cm ‡ "Philippe Parreno," February 1st March 7, 1992, Claudine Papillon Gallery, Paris, France || 1 edition ♦ **Vous la connaissez ? [Do You Know This One?], 1992** ◁ Installation: ¬ deflated inflatable sex doll • a joke told to the visitor; approx. 170 × 70 cm ‡ "Philippe Parreno," February 1st–March 7, 1992, Claudine Papillon Gallery, Paris, France || 1 edition ʃ Private collection, Monaco ♦ **Vous la connaissez ? [Do You Know This One?], 1992** ◁ Installation: ¬ stuffed animal (lamb) • antiseptic • a joke told to the visitor; 40 × 50 × 20 cm ‡ "Philippe Parreno," February 1st–March 7, 1992, Claudine Papillon Gallery, Paris, France || 1 edition ʃ Private collection, Stockholm, Sweden ♦ **Vous la connaissez ? [Do You Know This One?], Paf le chien, 1992** ◁ Installation: ¬ stuffed black and white cocker spaniel • a joke told to the visitor; 70 × 16 × 50 cm ‡ "Philippe Parreno," February 1st–March 7, 1992, Claudine Papillon Gallery, Paris, France || 1 edition ʃ Private collection, Monaco ♦ **Vous la connaissez ? [Do You Know This One?], 1992** ◁ Installation: ¬ table, 60 × 100 × 100 approx. • 7 table napkins • pale pink cotton, 25 × 25 cm approx. • a joke told to a visitor ‡ “Mami,” April 25–June 25, 1992, Esther Schipper Gallery, Cologne, Germany || 1 edition § Courtesy Esther Schipper, Berlin

Meubles de synthèse [Synthetic Furniture], 1992 With Pierre Joseph ◁ Group of varnished sculptures: ¬ armchair, 90 × 80 × 80 cm • coffee table, 40 × 110 × 60 cm • lamp, 190 × 45 × 33 cm ‡ February 15–23, 1992, Air de Paris booth, Découvertes 92, Paris, France || 1 edition § Courtesy Air de Paris, Paris **The *Meubles de synthèse* are the materialization of virtual images inspired by domestic furniture.**

Snaking, 1992 With Pierre Joseph ◁ 8 mm film transferred onto Beta cam SP, black and white, sound, 3’10”; direction: Olivier Venturini; production: Gió Marconi ‡ “Le Dimanche de la vie” [The Sunday of a Life], March 10–end April, 1992, Gió Marconi Gallery, Milan, Italy (exhib. cat.) || 50 VHS editions for private use; U-matic edition with broadcasting rights for the institution ʃ First public collection: Collection of the Centre Pompidou, Mnam, Paris, France § Courtesy Air de Paris, Paris **At the time of the burgeoning surf culture movement alongside the emergence of new urban sports, Parreno and Joseph invented a new abject “sport,” called *snaking*. ◊ This video parodies advertising techniques by showing a *snaker* in a neoprene suit moving to the music of Snakefinger, the guitarist from the group The Residents. Existing in three versions including one for a child, this neoprene suit is similar to a straight-jacket and forces the performer to crawl. ◊ The project was inspired by a trip to New York (more specifically a Sunday spent in Central Park): “Roller blades, streamlined protection helmets equipped with mirrors allowing for 360° vision, the colors of jumpsuits so well calculated that they have become a language, like the war paint of Indian tribes; … we remember the television program [we watched] the day before on CNN where we could see GIs crawling across the Saudi sands; finally, the ground and the trash cans so rummaged [through] by the homeless that it felt like we were walking on their culture or on their snacks. In short, *snaking*, the sport which consists [of] crawling on the ground in clothes carefully designed for living what we see and no longer being surprised by anything, remains to be invented.”[20] “Are you tired of blading, trekking, jogging, rafting… try snaking!” exclaims the exhibition flyer. This parody of the advertising world and leisure culture echoes Serge Daney’s remark on water as a metaphor for public space and “The Swimmer” as a figure of the contemporary individual.[21] In Postmodern times, we must crawl, surfing the real, thus creating a new relationship with the city, a relationship of slowness and solitude.**

The Imitator. Jean-Luc Godard, 1992 ◁ My First Sony red Walkman • audio tape, French, 12’ ‡ “Mami,” April 25–June 25, 1992, Esther Schipper Gallery, Cologne, Germany || 1 edition § Courtesy Esther Schipper, Berlin **In this sound track offered to visitors, Parreno imitates Jean-Luc Godard for the first time. He will use this voice several times until 1994.**

20. Text presenting the exhibition “Snaking” at the Air de Paris Gallery in Nice in 1991, reproduced in Philippe Parreno, *Speech Bubbles*, Dijon: Les presses du réel, 2001, p.9.

21. Serge Daney, “Notes sur *Palombella Rossa* avant que le film ne devienne à lui seul tout le cinéma,” *L’Exercice a été profitable*, Monsieur, Paris: P.O.L, 1993, p.165-169.

Filippo Lippi, 1992 ◁ *My First Sony* red Walkman • audio tape • French, 15' ‡ "Mami," April 25–June 25, 1992, Esther Schipper Gallery, Cologne, Germany || 1 edition § Courtesy Esther Schipper, Berlin **In this sound track, Philippe Parreno imitates the fictional character Salvatore from the film "The Name of the Rose." He uses this voice to embody Filippo Lippi, the 15th century Italian painter.**

Untitled, 1992 ◁ 2 sheets of white paper: ¬ 1 typewritten (text in black, laser print, 21 × 29.7 cm) • 1 drawing in black and colored pencils (21 × 29.7 cm) ‡ "Tattoo Collection," June 3–July 18, 1992, organized by the Air de Paris and the Urbi & Orbi Galleries at the Jennifer Flay Gallery, Paris, France || 1 edition § Courtesy Air de Paris, Paris **Philippe Parreno writes a text recounting a legend from the Marquesas Islands in which the main character tattoos a picture of himself on his chest.**

Pubblico di merda, 1992 With Philippe Perrin Previous title: *Hommage à Nanni Moretti* ◁ Installation: ¬ 2 groups of screen printed posters (80 × 145 cm each) stuck side-by-side • beneath, a red border situated at 72 cm from the ground (paper; H: 12) • automatic tracking projector • sound system • sound track (on a loop); overall dimensions: 150 to 300 m², H.: 4 to 8 m ‡ "I, Myself and Others," September 26–November 15, 1992, Le Magasin, Grenoble, France; exhibition curator: Thierry Ollat || 1 edition ʃ Frac Rhône-Alpes collection, Villeurbanne, France **A series of screen print posters cover the walls showing the two artists clapping. A sound track on a loop plays clapping to a song by Marino Marini. A theatrical tracking light sweeps around the room.**

Pubblico di merda, 1992 With Philippe Perrin Previous title: *Hommage à Nanni Moretti* ◁ 2 groups of 6 screen printed posters (80 × 145 cm each) || 8 editions § Courtesy of the artists and Le Magasin, Grenoble, France **This version of the installation presented at the Magasin in Grenoble proposes a group of 12 silk screen posters**

Affective Freaks, 1992 ◁ Dried clay, 20 × 25 × 25 cm ‡ "Time Bandits," October, 1992, Galleria Fac Simile, Milan, Italy || 1 edition ʃ Private collection, Brussels, Belgium **This molded clay sculpture represents a mixture of Maurizio Cattelan's physionomy.**

The Imitator, 1992 ◁ Walkman • infrared headphones • wireless terminal • sound track on audio tape, English, 48' ‡ "Postcards From Alphaville: Jean-Luc Godard in Contemporary Art, 1963–1992," October–November, 1992, P.S.1, Long Island City, New York, United States || 1 edition § Courtesy Air de Paris, Paris, and Esther Schipper, Berlin

L'Imitateur [The Imitator], 1992 ◁ *My First Sony* red Walkman • infrared headphones • wireless terminal • sound track on audio tape, French and German, 50'16" ‡ "Interventions," November 13, 1992, Esther Schipper Gallery, Cologne, Germany || 1 edition § Courtesy Esther Schipper, Berlin **Already having asked visitors**

to wear infrared headphones during the exhibitions "French Kiss" in Geneva (*Untitled*, 1990), and "Mami" in Cologne (The Imitator. Jean-Luc Godard, 1992, and *Filippo Lippi*, 1992), Parreno elaborates upon the idea of an extended guided tour with *L'Imitateur*, made in 1992 for the exhibition "Postcards from Alphaville." Parreno synthesizes the easily consumable language of museum wall texts and the format of audio guides—as he would later do with the video label (*La Narratrice* [The Narrator], in 1998 with Dominique Gonzalez-Foester) and the luminous label (*Alien Seasons*, in 2002). Originally made in 1990, this exploration into the language of exhibitions has multiple subsequent versions (six to date), all unique in execution but related conceptually. ◊ Jean-François Lyotard's exhibition "Les Immatériaux" [The Immaterials], at the Centre Pompidou in 1985, was a central influence on Parreno's malleable conception of exhibitions.[22] Lyotard, Parreno's teacher at the *Institut des hautes études en arts plastiques*, greatly influenced all of the French artists of Parreno's generation with his ideas on the "post-modern condition," and the end of "grand narratives."[23] The philosopher analyzes with precision the evolution of science and technology as an extension of language in an increasingly mechanized society.[24] ◊ *L'Imitateur* was followed by *Soundtrack #4* (a guided tour of the Frac Paca collection), and then in 1993, by *Visite commentée* (a guided tour of a private collection in Monaco with the artist imitating the voice of Jean-Luc Godard) and finally *L'Imitateur* (made at Emmanuel Perrotin's MA Gallery for an exhibition of the same name). The choice of Godard's voice for the narrative was a reference by the filmmaker's talent for deconstructing narrative. ◊ Parreno also evokes the creation of personality through models that disturb the feeling of being "of one's time." As a child, he spent his time imitating his role models. "Later we have the impression of having been born at the wrong time, to have been born too early or too late to be able to share our role model's commitments. We are always born under the wrong sign and we correct our horoscope day by day," he writes, questioning the notion of historicity which becomes central to his later pieces.

Vous la connaissez ? [Do You Know This One?], 1992 ◁ Installation: ¬ plastic Berjusa doll, 50 × 30 × 30 cm approx. • a joke told to a visitor ‡ "Les Mystères de l'auberge espagnole," December 19, 1992–January 17, 1993, Villa Arson, Nice, France || 1 edition § Courtesy of the artist and Air de Paris, Paris, France

Chaises de synthèse [Synthetic Chairs], 1993 With Pierre Joseph ◁ 2 chairs, green painted wood; 45 × 46 × 98 cm ‡ "Domorama," March 27–May 7, 1993, La Criée, Rennes, France; exhibition curators: Yannick Miloux and David Perreau || 1 edition § Courtesy Air de Paris, Paris *Chaises de synthèse* is a materialization of virtual images, giving these familiar objects a strange feel.

La Nuit des héros [The Night of Heroes], 1993 ◁ Installation: ¬ elements from the film set • advertisement for *La Nuit des héros*

22. Seven hundred infrared headphones specially made for this project had to be worn during the visit in order to materialize the spaces through sound effects mixed in with quotes read by actors.

23. Jean-François Lyotard's questioning of the artist's conceptual mastery as author, his thoughts on exhibitions and his criticism of the notion of subject clearly influence Parreno. Parreno often consulted the catalogue of the exhibition "Les Immatériaux" in 1985 at the Centre Pompidou.

24. "Le champ : le savoir dans les sociétés informatisées" [The field: knowledge in computerized societies] in Jean-François Lyotard, *La Condition postmoderne*, *op. cit.*, p.11-17.

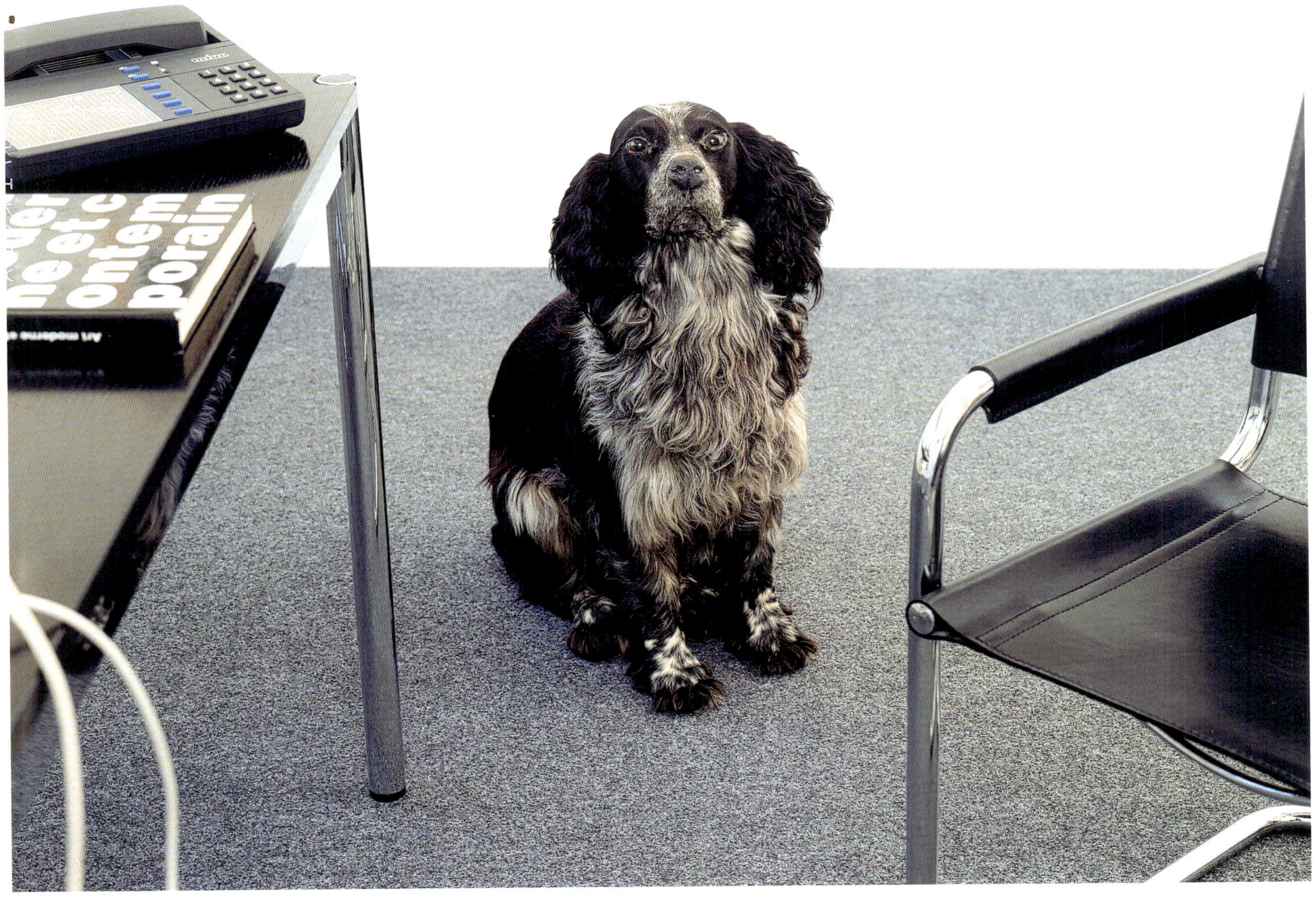

Vous la connaissez? Paf le chien, 1992

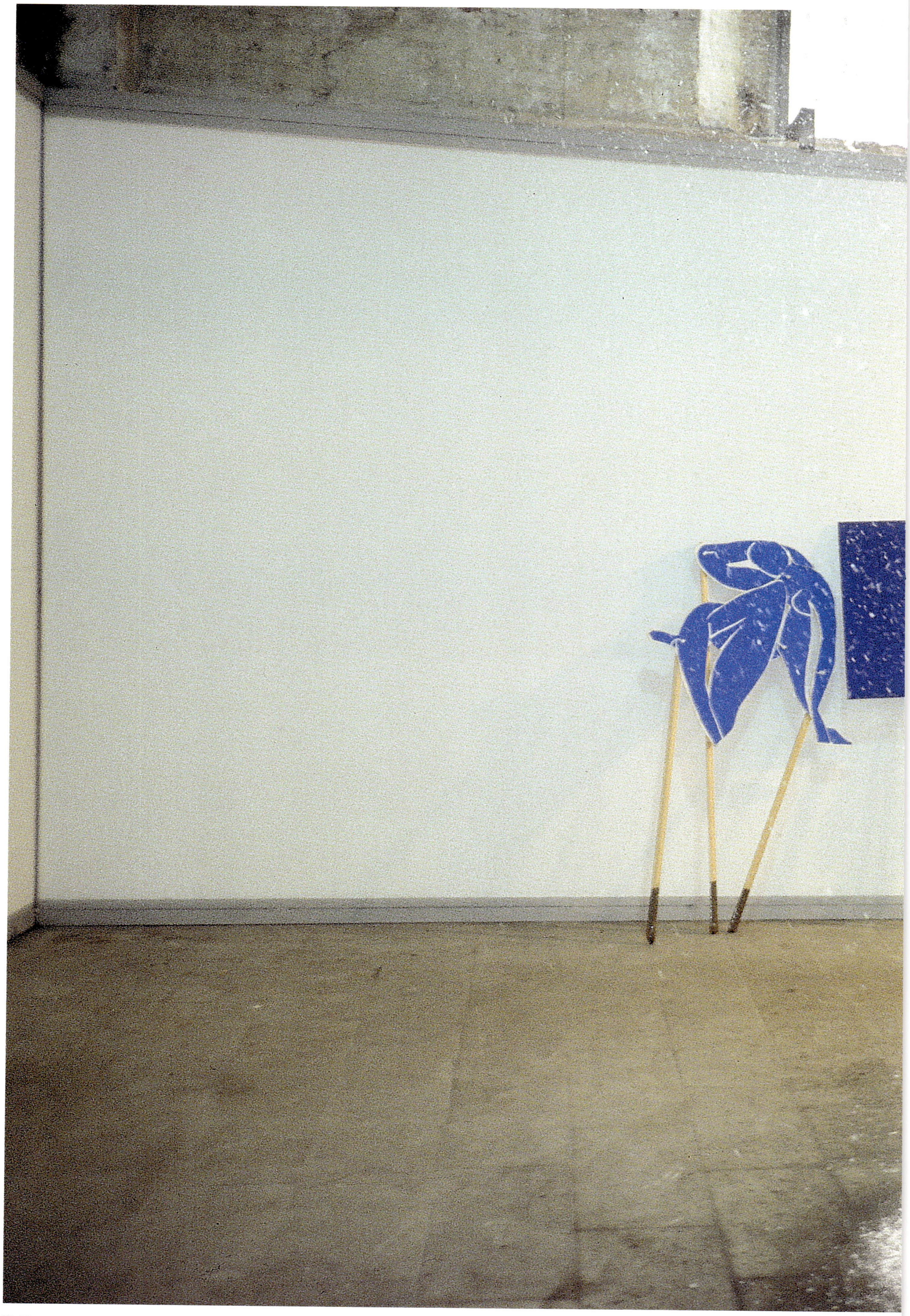

No More Reality (suite et fin), 1993, exhibition view "Aperto 93", 45th Venice Biennial

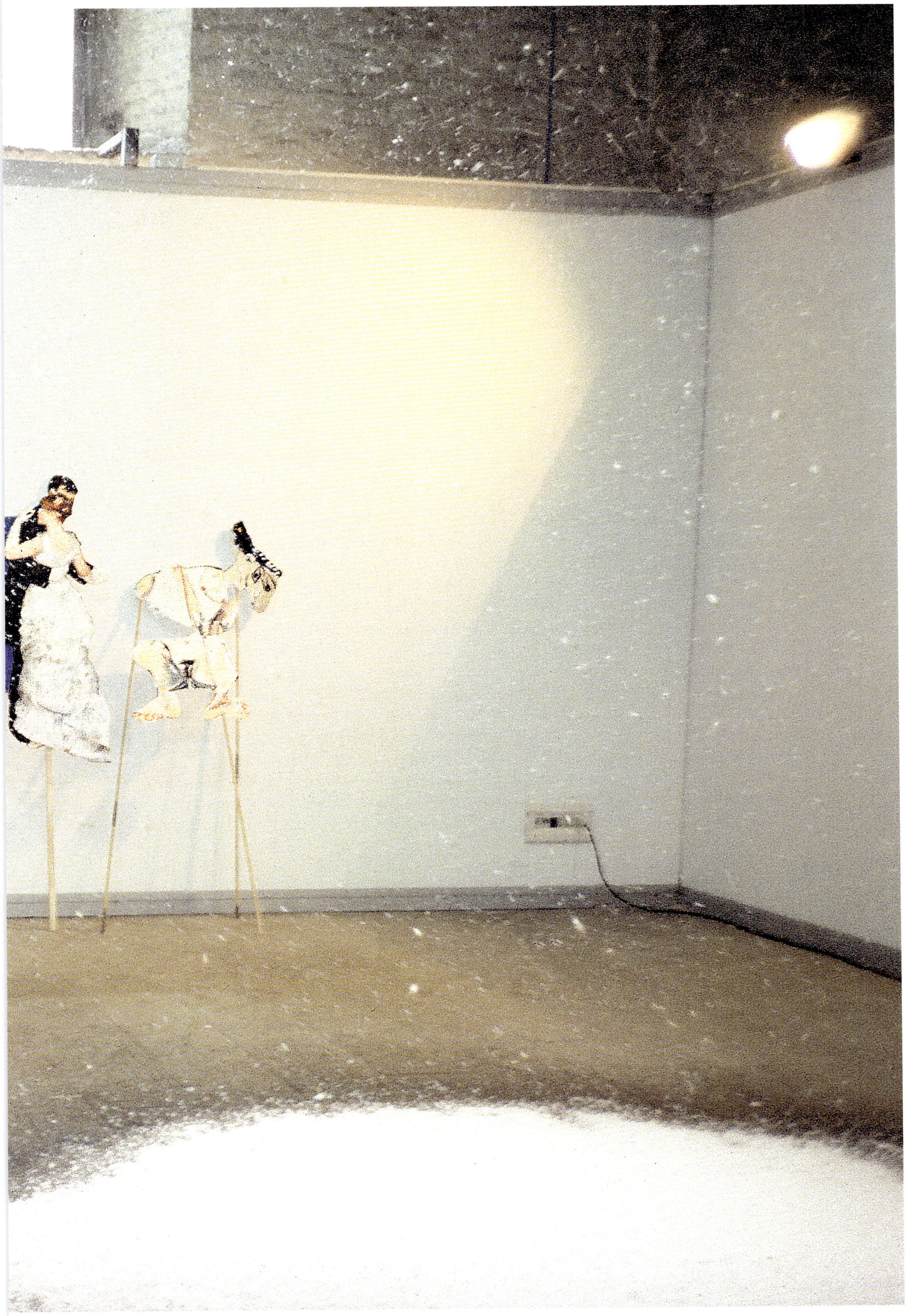

(1994), sound, color, 10' ‡ "Unité 1," June 1–September 30, 1993, Firminy, France (exhib. cat.); exhibition curator: Yves Aupetitallot || 1 edition ʃ Frac Poitou-Charentes, Angoulême, France **This film, co-written with Nicolas Bourriaud and shot in the Le Corbusier building in Firminy during the exhibition curated by Yves Aupetitallot, fictionalizes an art historian, Dante (played by Yves Lecoq), who retired to a deserted building to write the history of modern art. Dante amuses himself by making the important modern figures, from Cézanne to Yves Klein, speak with the voices of known celebrities such as Jean-Paul Belmondo or Françoise Sagan. Alone in his apartment, where each room's theme is informed differently by a modern artist, the historian rants while his neighbor Béatrice tries to reason with his madness by showing him films of everyday life. ◊ For the group exhibition, Parreno left the film set intact. On a monitor the trailer for "Unité 1" is shown, because the editing of the film was not yet completed. Parreno also organized a workshop with children who reenact the narrative.**

No More Reality (suite et fin) [No More Reality (concluded)], 1993 ◁ Installation: ¬ 4 shadow puppets (made from 4 posters reproducing works by Yves Klein, Matisse, Picasso, Renoir, cardboard, 8 wooden sticks) • artificial snow machine • fan; variable dimensions ‡ "Aperto 93," June 9–October 10, 1993, 45th Venice Biennial, Venice, Italy (exhib. cat.) || edition of 1 and 1 artist's proof ʃ Musée d'Art contemporain de Lyon collection, Lyons, France **The Matisse-like cut-outs of Centre Pompidou exhibition posters feature images such as, Renoir's dancing couple, a woman by Picasso, a collage by Matisse and a monochrome by Yves Klein and are placed against a wall inviting the viewer to participate in a shadow play at a festival. Artificial snow falls intermittently, blanketing the space in order to introduce a time-based tactile element. The snow functions as a kind of filmic special effect, exploring the possibility of looped time.**
♦ No More Reality, 1993 Other title: *125 Frames From Hook* ◁ Installation: ¬ black ink • parchment • metal sword (59 × 38 × 130 cm approx.) ‡ "Le Principe de réalité" [The Principle of Reality], July 3–October 3, 1993, Villa Arson, Nice, France (exhib. cat.) || 1 edition ʃ Private collection, Monaco **A piece of parchment paper bears a text written by Captain Hook, from Steven Spielberg's film *Hook* (1991).**
♦ No More Reality, 1993 Alternate title: *75 Frames From Batman Returns* ◁ Installation: ¬ Vinyl balloon (ø: 300 cm) • Acrylic paint • nylon ‡ "Le Principe de réalité" [The Principle of Reality], July 3–October 3, 1993, Villa Arson, Nice, France (exhib. cat.) || 1 edition ʃ Private collection, Cologne, Germany **The balloon of a screaming baby's head references a scene in Tim Burton's film *Batman Returns* (1992). It fills an entire room so that no one can enter.**

Vous la connaissez ? [Do You Know This One?], 1993 ◁ Installation: ¬ sculpture (resin, toilet paper, 31 × 13 × 11 cm) • a joke told to the visitor ‡ "Le Principe de réalité" [The Principle of Reality], July 3–October 3, 1993, Villa Arson, Nice, France (exhib. cat.) || 1 edition ʃ Private collection, Vienna, Austria **This work belongs**

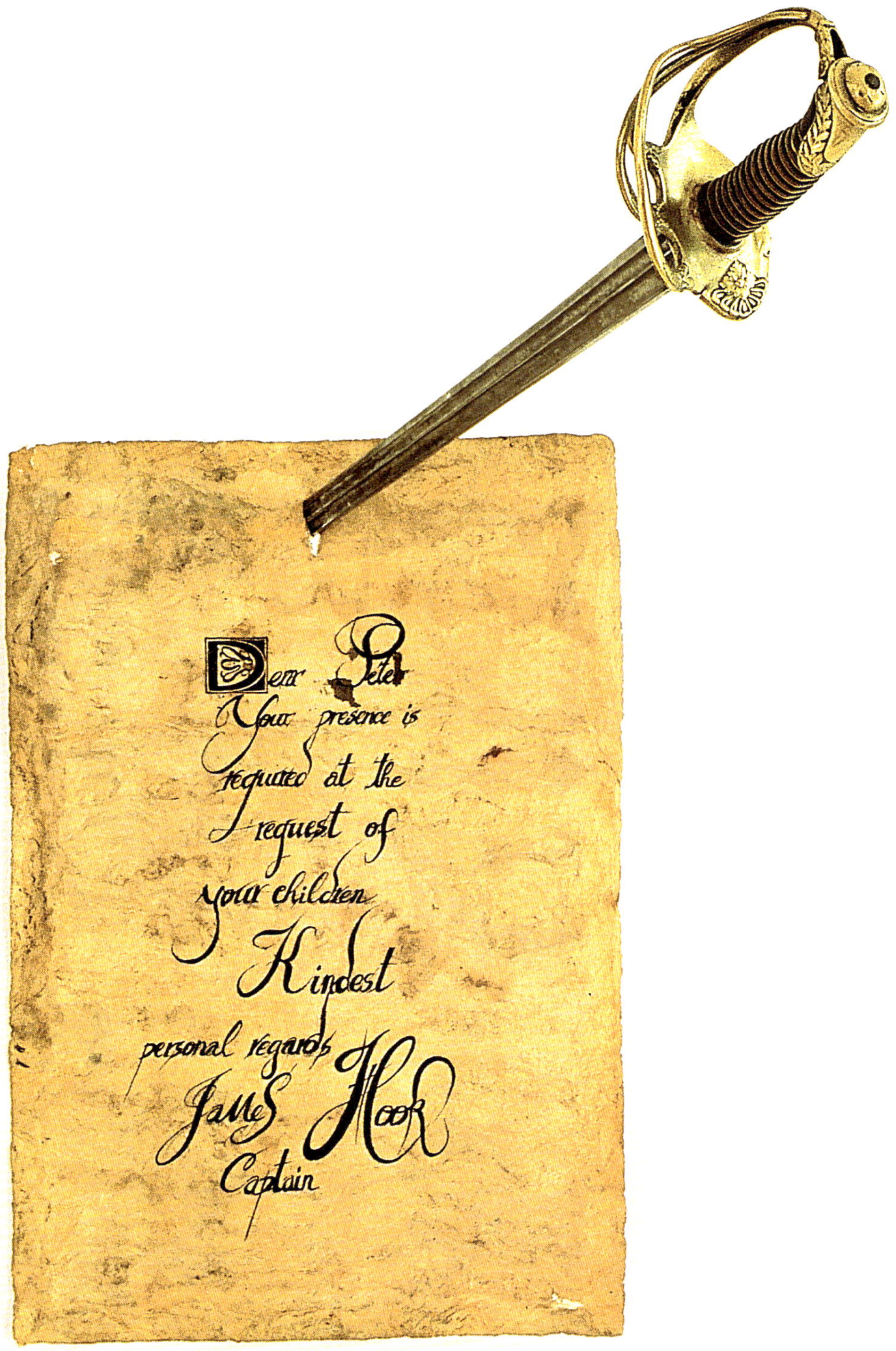

No More Reality, 125 Frames From Hook, **1993**

to the *Vous la connaissez ?* [Do You Know This One?], series which is based on jokes. During the exhibition the gallery staff approaches visitors and asks, "Do you know this one?" before telling them the humorous anecdote to which the object refers. The humor of the narrative is dependent upon timing and intonation.

L'Article des lucioles [The Firefly Article], 1993 ◊ Installation: ¬ LEDs and electrical system (3.50 × 18 × 5 m during the first exhibition) • black and white photocopy under glass (21 × 29.7 cm); variable dimensions ‡ "Le Principe de réalité" [The Principle of Reality], July 3–October 3, 1993, Villa Arson, Nice, France (exhib. cat.) || 1 edition ∫ Private collection, London, United Kingdom *L'Article des lucioles* [The Firefly Article], is a string of LED lights installed in the garden of the Villa Arson and visible only at night thus viewable only by the nearby residents. In a passage of the "Corsair Writings"—an article published in the *Corriere della Sera* in February 1, 1975 under the title "The Emptiness of Power in Italy"[25]—Pier Paolo Pasolini uses the disappearance of fireflies in Europe at the beginning of the 1960s from the pollution of the water as a metaphor for the fall of ideology, the paradigmatic shift to mass consumerism, and the emptiness of Christian democratic discourse. In this work, artificial fireflies symbolize a dehumanized society of mass consumerism. The reproduction of Pasolini's text hung in the Villa Arson's small entrance room is framed under glass. During the day, visitors can see a label in place of the exhibition as the installation is only visible at night when the museum is closed.

25. Pier Paolo Pasolini's articles published in the *Corriere della Sera* from January 7, 1974 to February 18, 1975 were brought together in his book *Corsair Writings* (Paris: Flammarion, 1976, for the French Edition).

La Peur des anges [The Fear of Angels], 1993 ◊ Sound track, French, 13'21" • small speakers • sound system; variable dimensions ‡ "Le Principe de réalité" [The Principle of Reality], July 3–October 3, 1993, Villa Arson, Nice, France (exhib. cat.) || 1 edition § Courtesy Air de Paris, Paris The artist invited specialists of the occult sciences (diviner, clairvoyant, psychic, fortune-teller, exorcist, healer, astrologer) to visit the exhibition before the opening. He brought them together afterwards to interpret the empty space discussing, what they had "seen." The recording is played on a loop in several spaces throughout the exhibition.

La Peur des anges [The Fear of Angels], 1993 ◊ ¬ Pencil on paper, wood • opal glass • signature in red pencil "O.T"; 69 × 56 × 7 cm (49 × 62 cm unframed) ‡ "Summer 93," August, 1993, Air de Paris Gallery, Nice, France || 1 edition § Courtesy Air de Paris, Paris A pencil drawing was made by a psychic during the discussion recorded the evening before the opening of the exhibition Summer '93.

La Peur des anges [The Fear of Angels], 1993 ◊ ¬ Ball point pen on paper • wood • opal glass • signature in red pencil "O.T"; 69 × 56 × 7 cm (49 × 62 cm unframed) ‡ "Summer 93," August, 1993, Air de Paris Gallery, Nice, France || 1 edition § Courtesy Air de Paris, Paris A ballpoint pen drawing made by a psychic

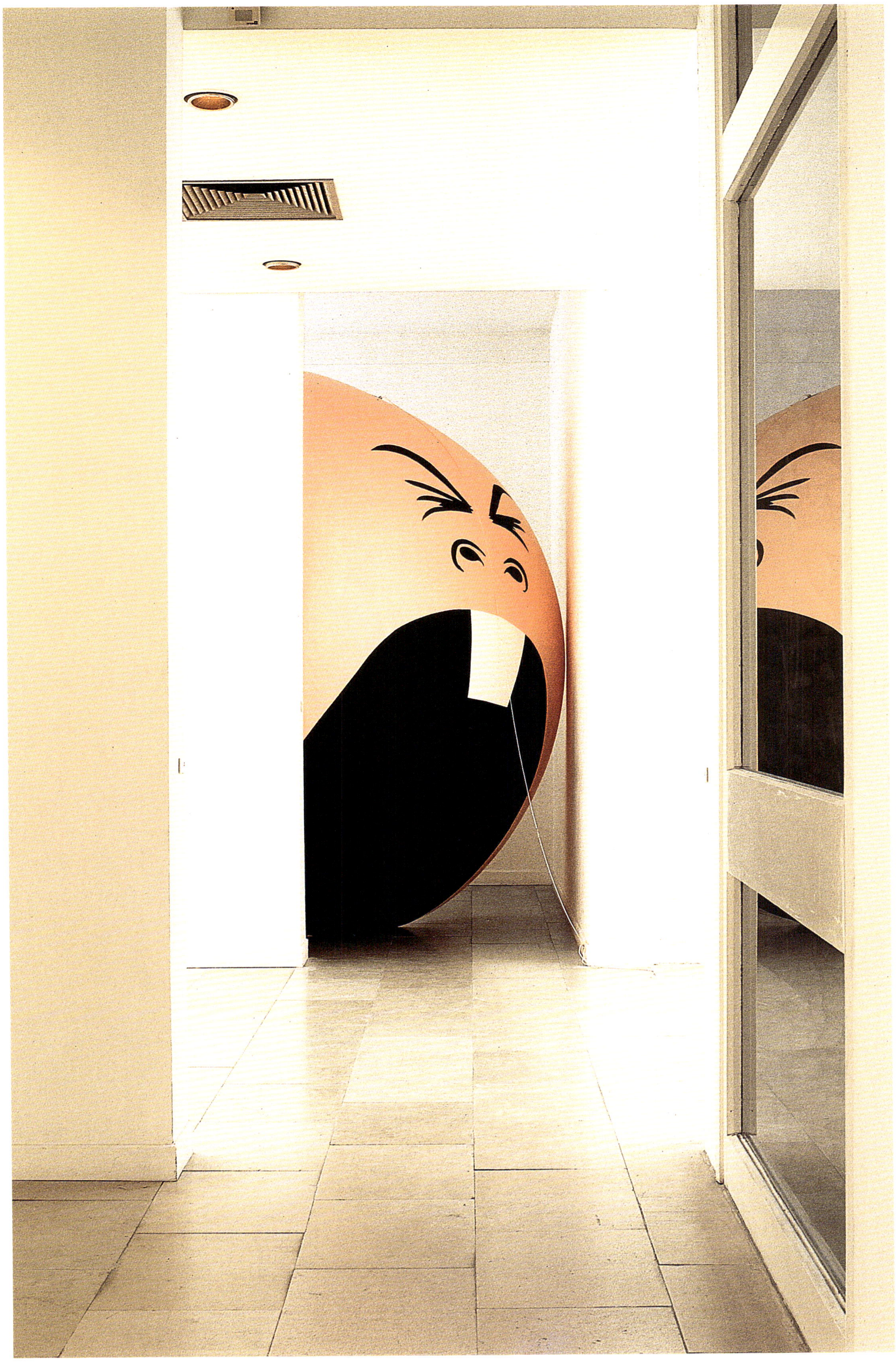

No More Reality, 75 Frames From Batman Returns, **1993,** exhibition view "Le Principe de réalité", Villa Arson, Nice

100

Scritti corsari p. 160

"La distinzione tra fascismo aggettivo e fascismo sostantivo risale niente meno che al giornale Il Politecnico, cioè all'immediato dopoguerra..." Così comincia un intervento di Franco Fortini ("L'Europeo", 26-12-1974): intervento, come si dice, io sottoscrivo tutto e pienamente. Non posso sottoscrivere l'esordio. Con esso Fortini cerca di rimuovere (respingendola indietro nel tempo) la realtà di un problema impostato (almeno sul piano della grande opinione pubblica) da una persona "innominabile": cosa che non ha mancato di suscitare lo scandalo dei pedanti di cui portavoce Giorgio Bocca. Questa persona "innominabile" sono io. Ritengo perciò necessaria una ulteriore chiarificazione, magari semplificante, del famoso problema.

La distinzione fra "fascismi" fatta sul "Politecnico" non è pertinente nè attuale. Essa poteva valere ancora fino circa una decina di anni fa: quando il Regime democristiano era ancora la continuazione del Regime fascista.

Ma una decina di anni fa, è successo "qualcosa". "Qualcosa" che non c'era e non era prevedibile non solo ai tempi del "Politecnico", ma nemmeno un anno prima che accadesse (o addirittura, mentre accadeva).

Il confronto reale tra "fascismi" non può essere dunque cronologicamente, tra il fascismo fascista e il fascismo democristiano: ma tra il fascismo fascista e il fascismo radicalmente, totalmente, nuovo che è nato da quel "qualcosa" che è successo una decina di anni fa.

Poichè sono uno scrittore, e scrivo in polemica, o almeno discuto, con altri scrittori, mi si lasci dare una definizione di carattere poetico-letterario di quel fenomeno che è successo. Ciò servirà a semplificare e ad abbreviare il nostro discorso (e probabilmente a capirlo anche meglio).

Una decina di anni fa, a causa dell'inquinamento dell'aria, e, soprattutto, in campagna, a causa dell'inquinamento dell'acqua (fiumi e rogge) sono cominciate a scomparire le lucciole. Il fenomeno è stato fulmineo e folgorante. Dopo pochi anni le lucciole non c'erano più. (Sono, ora, un ricordo, abbastanza straziante, del passato: e un uomo anziano che abbia un tale ricordo, non riconosce nei nuovi giovani se stesso giovane, e dunque non può avere più i bei rimpianti di una volta).

Quel "qualcosa" che è accaduto una decina di anni fa lo chiamerò dunque "scomparsa delle lucciole".

Il Regime democristiano ha avuto due fasi assolutamente distinte, che non solo non si posso=

First page of the original manuscript of "Il vuoto del potere" [The firefly article] written by Pier Paolo Pasolini, 1975
L'Article des lucioles, 1993, exhibition view "Le Principe de réalité", Villa Arson, Nice

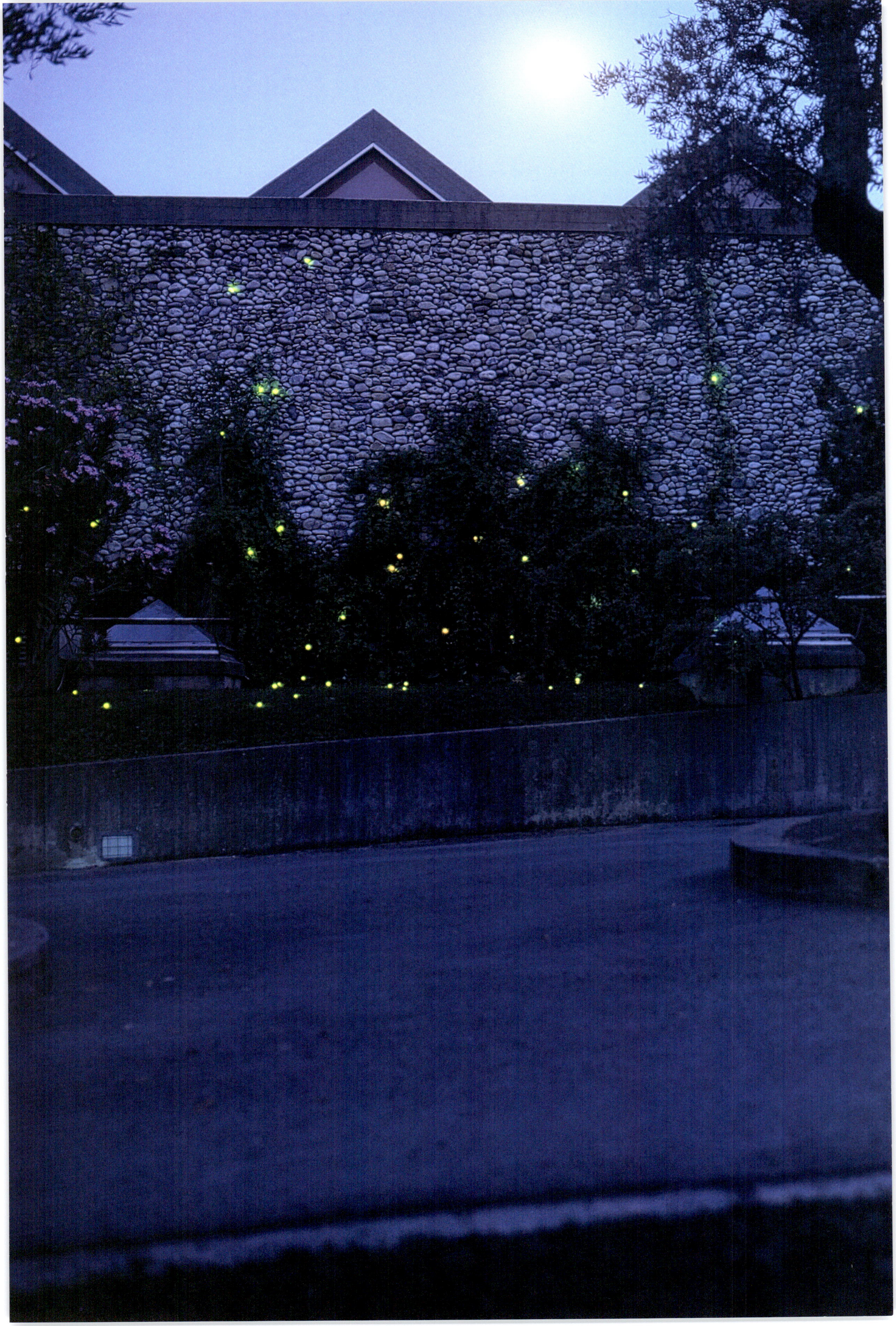

during the discussion recorded the evening before the opening of the exhibition *Summer 93*.

La Peur des anges [The Fear of Angels], 1993 ◁ ¬ Red pencil on paper • wood • opal glass • signature in red pencil "O.T"; 69 × 56 × 7 cm (49 × 62 cm unframed) ‡ "Summer 93," August 1993, Air de Paris, Nice, France || 1 edition § Courtesy Air de Paris Gallery, Paris A red pencil drawing made by a psychic during the discussion recorded the evening before the opening of the exhibition *Summer 93*.

Vous la connaissez ? [Do You Know This One?], 1993 ◁ Installation: ¬ display case with various chocolates placed on a glass shelf positioned 3 m high (60 × 20 × 5 cm) • a joke told to the visitor ‡ "Summer 93", August 1993, Air de Paris Gallery, Nice, France || 1 edition § Courtesy Air de Paris, Paris, This work belongs to the *Vous la connaissez ?* [Do You Know This One?], series which is based on jokes. During the exhibition the gallery staff approaches visitors and asks, "Do you know this one?" before telling them the humorous anecdote to which the objects refer. The humor of the narrative is dependent upon delivery, timing and intonation. ♦ Vous la connaissez ? [Do You Know This One?], 1993 ◁ Installation: ¬ black and white material nailed to the wall at a height of 170 cm; 130 × 160 cm • a joke told to the visitor ‡ "Summer 93," August 1993, Air de Paris Gallery, Nice, France || 1 edition § Courtesy Air de Paris Gallery, Paris

C'est une œuvre d'art pendant onze mois de l'année et en décembre c'est Noël [It is an artwork during eleven months of the year and in December it is Christmas], 1993 ◁ Installation: ¬ Plastic Christmas tree • plastic tinsel • electric string of LED lights • 2 wrapped presents (metallic pink and purple paper); 120 × 90 × 90 cm approx. ‡ exhibition at collectors' house, summer 1993, Monaco || 1 edition ʃ Private collection, Monaco

Visite commentée [Guided Tour], 1993 ◁ Walkman • infrared headphones • wireless terminal • sound track on audio tape ‡ Exhibition at collectors' home, summer 1993, Monaco || 1 edition ʃ Private collection, Monaco The artist impersonates the voice of Jean-Luc Godard, commenting on selected works from the collection.

No More Reality, 1993 Other title: *Hell[o t]here 168 Frames from Batman Returns* ◁ Pink neon lights • electrical system, 120 × 200 cm approx. • letters O and T switched off ‡ exhibition at collectors' home, summer 1993, Monaco || 1 edition ʃ Private collection, Monaco This neon "hell[o t]here" references a scene from Tim Burton's *Batman Returns* (1992).

Untitled (J.-L. Godard), 1993 ◁ Installation: ¬ live Christmas tree, variable dimensions (250 × 130 approx. during the first exhibition)

• 11 teddy bears, 13 × 10.5 cm approx. each • 18 Christmas tree balls, pearlescent plastic, diam.: 0.9 cm • 3 strings of LED lights • 28 presents wrapped in brown marbled paper • folding Lafuma stools, blue fabric, white painted metal • 1 Sony Mega Bass radio tape, 68 × 21 × 21 cm • 2 audio tapes, *The Imitator,* 29'49" and *Untitled,* length unknown ‡ "Backstage," September 9–October 24, 1993, Kunstverein in Hamburg, Hamburg, Germany || 1 edition

No More Reality (suite et fin) [No More Reality (concluded)], 1993 ◁ Installation: ¬ 4 puppets cut out of posters representing works by Dalí, Matisse, Miró, Keith Haring • cardboard • 8 wooden sticks • artificial snow; variable dimensions ‡ "Plädoyer," October 15–27, 1993, Esther Schipper Gallery, Cologne, Germany || 1 edition § Courtesy Esther Schipper, Berlin

Anna, 1993 ◁ Video on VHS tape, color, sound, 4' ‡ "Plädoyer," October 15–27, 1993, Esther Schipper Gallery, Cologne, Germany || Number of editions ***Anna*** **consists of a single sequence, shot in close up of the face of Esther Schipper's new-born baby.**

Le Fan-club de Stevie Wonder [Stevie Wonder's Fan Club], 1993 ◁ ¬ 1 sheet of paper stuck to orange cardboard and framed 21 × 29.7 cm (unframed) • 10 photocopies of Stevie Wonder's autograph ‡ "Plädoyer," October 15–27, 1993, Esther Schipper Gallery, Cologne, Germany || 1 edition ∫ Private collection, London, United Kingdom

L'Imitateur [The Imitator], 1993 ◁ Installation: ¬ audio tape • infrared headphones • wireless terminal • *My First Sony* Walkman (unknown length) ‡ December 18, 1993, MAgalerie [Emmanuel Perrotin], Paris, France || edition of 1 and 1 artist's proof § Courtesy Air de Paris, Paris, France and Esther Schipper, Berlin **On the audio guide the artist mimics the voice of Jean-Luc Godard.**

Affective Freaks, 1993 Alternate title: *Affective Freak (Lothi)* ◁ Dried clay, 16 × 16 × 25 cm ‡ Unfair, Esther Schipper booth, November 10–15, 1993, Cologne, Germany || 1 edition ∫ Private Collection, Vienna, Austria **The molded clay sculpture is a portrait of the artist Lothar Hempel's physionomy.**

Affective Freaks, 1994 Alternate title: *Affective Freak (Carsty)* ◁ Dried clay, 20 × 25 × 20 cm approx. ‡ "Handmade," January 29–March 5, 1994, Esther Schipper Gallery, Cologne, Germany || 1 edition § Courtesy Esther Schipper, Berlin **This molded clay sculpture is a portrait of the artist Carsten Höller's physionomy.**

Affective Freaks, 1994 Alternate title: *Affective Freak (Dominique)* ◁ Dried clay, 20 × 25 × 20 cm approx. ‡ "Handmade," January 29–March 5, 1994, Esther Schipper Gallery, Cologne, Germany || 1 edition ∫ Private collection, Mulhouse, France **The molded clay sculpture is a portrait of the artist Dominique Gonzalez-Foerster's physionomy.**

Innocent et emprisonné : mais ce que vous avez contre moi c'est que j'ai abandonné mon premier amour [Innocent and emprisoned: but what you have against me is that I abandoned my first love], 1994 With Carsten Höller ◊ Installation: ¬ *La Pause de la mécanique* [The Mechanical Pause] (Carsten Höller and Philippe Parreno) • 8 bottles of *Champagne Amour* [Love Champagne] (Carsten Höller and Philippe Parreno) • sprays of fresh flowers • petition forms • posters (black photocopies on colored paper 60 × 85 cm approx., either fixed to the outside wall or on a wooden panel) • awning (red oilskin fabric, white screen print, 40 × 250 cm approx.) • water supply • pierced hose • red rug (0.8 × 15 m approx.) • sound system • sound track (on a loop) ‡ "Innocent et emprisonné: mais ce que vous avez contre moi c'est que j'ai abandonné mon premier amour," January 22–March 1, 1994, Air de Paris Gallery, Paris, France || 1 edition § Courtesy Air de Paris, Paris, France **The gallery is transformed into a support group, where one can sign a petition for the freedom of something or to free someone imprisoned in the abandoned building opposite the gallery. Flowers and champagne bottles are ready and waiting for their liberation.The opening takes the form of a demonstration for the release of an imaginary prisoners.**

La Pause de la mécanique [The Mechanical Pause], 1994 With Carsten Höller ◊ Unique offset color poster; 98.5 × 130 cm ‡ "Innocent et emprisonné: mais ce que vous avez contre moi c'est que j'ai abandonné mon premier amour," January 22–March 1, 1994, Air de Paris Gallery, Paris, France || 1 edition § Courtesy Air de Paris, Paris **The poster is a photographic reproduction of a demonstration held in Paris in defense of state schools. At the center of the image, two hands holding a sheet of white paper on which is written "amour" emerge from beneath umbrellas and banners.**

Champagne Amour [Love Champagne], 1994 With Carsten Höller ◊ 8 champagne bottles with offset labels (11 × 15 cm) ‡ "Innocent et emprisonné: mais ce que vous avez contre moi c'est que j'ai abandonné mon premier amour," January 22–March 1, 1994, Air de Paris Gallery, Paris, France || editions of 8 and 2 artist's proofs ʃ First private collection: private collection, Paris, France § Courtesy Air de Paris, Paris ***La Pause de la mécanique*** **poster is reproduced on a champagne bottle's label. Above the image is the inscription: "And here is some Love Champagne for the day of his liberation," The signatures of the artists are reproduced on the righthand side of the label.**

La Nuit des héros [The Night of Heroes], 1994 ◊ 35 mm, color, sound, 13' With Yves Lecoq, Delphine Grange, Charles de Meaux and Erik Dietman; original screenplay: Nicolas Bourriaud and Philippe Parreno; direction: Philippe Parreno; Production Air de Paris, Plus de Lumière! and Les Films du requin; images: Jean-Louis Vialard; sound: Emmanuel Crosset and Éric Lesachet; scenery: Emmanuelle Duplay; costumes: Daniel Jasiak; music: Vincent

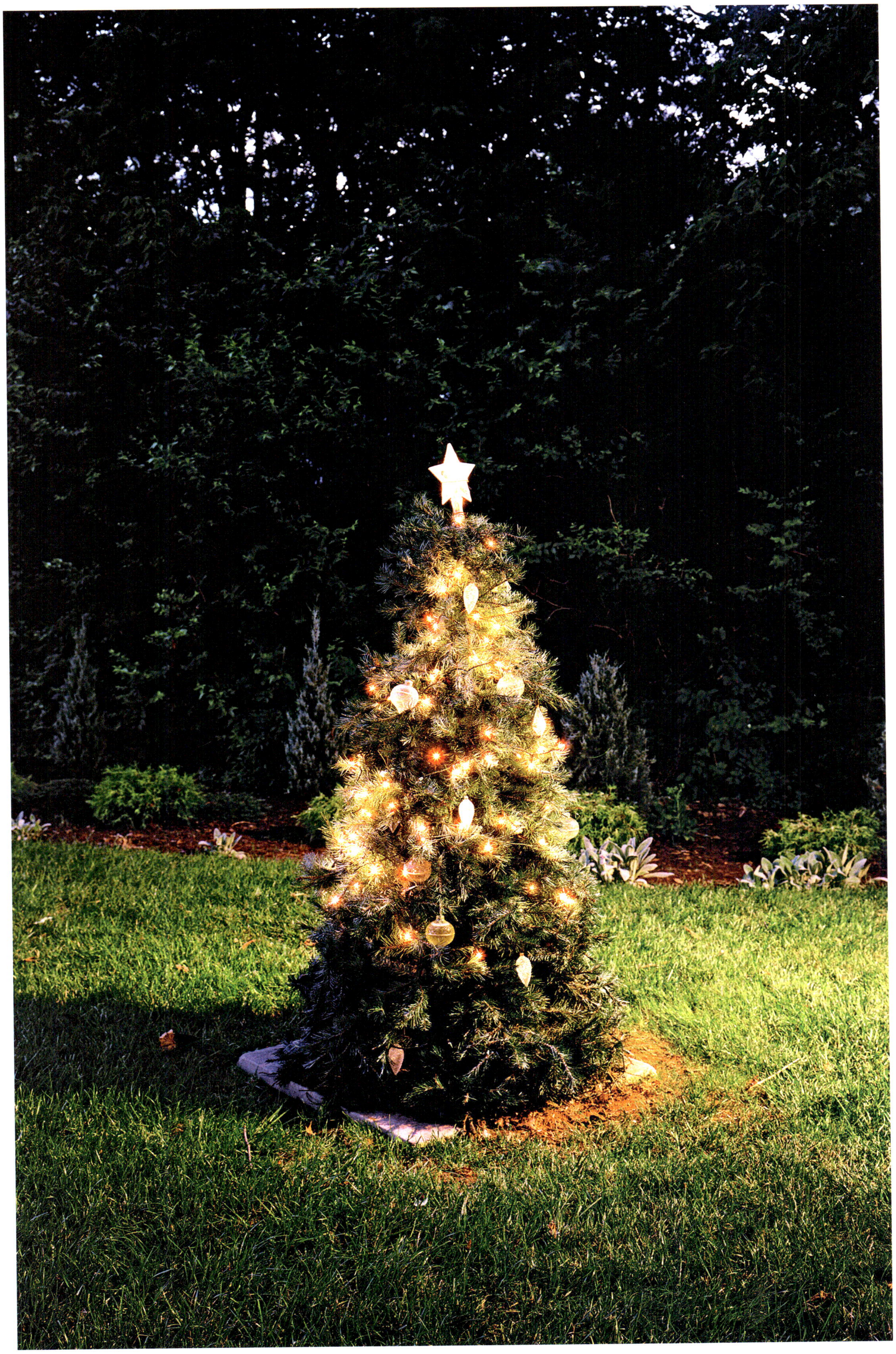

C'est une œuvre d'art pendant onze mois de l'année et en décembre c'est Noël, 1998, private collection, Cincinnati

Burgala; editing: Anne Arbouse and Nicolas Fagart; sound mixing: Stéphane Bauer ‡ First screening: February 10, 1994, Frac Poitou-Charentes, Angoulême || Unedited ʃ First public collection: Frac Paca, Marseilles, Paris ***La Nuit des héros*** **is the story of an art critic (Yves Lecoq) who, isolates himself in order to write the history of modern art. Haunted by artists and artworks, he withdraws into his imagination.**

La Pierre qui parle [The Speaking Stone], 1994 ◁ Installation: ¬ synthetic stone • infrared loudspeaker • DataWave sound transmitter • sound track (40') • 12 drawings (variable techniques and formats) • 1 drawing by the artist (64.5 × 49.6 cm); variable dimensions ‡ "Backstage: Topologie zeitgenössischer Kunst," February 5–April 4, 1994, Kunstmuseum Luzern, Luzern, Switzerland || 1 edition § Courtesy Esther Schipper, Berlin ♦ **La Pierre qui parle [The Speaking Stone], 1994** ◁ Installation: ¬ synthetic stone • infrared loudspeaker • DataWave sound transmittor • 1 Walkman • sound track (40') • group of 30 drawings; variable dimensions ‡ "France. Une nouvelle génération" [France: A New Generation], February 10–April 30, 1999, Circulo de Bellas Artes, Madrid, Spain; exhibition curator: Jean-Marc Prévost || 1 edition ʃ Private collection, Lille, France ♦ **La Pierre qui parle [The Speaking Stone], 1994** ◁ Progressive sound installation: ¬ synthetic stone • autorewind Sony Walkman • transformer • DataWave sound transmitter • sound track (40') • 25 folding stools • group of drawings (number of drawings increases with each class); variable dimensions ‡ "Nouvelle Vague" [New Wave], February 18–April 4, 1994, Mamac, Nice, France || 1 edition ʃ Fonds national d'art contemporain (Fnac), Puteaux, France **A synthetic stone containing a wireless speaker and an audio tape is placed in the center of the installation. Similar to previous works exploring language and imitation (*No More Reality, une vidéoconférence, L'Homme public…*), the stone gives a lecture spoken by Philippe Parreno imitating the voice of Godard. The lecture begins by describing the exhibition "Backstage: Topologie zeitgenössischer Kunst" in Lucerne, where the work was presented for the first time and makes a comparison between the whiteness of museum walls and of the snow in the film. This line of thought corresponds to a change in point of view which occurred in the 1990s, when "finally, going to a museum is like going to Disneyworld, to the movies or to see a football match." The questions arise of illusion or hallucination in film, of love, of the mystery of consciousness and finally the cognitive side of the status of representation. "Find your metaphors," concludes the monologue, as if to free consciousness. It is to this command that the children reply, invited to sit on blue folding chairs around the speaking stone. Indeed, twice a week classic drawing lessons are organized with schools. At each lesson, the students have to draw the stone under the influence of this voice like many anonymous authors giving their interpretation.** ◊ **The group of drawings is later exhibited around the stone continuously modifying this work forever in progress. As Parreno remarked,**

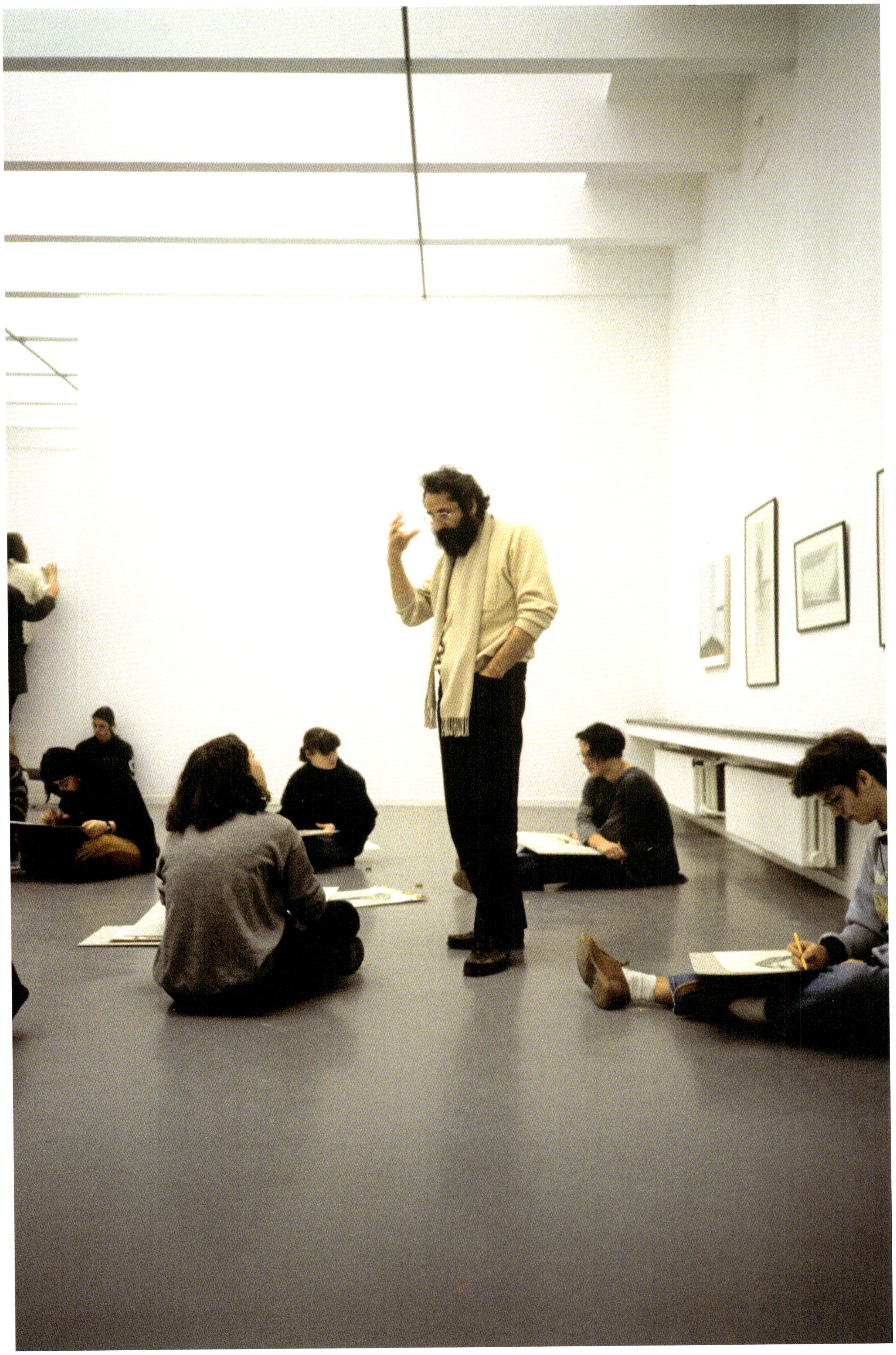

La Pierre qui parle, 1994, exhibition view "Backstage : Topologie zeitgenössischer Kunst ", Kunstmuseum Luzern, Lucerne

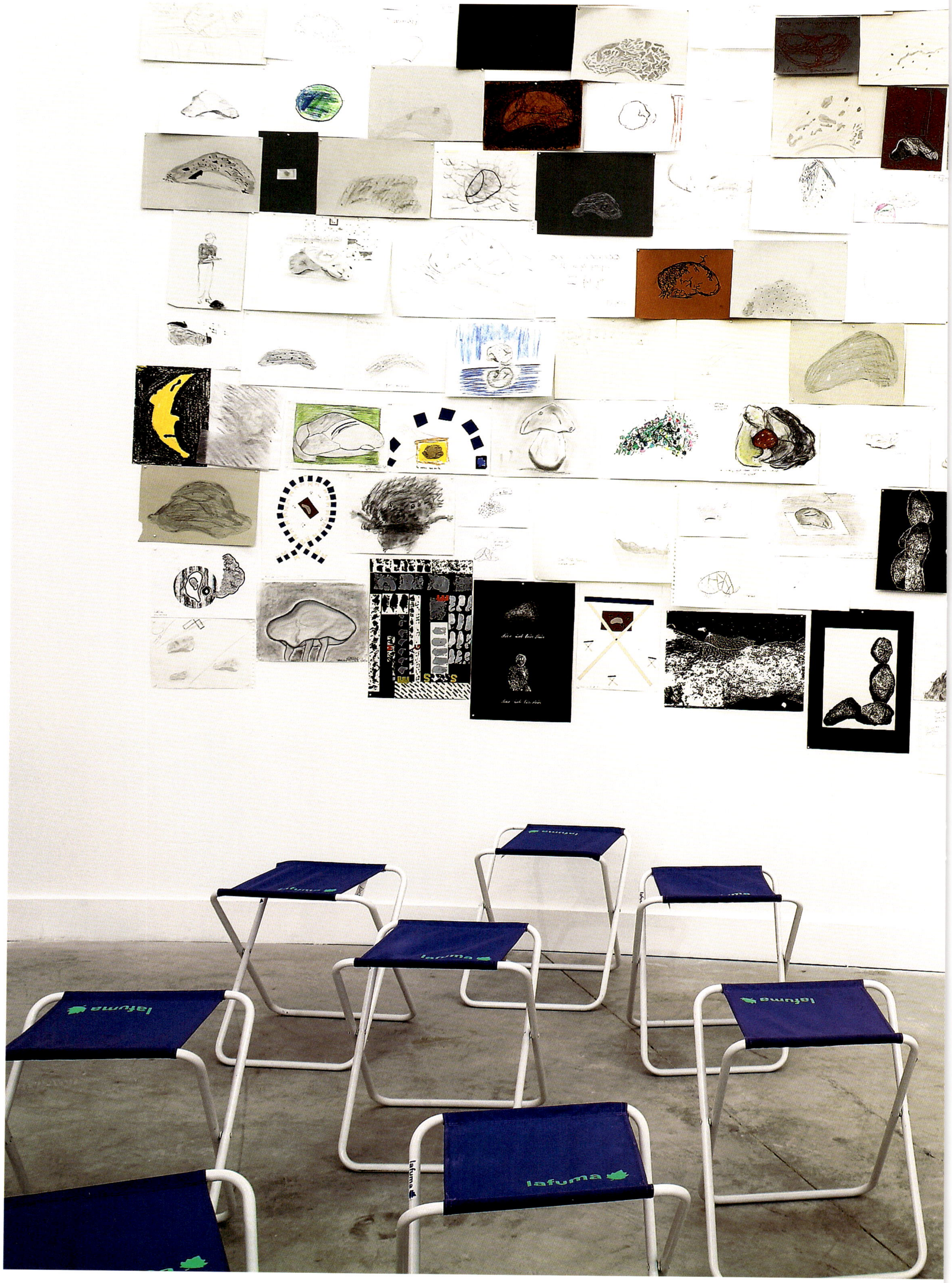

La Pierre qui parle, 1994, exhibition view "Cinema(s)", Le Magasin, Grenoble, 2006

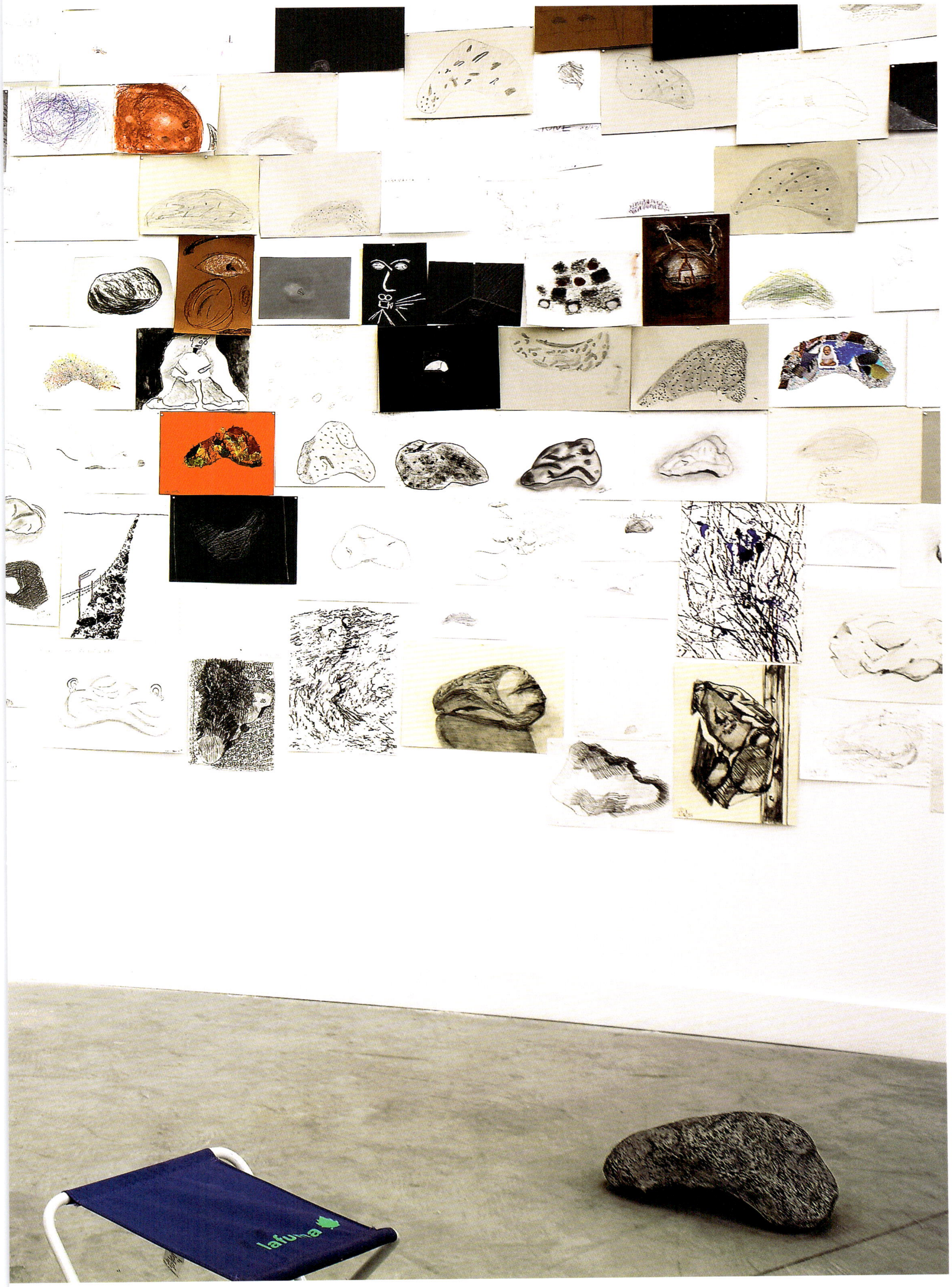
lafuma

26. Philippe Parreno, "Facteur Temps," *Documents sur l'art*, no.6, Fall 1994, p.22-23; reproduced in *Speech Bubbles*, op. cit.

"cinema teaches patience; we must wait for the words THE END. In art, the words THE END never come."[26] This work therefore also questions the projected image and cinemagraphic language which inhabit Parreno's thoughts.

Vingt années-lumière [Twenty Light Years], 1994 Alternate title: *Dix années-lumière* [Ten Light Years] ◁ Installation: ¬ 10 Ikea lamps (model *Pia*) • electrical system with timer and on-off system; variable dimensions ‡ "Sonne München," April 29–June 4, 1994, Daniel Buchholz Gallery, Cologne, Germany || 3 editions § Courtesy Air de Paris, Paris, and Esther Schipper, Berlin, Germany Parreno imagined that the newly opened gallery would switch its lights on and off twice a day for twenty years. In this room, the gallery's lights switch on and off the same number of times a day but only for a month.

Hypnose [Hypnosis], 1994 ◁ 7 stapled A4 format pages ‡ "Grand Prix, Monaco," May 7–25, 1994, Évelyne Canus Gallery, La Colle-sur-Loup, France; May 9–June 5, 1994, Pierre Nouvion Gallery, Monaco; May 10–15, 1994, Air de Paris Gallery, Nice, France; May 10–15, 1994, Art:Concept Gallery, Nice, France; May 10–June 15, 1994, Nice Fine Arts Gallery, Nice, France § Courtesy of the artist and Air de Paris, Paris Philippe Parreno initially wanted to have a hypnotist read a text which he would then broadcast via the loudspeakers of the Monaco Grand Prix. Due to a lack of authorization, only the printed text is distributed in five exhibition spaces.

27. Yves Lecoq does the voices of the political satire "Guignols de l'info" on the television channel Canal +.

L'Homme public, l'ordre du discours (partie 1) [The Public Man, The Order of Speech (part 1)], 1994 ◁ Performance with Yves Lecoq ‡ May 28, 1994, during the inauguration of the Museum of Contemporary Art (Mac), Marseilles, France § Courtesy of the artist and Air de Paris, Paris The 28th of May 1994 (just before the Minister of Culture Jacques Toubon's speech planned for the inauguration of the Mac (Museum of Contemporary Art) in Marseilles, the famous impersonator Yves Lecoq[27] walks up to the official speaker's platform. While impersonating one by one the voices of the television presenter Patrick Poivre d'Arvor, of Jacques Toubon and of Sylvester Stallone, he recites a satirical speech on the new museum of contemporary art: "You watch too much television and do not look at enough contemporary art. Good evening…" With Jacques Chirac's voice he concludes "What is an art museum? It is a park for the real, a protected space, not a place for escaping from the real, no, far from the public gaze and opinion polls, but on the contrary a place where the real is preserved in all that is fundamentally fragile about reality itself." Then he cuts the ribbon and disappears just before Jacques Toubon officially inaugurates the museum. ◊ The parody of the museum opening therefore took place before the event.

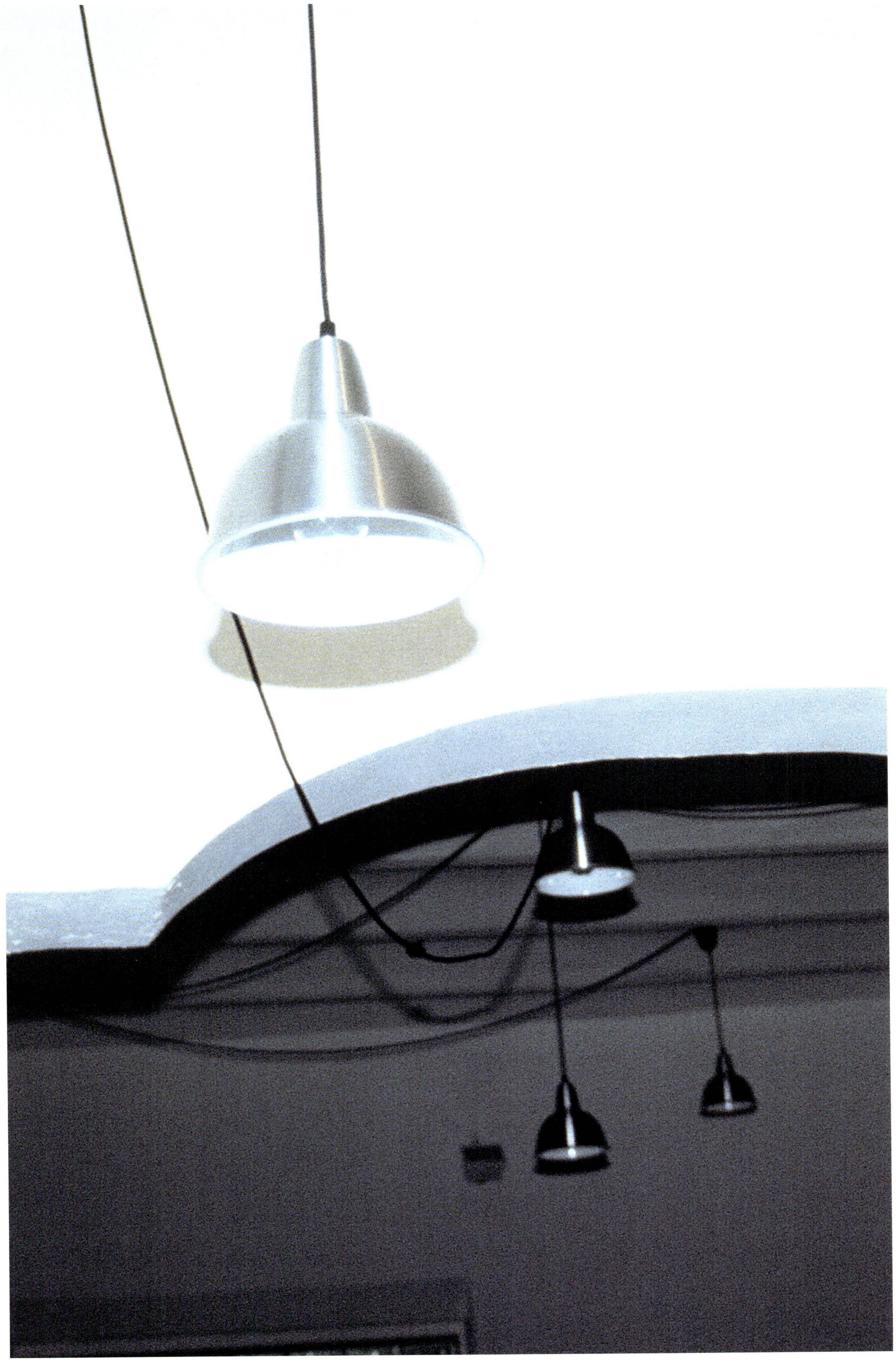

Vingt années-lumière, Dix années-lumière, **1994,** exhibition view "Sonne München", Galerie Daniel Buchholz, Cologne

La Peur des anges [The Fear of Angels], 1994 ◊ Installation: ¬ 2 loudspeakers (120 × 60 × 30 cm approx.) • sound system • CD audio stereo French/English, 29' ‡ "Soggetto-Soggetto," June 24–August 28, 1994, Museo d'arte contemporanea, Rivoli castle, Turin, Italy (exhib. cat.); exhibition curators: Francesca Pasini and Giorgio Verzotti || 1 edition § Courtesy of the artist and Air de Paris, Paris **For this bilingual version of the installation of the same name presented during the "Le Principe de réalité" [The Principle of Reality] exhibition at the Villa Arson, during the summer of 1993, the first loudspeaker plays the descriptions of specialists in the occult sciences, and the second simultaneously plays the English translation.**

L'Arbre anniversaire [The Birthday Tree], 1994 ◊ Installation: ¬ dead tree (100 × 70 × 70 cm approx.) • a hundred birthday candles (white wax; H: 10 cm approx.) • base (black lacquered wood, 15 × 15 cm approx.) ‡ October 8–16, 1994, Air de Paris booth, Fiac, Paris, France || 1 edition § Courtesy of the artist and Air de Paris, Paris

Facteur Temps / Postman Time, 1994 ◊ Installation: ¬ helium inflated balloons • flyers • projectors • parachute tent (300 × 300 cm env.) • an actor in postman's costume • pile of flyers ‡ "Lost Paradise," October 21–December 11, 1994, Kunstraum, Vienna, Austria; exhibition curator: Barbara Steiner § Courtesy of the artist and Esther Schipper, Berlin ♦ **Facteur Temps / Postman Time, 1994** Alternate title: *Postman Time Helium* ◊ Installation: ¬ cardboard box covered with turquoise fabric (40.7 × 25.7 × 51 cm), brown leather buckle • blue false leather cover, photo album (34 × 43 × 6 cm), photographs • 17 Mylar helium inflated balloons (1 beige, 2 white, 2 blue, 1 light blue, 2 gold, 1 magenta, 2 crimson, 2 red, 2 green, 2 purple; diam. deflated: 88 cm • 5 deflated balloons (yellow, blue, orange, red, green), plastic; diam.: 56 cm) • light green gauze, 750 × 170 cm approx. • white gauze, 400 × 270 cm approx. • 4 brochures and technical manuals • audio tape *Facteur Dimanche* [Sunday Postman] 26'54" • audio tape *Mixing Tape*, 30' • silver bag (10 × 111 × 18.5 cm) • Contents of silver bag: 5 deflated plastic balloons (yellow, blue, orange, red, green; diam.: 40.5 cm) • a folded light green canopy, nylon, 285 × 385 cm (unfolded) • 5 metal rings, diam.: 1.5 cm • 4 tent props, variable lengths and materials • 5 flexible tubes, PVC, diam.: 0.9 cm, variable lengths • 1 spare set of props, aluminum ‡ November 10–15, 1994, Schipper & Krome Gallery booth, Art Cologne, Cologne, Germany || 1 edition § Courtesy Esther Schipper, Berlin ***Facteur Temps* translates literally to "Postman Time" and also refers to the phrase "time is of the essence." The exhibition space was transformed into the set of a sitcom set with lights, balloons and soundtrack. An actor, dressed as a postman, distributed flyers and other advertisements to the inhabitants of a fictional town chatting with "the inhabitants" and distracting them from their own affairs, thereby "stealing" a bit of their time. Parreno describes the comedic**

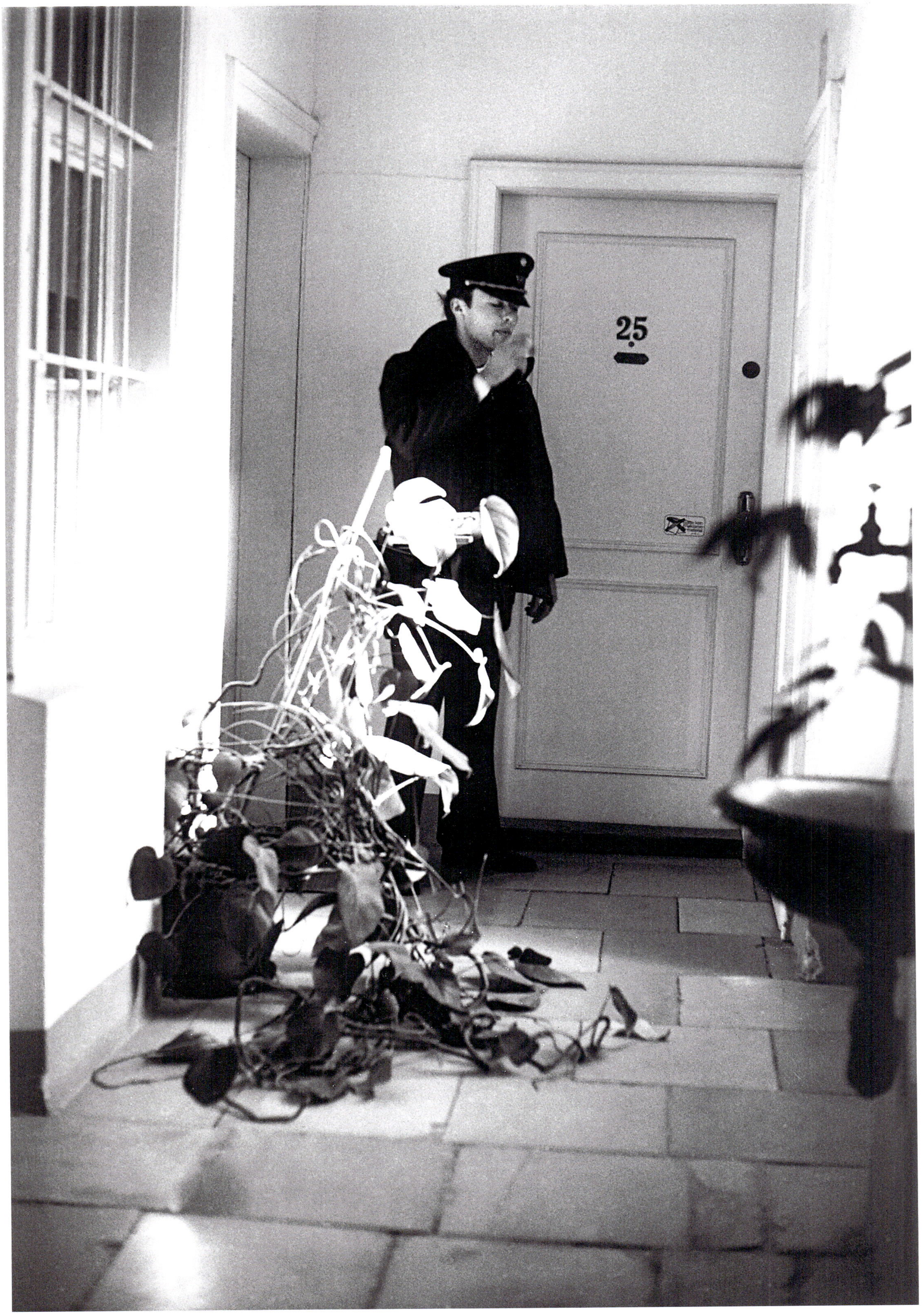

Facteur Temps / Postman Time, 1994, exhibition "Lost Paradise", Kunstraum, Vienna

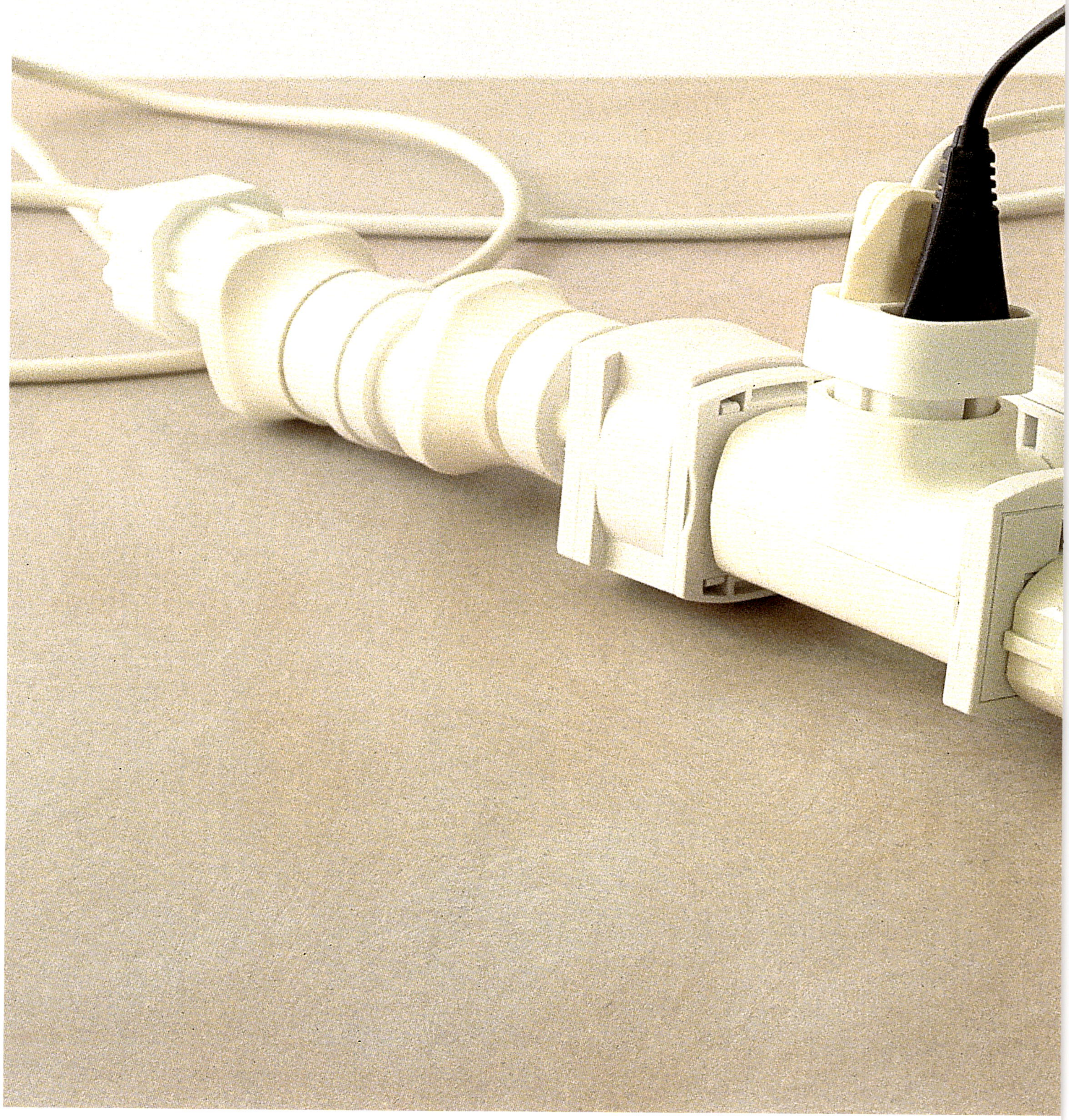

AC/DC Snakes, 1995, private collection, Paris

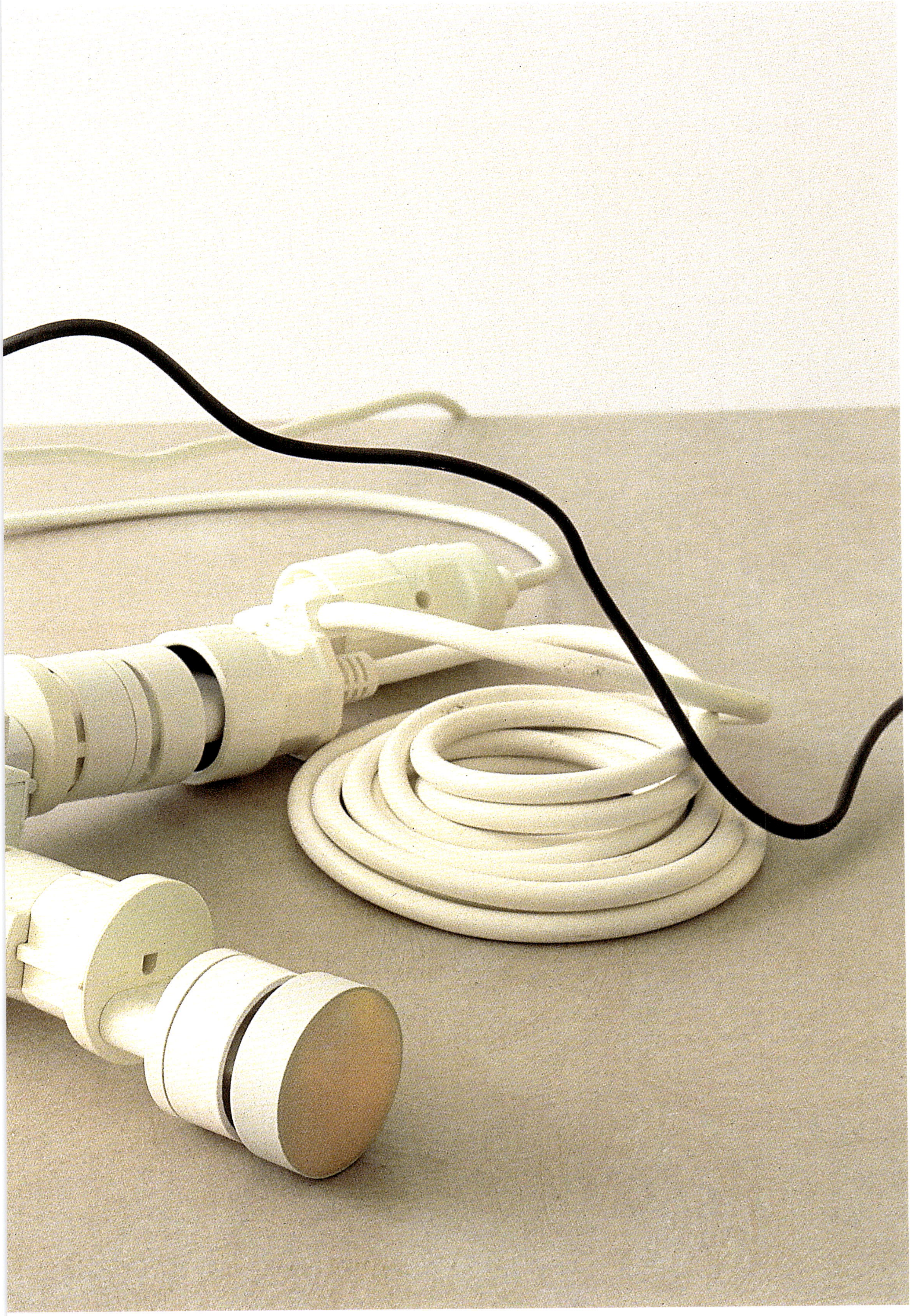

implications of this project: "The artist wants the viewer to imagine a postman giving things to people for no reason, things that do not have a particular address, such as those flyers or leaflets that we find everywhere. Very colorful, they contain many images and that can be easily the subject of a conversation. ... the postman acts like a television newscaster, he rings at different doors, and presents certain current events. ... Parreno speculated at the end of a text he wrote that if the work were a sitcom it would be called *Postman Time Helium*. This imaginary sitcom without a camera has multiple titles including *Postman Helium* or *Postman Helium Maxi Disco 45*."[28] Subsequently the work was made for Schipper & Krome Gallery's booth at Art Cologne.

28. Philippe Parreno, "Facteur Temps," *Speech Bubbles*, Dijon: Les presses du réel, 2001, p.22-23, translated from the English by Éric Troncy.

Un Homme public [A Public Man], 1994 ◁ Installation: ¬ unplugged microphone, microphone stand, 6 empty loudspeakers, Walkman, audio tape (29'45"), printed text; variable dimensions ‡ "Surface de réparations 2" [Surface of Repairs 2], October 29, 1994, Frac Bourgogne, Dijon, France (exhib. cat.); exhibition curator: Éric Troncy || 1 edition ∫ Frac Bourgogne collection, Dijon, France

L'Homme public (partie 2) [The Public Man (part 2)], 1994 ◁ Performance: ¬ unplugged microphone, microphone stand, 6 empty loudspeakers • speech by Yves Lecoq ‡ Opening of "Surface de réparations 2" [Surface of Repairs 2], October 29, 1994, Frac Bourgogne, Dijon, France (exhib. cat.); exhibition curator: Éric Troncy § Courtesy of the artist During the opening of "Surface de Reparations 2" at the Fnac Bourgogne collection in Dijon, the French impersonator Yves Lecoq stands behind an unplugged microphone near fake loudspeakers, telling the adventures of Son Goku, a small child with great powers from the Japanese cartoon *Dragon Ball Z* (broadcast on the famous children's program "Club Dorothée" on TF1). The story is told in the voices of different stars such as Johnny Hallyday, Jean-Pierre Foucault and Bernard Tapie.[29] Since his words are not amplified, the spectators must draw close to hear him. There are three parallel representations: the cartoon broadcasted on TF1, the live performance at the Frac and its simultaneous broadcast on Lecoq's television program "Guignols de l'info" on Canal+—giving the impression that the television persona has spontaneously manifested itself. *L'Homme public* (partie 2) presented the physical elements of the performance such as the microphone and the empty speakers, as well as the audio tape of the Lecoq's performance, which could be listened to on a Walkman. ◊ "My work with Yves Lecoq ... comes from a fascination with him which goes back to my childhood: he was for me television incarnate, as he could reproduce all the voices ... but the project, in the end, revolves around Lecoq as a public man. What interested me as much as Lecoq's presence was the movement of the audience around him, to see the audience approach him when he spoke into the unplugged microphone. It is a question of total dependence, between television (Lecoq) and the audience (me)."[30]

29. The text is reproduced in the exhibition catalogue *Surface de réparations*, *op. cit.*, p.77-79.

30. "Philippe Parreno, réalité virtuelle," Philippe Parreno interviewed by Nicolas Bourriaud, *Art press*, no.208, December 1995, p.42.

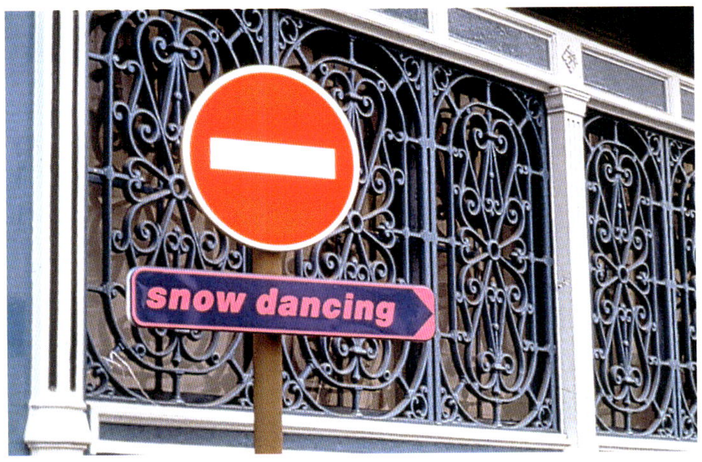

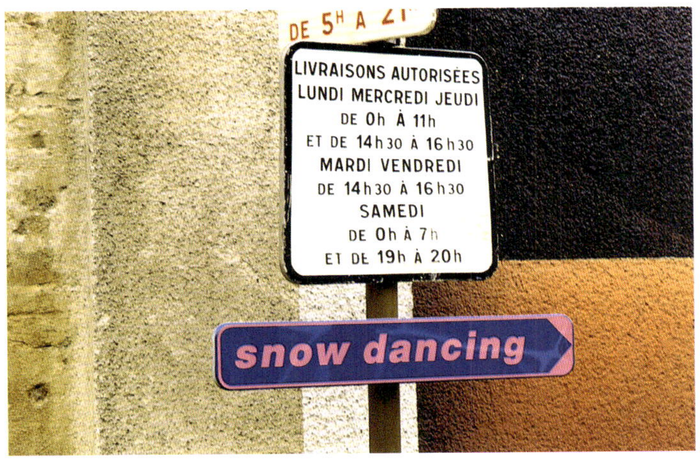

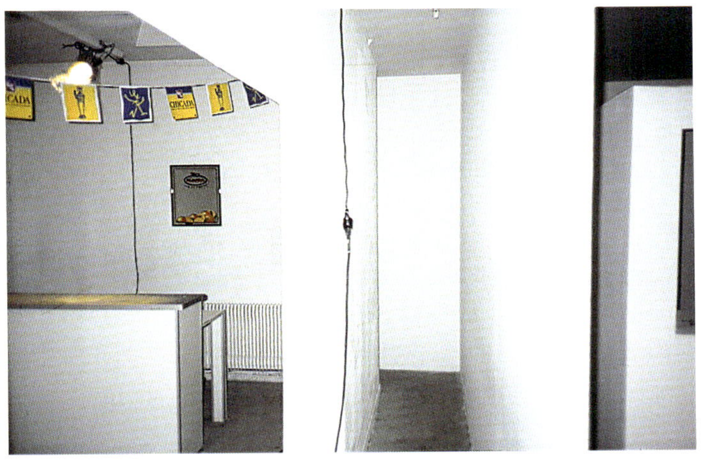
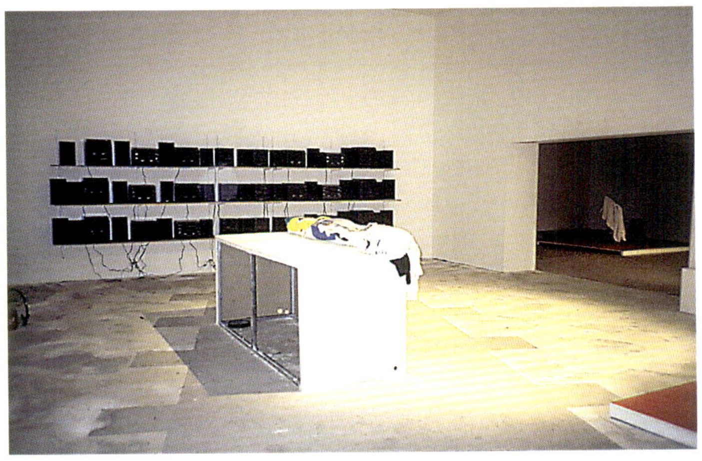
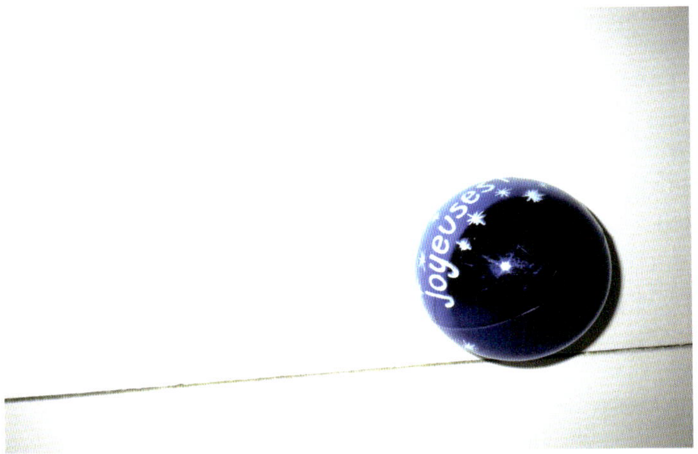

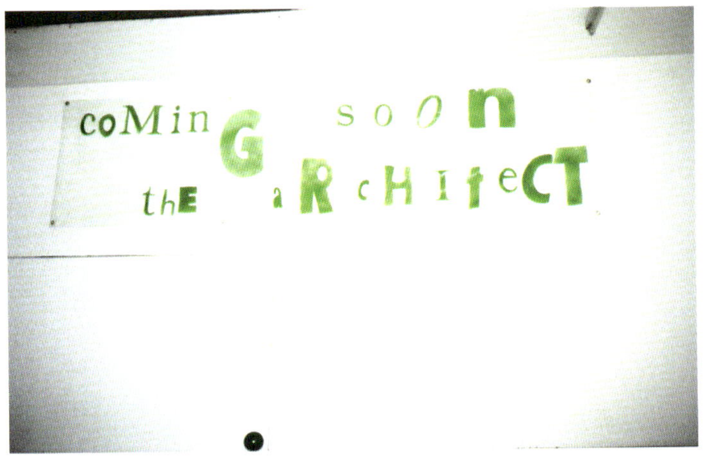

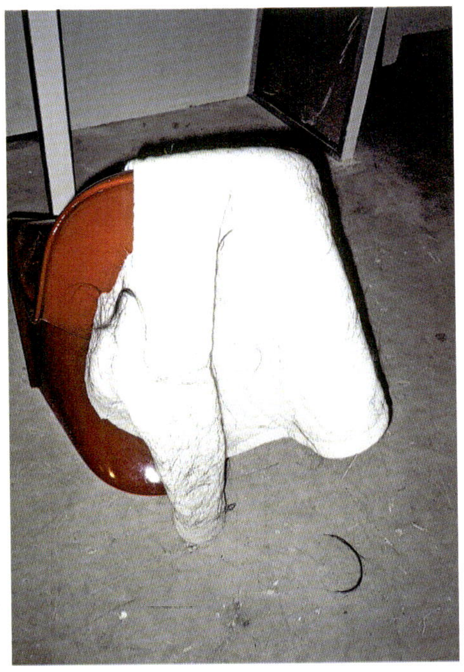
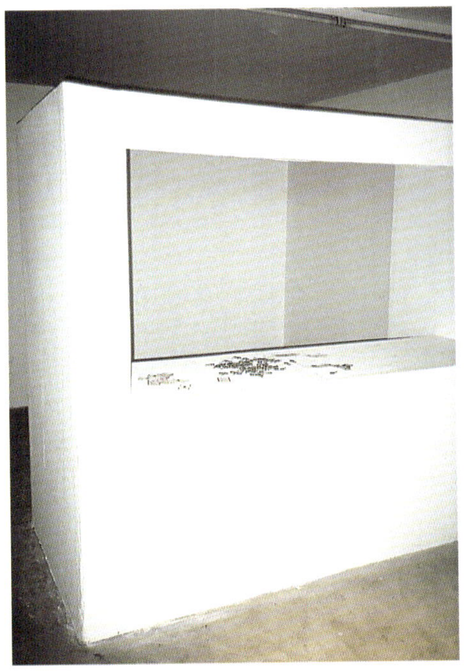

Snow Dancing, Consortium, Dijon, 1995

31. *Philippe Parreno. Alien Affection*, Arc/Musée d'Art moderne de la Ville de Paris, Paris-Musées/Les presses du réel, 2002.

Snow Dancing, 1995 ◁ Work in three parts: ¬ a book • an event (January 19, 1995) enacting the scenario described in the book • an exhibition (traces of the event) ‡ "Snow Dancing," January 20–March 8, 1995, Le Consortium, Dijon, France (exhib. cat.) ʃ Le Consortium Collection, Dijon § Courtesy of the artist ♦ **Snow Dancing, 1995** ◁ Book (text and drawings by Philippe Parreno), 20 × 14 cm, 54 pages, paperback, black and white, GW Press Ltd., London, United Kingdom; cover illustration printed in four colors: Alison McLaughlin ♦ **Snow Dancing, 1995** ◁ Road sign: color print (pink and purple) on aluminum, 20 × 80 cm approx. ‡ "Snow Dancing," January 20–March 8, 1995, Le Consortium, Dijon, France (exhib. cat.) || 1 edition ʃ Private collection, Dijon, France ***Snow Dancing***, **a book written by Parreno (published in English in 1995, currently out of print) tells the story of a promotional book launch that takes place for an hour-and-a-half at the Consortium in Dijon, which is the approximate amount of time that it takes to read the book. The book launch guests, invited by the random distribution of flyers in the streets, find themselves both actors and spectators at an event that, as Liam Gillick, one of the actors/spectators, wrote:[31] " … it had no end as it had no beginning." ◊ During the opening of the exhibition which cleverly addresses the architectural elements of the building, only traces of the book launch event remain. In keeping with Parreno's absurdist style, the exterior facade is wrapped in denim and the interior staircase is covered in a layer of Styrofoam, which guests jump upon, leaving footprints marked with Italian phrases—*sono diverso* or *sono uguale* ["I am different" or "I am the same"]. The soles of the shoes were imprinted with the phrases before the exhibition. Visitors are invited to have keys made at a station within the exhibition adjacent to padded walls which unlock all of the doors of the Consortium. Watersport equipment—eg. surfboards, balls, flippers and masks—are arranged in one room. Or visitors can chose to put on a wig and get a "hooligan" haircut from a stylist at a station near a speaker-equipped dance floor that plays music from Japanese sitcoms. A few "mutant objects," such as Christmas tree ornaments, made into door handles, further disrupt the logic of the architectural convention of the space. In further keeping with Parreno's absurdist position, *Radio Reality—Snow Dancing*, broadcast waves which are transmitted continuously on the evening of the opening and are purported to survive the end of the world. They continue to be broadcast for an hour daily, indefinitely. ◊ With this work, Parreno generates a situation that distorts the normative conception of exhibition time. *Snow Dancing* is an inverted chronology of events, which create an absence—instead of a presence—thereby subverting the established highly structured conceptual construct of time in the gallery. In this work, Parreno's interests extend beyond a concern with discreet objects, as defined by the traditional space of the museum, and more toward situations or happenings generated for, and from within an indefinite social space. As Parreno observes, in reference to a remark by Daniel Buren, "if art is interested in space it is curiously never interested in time" leaving this arena to**

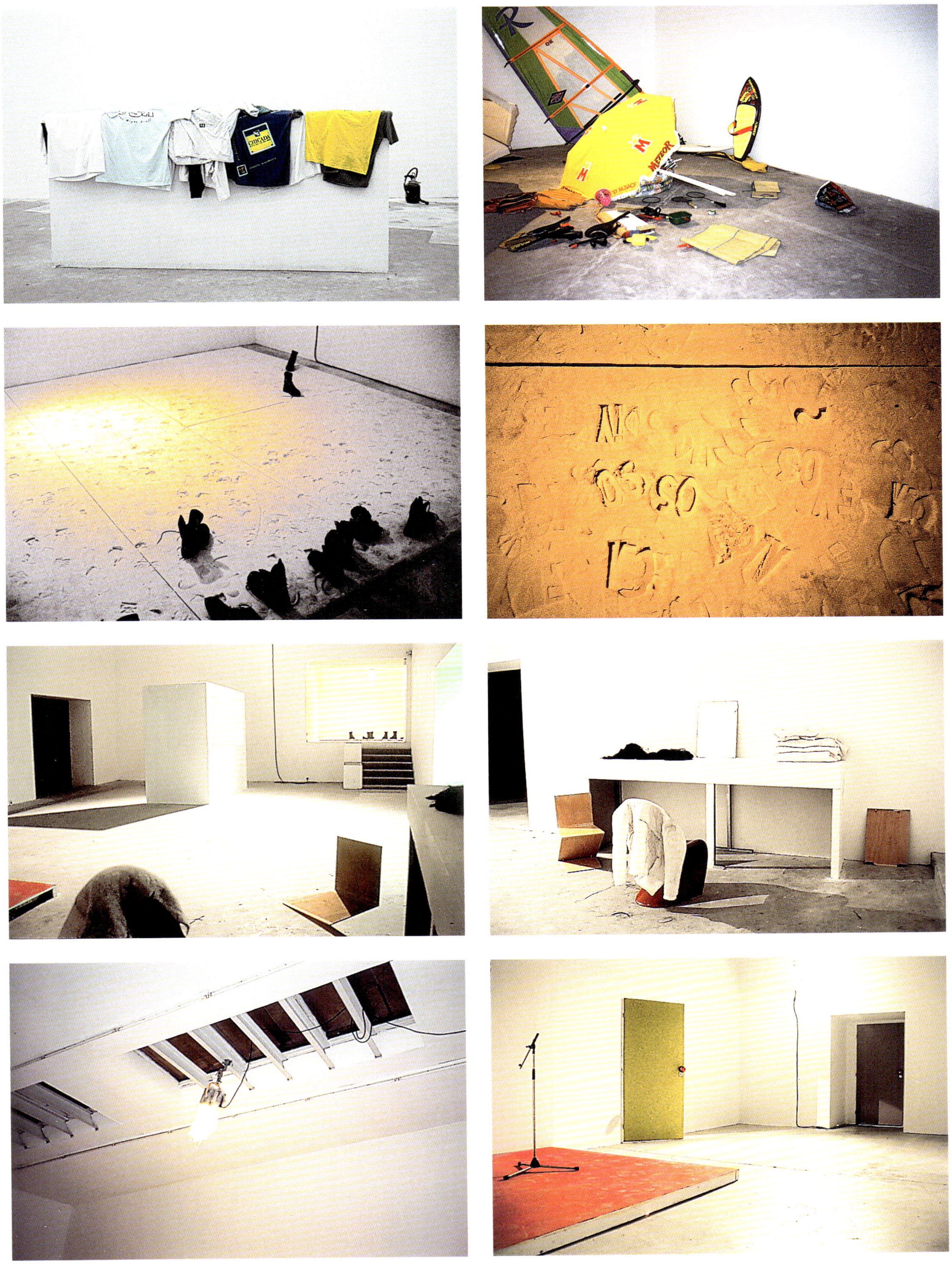

Snow Dancing, Consortium, Dijon, 1995

institutions "who decide on the work's visibility time."[32] He deliberately works against sequential or narrative expectations that are culturally, or more specifically, institutionally ascribed to an activity or gathering. The film, *Les Ateliers du Paradise*, reflects this new direction. The work is made without a camera[33] and therefore functions solely as theater for the artist.[34]

Eva, 1995 ◁ DV video transferred onto VHS, color, sound, 30' ‡ "Possessions," January 28–February 18, 1995, NZET Projekt, Gand, Belgium [temporary gallery of Air de Paris, Météo & Philippe Rizzo] || 1 edition § Courtesy Air de Paris, Paris **A young girl, filmed in a studio at the local television channel AVS TV in Gand, presents a special program of Lecoq's different performances made for the project *L'Homme public.***

Cinemascope / Visitors vs Home, 1995 With Rirkrit Tiravanija ◁ Performance (football match) and installation ¬ Installation: video projector, 20 hours approx. of Hi8 video recording ‡ "Volatile Colonies," February 28–April 30, 1995, 1st Johannesburg Biennial, South Africa; exhibition curator: Kendell Geers § Courtesy of the artists **Parreno and Rirkrit Tiravanija organized a football match between a team of international artists all of whom participated in the 1st Johannesburg Biennial and a team of local artists. Each participant wore a printed T-shirt reproducing the headlines of South African newspapers at the time. The video projection presented during the Biennial documented almost 20 hours of this project.**

Cinemascope, 1995 With Rirkrit Tiravanija ◁ Installation: projection screen, 122 × 250 cm • curved structure mounted on wooden stand • Hi8 master video, color, sound, 7 hours approx. • rough wooden table • 1 poster • 4 printed T-shirts ‡ Frac Lorraine, Metz, France || 1 edition ʃ Frac Lorraine collection, Metz, France **This installation presents documentation of *Cinemascope / Visitors vs Home* project made during the 1st Johannesburg Biennial.**

The Factory of Clouds, 1995 ◁ One week workshop with 10 participants ‡ From April 25 to May 4, 1995, at the Kunstverein in Hamburg, Germany § Courtesy of the artist **The workshop participants spend a week together planning the elements of the Kunstverein exhibition "While…."**

While…, 1995 ◁ Installation: ¬ chairs and round tables • 1 television playing 1 VHS video, color, sound, 5'30" • 1 radio • daily edition of *Tageszeitung* (several copies replaced every day); variable dimensions ‡ "Philippe Parreno," May 30–June 29, 1996, Robert Prime Gallery, London, United Kingdom || 1 edition § Courtesy Esther Schipper, Berlin **Over the course of the exhibition the same information is published in the *Tageszeitung* daily. At 4 pm everyday, the same radio programme (newscaster: Ditman Mues) is broadcast, and at 5 pm everyday the same television programme (newscaster: Dagmar Berghoff) is broadcast.**

32. *Speech Bubbles*, *op. cit.*, p. 20.

33. Barbara Steiner, "Film as a Method of Thinking and Working," *Paletten*, no.224, p.53.

34. Nicolas Bourriaud wrote: "In their desire to leave the peripheries (of representation and metaphor) for the centre (of power), artists brought more visible professional activities into their practices: they were company managers, communicators, designers or film directors. And some built strong artwork upon this premise, from Carsten Höller to Philippe Parreno." ("Topocritique. L'art contemporain et l'investigation géographique") (Topocritic. Contemporary Art and Geographical Investigation), *GNS, Global Navigation System*, Paris: Palais de Tokyo, Site de création contemporaine / Cercle d'art, 2003).

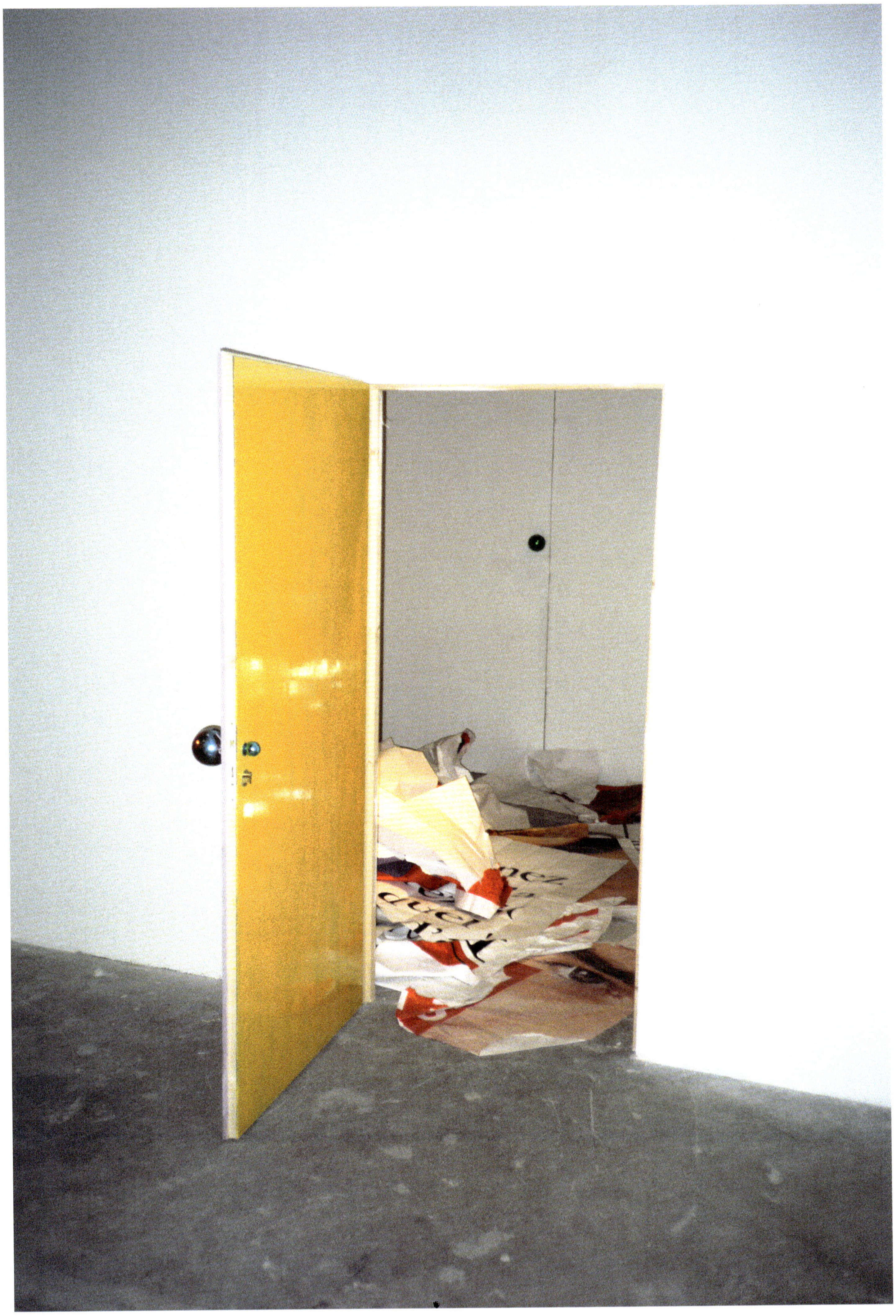

Snow Dancing, Consortium, Dijon, 1995

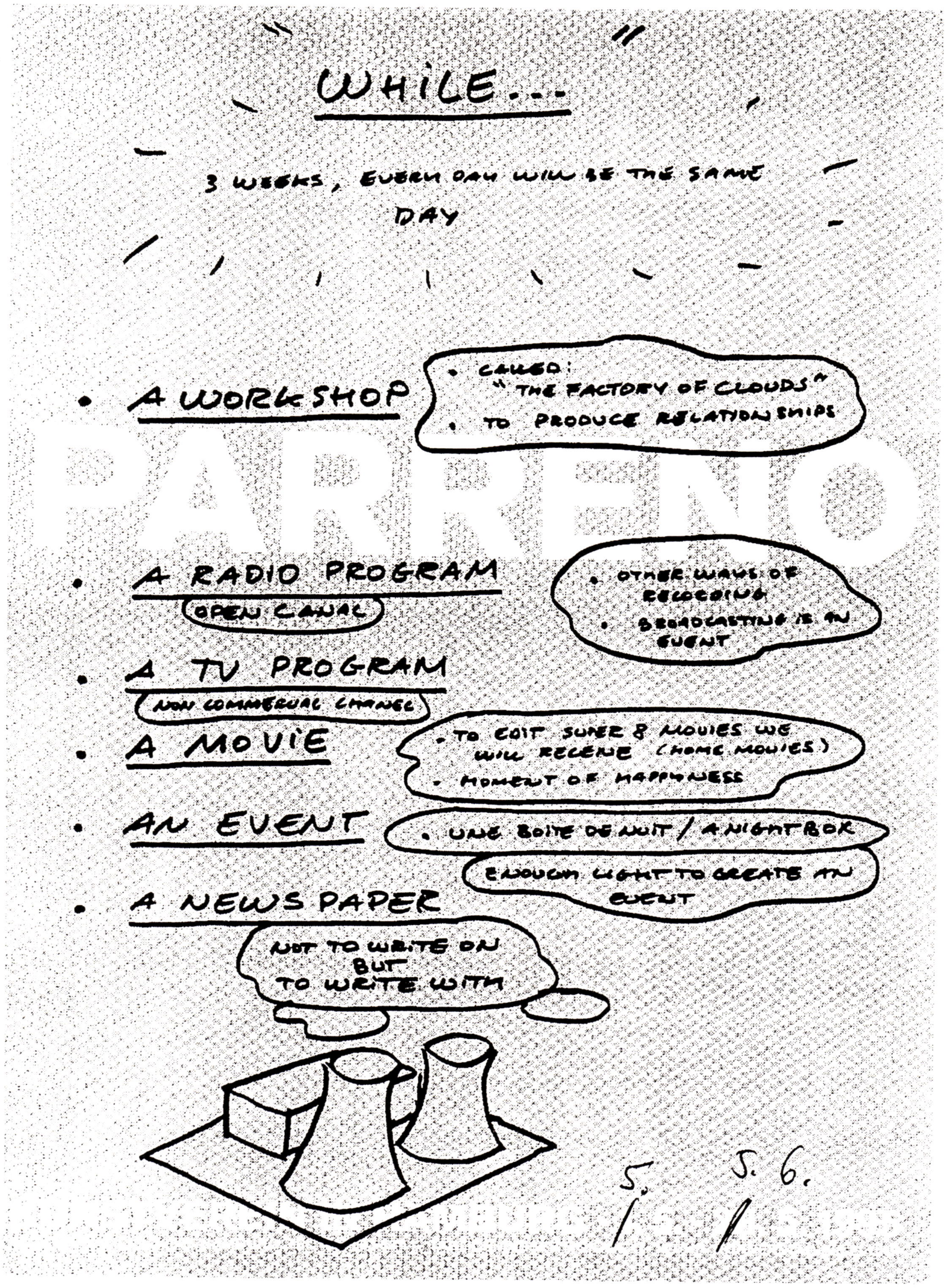

Exhibition poster "While… ", Kunstverein, Hamburg
While…, 1995, exhibition view "While… ", Kunstverein, Hamburg

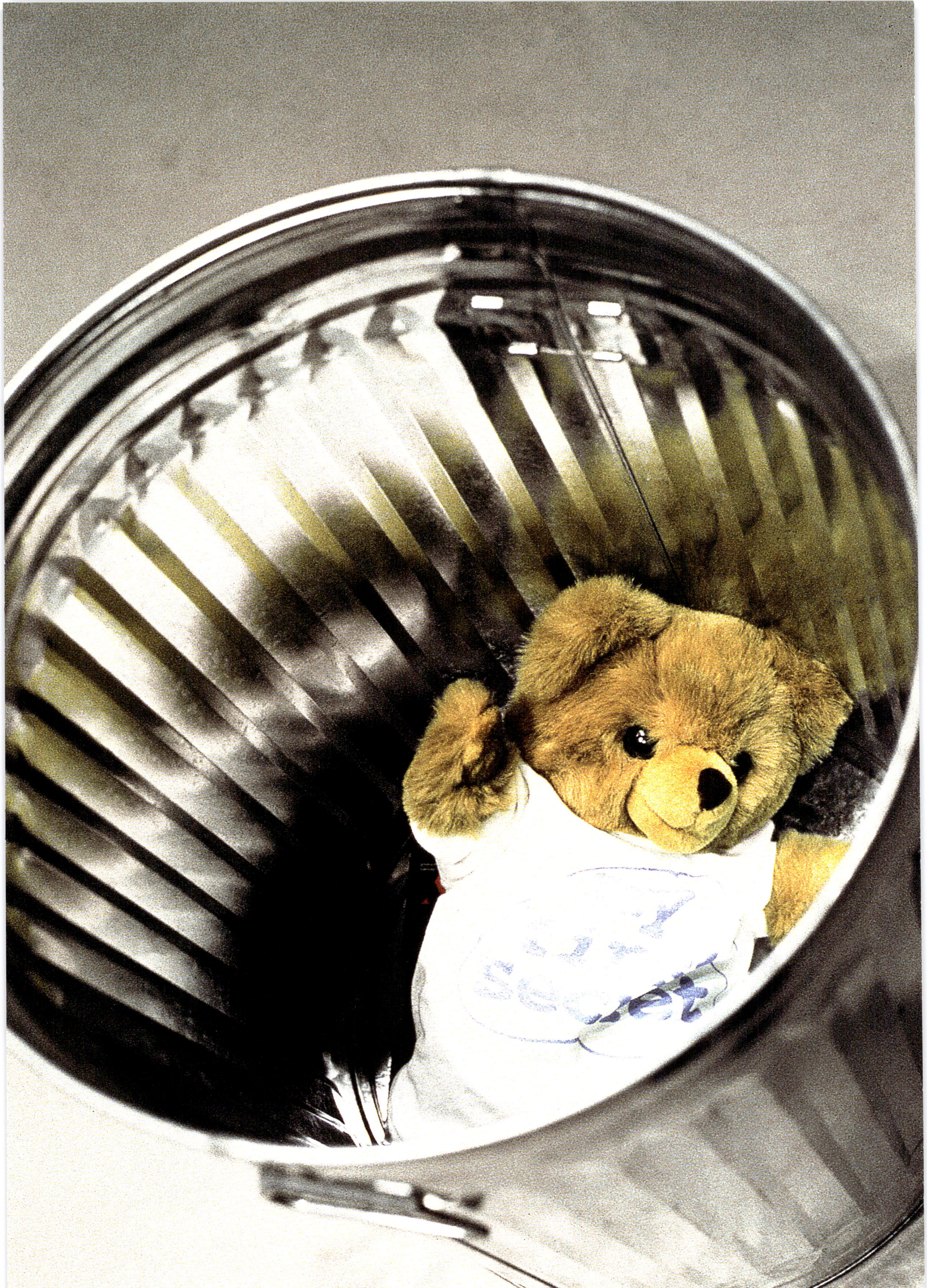

While (Dagmar Berghoff), 1995 ◁ Installation: ¬ black and white television monitor (50 × 50 cm approx.), VHS video, color, sound, 5'30" • mirror, 220 × 200 cm ‡ "While…," May 5–June 5, 1995, Kunstverein in Hamburg, Hamburg, Germany; exhibition curator: Stephan Schmidt-Wulffen || 1 edition § Courtesy Esther Schipper, Berlin **The video of the exhibition "While…," in which the newscaster Dagmar Berghoff reads the news written by the participants of *The Factory of Clouds* workshop, is shown on a television placed on the ground facing a large mirror.**

Werktische [Made on the First of May], 1995 Alternate title: *L'Établi* [The Established] ◁ Performance: ¬ a dozen participants • 2 round tables (H.: 85 cm; diam.: 160 cm) • chairs • teddy bear • microchip with recorded message • *My First Secret* printed T-shirts • various tools ‡ May 1st, 1995 at the Schipper & Krome Gallery, Cologne, Germany § Courtesy of the artist **Members of different labor unions work on an assemby line to make teddy bears in celebratation of May day. These teddy bears wear a T-shirt that reads: *"My First Secret"* and contain a microchip in their right paw which allows the teddy bears to record and then to repeat short messages. The video documenting this performance is entitled *Werktische (Made on the First of May)*.**

Werktische I, 1995 ◁ Installation: ¬ round table (H.: 85 cm; diam.: 160 cm) • 8 teddy bears with *My First Secret* printed T-shirts • microchip with pre-recorded message and white cotton label printed with "Made on the First of May" ‡ "Werktische," May 5–June 16, 1995, Schipper & Krome Gallery, Cologne, Germany || 1 edition § Courtesy Esther Schipper, Berlin **This installation consists of a series of elements from the exhibition "Werktische." Eight teddy bears containing messages recorded by the workers were assembled during the performance on the first of May.**

Werktische II, 1995 ◁ Installation: ¬ projection screen (180 × 130 cm) • compact video projector • 2 VHS tapes and 1 Beta cam SP master of the video *Werktische (Made on the First of May)*, color, sound, 2'40", round table (H.: 85 cm; diam.: 160 cm) ‡ "Werktische," May 5–June 16, 1995, Schipper & Krome Gallery, Cologne, Germany || 1 edition ∫ Private collection, Milan, Italy **This second installation presents the video *Werktische (Made on the First of May)* documenting the performance and includes the table used to fabricate the teddy bears.**

Ice Man in Reality Park, 1995 ◁ Exhibition: ¬ sculpted ice, replaced each day • pink balloons, (plastic, diam.: 100 cm approx.) • ten cushions (material, stuffing, 50 × 50 cm each approx.) ‡ "Ripple Across the Water," September 2–October 1, 1995, Minami Aoyama, Tokyo (exhib.cat); exhibition curator: Jan Hoet || 1 edition § Courtesy of the artist **Everyday, just before the lunch break in the private park of the Kirin Brewery Company in Minami**

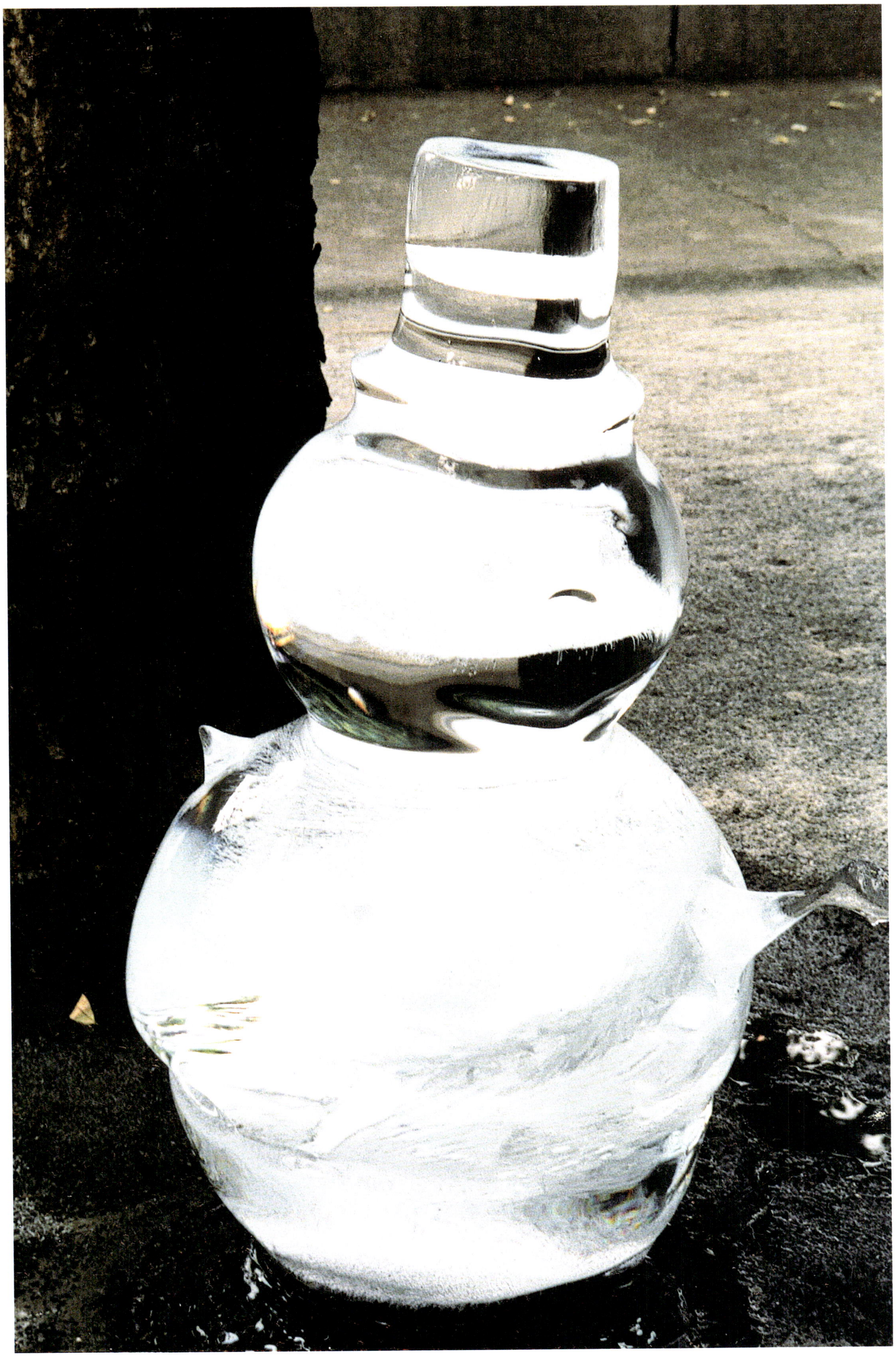

Ice Man in Reality Park, 1995, exhibition view "Ripple Across the Water", Minami Aoyama, Tokyo

Aoyama, Tokyo, a refrigerated truck drops off an ice sculpture of a snowman. Large pink balloons float on the park's water fountains. Cushions are placed on the riverbank for the employees to sit during their lunch hour.

Ice Man in Reality Park, 1995 ◁ 2 drawings pencil on paper || 1 edition ʃ Watari-Um Collection, Watari Museum of Contemporary Art, Tokyo, Japan Two pencil drawings explain, in comic-strip format, the *Ice Man in Reality Park* project.

Le Labyrinthe moral / Moral Maze, 1995 ◁ Exhibition made with Liam Gillick, June 22–August 12, 1995, Le Consortium, Dijon, France ¬ Invited artists: Angela Bulloch, Maurizio Cattelan, Liam Gillick, Dominique Gonzalez-Foerster, Douglas Gordon, Lothar Hempel, Carsten Höller, Pierre Huyghe, Jorge Pardo, Philippe Parreno, Rirkrit Tiravanija, Xavier Veilhan § Courtesy of the artists *Le Labyrinthe moral / Moral Maze* uses the conceptual framework of the series *The Moral Maze*, broadcast beginning in 1990 on Radio 4, BBC. This talk radio series features an "expert" whom listeners query with a "question of the day." Daily, prior to the opening the exhibition, a guest is questioned by the artists. The exhibition features recordings of these interviews.

Vicinato, 1995 With Carsten Höller and Rirkrit Tiravanija ◁ 16 mm film, black and white, sound, 12'47"; original version in Italian, other versions with English sub-titles. ‡ "Vicinato," October 5–November 18, 1995, Studio Guenzani, Milan, Italy || 12 editions and 3 artists' editions ʃ First public collection: Frac Languedoc-Roussillon, Montpellier, France (2/12) § Courtesy Studio Guenzani, Milan; Air de Paris, Esther Schipper, Berlin Invited by the Guenzani studio in Milan to participate in a group exhibition, Carsten Höller, Philippe Parreno and Rirkrit Tiravanija make a 16mm black and white film (directed by Parreno in Milan in early Fall 1995). They asked "What is this proximity of thought which justifies our presence together?"[35] This dialogue, in the form of a film—a closed and timeless scene written in English by three different hands—functions as the exhibition and replaces the traditional role of objects that the artists could have made.[36] The dialogue is transcribed, translated into Italian and then randomly distributed between three actors who play the three artist/friends sitting around a patio table on a terrace. Each actor has the same number of words, as they pose questions to each other on the nature of reality, art and language in a cinematic style evocative of Italian realist films of the 1950s. This work is an attempt to bring together a group within an image, to "see what there is that is singular in that which is plural and to see in a singular work that which is plural."[37] ◊ *Vicinato 2*, which followed in 2000, stages four actors based on a conversation between Gillick, Douglas Gordon, Höller, Pierre Huyghe, Parreno and Tiravanija about their role in consumer society and possible alternatives with the commentary of a narrator. The narrator in *Vicinato 2* who *(see page 110)*

35. Philippe Parreno, interview with Philippe Vergne, *Art Press*, no.264, January 2001, p.26.

36. See the book *Vicinato, The Transcription of a Film by Carsten Höller, Philippe Parreno, Rirkrit Tiravanija*, London: GW Press Ltd., 1996.

37. *Ibid.*

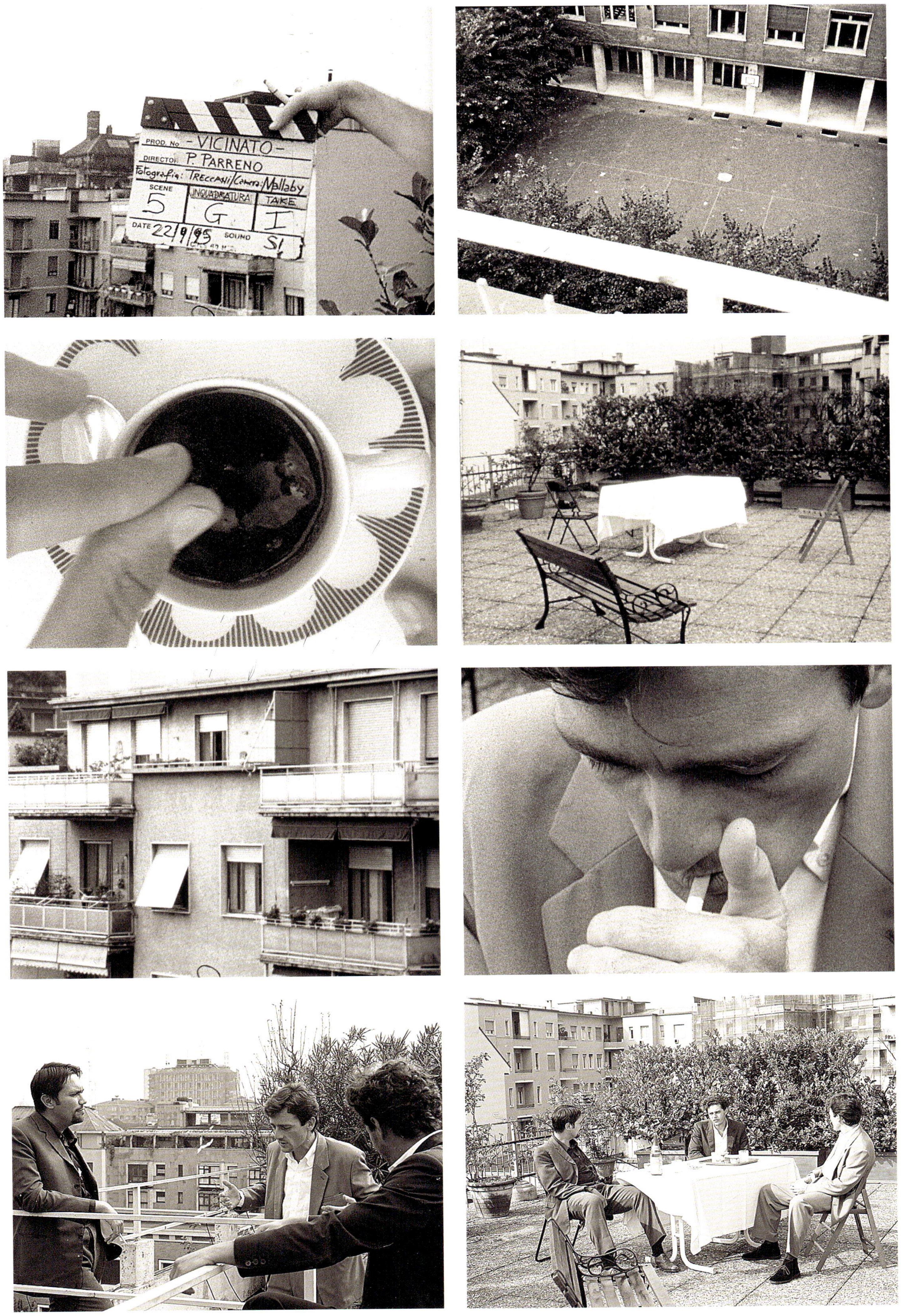

Vicinato, 1995, film

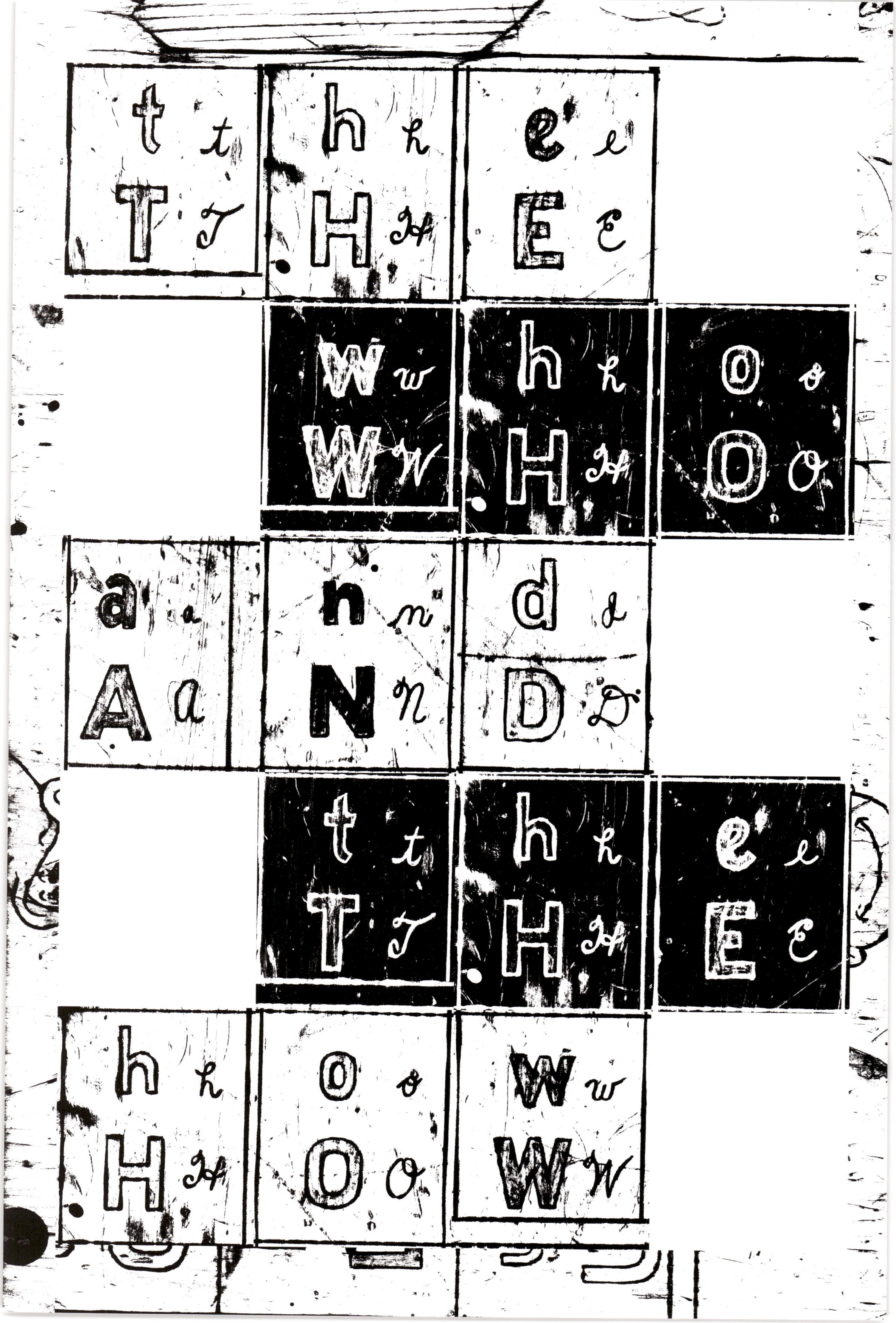
the
THE
who
WHO
and
AND
the
THE
how
HOW

The Who and the How: thoughts on Philippe Parreno's work

Maria Lind

A group of young men engage in the same activity. Each of them is carrying a heavy weapon. They are in the middle of a dance of death, surrounded by tall apartment buildings and posters of the angular face of a man. We are thrown into a fierce battle and the men argue about who gets to use the biggest gun. "If I don't get it we are not going to make it across the street and then we are lost." The men are rendered like figures in a 1930s expressionist ink drawing; with simplified features and thick contours.

Then switch to a rooftop where three men dressed in slightly over-sized suits sit around a table, sometimes they get up to walk around. They talk, drink and smoke one cigarette after another. Love, friendship and work are discussed animatedly in Italian. We glimpse an affluent residential neighborhood as the camera restlessly circles around the men as if they were crime suspects. *Film noir* is the appropriated aesthetic.

Another switch, we see four handsome young men lounging in the sun on a terrace perched high on a promontory, the sea is visible in the distance. Again there is talk about how to live life, about leisure and things they don't understand. They ask each other to what degree is it advisable to represent the here and now. They wonder if you destroy something, when you talk about how lovely it is to go for a walk in the snow, while you are going for a walk in the snow. The images are filtered through the visually voluptuous style of Brian de Palma's Hollywood suspense movies.

All three films are based on real conversations between men who know each other and share some form of actual experience. *Vicinato* (1995), a collaboration between the artists Carsten Höller, Philippe Parreno and Rirkrit Tiravanija, is drawn from discussions between the artists, turned into a script and then staged with actors on top of a building in Milan. *Vicinato 2* (2000) is a collaboration between the aforementioned artists plus fellow artists: Liam Gillick, Douglas Gordon and Pierre Huyghe. The film pulls together comments and questions from colleagues and friends who were specially brought together by Parreno to produce the piece. The voice over retells their stories with a strange metallic computer-generated voice. Exhibitions and art world screenings are the primary venues for both films.

Ari Folman's acclaimed feature length documentary *Waltz With Bashir* (2008) is an autobiographical account of an Israeli man who has forgotten what he did as a soldier in the 1982 Lebanese War. This animated film follows him on his quest for remembrance, through meetings with fellow soldiers and a psychologist friend who explains the mechanisms of trauma and forgetting. The narrator's repression of his deeds most likely originates in finding himself in the same position as the Nazi camp guard who persecuted his parents during the Second World War. Strikingly different from the kind of media reports of similar events with which we are usually bombarded, the film's highly transformed visual appearance allows for affective responses. It is deeply touching.

Male bonding is at the core of these three rather different works. Bonding which is direct and basic, mediated and de-familiarized at the same time. Men spend time with each other talking about personal and existential issues, traditionally understood as "feminine." A group of what appears to be straight guys embraces something clearly connected to notions of femininity. What kind of gender bending is going on here?

1. In the case of Liam Gillick it is "the decorative" and in the work of Douglas Gordon "the emotional."

Women are part of the mix in the children's television series ***The Power Rangers,*** from which the Italian dub actors were borrowed and the Hollywood film ***The Beach,*** in which two of the actors in ***Vicinato 2*** were working together. In both films no women are present in the discussions, they are not even in sight. With women absent it becomes if not homoerotic then at least openly homo-social, which is arguably already all too common within contemporary culture. A deep-seated desire to engage with the intimate and emotional, but also with magic and the fantastical seems to lie behind these, and numerous other works by Parreno. Although the works may themselves appear more or less straightforward and mundane, the television series and the movie from which Parreno and the others drew the actors in the ***Vicinato*** films are both about supernatural powers and extrasensory experiences. Yet the masculinities at play are far from monolithic. Like in other works of some of the artists involved in these two projects, phenomena that have been understood, historically speaking, to be connected to femininity are placed at the center.[1] Rather than talking about gender bending we can think in terms of gender tweaking. A form of mild, and possibly unconscious, identity politics.

2. The main point of narrative rupture in *Waltz With Bashir*, when "the other" enters, occurs at the very end when footage from either Shabra or Shatila is introduced. We are confronted with crying women and children surrounded by dead bodies and other forms of devastation. This is also the moment when Arabic and Arabs enter the story. Women do appear before this moment but remain in the background.

Another instance of confusion of traditional notions of femininity and masculinity happens when Zidane in the feature length film with the same title, directed by Parreno and Gordon, is portrayed not only as an outstanding football player but as an exotic object of desire. In the film, he is on the one hand celebrated as the perfect image of an alpha male super ego. A man whose every body movement, every little gesture is deemed not only important but also pleasurable to watch. On the other hand an abundance of cameras make his facial features become a miniature landscape in transition. If we didn't know what his playing style is before we watched the film we remain just as ignorant afterwards, but we do learn that Zidane is a man of many emotions. A similar strategy was used in 1930s film melodramas, which focused on love, relationships and other intimate issues and whose main audience consisted of women. However, there it was close-ups of the faces of the female stars, which functioned as screens for dramatic events.[2]

Even more particular is Parreno's commitment to the actual process of making a work of art and to the very conditions of its production. At one point this led him to co-found a film production company, Anna Sanders Films, which opened up the possibility of collaborations beyond the art world. While interesting ideas are not that unusual with art, neither are funny ones—even brilliant ideas abound—they are rarely matched by the outcome. This discrepancy between the intention and the final artwork can often be painful. A particular feature of Parreno's work is not only a special focus on the methodologies of production but also on elaborate production processes, which sometimes are extremely complex. At first glance a project can appear awkwardly complicated and unnecessarily costly but in the end it is clear that it is necessary to proceed in this way. The finished project, so to speak, stands up to the idea and the production.

But the very foundational question comes from another realm, from the ontology of semiotics: what is the nature of an image? "An image is many things," is the quick answer in Parreno's universe. Many unexpected things, to be more precise. It is something that you can walk through, if you look at *No More Reality, une vidéoconférence* (1991) where a video projection of a close up of the face of a man who is trying to portray a character from the film *The Name of the Rose* (1986) is projected on to a curtain covering the entrance to the exhibition. But an image can also be an image of another image, like the transparent Eero Saarinen glass lamp, *Happy Ending, Stockholm, 1997-1996* (1997), which turns out to bear no resemblance to the original. To add to the opacity of the piece the light is on although the lamp remains unplugged. An image can even be a short film in constant pre-production, filmed at the sunrise on an island above the Arctic Circle like in *El Sueño de Una Cosa* (2001). This science-fiction like pastoral creates new stories in each new presentation, whether inserted among commercials for Coca Cola and Ikea in Swedish cinemas or projected onto a reproduction of a painting from Robert Rauschenberg's *White Paintings* series (1951) and accompanied by John Cage's *4'33* (1952) in an exhibition space.

This sense of play is a recurring feature in Parreno's work and one which informs the frequent question, namely: How do you make such an image collectively? Enticement with collaborative practices is something that Parreno shares with many of his contemporaries. Close attention must be paid to the procedures, building blocks and not least as has been shown, to the makers themselves. Every detail is potentially significant and yet the work does not come across as anal. Take for example *Vicinato* which means neighborhood in Italian, that which is close to you and readily at hand, in this case, a peer group of the same generation. Parreno has collaborated with the other artists involved who to some degree also make up a group of friends. The two sets of actors in the *Vicinato* films have in turn worked together for *The Power Rangers* and in *The Beach* respectively, which indeed also deal with collective activity and group dynamic.

Besides the many examples of collaborations in Parreno's body of work, ideas of connectivity abound; "multiple takes," "a variety of links," "the chain" are phrases which often crop up in interviews with him.

It can be argued that the last two decades have witnessed a collaborative turn within contemporary art. This is by no means an entirely new phenomenon. On the contrary, it is a well-trodden trajectory from baroque masters large-scale studios to the romantic Nazarenes in Rome around 1820, Surrealist experiments and Andy Warhol's factory. The transition from modernism to postmodernism may not even have been possible without the abundance of collaborations and challenges to conventional concepts of authorship on which conceptual art, fluxus festivals and feminist practices insisted. More recently various forms of collaborations have surfaced among artists, curators, architects and other cultural producers, some of which are new. Think of the many collective activities imbued with notions of solidarity and characterized by shared decision-making processes; participatory projects where the overall structure is decided by one or several people for others to interact with or be a part of; teamwork and outsourcing within commercially defined initiatives. And these are just a few examples of frequently used methods.

Parreno seems to be obsessed with collectivity, community and the common. If the *Vicinato* films are not aiming for an existential union between their characters then they at least put forth sharing as a principle and having something in common. But the common always goes in tandem with how the individual can participate in the common. How to be part of the collective and simultaneously contribute individually. How to grant the whole and at the same time its parts equal shares. In *Vicinato,* queries of this kind operate both on the level of "motive," that which is to be seen and heard in the films, and on a structural level. In the production process, the films "perform" their subject matter. Therefore it is important to look at not only motivation but also at production processes: the first *Vicinato* came about as a response to an invitation for a group exhibition from an Italian gallery. Having often been asked to exhibit in the same shows the artists instead made a collective film, based on contributions by each of them, thereby replacing one group format with another, which, in this case, was self-organized. The resulting films end up thematizing and to a degree performing the old feminist dictum: difference without hierarchies.

Deeply embedded in current social, political and economic situations Parreno's work needs to be considered as part of that foil. Contrary to popular belief that community is weakening and vanishing today, it can be claimed that "coming together," "bonding" and "caring" are more vital than in a long time. In fact, if we resist the temptation to understand community as the foundation of the formation of society, we make possible something that is non-essential and non-absolute. Community as relational if you wish, which emerges in the wake of society rather than the other way around and which is resistant to immanent power. Here the urge to account for the specific, for the individual, in order to avoid subsumption into the larger context is crucial. Notions such as "multitude" and "the common" are distinguished by the balance between on the one hand the group, moving away from the mass or mob, and on the other hand the single person. Among the most striking manifestations of this resurgence of social interests is the new wave of activism over the last decade and its media presence through anti—or alter—globalization events from Seattle in 1999 to Genoa in 2003 but also more discrete self-organized projects. Movements like the collective Reclaim the Streets (RTS) and other tactical media have clearly made their mark in how acting together and joining forces can be reinvented and understood today.

Parreno's work involves all the above approaches to collaboration. To the degree that research-based projects are intrinsically collaborative, *Michel Amathieu, Djamel Benameur, Jacques Chaban-Delmas, James Chinlund, Maurice Cotticelli, Hubert Dubedout, François Dumoulin, Ebezeber Howard, M/M (Paris), Pierre Mendès-France, Miko, Neyrpic, Alain Peyrefitte, Inez van Lamsweerde & Vinoodh Matadin, Anna-Léna Vaney, Angus Young,* called *Credits* (2000) can be characterized by collaboration with numerous individuals. This work was based on non-documented interviews made by the artist who assembled multiple voices talking about the shared experience of living in 1970s suburban housing projects in France, which eventually converges in one image. Having grown up in ZUP, the artist could easily recognize them as long-standing blind spots within Western culture. This moving image shows a set with a handful of young slender trees adorned with colorful plastic bags in front of a block of apartments where the windows are lit at the end. Combined with a brief soundtrack by AC/DC's Angus Young and a large color photograph of a boy by Inez van Lamsweerde and Vinoodh Matadin, it extends into a mini-exhibition of sorts. In one of its incarnations this work was timed so that at the end of the projection of the short film, a light went on which illuminated the photograph, which functioned as a credit line for the project. The boy in the photograph could very well have lived in the neighborhood. Maybe he even tied the plastic bags to the trees causing the branches to break in the wind so that the trees would die and its original users could reclaim the green area.

In comparison *Snow Dancing* (1995) was more participatory. A book was the basis for an archetypically participatory event —a party/promotion— with many activities, services and products; the residue became the exhibition, which in and of itself is one of the oldest forms of public participation. Like so many art venues, Le Consortium in Dijon is a big old building which once had an entirely different function. There were people wearing T-shirts with Marlboro logos and pants with Agfa signs. The slogan "identical and different" could be seen here and there. A young postman was distributing information and someone was comparing the effect of two different washing powders. A shoemaker was cutting revolutionary slogans into the soles of shoes, which left an imprint in the expanded foam flooring. Simultaneously, a lot of dancing was going on. Like at Euro Disney it was unclear who was paid to participate and who was not. Before leaving it was a good idea to double-check the routes as the entrance and exit signs had been exchanged. The book itself was generated by the narrative as written by the artist and eventually published. It takes about an hour and a half to read the book out loud, which is also how long the party lasted.

The project which is perhaps most quintessentially of our time in regards to its collaborative production process is *No Ghost Just a Shell* (1999–2003), initiated by Huyghe and Parreno and eventually involving a dozen artists. An inexpensive and simple Manga figure was acquired in Japan and this relatively empty sign, consisting only of the name Annlee and a face, was used as a vessel to be filled by the contributors's desires and personal trajectories. Many of them made videos, others produced objects and sound. It should be remembered that a majority of the invited contributors were men shaping the sign of a woman. In Parreno's own episode, *Anywhere Out of the World,* the sign becomes a pure product whose voice belongs to a model who normally earns a living from selling images of herself. The episode recounts Annlee's creation story, once again putting the conditions of production in basic materialist terms, and how she was "salvaged" from almost certain disappearance within the entertainment industry and given new life within an art project. Otherwise, with only a name and a face she would most likely have been an extra appearing briefly in a production. Instead, like a contemporary Pygmalion, she is granted a new existence, freed from the marketplace by Parreno and Huyghe.

By outsourcing the production to a loose network of friends and colleagues a temporary community with a best-before date was created, namely when the product which was taken out of one commercial context and moved to the next—Annlee—was sold for one euro to a legal entity whose only purpose is to prevent the use of this sign again. The circulation of this "flashing sign" was halted and the community dissolved. Attribution, authorship and ownership are obviously essential here. In line with Parreno's distinctly non-didactic approach to art making *No Ghost Just a Shell* does not just celebrate collaboration—a "collaborateur" is after all a traitor not to be trusted. Neither does he promote salutary professional relationships but rather taps into many of the problematic aspects of working conditions under neo-liberalism. On a post-Fordist deregulated job market the worker/producer gains independence as well as insecurity, flexibility as well as self-exploitation. S/he becomes a member of the precariat that encompasses anyone whose working conditions are precarious, regardless of social and cultural status. Here the artist as a figure representing self-motivation, unconventionality and endless creativity is the very role model for the contemporary worker.

In Parreno's projects real conditions, including working conditions, are articulated and yet the odd, illogical and quirky are taken in earnest. His most recent project, the creation of a group of monsters, is a collaboration with the illustrator Johan Olander who is the inventor of "monstrology" and the author of the children's book *A Field Guide to Monsters*. In another work, there is a commercial for a product which does not exist anymore but which at the same time is an advertisement of itself. He also made a promotional video for a sport that does not yet exist, as well as a demonstration with children for snow in the summer and Christmas during the fall and objects dissolving into the walls. Another simple but striking example is a sculpture of a fir tree that is merely a fir tree for the whole year apart from December when it turns into a Christmas tree.

In this way some of our most fundamental concepts and phenomena are being reinterpreted and remodeled in Parreno's work. Against the "tyranny of time" he has repeatedly shifted focus and made time the prime site for his work. But one where preconceptions of how to structure time get a blow. *Snow Dancing* is only one example of how sequencing and duration enter his work in ways that we use to consider space. *Il Tempo del Postino* (2007) in Manchester co-curated with curator Hans Ulrich Obrist, took the logic of time to an extreme by transforming an exhibition into a single evening at the opera. Fifteen artists were asked to contribute performative pieces, which would take place on and off stage, more or less theatrically.

The work is rigorous but not academic, serious but not didactic. It is even distinctly non-didactic which in this context among other things implies restricted transparency. If critical paradigms since the advent of Enlightenment have been imbued with transparency, Parreno tends to muddle things up. The affective is embraced and in *The Invisible Boy*, his most recent film project, he turns like Folman to animation to tell the real story of an illegal Chinese boy living in NYC. We know that animation can produce immersive films, who has not cried to *Dumbo* and been scared by *Snow White*, but the achievement here is to address biographical material of a painful nature. Drawing as therapy is evoked and yet no real catharsis is offered in these works. Instead opacity becomes one of his favored features and while rejecting resolutions he is calling for more proceedings. If we can imagine emancipatory impulses imbued with magic we are probably coming closer to his work, in which doing and reflecting tend to happen at the same time. Here, performance and analysis are simultaneous operations, immersion and distance go hand in hand without collapsing into each other.

We are situated in an artistic world brimming with an urge to touch the real, and yet it never lets go of the poetic. Therefore, the early series of works entitled *No More Reality* (1991–1993) should rather be understood as "no more reality as we know it" as a call for change, a refusal of pleasure the way culture imposes it on us. Rejecting the idea of equilibrium as an ideal and challenging status quo. Saying no to desire as it is being offered to us.

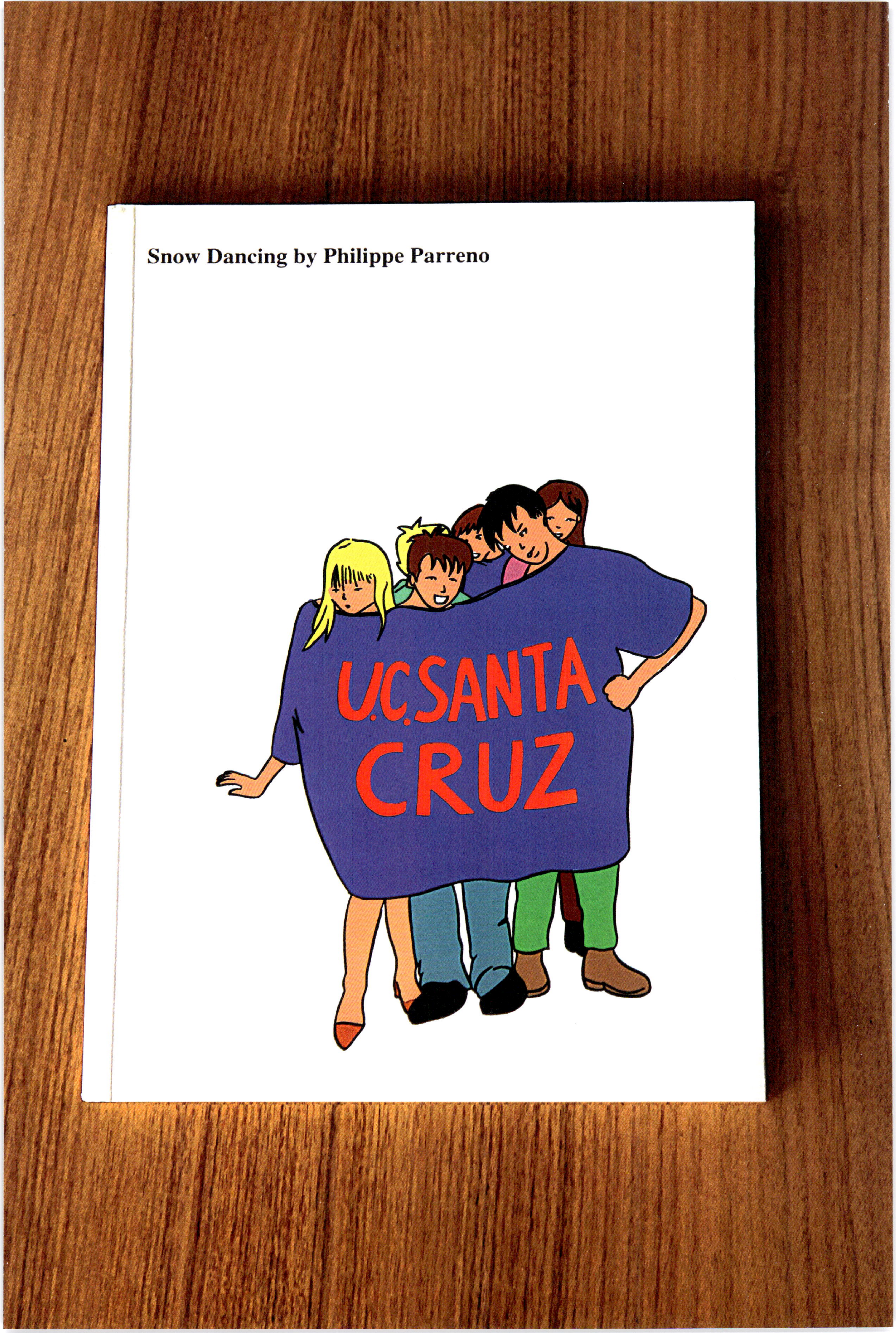
Snow Dancing by Philippe Parreno
U.C. SANTA
CRUZ

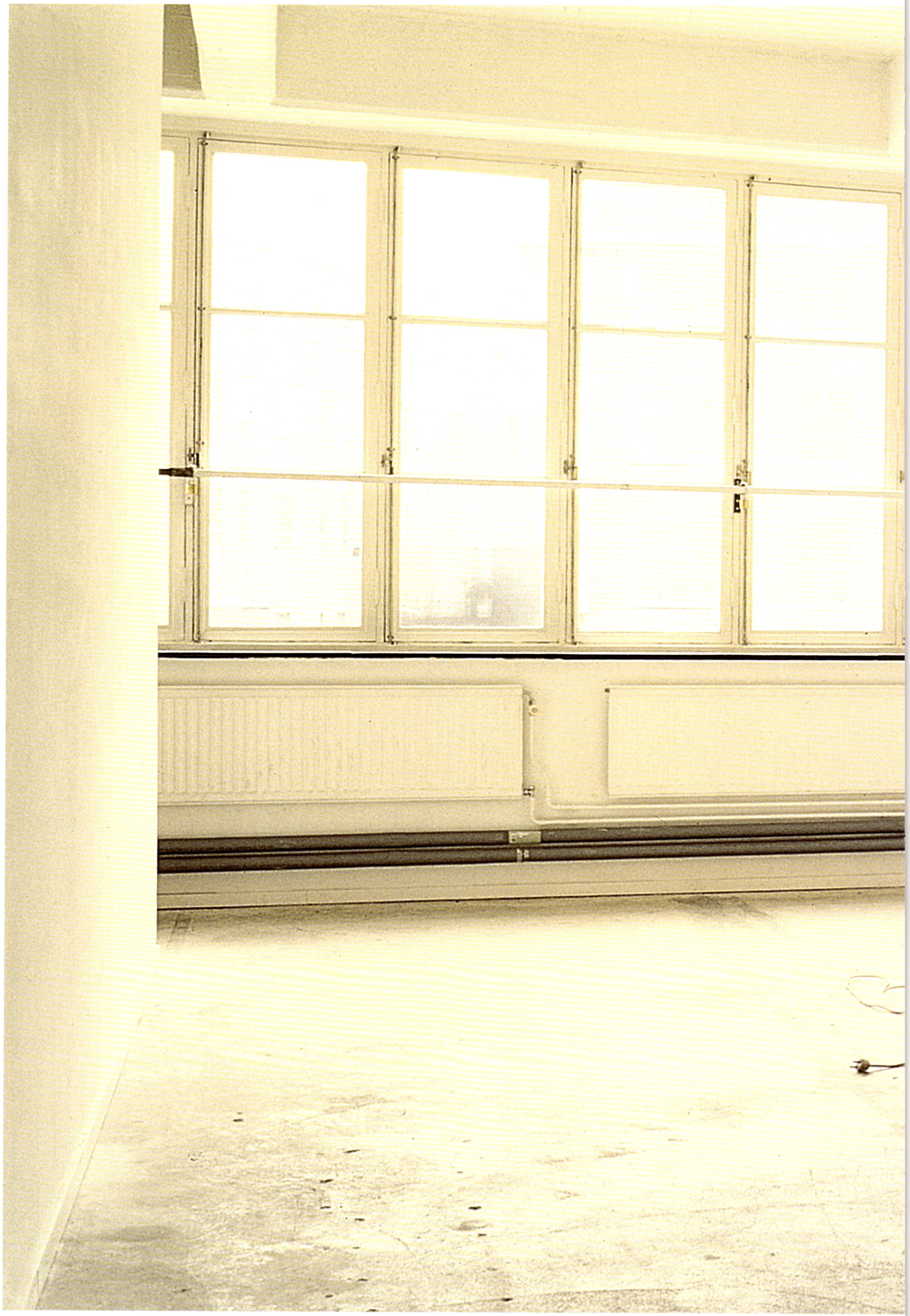

Happy Ending, 1996, exhibition view, Ynglagatan, Stockholm

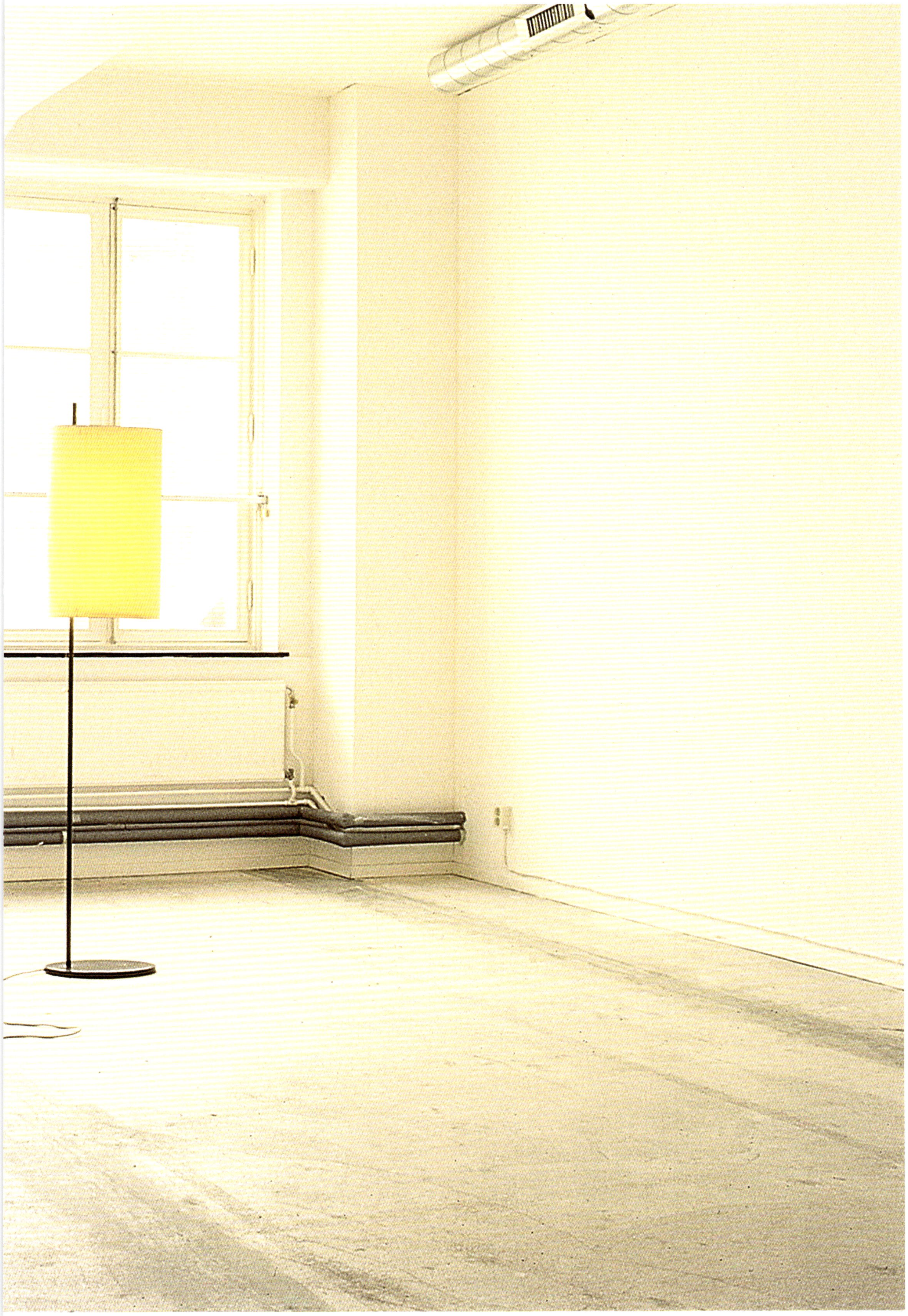

(Continued from page 96) **represented a non-physical presence in the film precedes the *Annlee* project which brought together a group of artists who as collaborators create the context which is the work.**

Atomic Explosion; Snowman; Wok, 1995 With Carsten Höller and Rirkrit Tiravanija ◁ Blown glass, 60 × 80 × 40 cm ‡ "Vicinato," October 5–November 18, 1995, Studio Guenzani, Milan, Italy || 3 editions ʃ First private collection: collection SudwestLB, Stuttgart, Germany **Each artist makes a blown glass sculpture referring to one of his past works which are collapsed into a co-signed work.**

AC/DC, 1995–2002 ◁ A group of 32 electrical plugs and adapters corresponding to the electrical receptors of different countries, 3 power cables and electrical extension cords, 1 adapter, 3 electrical light bulbs; variable dimensions ‡ "Urbanités," June 5–December 31, 2000, Frac Languedoc-Roussillon, Monpellier, France || 1 edition ʃ Frac Languedoc-Roussillon Collection, Montpellier, France

Snow Job, 1995 ◁ Installation: ¬ building of sand castles by children • plastic toys ‡ "Snow Job," December, 1995–January, 1996, Espace Forde, Geneva, Switzerland; exhibition curators: Lionel Bovier and Christophe Cherix § Courtesy of the artist **Sand, spades and plastic molds are available during the opening for children to build two sand castles. This performance leads to the 1997 glass sculpture of the same name, *Snow Job*, as well as an edition of postcards in 1998.**

CPC Channel, 1996 With Maurizio Cattelan ◁ Archive boxes, variable dimensions ‡ "Traffic," January 26–March 24, 1996, CAPC, Bordeaux, France; exhibition curator: Nicolas Bourriaud (exhib. cat.) || 1 edition § Courtesy of the artists

Dolce Utopia, 1996 With Maurizio Cattelan ◁ Installation: ¬ vinyl sphere (diam.: 120 cm) • helium • nylon ropes • chandelier • electrical system ‡ "Traffic," January 26–March 24, 1996, CAPC, Bordeaux, France; exhibition curator: Nicolas Bourriaud (exhib. cat.) || 3 editions ʃ First public collection: Frac Poitou-Charentes, Angoulême, France (1/3: version with blue balloon) **Made of an illuminated chandelier suspended from an inflated balloon, *La Dolce Utopia*, through its poetic presentation, evokes a building at night where a dimly lit window glows, conjuring the image of a person illuminated by a television. Conceived by Maurizio Cattelan and Parreno, *CPC Channel* is a hypothetical television station which broadcasts only to one person—the astronaut Patrick Baudry. Curated by Nicolas Bourriaud at the CAPC in Bordeaux in 1996 for the exhibition "Traffic," this project was intended for distribution as a 24-hour program, and the later exhibition of the videotapes which served as documentation of the broadcasts was presented in cardboard boxes. The catalogue reproduces a number of CPC channel flyers as well as Parreno and Cattelan's thoughts on the project where they question the nature of television through** "this first cable TV without cable, camera or studio ... A 'sweet utopia' for everyday life to replace dead ideologies" (Cattelan).

The Swimmer, 1995 ◁ Vinyl, 100 × 60 × 25 cm approx. ‡ "Ou" [Or], April 20–May 25, 1996, Air de Paris Gallery, Paris, France || 1 edition ʃ Private collection, Paris **This comic-strip bubble is the prototype of *Speech Bubbles* (1997).**

Ou [Or], 1996 Alternate title: *Grenadine. Le grand paradoxe* [Grenadine. The Great Paradox] ◁ Installation: ¬ flat screen (video projection for the first exhibition) • 16 mm film transferred on digital Beta cam, color, sound, 6'; variable dimensions ‡ "Ou," April 20–May 25, 1996, Air de Paris Gallery, Paris, France || editions of 2 and 1 artist's proof ʃ First private collection: private collection, Venice, Italy **A twenty second sequence with a list of credits ten minutes in duration, played at the beginning and end. The credits list technicians, books, encounters, people, music and places who produced, or which informed the sequence.**

Speech Bubbles, 1996 ◁ Gouache on celluloid; 30 × 40 cm ‡ "Philippe Parreno," May 30–June 29, 1996, Robert Prime, London, United Kingdom || 1 edition ʃ Private collection, London, United Kingdom **This cartoon shows a group of people holding balloons in the shape of comic-strip bubbles.**

Snow Dancing While U Wait, 1996 ◁ Table with the keys of the Robert Prime Gallery placed on it ‡ "Philippe Parreno," May 30–June 29, 1996, Robert Prime, London, United Kingdom || 1 edition

Happy Ending, 1996 ◁ Installation: lamp with Eero Saarinen lampshade (H: 160 cm approx.; diam.: 50 cm), electrical system, electrical wire and plug; variable dimensions ‡ "Happy Ending Sweden," 1996, Ynglagatan, Stockholm, Sweden § Courtesy of the artist **This lamp by Eero Saarinen was made for a hotel in Stockholm that was never built. The hotel would have been located on the site of the gallery where the lamp is shown. The lamp is lit without being visibly plugged in, by means of a power source hidden beneath the floor of the gallery.**

Soundtrack #4, 1992–1996 Previous title: *Visite commentée de la collection du Frac Provence-Alpes-Côte d'Azur* [A Commented Visit of the Frac Provence-Alpes-Côte d'Azur Collection] ◁ Installation: ¬ DAT audio tape (94') • Walkman at the public's disposal ‡ "Inventaire" [Inventory], Frac Provence-Alpes-Côte d'Azur, Marseilles, November 15, 1996–January 5, 1997 || 1 edition ʃ Frac Paca Collection, Marseilles, France

Birthday Zoe, 1996 ◁ Hi8 video transferred onto digital Betacam, color, sound, 4' || 1 edition ʃ Private collection, Cincinnati, United States **In this home video, a twelve year old girl, Zoe Stillpass, imagines her twentieth birthday with her family.**

Philippe Parreno, Air de Paris, rue Louise Weiss, ‡ April 1st–May 17, 1997, Air de Paris Gallery, Paris, France

Philippe Parreno, Air de Paris, rue Louise Weiss, 1997
◊ Installation: group of glass pieces (*Snow Dancing, 1997–1995*; *Snow Dancing, Footsteps, 1997–1995*; *Happy Ending, Stockholm, 1997–1996*; *Grand Prix, Monaco, 1997–1995*, 1997) ‡ April 1st–May 17, 1997, Air de Paris Gallery, Paris, France § Courtesy of the artist and of Air de Paris, Paris **For his solo show at the Air de Paris Gallery's new space on rue Louise Weiss in Paris, Parreno decides to leave the space nearly empty, excepting a few "phantom" objects which reappear from previous projects. The exhibition, as well as each of its elements function as individual works.**

Snow Dancing, 1997–1995, 1997 ◊ Installation: ¬ group of 6 door handles in colored blown glass and brass • cardboard • Styrofoam chips, 65 × 50 × 50 cm approx. ‡ "Philippe Parreno, Air de Paris, rue Louise Weiss," April 1st–May 17, 1997, Air de Paris Gallery, Paris, France || 1 edition ∫ Private collection, Zurich, Switzerland **Christmas tree balls made into door handles that interrupt the architecture of the Consortium in Dijon are shown in *Snow Dancing, 1995–1997* as six blown glass Christmas tree balls presented in a cardboard box full of Styrofoam chips.**

Snow Dancing, Footsteps, 1997–1995, 1997 ◊ 3 sheets of poured glass, variable dimensions ‡ "Philippe Parreno, Air de Paris, rue Louise Weiss," April 1st–May 17, 1997, Air de Paris Gallery, Paris, France || 1 edition ∫ Private collection, Paris, France **The footprints made for *Snow Dancing* two years earlier reappear in the form of a poured glass object.**

Happy Ending, Stockholm, 1997–1996, 1997 ◊ Lamp in blown glass, electrical system, lightbulb; 51.5 × 21.5 × 27.5 cm ‡ "Philippe Parreno, Air de Paris, rue Louise Weiss," April 1st–May 17, 1997, Air de Paris Gallery, Paris, France || 3 editions ∫ First public collection: Design collection of the Fonds national d'art contemporain (Fnac), Puteaux, France (2/3) **This work in blown glass is a homage to the lamp designed for a hotel in Stockholm which was never built but presented in the exhibition "Happy Ending," 1996.**

Grand Prix, Monaco, 1997–1995, 1997 ◊ 2 loudspeakers in blown and poured glass, 50 × 30 × 30 cm each ‡ "Philippe Parreno, Air de Paris, rue Louise Weiss," April 1st–May 17, 1997, Air de Paris Gallery, Paris, France || editions of 2 [edition 2/2 detailed in loudspeaker A and loudspeaker B] and 1 artist's m ∫ Private collection, Paris, France **Two loudspeakers in blown and poured glass refer to a project in 1994 entitled "Hypnose" [Hypnosis]. For this project, Parreno wrote a text for a hypnotist which was to be broadcast by two loudspeakers at the Grand Prix in Monaco.**

Listen to That Picture, 1997 ◊ 1 loudspeaker in blown and poured glass, 50 × 30 × 30 cm || Edition 2/2 of *Grand Prix, Monaco, 1997–1995*, loudspeaker A ∫ Private collection, Paris, France

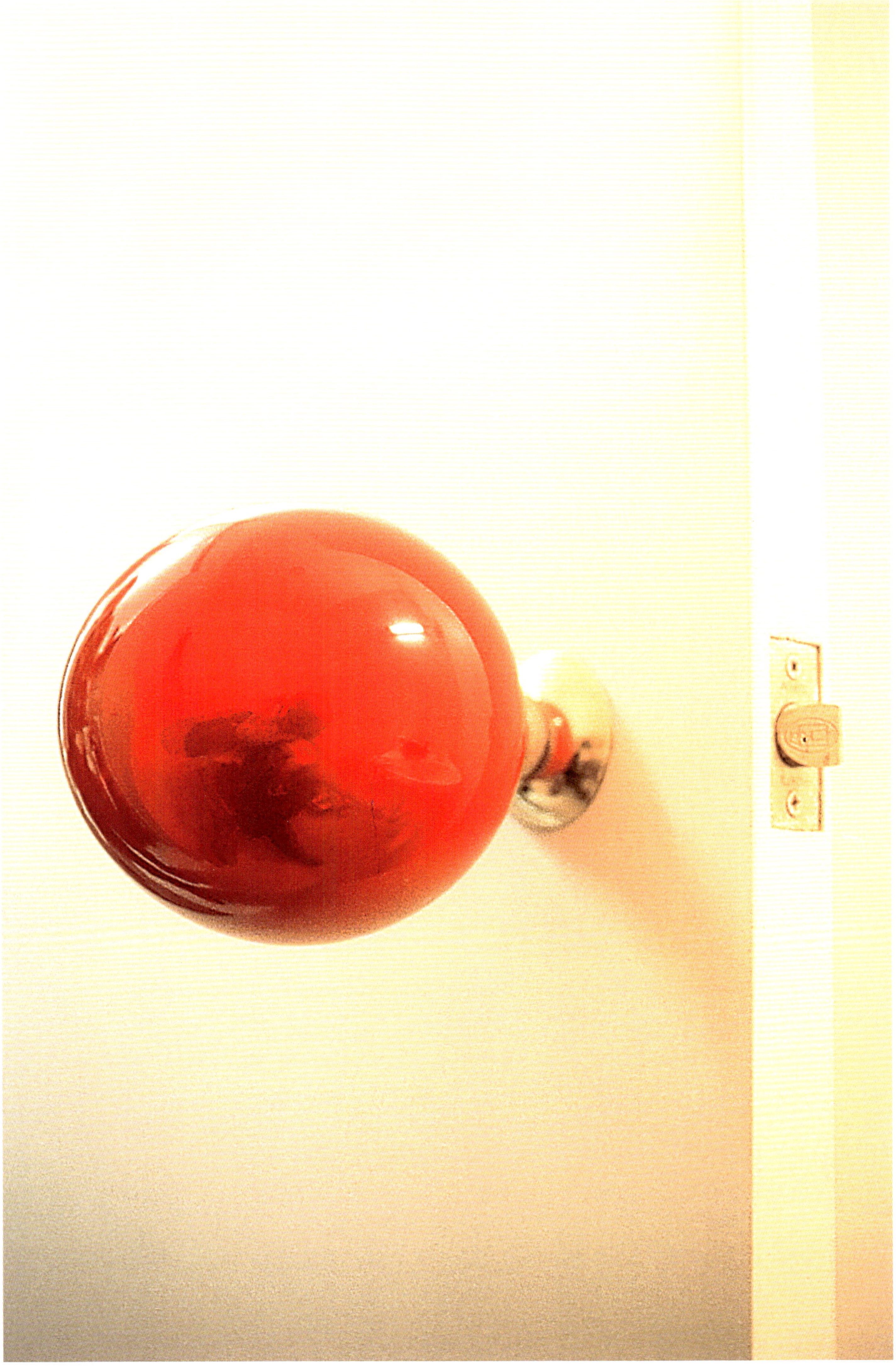

Snow Dancing, 1997-1995, 1997

Diskussion Zwischen einem Touristen und einem Arbeitlosen, Nürnberg, 1997 🔈 1 loudspeaker in blown and poured glass, 50 × 30 × 30 cm ‡ "Listen to That Picture," April 18–May 20, 1998, Schipper & Krome Gallery, Berlin, Germany || Edition 2/2 of *Grand Prix, Monaco, 1997–1995*, loudspeaker B ʃ Private collection, New York, United States

Snow Job, 1997–1995, 1997 🔈 Molded glass, 70 × 70 × 70 cm approx. || 1 edition ʃ Private collection, Monaco

Speech Bubbles, 1997 🔈 Installation: white Mylar balloons, helium; variable dimensions (up to 100 m^2) ‡ "Moment Ginza" (invited by Dominique Gonzalez-Foerster), April 6–September 7, 1997, Le Magasin, Grenoble, France || 1 edition ʃ Frac Nord-Pas-de-Calais Collection, Dunkirk, France **White Mylar helium inflated balloons are offered to the trade Union CGT. During a demonstration—which is not documented—everyone is invited to write their own statement or slogan. In the *Speech Bubbles* installation, white helium balloons form a cloud of bubbles without text collecting on the ceiling, like suspended or potential discourse.**[38]

38. In the text "Sitcom Ghost," Parreno writes: "All your stories formed white clouds above you, like comic-strip balloons. I could actually see these words in the air, until somebody rubbed them away with a frost-rimmed finger" in *A Retrospective (Tomorrow is Another Fine Day), Bruce Sterling, Rirkrit Tiravanija, Philippe Parreno*, exhibition catalogue, Rotterdam, Museum Boijmans Van Beuningen, p.107.

Anna Sanders. L'Histoire d'un sentiment [Anna Sanders. The Story of a Feeling], 1997 With Pierre Huyghe 🔈 Color printed magazine, 27.5 × 21 cm, 64 pages, French/English bilingual text; graphic design: Lily Fleury ‡ "X-squared," July 23–September 14, 1997, Secession, Vienna, Austria || Printed in 2 000 copies ***Anna Sanders. L'Histoire d'un sentiment* is a magazine which describes the life of the fictional character *Anna Sanders*.**

Visitors vs Home, 1995–1998 With Rirkrit Tiravanija 🔈 Edition of screen printed cardboard boxes in 3 colors bearing the inscription *"Visitors vs Home"* and containing 11 white printed T-shirts (black text); 44 × 32 × 17.5 cm ‡ "Bonne Année !" [Happy New Year!], January 5–February 28, 1998, Air de Paris Gallery, Paris, France || editions of 11 and 2 artist's proofs ʃ First private collection: private collection, Lille, France (2/11) § Courtesy Air de Paris, Paris, France

AC/DC Snakes, 1998 🔈 ¬ Group of 19 adapters, electrical plugs and warning lights • connecting wires; 62 × 6 × 6 cm ‡ "Bonne Année !" [Happy New Year!], January 5–February 28, 1998, Air de Paris Gallery, Paris, France || 1 edition ʃ Private collection, Paris, France

AC/DC Snakes, 1998 🔈 ¬ Group of 17 adaptaters and electrical plugs • 1 electric light bulb • connecting wires; variable dimensions || 1 edition ʃ Private collection, Brussels, Belgium

AC/DC Snakes, 1998 🔈 ¬ Group of 15 adapters and electrical plugs • 2 electric light bulbs • connecting wire; 40 × 30 × 8 cm ‡ "La Table" [The Table] September 10–October 17, 1998, Air de Paris Gallery, Paris, France || 1 edition ʃ Private collection, Paris, France

Snow Dancing, Footsteps, 1997-1995, 1997, exhibition view "Philippe Parreno, Air de Paris, Rue Louise Weiss", Air de Paris, Paris
Grand Prix, Monaco, 1997-1995, 1997, exhibition view "Philippe Parreno, Air de Paris, Rue Louise Weiss", Air de Paris, Paris
Snow Job 1997-1995, 1997, exhibition view "Philippe Parreno, Air de Paris, Rue Louise Weiss", Air de Paris, Paris

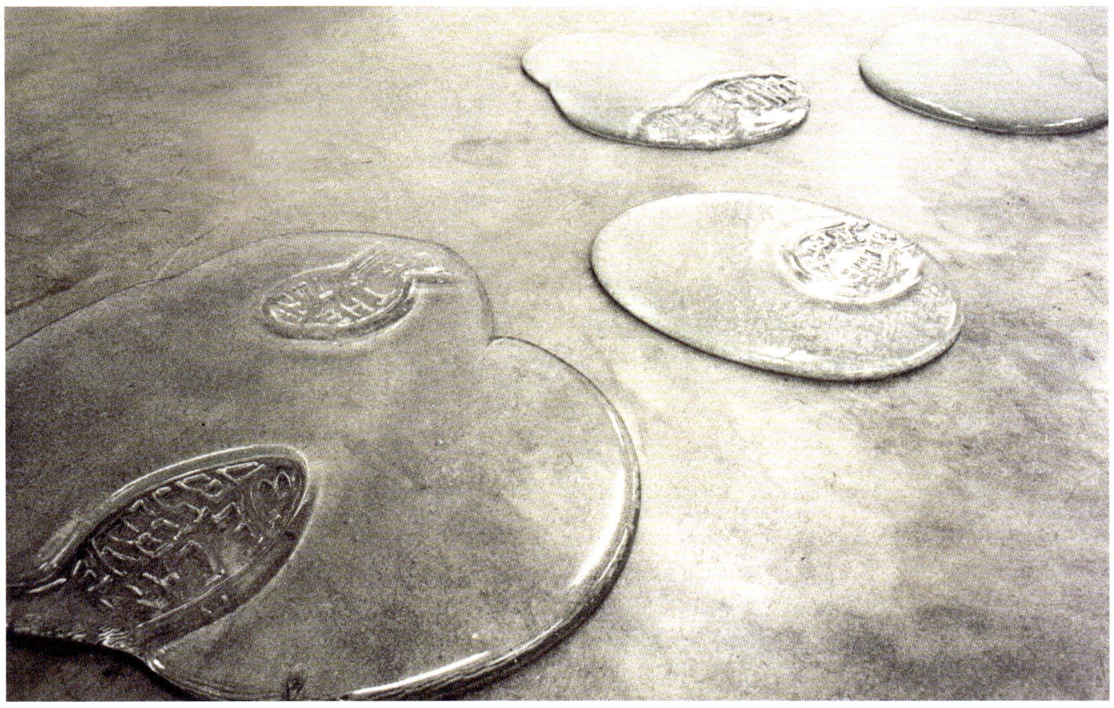

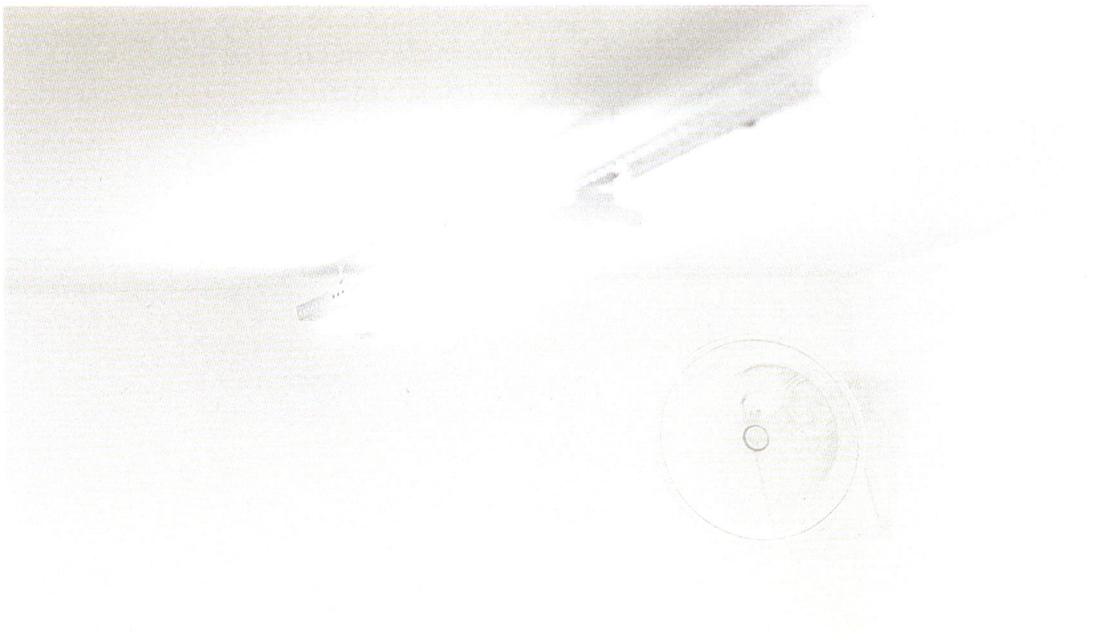

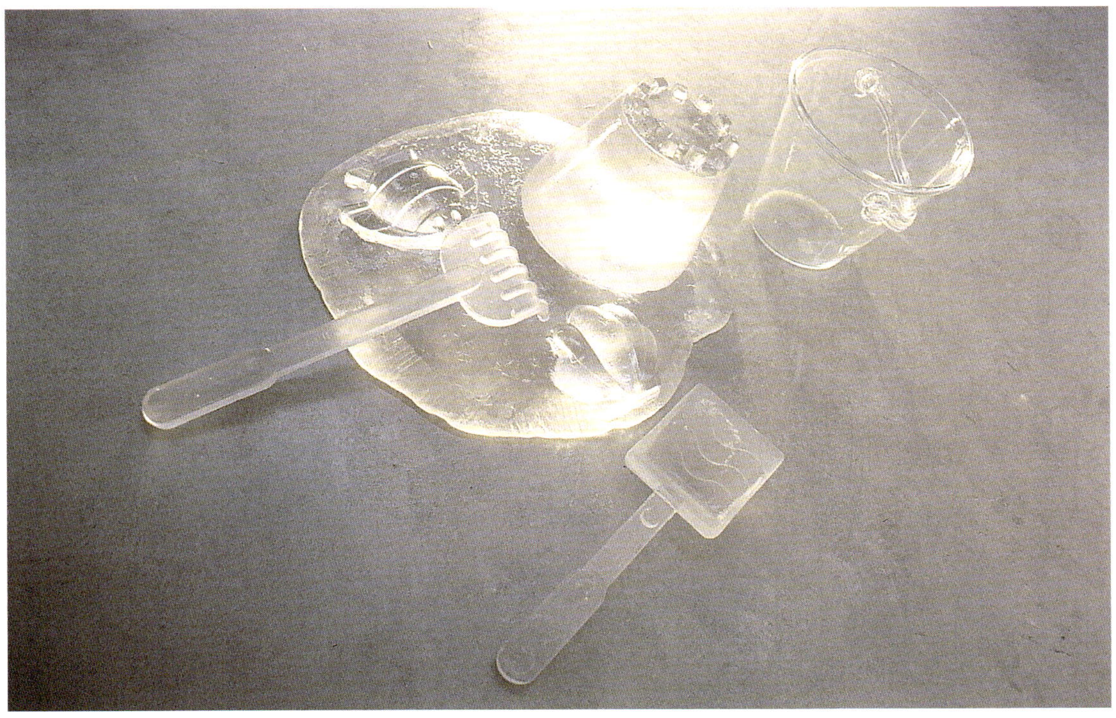

Esther, 1998 ✧ Glass tube, socket, Deco Classics 60W Philips lightbulb, electrical cable; H.: approx. 40 cm ‡ First exhibition: "Listen to the Picture," April 18–May 20, 1998, Schipper & Krome Gallery, Berlin, Germany || Edition of 50 examples ʃ First private collection: private collection, Berlin, Germany § Courtesy Esther Schipper, Berlin

TV Channel (We Sit in Front of Stories Like a Player Without a Joystick), 1998 ✧ Installation: ¬ reflecting adhesive letters indicating "We sit in front of stories like...," • portable screen • projector • digital Betacam videotape, color, sound, 45' ‡ "Blue almost transparent," June 28–July 19, 1998, Kunstverein Ludwigsburg, Ludwigsburg, Germany; exhibition curator: Barbara Steiner || edition of 1 and 1 artist's proof ʃ Landesbank Baden-Württemberg Collection, Stuttgart, Germany **This video collages clips from several of the artist's films: *No More Reality, une vidéoconférence* (1991), *Snaking* (1992, with Pierre Joseph), *La Nuit des héros* (1994), *Werktische (Made on the First of May)* (1995), *While...* (1995), *Vicinato* (1995, with Carsten Höller and Rirkrit Tiravanija), *Ou* (1996) and *Birthday Zoe* (1996) in the style of a television program.**

La Peur des anges [The Fear of Angels], 1993–1998 ✧ Installation: ¬ 2 flat loudspeakers (wood and material, 75 × 100 cm) • sound system • sound track on audio stereo CD French/English, 29' ‡ "Dominique Gonzalez-Foerster, Pierre Huyghe, Philippe Parreno," October 30, 1998–January 10, 1999, Arc/Musée d'Art moderne de la Ville de Paris (exhib. cat.) || 2 editions ʃ First public collection: Frac Paca, Marseilles, France

La Narratrice [The Narrator], 1998 With Dominique Gonzalez-Foerster and Pierre Huyghe ✧ Video labels: 10 active matrix screens, 10 DVD players, 10 DVD discs ‡ "Dominique Gonzalez-Foerster, Pierre Huyghe, Philippe Parreno," October 30, 1998–January 10, 1999, Arc/Musée d'Art moderne de la Ville de Paris (exhib. cat.) || 1 edition § Courtesy of the artists

Some Products, 1998 ✧ Installation: ¬ glass showcase (H.: 300 cm approx.) • screen • projector • Beta cam video, color, directional sound, 3'10" ‡ "Dominique Gonzalez-Foerster, Pierre Huyghe, Philippe Parreno," October 30, 1998–January 10, 1999, Arc/musée d'Art moderne de la Ville de Paris (exhib. cat.) || editions of 2 and 1 artist's proof ʃ First private collection: private collection, London, United Kingdom (1/2) ***Some Products* is both a music video made for the promotion of an album by Dave Stewart and an advertisement for a product that no longer exists.**

Le Procès de Pol Pot [Pol Pot's Trial], 1998 ✧ Exhibition made with Liam Gillick ¬ Invited artists: Terry Atkinson, Zeigam Azizov, Douglas Gordon, Rebecca Gordon-Nesbitt, Carsten Höller, Pierre Huyghe, Ronald Jones, Pierre Joseph, Gabriel Kuri, Thomas Mulcaire, Josephine Pryde, Adrian Schiesser, Rirkrit Tiravanija ✧ Installation:

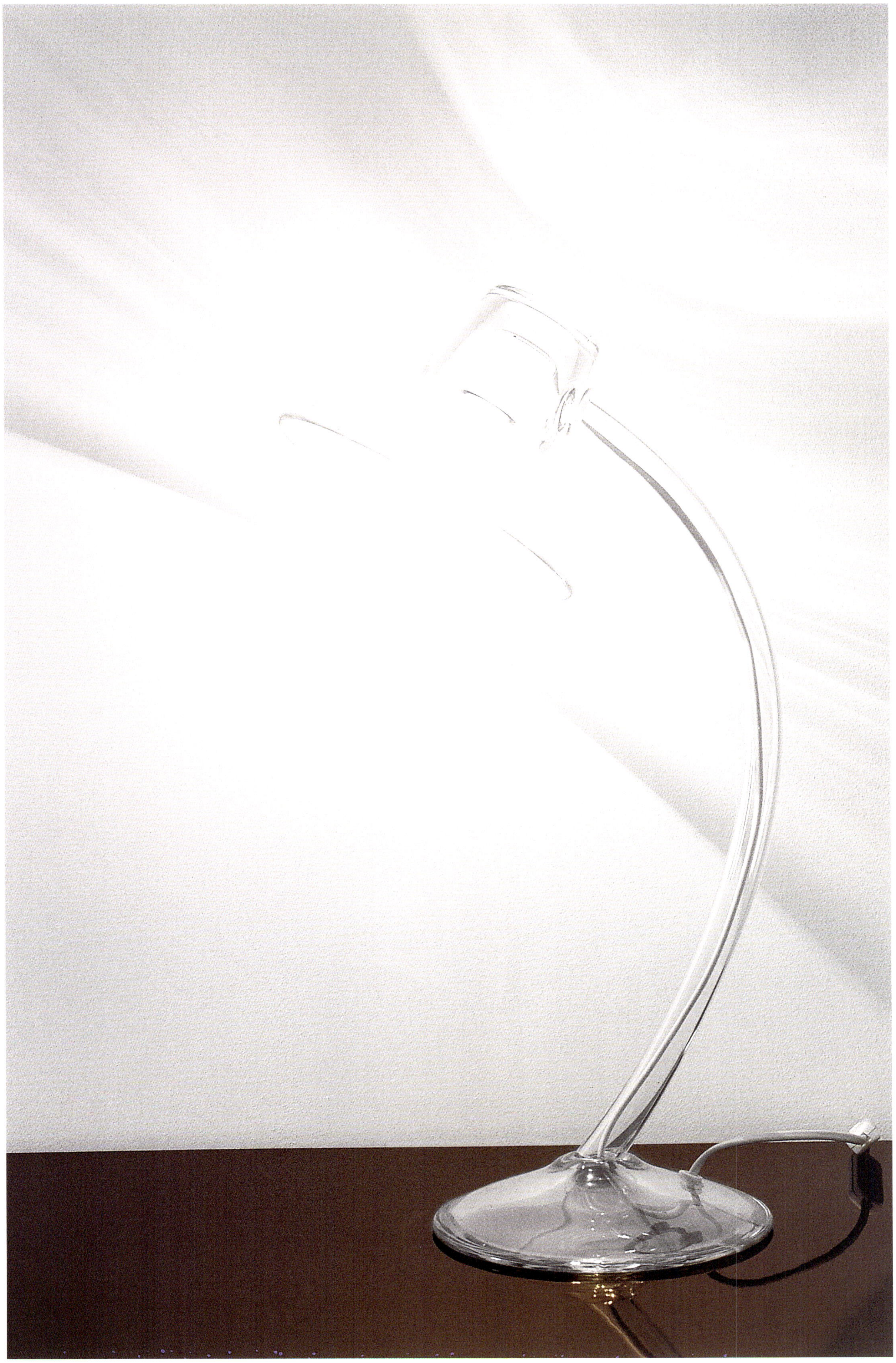

Happy Ending, Stockholm, 1997-1996, 1997, exhibition view "Philippe Parreno, Air de Paris, Rue Louise Weiss", Air de Paris, Paris

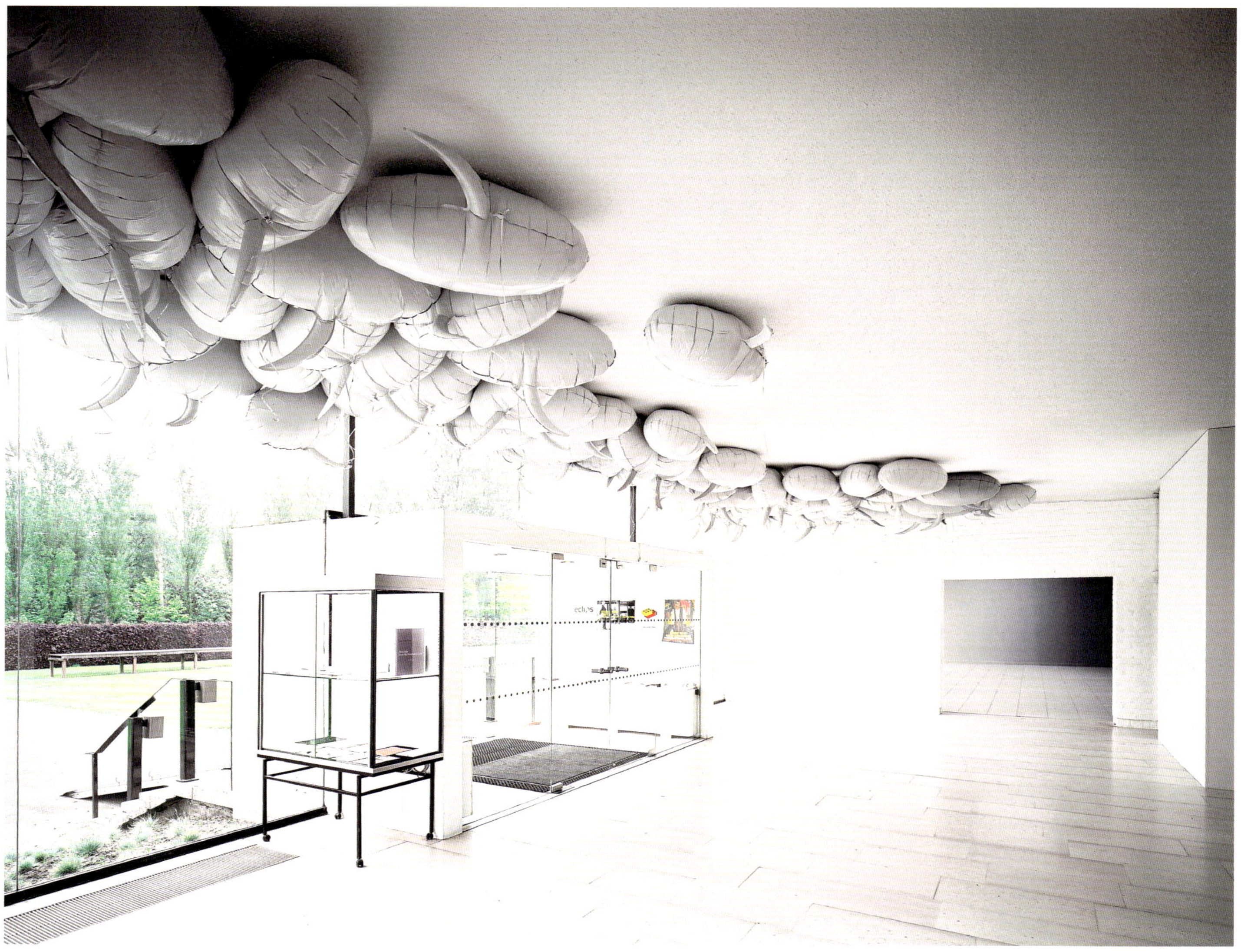

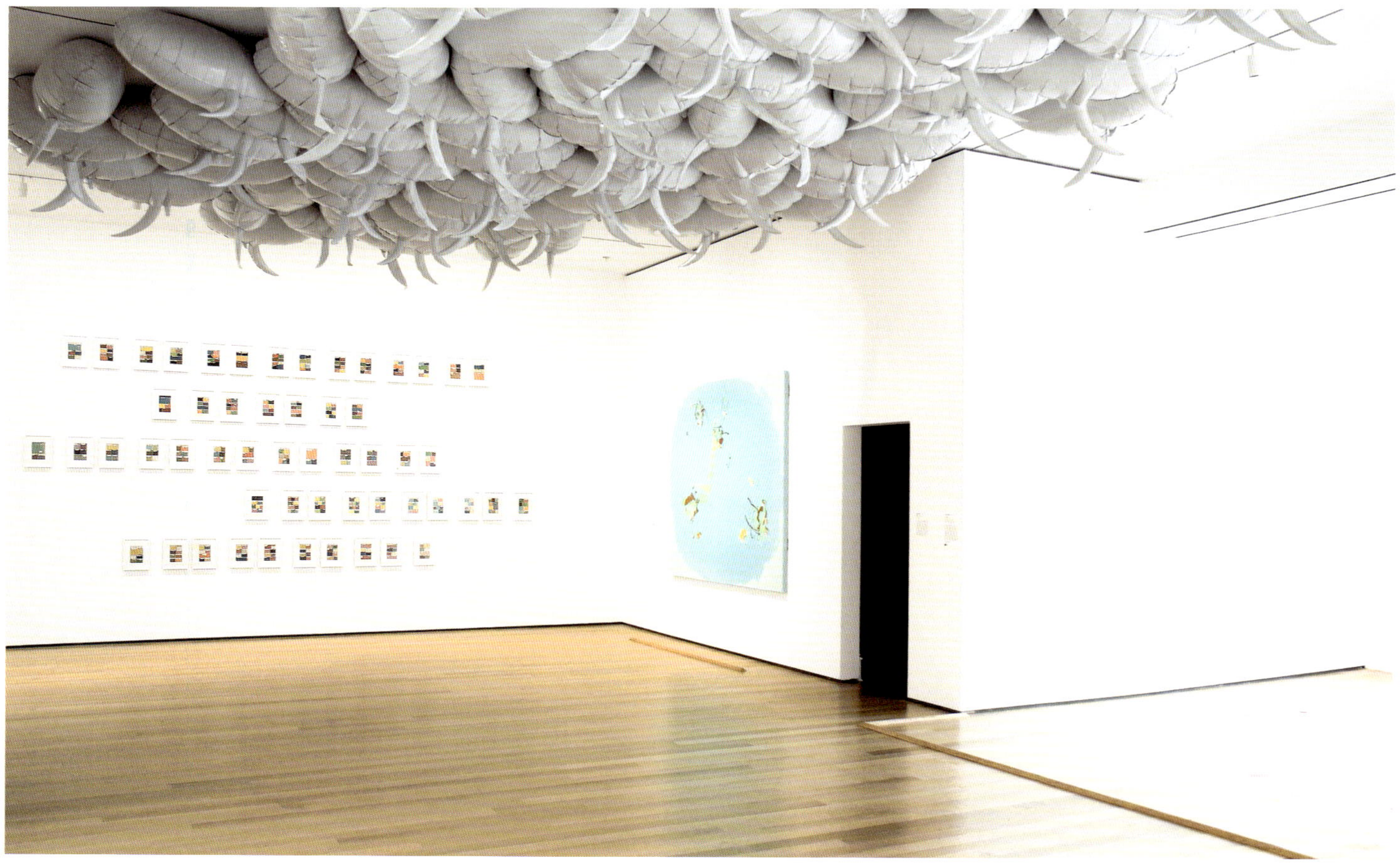

Speech Bubbles, 1997, exhibition view "Across the border", Museum Dhondt-Dhaenens in Deurle, 2004
Speech Bubbles, 1997, exhibition view "Comic Abstraction", MoMA, New York, 2007

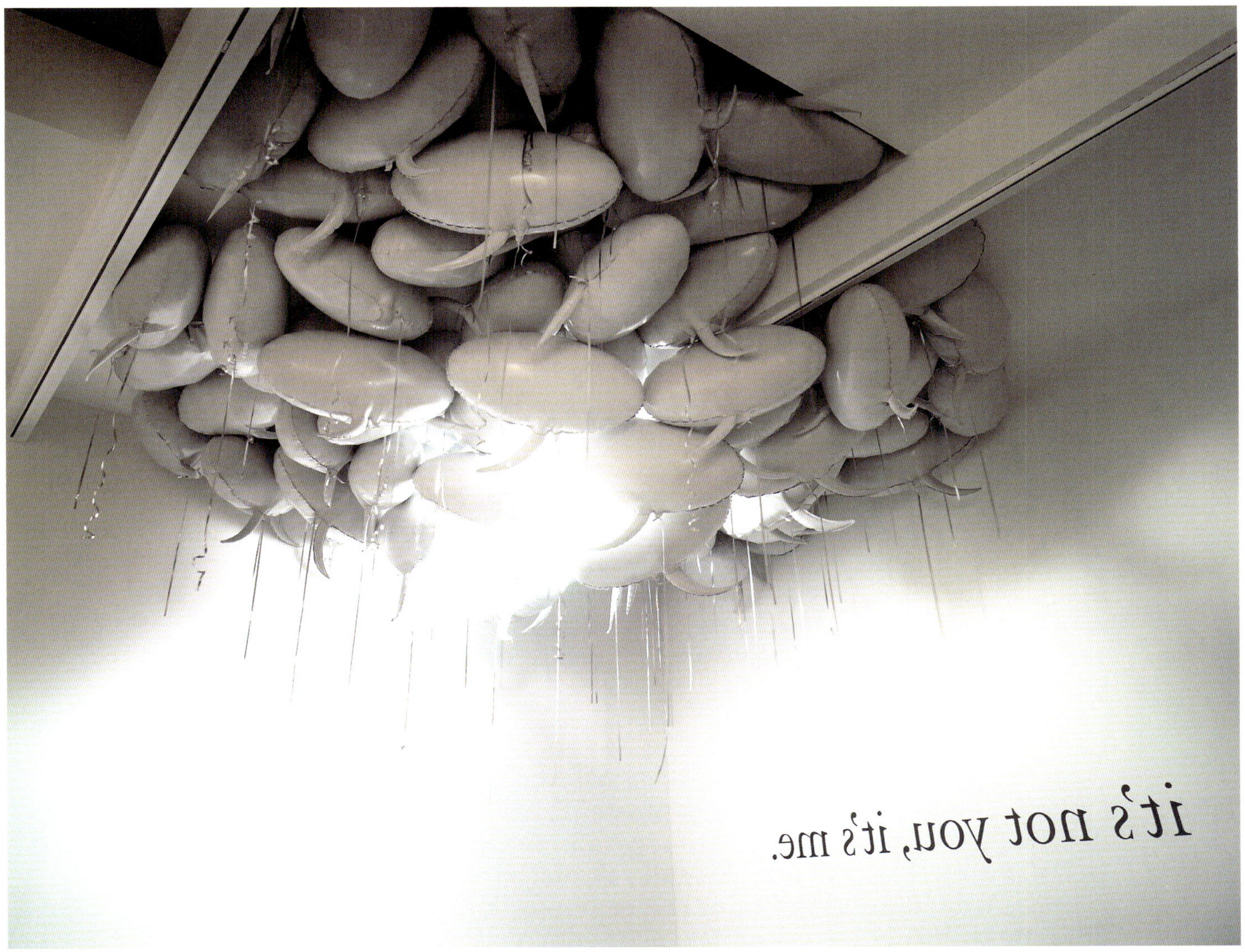

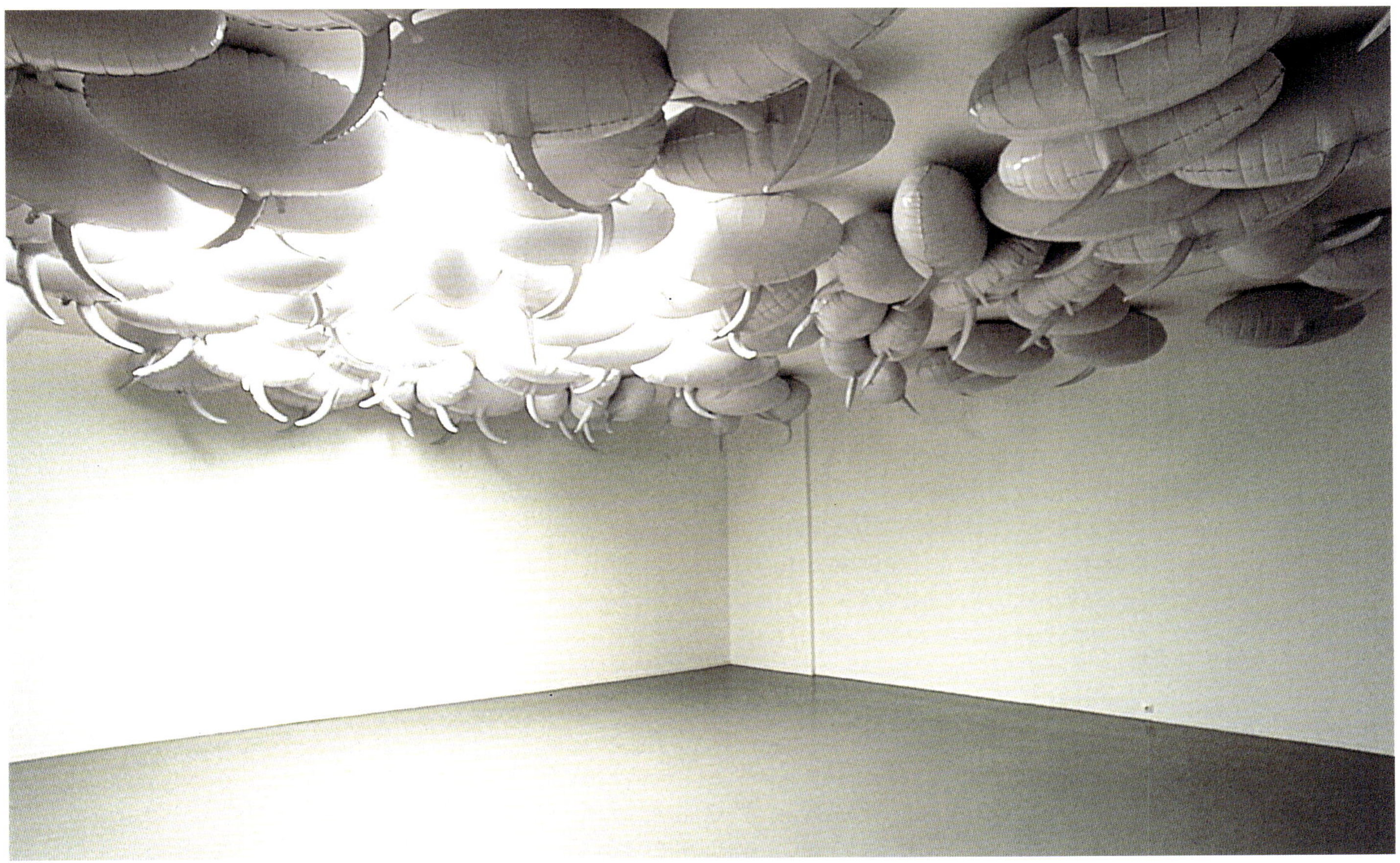

Speech Bubbles, 1997, exhibition view "You and Me – Me and You", Fondazione Davide Halevim, Milan, 2005-2006
Speech Bubbles, 1997, exhibition view "Dominique Gonzalez-Foerster, Pierre Hyughe, Philippe Parreno", Musée d'Art moderne de la Ville de Paris, 1998

¬ white walls • black adhesive letters • printed veil • theatre tracking lights • puppet show which once a week explains the exhibition to children. ‡ "Le Procès de Pol Pot" [Pol Pot's Trial], November 8, 1998–January 3, 1999, Le Magasin, Grenoble, France || 1 edition § Courtesy of the artists **The exhibition organized by Parreno and Gillick does not attempt to document Pol Pot's trial in the Cambodian jungle, rather, the way in which criminal identity is mediatized. The project occupies a space between documentary film and fiction. The installation hung texts on the wall illuminated by colored lights.**

C'est une œuvre d'art pendant onze mois de l'année et en décembre c'est Noël [It is an Artwork for Eleven Months of the Year and in December it is Christmas], 1998 ◁ Installation: Christmas tree, artificial snow, transparent decorations, string of LED lights; variable dimensions || 1 edition ∫ Private collection, Cincinnati, United States

Le Pont du trieur, 1999 With Charles de Meaux ◁ 35 mm film, color, sound, 74'; with: Thibault de Montalembert, Camille Japy and Ogonozar Aknazarov; original music: Dave Stewart; script: Charles de Meaux and Philippe Parreno; production: Anna Sanders Films || DVD edited by MK2 § Courtesy Anna Sanders Films, Paris, France **A documentary about the region of Pamir in Tadjikistan devastated by civil war and the economic crisis caused by the dissolution of the USSR in the 1990s.**

About, 1999 With Dominique Gonzalez-Foerster and Pierre Huyghe ◁ Video: Digital Beta cam transferred onto DVD, color, sound, 27'40" ‡ "D'Apertutto," June 13–November 7, 1999, 48th Venice Biennial, Italy (exhib. cat.); exhibition curator: Harald Szeemann || 1 edition ∫ Private collection, Cincinnati, United States **The videos *Riyo* (sound, color, 10'), *L'Ellipse* (1998, sound, color, 13') and *Some Products* (1998) are edited together with short film sequences shot before the opening of the 48th Venice Biennial.**

No Ghost Just a Shell, 1999–2003 With Pierre Huyghe ◁ Purchase of the manga character Annlee who under copyleft is free to be used for various artistic projects. ‡ "No Ghost Just a Shell," August 24–October 27, 2002, Kunsthalle Zürich, Zurich, Switzerland ∫ Public collection of all the works in the project: Van Abbemuseum Collection, Eindhoven, The Netherlands **Anywhere Out of The World, 2000** Philippe Parreno ◁ Installation: video projector, digital video on DVD (sound, color, 4'), Dolby Surround Digital 5.1 sound system, loudspeakers, blue wool; variable dimensions ‡ "No Ghost Just a Shell: Anywhere Out of the World," June 15–July 24, 2000, Air de Paris Gallery, Paris, France || 4 editions and 2 artist editions ∫ First public collection: Frac Poitou-Charentes, Angoulême, France (1/4) ♦ **Skin of Light, 2001** With Pierre Huyghe ◁ Installation: neon, electrical system, 80 × 58 × 1.4 cm ‡ "In Many Ways the Exhibition Already

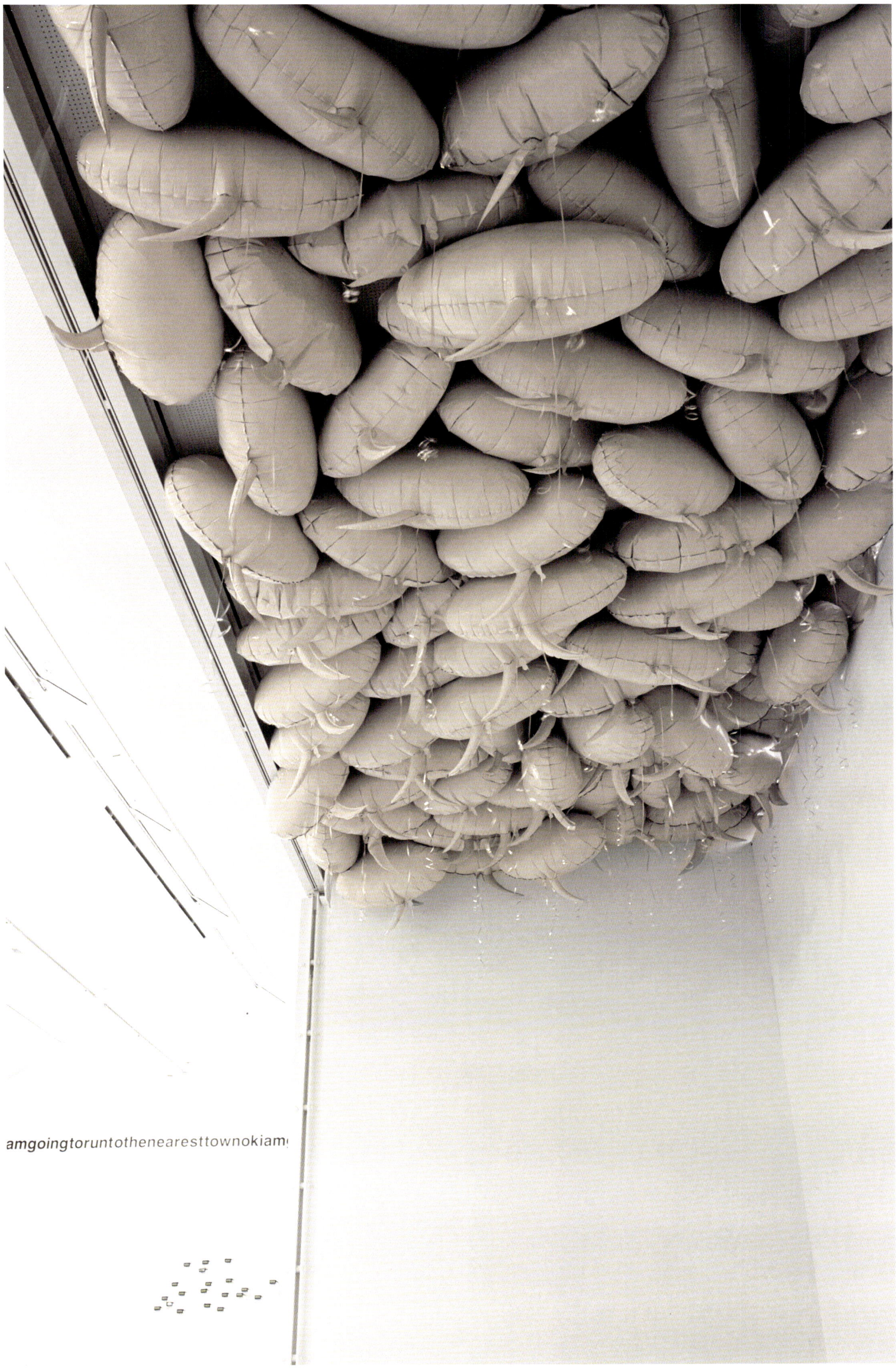

Speech Bubbles, 1997, exhibition view "III Communication", Dundee Contemporary Arts in Dundee, 2003

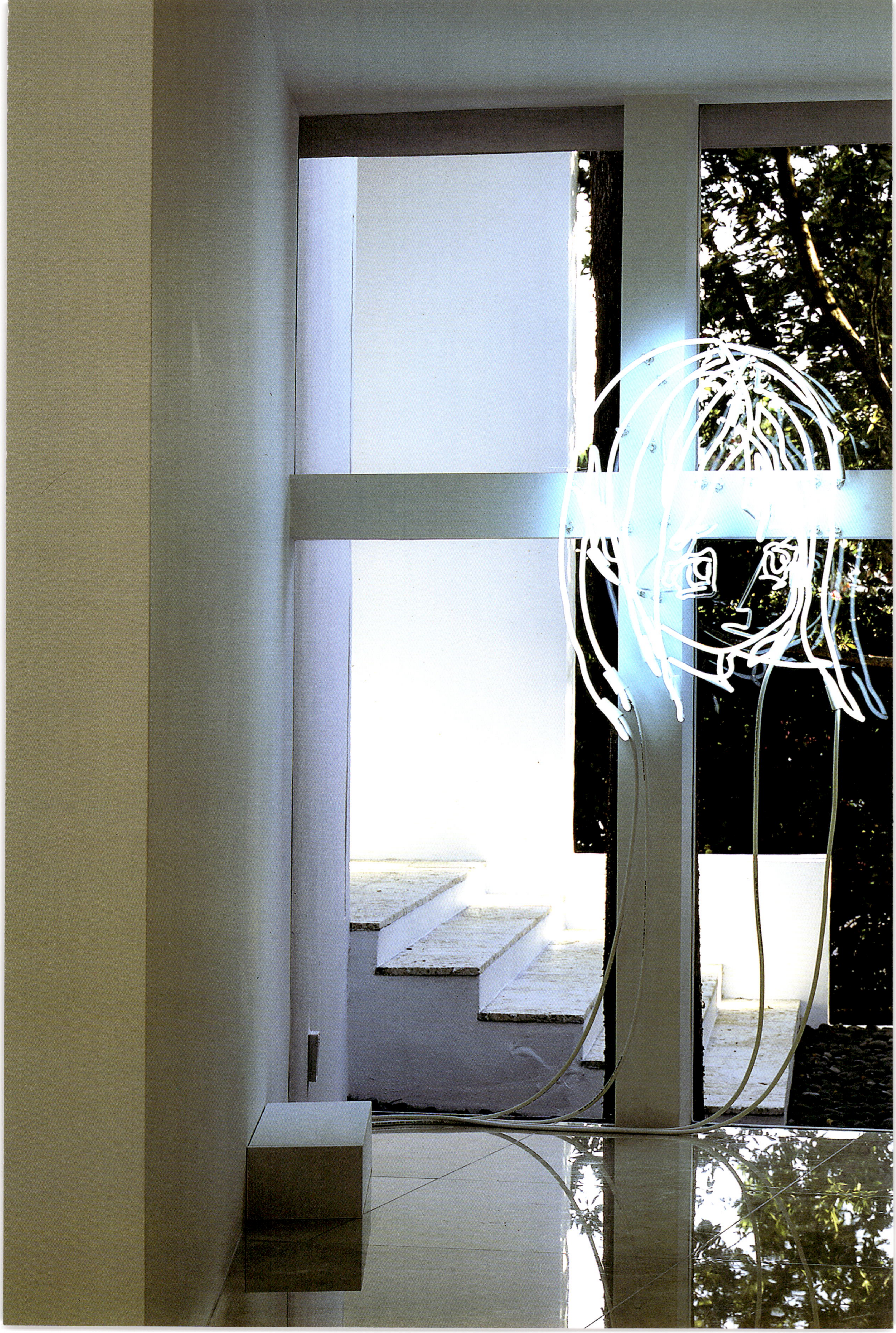

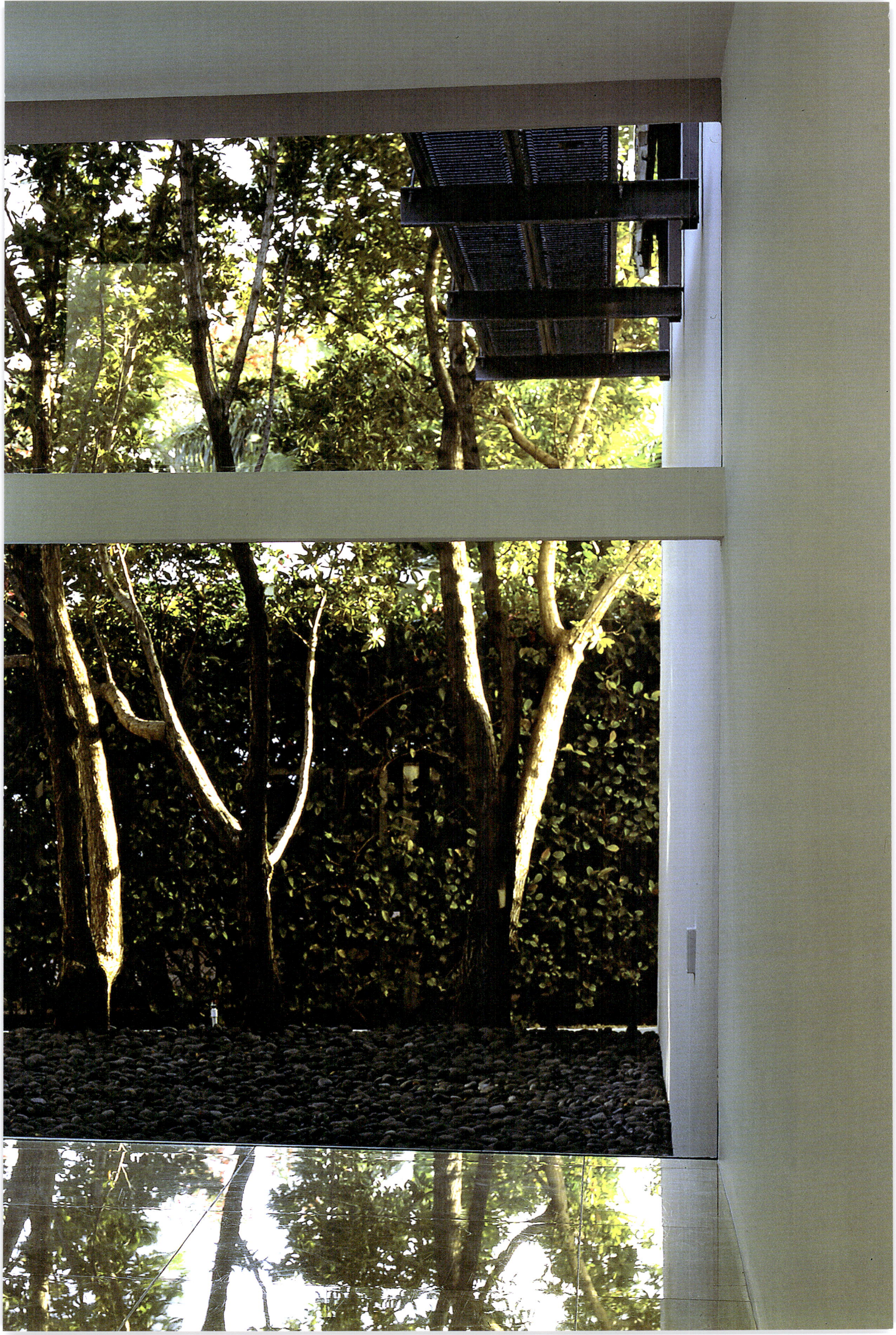

Happened," December 1st, 2001–January 20, 2002, Institute of Contemporary Art (ICA), London, United Kingdom || 12 editions and 2 artist editions ∫ First private collection: private collection, Monaco ♦ **No Ghost Just a Shell, 2003** Pierre Huyghe and Philippe Parreno ◁ Book: 304 pages, 23 × 29 cm, 150 ill. color, hardback, Cologne: Publisher Walther König; Editorial direction: Pierre Huyghe and Philippe Parreno, with the contribution of Stefan Kalmar, Beatrix Ruf and Hans Ulrich Obrist ◊ Summary: Maurizio Lazzarato, "Dialogism and Polyphony," 2002; Molly Nesbit, "Done," 2002; Israel Rosenfeld, "Dr. Arnold T.P. West's Thoughts On The Annlee Case," 2002; Maurice Pianzola, "Painters and Villains," 1993; Jan Verwoert, "Copyright, Ghosts and Commodity Fetishism," 2002; Kathryn Davis, "Annlee Darling," 2002; Hans Ulrich Obrist, "How Annlee Changed Its Spots," 2002; Jean-Claude Ameisen, "To Be or Not To Be...Nothing More...Perchance To Dream," 2002; Luc Saucier, "Annlee Association Articles" (legal contract), 2003 ‡ "No Ghost Just a Shell," January 19–August 30, 2003, Van Abbemuseum, Eindhoven, The Netherlands (exhib. cat.) ♦ **Travelling Pod, 2003** Pierre Huyghe and Philippe Parreno ◁ Robot: ¬ polyurethane resin shell • projector • DVD players; 110.5 × 91 × 86.5 cm ‡ "No Ghost Just a Shell," January 19–August 30, 2003, Van Abbemuseum, Eindhoven, The Netherlands (exhib. cat.) || 1 edition ∫ Van Abbemuseum collection, Eindhoven, The Netherlands **In 1999, Huyghe and Parreno with Anna Sanders Films,[39] purchased the Manga character Annlee from KWorks for the modest sum of 46,000 Yen (US$483.15) with the intention of placing the avatar under copyleft. Eighteen artists, Parreno and Huyghe initially, but soon followed by Dominique Gonzalez-Foerster, François Curlet, Liam Gillick, Rirkrit Tiravanija, Mélik Ohanian among others made twenty-eight distinct works. *No Ghost Just a Shell* (1999–2002) (produced by Anna Léna Vaney), of which the title refers to the famous Manga character, *Ghost in the Shell*, is exhibited first at the Kunsthalle in Zurich, next at the Rosa and Carlos de la Cruz collection in Miami, and then in 2003, at the Van Abbemuseum in Eindhoven. The latter two venues showed the group exhibition as a single work. ◊ Annlee develops from the story of a manga character, a purely commercial product, to that of a anthropormorphized character with a voice and a presence created by the collective imagination of the eighteen artists who collaborated with her. In the first episode, Parreno's video *Anywhere Out of the World* (2000), Annlee presents herself as a product, explaining the process of her birth, and questions the modalities of her existence: "I am a product ... . I was bought, but strangely enough I do not belong to anybody. I belong to whoever is able to fill me with any kind of imaginary material. Anywhere out of the world. I am an imaginary character. I am no ghost, just a shell," Annlee says. The graphic designers M/M (Paris) contribute to the project in 2000 with a poster that appropriates the Shell Oil logo. ◊ For the exhibition at the Van Abbemuseum in Eindhoven, Huyghe and Parreno create the motorized robot *Travelling Pod*, which moves around the space showing various films which feature Annlee. The *No Ghost Just a Shell* book explores the different facets of the**

39. Anna Sanders Films is a production company founded in 1998 by Charles de Meaux, Pierre Huyghe and Philippe Parreno, with Xavier Douroux and Franck Gautherot, joined by Dominique Gonzalez-Foerster.

Previous pages: **Skin of Light, 2001,** exhibition view "No Ghost, Just a Shell", collection Rosa and Carlos de la Cruz, Miami, 2005

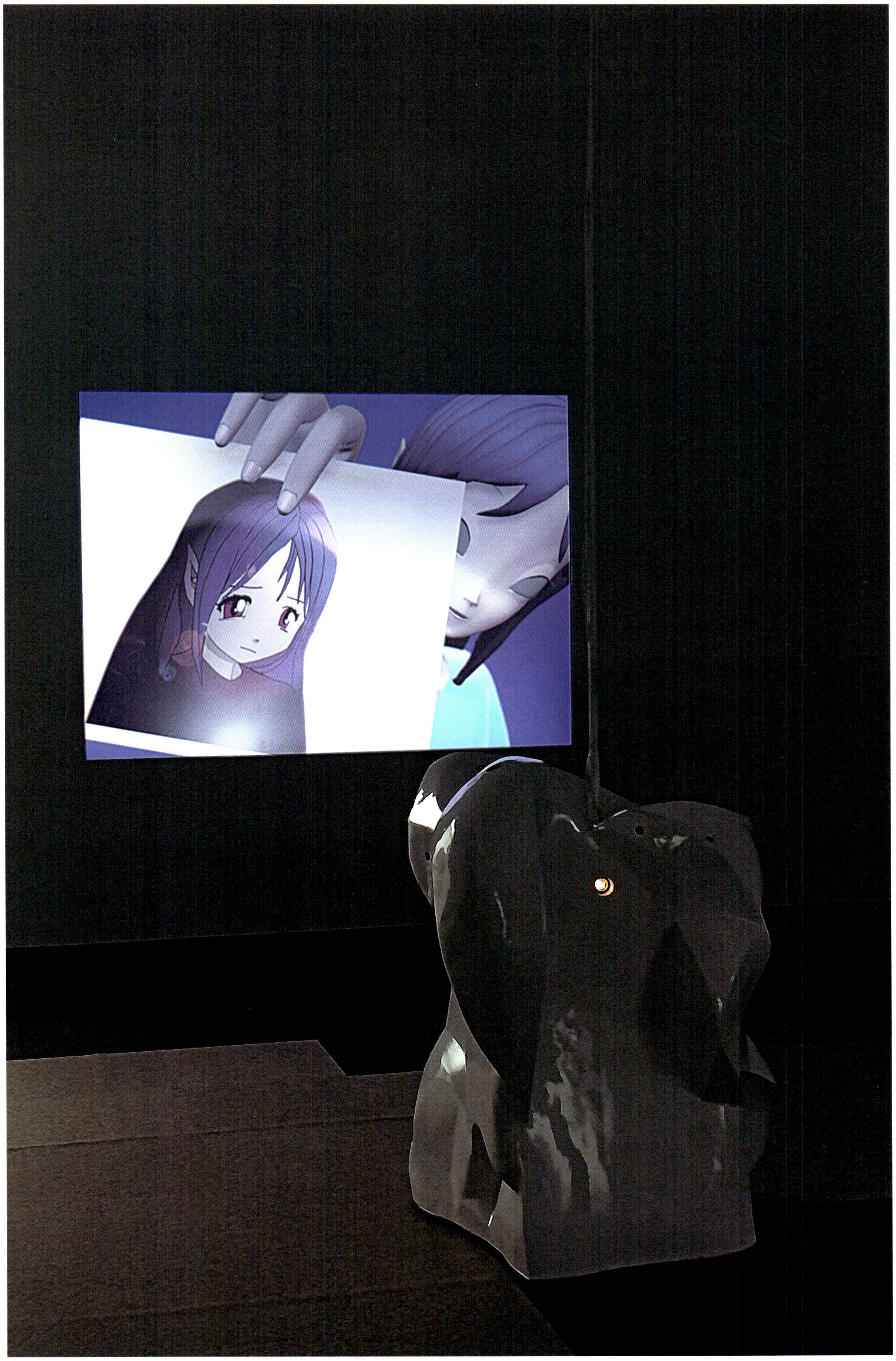

Anywhere Out of The World, 2000 and **Travelling Pod, 2003,** exhibition view "No Ghost, Just a Shell", Van Abbemuseum, Eindhoven, 2002

collaborations, including contributions on the question of copyright, thereby enriching the project's polyphony.[40] As Parreno points out, if liberalism needs the recognition of authors through copyright, Annlee inverts the process. Indeed, here each artist produces an artwork from the same image which they did not author. ◊ The project *A Smile Without a Cat (Celebration of Annlee's Vanishing)*, made by Huyghe and Parreno in 2002, is Annlee's last appearance. On Miami Beach at night, the Manga character is ignited by numerous fireworks exploding from a metallic structure. Inspired by the passage from Lewis Carroll's *Alice in Wonderland* in which the Cheshire cat disappears leaving behind only its smile—so to speak, "a smile without a cat" or an image without body—, Annlee's final moments are photographed and documented in 35 mm film. Annlee is liberated through a legal document cosigned by Huyghe and Parreno, in which the two artists relinquish their rights to the Annlee estate founded with Luc Saucier.

Michel Amathieu, Djamel Benameur, Jacques Chaban-Delmas, James Chinlund, Maurice Cotticelli, Hubert Dubedout, François Dumoulin, Ebezeber Howard, M/M (Paris), Pierre Mendès-France, Miko, Neyrpic, Alain Peyrefitte, Inez van Lamsweerde & Vinoodh Matadin, Anna-Léna Vaney, Angus Young, 1999, called *Credits* ◁ 35 mm film transferred onto DVD, color, sound, 6'30" || 1 artist's proof ʃ Fondation Louis Vuitton pour la création collection, Paris, France ♦ Michel Amathieu, Djamel Benameur, Jacques Chaban-Delmas, James Chinlund, Maurice Cotticelli, Hubert Dubedout, François Dumoulin, Ebezeber Howard, M/M (Paris), Pierre Mendès-France, Miko, Neyrpic, Alain Peyrefitte, Inez van Lamsweerde & Vinoodh Matadin, Anna-Léna Vaney, Angus Young, 2000, called *Credits* ◁ Installation: ¬ video projector, video, photograph, dimmer switch • Video: 35 mm film transferred onto DVD, color, sound, 6'30" • Photograph: *Gérard Philippe (Title Sequence for a Film by Philippe Parreno)*, Inez van Lamsweerde & Vinoodh Matadin, 2000, C-print mounted on aluminum, 169.4 × 134.2 cm (framed) ‡ "Let's Entertain," February 12–April 30 2000, Walker Art Center, Minneapolis, United States || editions of 3 and 2 artist's proofs ʃ First public collection: Walker Art Center, Minneapolis, United States (1/3) Parreno grew up in a ZUP (Urban Priority Zones) housing project with a children's playground in Échirolles in the late 1970s. The apartment building no longer exists, so in an attempt to piece together memories of the urban wasteland of his childhood, Parreno asked a few old friends to help him make a film. The work's title consists of seventeen names, not only his childhood friends but those who were involved in the adminstration of the project and the politicians involved in the construction of the ZUP. Greater than the sum of these subjective viewpoints, *Credits* goes beyond the simple descriptive event.[41] Made of hazy recollections, this work is the imperfect result of research conducted on a place, and a memory of a place. For example, as a boy, Parreno and his friends would hang plastic bags on trees which had been planted in an attempt to make the playground more green. The boys resented the trees because

40. Pierre Huyghe, Philippe Parreno, *No Ghost Just a Shell*, with the contributions of Maurizio Lazarato, Maurice Pianzola, Jan Verwoert, etc. The founding act of the Annlee association is reproduced in the German edition, published by Walther König, Cologne, in 2003.

41. This interest in multiple view points and their necessary harmonization in order to observe a situation comes from Pier Paolo Pasolini's *L'Expérience hérétique* [The Heretic Experience]. Pasolini mentions here the model of the hologram as the most accurate image of the real (Philippe Parreno, Hans Ulrich Obrist, *The Conversation Series, op. cit.*, p.37).

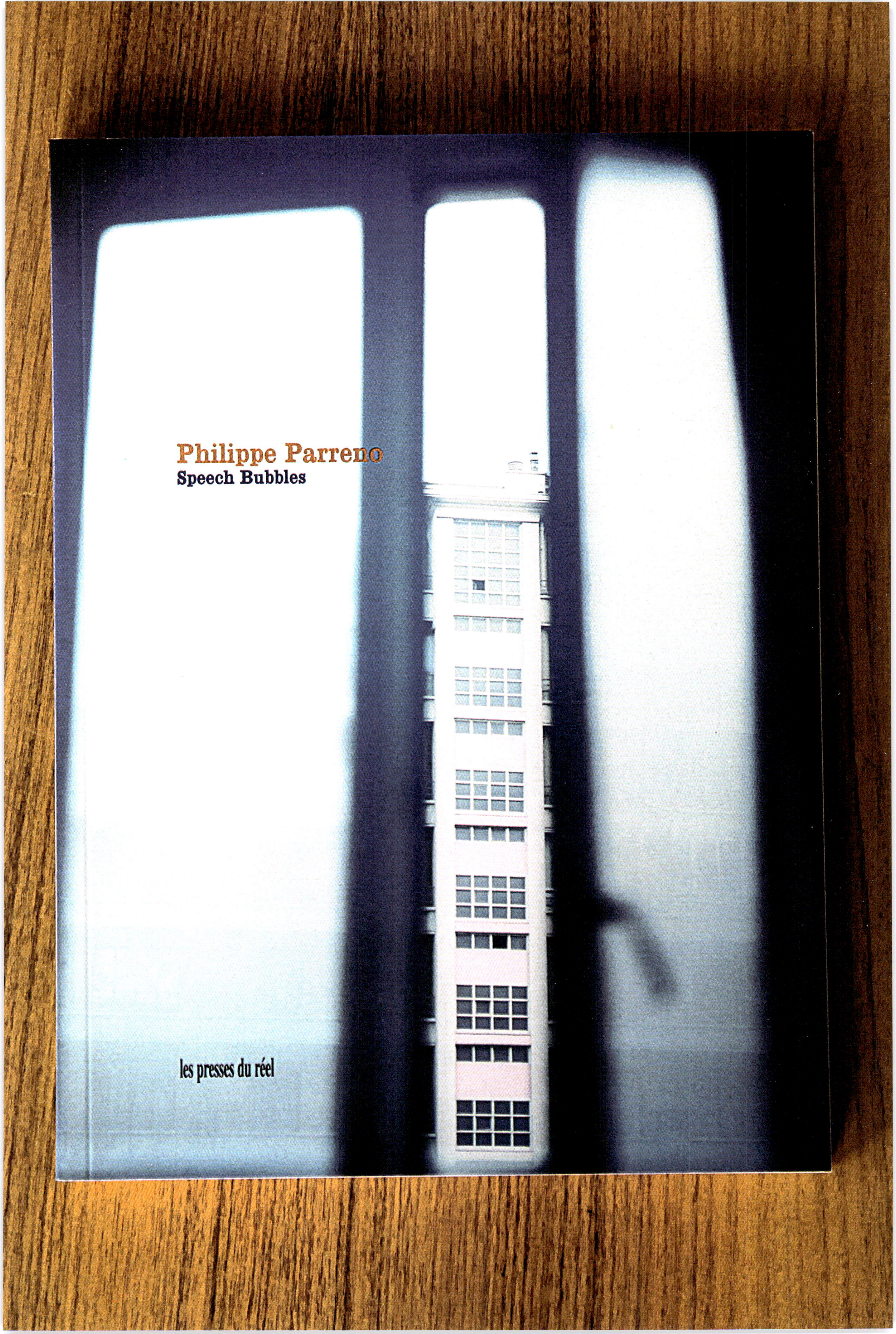
Philippe Parreno
Speech Bubbles
les presses du réel

they prevented them from playing soccer. ◊ The film is accompanied by the guitar riffs of Angus Young, the lead guitarist of AC/DC, an idol of Parreno in the late 1970s, and a photograph by Inez van Lamsweerde and Vinoodh Matadin of an adolescent with a child's head on an adult's body, the French designers M/M (Paris) used the photograph for the film's poster. ◊ At the end of each showing, the light comes back on for the same length of time as the duration of the film, then goes out when the film starts again, evoking an endless screening. The work questions the authorship and the construction of the solo show, which Parreno replaces here with "a group solo show."

Vicinato 2, 2000 With Liam Gillick, Douglas Gordon, Carsten Höller, Pierre Huyghe and Rirkrit Tiravanija ◁ 35 mm film transferred onto digital Betacam, color, Dolby stereo sound, 11'30"; production: Anna Sanders Films, Dijon, France; coproduction: Air de Paris, Paris, France/Yvon Lambert Gallery, Paris, France/Lisson Gallery, London, United Kingdom/Marian Goodman Gallery, New York, United States/Neugerriemschneider, Berlin, Germany/Schipper & Krome Berlin, Germany/Studio Guenzani, Milan, Italy ‡ June 2000, MK2 Beaubourg movie theater, Paris, France || editions of 12 and 6 artist's proofs ʃ First private collection: Private collection, Paris, France (1/12) § Courtesy Air de Paris, Paris; Yvon Lambert, Paris; Studio Guenzani, Milan; Esther Schipper, Berlin; Lisson Gallery, London; Neugerriemschneider, Berlin **Based on a conversation between Liam Gillick, Douglas Gordon, Carsten Höller, Pierre Huyghe, Philippe Parreno and Rirkrit Tiravanija, *Vicinato 2* presents four actors in Monaco.**

Anywhere Out of the World (After Leipzig Floor Plan), 2000 ◁ Thick yellow woolen rug, 200 × 500 cm ‡ "I Love You Too, But...," June 4–July 23, 2000, Galerie für zeitgenössische Kunst, Leipzig, Germany; exhibition curator: Jan Winckelmann || 3 editions and 1 artist edition § Courtesy Air de Paris, Paris and Esther Schipper, Berlin

Anywhere Out of the World (After Air de Paris Floor Plan), 2000 ◁ Thick blue wool rug, 200 × 380 cm ‡ June 21–26, 2000, Air de Paris booth, Art Basel, Basel, Switzerland || 3 editions and 1 artist edition ʃ First private collection: Private collection, Monaco (1/3) § Courtesy Air de Paris, Paris and Esther Schipper, Berlin

6 pm, 2000 Work "shared" with Pierre Huyghe ◁ Installation: carpet pattern, three colors, variable colors and dimensions ‡ "One Thousand Pictures Falling from One Thousand Walls, 1997–2000," October 25, 2000–January 21, 2001, Mamco, Geneva, Switzerland || 5 different versions and 1 artist edition ʃ First public collection: Daimler Art Collection, Stuttgart and Berlin, Germany (1/5: grey version) § Courtesy Air de Paris, Paris; Friedrich Petzel, New York; Esther Schipper, Berlin **This tri-color carpet represents**

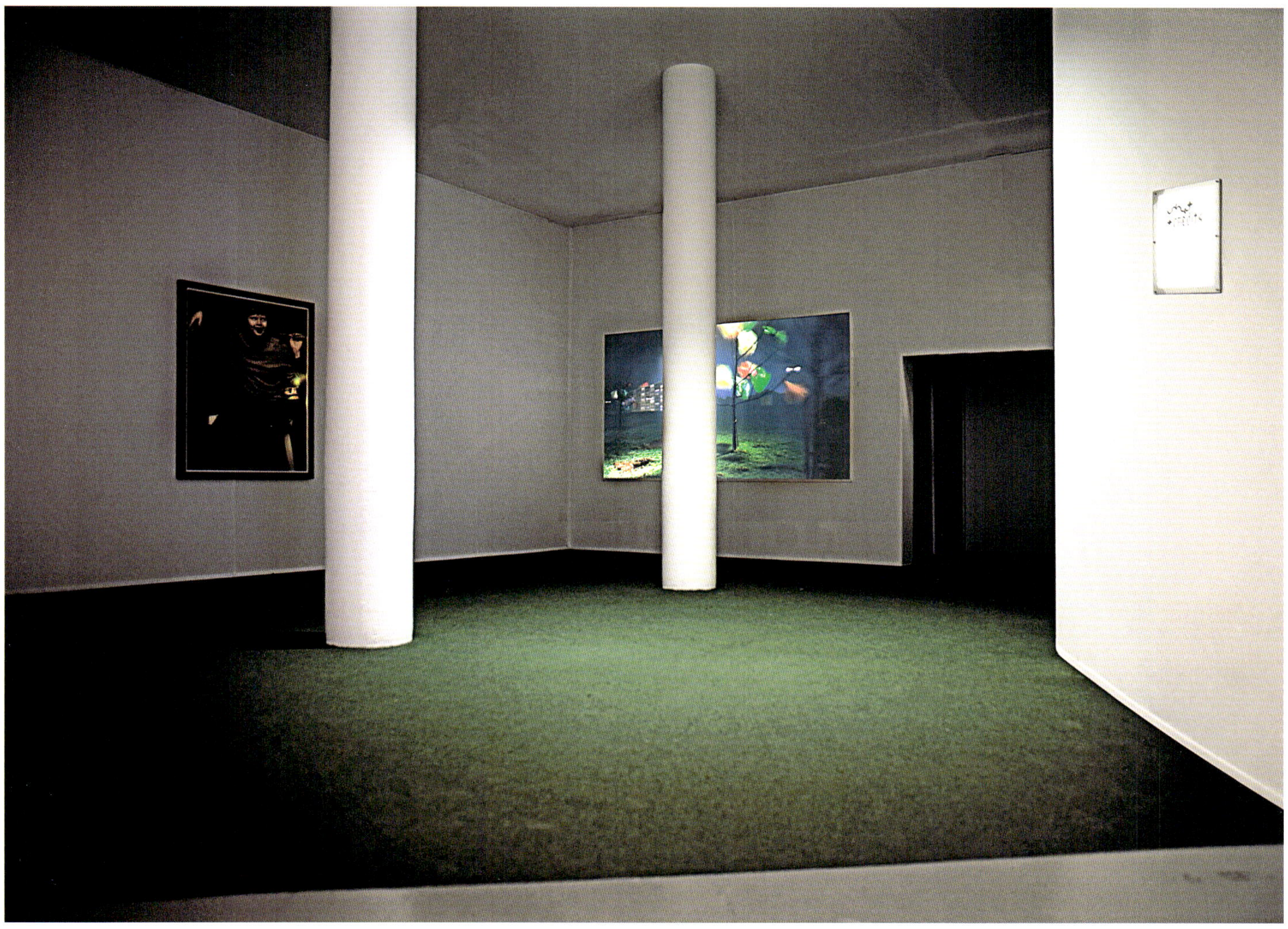

Michel Amathieu, Djamel Benameur, Jacques Chaban-Delmas, James Chinlund, Maurice Cotticelli, Hubert Dubedout, François Dumoulin, Ebezeber Howard, M/M (Paris), Pierre Mendès-France, Miko, Neyrpic, Alain Peyrefitte, Inez van Lamsweerde & Vinoodh Matadin, Anna-Léna Vaney, Angus Young, called Credits, 1999, exhibition view "Alien Seasons", Musée d'Art moderne de la Ville de Paris, 2002
Following pages: Michel Amathieu, Djamel Benameur, Jacques Chaban-Delmas, James Chinlund, Maurice Cotticelli, Hubert Dubedout, François Dumoulin, Ebezeber Howard, M/M (Paris), Pierre Mendès-France, Miko, Neyrpic, Alain Peyrefitte, Inez van Lamsweerde & Vinoodh Matadin, Anna-Léna Vaney, Angus Young, called Credits, 1999, film

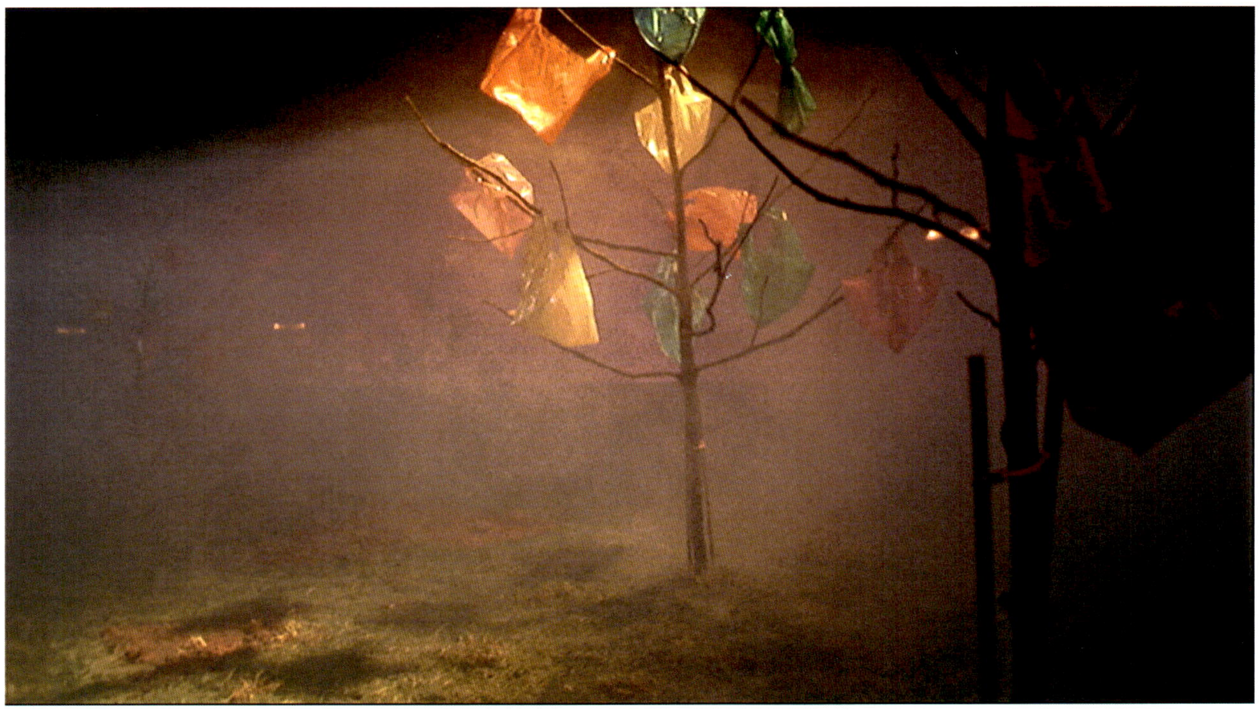

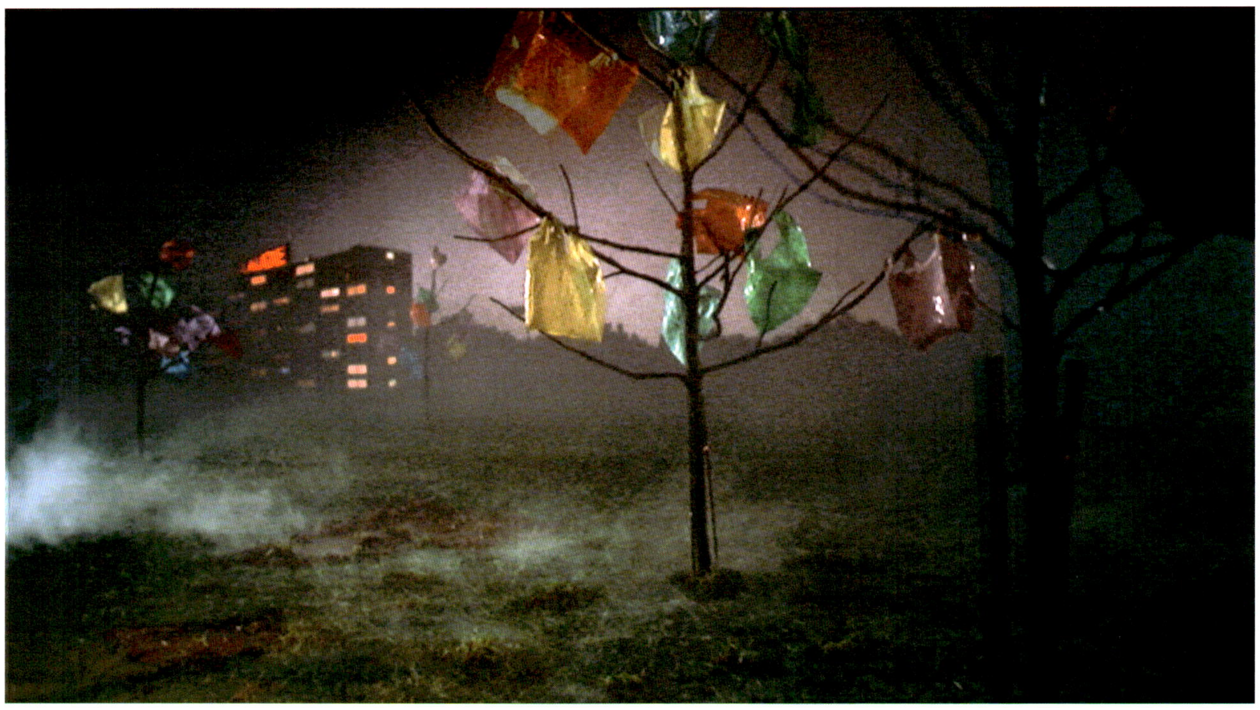

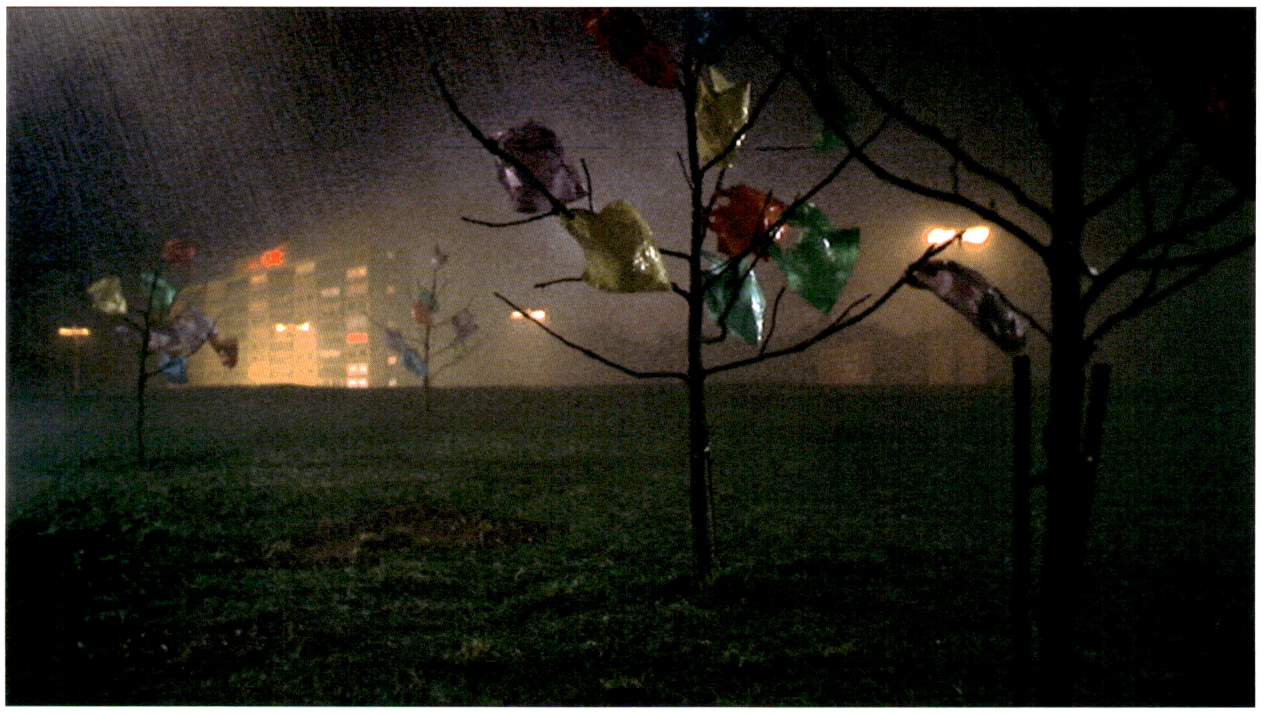

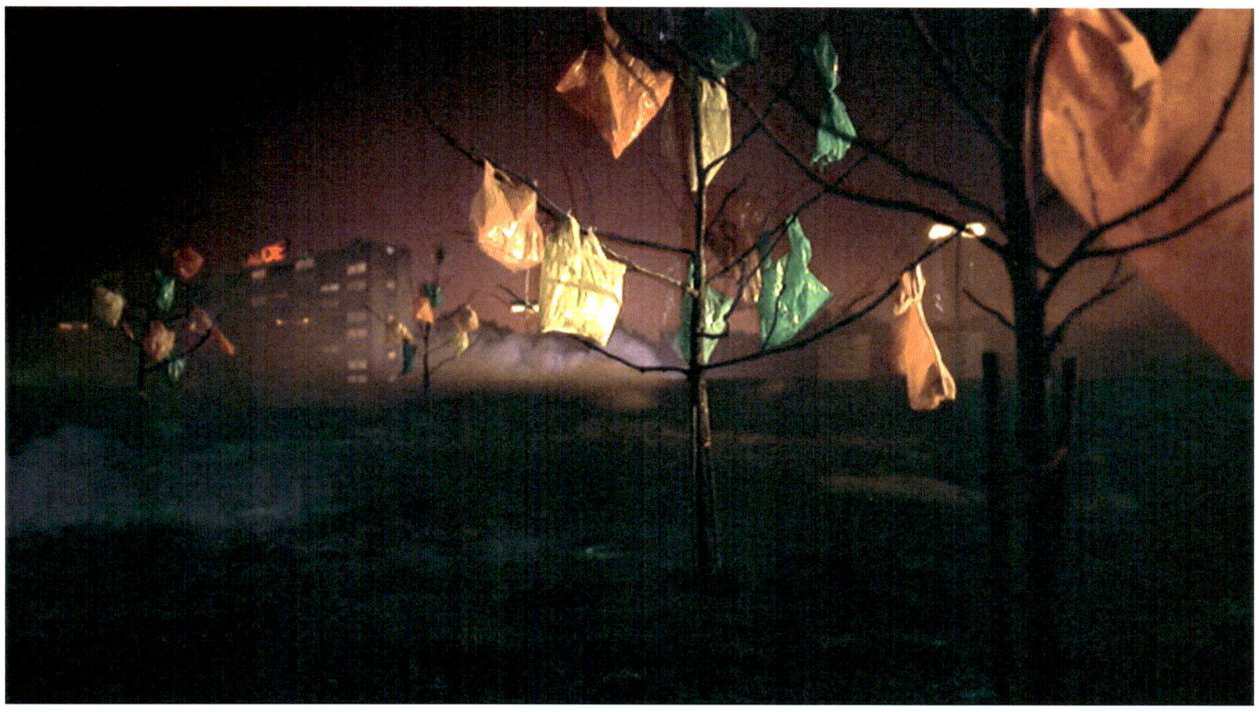
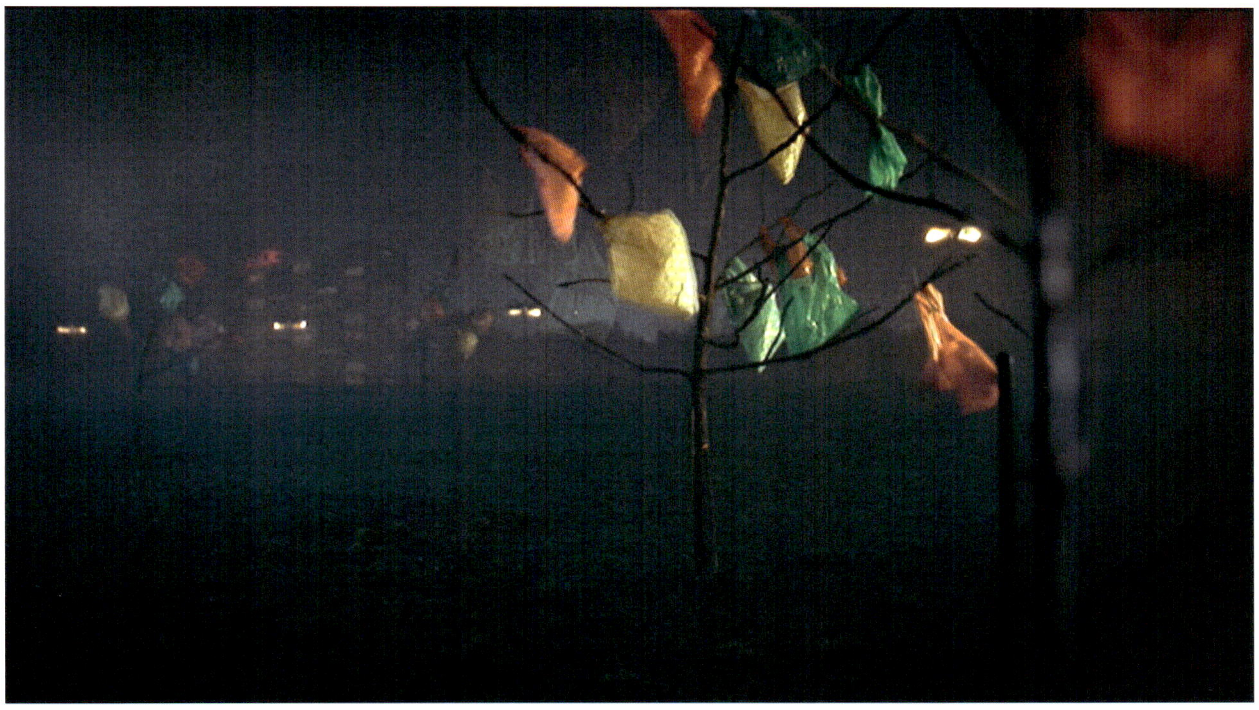
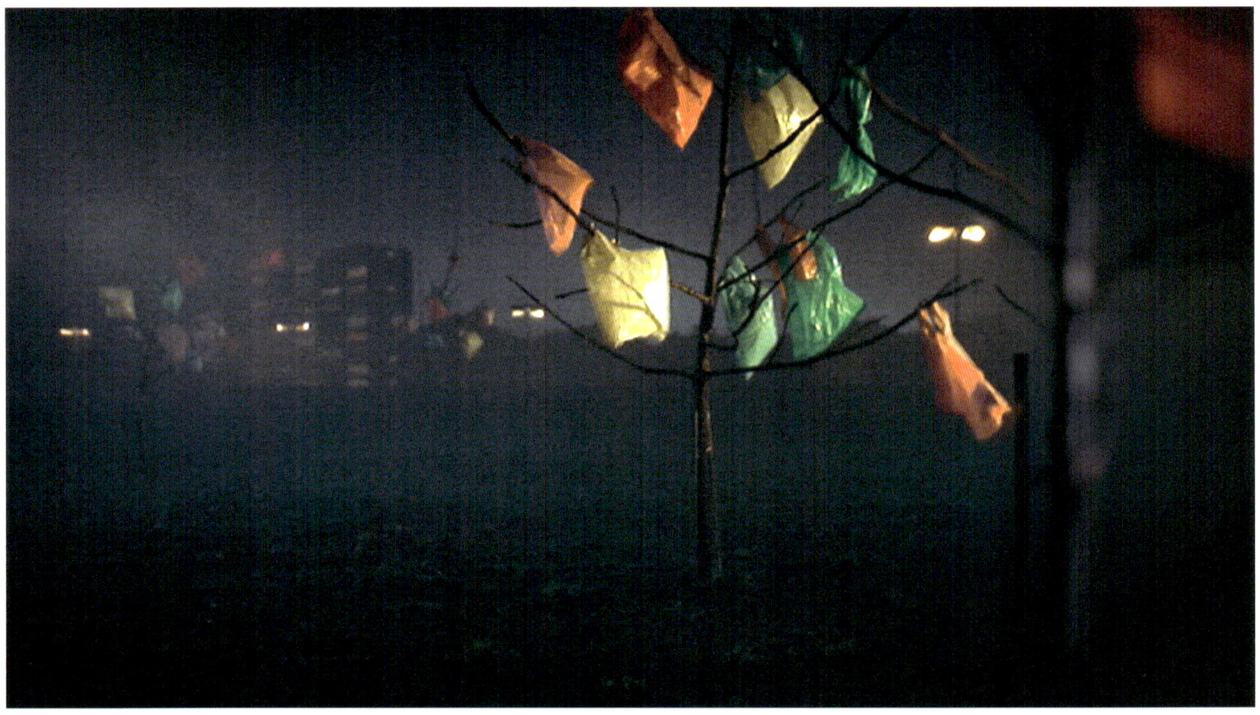

the shadow cast by a virtual window. The five editions made by Parreno were produced in a variety of different colors.

Prototype de luminaire [Light prototype], 2001 With Pierre Huyghe and M/M (Paris) ◊ Luminous furniture prototype: ¬ *Carrousel* seat (white fiberglass, 6 seat model, diam.: 190 cm, design by Elsie Crawford for the Sintoform company, 1972) • luminous structure (24 units in blown glass, white painted aluminum, plastic, resin, electrical wires): minimum dimensions of the whole structure: 700 × 900 cm ‡ "Pierre Huyghe," June 10–November 4, 2001, French Pavillion of the 49th Venice Biennial, Venice, Italy || 1 edition ʃ Fonds national d'art contemporain (Fnac) collection, Puteaux, France
Only one (of three editions initially planned) was produced in 2001 for the Café Étienne-Marcel, in Paris. It consists of a fiberglass base made for *Carrousel*, 1972, by Elsie Crawford, six seats and a network of lights. For the prototype, 24 blown glass units each containing a light (or "monster" in pink resin) were made with the help of the Cirva, in Marseilles.

Information Is Leaking A, 2001 ◊ Pencil on paper || 1 edition

Information Is Leaking, 2001 ◊ Pigmentary print, 29.8 × 41.9 cm ‡ June 13–18, 2001, Air de Paris and Esther Schipper booths, Art Basel, Basel, Switzerland || 12 editions and 1 artist edition ʃ First private collection: private collection, Monaco (1/12) § Courtesy Air de Paris, Paris; Friedrich Petzel, New York; Esther Schipper, Berlin

El sueño de una cosa, 2001 ◊ Pigmentary print, 26 × 41 cm (image), 33 × 48 cm (paper) ‡ June 13–18, 2001, Air de Paris and Esther Schipper booths, Art Basel, Basel, Switzerland || 12 editions and 1 artist edition ʃ First private collection: private collection, Monaco (1/12) § Courtesy Air de Paris, Paris; Friedrich Petzel, New York; Esther Schipper, Berlin ♦ **El sueño de una cosa, 2001** ◊ Installation: ¬ 35 mm film, color, sound stereo, variable length • music: Edgar Varèse; production: Moderna Museet, Stockholm, Sweden; variable dimensions ‡ First showing: September 6, 2001, "The Astoria" movie theater, Stockholm, Sweden, during the exhibition "MMP: Philippe Parreno," September 7–October 4, 2001 at the Moderna Museet, Stockholm, Sweden (exhib. cat.) || 1 edition § Courtesy Air de Paris, Paris ♦ **El sueño de una cosa, 2001–2002** ◊ Installation: ¬ Show Controller, HD player, video projector, 35 mm film transferred onto master digital HD (color, stereo, 1'), electric curtains, sound system • *White Painting Series* (Robert Rauschenberg, 1951) • *4'33"* (John Cage, 1952) • music: Edgar Varèse, *Deserts*, 1954; production: Moderna Museet, Stockholm, and musée d'Art moderne de la Ville de Paris, Paris ‡ "El sueño de una cosa," February 2–March 10, 2002, Portikus, Frankfurt, Germany || 1 edition ʃ Solomon R. Guggenheim Museum Collection, New York, United States
♦ **El sueño de una cosa, 2001** ◊ Installation: ¬ computer program, Show Controller, video projector, 35 mm film transferred onto Master digital HD (color, stereo, 1') • sound system • music: Edgar

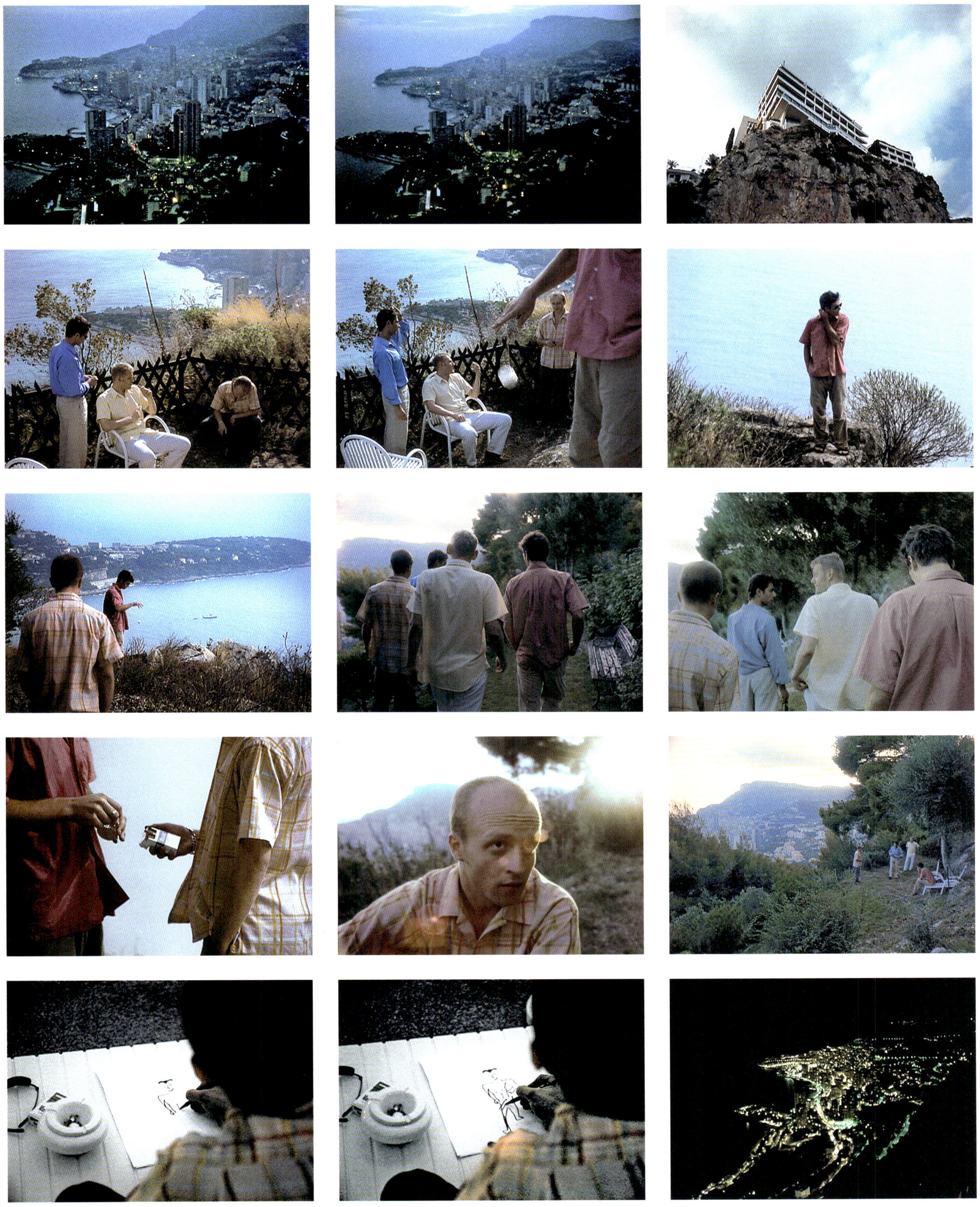

Vicinato 2, 2000, with Liam Gillick, Douglas Gordon, Carsten Höller, Pierre Huyghe and Rirkrit Tiravanija, film

42. Philippe Parreno, Hans Ulrich Obrist, *The Conversation Series*, op. cit., p.35.

Varèse, *Deserts*, 1954; production: Moderna Museet, Stockholm, and musée d'Art moderne de la Ville de Paris, Paris || 1 edition ʃ Centre Pompidou Collection, Mnam, Paris, France **This one-minute film was shot in Svalbard, a Norwegian island situated above the Arctic Circle. In the green mountainous landscape, a bed of yellow flowers springs from the ground, and blossoms at an accelerated speed right before our eyes. Music by Edgar Varèse, *Désert* (1954) accompanies this improbable and magical spectacle. *El sueño de una cosa* [The Dream of a Thing] is shown in several different ways. First, the film was screened in a number of movie theaters throughout Sweden as an advertisement or as a trailer for a movie. However, instead of an object or feature length film, an image of a dream which encourages the spectator to imagine his own object of desire is offered.**
The film was next presented at Portikus in Frankfurt, projected on a white painting by Robert Rauschenberg (*White Painting Series*, 1951) as part of an installation. Curtains are lowered, the film is projected for its duration of one-minute followed by four-minutes-and-thirty-three-seconds of silence, exactly the same length as John Cage's score *4'33"* (1952) which was made for Rauschenberg's painting. The work was also presented in a third version at the entrance of the "Alien Seasons" exhibition at l'Arc in 2002 which is now in the collection of the Solomon R. Guggenheim Museum in New York. The Centre Pompidou owns the third edition, for which a computer program generates a random ordering of sequences during each playback so that the film is always different. "It is a film in constant post-production," comments Parreno.[42] ◊ Revisiting the notions of collaboration and of the palimpsest, this work also establishes a new dialectic between the film's *black box* and the museum's *white cube*.

Mont Analogue, 2001 ◊ Installation: video projector without lens, Beta cam digital video transferred onto DVD, color, silent, 62'; variable dimensions ‡ "Mont Analogue," December 22, 2001– January 2, 2002, simultaneously in three spaces: Air de Paris Gallery, Paris; Friedrich Petzel Gallery, New York, Rirkrit Tiravanija's studio, Bangkok, Thailand || 12 editions and 2 artist editions ʃ First public collection: Musée d'Art moderne de la Ville de Paris, Paris, France (2/12) § Courtesy Air de Paris, Paris; Friedrich Petzel, New York; Esther Schipper, Berlin **Projected color sequences from a passage of René Dumal's novel, *Le Mont Analogue* (1952) translated into Morse code.**

El sueño de una cosa, 2002 ◊ Digital print on cotton paper, 30.5 × 44.7 cm ‡ "El sueño de una cosa," February 2–March 10, 2002, Portikus, Frankfurt, Germany || 30 editions ʃ First private collection: private collection, Frankfurt, Germany § Courtesy Portikus, Frankfurt

Alien Seasons, 2002 ‡ May 31–September 12, 2002 Arc/Musée d'Art moderne de la Ville de Paris, France
Alien Seasons, 2002 ◊ Installation: show Controller, DVD player, flat screen, 16 mm film transferred onto Beta cam digital, color, mute, 5', on a loop (5 sequences of 10" to 30") ‡ "Alien Seasons," May

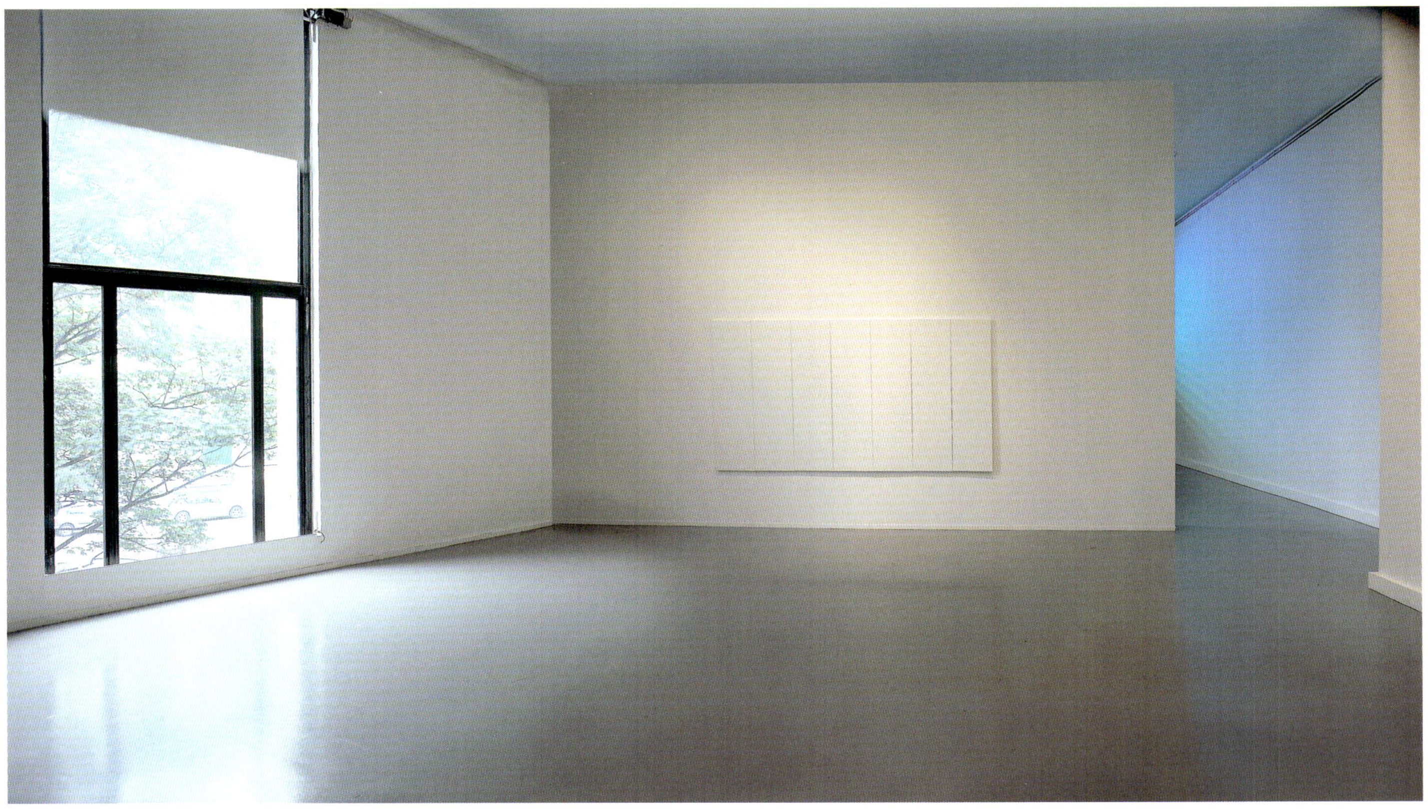

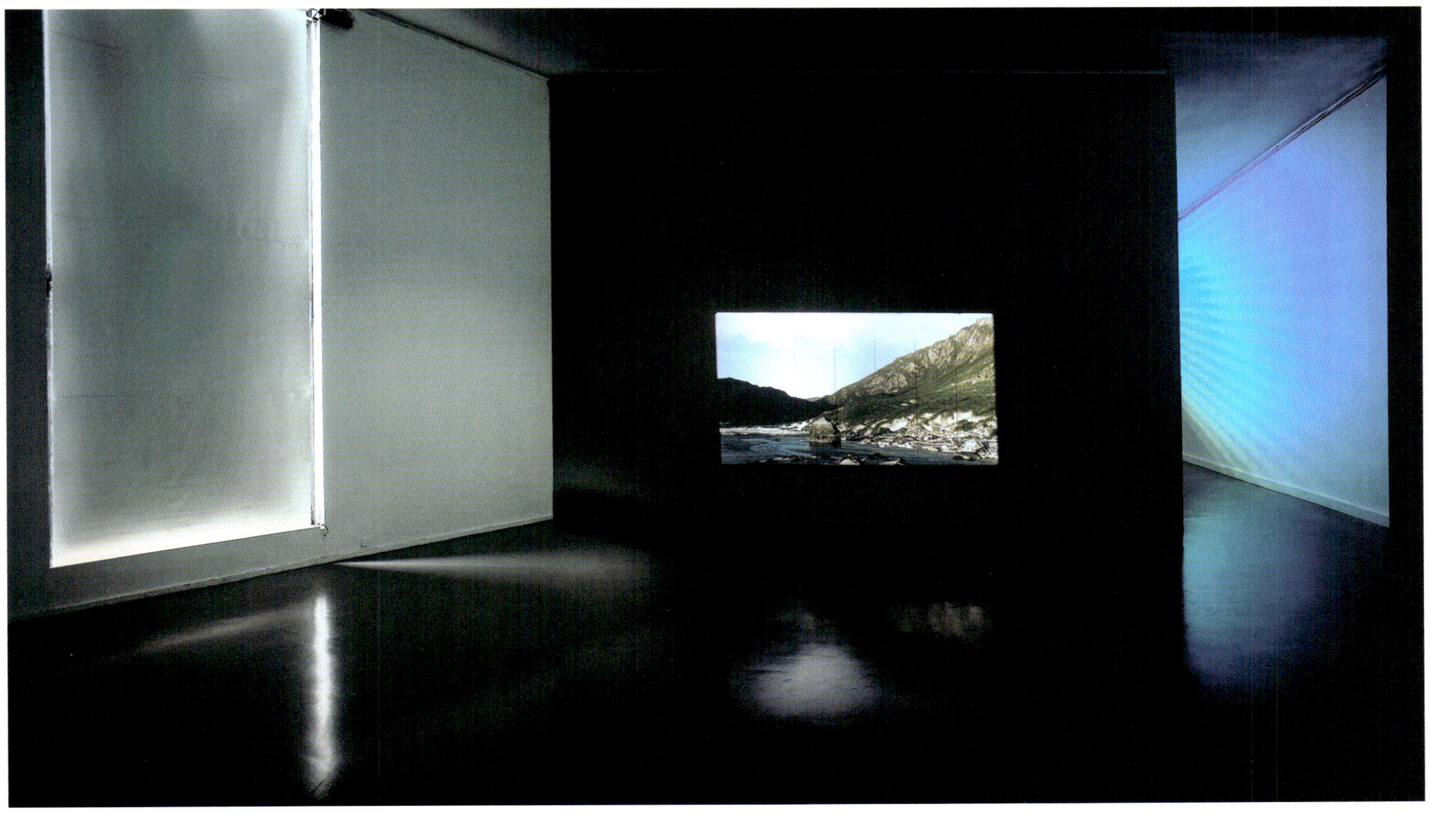

El sueño de una cosa, 2001-2002, exhibition view "Alien Seasons", Musée d'Art moderne de la Ville de Paris, 2002

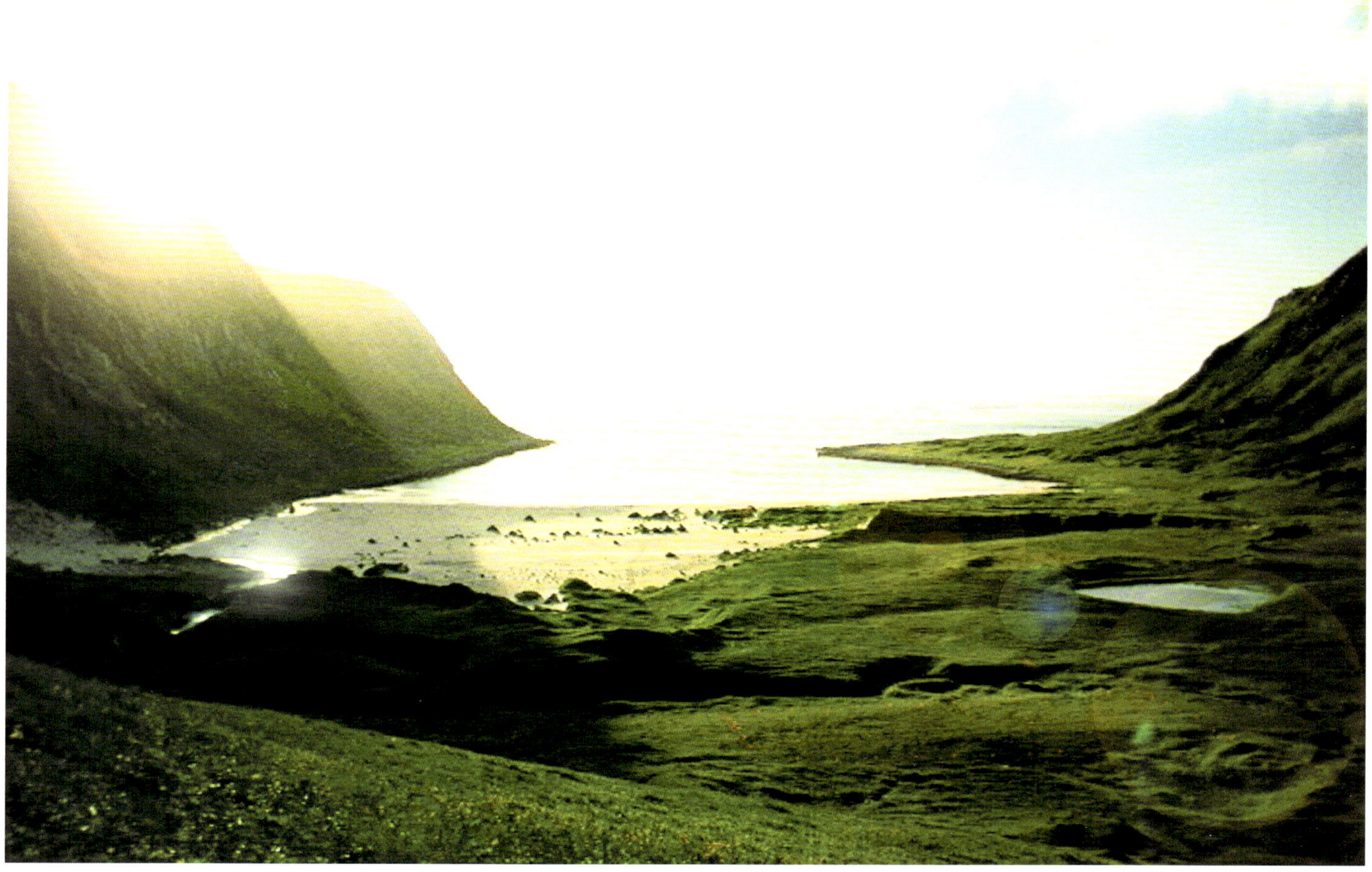

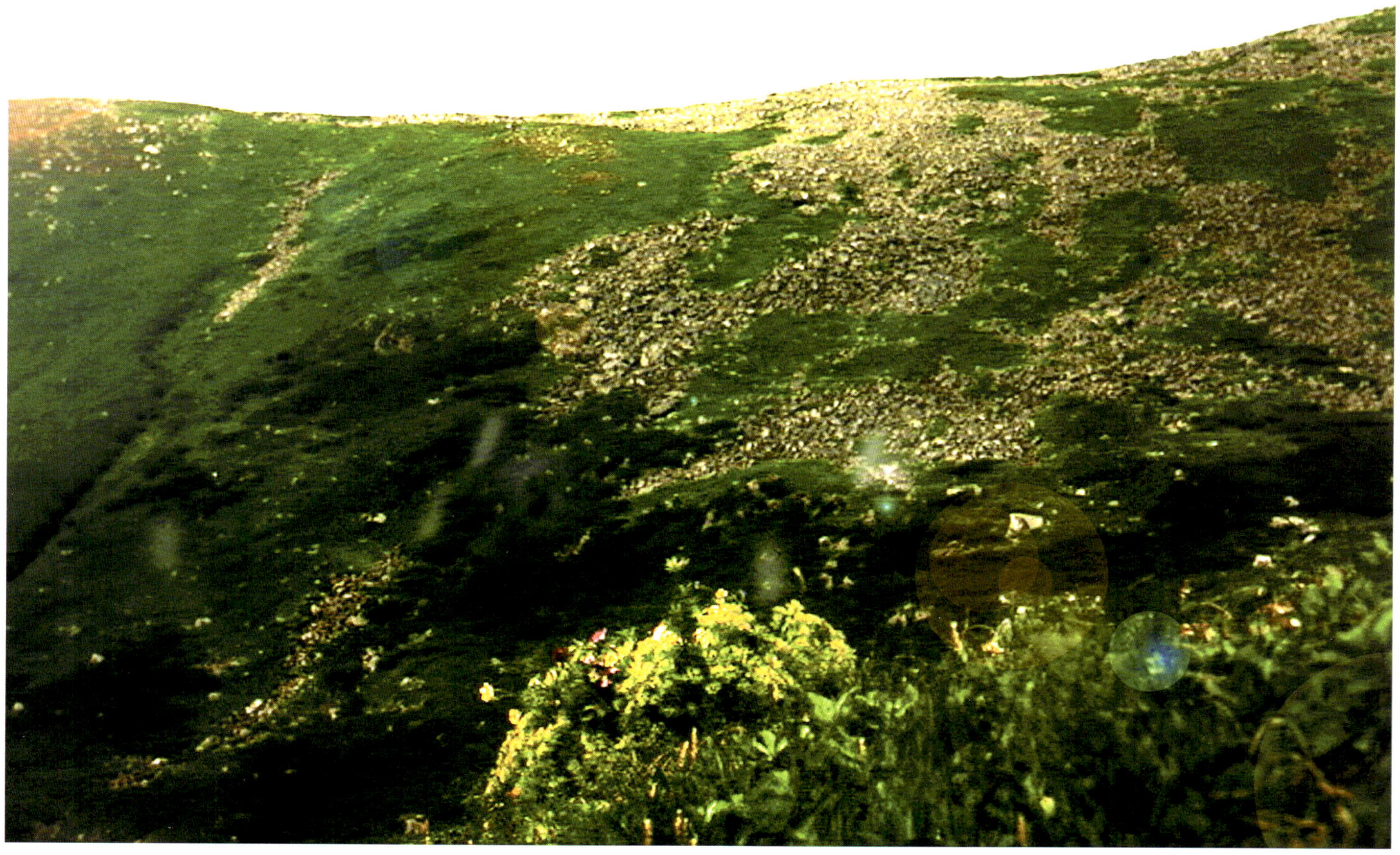

El sueño de una cosa, 2001, film

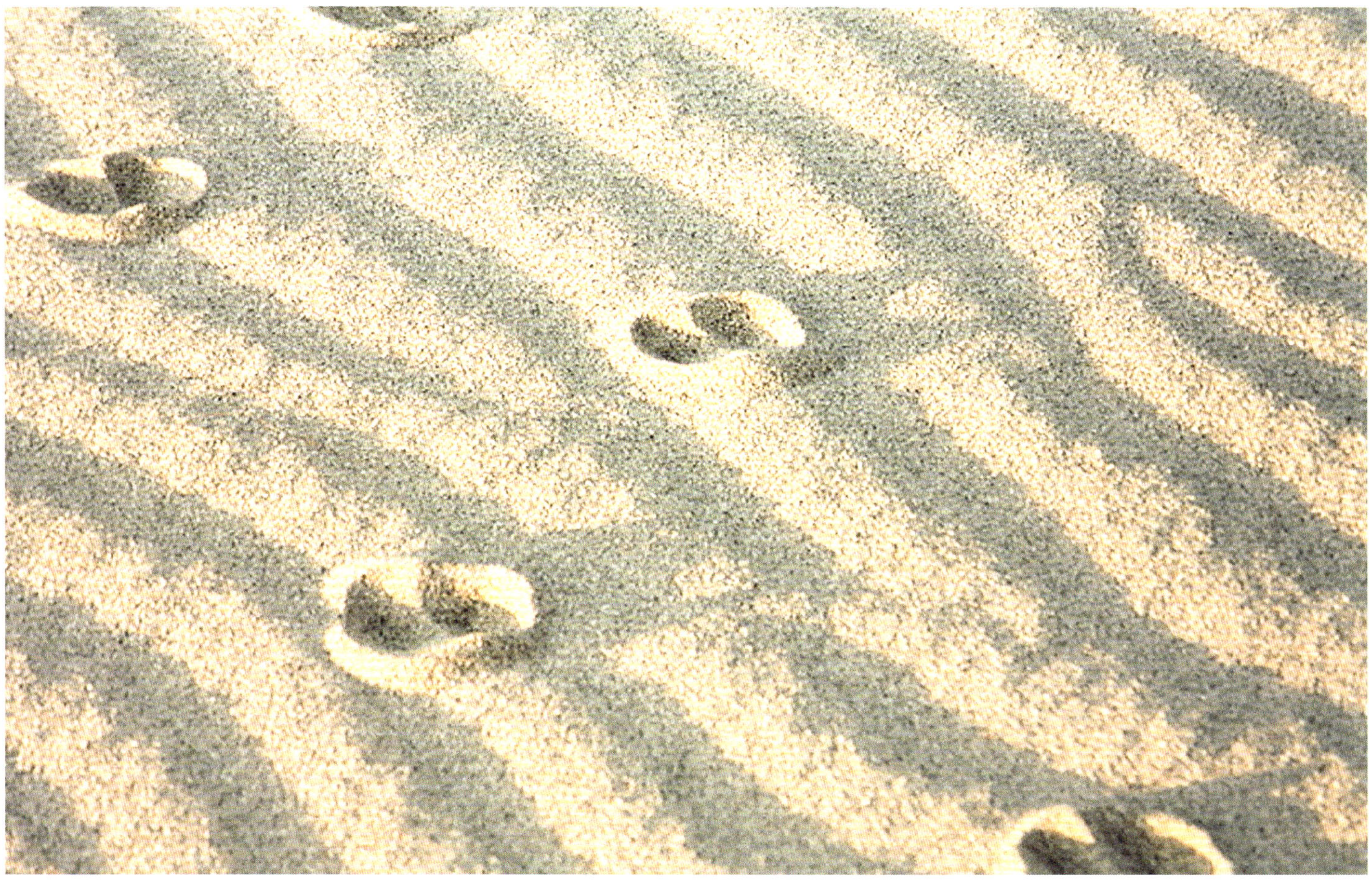

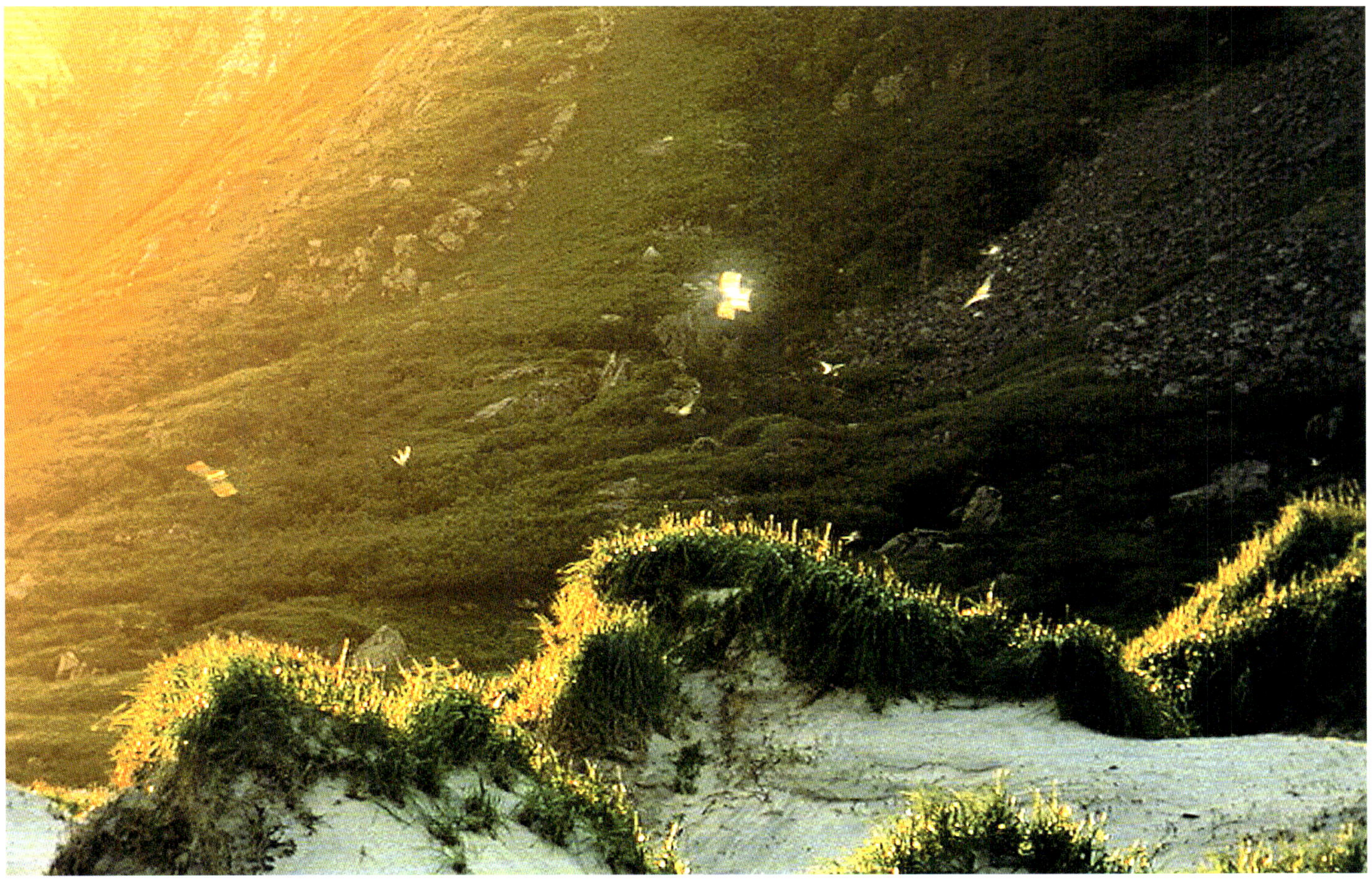

43. Philippe Parreno in Philippe Parreno, Hans Ulrich Obrist, *Conversation Series*, *op. cit.*, p.63, and also *Philippe Parreno. Alien Affection*, *op. cit.*

31–September 12, 2002, Arc/Musée d'Art moderne de la Ville de Paris, France (exhib.cat.) || 4 editions and 1 artist edition ʃ First public collection: Fonds national d'art contemporain (Fnac), Puteaux, France (1/4) § Courtesy Air de Paris, Paris; Friedrich Petzel, New York; Esther Schipper, Berlin ♦ **Orange Bay (After Gabriel Tarde's Fragment of Future History), 2002** ◁ 4 bays in orange Plexiglas, variable dimensions ‡ "Alien Seasons," May 31–September 12, 2002, Arc/Musée d'Art moderne de la Ville de Paris, France (exhib.cat.) § Courtesy Air de Paris, Paris; Friedrich Petzel, New York; Esther Schipper, Berlin ♦ **Battery House, 2002** With Roche & Sie ◁ Prototype of *Hybrid Muscle*: aluminum structure, recycled plastic leaves, inflatable muscle (523 × 280 cm) ‡ "Alien Seasons," May 31–September 12, 2002, Arc/Musée d'Art moderne de la Ville de Paris, France (exhib.cat.) || 1 edition ʃ Mudam Collection, Luxemburg § Courtesy of the artist and Roche & Sie ♦ **7 juillet 2002, 2002** ◁ Radio work ‡ "Alien Seasons," May 31–September 12, 2002, Arc/Musée d'Art moderne de la Ville de Paris, France (exhib. cat.) § Courtesy of the artist "Alien Seasons" was conceived in collaboration with Jaron Lanier as a sequence of events occurring in a space. Lanier proposed that the exhibition be controlled by a video of a cephalopod. Parreno has always been fascinated by cephalopods. "I always had this dream as a child, that I could open my mouth and that a projector beam would come out of it, that my imagination would transfer itself quite easily into images available for others. Or maybe that I could have an image on my skin like the giant Cuttlefish."[43] This cephalopod, which lives next to the Palau Islands in the Pacific, is photochromic, and therefore capable of producing images on the surface of its skin. The Cuttlefish's nervous system produces real images from imaginary nervous-impulses. This advanced animal has developed a post-symbolic way to communicate. ◊ The silent film *Alien Seasons*, five sequences of different lengths, is run by a *show controller*, a kind of metallic closet linked by a visible network of electrical wires. The *show controller* functions as a "switch," orchestrating the appearance of image sequences and activating the other works in the exhibition. Many possibilities exist for synchronizing the film within the context of an exhibition. *Le Fonds national d'art contemporain*, for example, showed it with the first *Fade to Black* series from 2003. A system was set up where a synchronizer triggered alternately the projection of the film and the lighting of the room where the phosphorescent screen prints were displayed. ◊ With the activation of the exhibition's *mise en scène*, the installation generates a new exhibition temporality as well as a unique form of interactivity. The exhibition *Alien Seasons* contains the installation *El sueño de una cosa (version 2)*, the prototype of *Battery House* made with Roche & Sie for *The Land* by Tiravanija at Chiang Mai in Thailand—a moving curtain of leaves covered in recycled plastic and powered by an air-filled muscle—and the *Mont Analogue*. This projection of luminous colors is only visible from the outside of the museum through a bay window from 10pm until 6am. The unfinished radio piece *7th July 2002* was meant to be broadcast on Radio France from 10:45pm until midnight everyday.

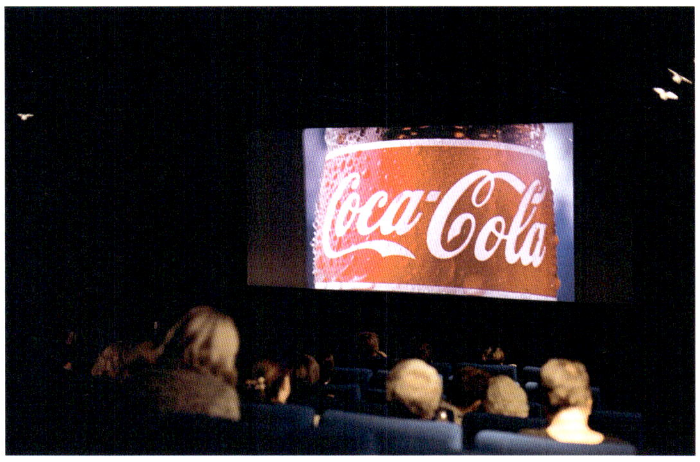

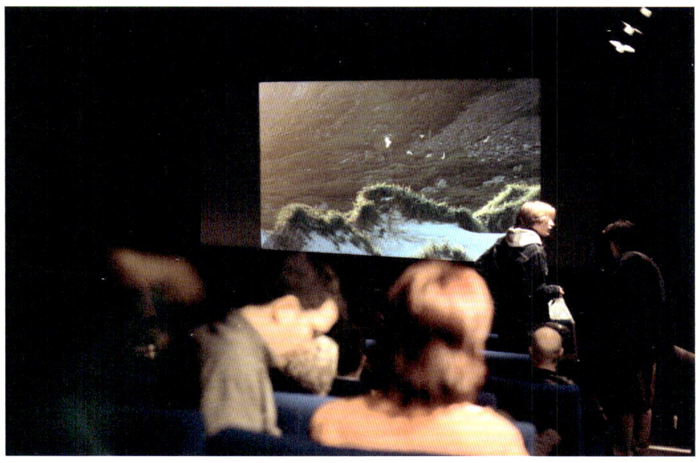

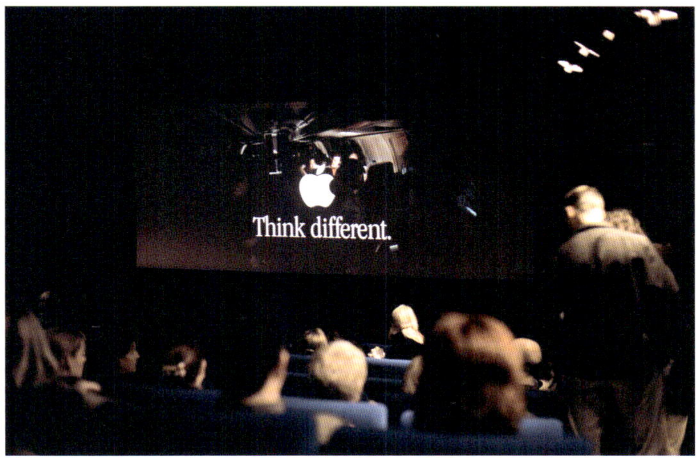

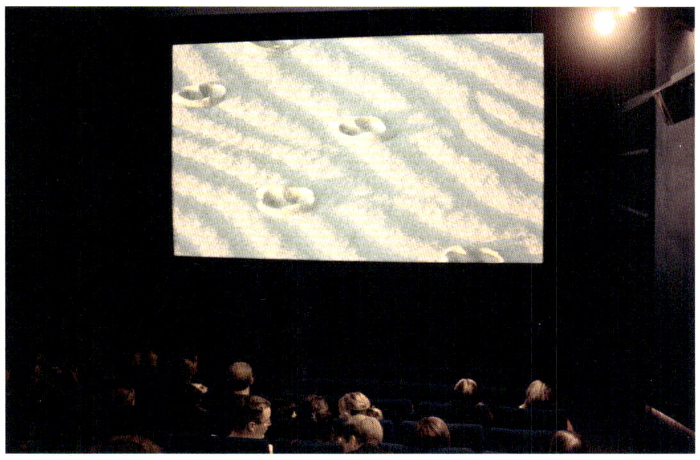

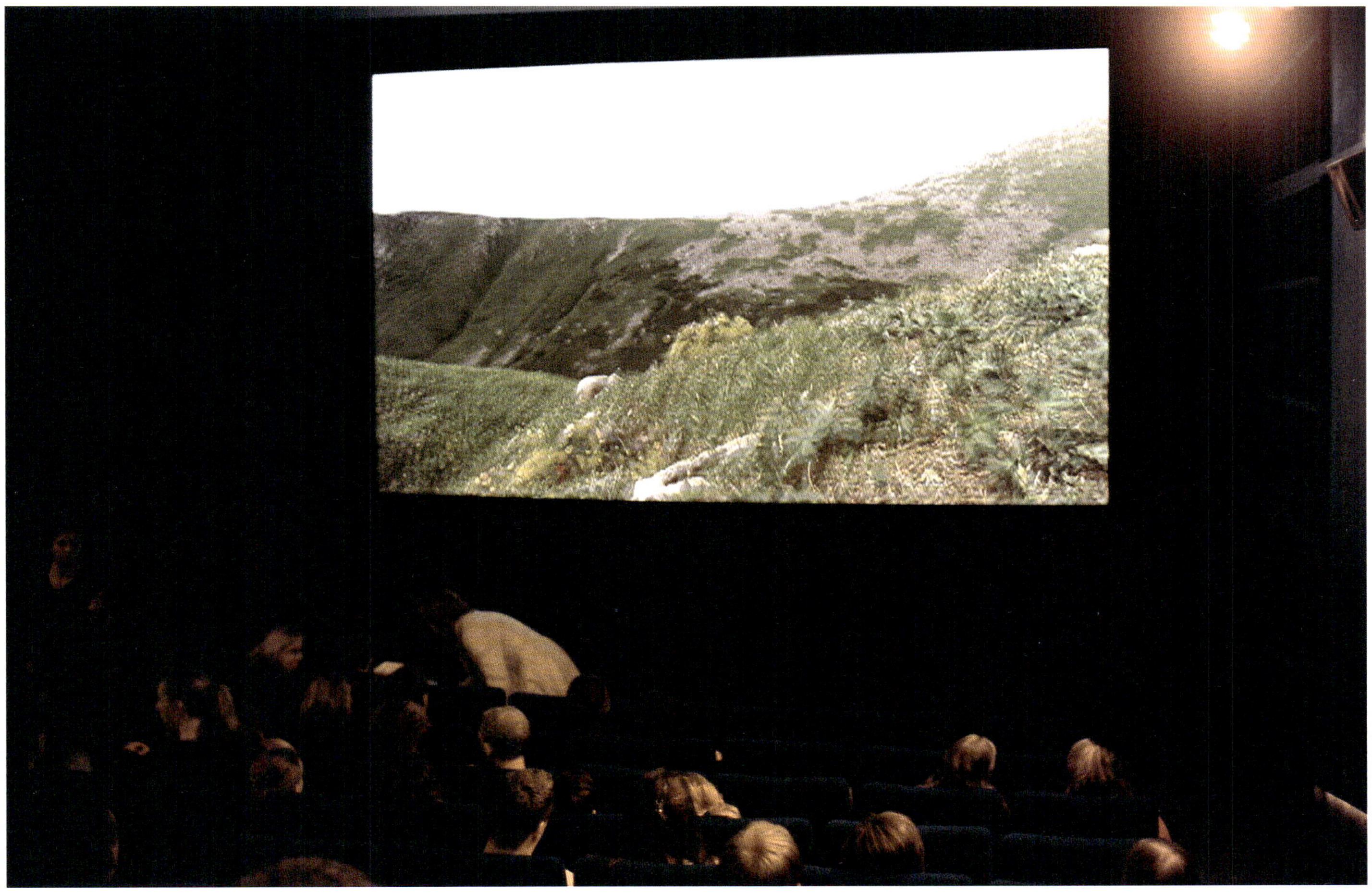

El sueño de una cosa, 2001, exhibition view "MMP : Philippe Parreno", Moderna Museet, Stockholm
Following pages: **"Alien Seasons",** exhibition view at the Musée d'Art moderne de la Ville de Paris, 2002

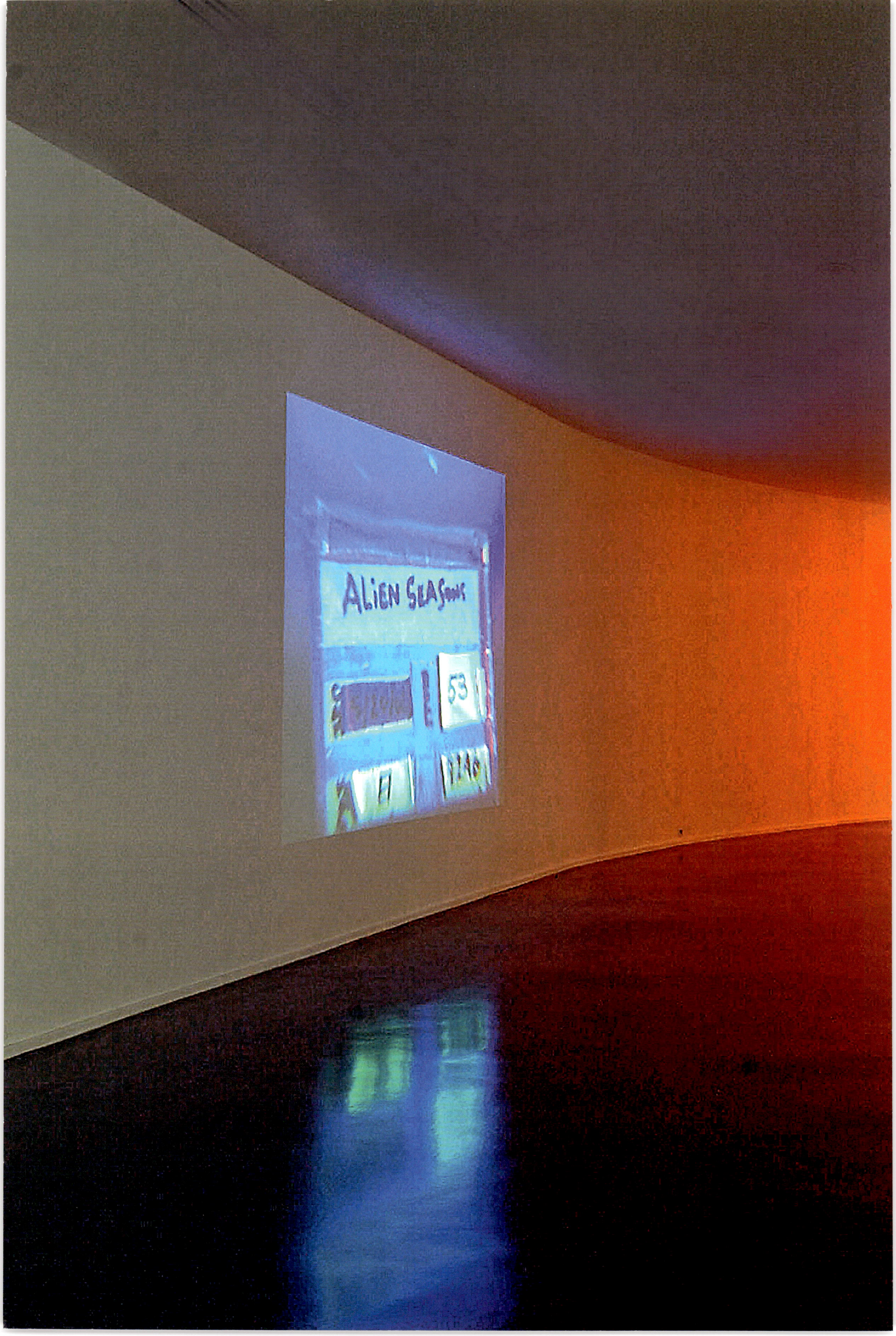
ALIEN SEASONS
53

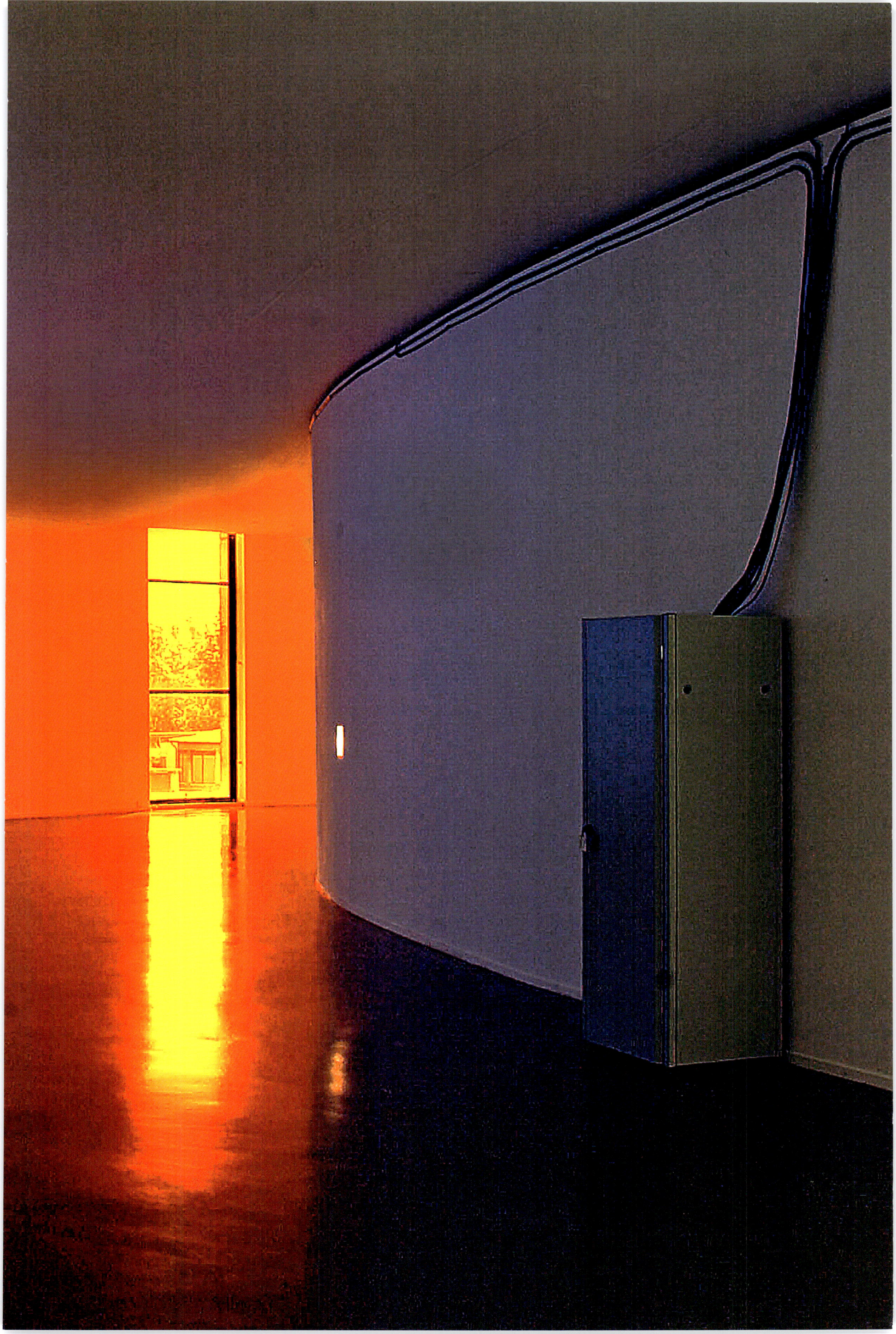

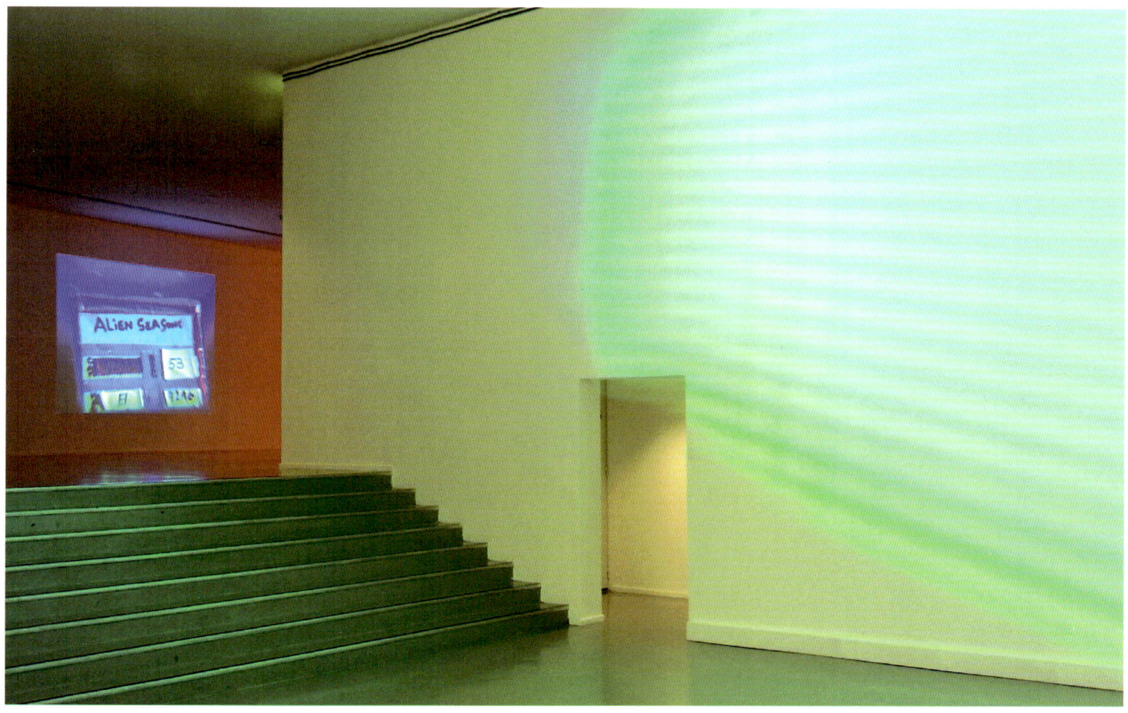
ALIEN
53

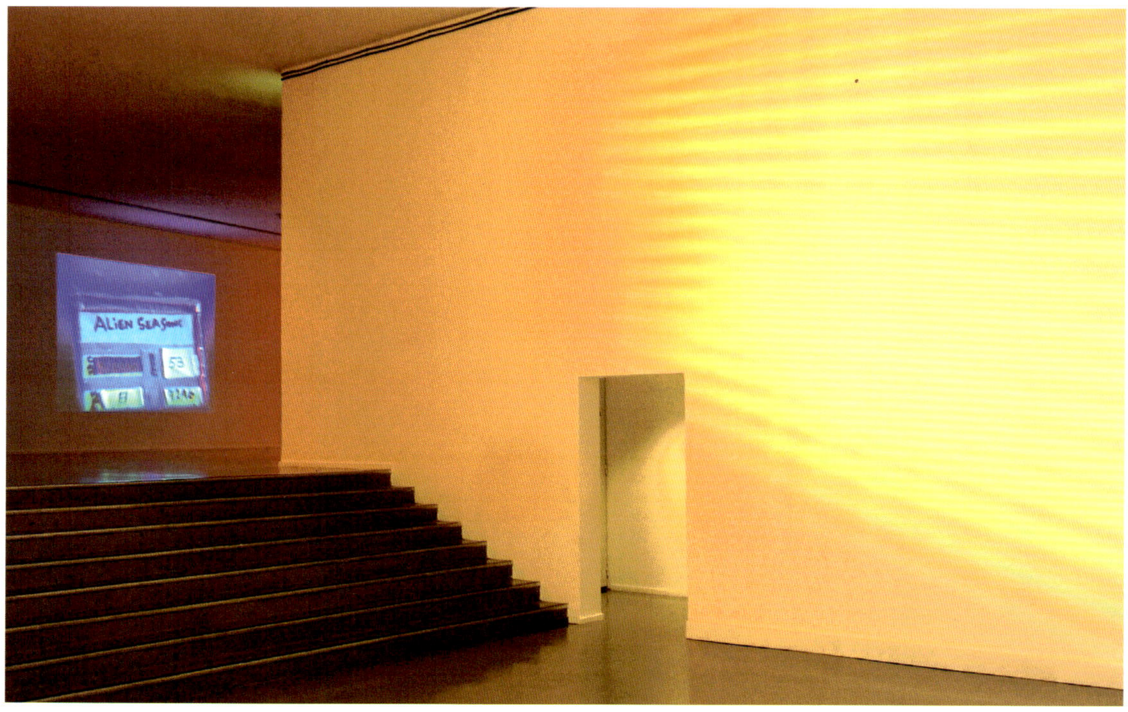

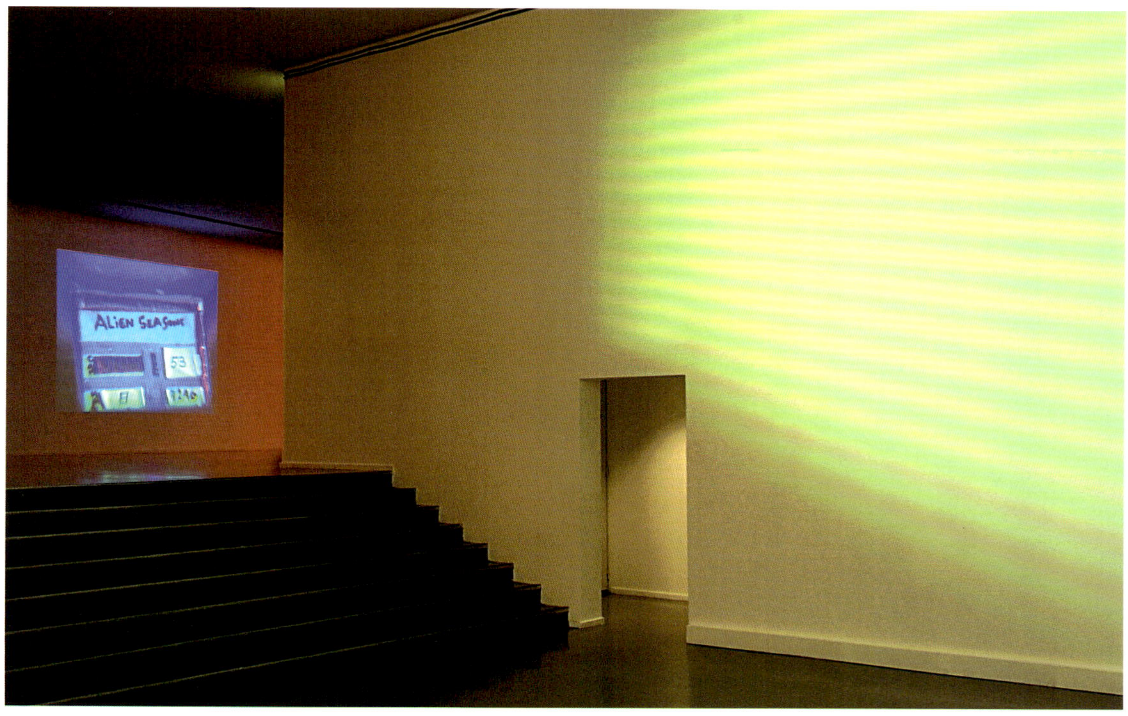

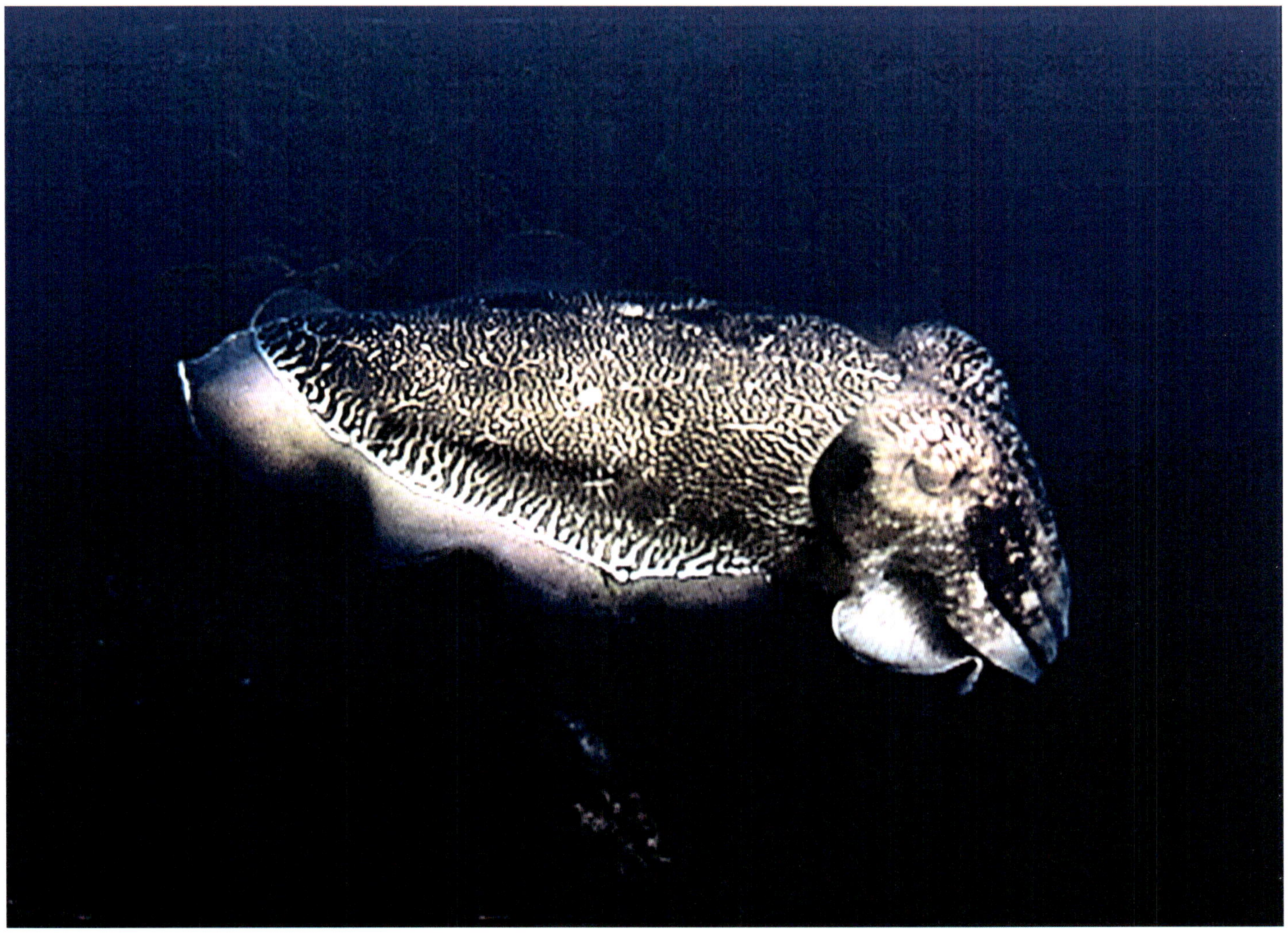

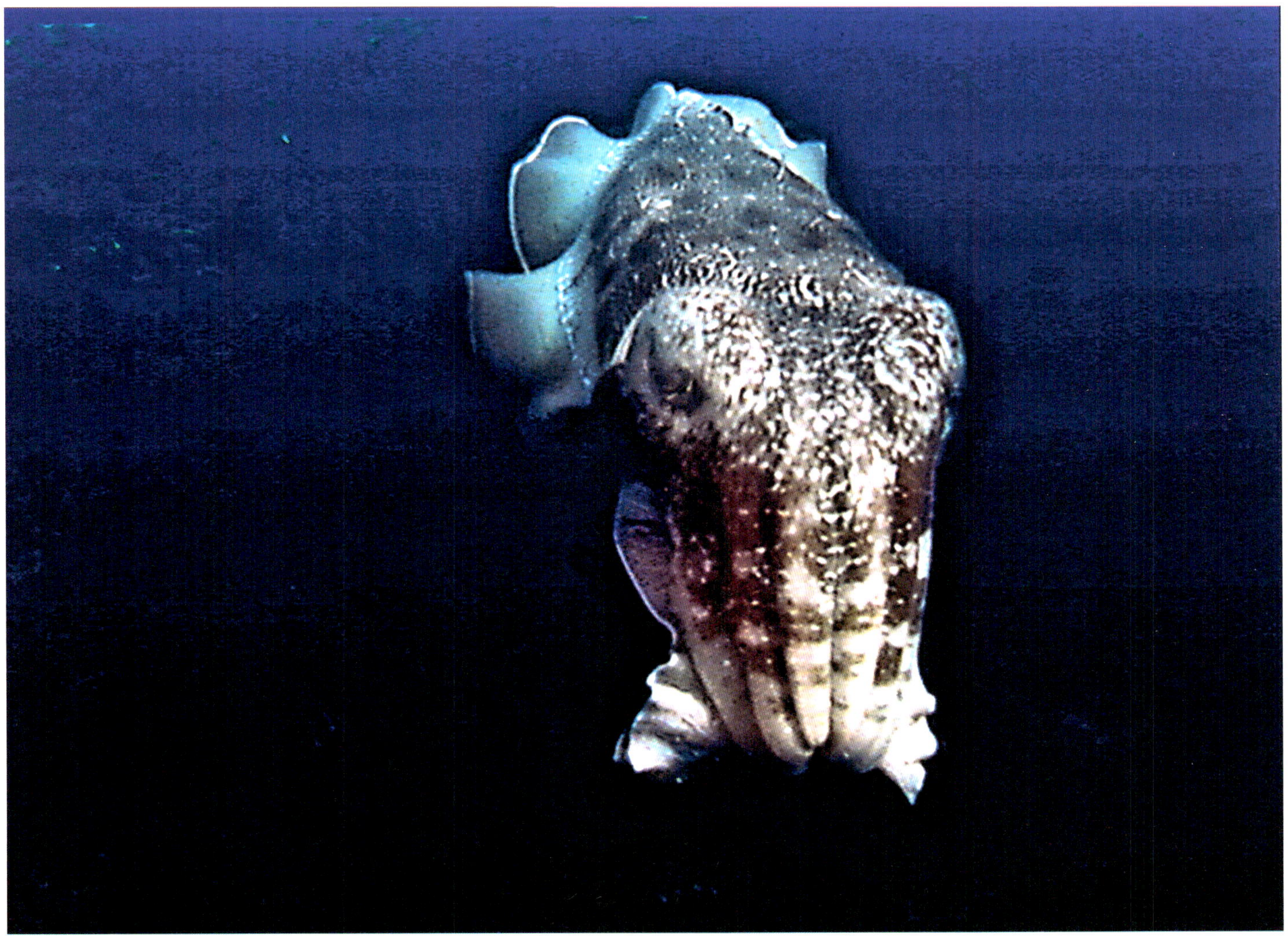

Alien Seasons, 2002, film
Alien Seasons and **Mont Analogue, 2001,** exhibition "Alien Seasons", Musée d'Art moderne de la Ville de Paris, 2002

These few minutes of silence were meant to represent the sound of the stars. Finally, the windows were replaced with orange Plexiglas for the work, *Orange Bay (After Gabriel Tarde's Fragment of Future History)*, which bathed the space in a surreal light. The work *Credits* (1999) completed the scenographic intervention into exhibition time.

L'oiseau, le chien, le chat [The Bird, the Dog, the Cat] 2002 With Jorge Pardo ⊲ Installation: 3 PVC molded shells, light bulbs and electrical system; 85 × 50 × 27 cm (the "bird") 85 × 63 × 51 cm (the "dog"), 72 × 52 × 20 cm (the "cat"); variable dimensions ‡ "Jorge Pardo, Philippe Parreno," November 9–December 31, 2002, 1301PE, Los Angeles, United States || 10 editions and 2 artist editions ʃ First public collection: Frac Poitou-Charentes, Angoulême, France (5/10) § Courtesy 1301PE, Los Angeles; Air de Paris, Paris; Friedrich Petzel, New York These lamps are made in collaboration with Jorge Pardo. Shown for the first time in the Brian Butler Gallery in Los Angeles (1301PE) in 2002, then at Air de Paris Gallery in 2003, the work consists of three lamps linked together and plugged into the same electrical source –forming a representation of immaterial architecture. During an interview with Claude Parent, the architect spoke to Parreno of Yves Klein's notion of immaterial architecture defined simply by three points of light: an external point in a city at night, a point in a lit bedroom and another in a neighboring room. For *Untitled*, 2002 the three lamps were placed in three rooms on the floor and mounted on the wall. The work makes a shift from functional design to sculpture, while introducing a fiction, a possibility of "projection," thereby blurring the boundaries between art and design. Indeed, the organic and zoomorphic forms of the lamps are suggestive of animals, such as a bird, dog or cat– and moreover, together create a kind of *alien* presence, reminiscent of the cephalopod in "Alien Seasons."

A Smile without a Cat, 2002 With Pierre Huyghe ⊲ Firework on metallic structure; production: *TRANS>* Sandra Antelo-Suarez ‡ December 7, 2002, Art Basel Miami, Miami Beach, United States § Courtesy of the artists ♦ **A Smile without a Cat, 2002** With Pierre Huyghe ⊲ 35 mm film transferred onto DVD; production Sandra Antelo-Suarez; Friedrich Petzel Gallery, New York, and Marian Goodman Gallery, New York ‡ Armory Show, February 23–26, 2007, New York, United States || 10 editions and 3 artist editions ʃ First private collection: Collector's Circle, New York, United States (1/10) § Courtesy Sandra Antelo-Suarez; Friedrich Petzel, New York; Marian Goodman Gallery, New York

Information is Leaking, 2003 ⊲ Pigmentary print; 29 × 42 cm (print), 33 × 48 cm (paper) || 12 editions and 1 artist edition ʃ First private collection: private collection, Miami, United States (1/12) § Courtesy Air de Paris, Paris; Friedrich Petzel, New York; Esther Schipper, Berlin

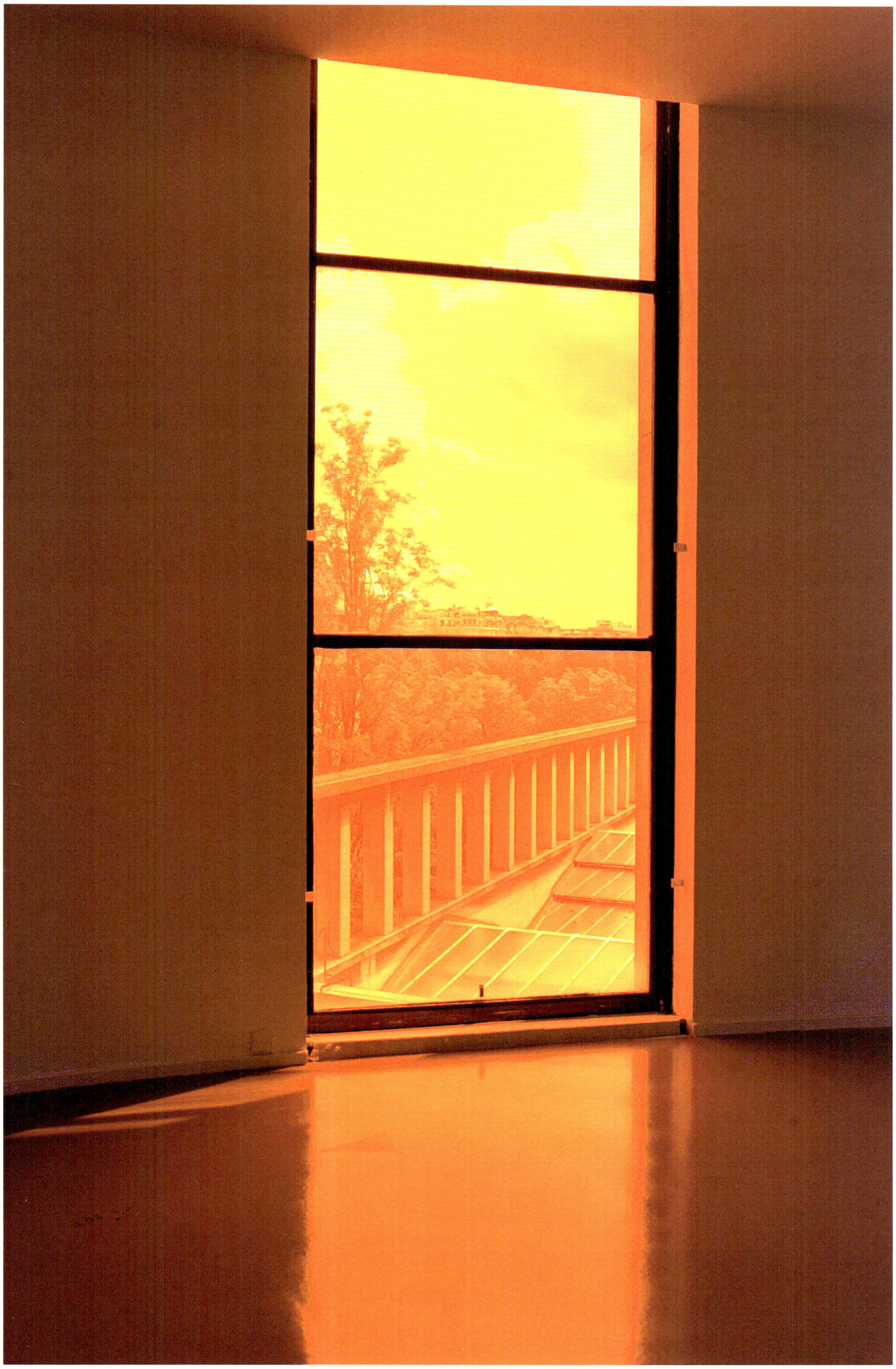

Orange Bay (After Gabriel Tarde's Fragment of Future History), 2002, exhibition view "Alien Seasons" at the Musée d'Art moderne de la Ville de Paris, 2002

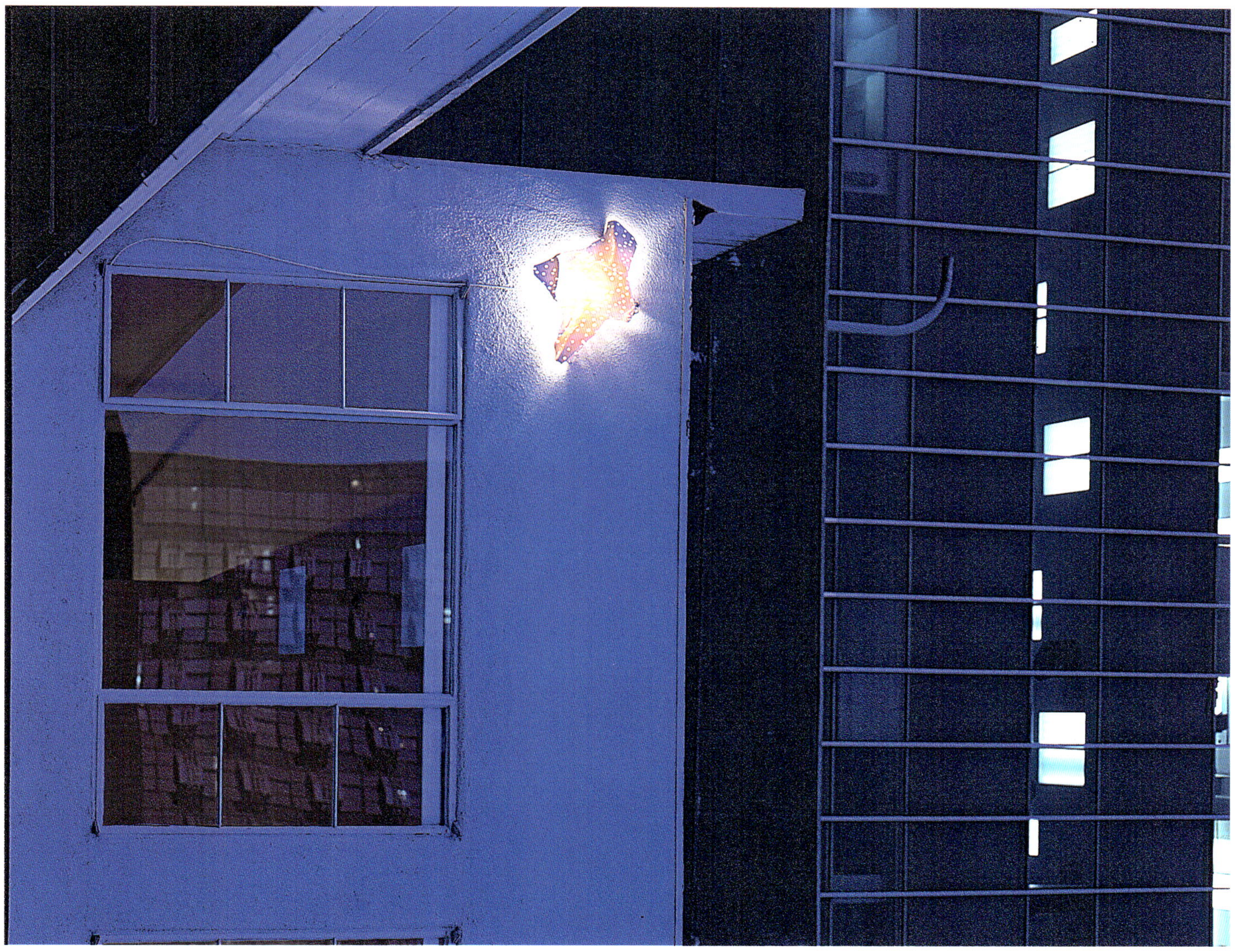

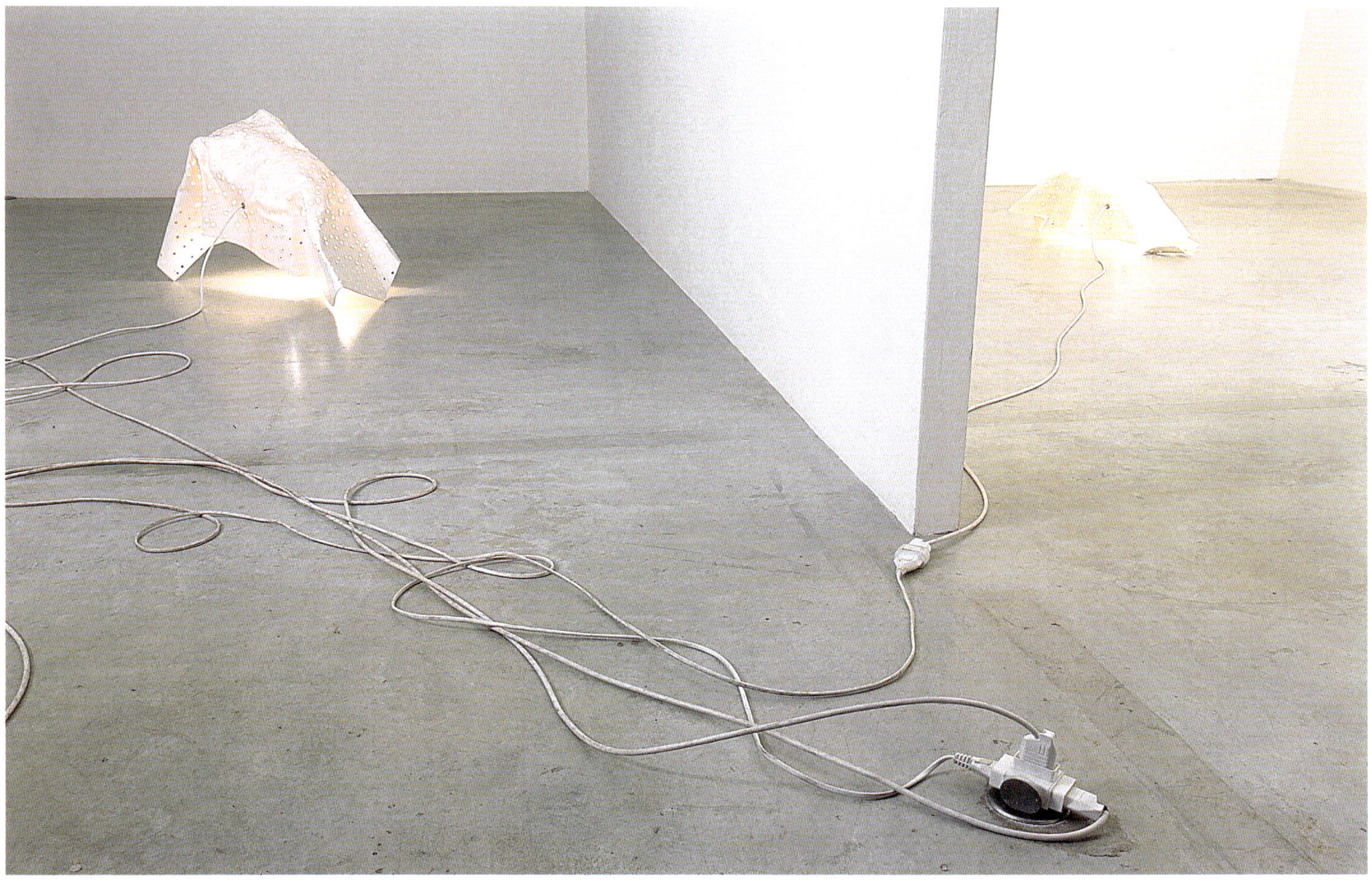

L'oiseau , Le chien, Le chat, 2002, with Jorge Pardo, exhibition view "Jorge Pardo, Philippe Parreno", 1310PE Gallery, Los Angeles
L'oiseau , Le chien, Le chat, 2002, with Jorge Pardo, exhibition view "Jorge Pardo, Philippe Parreno", Air de Paris, Paris

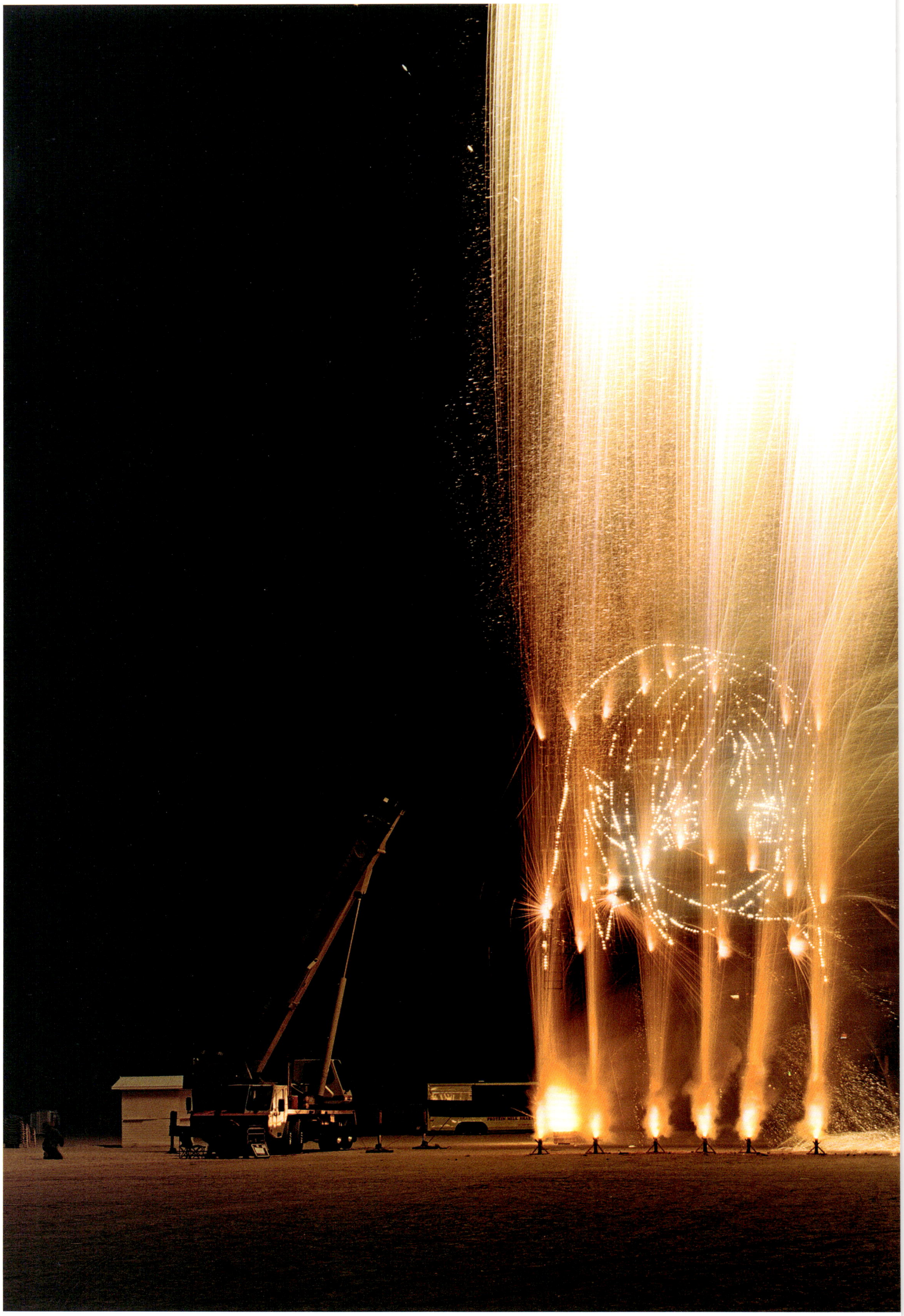

A Smile Without a Cat, 2002, with Pierre Huyghe, Art Basel, Miami Beach

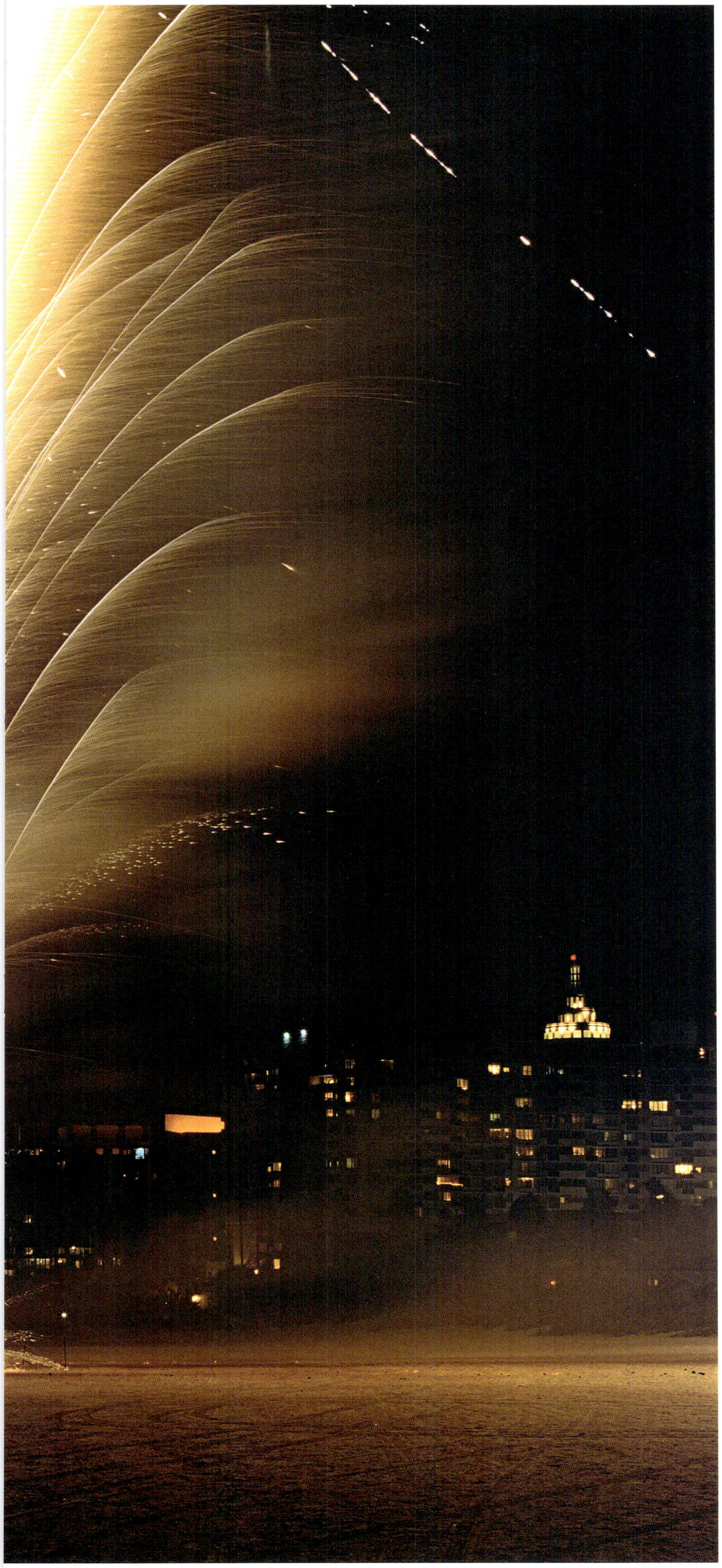

Untitled, 1997–2003 ◊ Group of 20 door handles in the form of decorated Christmas tree balls, blown glass ‡ 50th Venice Biennial, Italy, June 15–November 2, 2003 || 12 editions and 1 artist edition § Courtesy Air de Paris, Paris, and Friedrich Petzel Gallery, New York

Image vexée [Annoyed Image], 1994–2003 With Carsten Höller ◊ Extra-white hardened glass, 180 × 120 cm ‡ June 18–23, 2003, Air de Paris booth, Art Basel, Basel, Switzerland || 5 editions and 2 artist editions § Courtesy Air de Paris, Paris, and Esther Schipper, Berlin

Hybrid Muscle, 2002–2003 With François Roche ◊ Wood, aluminum structure, recycled plastic leaves, inflatable muscle; variable dimensions ‡ Made for *The Land* [The Land Foundation], Chiang Mai, Thailand; project initiated by: Kamin Lertchaiprasert and Rirkrit Tiravanija § Courtesy of the artists

The Boy From Mars, 2003 ◊ Installation: ¬ screen or flat screen, video projector • 35 mm film transferred onto HD video, (color, Dolby SR sound 10'39") • acoustic foam, grey paint, carpet • music: Devendra Banhart; production: Anna Sanders Films ‡ "C'est arrivé demain," September 18, 2003–January 4, 2004, 7th Lyons Biennial, France; exhibition curated by: Le Consortium in Dijon || 4 editions and 3 artist editions ʃ First public collection: Mudam, Luxemburg (1/4) **Parreno's 35 mm film *The Boy From Mars* was shot in the village of Sanpatong near Chiang Mai in Thailand, at the heart of Tiravanija's and Kamin Lertchaiprasert's *Land* project. Begun in 1998, *Land* is both a project for a self-organized and self-sufficient community, as well as a means of exploring new relationships between art and life. François Roche designed *Hybrid Muscle*, a shelter covered by leaves wrapped in recycled plastic for people who visit the *Land* project. A prototype of the facade was included in the exhibition "Alien Seasons," 2002. The basis for the film, *The Boy From Mars* was a fictional narrative about a human colony in another solar system, in reality the shooting of the film facilitated the construction of an actual building for students. *Battery House* generates its own electrical energy by means of buffalos harnessed to a pulley system. This same system also supplied power for the shooting of the 35 mm film. Parreno and Roche collaborated on this project, which they called "The Game." The film ends with a song written and sung by Devendra Banhart, *The Boy From Mars*, from which the film takes its title.[44] The film produced architecture and architecture produced a film.**

44. The film also gave rise to a text "The Boy From Paris," written by the science-fiction writer Bruce Sterling, in which the building triggers a digression (see the exhibition catalogue *A Retrospective (Tomorrow is Another Fine Day). Bruce Sterling, Rirkrit Tiravanija, Philippe Parreno*, Rotterdam, Museum Boijmans Van Beuningen, 2004). In order to continue this game of ping pong, Philippe Parreno published the book *The Boy From Mars* with the Kitakyushu Art Center, in 2004, made of images from the film.

Fade to Black 2003

Fade to Black (The Day After, Kitakyushu 2003), 2003 ◊ ¬ 1 color screen print on paper, phosphorescent ink, 185 × 120 cm • CD-Rom with digital files for reprint ‡ "C'est arrivé demain" [It Happened Tomorrow], September 18, 2003–January 4, 2004, 7th Lyons Biennial, Lyons, France; ***(See page 170)***

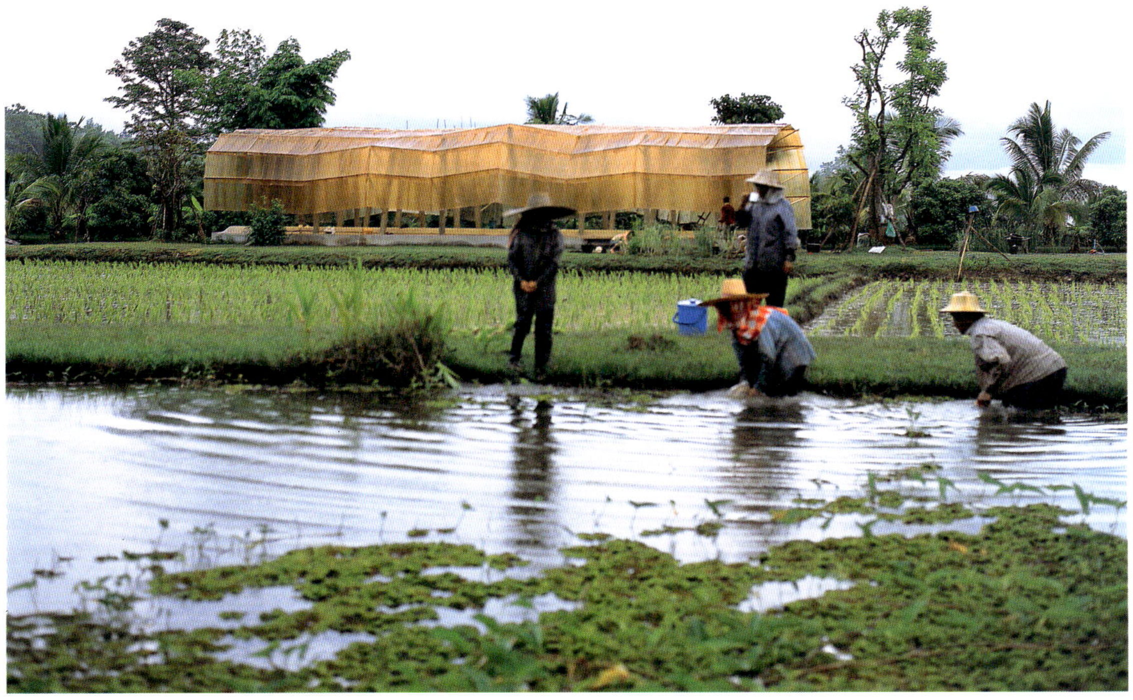

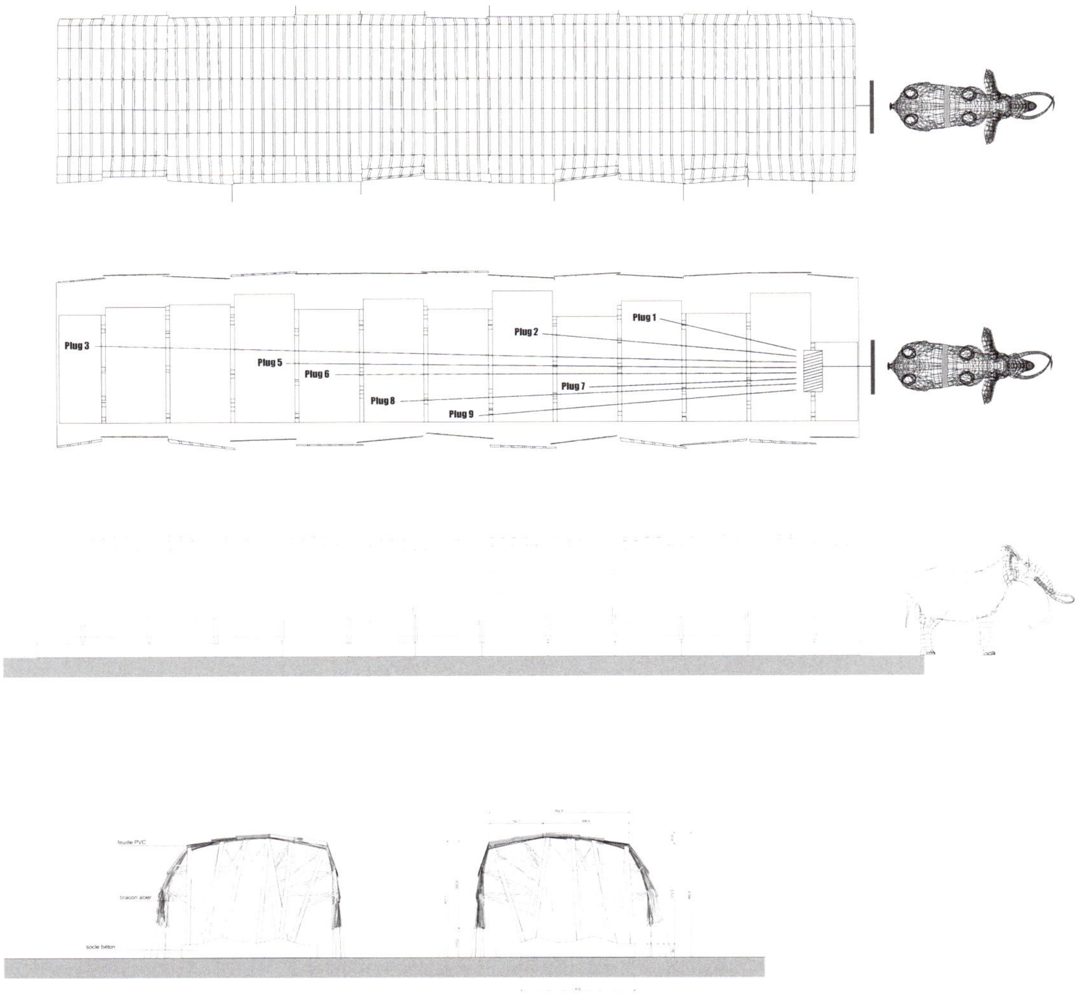

Le Jeu with Roche & Sie **(Hybrid Muscle** and **The Boy From Mars), 2002-2003,** The Land, Chiang Mai, Thailand

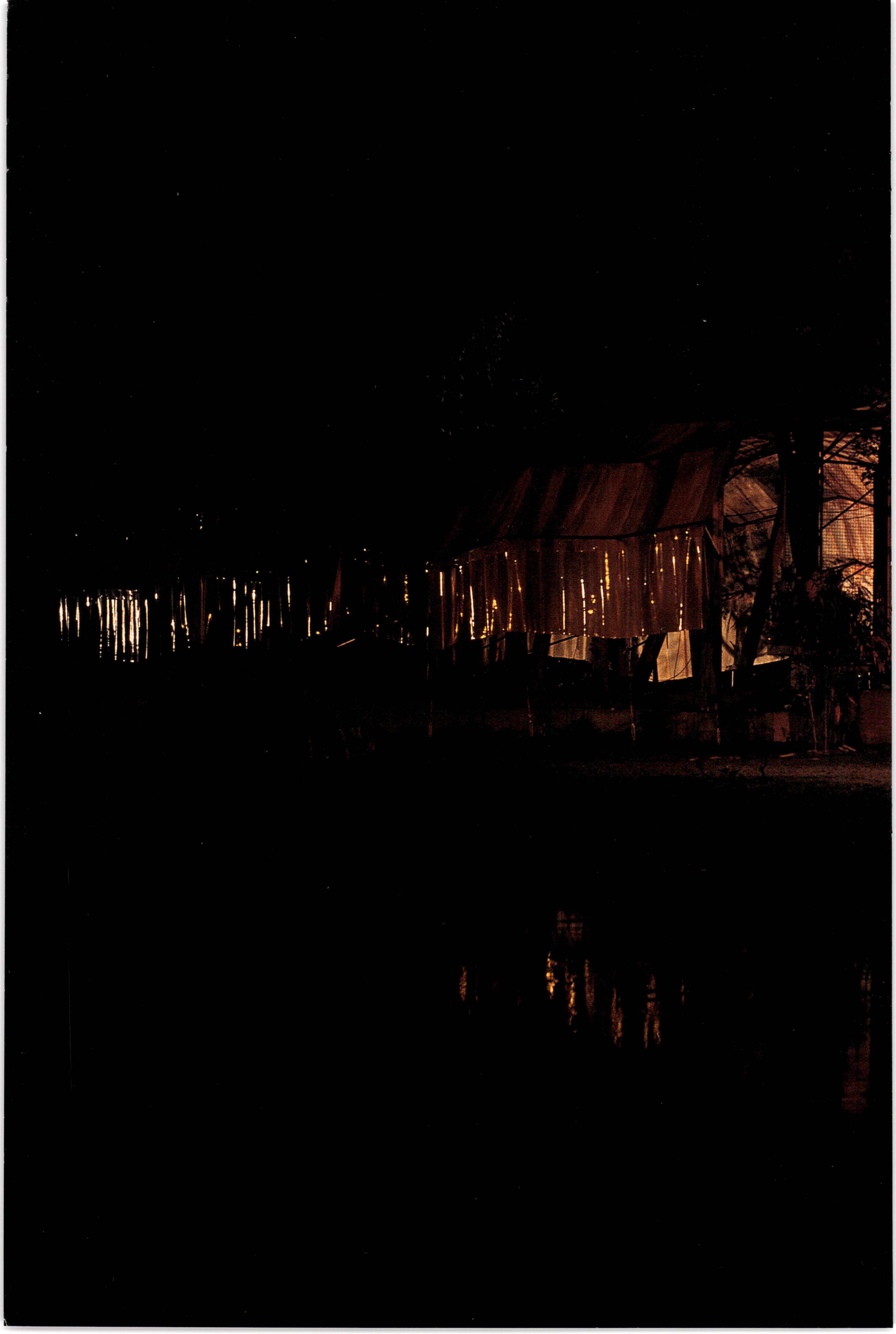

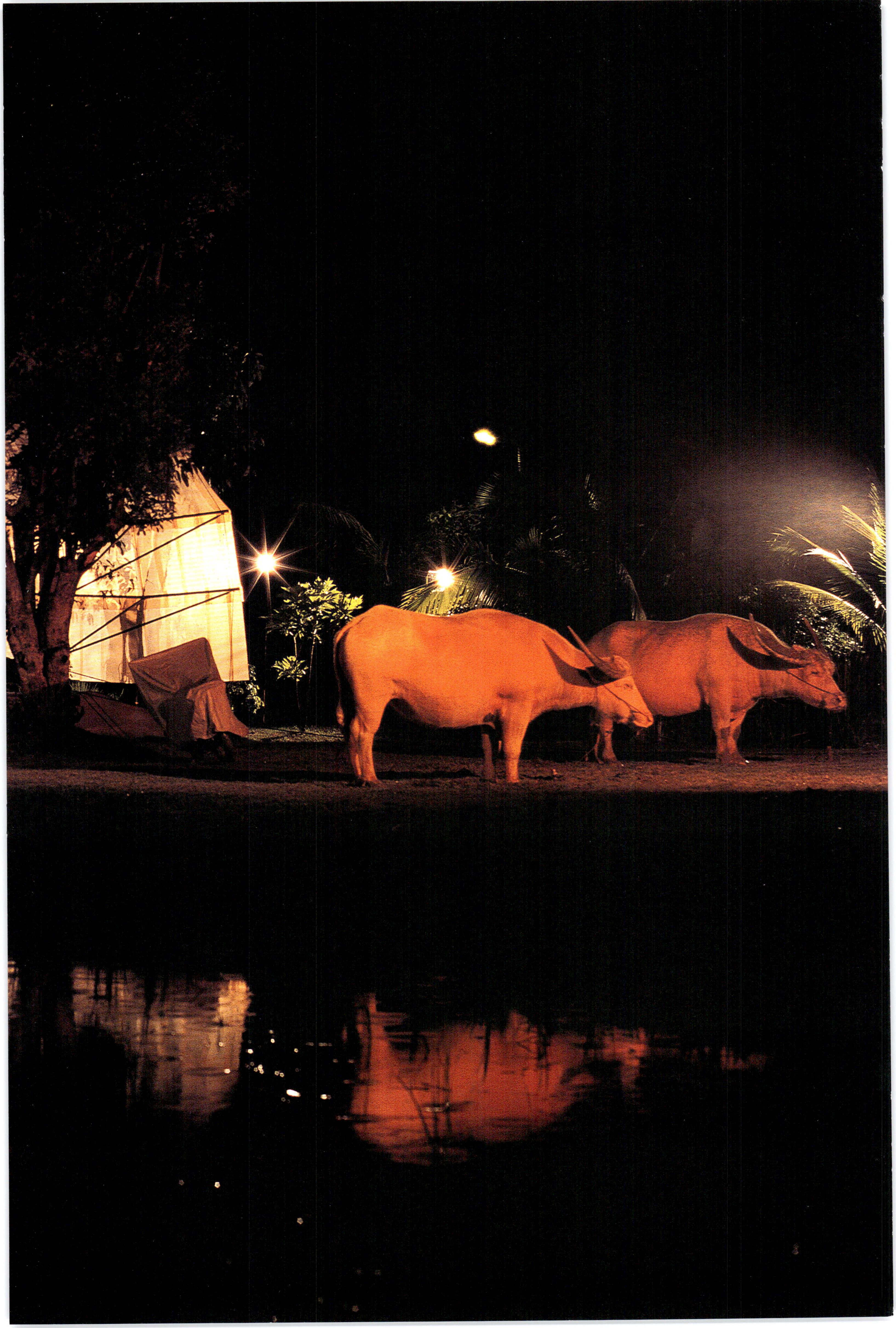

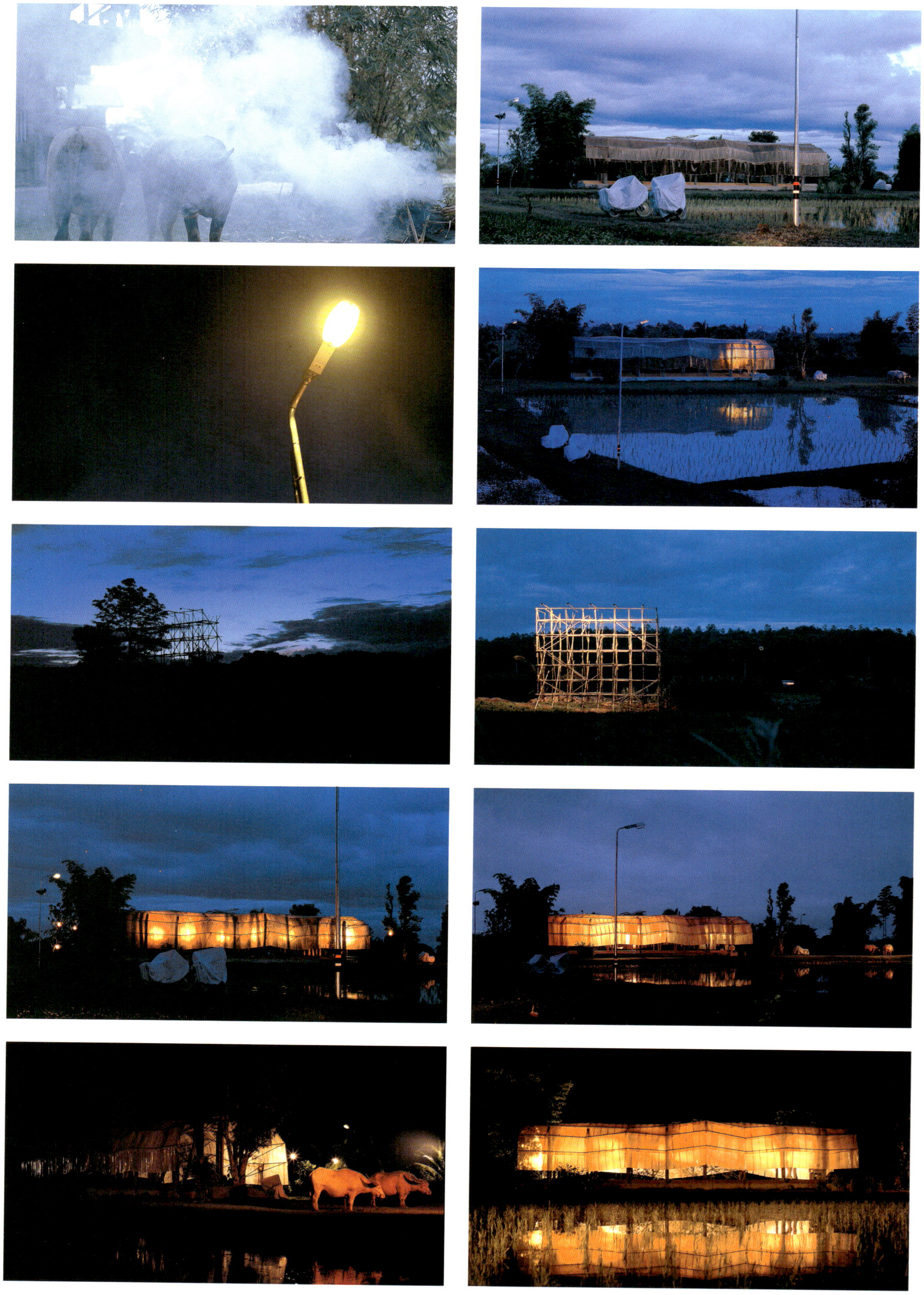

Previous pages: **The Boy From Mars, 2003,** film
The Boy From Mars, 2003, film

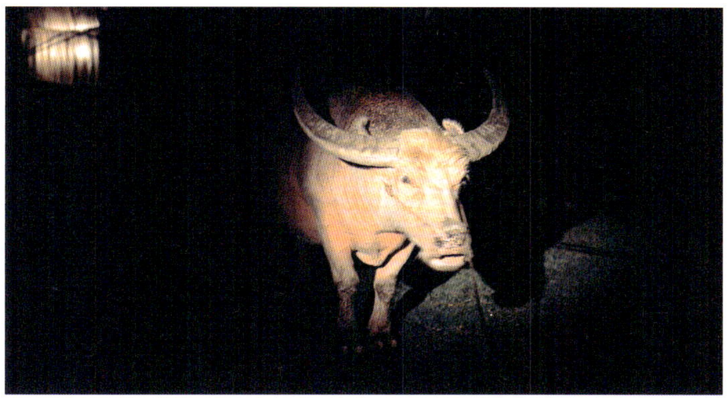
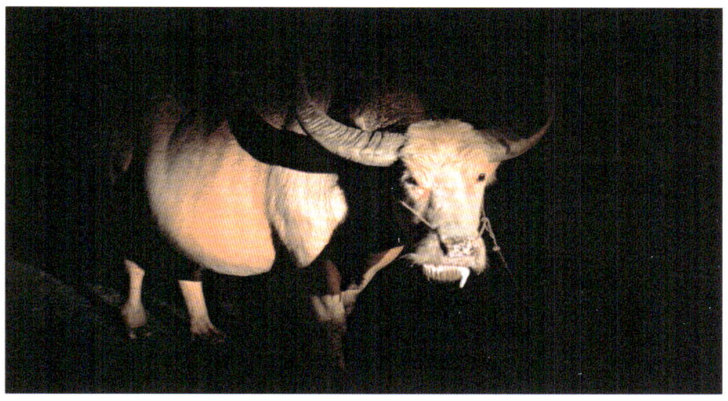
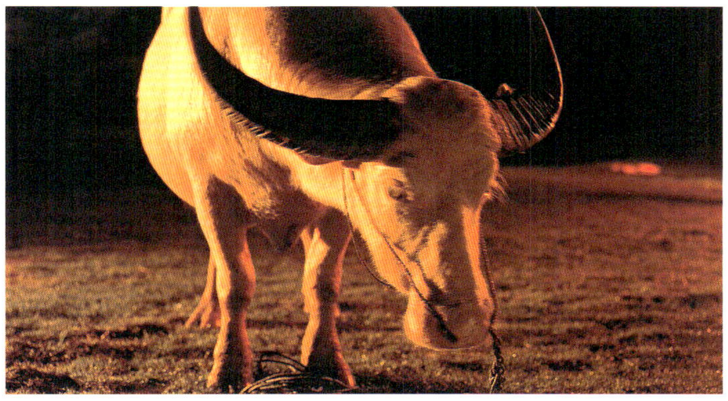
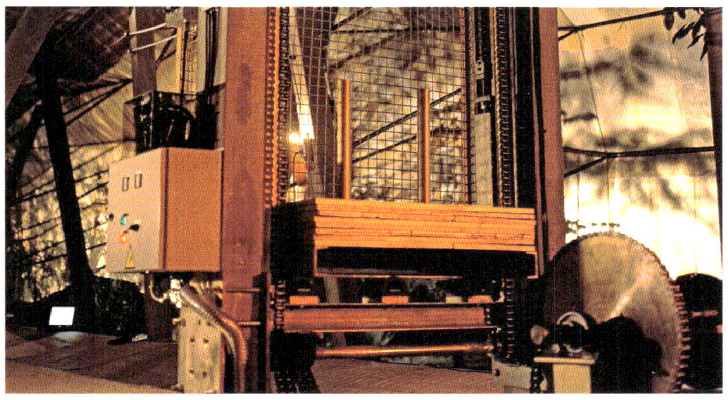
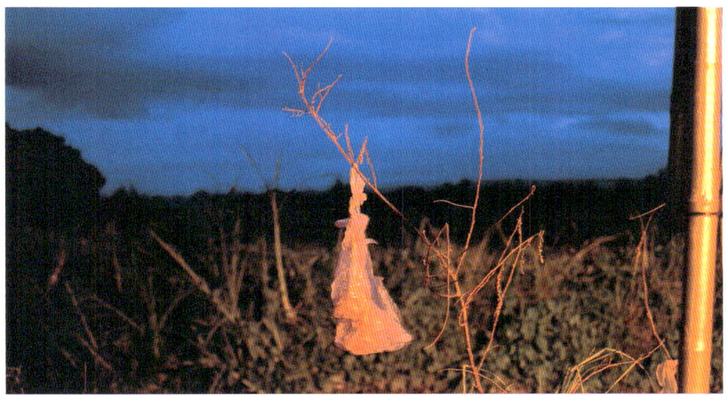
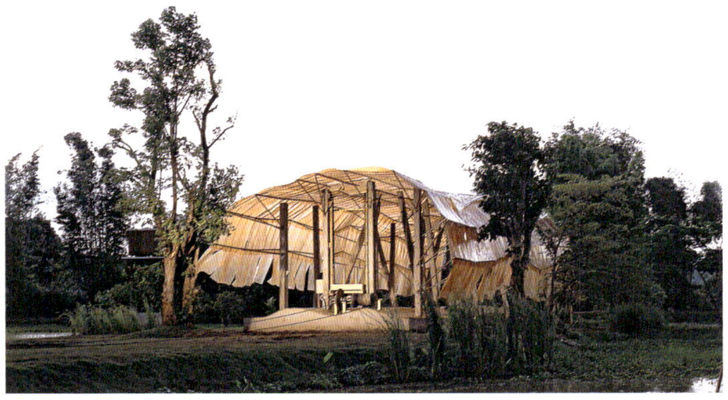
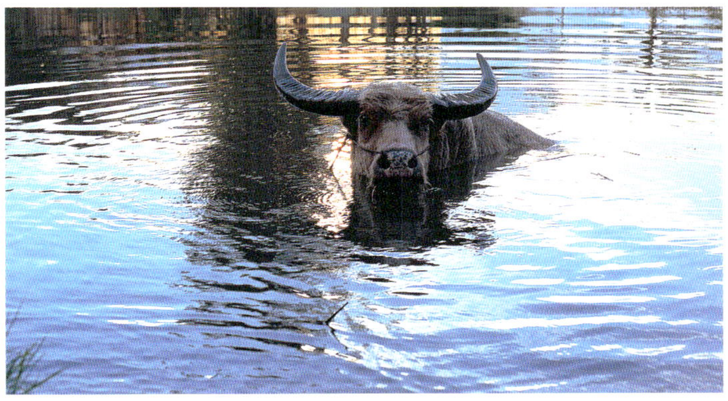
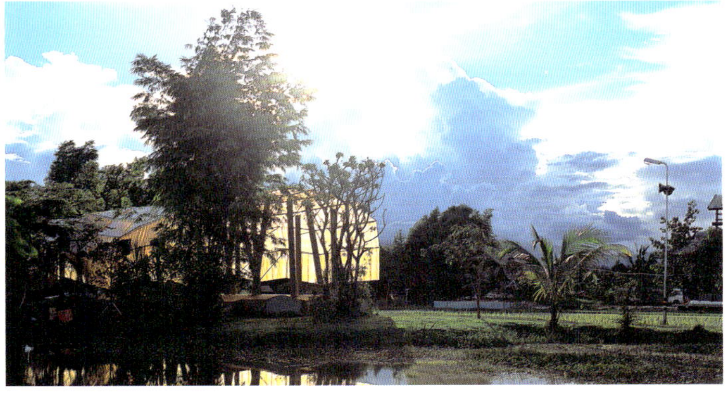
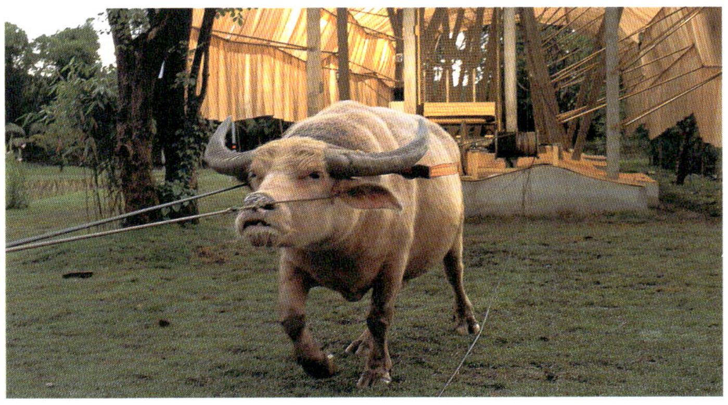
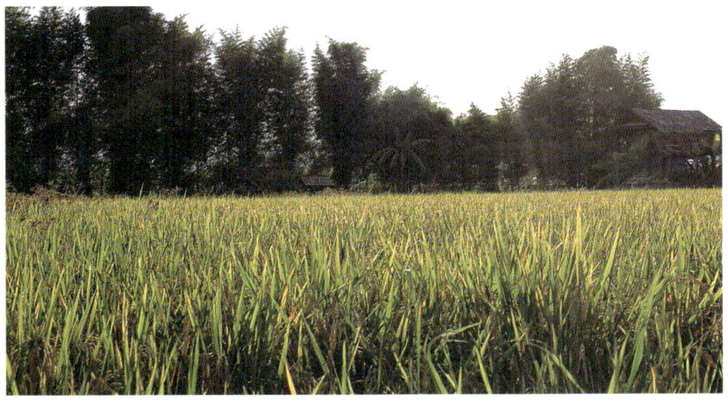

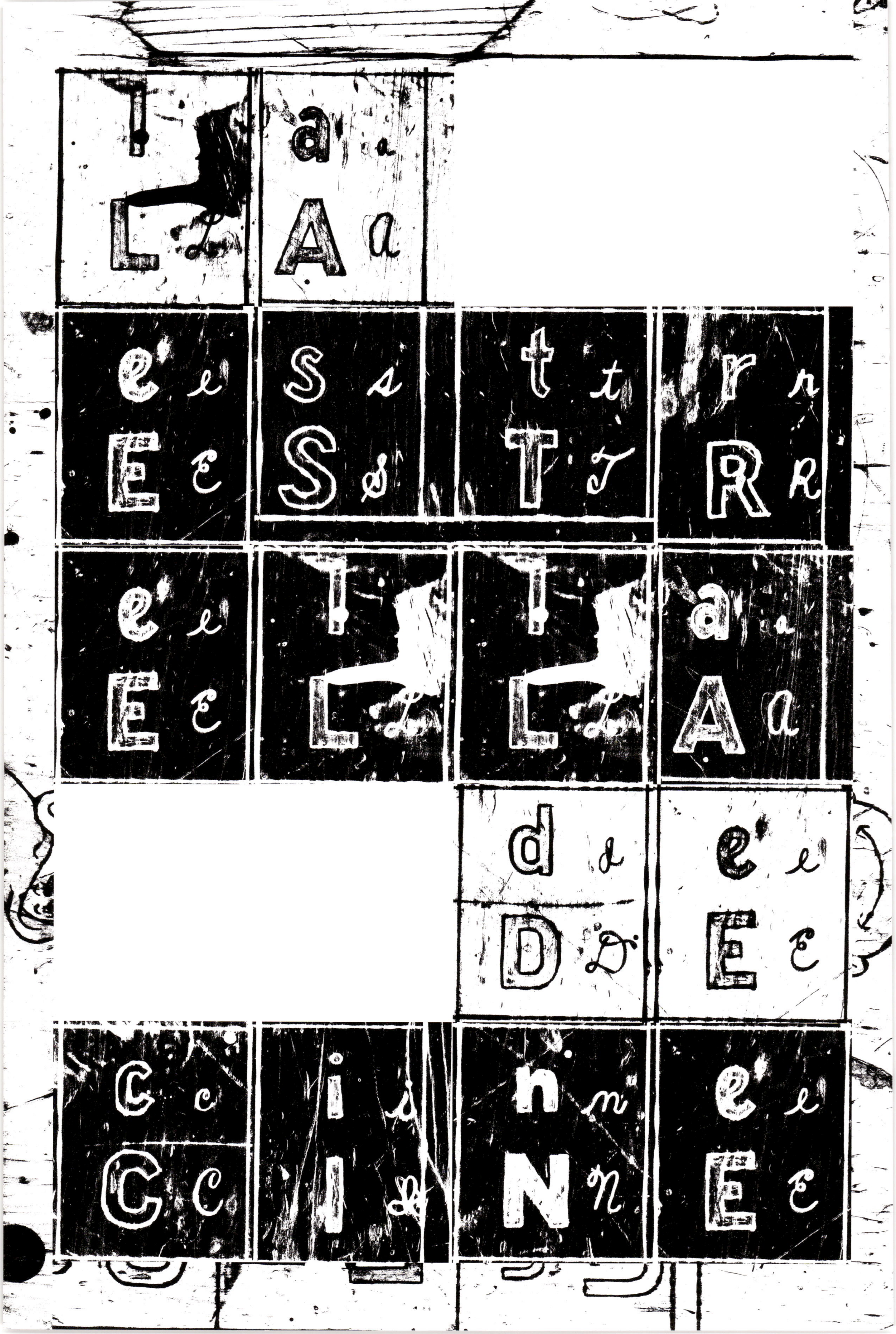
LA
ESTR
ELLA
DE
CINE

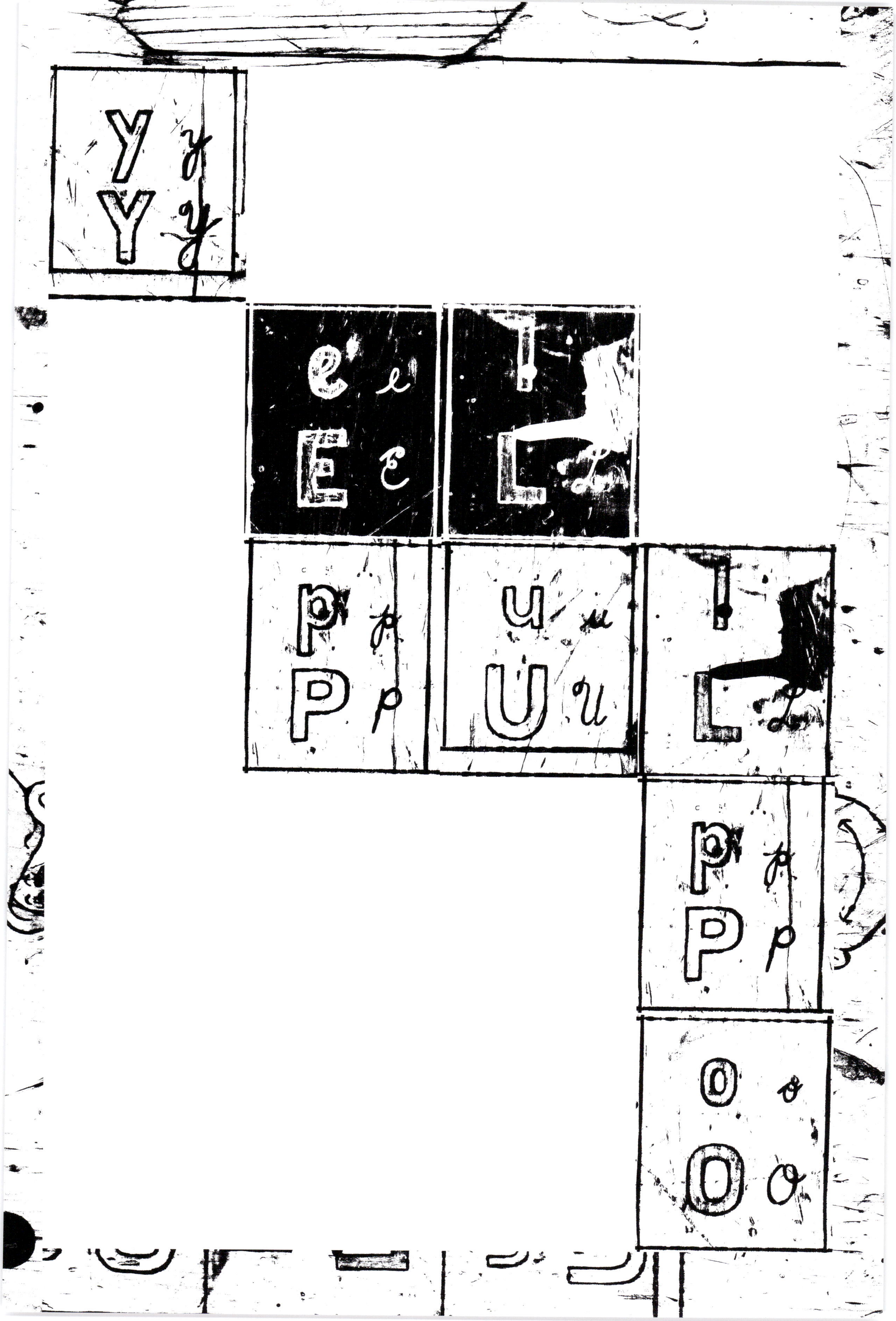
Y y
Y y
e e
E E
L L
p p
P p
u u
U u
L L
p p
P p
o o
O o

The Film Star and the Octopus

Enrique Juncosa for Philippe Parreno

In unmistakable Parrenian fashion, Philippe asked me nicely but firmly to write fiction for this book rather than a critical essay. We share many interests including a fascination with cephalopods. As a child, in the late 1960s, I used to fish for them every summer in Majorca, so I set the story there and at that time. Also, in the summers of 1969 and 1970, my family was living close to the house of the writer Romain Gary and the actress Jean Seberg. Philippe and I both love French Nouvelle Vague cinema, so it somehow made sense to include my neighbors in the story. I may have seen her at the time but have no recollection of this. In 1970, Seberg was the victim of a viscious C.I.A. conspiracy to destroy her reputation. They spread rumors that she was pregnant by a leader of the Black Panthers. Finally, the Jean Seberg of my story reads books that I know Philippe likes. I have written this text as a homage to him.

Jean woke alone, naked and sweating. Her mouth felt furry and she had a splitting headache. She knew from experience that it would pass as soon as she came into contact with water. Light filtered through the green shutters drawing vivid lines across the room. She loved how these zebra shadows fell across her legs, announcing what was bound to be another warm azure day. It must be one o'clock, she said to herself, which meant that she had not slept enough. The sound of cicadas roared above the monotonous breathing of the sea. She stroked her belly with her fingertips, paying attention to the liquid sounds inside her, and imagined her skin absorbing the almost imperceptible breeze that entered through the open window. Romain was no longer beside her, he must be upstairs writing. She concentrated, trying to hear the tapping of his typewriter, but she couldn't hear anything over, or under, the sounds of nature. She drank slowly from the glass of water that he must have left for her on the bedside table and loosened her limbs, stretching out her arms and legs. Then she lay still for a few minutes. She fantasized idly that she could hear the most intimate sounds—blades of grass sprouting, the excited comings and goings of ants. The first sound was squishy, almost obscene; the next was crystal clear, rapid, insistent.

Still conscious of her meandering thoughts, she got out of bed, almost tumbling from the sheets onto the floor. Once standing, she seemed to regain energy and noticed her paperback copy of René Daumal's *Le Mont Analogue* which was lying on the rug on the floor. Avoiding looking at herself in the mirror just yet, she climbed straight into the shower. She stayed there for a long time, enjoying the water and thinking of Daumal's story about the hollow men and the bitter rose. The bubble men evolved on ice, danced by the light of the moon and were doomed to burst if they came into contact with sunlight. Allowing the water to flow into her ears, she felt cocooned from the world and wondered if she would feel the same way if she too were a floating bubble about to burst.

Afterwards, she put on a black bikini with white stripes (or was it a white bikini with black stripes? she could never decide) an old straw hat and some dark sunglasses. She took her keys, cigarettes, the Daumal book and a towel and put everything into an enormous white leather bag. Feeling sufficiently glamorous she went out onto the street barefoot. As she made her way down to the cove, she tried not to think about the stupid argument she had with Romain the night before, after a somewhat boring dinner with his French friends and an obscene amount of anxiously consumed cocktails. Romain couldn't stand when she drank, and she was thoroughly sick of those friends of his who seemed incapable of surviving without them. However, she was not going to let herself dwell on this. The path burned beneath her feet and she quickened her pace to arrive at her favorite spot near the water's edge, a great flat rock that remained in the shade during the midday sun and from which she could dive into the sea. She wanted to continue reading the story about the rose which was also a huge multi-colored lichen and a cloud of butterflies.

The white house with its green shutters stood beside two other identical houses with large sun terraces draped with fronds of jasmine and honeysuckle. The three houses looked onto the sea beyond a small pine forest one had to cross to go down to the cove. Even in August the beach was nearly always empty—this was the summer of 1969. In fact, one of the houses had still to be rented. In the other house a young local family spent the summer. They had four children —two boys and two girls—luckily they weren't too noisy. The beach was now deserted, apart from one of the boys who was fishing from the spot that she considered hers. Of course, she was not going to relinquish her place. She walked across the sand towards the rock and laid out her towel, as if marking her territory, just one meter from the boy. It was the older of the neighbors' boys, he was six or seven, and he had caught her attention from the first day on account of his enormous blue eyes. Completely ignoring him, despite his direct and bright smile, Jean dived into the water. She swam confidently away from the shore. The sea was flat like a swimming pool and the water so transparent that one could clearly see the rocks, seaweed and sea urchins below. She imagined herself, Daumal-like, in search of something of unbearable brilliance; something far away in a place where everything burns and only eternal incandescence can live. Finally she stopped and, floating on her back, breathed deeply for several minutes. She was certain that she would be happy as a bubble. After a while, she returned to the shore and stepped out of the water. Feeling refreshed, she removed her top, lay down on the towel and was soon asleep. She dreamt that she was having a drink with her friend James Baldwin in a jazz club in Paris full of people and smoke. Wearing a fur coat over her naked body, she was engrossed in a performance of a young saxophonist. After an exhilarating solo, the place filled with a galloping herd of wild horses that knocked tables to the ground and frightened everyone. Baldwin then turned to her and said: *"That's the trouble with all you white bastards."*

The moment she awoke, she noticed that the boy had a hook stuck in his hand. With great beads of sweat on his forehead, and hands soaked with blood, he was trying to free himself, but without much success. Realizing that Jean had woken up, he tentatively held his wounded hand towards her while keeping his head bowed. Jean was irritated, thinking that any minute she would end up being his nanny. She gazed around at the still empty beach. Majorcan families preferred to come late in the afternoons when the sun was less harsh. She found herself having to stand up, topless, and walk over to the boy. She asked him in English and in French if she could help him; however, he only managed to blush and, raising his hand again, murmur something incomprehensible. Jean crouched down to take a closer look at his injury. The hook had become lodged under his thumbnail and the slightest touch caused blood to start gushing. Jean grabbed the bucket that the boy had been using to collect fish and emptied its contents onto the sand. She went to the water and filled the bucket halfway. She poured the salty water onto his wound. She never could stand to see others suffer. The skin under his nail had turned violet. The boy was extremely embarrassed, as if her touch was more terrifying than the butchery already taking place. In an attempt to calm him down, Jean grabbed him by the shoulders and kissed him on the forehead. This had an amazing effect on the child. At last he was quiet, almost paralyzed. She seized the opportunity to rip out the hook in one go. She bathed the wound again with saltwater and kissed the hurt thumb and his forehead once again. The child turned a bright tomato red and after hurriedly putting his fish back into the bucket, ran off without saying a word.

Late that evening, Romain's friends Sophie and Antoine showed up at the house unannounced—an annoying habit that seemed rapidly to be becoming the norm. Sophie was a French book publisher and her husband Antoine a pianist. They had brought two bottles of champagne and suggested going for dinner in Palma and then drinks at a club with live music. Sophie had a rather large nose, which gave her a decidedly bird-like appearance, and she always wore brightly colored make-up, thus earning the nickname *The Toucan*. Having just turned forty, she was petite, attractive and with a nice figure. She had long curly hair, which was always artfully disheveled and adorned with a flower. Her clothes seemed to have been chosen to create, through complex print patterns, the most curious optical phenomena, and she wore brightly colored patent leather platforms to compensate for not being tall. She utterly lacked discretion. She loved talking about sex but whenever she noticed that somebody was becoming irritated by her tales of the supposed private lives of Jean-Luc Godard or Alain Robbe-Grillet (to mention a couple of the names she loved to drop into the conversation) she would try to remedy the situation by blurting out something like the fact that she loved anal penetration and that her husband the pianist would confirm this. What was unbelievable was that he, who had not opened his mouth up to this point, would confirm whatever she said without a word of complaint. Her husband, Antoine, was tall, thin and pale. Somewhat younger than her, he always wore jeans and, in spite of the heat, a shirt buttoned fastidiously right up to his neck. His long lank black hair was carefully gathered in a ponytail. At some point, Romain had told Jean about a well-received recording he had made recently of Rachmaninov's famous *Piano Concerto no. 3*, so Jean, who claimed to be incapable of remembering his name, always called him Rachmaninov. He didn't talk much and always followed The Toucan's orders. He drank alcohol with an almost metaphysical thirst but it did not seem to affect him in the slightest. Jean would tell Romain that she was sure he played better when he was drunk.

The club they went to after dinner was whitewashed like the inside of an old farmhouse, yet the place had a futuristic feel to it because of the primary-colored plastic furnishings and especially the many extravagant lamps. It boasted spectacular views over the bay through enormous windows adorned with geometrically patterned curtains. All in all, the place seemed to have been designed with The Toucan specifically in mind. She had arranged to meet two other French couples there—Dora and Claude, and Régine and Pierre. They were spending a few days at the island in a yacht moored in the harbour. The two women were sisters, although they never mentioned their family connections. They were both very beautiful—Dora blonde and Régine brunette—and their husbands looked like powerful businessmen. The club bustled with people coming and going to and from the dance floor, most of them tourists. The conversation began with a long and tedious interrogation of Jean and Romain—their artistic projects seemed to be of particular importance to both Dora and Régine. Romain answered for both of them, conscious that Jean was feeling uncomfortable because they had no qualms in saying that they didn't like the last film he had directed Jean in, *Les oiseaux vont mourir au Pérou*. But after a few more drinks he was able to take revenge on them, by steering the conversation towards a Stanislaw Lem book called *Absolute Perfection*. Claude had previously let drop that he detested science fiction, but who knows why, perhaps to stop contradicting Romain, he conceded that this was the exception that proved the rule. Of course, he didn't realize that the book did not exist. Jean, wearing a t-shirt that said *The Girl from Mars,* had stopped following the conversation some time ago but was now enjoying watching Claude come up with reasons for liking the book which he described as strange and magnificent. However, she soon tired of listening to his nonsense and began to watch what was going on at the other tables. She took pleasure in staring intensely at people, delighting in the disarming effect that her extraordinary beauty had on them. Also proud of this phenomenon, Romain stroked her leg as he spoke. Just then, a young man sporting a flashy gold watch, which Jean must have been staring at, approached the table. Wearing a shirt unbuttoned to the navel, he offered to light her cigarette. He stood very close to her as he did it, in a way that was clearly intended to be flirtatious, so close in fact that the conversation at the table stopped. Dora remarked that this was incredibly vulgar since it was so obvious that she was not alone. Jean allowed the young man to light her cigarette. She inhaled slowly, blew the smoke in his face, and then proceeded to ignore him completely.

The Toucan, who hated playing second fiddle to anyone, took advantage of the lull to monopolize everyone's attention with an abrupt anecdote about the private life of Anna Karina. The smoke blown in the face of the macho who loved precious metals reminded her of a story that she had heard from a friend of the filmmaker Jacques Rivette. Meanwhile, a waiter brought another bottle of champagne to the table and, as he opened it, stared at The Toucan's generous cleavage without making any attempt to disguise where he was looking. Régine remarked that all Mediterranean men seemed to go around in a permanent state of semi-erection and had she been a little younger, she might have found it rather exciting. As far as she could tell, they were practically being hunted down in the presence of their partners. The Toucan claimed that it was all for show and that in actual fact, Parisian men were the best in bed and that she had sufficient international experience to back up her claim. Pierre and Claude's reaction was comic; they agreed in unison. The Toucan, now drunk, was becoming increasingly vociferous as she spoke. She was wearing a tight miniskirt which up until now had kept her quite occupied—stretching it down towards her pretty knees continuously during the evening. However, without warning, just as the waiter was filling her glass, she reached down and pulled it up to show that she was not wearing any knickers and, on top of that, she was completely shaved. Jean mused to herself that at last The Toucan was revealing her true colors, although the long wait had diminished somewhat her ability to shock. The waiter was a true professional. He managed to finish pouring her glass without spilling a drop while shamelessly examining, at close quarters, this recently revealed show of French exuberance. Suddenly, before anyone had even the chance to react, Rachmaninov began explaining how The Toucan loved to show her sex not only in bars and restaurants but also in other public places, that he was used to it and loved her just the way she was. In contrast, a bald fifty-year-old man, seated with a group of people at a nearby table, was not used to it—at least not quite yet—but at that moment, nothing else in the world existed for him. His gaze was firmly fixed between The Toucan's legs. Jean was delighted with this new turn of events as were the tourists from the yacht who had not stopped nudging each other, making strange hand gestures and joking remarks. They seemed to have realized that they would have something to talk about for the next few months. The Toucan talked and talked with her legs wide open, as the waiter came to change the ashtrays. The people at the neighboring table seemed unable to believe what they were seeing. Their faces expressed the whole emotional gamut—laughter, surprise, embarrassment and indignation. They spoke animatedly, with the exception of the gentleman who remained hypnotized by this mysterious part of the female anatomy that, unless one is a doctor or nurse, is normally only seen in private. His eyes were practically popping out. He was almost drooling. Jean mused on how women could only hold this kind of sway over men at the beginning of relationships. She was certain that, if she were to start flashing her bits around the house, Romain would end up begging her to put her clothes on. Now however, he had clearly decided to take advantage of the opportunity to get to know this part of The Toucan which had starred in so many of her endless stories. After a while, one of the women from the nearby table, who was seated beside the bald man, stood up and approached them. It was obvious, from the expression on her face, that she was furious. She grabbed the bottle of champagne and emptied the remaining contents, of which there was quite a lot, over The Toucan's pussy with a calmness and relish that bordered on cruelty. Her reaction was astounding. Now in her element, without flinching, The Toucan asked the woman if she would allow her husband to dry her between the legs with his tongue. She promised that he would arrive home still feeling horny and perhaps then she would discover new things. No one knew if she understood French, but what was very clear was that she reacted immediately with a few resounding slaps to The Toucan's face.

The following afternoon, while Jean lay drowsing in her usual spot with an English translation of Edouard Dujardin's *Les Lauriers sont coupés* propped open on her belly, her Majorcan neighbour approached her and addressed her in proper French. Her son, Toni had told her how she had freed him from the hook and she wished to thank her. He watched them from a distance looking obviously embarrassed and half hiding behind his brothers and sisters who were settling on the beach. Jean explained what had happened, casually pretending that she had almost forgotten about it, adding that it was nothing and anyway that is what neighbors were for. To rid herself of this woman because she was petrified by the thought of having to make friends in a place that she liked so much precisely because nobody knew her there, she looked in her bag and dug out some mint chewing gums for the children. The woman felt obliged to thank her again and this time she called her children over to do the same, shouting with exasperation. Toni's three siblings came over without any problem. He however turned red and, ignoring the pestering of his mother, remained where he was, pretending to be attending to something of the utmost importance with the prongs of a trident which he had been brandishing ever since he arrived at the beach. Jean, in turn, insisted repeatedly that it was unnecessary for him to come over. Nevertheless, his mother went over and shook him vigorously while berating him for his shyness. Then she dragged him over to Jean. The whole episode must have been excruciating for the poor creature, and Jean felt equally uncomfortable but she was at a loss as to how to put a stop to the scene which she had unwittingly instigated. At last Toni showed her his bandaged thumb, as if to divert attention from himself to something more concrete. He then withdrew quickly to conceal himself behind his brothers and sisters while his mother continued her tirade. Despite feeling angry, Jean decided not to get involved for fear of dragging out the child's suffering even longer. To compose herself, she gazed up at the blue sky and surrendered to her interior monologue, imagining horrible revenges involving mosquitoes, jellyfish and snakes.

Some time later, Toni proudly returned bearing a large octopus that he had just caught. It twisted and writhed, impaled on the child's trident. Since he was quite far away from the beach when he lifted the cephalopod out of the water, he started yelling in an attempt to get his family's attention. In doing so he had managed to capture his siblings' attention but not his mother's. She was deep in conversation with a friend of hers that Jean did not recall seeing before. As he left the water, his mother scolded him and told him to stop shrieking about the damn octopus and that by now the entire island had heard about what he had caught. Then she continued talking with her friend. Jean had heard the child's cries from her perch and observed the entire episode of the octopus. She wanted Toni to realize that she understood how irritating it was for him to be unable to obtain his mother's approval. So without being particularly interested in the octopus, she got up in an act of solidarity to admire it and to interrupt the women's conversation. The first thing that popped into her head was to ask how to cook it. The mother obligingly explained that she prepared them with a *sofrito* of onion and tomato, to which she later added raisins and pine nuts. Toni followed the whole discussion very closely. Jean stroked his head, while at the same time trying not to come across as a despicable adult. The mother then said that she should keep the octopus which seemed to please the boy to no end. Jean accepted, thanking him profusely, and this appeared finally to satisfy his pride. Then Jean began reading again, trying to drive the incident out of her mind: "*She gives a friendly smile; on her breast the lights glimmer, blonde and nocturnal.*"

A few minutes later, The Toucan made an unforgivable appearance on the beach accompanied by Dora and Régine. Jean was stunned by this unannounced visit. The Toucan was Romain's friend, not hers. After last night's episode she had hoped not to have to put up with her again for a while. She could not comprehend how The Toucan could show up for the umpteenth time without warning, and on top of that, bring her friends with her. She began by saying that they had come to rescue Jean from her boredom and that they didn't want her to spend all day alone on the beach while Romain was working. She even had the nerve to snatch the book from Jean's hands. As soon as she read the author's name, she exclaimed emphatically that she must really be in the depths of despair to read something like that. Dora was in full agreement and told her that she must hear how the event had ended last night. Jean and Romain had left abruptly last night after the slapping incident. Jean found Dora's use of the word "event" amusing; as if she were describing something of epic proportions. Meanwhile, Régine, unable to contain herself, began describing in tedious detail how she had screwed the waiter in the toilet without their husbands' knowledge. They begged her to come out with them again for fun this evening, without their partners. Finally, the three of them fell silent. Jean couldn't tell whether they were waiting for her to agree to go out with them or express her admiration for their sexual adventures. She took a deep breath, and then spoke slowly, savoring every word. She began by lamenting what was an obviously decadent state of the French education system (particularly since she had no doubt that they had all attended the best private schools). Were they aware that it was the height of bad manners to arrive unannounced on her beach and to disturb her with their stupid, crass gossip? Did they not see that she was already busy anticipating the end of a novel that she found extremely interesting, perhaps because it was so Wagnerian? Jean added, particularly enjoying this part, that she had thought that after the well-deserved rebuke received in the club, The Toucan would have reflected on her behavior. It was true that it had been entertaining, and that her pussy was probably a most charming Bonsai version of the Amazon, but she found herself compelled to ask them to go and leave her in peace. She added that there was no shortage of beaches on the island and she was sure that they would find a place to their liking. Furthermore, there was no shortage of toilets or horny waiters either. The Toucan started complaining that no-one in her entire life had ever been so horrible to her and of course they would leave her alone although it was clear that she was hung over and didn't realize what she was saying. And just as they had arrived, perhaps with a little more haste, they left. Jean was stunned. She made up her mind to speak with Romain and tell him that she never wanted to see any of those women again. It was true that she had got on well with The Toucan, and she could continue to tolerate her company in small doses given that she was entertaining and eccentric, but as she just demonstrated in the club, she could also be completely over the top. And, of course, they could not accept these unannounced visits to the house every day, disturbing the calm summer she had so much looked forward to. If things continued in this way, they would end up living with them. She was certain that Romain would back her up. As for the four millionaires, she had only met them for the first time the previous evening and they were already telling her about what they did in their spare time in toilets. She could not get the scene out of her head so she threw herself into the water and began swimming energetically. The world seemed full of hysterical women. Swimming did not help her calm down, on the contrary, it left her feeling stronger and more determined. Unable to lie still on the rock and relax to the sound of the waves, she decided to return to the house. She gathered her things, including the octopus in the bucket, and said goodbye to Toni and his family. She walked up the hill with resolute strides, passing under the pine trees. A warm wind was blowing, appearing to announce an imminent storm, yet the sky remained a perfect blue. Not even a seagull in sight. Before speaking with Romain, she planned to make herself a huge gin and tonic filled with ice. They were through once and for all with all the pseudo-intellectual *soirées*.

To her great surprise, she found the three hysterical women sitting on her terrace of the house drinking gin and tonics with Romain. They had obviously disturbed him in the middle of his writing, something she would never even conceive of doing. Romain gave her a quizzical look and asked her how she was. As Jean looked surprised by the question, he explained that they had told him that she was not feeling well and because of this she had come out with shocking, offensive, nonsensical remarks but of course they had forgiven her. The Toucan looked at her, magnanimously, as if she had already accepted her apology, and smilingly offered her a packet of aspirins from her bag. Jean, who couldn't tolerate this situation a moment longer, resorted to marine life. She dug her hand into the bucket, grabbed the octopus and flung it full force at The Toucan. She tried to dodge it but was unsuccessful.
The tentacles made a pleasant slap as it hit her forehead, and the octopus went sailing over The Toucan's head to land on the street in front of the house. Jean was pleased with her aim but was too worked up to be around those people any longer. Without a word, she entered the house, slamming the door with seismic force. She went straight to bed and tried to calm herself. Shortly after, Romain came into the room. He found her face down on the bed and lay beside her, putting his arms around her. He kissed her neck softly. Then her ear. Jean thought that they loved one another so much that at times words were not necessary.

While all this was taking place, the Majorcan family had remained on the beach. Toni had returned to the water hoping to catch another octopus. His mother had been calling for him to come out so that he would have enough time to shower before dinner. Toni pretended not to hear her, which drove her up the wall. The time eventually came when he could no longer ignore her because of the almighty beating she threatened him with. Sure enough, when he reached the water's edge he received a few slaps. Even so, he took his time, drying himself and gathering his fishing equipment as his mother and siblings walked towards the house. He was livid. All he wanted to do was swim and fish and he couldn't understand what difference it made whether he finished at eight or nine. Anyway, he was not even hungry and had no intention of eating. He wished that his mother could be like the American woman who didn't seem to care about timetables and spent all day on the beach without speaking to anyone. When he will be older he would go to live in Africa. He had heard that children there did not go to school because there was no school to go to and they spent all day on the street doing whatever they wanted. Now that was a good plan. He was tired of being constantly told off. And he was sure that Africa would be good for fishing. Tomorrow morning he would return to fish from the flat rock beside his new friend and catch more octopi for her. She liked to be left in peace. He threw his towel around his neck and picked up his goggles, trident and flippers. He paused to gaze at the sunset. He liked to watch the sun suddenly disappear into the water and the sky turn all orange or violet. The American also liked this moving spectacle—on more than one occasion he had spied her contemplating the horizon from the rocks. He was definitely going to fish for more octopi for her. After the sun had set he began moving quickly, hoping to avoid another hypothetical thrashing. He climbed up through the pine trees, breathing in the aroma of pine leaves and sea iodine. A few cicadas could still be heard, sounding as if they were about to explode.

He saw it the moment he arrived at the road, just in front of the houses. In spite of the semi-darkness, it stood out on the tarmac. In smacking against the ground, the ink sack had ruptured and the tentacles spattered into a large, dense and viscous black stain. For some reason, the formless mass of octopus seemed to be moving. He went closer and saw that this was because thousands of ants were now feasting on it. By morning, the carcass would have attracted flies and wasps too. He remained motionless, struggling to understand the meaning of this. It had to be the same octopus he had given Jean as a present. She had not even bothered to conceal it. His body felt as heavy as stone and the earth seemed to lurch. He felt like he was walking on water. Suddenly his mouth went completely dry and he found it difficult to swallow. Everything around him was spinning and his eyes filled with tears. He trembled. In the pine forest a multitude of glow-worms became a battalion of hostile spacecrafts.

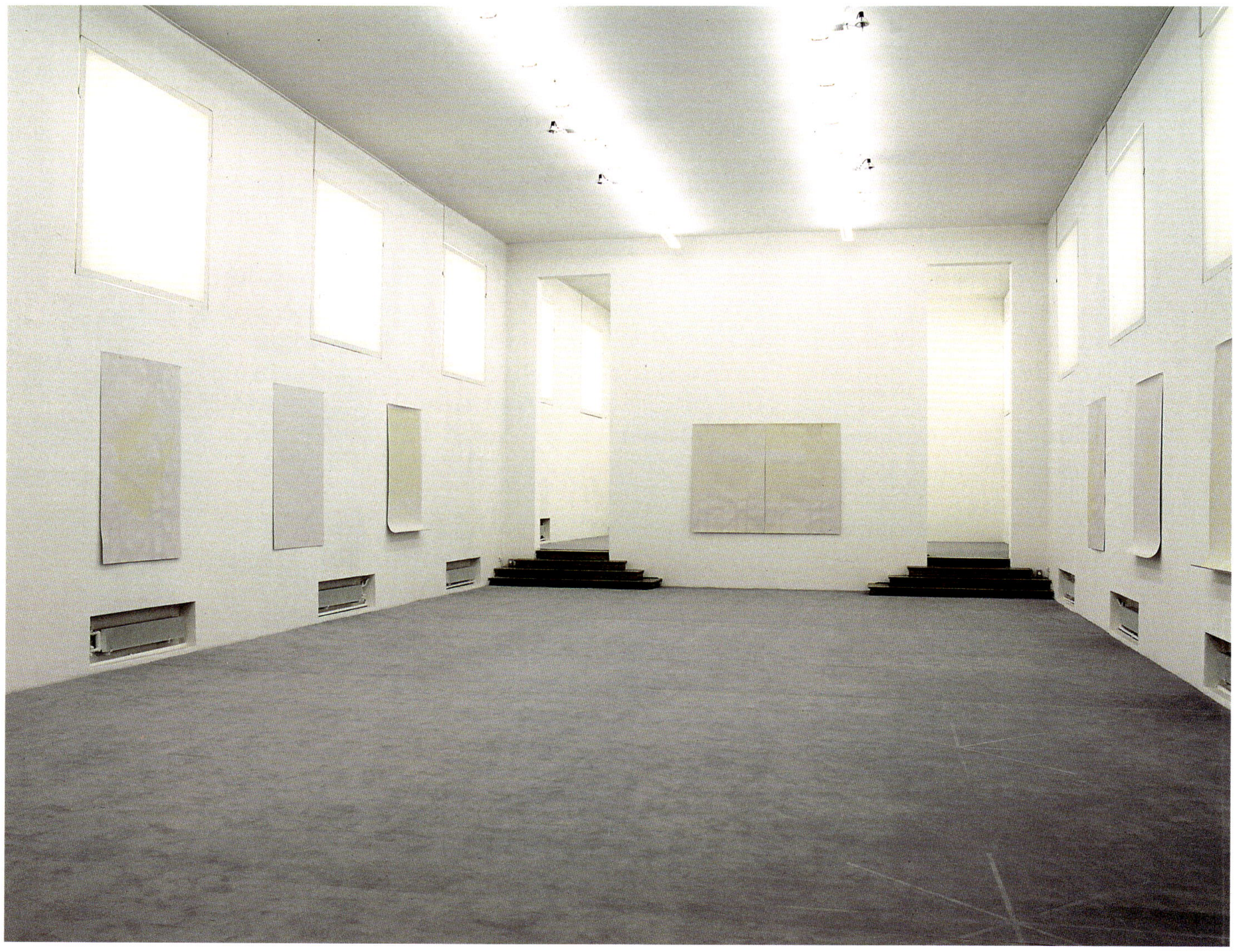

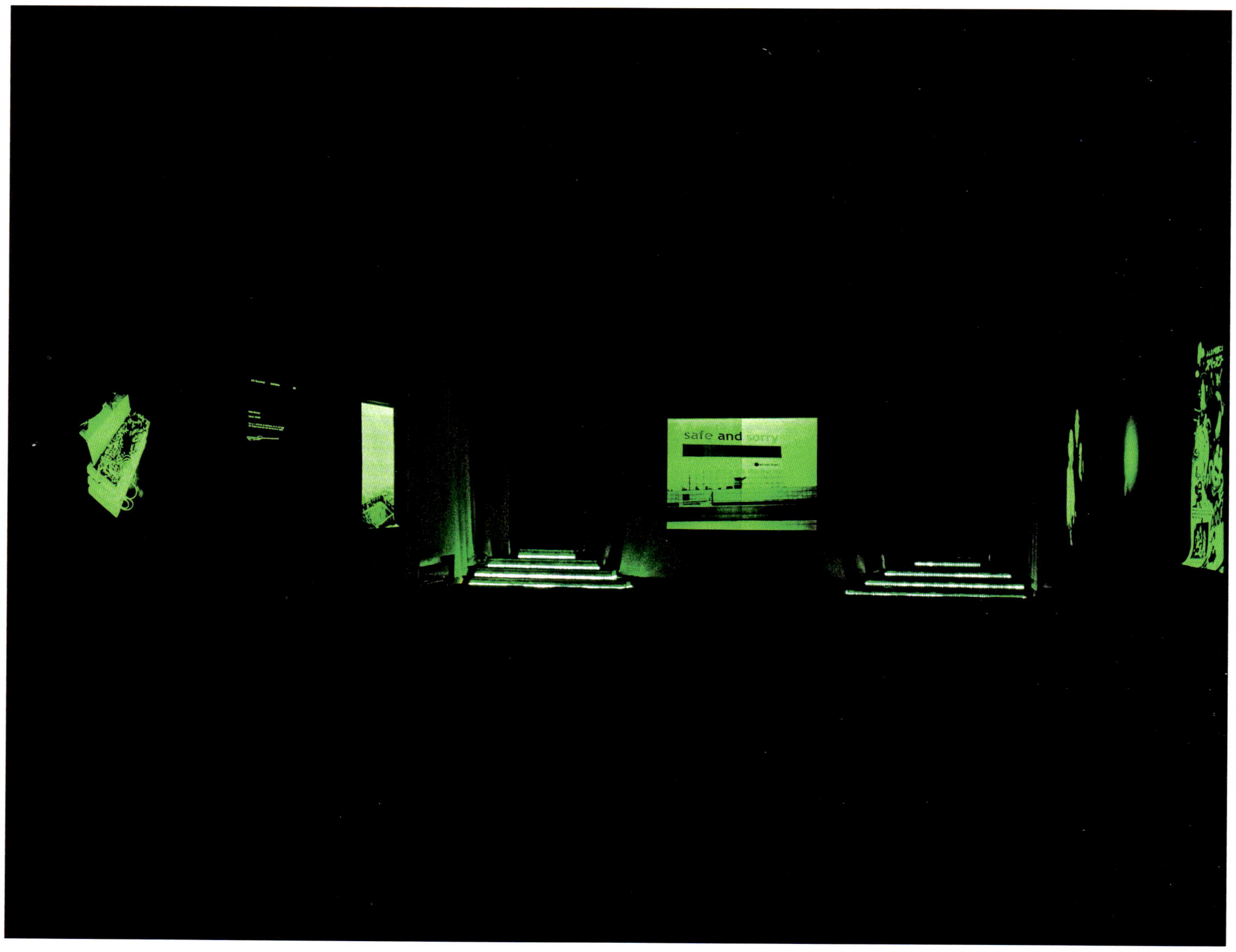
safe and sorry

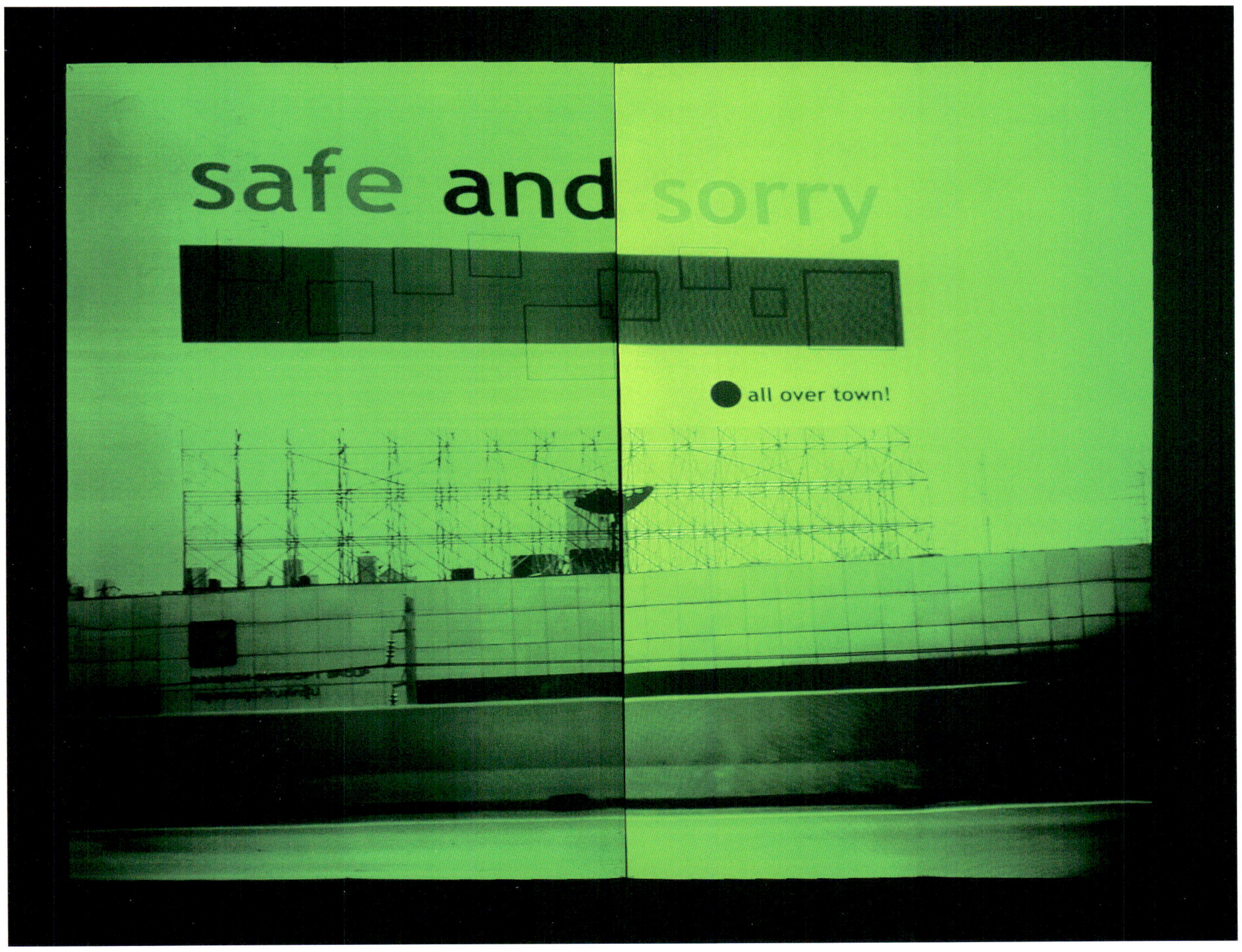

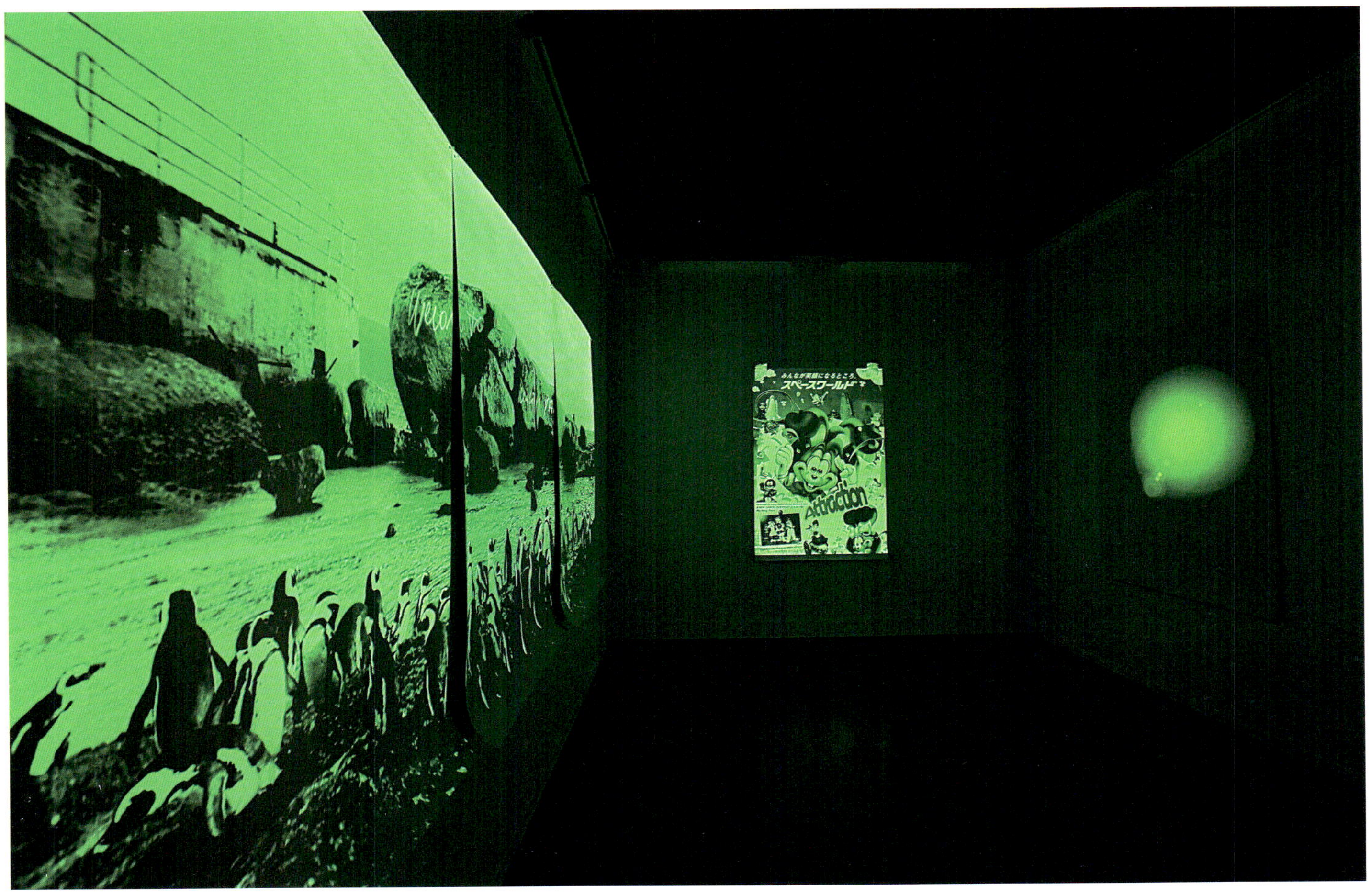

Left: posters **Fade to Black, 2001,** exhibition views "Fade Away", Kunstverein München, 2004
Top: **Fade to Black (Liam Gillick 2003), 2003**
Bottom: **Fade to Black (Boulders Beach 2003), 2003, Fade to Black (Space World, Kitakyushu 2003), 2003** and **Fade to Black (Sound Pan, Paris 2002), 2003,** exhibition view "The Expanded Eye", Kunsthaus Zürich, 2006

(Continued from page 150) exhibition curated by Le Consortium in Dijon || 6 editions and 2 artist editions ∫ First public collection: Fonds national d'art contemporain (Fnac), Puteaux, France (6/6) § Courtesy Air de Paris, Paris; Esther Schipper, Berlin ♦ **Fade to Black (The Ice Man, Tokyo 1995), 2003** ✇ ¬ 1 color screen print on paper, phosphorescent ink, 185 × 120 cm • CD-Rom with digital files for reprint ‡ "C'est arrivé demain" [It Happened Tomorrow], September 18, 2003–January 4, 2004, 7th Lyons Biennial, Lyons, France; exhibition curated by: Le Consortium in Dijon || 6 editions and 2 artist editions ∫ First public collection: Fonds national d'art contemporain (Fnac), Puteaux, France (6/6) ♦ **Fade to Black (Sound Pan, Paris 2002), 2003** ✇ ¬ 1 color screen print on paper, phosphorescent ink, 185 × 120 cm • CD-Rom with digital files for reprint ‡ "C'est arrivé demain" [It Happened Tomorrow], September 18, 2003–January 4, 2004, 7th Lyons Biennial, Lyons, France; exhibition curated by: Le Consortium in Dijon || 6 editions and 2 artist editions ∫ First public collection: Fonds national d'art contemporain (Fnac), Puteaux, France (6/6) ♦ **Fade to Black (Space World, Kitakyushu 2003), 2003** ✇ ¬ 1 color screen print on paper, phosphorescent ink, 185 × 120 cm • CD-Rom with digital files for reprint ‡ "C'est arrivé demain" [It Happened Tomorrow], September 18, 2003–January 4, 2004, 7th Lyons Biennial, Lyons, France; exhibition curated by: Le Consortium in Dijon || 6 editions and 2 artist editions ∫ First public collection: Fonds national d'art contemporain (Fnac), Puteaux, France (6/6) ♦ **Fade to Black (Argentina vs. Netherlands 1978, Medina 2003), 2003** ✇ ¬ 1 color screen print on paper, phosphorescent ink, 185 × 120 cm • CD-Rom with digital files for reprint ‡ "C'est arrivé demain" [It Happened Tomorrow], September 18, 2003–January 4, 2004, 7th Lyons Biennial, Lyons, France; exhibition curated by: Le Consortium in Dijon || 6 editions and 2 artist editions ∫ First public collection: Fonds national d'art contemporain (Fnac), Puteaux, France (6/6) § Courtesy Air de Paris, Paris; Friedrich Petzel, New York; Esther Schipper, Berlin ♦ **Fade to Black (Rirkrit Tiravanija, 1993), 2003** ✇ ¬ 1 color screen print on paper, phosphorescent ink, 185 × 120 cm • CD-Rom with digital files for reprint ‡ "Fade Away," January 17–February 29, 2004, Kunstverein München, Munich, Germany; exhibition curator: Maria Lind || 6 editions and 2 artist editions ∫ First public collection: Frac Corse, Corte, France (5/6) § Courtesy Air de Paris, Paris; Friedrich Petzel, New York; Esther Schipper, Berlin ♦ **Fade to Black (Pierre Huyghe, 1996), 2003** ✇ ¬ 1 color screen print on paper, phosphorescent ink, 185 × 120 cm • CD-Rom with digital files for reprint ‡ "Fade Away," January 17–February 29, 2004, Kunstverein München, Munich, Germany; exhibition curator: Maria Lind || 6 editions and 2 artist editions ∫ First public collection: Frac Corse, Corte, France (5/6) § Courtesy Air de Paris, Paris; Friedrich Petzel, New York; Esther Schipper, Berlin ♦ **Fade to Black (Rirkrit Tiravanija, 2003), 2003** ✇ ¬ 1 color screen print on paper, phosphorescent ink, 185 × 120 cm • CD-Rom with digital files for reprint ‡ "Fade Away," January 17–February 29, 2004, Kunstverein München, Munich, Germany; exhibition curator:

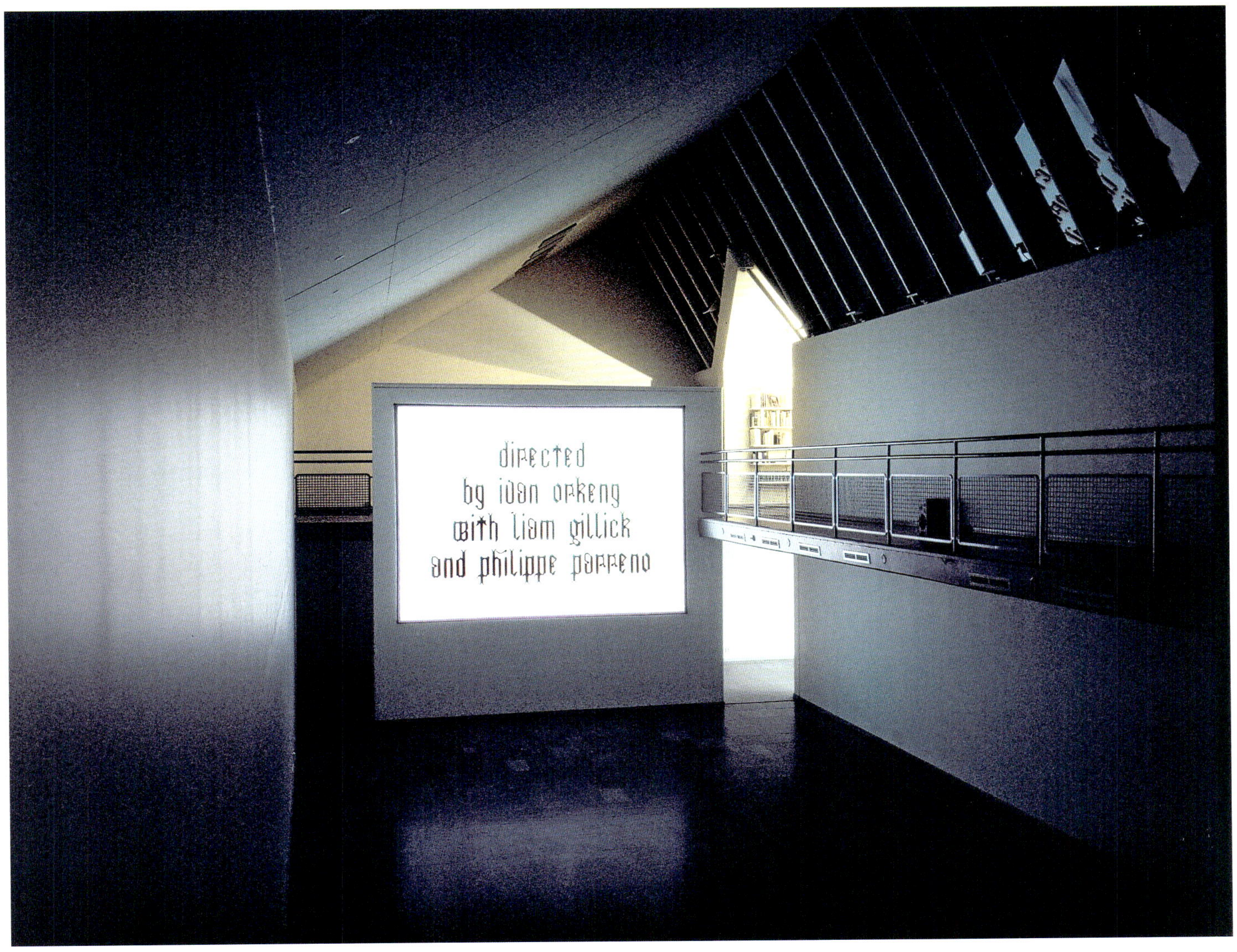

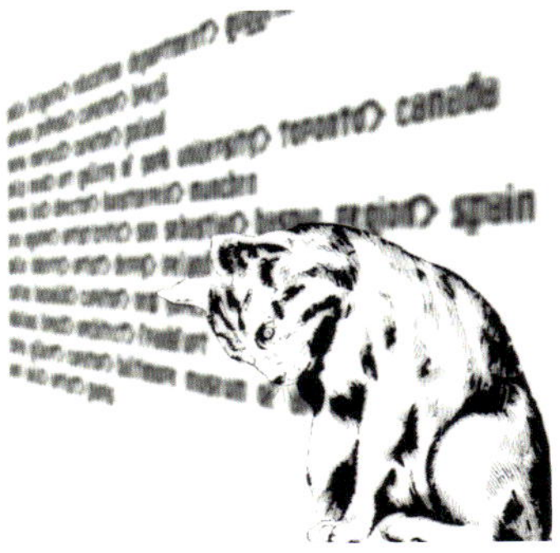
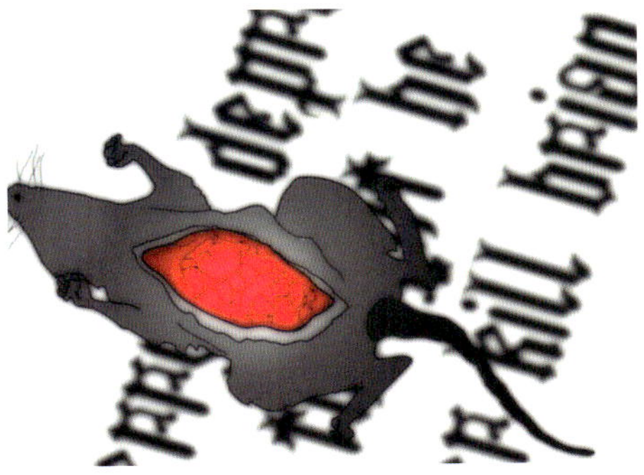

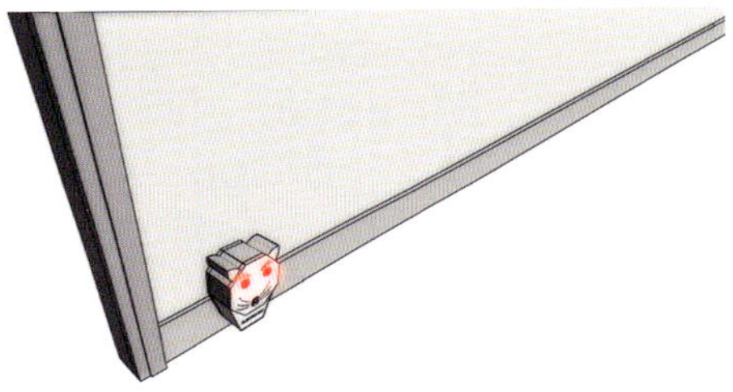
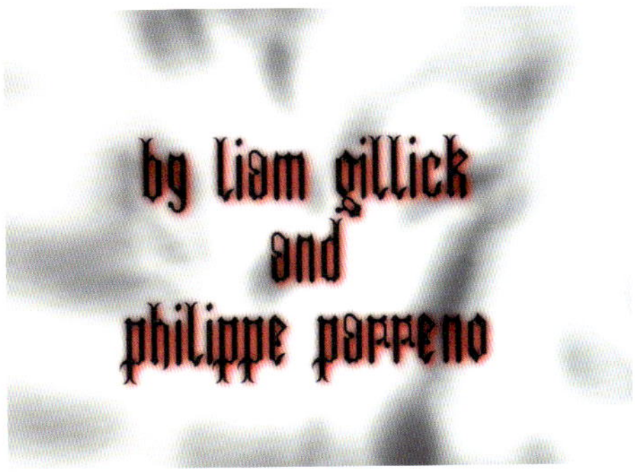

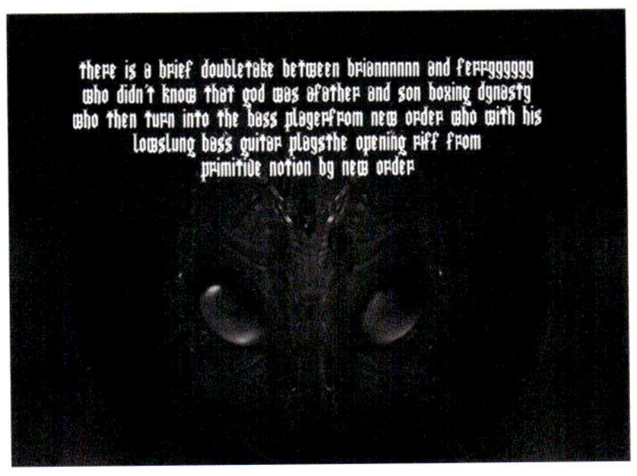

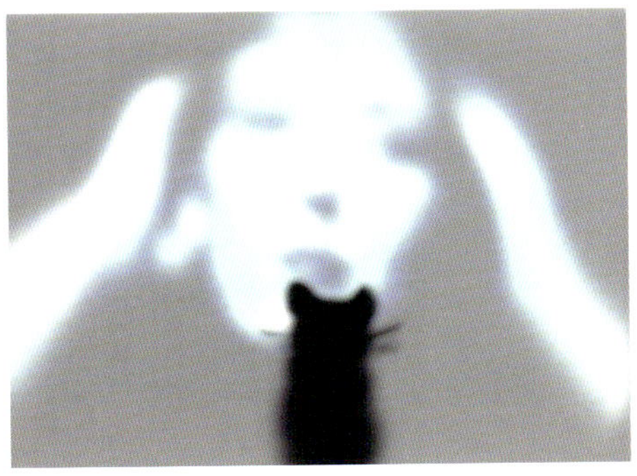
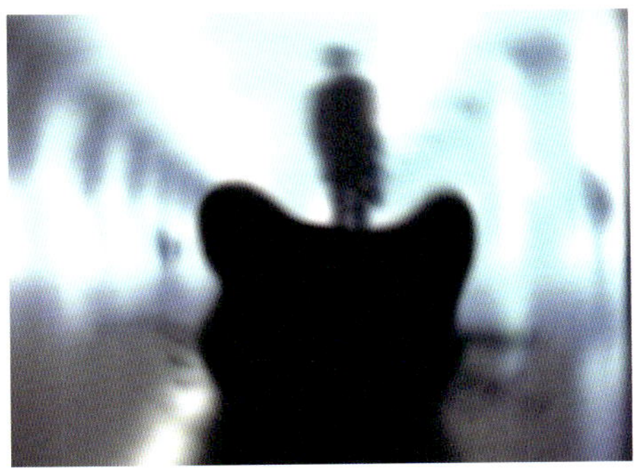
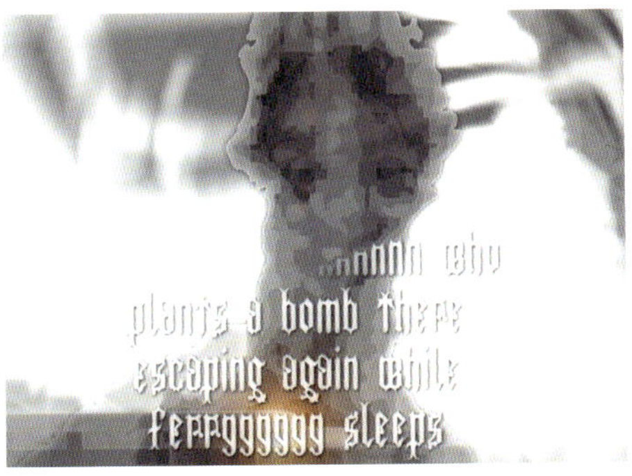

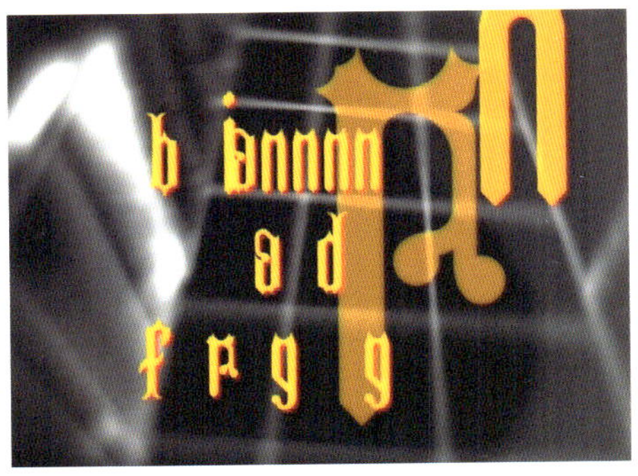

Briannnnnn & Ferryyyyyy, 2004, exhibition view "Law and Creativity", Lunds Konsthall, Lund, 2004; **Briannnnnn & Ferryyyyyy, 2004,** video

Maria Lind || 6 editions and 2 artist editions ∫ First public collection: Frac Corse, Corte, France (5/6) § Courtesy Air de Paris, Paris; Friedrich Petzel, New York; Esther Schipper, Berlin ♦ **Fade to Black (The Sky of Seven Colors, 1997), 2003** ◁ ¬ 1 color screen print on paper, phosphorescent ink, 185 × 120 cm • CD-Rom with digital files for reprint ‡ "Fade Away," January 17–February 29, 2004, Kunstverein München, Munich, Germany; exhibition curator: Maria Lind || 6 editions and 2 artist editions ∫ First public collection: Frac Corse, Corte, France (5/6) § Courtesy Air de Paris, Paris; Friedrich Petzel, New York; Esther Schipper, Berlin ♦ **Fade to Black (Liam Gillick), 2003** ◁ ¬ 1 color screen print on paper, phosphorescent ink, 185 × 120 cm • CD-Rom with digital files for reprint ‡ "Fade Away," January 17–February 29, 2004, Kunstverein München, Munich, Germany; exhibition curator: Maria Lind || 6 editions and 2 artist editions ∫ First public collection: Frac Corse, Corte, France (5/6) § Courtesy Air de Paris, Paris; Friedrich Petzel, New York; Esther Schipper, Berlin ♦ **Fade to Black (Boulders Beach, 2003), 2003** ◁ ¬ 1 color screen print on paper, phosphorescent ink, 185 × 120 cm • CD-Rom with digital files for reprint ‡ "Fade Away," January 17–February 29, 2004, Kunstverein München, Munich, Germany; exhibition curator: Maria Lind || 6 editions and 2 artist editions ∫ First public collection: Frac Corse, Corte, France (5/6) § Courtesy Air de Paris, Paris; Friedrich Petzel, New York; Esther Schipper, Berlin ♦ **Fade to Black (Mont Analogue, 2003), 2003** ◁ ¬ 1 color screen print on paper, phosphorescent ink, 185 × 120 cm • CD-Rom with digital files for reprint ‡ "Fade Away," January 17–February 29, 2004, Kunstverein München, Munich, Germany; exhibition curator: Maria Lind || 6 editions and 2 artist editions ∫ First public collection: Frac Corse, Corte, France (5/6) § Courtesy Air de Paris, Paris; Friedrich Petzel, New York; Esther Schipper, Berlin ♦ **Fade to Black (Sequences), 2003** ◁ ¬ 1 color screen print on paper, phosphorescent ink, 185 × 120 cm • CD-Rom with digital files for reprint ‡ "Fade Away," January 17–February 29, 2004, Kunstverein München, Munich, Germany; exhibition curator: Maria Lind || 6 editions and 2 artist editions ∫ First public collection: Frac Corse, Corte, France (5/6) § Courtesy Air de Paris, Paris; Friedrich Petzel, New York; Esther Schipper, Berlin **This group of fifteen screen prints in phosphorescent ink is only visible in the dark and evokes different moments in Parreno's work between 1993 and 2003. Unfinished or ephemeral projects come to mind such as *The Ice Man* (a banner created in 1995 by Gillick for a film), or *Sound Pan* (a 2002 project where the sound of stars presented as the image of an explosion was broadcast on the radio). ◊ The first five screen prints, exhibited for the first time at the 7th Lyons Biennial in 2003–2004, are accompanied by seven additional prints, like the ghosts of vanished works, at the Kunstverein in Munich in 2004 for "Fade Away." In daylight, the white surface of the posters reveals only pale traces, but when the room is plunged into darkness images appear only to fade away when the lights are turned on. In an exploration of the conditions of visibility, *Fade to Black* questions the recording of memory.**

The Boy From Mars, 2005, exhibition view "The Boy From Mars", Friedrich Petzel Gallery, New York, 2005
The Boy From Mars, 2005, exhibition view "The Parallel Action", Cieszyn, 2004

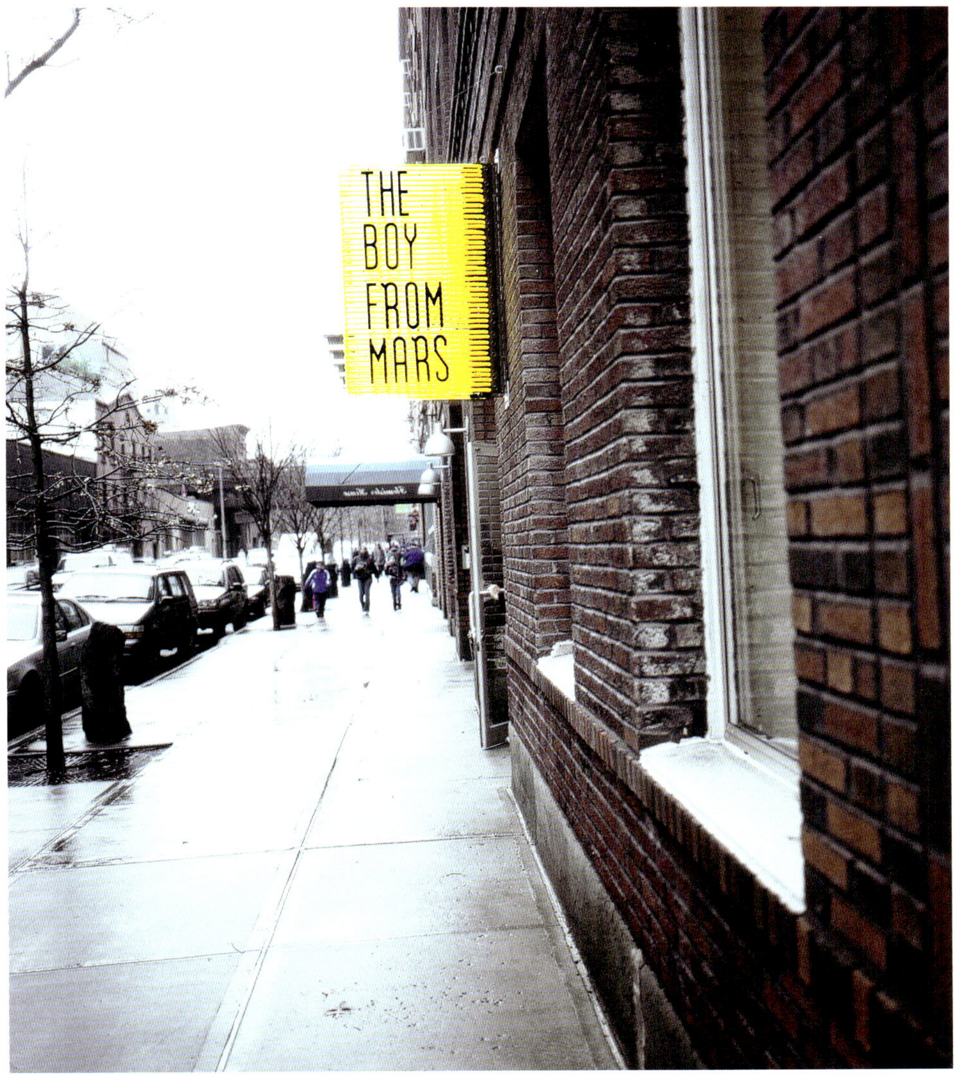
THE
BOY
FROM
MARS

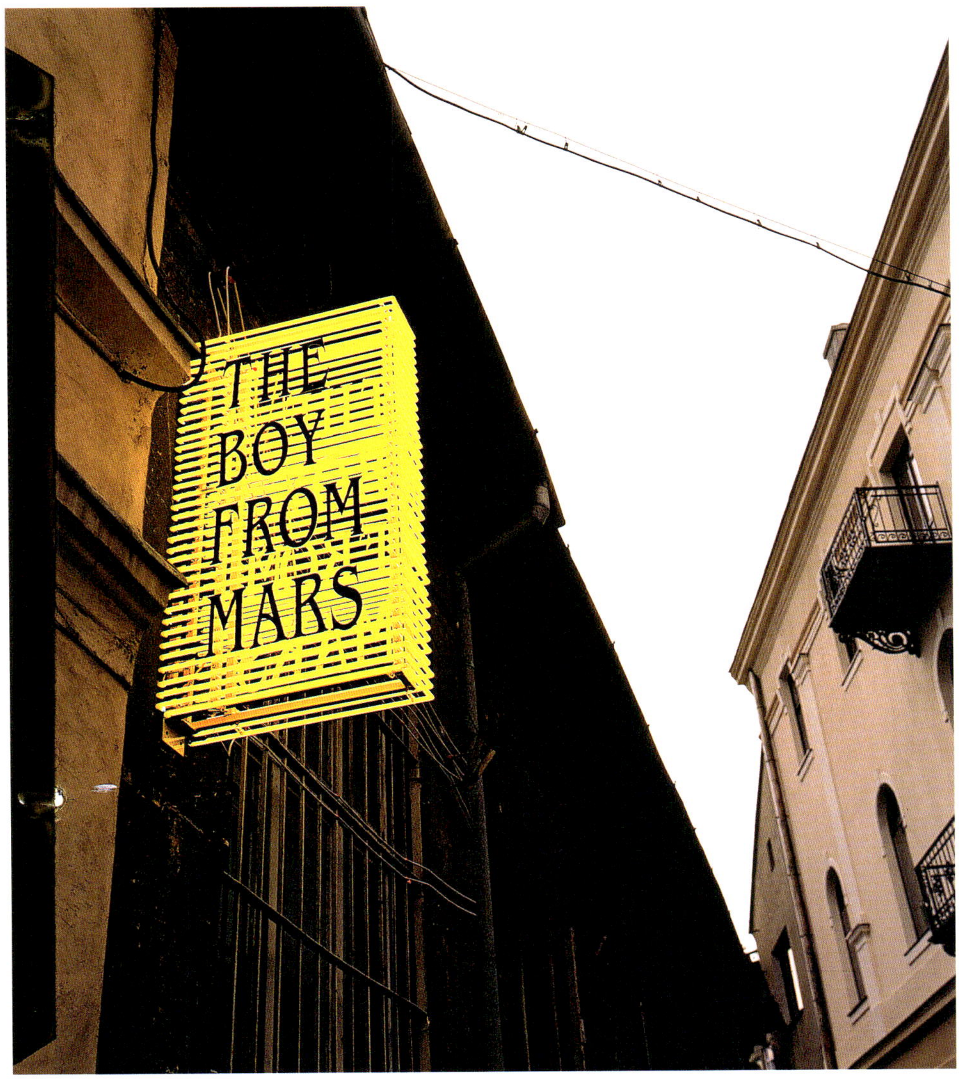
THE
BOY
FROM
MARS

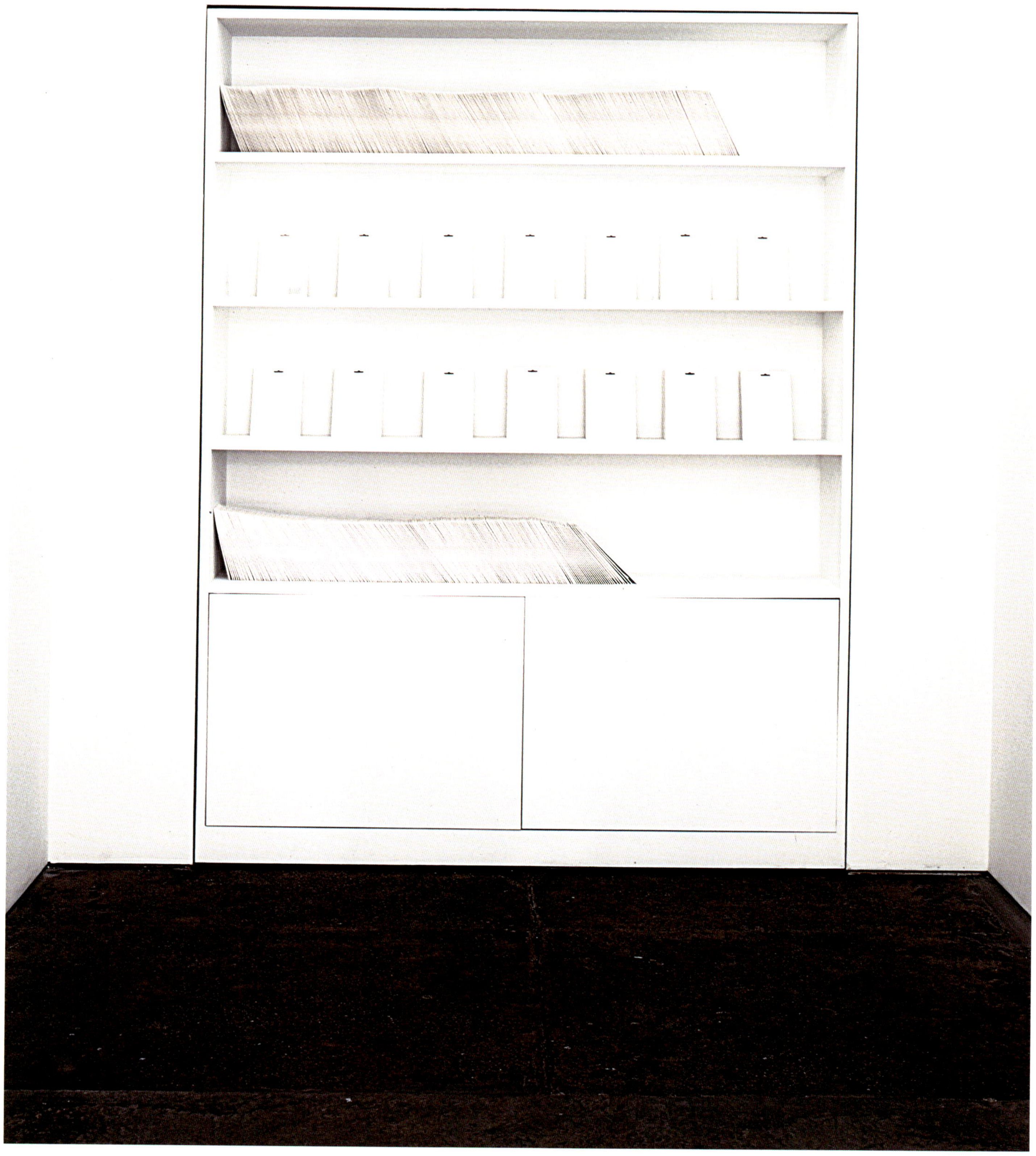

The Boy From Mars, 2005, exhibition view “The Boy From Mars”, Friedrich Petzel Gallery, New York, 2005

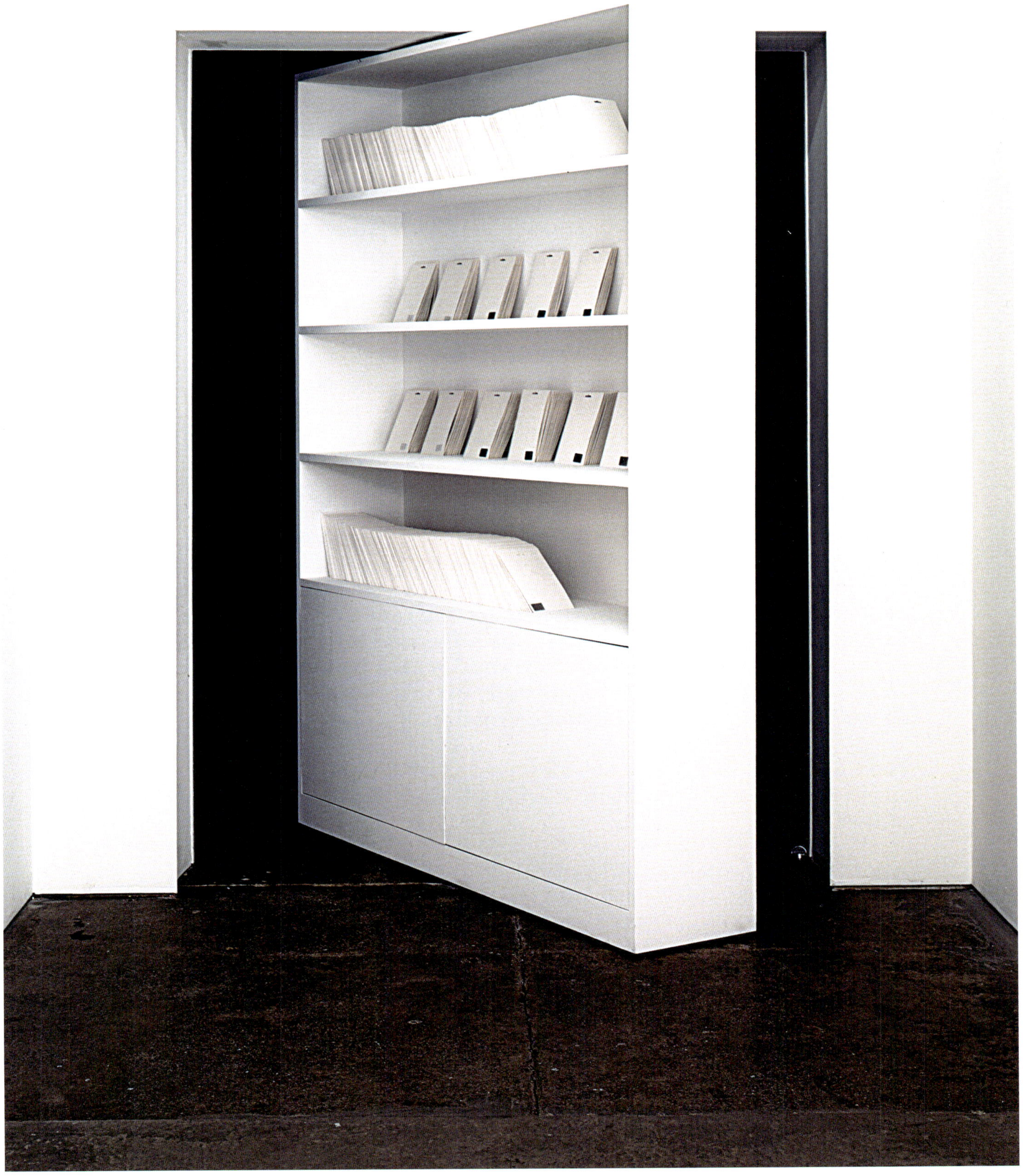

45. "Maybe posters are so good because they are like one-offs, like an exhibition," in Philippe Parreno, Hans Ulrich Obrist, *The Conversation Series*, *op. cit.*, p.106.

In a rejection of photography, Parreno uses the format of the poster[45] as a mnemonic image. "What I like [about these images] is that they are like a hangover from the 1970s." In this work, Parreno creates images that are both present and absent, depending upon the moment of seeing—once again—playing with the *time code*.

The Boy from Mars, 2004 ◁ Book: 164 pages, 21 × 15 cm, color; publisher: CCA Kitakyushu, Kitakyushu, Japan ***The Boy From Mars*** **book consists of full page photographs documenting the construction of *Hybrid Muscle* (2002) and the shooting of the film *The Boy From Mars* (2003).**

Radio Réalité, 2004 First project 1991, émetteur radio, LED, lecteur son ‡ "Utopia Station: auf demweg nach porto alegre," October 7, 2004–January 16, 2005, Haus der Kunst, Munich, Germany, curator: Molly Nesbit, Hans Ulrich Obrist and Rirkrit Tiravanija || 1 edition § of the artist

Briannnnnn & Ferryyyyyy, 2004 With Liam Gillick ◁ Video, color, sound, 30'; production: Anna Sanders Films ‡ "Law and Creativity," November 27, 2004–February 13, 2005, Lunds Konsthall, Lund, Sweden || 4 editions and 3 artist editions ʃ First private collection: private collection, Athens, Greece § Courtesy Air de Paris, Paris; Casey Kaplan Gallery, New York; Friedrich Petzel, New York; Esther Schipper, Berlin **Using the cat and mouse theme often found in cartoons, Parreno and Gillick created two characters: Briannnnnn and Ferryyyyyy, in homage to the British singer Brian Ferry. *Alien Gothic,* an animated film, presents a simple action in ten scenes: the cat chases the mouse, the cat catches the mouse, etc. The end credits of each episode list quotations, ideas, and the names of both imaginary and real people. The episodes were written by Gillick, drawn by Parreno and animated by a young New York based artist, Ivan Orkney. The typography was originally designed by M/M (Paris) for Parreno's "Alien Seasons" exhibition. The Anna Sanders Films animated logo that appears at the beginning of each sequence was created by Gillick and Sean Dack. ◊ This work reflects humorously on intellectual property rights, as well as on popular and artistic creation.**

Fade to Black, 2004 ◁ Book: 32 pages, 34 × 24 cm, 11 ill. color, spiral cover; publisher: MFC-Michèle Didier, Brussels, Belgium || 600 copies

A Smile Without a Cat, 2005 With Pierre Huyghe ◁ 4 C-prints mounted on aluminum; 33 × 40.6 cm (unframed); 37.2 × 44.8 cm (framed) ‡ February 23–26, 2007, Armory Show, New York, United States || 10 editions and 3 artist editions ʃ First private collection: Private collection, New York, United States (1/10) § Sandra Antelo-Suarez; Friedrich Petzel Gallery, New York; Marian Goodman Gallery, New York

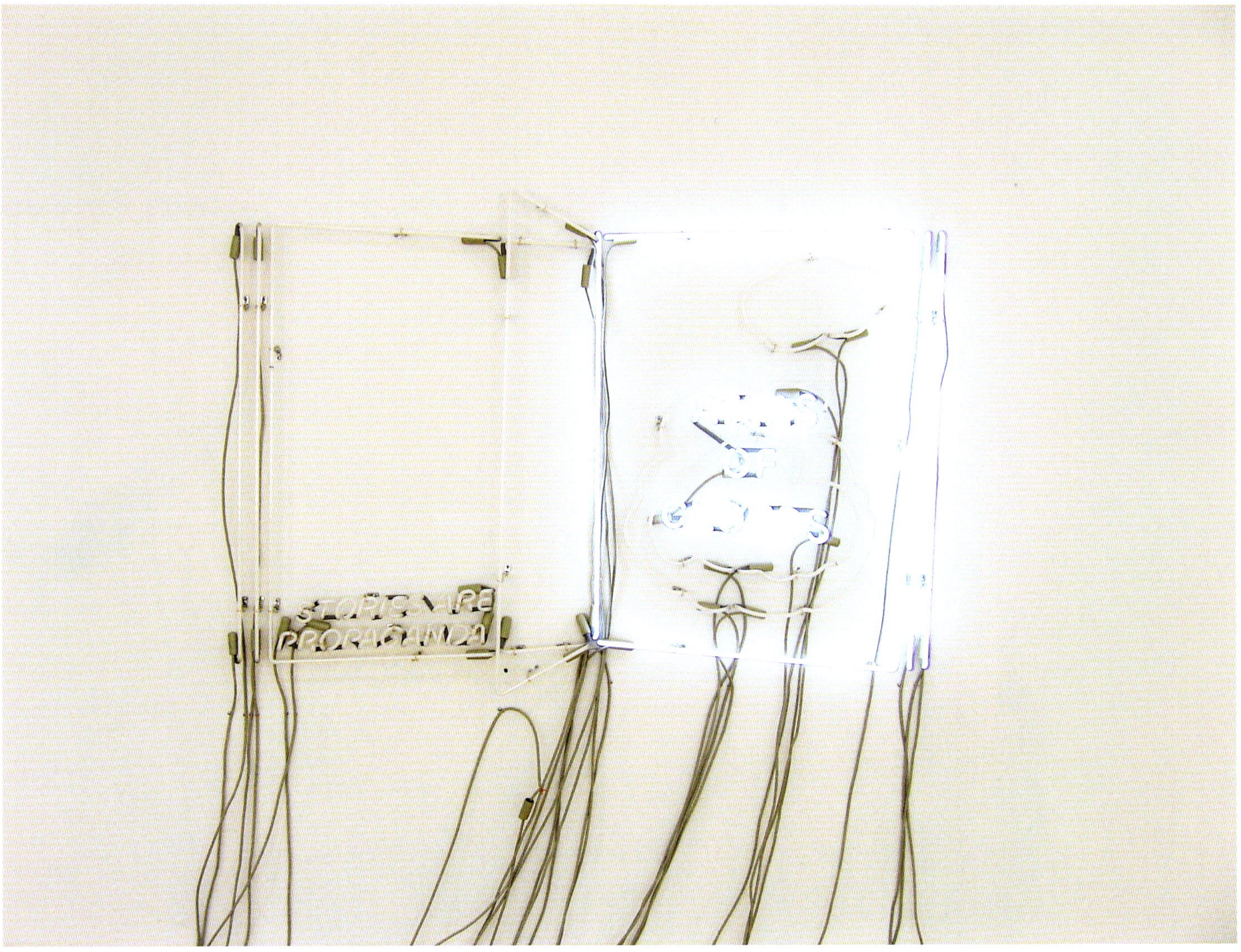

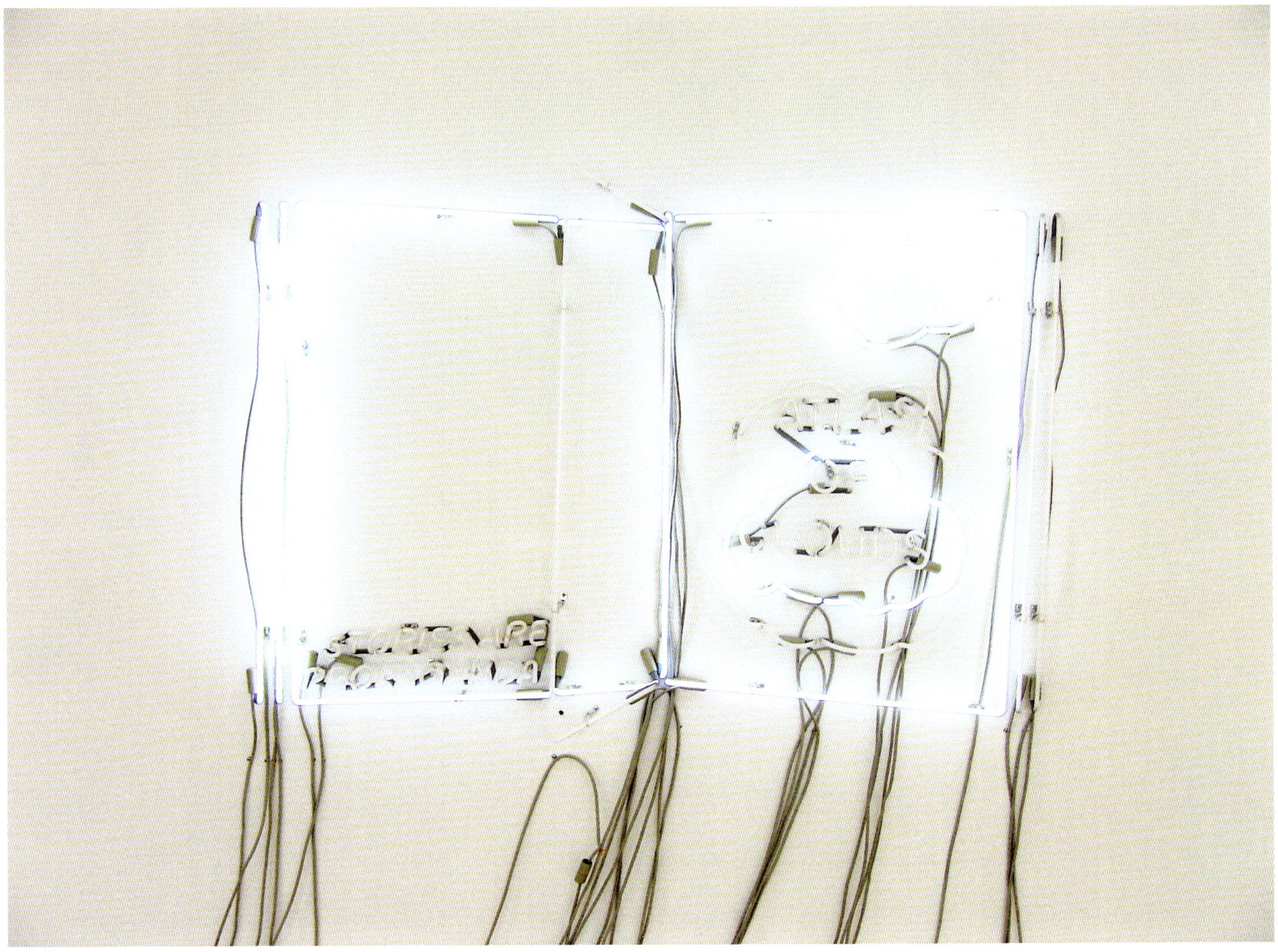

Atlas of Clouds, 2005

Population Size of Imaginary Friends for Countie

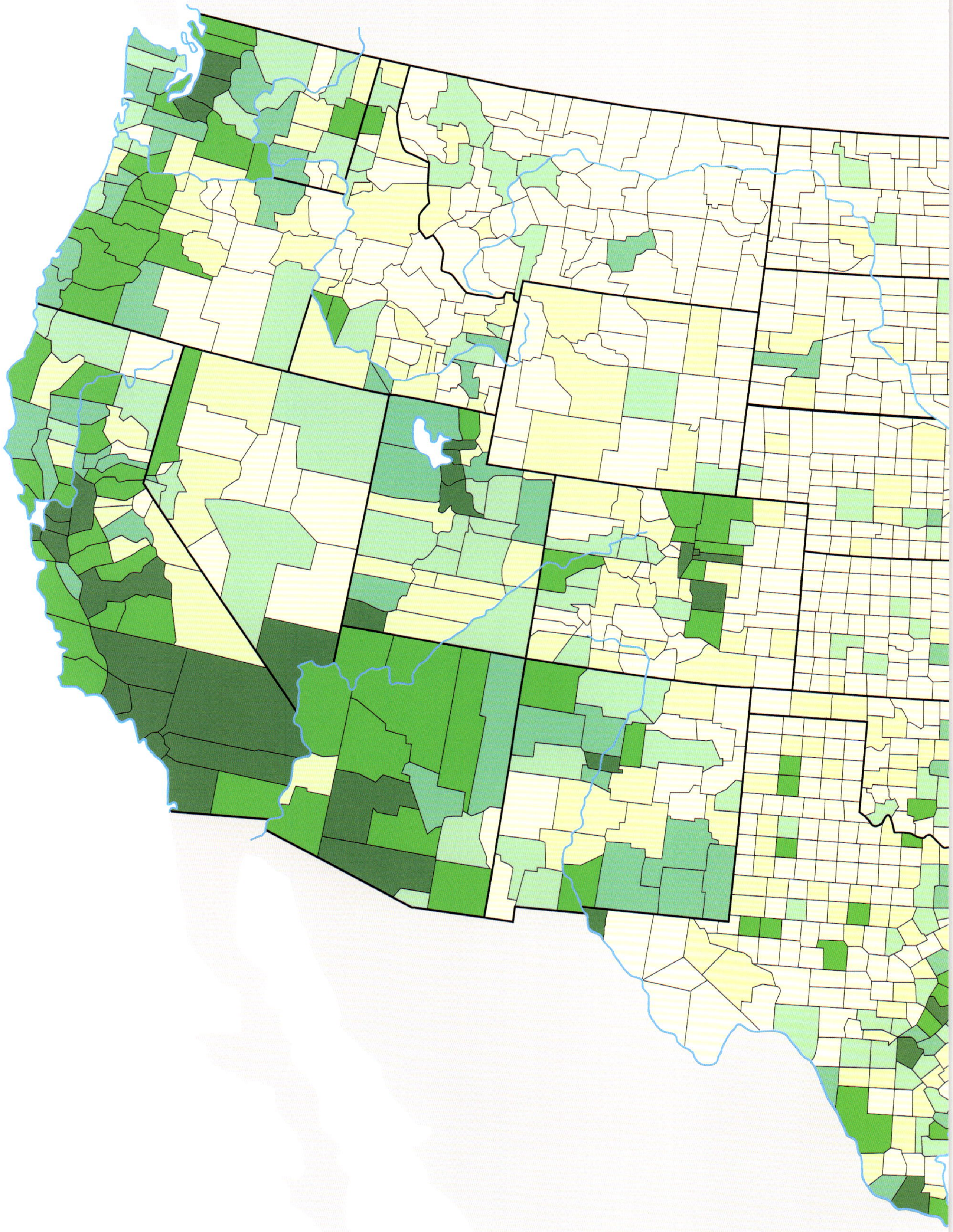

Sources: U.S. Census Bureau, Population Estimates Program; University of Washington, Social Studies Department

ebruary 1, 2005 **Total Population Estimates: 23,644,174**

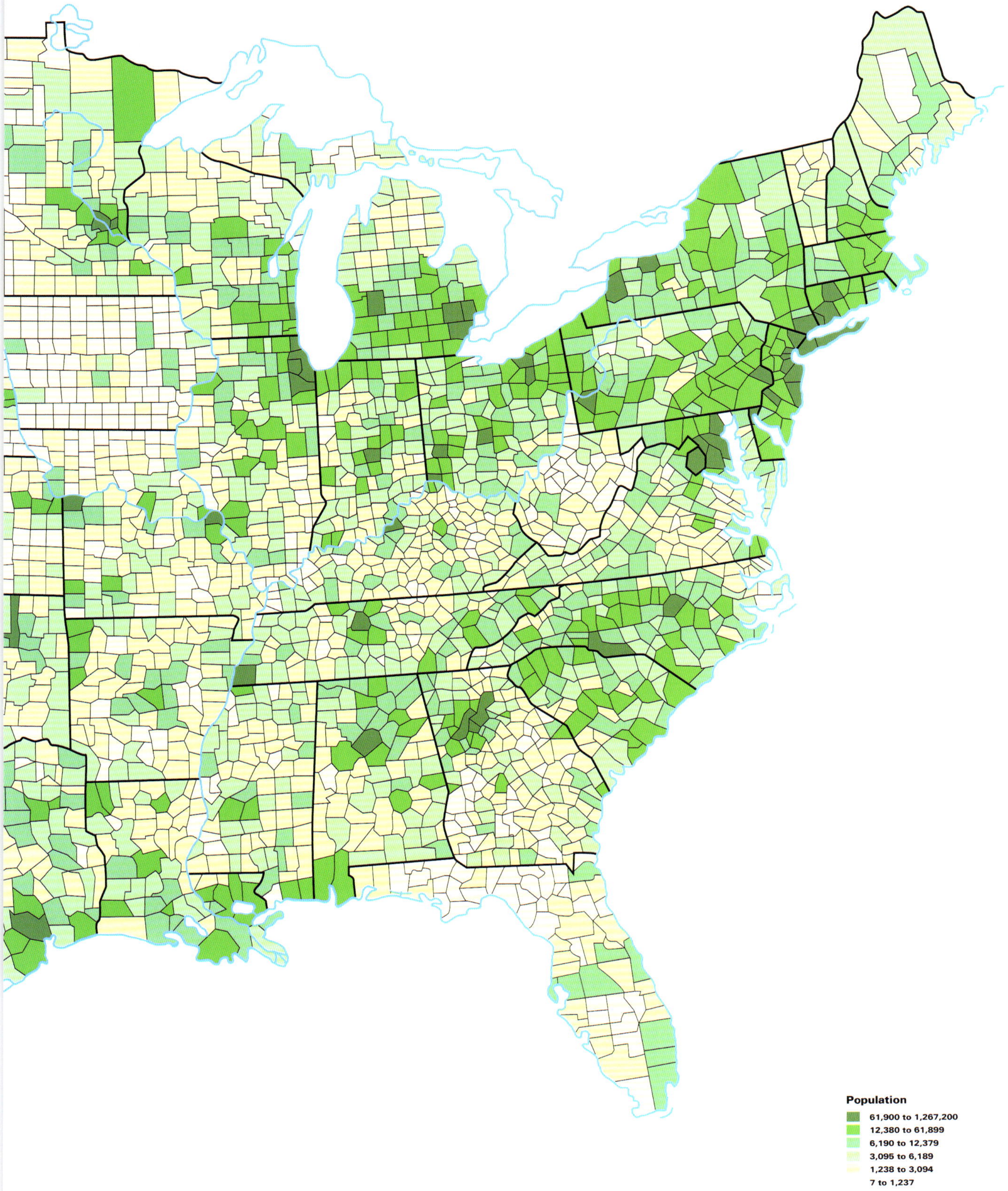

The Boy From Mars, 2005 ◁ Installation: ¬ swinging bookshelf (241 × 178 × 38 cm) • deletable DVDs of the film *The Boy from Mars* (2003) packaged in white cardboard sleeves ‡ "The Boy From Mars," April 2–May 7, 2005, Friedrich Petzel Gallery, New York, United States § Courtesy Friedrich Petzel Gallery, New York ♦ **The Boy From Mars, 2005** ◁ Light sign: 44 yellow neons, metal stucture, Plexiglas, 5 transformers (37 mA, 10 000 V), electrical system; 148 × 90.2 × 41.9 cm ‡ "The Boy From Mars," April 2–May 7, 2005, Friedrich Petzel Gallery, New York, United States || 5 editions and 1 artist edition ʃ First public collection: Musée d'Art moderne de la Ville de Paris, Paris, France (3/5) § Courtesy Air de Paris, Paris; Friedrich Petzel, New York; Esther Schipper, Berlin **Parreno continues *The Boy From Mars* project with an exhibition at the Friedrich Petzel Gallery, in New York. Outside, a neon sign displays the exhibition's title. Inside, *The Boy From Mars* is shown on a television placed behind a swinging bookshelf. The bookshelf holds DVD copies of the 35 mm film packaged in white cardboard sleeves. Once the packages are unsealed, the DVD is only viewable for 48 hours before the chemically treated surface oxidizes and erases the recording. This work recalls the disappearing images in *Fade to Black*.**

Imaginary Friends, 2005 ◁ Glossy Lambda print mounted on aluminum, 126.5 × 163.5 cm (framed) ‡ June 16–21, 2005, Air de Paris booth, Art Basel, Basel, Switzerland || 5 editions and 2 artist editions ʃ First public collection: Solomon R. Guggenheim Museum, New York (1/5) **Based on real statistics, this map of the United States represents the geographical distribution, by state, of the number of imaginary friends invented by children aged seven to thirteen. The number of these imaginary friends is more than 23 million and growing.**

Welcome to Reality Park, 2003–2005 ◁ Lambda print mounted on aluminum, 123.6 × 145.3 × 4.5 cm (framed) ‡ June 16–21, 2005, Air de Paris booth, Art Basel, Basel, Switzerland || 5 editions and 2 artist editions ʃ Fondation Louis Vuitton pour la création Collection, Paris, France (2/5) **The photograph documents a penguin reserve at Boulders Beach in South Africa where Philippe Parreno marked the entrance with the words "Reality Park."**

Atlas of Clouds, 2005 ◁ Animated neon sign, electrical system; 100 × 156 cm ‡ "Atlas of Clouds," July 30–August 27, 2005, 1301PE Gallery, Los Angeles, United States || 7 editions and 2 artist editions ʃ First private collection: private collection, Mexico City, Mexico (1/7) § Courtesy 1301PE, Los Angeles; Air de Paris, Paris; Friedrich Petzel, New York; Esther Schipper, Berlin

Untitled, 2005 With Rirkrit Tiravanija ◁ Five puppets: heads in painted terracotta; synthetic feet, hands and hair clothes, stuffing;

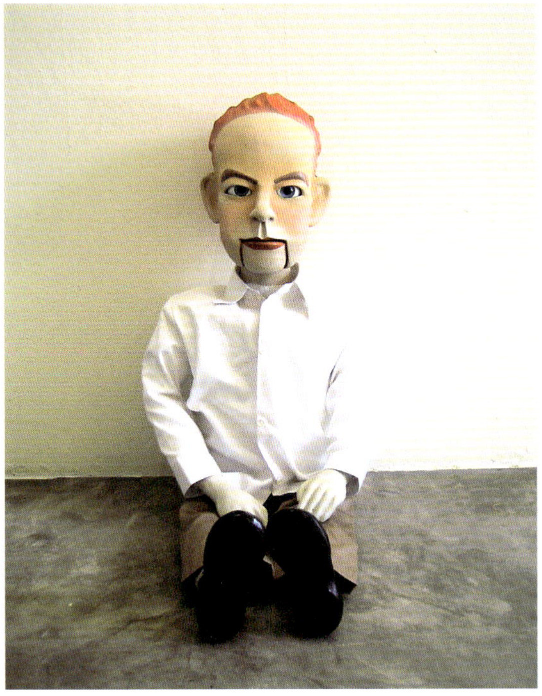
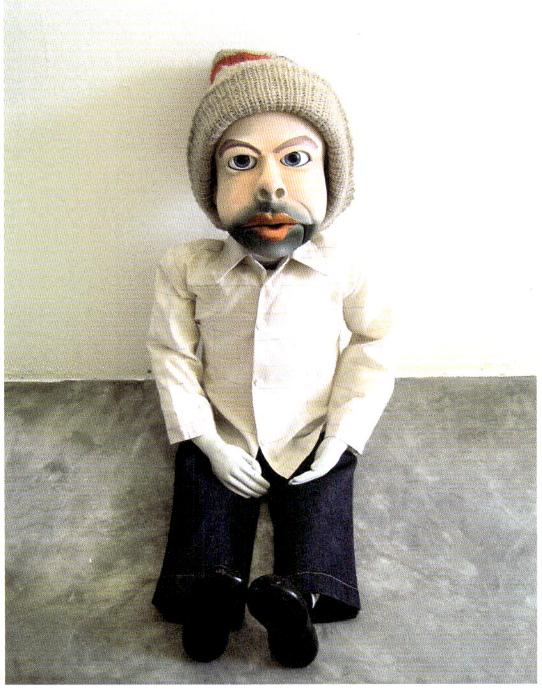
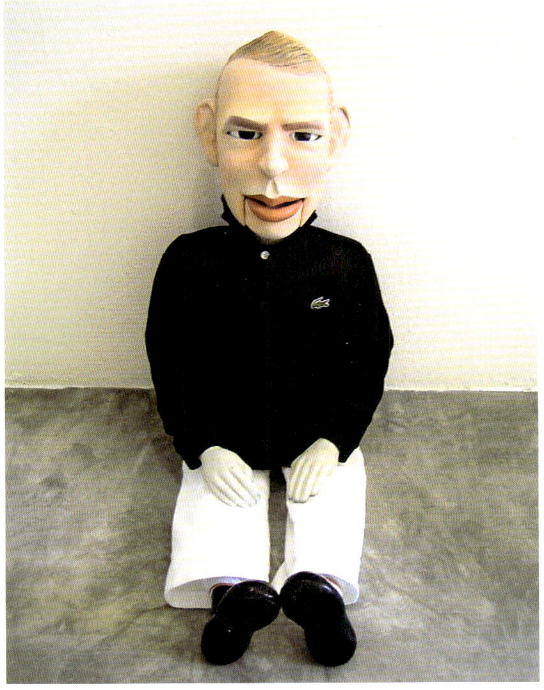
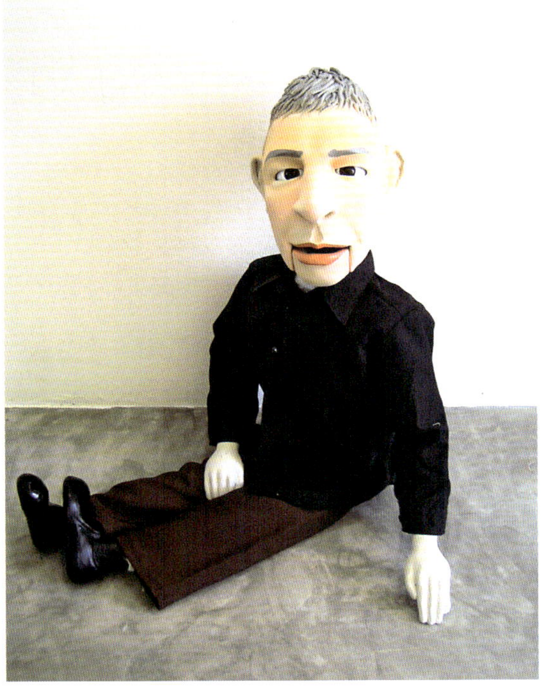
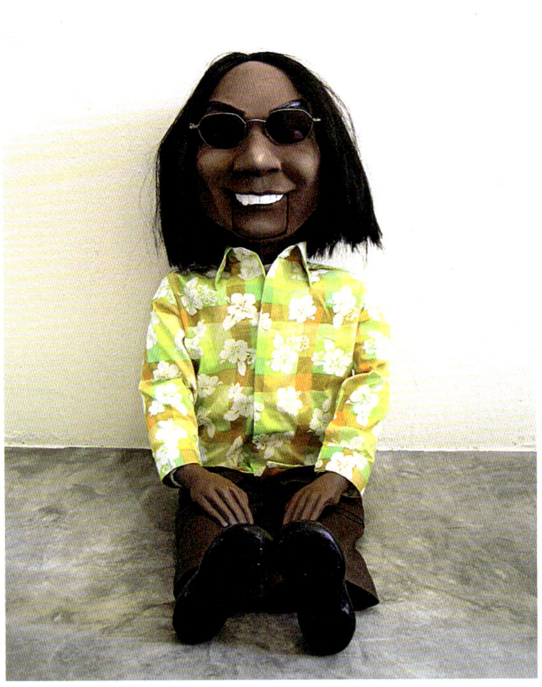

Untitled, 2005, with Rirkrit Tiravanija

46. Hans Ulrich Obrist, *Interviews*, Milan, Charta, 2003.

variable dimensions ‡ "Philippe Parreno & Rirkrit Tiravanija," April 27–29, 2006, Friedrich Petzel Gallery, New York, United States || 4 editions ʃ First private collection: private collection, New York, United States (1/4) **These ventriloquist puppets represent five artists (Liam Gillick, Pierre Huyghe, Rirkrit Tiravanija, Philippe Parreno) and the curator Hans Ulrich Obrist.**
Untitled (Ventriloquist Performance no. 1), 2005 With Rirkrit Tiravanija ◁ 16 mm black and white film, sound, 12' ‡ "Philippe Parreno & Rirkrit Tiravanija," April 27–29, 2006, Friedrich Petzel Gallery, New York, United States || 3 editions ʃ First private collection: private collection, New York, United States (1/3) § Courtesy Friedrich Petzel, New York **The film was shot during a conversation in 2005, where the two artists were invited to participate in the launch of Hans Ulrich Obrist's book *Interviews Volume 1*.[46] Instead of attending, they sent two puppets made in Thailand of their likeness and a ventriloquist. The ventriloquist performed a dialogue written by Parreno in advance and based on past conversations with Obrist about experience, memory, theatricality and human relations. The conversation or performance takes on a new form in this film. The ventriloquist repeats the dialogue on a loop, making the two puppets converse and tease one another, and finally laud Obrist's *Interviews* project: "a novel!," "a human comedy!," "a symphony!," "a polyphony!."**

Stories Are Propaganda, 2005/2007 ◁ Installation: ¬ screen, video projector (2005 version) or flat screen (2007 version) • 35 mm film transferred onto DVD (color, sound, 8'40") • red velvet curtain, inscription "Stories are propaganda" (golden paint or spray paint); coproduction: Guangdong Museum of Art, Guangzhou, China, and Lyons Biennial, Lyons, France ‡ "Expérience de la durée," September 14–December 31, 2005, 8th Lyons Biennial of contemporary art, Lyons, France (exhib. cat.); exhibition curators: Nicolas Bourriaud and Jérôme Sans || 5 editions ʃ First private collection: private collection, Hamburg, Germany (2/5) § Courtesy Air de Paris, Paris; Friedrich Petzel, New York **Invited to the Guangzhou Biennial, Parreno and Tiravanija documented the new city under construction. A red curtain with the words "Stories are propaganda" unveiled at regular intervals a 35 mm film written by Parreno and read by a child with an eerily sage voice. *Stories Are Propaganda, 2005* creates a feeling of melancholy through its evocation of the end of the world's ideologies. A succession of fixed shots show black factory smoke, piles of trash, words written in the sand ("vermillon sands" [sic]) and trees swaying in the wind. Several moments of poetic fragments unroll like snapshots: a Chinese magician makes watches and clocks appear at night, a small albino rabbit flounders in a muddy puddle, a snowman is made of mud, a wall bears the sentence: "*No amount of effort can save you from oblivion*." Finally, a rabbit's silhouette appears before a crescent moon as if a shadow formed by two hands.**

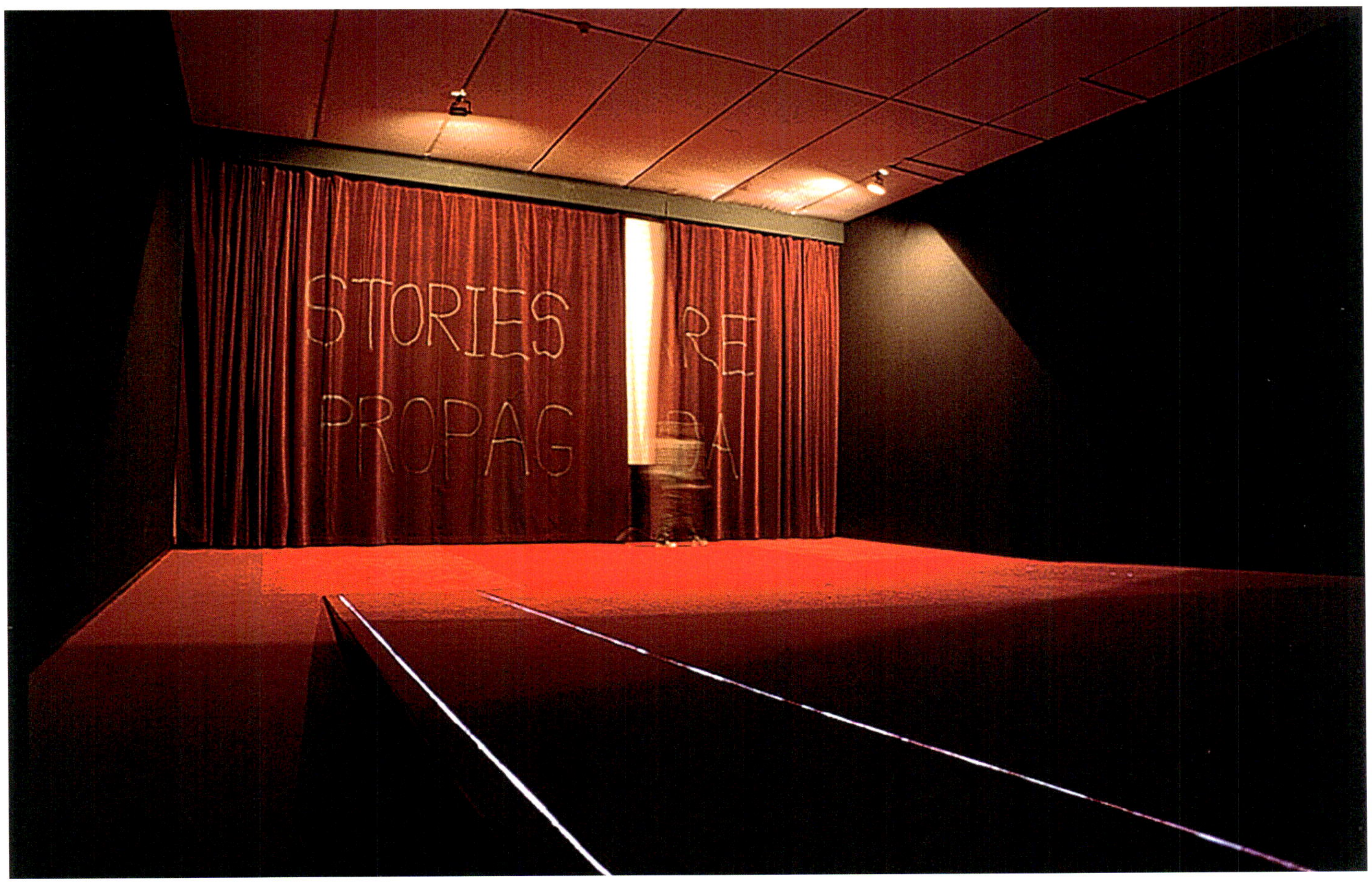

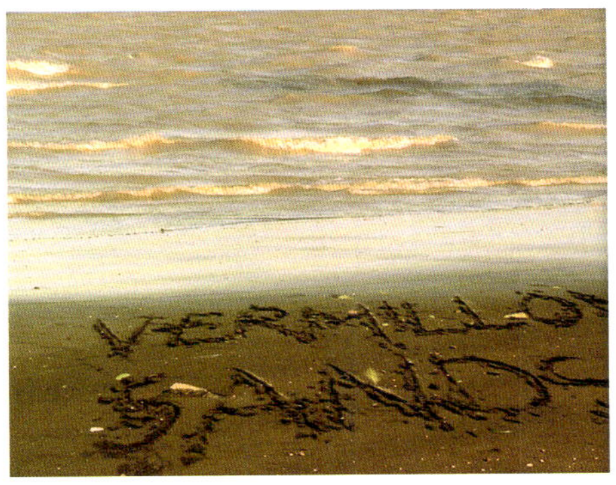
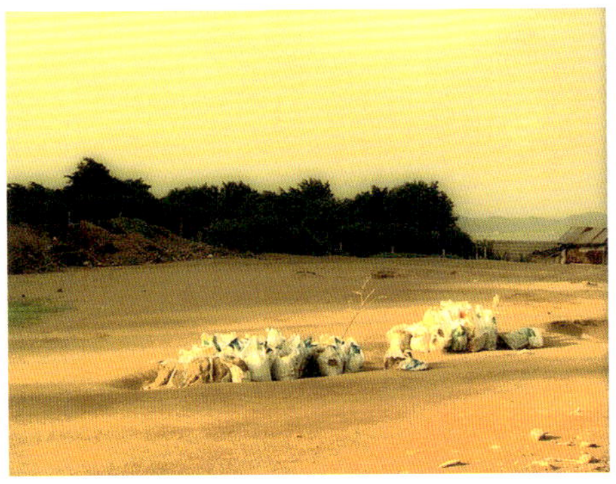
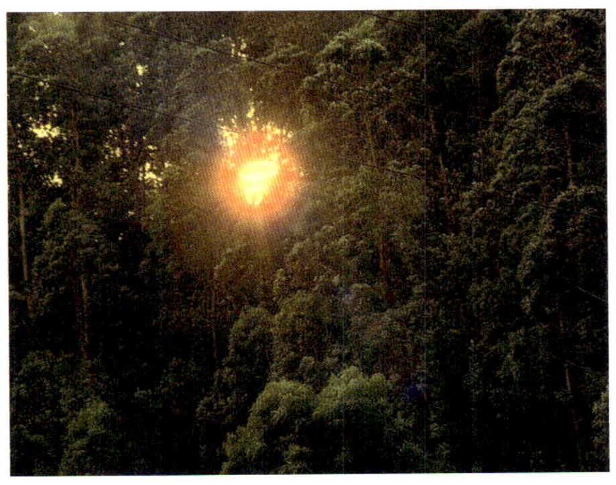
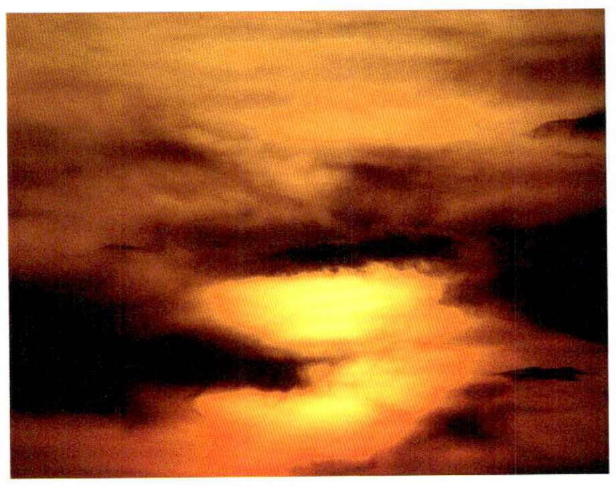
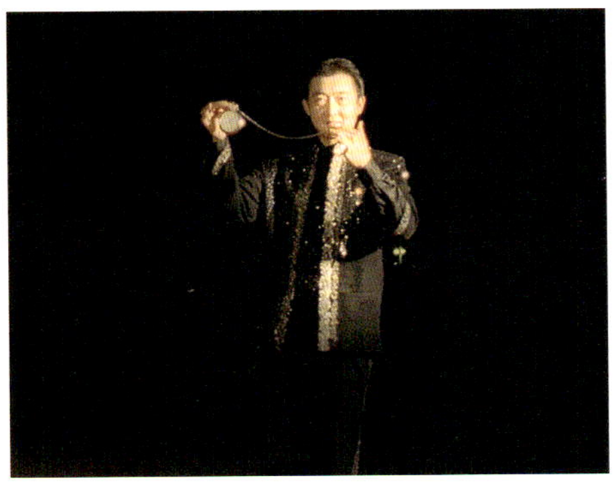
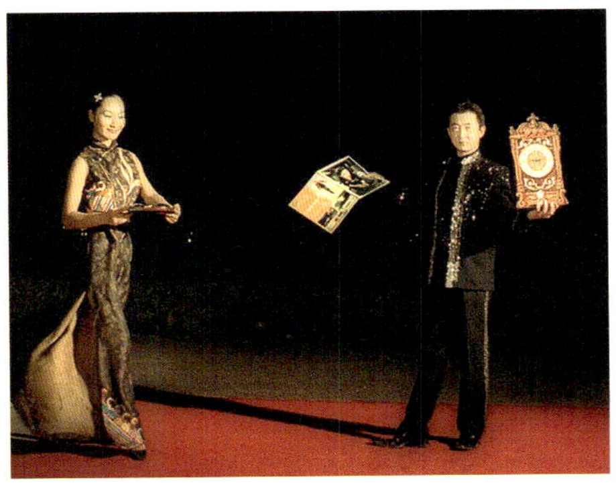
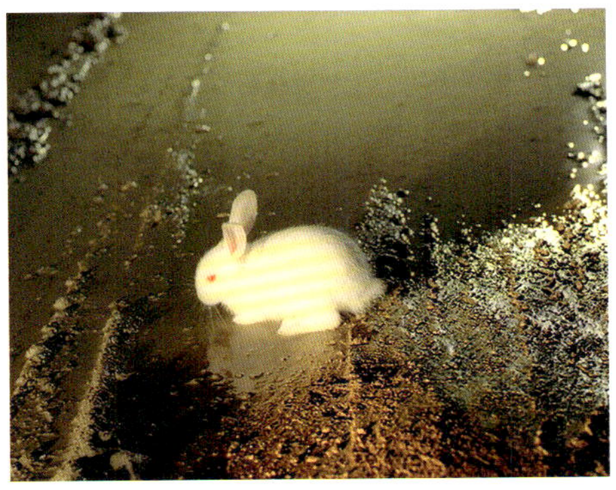
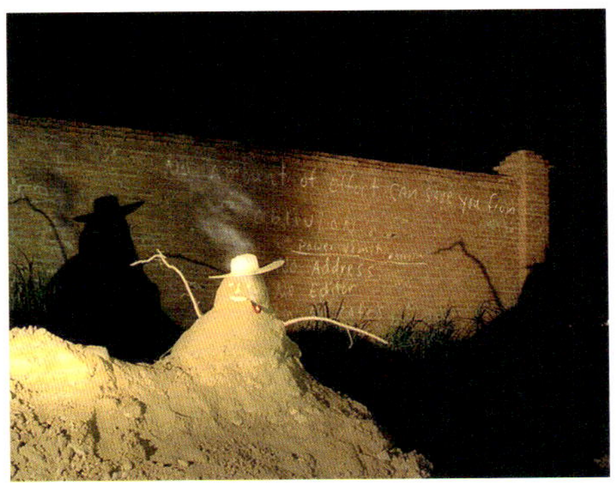
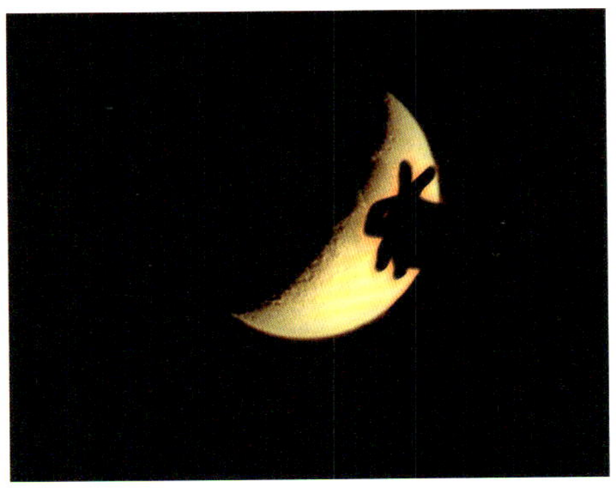

Stories Are Propaganda, 2005/2007, with Rirkrit Tiravanija, exhibition view "Expérience de la durée", 8th Biennial of Contemporary Art, 2005
Stories Are Propaganda, 2005/2007, with Rirkrit Tiravanija, film

No More Reality/Raise the Dead, 2005 With Douglas Gordon ◁ Wall painting (black and red spray paint), variable dimension ‡ "You and Me, Me and You," December 13, 2005–January 28, 2006, Fondazione Davide Halevim, Milan, Italy § Courtesy of the artists **"No More Reality" was the slogan used by Parreno in 1991 for a selected grouping of works, most of which were exhibited at the Villa Arson in Nice. "Raise the Dead" is the slogan written by Gordon on the facade of the Kunsthalle in Vienna in 1996, for a series of exhibitions entitled, "Large Scale Picture." This simple yet defiant phrase rejects the rationality of ideology which, according to Gordon, greatly influenced the construction of most of the cities of the 20th century.**

Zidane, un portrait du XXIe siècle [Zidane, a 21st Century Portrait], 2006 With Douglas Gordon ◁ 35 mm film, color, sound, 90'; production Anna Lena Films Palomar Pictures; coproduction with Arte France Cinema/Love Streams agnès b. Productions ‡ First showing: May 23, 2006 at the Cannes Festival, in the official selection, out of competition; film distribution May 24, 2006 ♦ **Zidane, un portrait du XXIe siècle [Zidane, a 21st Century Portrait], 2006** With Douglas Gordon ◁ Installation: ¬ 2 video projectors, 2 screens (either placed side-by-side or forming an angle of 90°), 2 videos • Video 1: *Zidane, un portrait du XXIe siècle*, 2006, 35 mm film transferred onto DVD, color, sound, 90'; variable dimensions • Video 2: sequence shot from one of the 17 cameras filming during the match, 90' ‡ "Zidane, A 21st Century Portrait," National Gallery of Canada, Ottawa, Canada, July 6–October, 2007 || 17 versions (each with a different video 2) ʃ First public collection: National Gallery of Canada, Ottawa, Canada (1/17) **Gordon and Parreno had wanted to do a project about Zidane since 1997. In 2005, they were finally able to make a 90-minute film, which is the approximate duration of a soccer game. The filming took place on April 25th, at the Santiago Bernabeu Stadium in Madrid, where the Real Madrid team played against the Villareal team. It was a prophetic moment, because Zidane was penaltied and thrown out of the game, forshadowing what would occur during the World Cup final that same year. ◊ Seventeen 35 mm cameras follow Zidane throughout the match. The film consists of seventeen points of view edited in real time. The result has a very "musical" structure, accentuated by a rich soundtrack composed by the band Mogwai. ◊ The question of time is central in this project,[47] as the work "interpret[s] the real in motion and reinvent[s] it."[48] Parreno's belief that everyday life can be deciphered through a *time code* informs the structure of the film. "In the editing of a film, there is a *time code* and we can fast forward or rewind, edit sequences, re-edit, and in the same way at certain moments of our existence, we edit sequences of our life in order to find their meaning, to re-edit and especially to understand them."[49] ◊ In Tiravanija's catalogue for l'Arc, Parreno wrote: "These time games are fascinating. It is really a question of how to think about the present. How to experiment with a present which is neither a temporal presence** *(See page 200)*

47. We note that the questions dealt with in this work, that of the portrait, of the image and of the moment, are those that characterize, out of compensation, the schizophrenic rupture of language and time proper to postmodernism, according to Fredric Jameson.

48. Philippe Parreno in Hans Ulrich Obrist, *Interviews*, *op. cit.*, p.334.

49. Philippe Parreno in "Peut-on exister sans produire de récit ?" [Can we exist without producing stories?], interview with Jean-Max Colard, *02*, no.37, Spring 2006, p.16-17.

Shooting of the film **Zidane: A 21st Century Portrait,** Santiago Bernabeu Stadium, Madrid, April 25, 2005

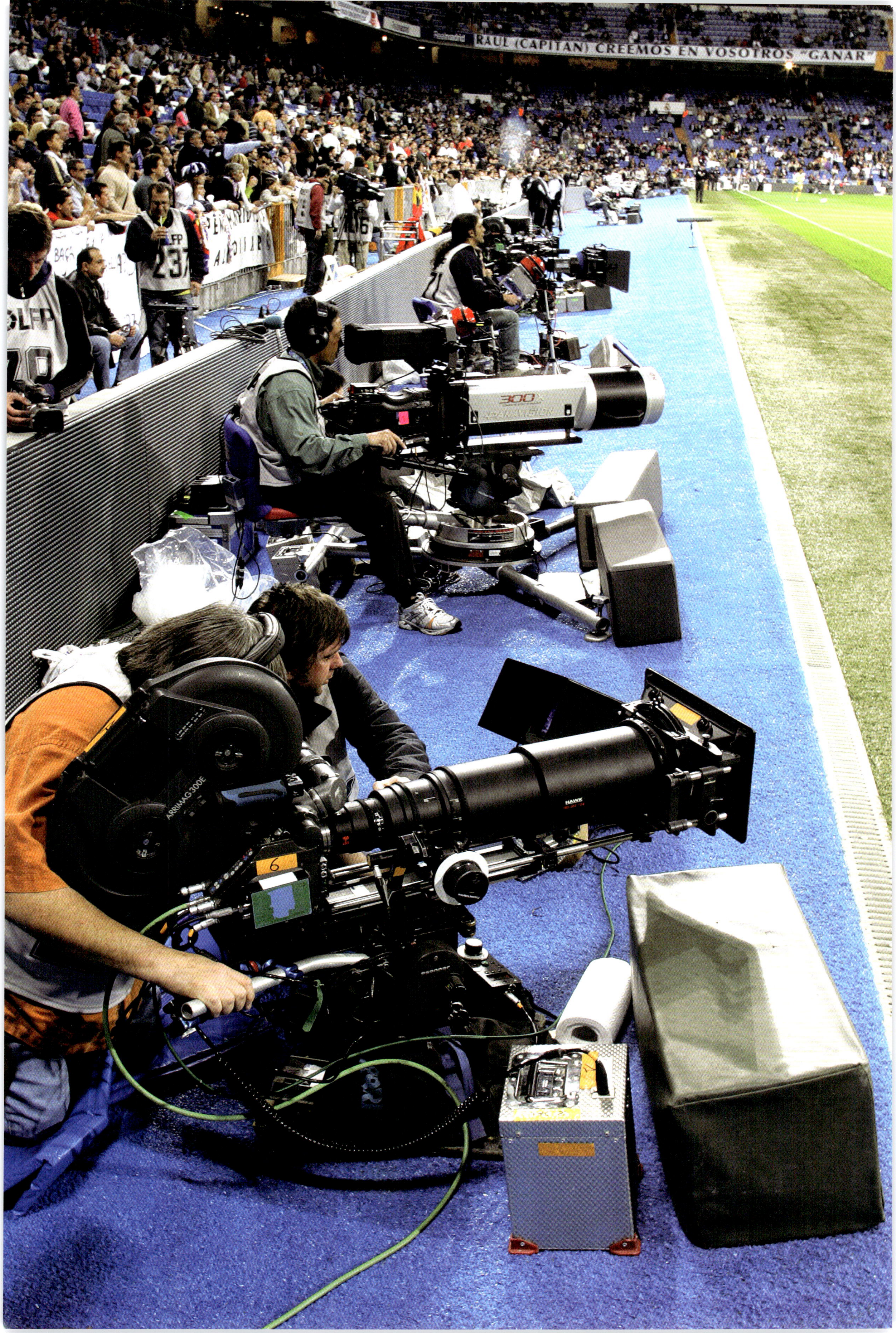
RAUL (CAPITAN) CREEMOS EN VOSOTROS "GANAR"
ARRIMAG300E

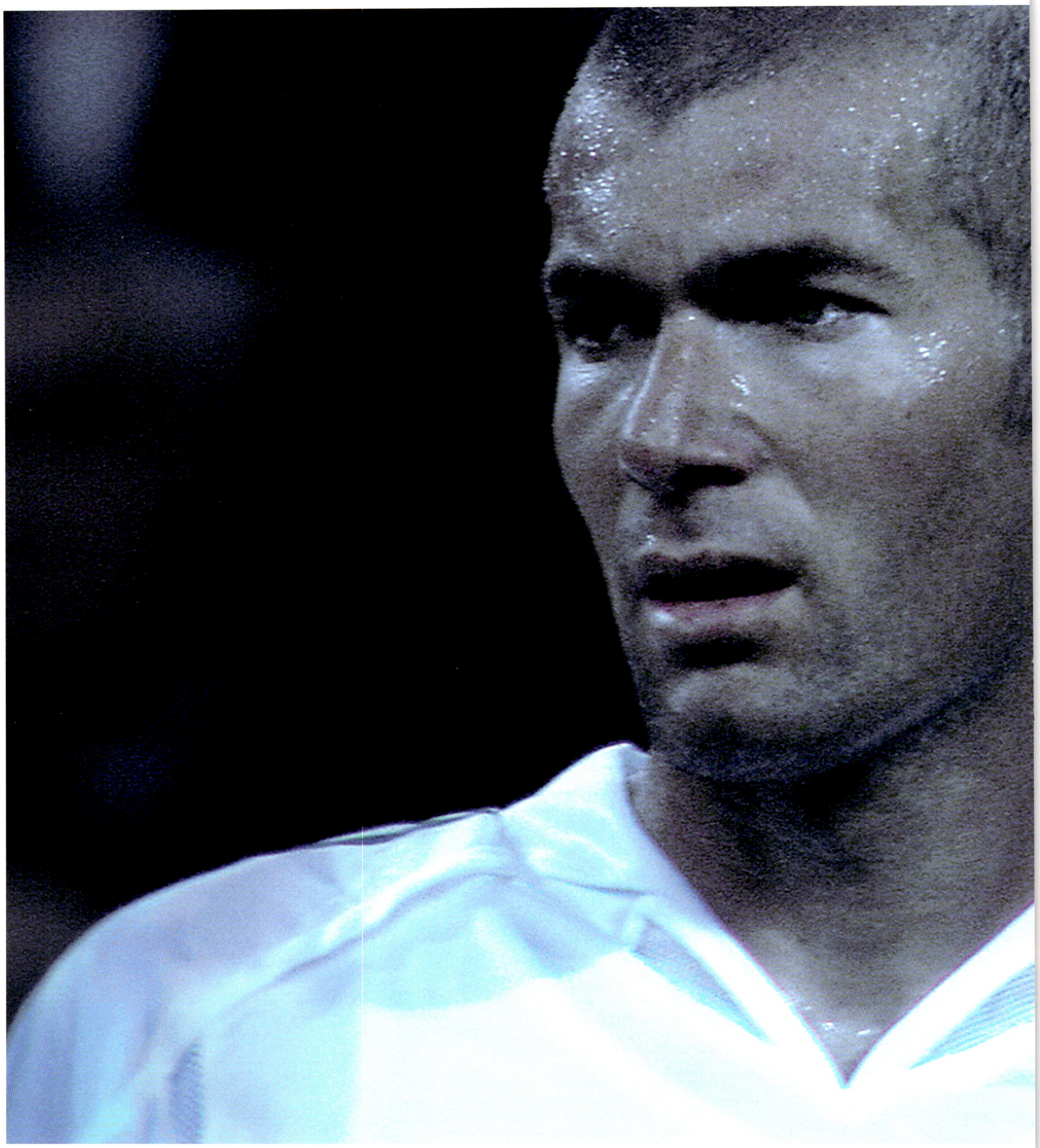

Zidane: A 21st Century Portrait, 2006, with Douglas Gordon, film

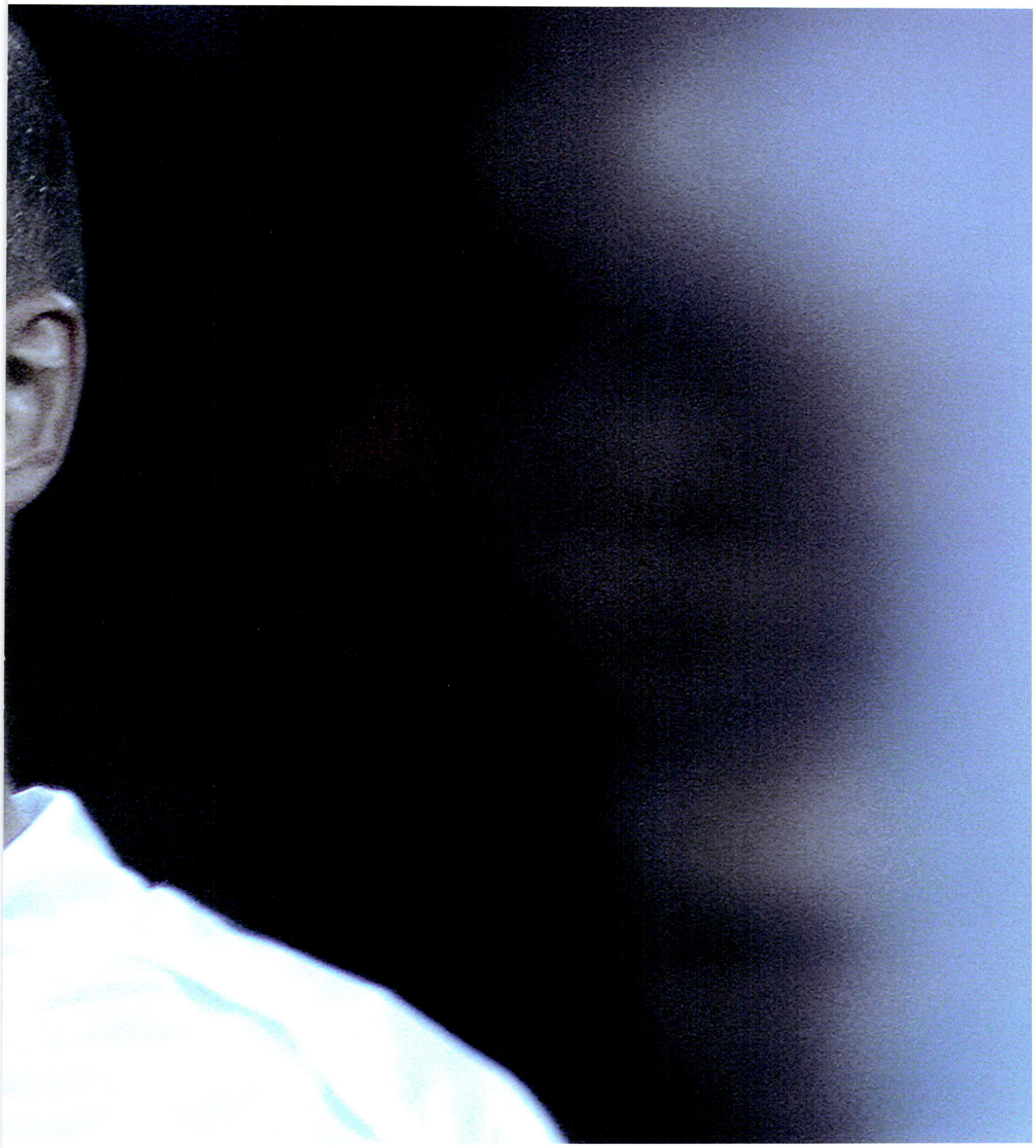

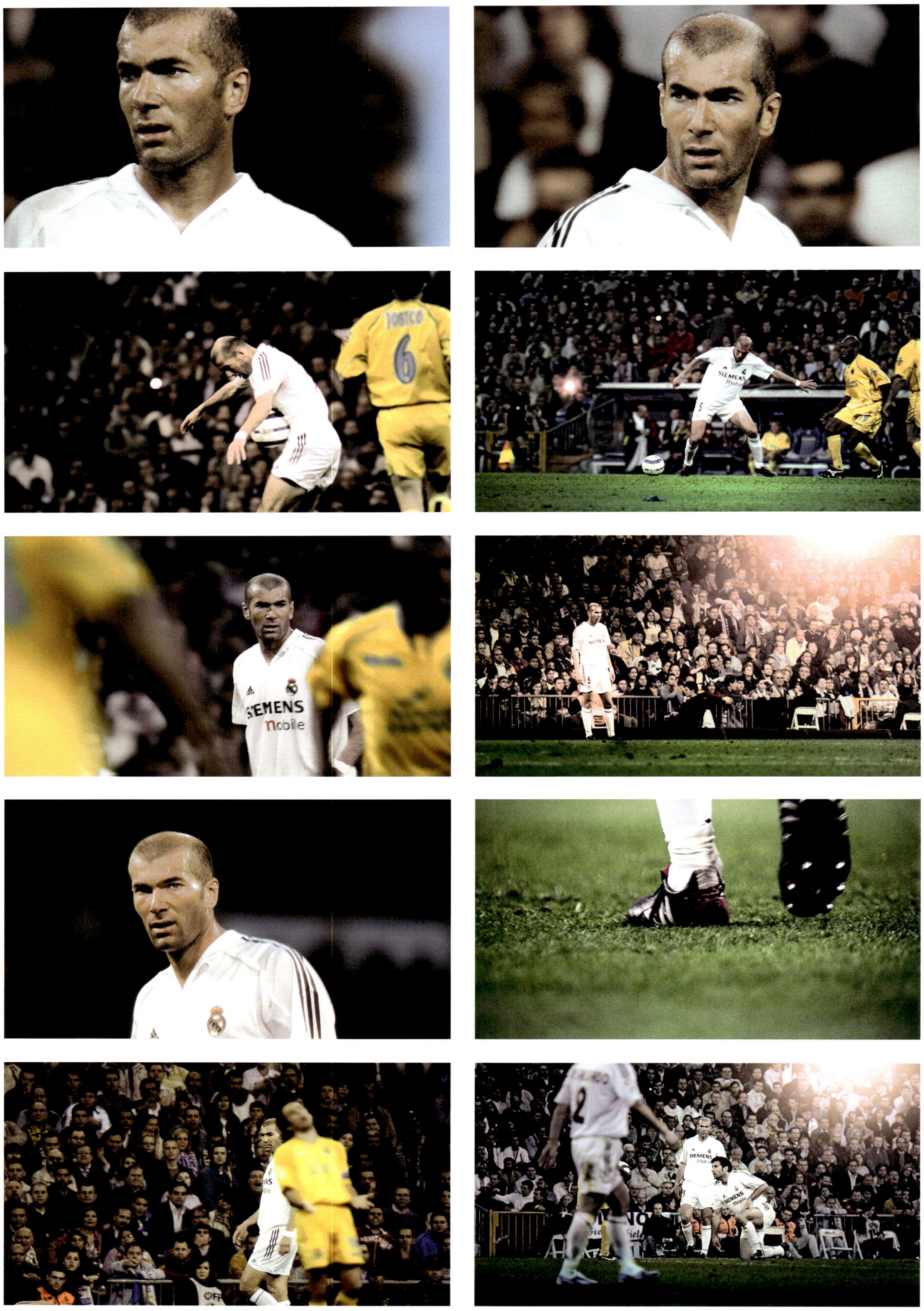

Zidane: A 21st Century Portrait, 2006, with Douglas Gordon, film

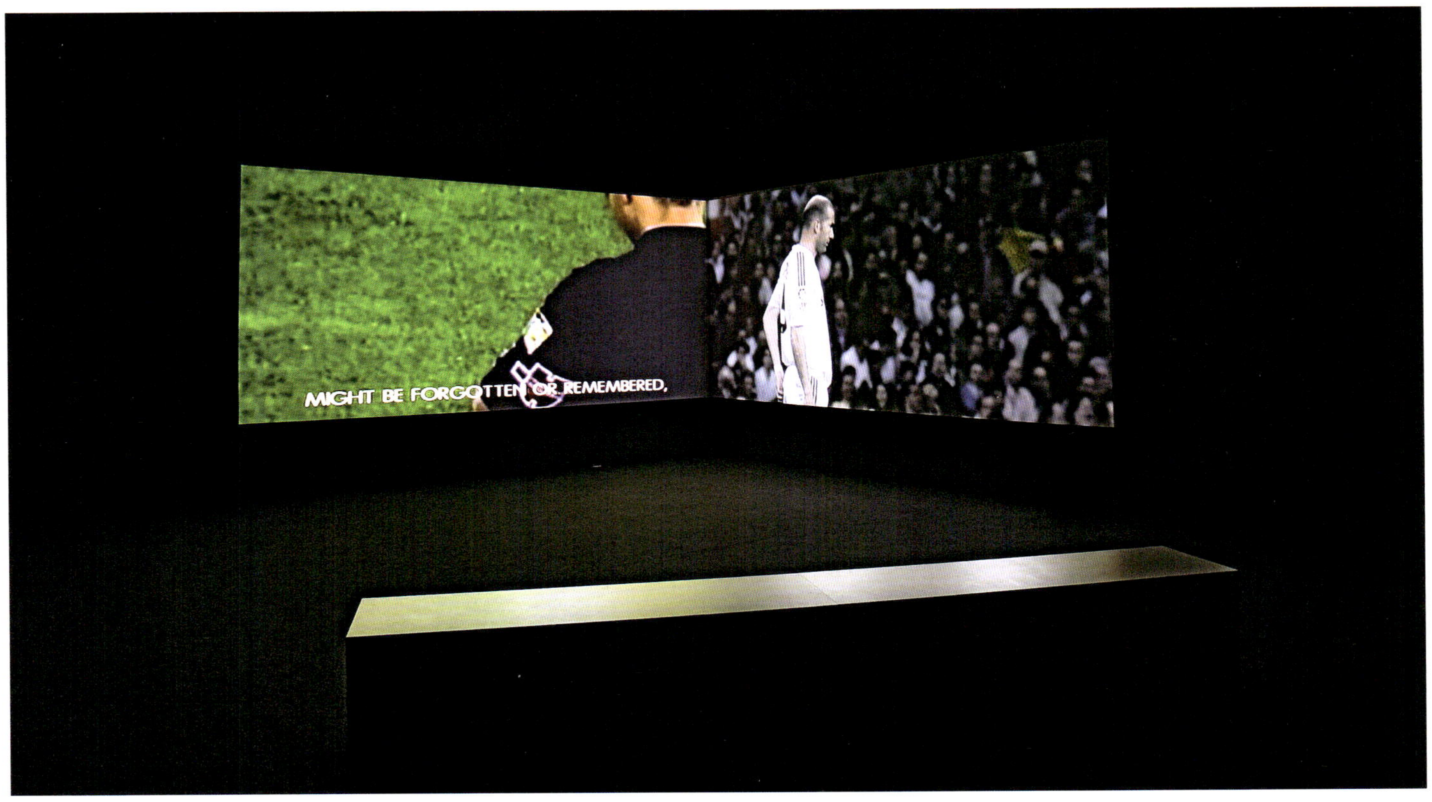

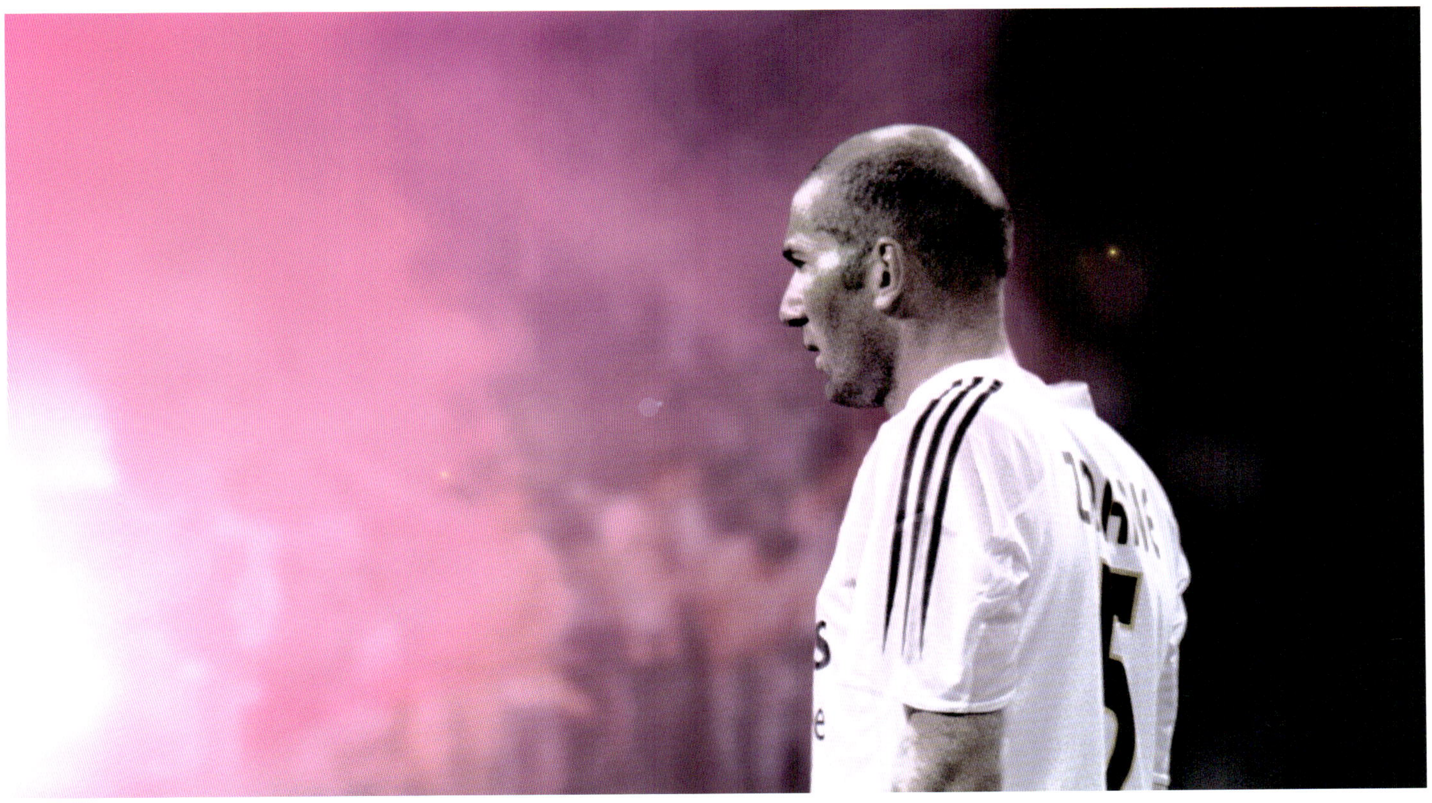

Zidane: A 21st Century Portrait, 2006, with Douglas Gordon, exhibition view, Fondazione Sandretto Re Rebaudengo, Turin, 2007
Zidane: A 21st Century Portrait, 2006, with Douglas Gordon, film

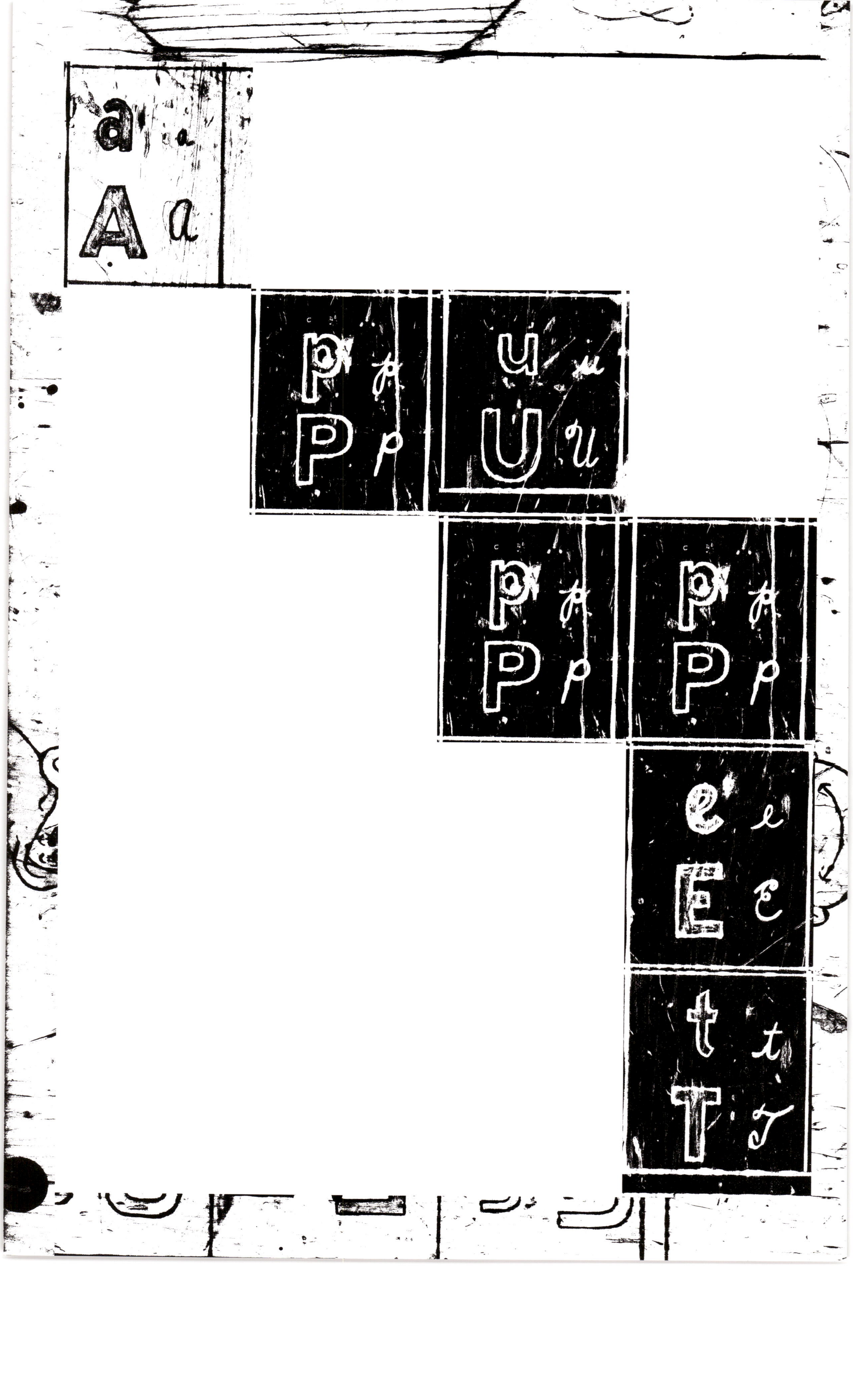
a a
A a
p p
P p
u u
U u
p p
P p
p p
P p
e e
E e
t t
T T

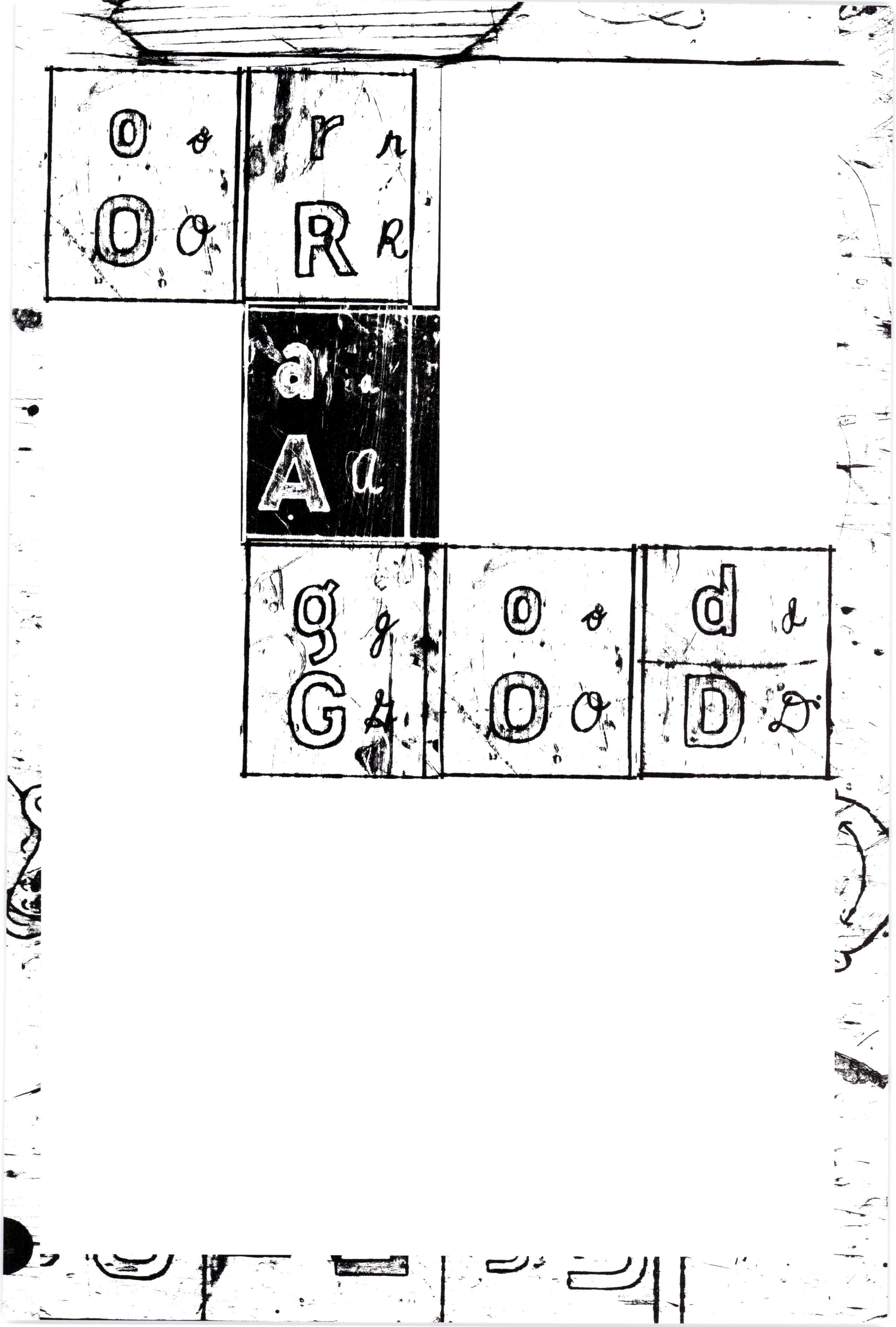

Oo Rr
Aa
Gg Oo Dd

A Puppet or a God? On Philippe Parreno's Films

Simon Critchley

A package arrived from Paris with a handful of DVDs from Philippe. As soon as I saw them I immediately said yes that I would write a text about the films for the book.

One sweaty summer afternoon last July, Philippe came around to my place in Brooklyn. My son Edward, who lives in England, was visiting me at the time and the three of us sat on the sofa drinking beer, watching Zidane and talking about football. I could see him testing Philippe's authenticity when it came to the beautiful game. Philippe talked us through various scenes and I remember looking at Edward's face as he described the way Zidane moved.

There is a strange process of creation in Philippe Parreno's films. Things are not created. Rather, a frame is established which allows something to happen. What interests me is the attention to things in their mineral quality, in their sheer materiality. By focusing intensely on a particular, by following the course of that particular in its randomness with an intense, Cyclops-like, cinematic eye, something necessary comes to pass. There is a happening where the order of intentionality flips around and things are somehow *thinging* irrespective of our will. In the scenario from *The Boy From Mars* (2003) Parreno calls it—with a strong whiff of spontaneist anarchism—"magic, in a process of non-authoritarian creation."

He deliberately points the camera towards things. But the camera is not the subject that inspects objects. On the contrary, it becomes the subject of the object's gaze. Things turn to look at us. In films like *The Boy From Mars*, whose seemingly random beauty recalls the series of oblique images that end Antonioni's *L'Eclisse* (both eclipse and ellipsis), there is a concern with nature in its sheer massive physicality in a way that rubs against the grain of the utter artificiality of the situation, of the fact of art. *The Boy From Mars* is an ode to light, the poetry of cataract-infected water buffalos and extra-terrestrial visitation.

1. Portrait

My focus in this essay will be *Zidane* (2006) because I want to write about football as I watch a lot of it and my only religious commitment is to Liverpool FC. *Zidane* is a meditation on the nature of the image and the endlessly mediated quality of reality. We begin *Zidane* by watching the usual, flat TV images and commentary of the game before being sucked into something else... but let's leave that something else for a moment.

At the most obvious level, *Zidane* is a portrait of the 21st century —which by the way is the movie's subtitle—reality has an utterly mediated quality. It is a world of celebrity and commodity, a world of smooth and shiny surfaces, a hallucinatory reality, nothing more. The 21st century is a portrait. Everything is a portrait. Zidane himself is a portrait, a perfect and magical fetish, a pure commodity that inspires desire, a product with rights owned by Adidas, Siemens or his whole panoply of sponsors. Zidane is a spectacle.

Sure. That's right. Point taken. We are all children of the Situationists and the world is a world of images. Nothing more. No more reality.

But there is more to a portrait than some dumb Situationist thesis about the society of the spectacle. Douglas Gordon—who collaborated on *Zidane* with Parreno—has spoken about the importance of silence and immobility in portraiture. This is crucial, I think. At one level, when we look at a portrait we look for something about ourselves in the image. In the interview he gave to accompany the film, Zidane recognizes this and acknowledges that people watching the film will perhaps be able to feel themselves in his place, *"un petit peu,"* he adds. Such is the nature of the image at the level of identification. This is fine. But there is more.

2. Grace

It's the *petit peu* that counts. The paradox of Zidane as a portrait is that he is constantly in movement and engulfed in the noise of the crowd and the game. And yet, in the firmness, closed-ness and severity of his face we see through the skin, through the image, to something else, what I want to call some truth, some darker truth, even some reality beyond the image. Somehow, in all the cacophonous noise and ceaseless movement of the film, there is a dark kernel of immobility and silence.

The model for this is Velázquez and I take it that *Zidane* is a kind of homage to and reenactment of the famous portrait of Pope Innocent X (Galleria Doria-Pamphili, Rome). As is well known, when the far from innocent looking Pope saw Velázquez's portrait, he said *"troppo vero,"* too true or too much truth. This is echoed in Zidane's remarks on his own image in the movie. First he says that his face looked *"un peu dure, un peu ferme,"* (A bit tough, a bit firm) and then he adds, *"c'était moi quoi ; voilà, c'était moi."* (What can I say? It was me. You see, it was me.)

Zidane is a portrait in a double sense, then. On the one hand, it gives us a sense of the capture of reality by commodified images in the century into which we are slowly slouching our way. But on the other hand, this portrait is true to Zidane in a way that exceeds the sensible content of the image. There is the suggestion, the adumbration of an inaccessible interiority, a reality that resists commodification, an atmosphere, something like Orpheus looking over his shoulder as Eurydice disappears into Hades. In a word, grace.

3. Time

The film begins and returns to the phrase *Un jour extraordinaire*. Of course, Saturday April 23, 2005—the day the movie was shot and the match between Real Madrid and Villareal was played—was a perfectly ordinary day. At half-time, we get a flash sequence of images from the outside world, in a chaotic muddle of the instantly forgotten. All that counts is what takes place in the stadium, on the face of Zidane. This has something to do with abandoning oneself to chance and the flow of time. As Zidane says, he might have been injured after five minutes or sent off at the beginning rather than the end of the match. The fact is that he wasn't. It is the act of submission to the order of time that is crucial. The 90-minutes of the game provide a frame, an order of counting and accounting within which the extraordinary can happen. Zidane keeps looking up at the clock during the match, checking the time. Such is the time of the line, of the frame, of the game. Vulgar clock-time.

But this submission opens another temporal order, a different experience of duration, not the linear flow of 90-minutes, but something else. In abandoning oneself completely to chance, something like necessity begins to appear, even a sense of fate. *Tyche* and *Ananke*, the Greeks understood this. In his commentary on the film, Zidane recalls the moment—it only happened once—when he received the ball and he knew exactly what was going to happen, he knew that everything had been decided. He knew he was going to score before the ball had even touched his foot.

This bifurcation in the order of time is also found in what Zidane says about his memory of a match. You don't really remember a game, he says. It's a series of fractured images that announce a different experience of duration: episodic, random, flickering. Memory flares up and catches hold of an image and sucks out its truth. This is time as ecstasy.

4. Smell/Sound

There are two things that totally escape you when you watch football on TV: smell and sound.

Football is all about smell: the crowd, the acrid piss stink of the toilets, beefy Bovril, cigarette smoke and meat pies. In the late 1950s, in the heyday of 3D cinema, there was an experiment in Scratch-n-Sniff cards that were given to moviegoers in order to intensify their experience. At a given prompt, they would scratch away at the card and sniff fresh mown grass, gunpowder, rotting alien flesh or whatever. I can smell this movie.

But there is also the smell of the earth, the earth that Zidane treats with such delicacy, carefully replacing divots of grass ripped out during play or the persistent light dragging noise of Zidane's foot against the pitch. There is something nostalgic, elegiac about this smell and when I think back to watching games with my Dad when

I was young or crying in the car driving home if Liverpool lost, then what I remember are smells, but most of all the smell of wet earth on the pitch that ascended into the terraces.

The movie is also all about sound. Zidane talks about his experience of sound when he is playing. Of being pulled in and out of the game through noises, of the vast presence of the crowd when you go onto the pitch. He has the most acute sense of hearing during a match. He can hear someone cough or whisper to his neighbor. *"Il y a du son,"* (There is sound) he says, and adds an extraordinary phrase, *"le son du bruit,"* (The sound of noise). In many ways, this movie is about the *il y a* of noise, the sheer being of noise as engulfing. This is what it is to be in a crowd—sensate ecstasy.

5. Image

It is something of a banality to suggest Parreno's work is preoccupied with the nature of the image. Rather, he is obsessed with chains of images, with life as an enchainment of images, with reality as a form of hallucination, a dream. One can sketch a line here, a kind of narrative arc.

It begins with the manifesto-like declaration of *No More Reality* (1991) and the compressed and comically manic meditation on the nature and force of images in *La Nuit des Héros* (1994); it continues with the total commodification of the image in the Manga character, Annlee, in the series *No Ghost Just a Shell*[1]; it ends, for the moment, with *The Writer* (2007) and the mechanically written but unfinished sentence "What do you believe? Your eyes or my words" (the last word is not spelled out). There is a sort of perfection and grace in such imaginary deception. Looking at the machine-marionette of *The Writer*, one is reminded of Kleist's remarks that grace will only appear in bodily form in a puppet or a god, that is, in a being with either no consciousness or infinite consciousness. Perhaps Zidane is both.

1. Of course, Annlee is not only a Manga character. She is a homonym for the enthused young woman, known as Mother Anne (1736-84), from Manchester who brought a select band of persecuted Shakers (more properly, The Church of Believers in Christ) from England to New York in 1774, before setting up communities in upper state New York and Western Massachusetts. Various divine visitations led her to declare celibacy and the imminent second coming of Christ. She was seen by some as the female equivalent of God, the female complement to the divine male principle. But that, as they say, is another story.

6. Atmosphere

Strange as it may sound, Parreno's films are about the happening of an atmosphere, a space of breath where some kind of stillness is possible in the turning world. A calm, an *ataraxia* of sorts is being cultivated here. This is nothing mystical or quasi-Buddhist, it is more Epicurean, it is simply the attempt to track material particulars in their course, to return authority from the author to the contingent massiveness of nature. Anarchic creation.

7. Mediation

Atmosphere is what counts. We only know football through commentary, through hugely inane commentary. There is no immediacy here. The whole experience is completely mediated and mediatized. Zidane recalls when he was a kid commenting on himself playing as he was playing. We all did this. It was as if only an act of ventriloquism and self-distancing could grant you access to what was of utmost importance to your being (recall Bill Shankly, "Football is not a matter of life and death. It's more important than that.") The film gets as close as possible to the immediacy of football mainly because it is made out of sheer love of the game. But we can only get so close. Zidane recalls running and sitting as near to the TV as he could in order to watch French *Téléfoot* and listen to the voice of the commentator, Pierre Cangioni. He says—and this is fascinating—that what attracted him was not the content of Mangioni's words, but the tone, the accent, the atmosphere. It is this atmospherics that Parreno tries to evoke, to draw us into, the evocation of space, a heavenly sphere, the time of breath and vapour. At times, it reminds me of the cinema of Terrence Malick.

8. Heroism

Is Zidane a puppet or a god? I couldn't possibly say. What he has is grace—which means that he could be both. It is the grace of Zidane's movements that astonishes: an utter containment and repose broken by bursts of controlled power.

It is unclear what meaning there is—if any—to heroism in the 21st century. The hero is an icon. We know that. But he is also something more. The true hero is possessed of fragility and solitude. Most of all, and here is where Zidane comes closest to the figure of the hero, he is wedded to self-ruination.

Zidane smiles once, maybe twice, in the movie. The second time is towards the end of the match when he exchanges some casual banter with Roberto Carlos. Real Madrid is winning after being a goal down to a stupid penalty. Zidane created the first goal *ex nihilo* with an extraordinary show of intelligence, power, speed and skill. He seems happy. But it's a menacing smile. Almost a grimace.

Darkness descends, the eyes darken and he seems engulfed in a claustrophobic intensity of doubt and self-loathing. A teammate is fouled badly, but not appallingly, Zidane runs across the pitch and whacks the guy and looks like he is going to hit him again until David Beckham pulls him off. Then some kind of world of pain breaks over Zidane. He is sent off and submits to the law, reluctantly, but he submits nonetheless, like at the end of the 2006 World Cup Final (when most of the civilized world was wishing that he had head-butted Marco Materazzi even harder). Heroism always leads to self-destruction and ruination. As he leaves the pitch, he knows that it is finished. He looks helpless. As Kleist says in the final words of his essay on the puppet theatre, "This is the final chapter in the history of the world."

9. Moths

Moths fly transfixed in the stadium floodlight. Indifferent to human display, they seem to support neither Villareal nor Real Madrid. They seek only their destruction in a tiny blaze of heat and light.

10. Reality

No more reality? Not really. Parreno is seeking a reality in relation to the world of images and shiny surfaces that we endure—from the spectacle world that fascinates and bores us, to the sheer being of things, to a kind of truth. His films are experiments in reversed intentionality, where we submit ourselves to the order of real time, to the law of chance, and through such submission something breaks through, something begins to happen, something necessary through that break with the random order of real time.

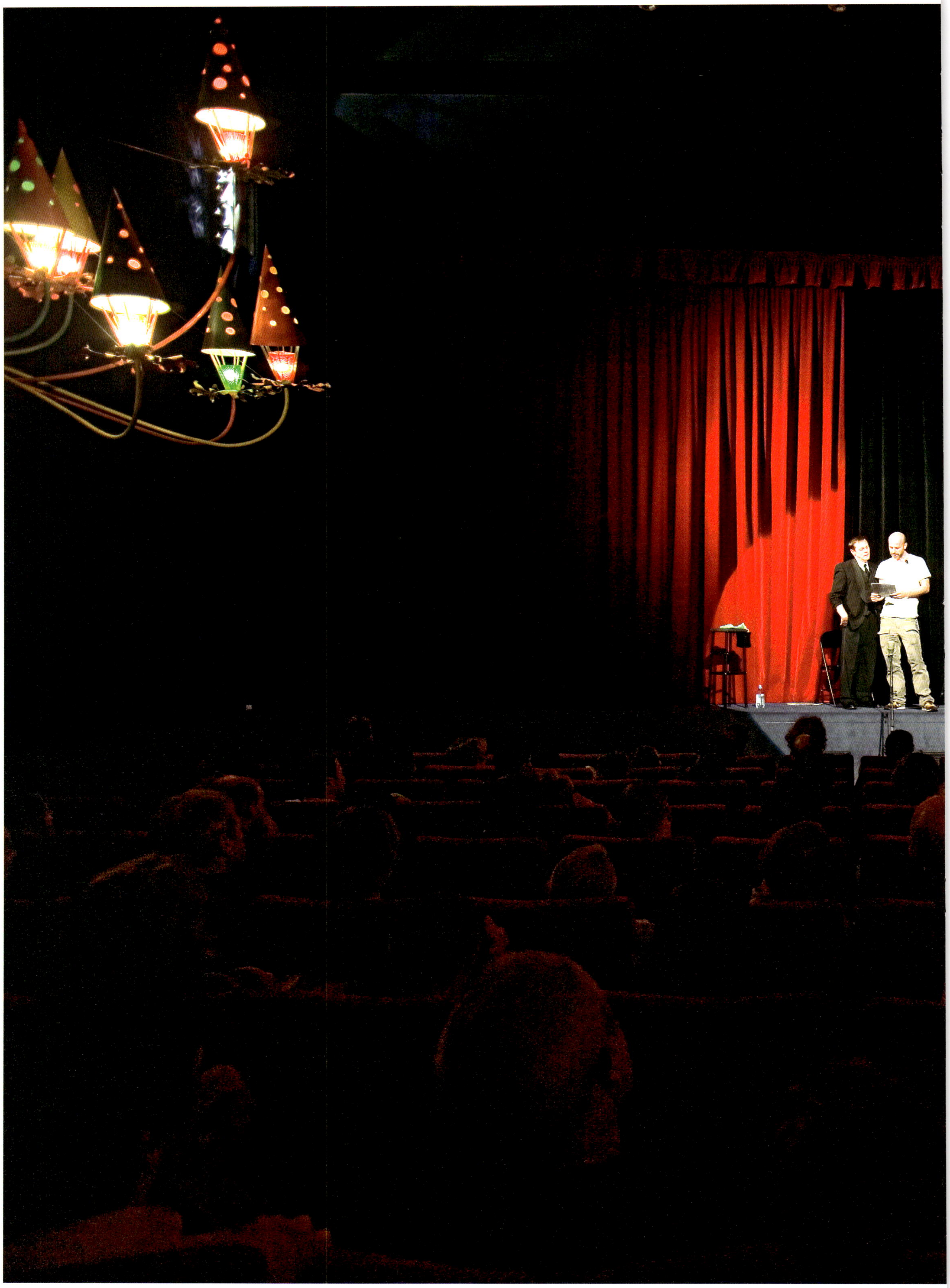

The Ultrasonic Scream of the Squirrel, Studio 28, Paris, September 18, 2006

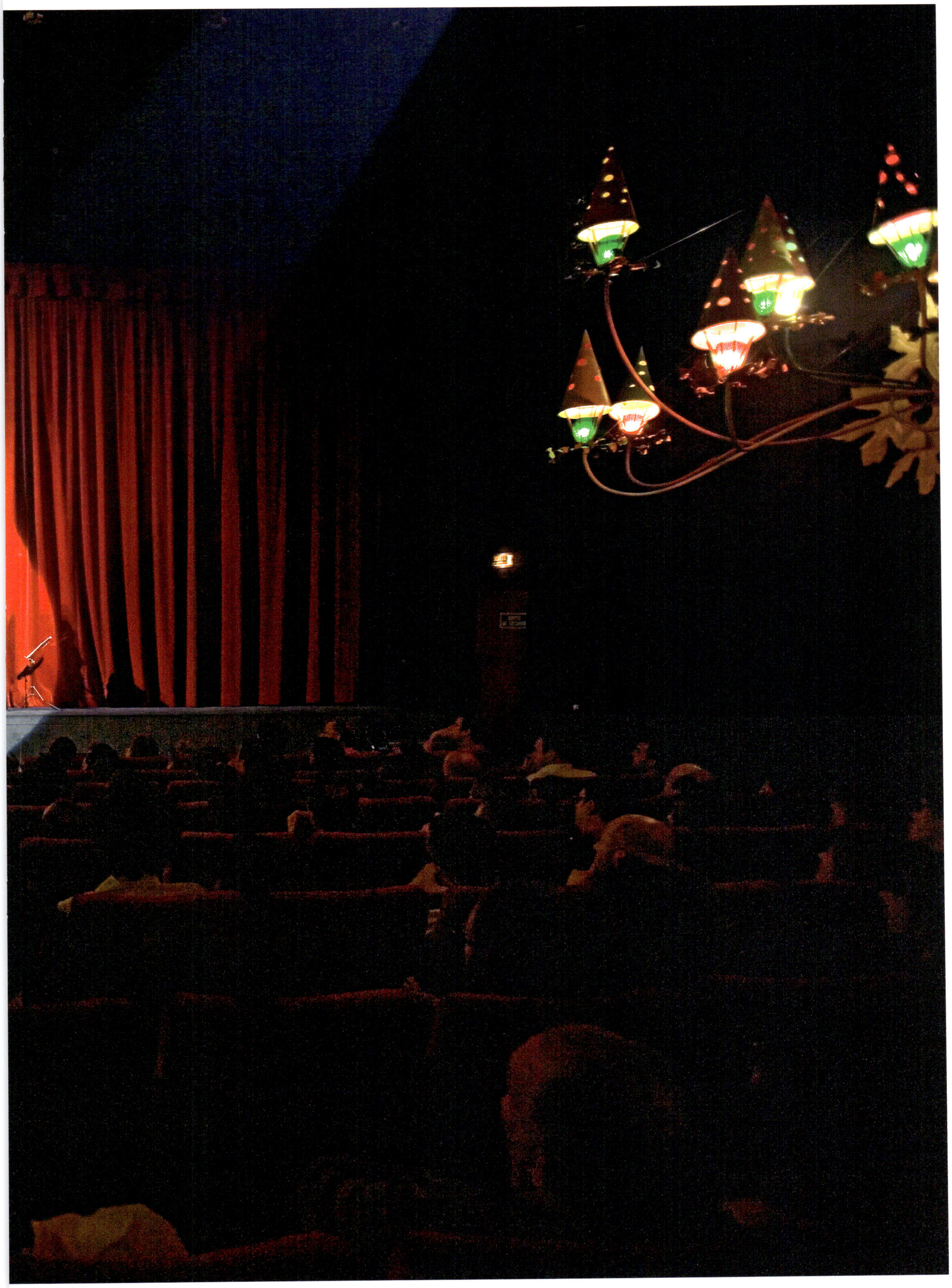

(Continued from page 184) **nor a virtual point on a temporal line, a point which has no other existence apart from a mathematical one, ... The present comes from the future and goes back to the past. ... The act is diluted with time as it is constantly updated."[50] ◊ *Zidane* also reflects Parreno's interest in portraiture, which can be seen in his work as early as the Anna Sanders and Annlee projects. The question of subjectivity haunts this 21st century portrait. Parreno believes that for his generation—coined by Douglas Coupland "Generation X"—the relationship to the present is problematic because it is "very melancholic and mediated."[51] Zidane is the "model fashioned by the artists" whose thoughts on how to create a portrait of this subject were influenced by Velázquez's painting of *Pope Innocent X*. Zidane emerges as a subject without a story, seems to be elusive and mutable, thereby becoming the perfect contemporary model. "How to look at a single face for 90 minutes? It is very Beckettian... This idea of a character with the persistent and dissatisfied desire for the ultimate story comes from Beckett,"[52] explains Parreno. The work was shown at the Cannes Festival, in a stadium at the Art Basel fair, and in movie theaters (both in France and in other countries). It was nominated for the César award in the Documentary film category as well as presented as an installation in art spaces and commercially distributed on DVD. ◊ *Zidane* has been commented on by Cyril Neyrat,[53] Simon Critchley and Michael Fried.[54] Fried writes that *Zidane* is part of a long tradition of portraiture in contemporary culture, and is moreover a remarkable film in its formal innovation and its engagement in the sphere of mass media.[55]**

50. Philippe Parreno, "Sitcom Ghost," in the exhibition catalogue *A Retrospective (Tomorrow is Another Fine Day)*, *op. cit.*, p.107.

51. Philippe Parreno, Hans Ulrich Obrist, *The Conversation Series*, *op.cit.*, p.46.

52. *Ibid.*, p.120.

53. Cyril Neyrat, "Rêverie d'un solitaire" [Dreams of a Solitary Person], *Cahiers du cinéma*, no.613, June 2006, p.29-30.

54. Michael Fried, "Absorbed in the Action," *Artforum*, no.1, September 2006, p.332-335.

55. See also "How Can You Look at One Face for 90 Minutes?" Conversation with Douglas Gordon about Zidane: A 21st Century Portrait, Paris, 2005-2006," Philippe Parreno, Hans Ulrich Obrist, *The Conversation Series*, *op. cit.*, p.111-120.

The Ultrasonic Scream of the Squirrel, 2006 ◁ Performance with the ventriloquist Ronn Lucas, 60' approx.; production: Air de Paris ‡ 18 September, 2006, at Studio 28, Paris, France § Courtesy of the artist and Air de Paris, Paris ♦ **The Ultrasonic Scream of the Squirrel, 2006** ◁ Installation: ¬ digital print on aluminum mounted beneath Plexiglas (120 × 180 cm) • LCD TFT screen • video on DVD (color, sound, 6'04") ‡ "Le cri ultrasonic de l'écureuil," January 27–March 21, 2007, Air de Paris Gallery, Paris, France || 5 editions and 2 artist editions ∫ First public collection: Frac Nord-Pas-de-Calais, Dunkirk, France (3/5) § Courtesy Air de Paris, Paris; Friedrich Petzel, New York; Esther Schipper, Berlin **Instead of an exhibition, Parreno creates his first staged performance with the ventriloquist Ronn Lucas entitled *The Ultrasonic Scream of the Squirrel*. In this commentary on collaboration and polyphony, the artist becomes a body emptied of speech, similar to the empty shell of Annlee. The exhibition becomes a performance where a body is deprived of its reality and communicates through a borrowed voice.**

Interior Cartoons Animation, 2006 ◁ Installation: "animated" exhibition space with 2 electric curtains, 2 large format aluminum frames enclosing vinyl plates, 2 door handles, 6 perfume diffusers (dust, vinyl, coffee, rain, grass, trees), ventilator, dimmer switch,

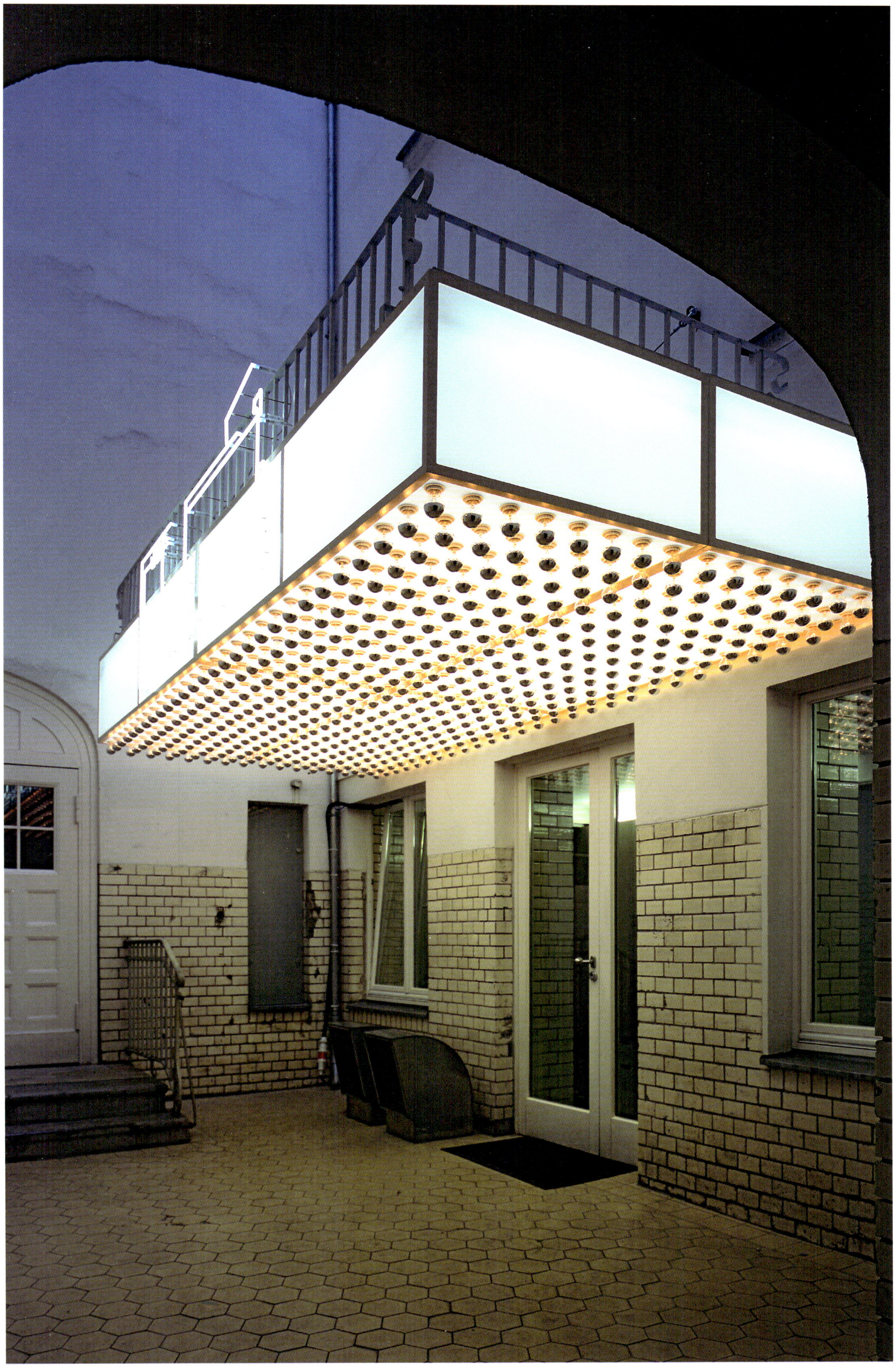

Marquee, 2006, exhibition view "Interior Cartoons", Esther Schipper, Berlin, 2006

Untitled, 2007, exhibition view “Interior Cartoons”, Esther Schipper, Berlin, 2007

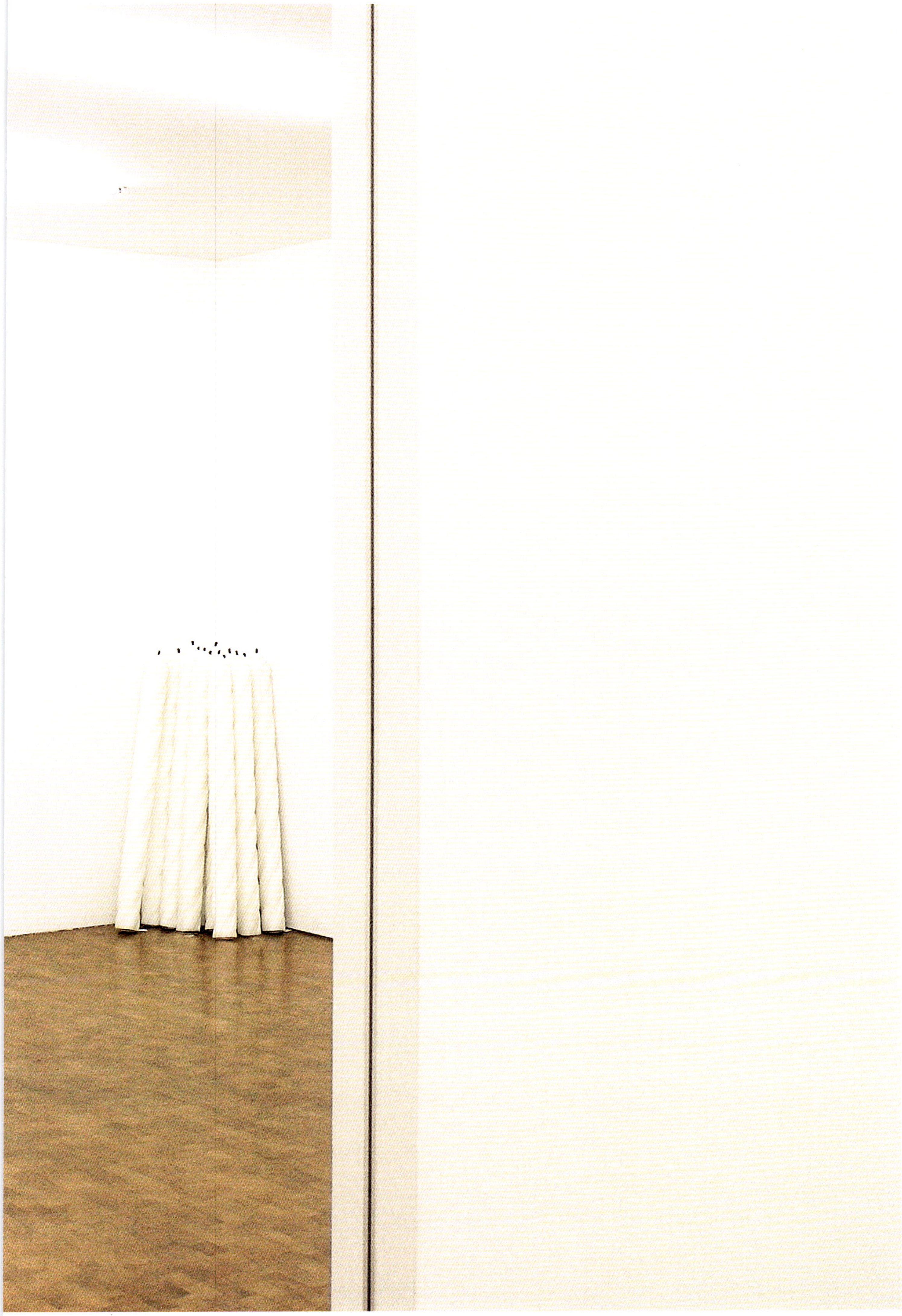

DMX control box, electrical system; variable dimensions ‡ "Interior Cartoons," September 30–October 28, 2006, Esther Schipper, Berlin, Germany || 1 edition § Courtesy Esther Schipper, Berlin
This installation, which humorously references interior design, responds to the gallery's desire to open up its space, which is traditionally otherwise inward looking. Parreno surrounded the windows with large aluminum frames outlined in pale white vinyl visually reminiscent of comic strip frames. In front of the windows, curtains equipped with electrical motors flutter, giving the impression that the space is breathing. When the curtains are down, special systems hidden behind the walls emit the smell of coffee, vinyl and dust. When the curtains are raised, the windows emit the smell of grass, rain and trees. The gallery lighting is timed to correspond to these emissions. The entire installation is automated by a DMX control box and synchronized with a *Marquee*, which hangs outside the gallery.

Marquee. Other title: Marquee (Esther Schipper Plans), 2006
◁ Anodized steel, aluminum, macralon, 448 reflecting light bulbs, (type E27, 40W), 28 fluorescent neon tubes (50 W), DMX control box, electrical system; 435 × 200 × 56 cm; (043) ‡ "Interior Cartoons," September 30–October 28, 2006, Esther Schipper Gallery, Berlin, Germany || 1 edition ∫ Private collection, Ostende, Belgium
The first *Marquee* by Parreno was made for "Interior Cartoons Animation." Inspired by the marquees which hang over the entrances to American movie theaters that advertise film titles and the names of the stars against a luminous background, this *Marquee* was hung in a small courtyard above the gallery's entrance. Instead of the name of a film, the gallery's floor plan is illuminated in neon. Parreno's marquee co-opts the language of film promotion and transforms the marquee into a signifier of space and time. In the continuation of the meaning of the trailer which is a promise of time to come, the marquee is scaffolding on which dreams are promised. At Arc in 2002, the marquee is an art object and a signifier of the self-reflective announcement of an exhibition.

Welcome to Reality Park (From the Other Side), 2003–2006
◁ Framed color C-print; 123.6 × 145.3 × 4.5 cm ‡ October 26–30, 2006, Air de Paris Gallery booth, Fiac, Paris, France || 5 editions and 2 artist editions ‡ Courtesy Air de Paris, Paris; Esther Schipper, Berlin; Friedrich Petzel Gallery, New York

. all hawaii eNtrées/LuNar reGGae, 2006 ◁ Exhibition curated with Rachael Thomas ¬ Invited artists: Doug Aitken, Bas Jan Ader, Carlos Congost, Keren Cytter, Thomas Demand, Cory Doctorrow, Peter Fischli et David Weiss, Liam Gillick, Dominique Gonzalez-Foerster, Douglas Gordon, Carsten Höller, Jim Lambie, Sarah Lucas, Sarah Morris, Grant Morrisson, Jorge Pardo, Philippe Parreno, Paola Pivi, Eva Rotschild, Anri Sala, Rirkrit Tiravanija, Kurt Vonnegut, Cerith Wyn Evans ‡ November 30, 2006–February 19, 2007, Irish Museum of Modern Art, Dublin, Ireland (exhib. cat.)

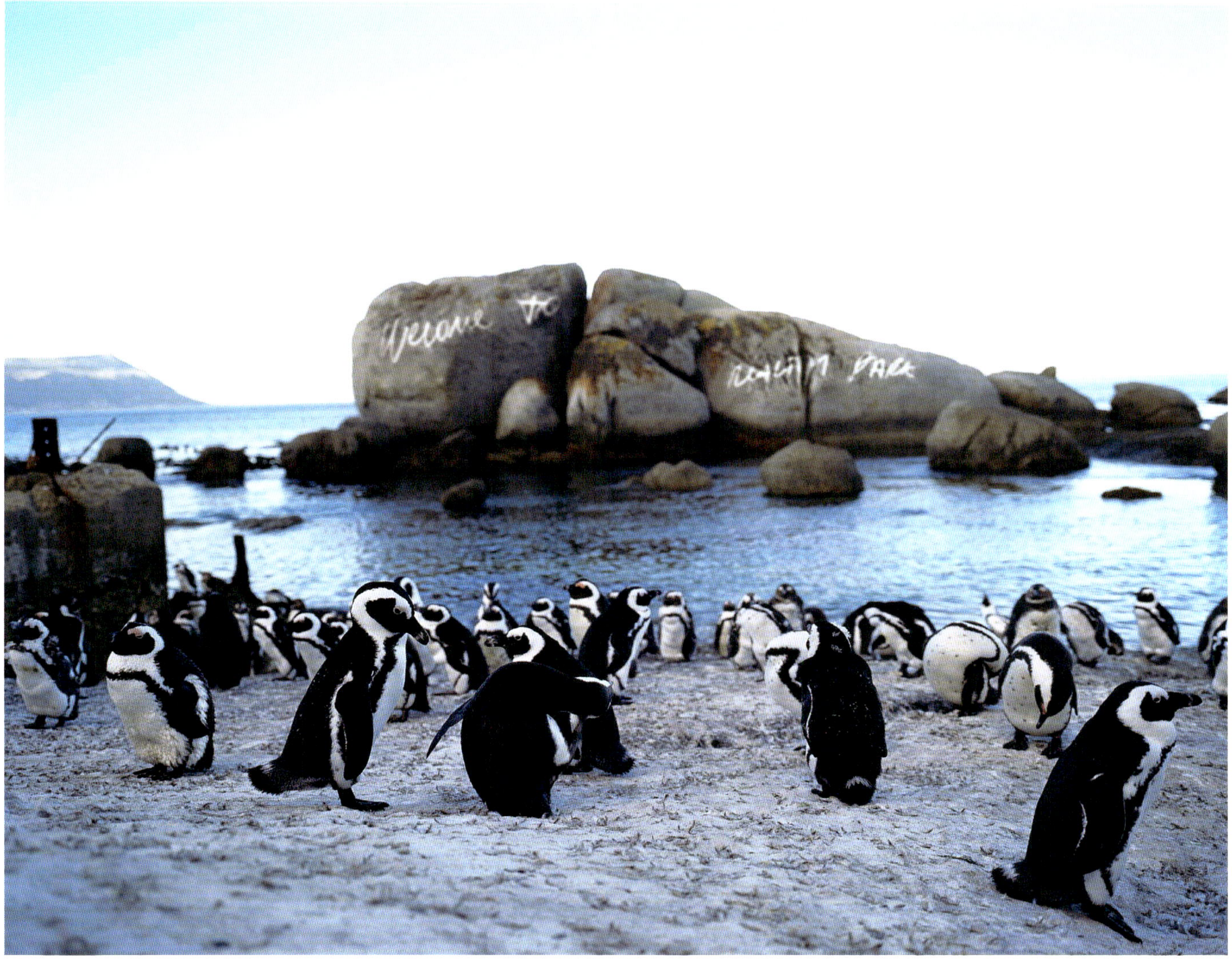

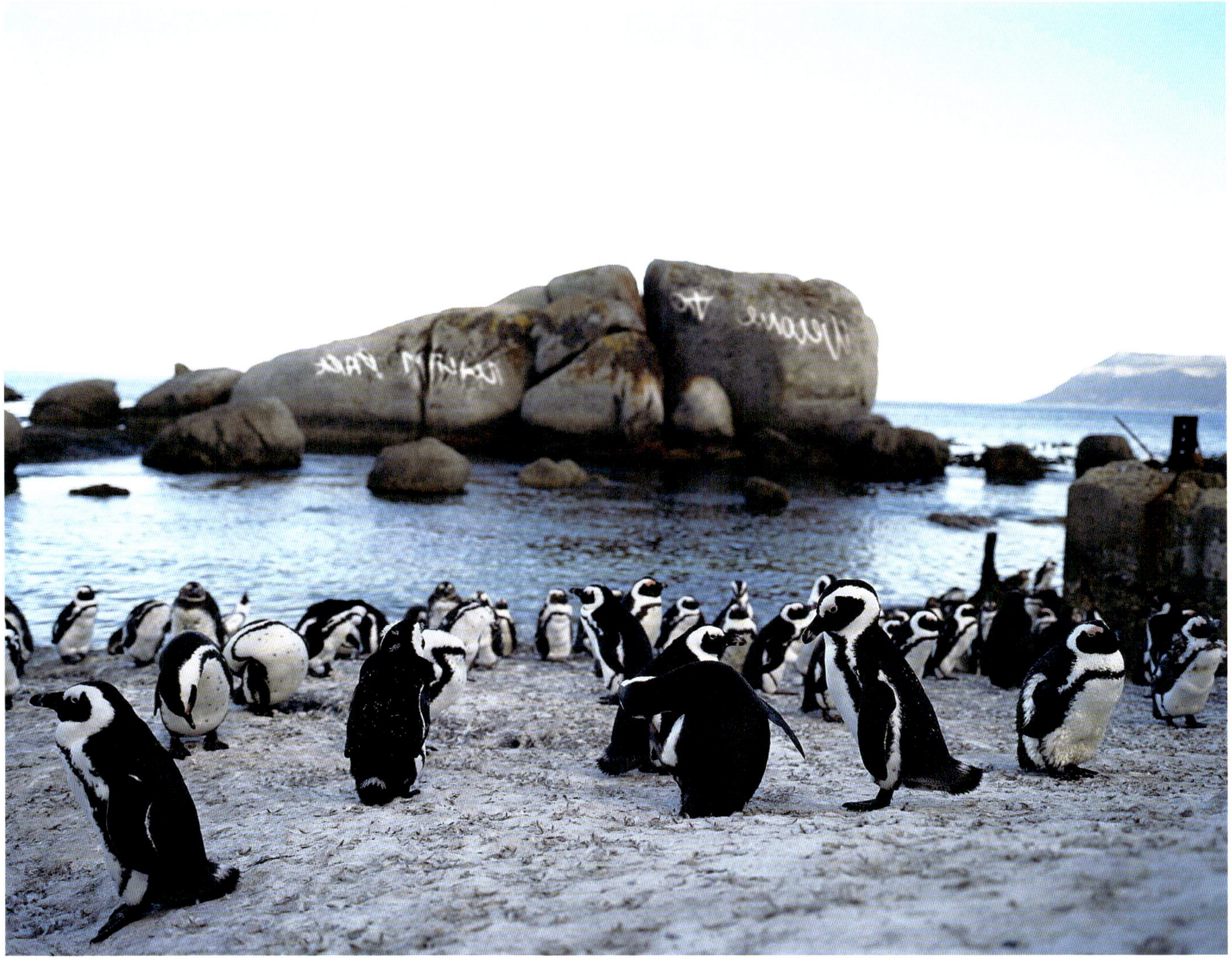

Welcome to Reality Park, 2003-2005; Welcome to Reality Park (From the Other Side), 2003-2006

♦ **Nail Sewer Legs, 2006** With Liam Gillick ◁ White plastic letters; variable dimensions ‡ ". all hawaii eNtrées/LuNar reGGae," November 30, 2006–February 19, 2007, Irish Museum of Modern Art, Dublin, Ireland || 1 edition ʃ IMMA collection, Dublin, Ireland ♦ **Nail Sewer Legs, 2006** With Liam Gillick ◁ White plastic letters; variable dimensions || 25 editions ʃ First private collection: Private collection, Dublin, Ireland § Courtesy Irish Museum of Modern Art, Dublin, Ireland ♦ **All Hawaii Entrées/Lunar Reggae, 2006** ◁ Blurred exhibition catalogue: 224 pages, 28.7 × 24.6 cm, color, hard back; Dublin: Irish Museum of Modern Art Publications, 2006 ‡ ". all hawaii eNtrées/LuNar reGGae," November 30, 2006–February 19, 2007, Irish Museum of Modern Art, Dublin, Ireland ***Nail Sewer Legs*** **made with Gillick refers to the exhibition title, which is an anagram in Gaelic and English for "new galleries." In an attempt to "readjust the gaze,"** ***All Hawaii Entrées/Lunar Reggae*** **questions the conventions of the exhibition, through collaborative practices. Inspired by a remark by Michael Faraday —the author of** ***The Chemical History of a Candle*** **(1861) which was quoted by David** ***Deutsch in The Fabric of Reality*** **(1997): "There are no more open doors by which to enter into the study of the philosophy of nature apart from the physical phenomenon of the candle"— Parreno explores the question of light as an entity in itself, which alters what we see and obscures what we do not see. Höller's** ***7.8 Hz*** **(2006) interferes with the exhibition's lighting by changing the frequency of the electric current to obtain a flickering effect. The catalogue, as important as the exhibition itself, is printed entirely out of focus from the cover to the bar code. The book includes texts by Gillick, Parreno and others, a comic-strip by Grant Morrison, and stories by Cory Doctorow and Kurt Vonnegut.**

Penguin Crossing, 2006 ◁ Reflecting vinyl on aluminum; diam.: 95.25 cm ‡ December 7–10, 2006, 1301PE booth, Art Basel Miami Beach, Miami, United States || 7 editions ʃ First private collection: private collection, Chicago, United States ‡ Courtesy 1301PE, Los Angeles; Air de Paris, Paris; Friedrich Petzel, New York; Esther Schipper, Berlin

Teranésie, Pudong, Hyperion, 2007 ◁ Installation: three blue signposts variable dimensions ‡ "Expérience Pommery #4. L'emprise du lieu," March 29th–November 1st 2007, Pommery domain, Reims, France; exhibition curator: Daniel Buren || 1 edition § Courtesy of the artist and Air de Paris, Paris

Speaking to the Penguins, 2007 ◁ Color silver print, aluminum under Plexiglas; 150 × 227 cm ‡ "What Do You Believe, Your Eyes or My Words?," April 5–May 12, 2007, Haunch of Venison Gallery, London, United Kingdom || 5 editions and 1 artist edition ʃ First private collection: private collection, Monaco (1/5) ‡ Courtesy Air de Paris, Paris; Friedrich Petzel, New York; Esther Schipper, Berlin, Pilar Corrias Inc., London

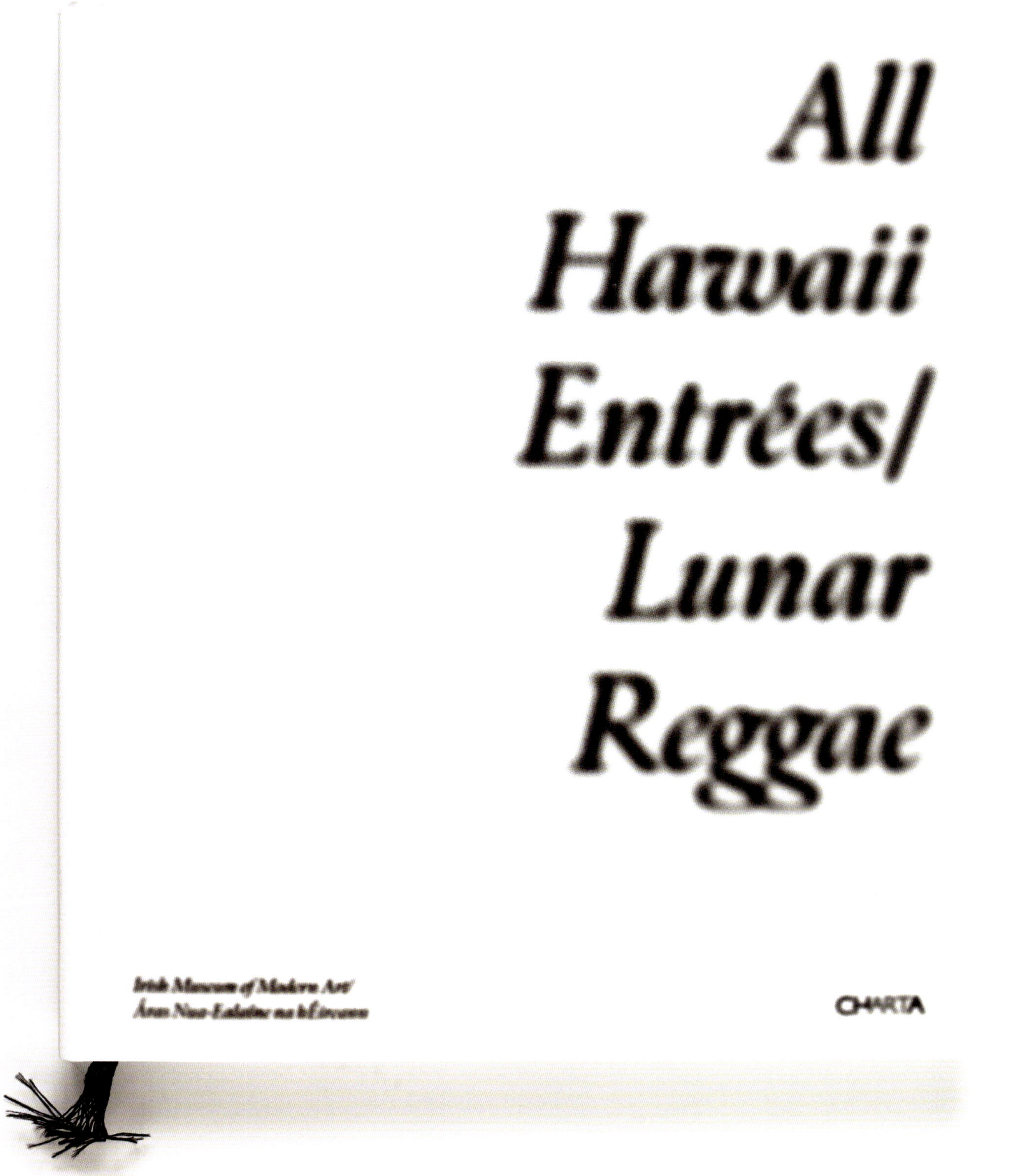

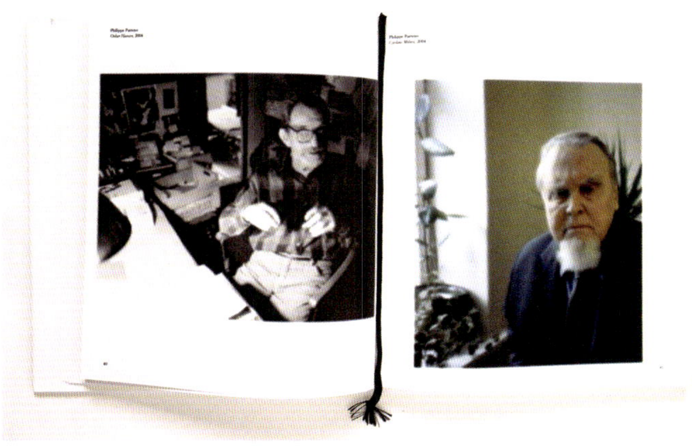

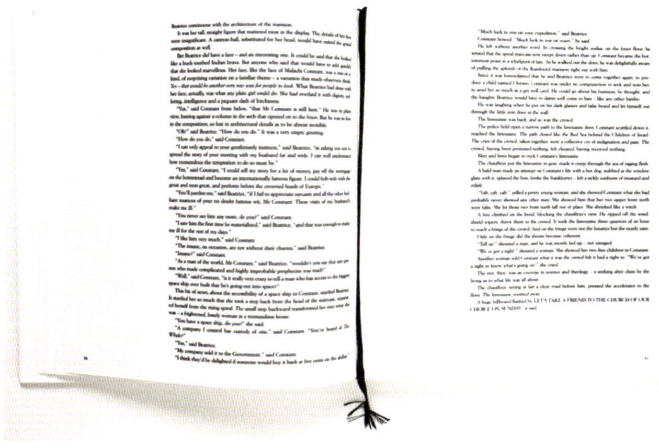

.all hawaii eNtrées / LuNar reGGae, 2006 Charta

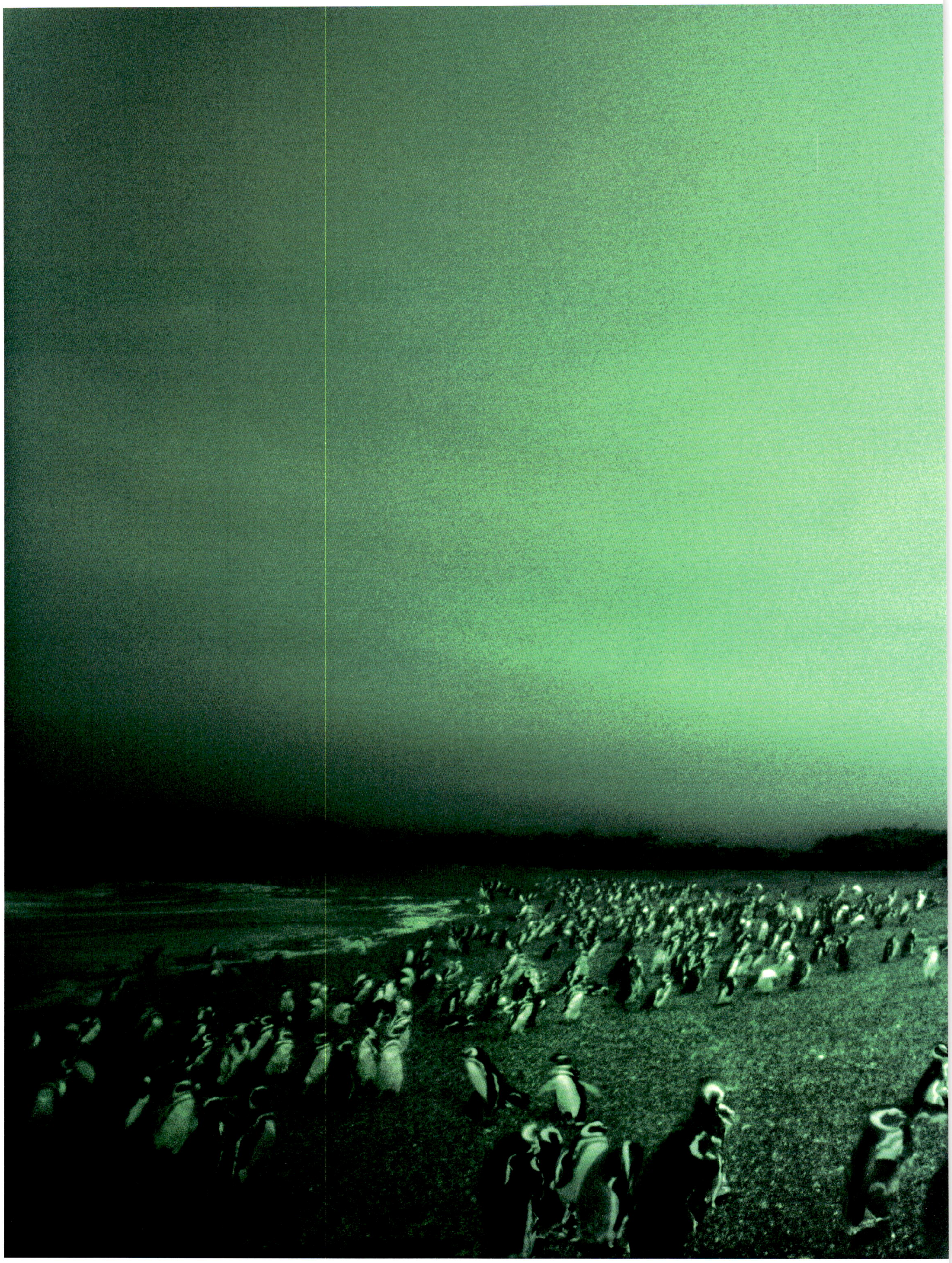

Speaking to the Penguins, 2007

This photograph document a performance during which Parreno spoke to penguins at night on a beach in Patagonia. In opposition to the tradition of painting from life, this piece is about speaking *to* life. ◊ Parreno read to the penguins "After Affects,"[56] a series of texts he had written for the Italian architecture magazine *Domus,* exploring man's relationship to nature and urban landscapes in contemporary society. Penguins, like humans, are social animals in constant communication with each other and live in large groups. We as humans project that penguins have the same theories and social conventions about the reality of their concerns with nature, urban sprawl and global warming.

56. Philippe Parreno, "After Affects," text published in several instalments in *Domus*, from no.866, January 2004, and reproduced in the exhibition catalogue *All Hawaii Entrées/Lunar Reggae*, Milan, Charta, 2006.

The Writer, 2007 ◊ Installation: LCD 7 inch screen, 17.4 × 12 × 2 cm, digital video on DVD, color, sound, 3'58" ‡ "What Do You Believe, Your Eyes or My Words?," April 5–May 12, 2007, Haunch of Venison Gallery, London, United Kingdom || 3 editions and 3 artist editions ʃ First private collection: Fondation Louis Vuitton pour la création, Paris (1/3) ♦ **Untitled (What Do You Believe, Your Eyes or My Words?), 2007** ◊ Color silver print, cardboard, passe-partout frame, wood and glass (frame); 68 × 86 cm ‡ "What Do You Believe, Your Eyes or My Words?," April 5–May 12, 2007, Haunch of Venison Gallery, London, United Kingdom || 10 editions ʃ First private collection: private collection, United Kingdom (2/10) § Courtesy Air de Paris, Paris; Friedrich Petzel, New York; Esther Schipper, Berlin, Pilar Corrias Inc., London ♦ **Untitled (What Do You Believe, Your Eyes or My Words?), 2007** ◊ Black and white print on drawing paper, 315 g; 150 × 255 cm || 5 editions and 1 artist edition ʃ First private collection: private collection, Milan, Italy (1/5) § Courtesy Air de Paris, Paris; Friedrich Petzel, New York; Esther Schipper, Berlin, Pilar Corrias Inc., London **In this four-minute film presented on a plasma screen, a Jacquet-Droz automaton from the musée d'Art et d'Histoire in Neuchâtel, made in 1772, slowly writes "What Do You Believe, Your Eyes or My Words?" on a white card with a feather pen. Beginning with a close up shot of the hand, before progressively backing up, the film ends before the automaton has time to answer the question and fully reveal the automatic nature of its answer. The sentence, which raises the question of trust between two individuals, is never answered, as if reality can never be fully put into words, but remains full of white spaces, breaks and even failures. ◊ In addition Parreno made two other works which included the same sentence—one a color photograph and the other a black and white print.**

Speech Bubbles, 2007 ◊ Installation: Black Mylar balloons, helium; variable dimensions ‡ "What Do You Believe, Your Eyes or My Words?," April 5–May 12, 2007, Haunch of Venison Gallery, London, UK || 1 edition ʃ Fondation Louis Vuitton pour la création collection, Paris, France

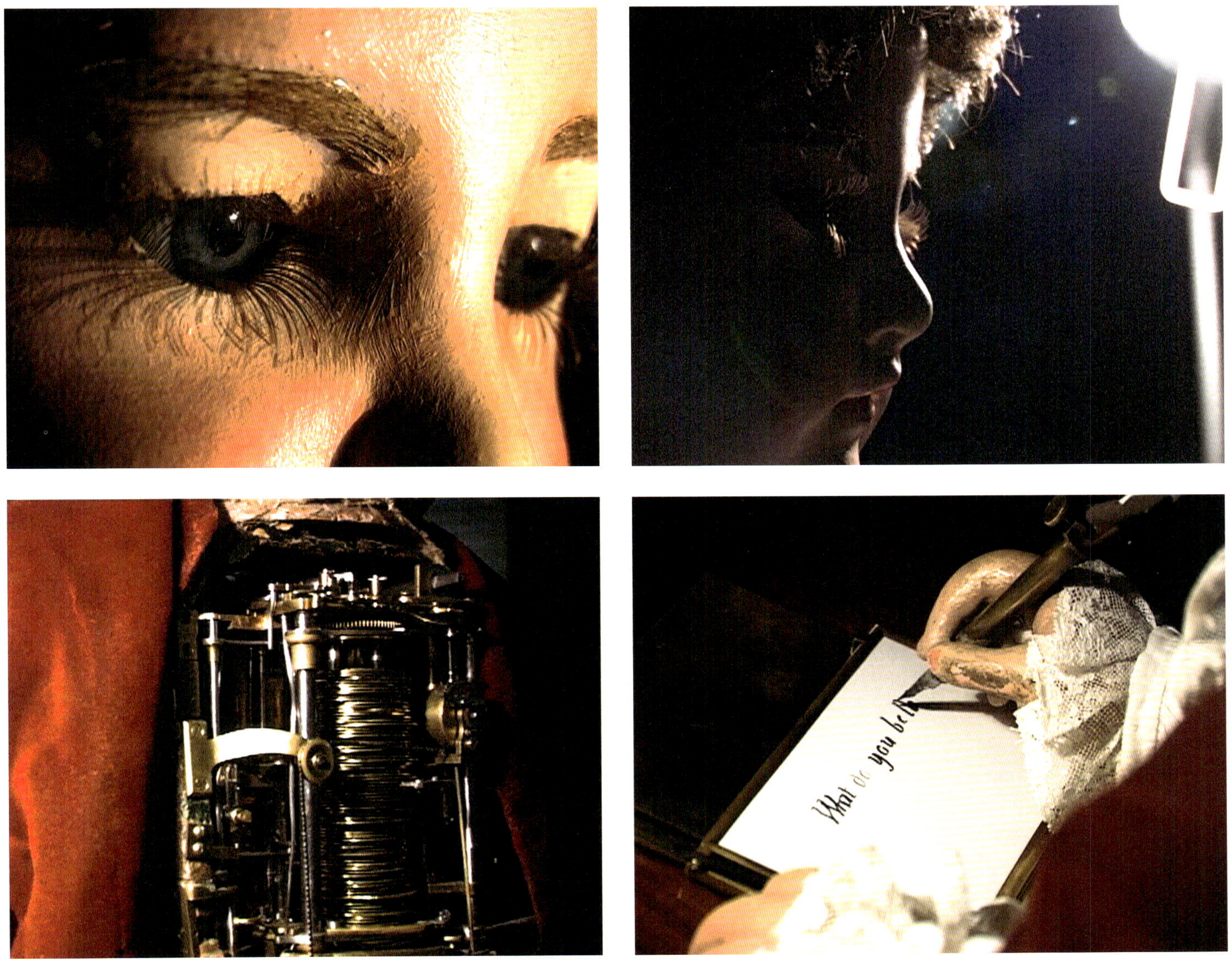

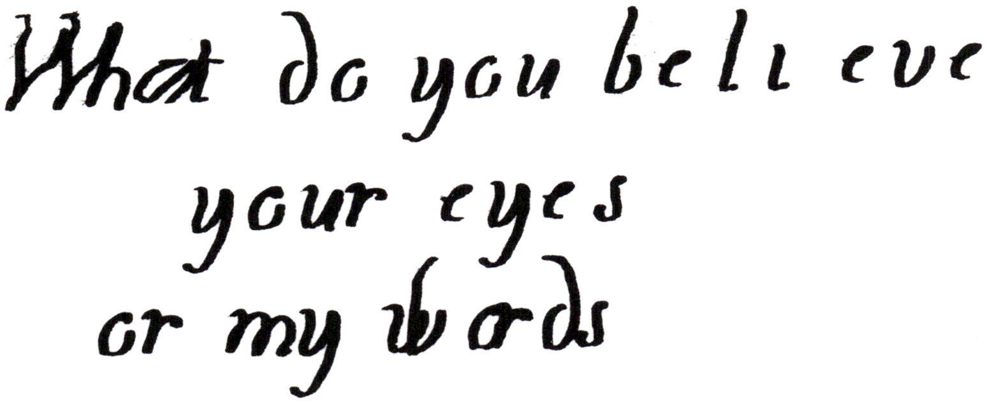

The Writer, 2007, video
Untitled (What Do You Believe, Your Eyes or My Words?), 2007

Il Tempo del Postino: A Group Show, 2007 ◁ Exhibition made with Hans Ulrich Obrist ¬ Invited artists: Doug Aitken, Matthew Barney and Jonathan Bepler, Tacita Dean, Trisha Donnelly, Olafur Eliasson, Liam Gillick, Dominique Gonzalez-Foerster, Douglas Gordon, Carsten Höller, Pierre Huyghe, Koo Jeong-A, Anri Sala, Tino Sehgal and Rirkrit Tiravanija • Direction: Philippe Parreno assisted by Ann-Christin Rommen • musical director and conductor: Ari Benjamin Meyers • orchestra: Royal Northern College of Music and RNCM Symphony Orchestra • lighting design: Darius Khondji • costume designer: Ramdane Touhami • graphic design: Peter Saville; Production: Manchester International Festival, UK ‡ From July 12 to 14, 2007 at the Opera House in Manchester, for the Manchester International Festival ♦ **Postman Time, 2007** ◁ Performance presented by the ventriloquist Jay Johnson, 15' (prologue of *Il Tempo del Postino*) ‡ From July 12 to 14, 2007 at the Opera House in Manchester, for the Manchester International Festival § Courtesy of the artist ***Il Tempo del Postino*, curated by Parreno and Obrist for the theatre on July 12, 2007 was commissioned by the first Manchester International Festival 2007. While the title in Italian refers to opera, it also comes from Parreno's 1994 text "Postman Time."[57] In this text, he calls into question both the delivery of the message, through the allusion to a postman, and the concept of variable time. Parreno studies the artwork's reception time, its length and the artist's control over these variables.[58] This piece is concerned with the occupation of time rather than space. As Obrist explains, the artists participating in the project choose to work in a direct, unmediated space. Fifteen artists created an act of different lengths. The show opens with Parreno's prologue, *Postman Time*, a monologue by the ventriloquist Jay Johnson about time-based architecture. For the opening act, choreographed by Tino Sehgal, the red curtain flies up and dances. For Olafur Eliasson's *Echo House*, a "mirror cloth" drops in front of the stage, while the spectators must guess which of the noises from the audience are being imitated by different instruments in the orchestra. Tacita Dean pays homage to Cage by filming the American composer's *4'33*." Performances directed by Doug Aitken, Anri Sala, Höller, Gordon, Gillick, Koo Jeong-A and Huyghe follow. Following the intermission was a performance by Matthew Barney, *Guardian of the Veil,* and Jonathan Bepler accompanied by a group of nearly ten people, which exceeded its alotted time by almost 45 minutes.[59] At the end of the second intermission, Gillick's performance, *Factories in the Snow*, recurs, while Tiravanija and Arto Lindsay begin theirs. Trisha Donnelly presents her performance *The Second Saint* made with the participation of a soprano, and Gonzalez-Foerster closes the show when the orchestra leaves the pit. ◊ *Il Tempo del Postino* not only hypothesizes that the artwork is a function of unmediated experience, a question which intrigues an entire generation of artists born in the era of the media, but also examines the notion of a collective subject of authorship. This opera can**

57. Philippe Parreno, "Postman Time," *Speech Bubbles*, Dijon, Les presses du réel, 2001, p.19.

58. *Ibid.*, p.19-20: "Visitors usually don't know how much time they've got to spend looking at a work of art. Nothing, nobody tells them. Have I got stay there 10 seconds or 2 hours? […] Museums manage the visitor's time as other organisations manage tourists' or old people's time […]. How much time do I have to spend with the other? For here is the question: Share a little time with another and not let his encounter be controlled by a third man who'll get rid of him […]."

59. See Jessica Morgan, "Il Tempo del Postino, Festival International de Manchester," *Frog*, no.6, January-June 2008, p.60-64. See also Élisabeth Lebovici, "Autant en emporte le temps" [Gone with the Time], *Art Press*, no.342, p.57-60: "Good old yesterday's team leaves each artist isolated in his or her personal magazine issue. But maybe one should not ask too much of friends we have known for twenty years."

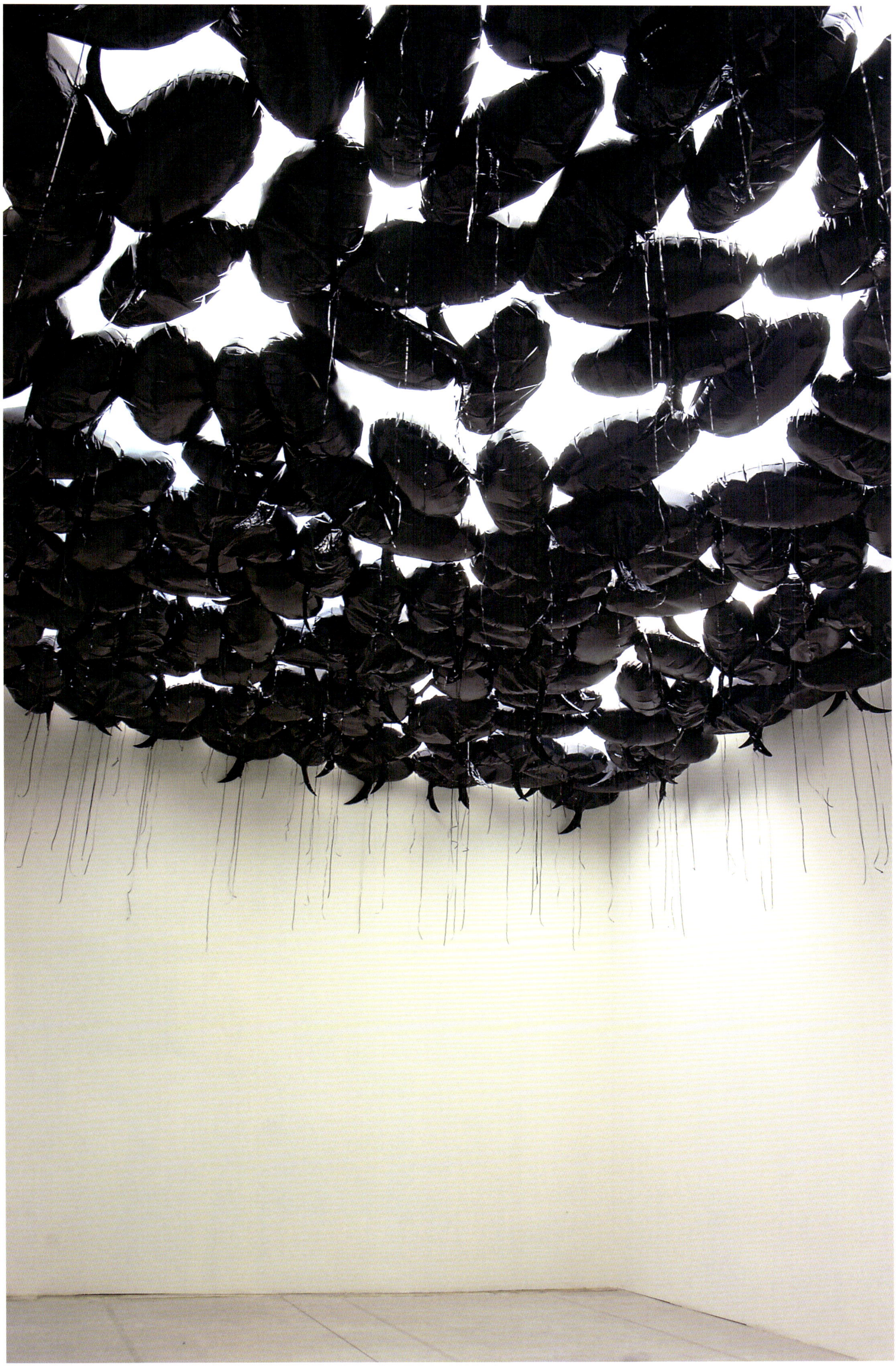

Speech Bubbles, 2007, exhibition view "What Do You Believe, Your Eyes or My Words?", Haunch of Venison Gallery, London, 2007

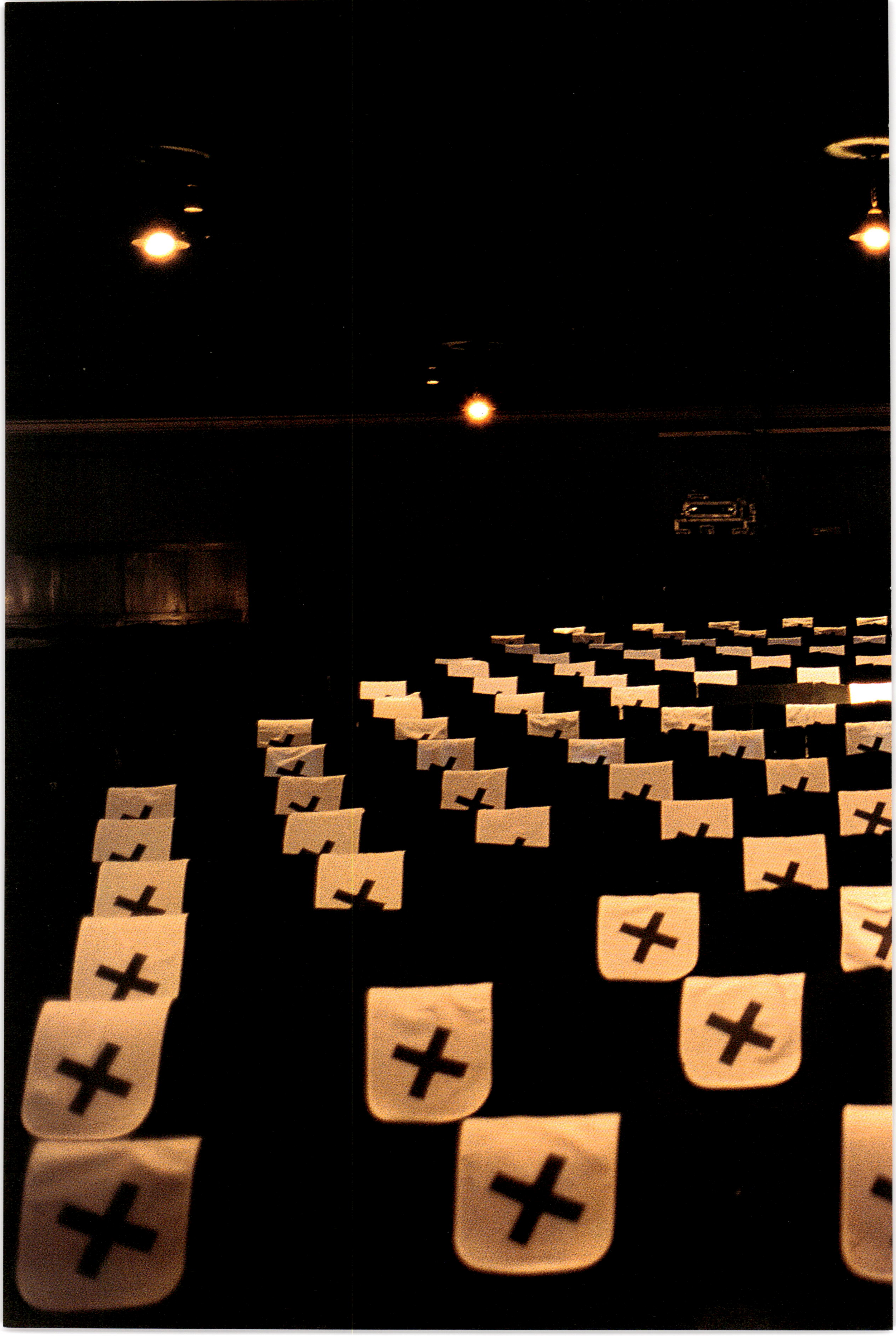

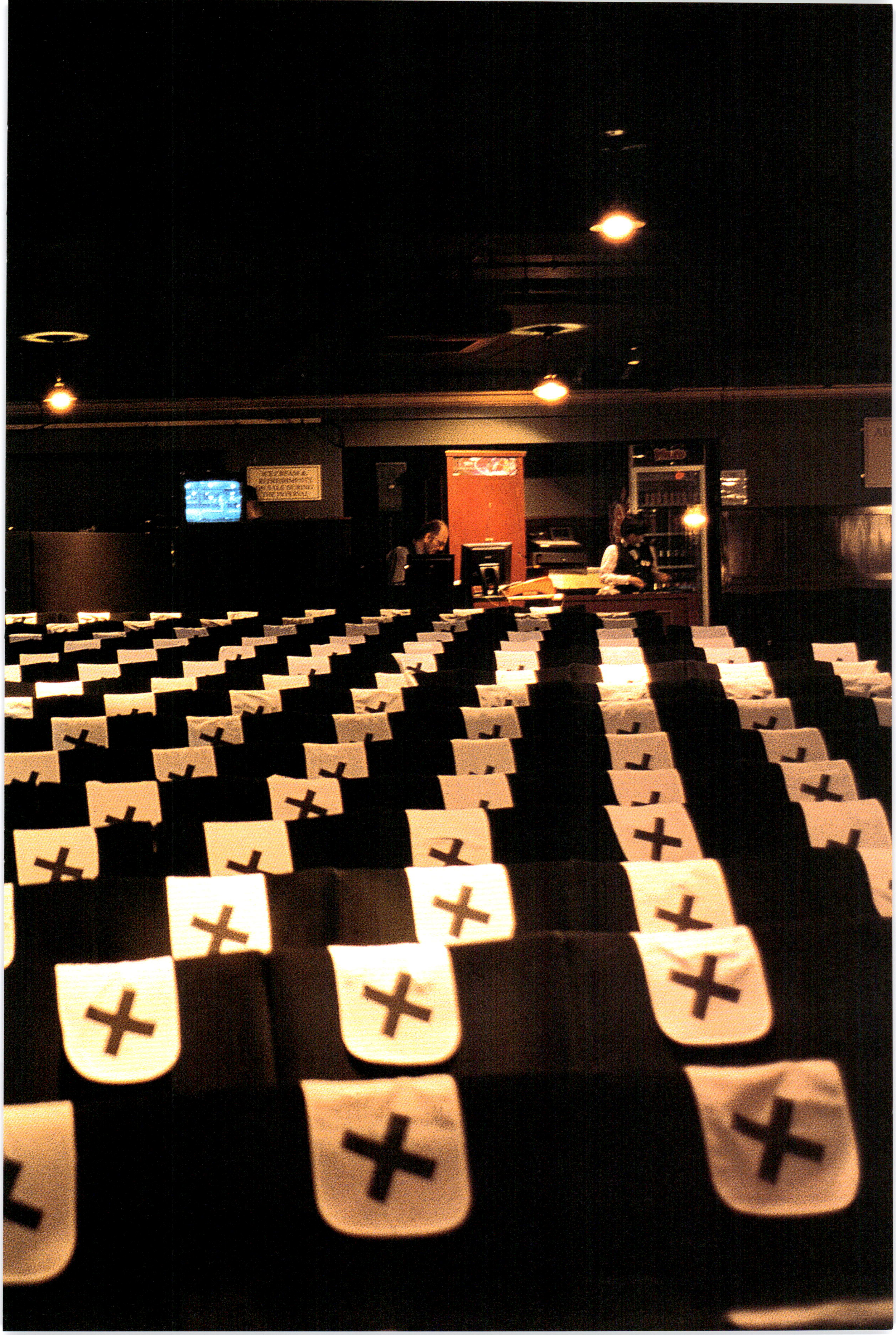

60. "The Score of a Score. Conversation with Pierre Boulez, Ircam, Paris 2003-2005," in Philippe Parreno, Hans Ulrich Obrist, *The Conversation Series*, *op. cit.*, p.123-141.

be performed again, and continually reinterpreted by a new generation of artists. The idea which catalyzed the work was Pierre Boulez's thoughts on "the score of the score"[60] which allows a work to be eternally replayed in different forms. Although a "replay" of this opera at the Théâtre du Châtelet in Paris was cancelled, the nature of these immaterial works demands that they be succeeded by new interpretations.

Are There Possibilities to Unify Dispersed Fragments in A Coherent Narrative Framework?, 2007 ✎ Group of seven drawings: Indian ink, gouache and felt pen; 48 × 33 cm each ‡ published in *Parkett No. 80: Jennifer Allora & Guillermo Calzadilla, Dominique Gonzalez-Foerster, Mark Grotjahn*, October 1st, 2007, Zurich: Parkett Verlag, p.88-92 ʃ Private collection, London
For an issue of *Parkett* magazine featuring her work, Gonzalez-Foerster invites Parreno to write a text on her work. Instead of writing a text, Parreno produces a group of drawings.

Untitled, 2007 ✎ 12 scented wax candles; H.: 120 cm; diam.: 10 cm (each) ‡ "Interior Cartoons," October 28–November 3, 2007, Esther Schipper Gallery, Berlin, Germany || 1 edition § Courtesy Esther Schipper Gallery, Berlin

Marquee, 2007 ✎ Plexiglas, metal frame, 8 neon lights, 11 incandescent light bulbs, (60 and 75 W); 5 light bulbs of 8 cm in diam., 4 of 9.5 cm in diam., 2 of 12 cm in diam.), electrical system; 140 × 100 × 65 cm; (048) ‡ "Interior Cartoons," October 28–November 3, 2007, Esther Schipper Gallery, Berlin, Germany || 1 edition ʃ Kunsthalle Weishaupt, Ulm, Germany
***Untitled* and *Marquee* are allusions to the exhibition "Interior Cartoons Animations" at the Esther Schipper Gallery in 2006. This time, twelve scented candles release similar fragrances: cold tobacco, fresh paint, cleaning products, men's perfume, sweat, etc. The exhibition creates a feeling of "déjà vu," despite the reduction in size of the *Marquee* at the entrance. The work functions both as a portrait of the gallery and a remake of the 2006 exhibition, both gestures satirizing the redundancy expected from an established artist's solo exhibition. *Interior Cartoons Animation* is the double portrait of the artist and his gallery—the ghost of a replayed event.**

Postman Time, 2007 ✎ Digital print mounted on aluminum, 2 signatures (white pen), metal frame, anti-glare and anti-UV glass; 152 × 101 cm (unframed), 153 × 102 cm (framed) ‡ March 27–30, 2008, Friedrich Petzel Gallery booth, The Armory Show, New York, United States || 8 editions and 2 artist editions § Courtesy Air de Paris, Paris; Esther Schipper, Berlin; Friedrich Petzel, New York; Pilar Corrias Inc., London

Federico, 2008 ✎ Acid on glass; variable dimensions ‡ "Everstill/ Siempre Todavía," May 24–July 3, 2008, La Huerta de San

Previous pages and right: **Il Tempo del Postino,** exhibition view at the Opera House, Manchester

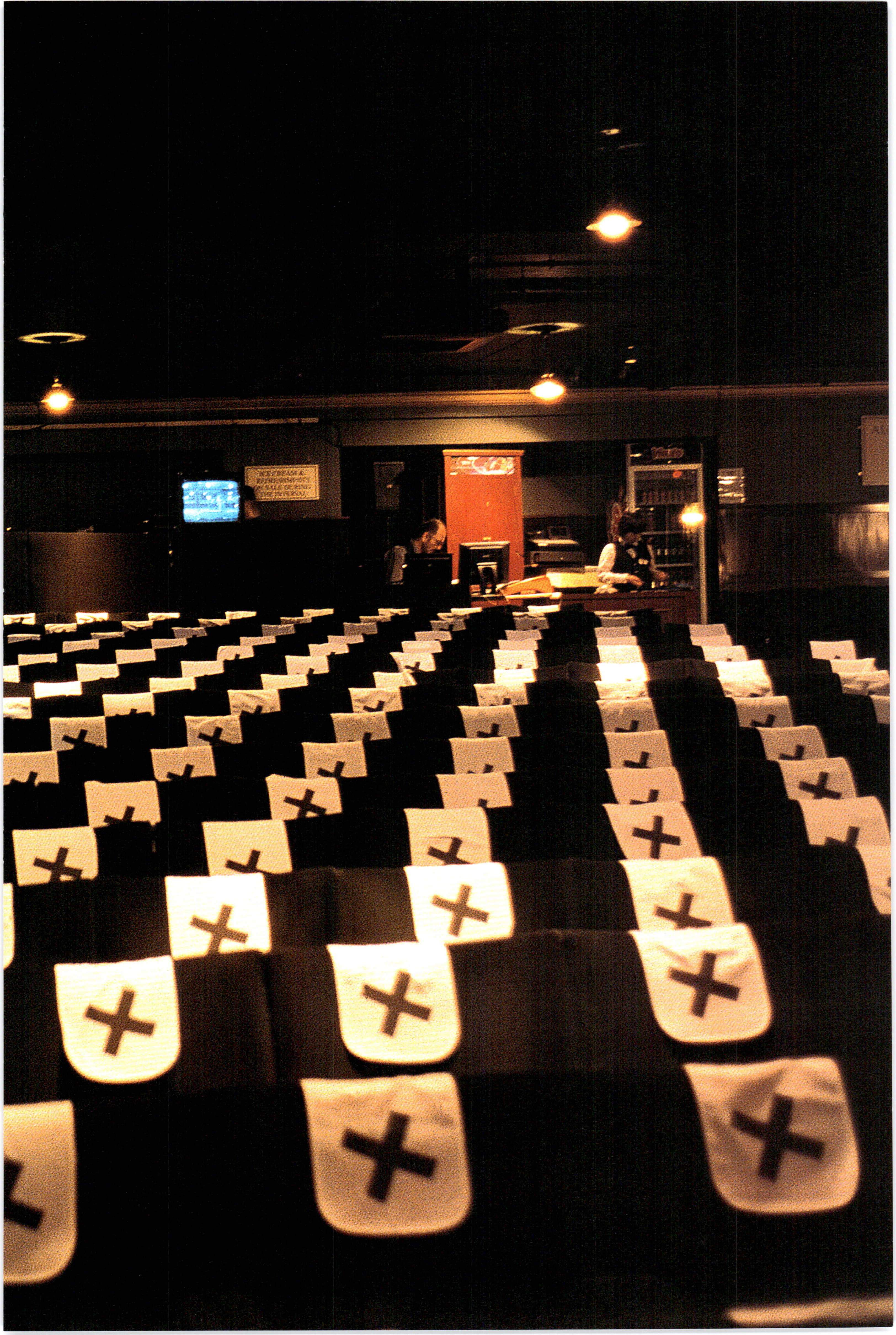

60. "The Score of a Score. Conversation with Pierre Boulez, Ircam, Paris 2003-2005," in Philippe Parreno, Hans Ulrich Obrist, *The Conversation Series, op. cit.*, p.123-141.

be performed again, and continually reinterpreted by a new generation of artists. The idea which catalyzed the work was Pierre Boulez's thoughts on "the score of the score"[60] which allows a work to be eternally replayed in different forms. Although a "replay" of this opera at the Théâtre du Châtelet in Paris was cancelled, the nature of these immaterial works demands that they be succeeded by new interpretations.

Are There Possibilities to Unify Dispersed Fragments in A Coherent Narrative Framework?, 2007 ⊲ Group of seven drawings: Indian ink, gouache and felt pen; 48 × 33 cm each ‡ published in *Parkett No. 80: Jennifer Allora & Guillermo Calzadilla, Dominique Gonzalez-Foerster, Mark Grotjahn*, October 1st, 2007, Zurich: Parkett Verlag, p.88-92 ʃ Private collection, London
For an issue of *Parkett* magazine featuring her work, Gonzalez-Foerster invites Parreno to write a text on her work. Instead of writing a text, Parreno produces a group of drawings.

Untitled, 2007 ⊲ 12 scented wax candles; H.: 120 cm; diam.: 10 cm (each) ‡ "Interior Cartoons," October 28–November 3, 2007, Esther Schipper Gallery, Berlin, Germany || 1 edition § Courtesy Esther Schipper Gallery, Berlin

Marquee, 2007 ⊲ Plexiglas, metal frame, 8 neon lights, 11 incandescent light bulbs, (60 and 75 W); 5 light bulbs of 8 cm in diam., 4 of 9.5 cm in diam., 2 of 12 cm in diam.), electrical system; 140 × 100 × 65 cm; (048) ‡ "Interior Cartoons," October 28–November 3, 2007, Esther Schipper Gallery, Berlin, Germany || 1 edition ʃ Kunsthalle Weishaupt, Ulm, Germany
Untitled and *Marquee* are allusions to the exhibition "Interior Cartoons Animations" at the Esther Schipper Gallery in 2006. This time, twelve scented candles release similar fragrances: cold tobacco, fresh paint, cleaning products, men's perfume, sweat, etc. The exhibition creates a feeling of "déjà vu," despite the reduction in size of the *Marquee* at the entrance. The work functions both as a portrait of the gallery and a remake of the 2006 exhibition, both gestures satirizing the redundancy expected from an established artist's solo exhibition. *Interior Cartoons Animation* is the double portrait of the artist and his gallery—the ghost of a replayed event.

Postman Time, 2007 ⊲ Digital print mounted on aluminum, 2 signatures (white pen), metal frame, anti-glare and anti-UV glass; 152 × 101 cm (unframed), 153 × 102 cm (framed) ‡ March 27–30, 2008, Friedrich Petzel Gallery booth, The Armory Show, New York, United States || 8 editions and 2 artist editions § Courtesy Air de Paris, Paris; Esther Schipper, Berlin; Friedrich Petzel, New York; Pilar Corrias Inc., London

Federico, 2008 ⊲ Acid on glass; variable dimensions ‡ "Everstill/ Siempre Todavía," May 24–July 3, 2008, La Huerta de San

Previous pages and right: Il Tempo del Postino, exhibition view at the Opera House, Manchester

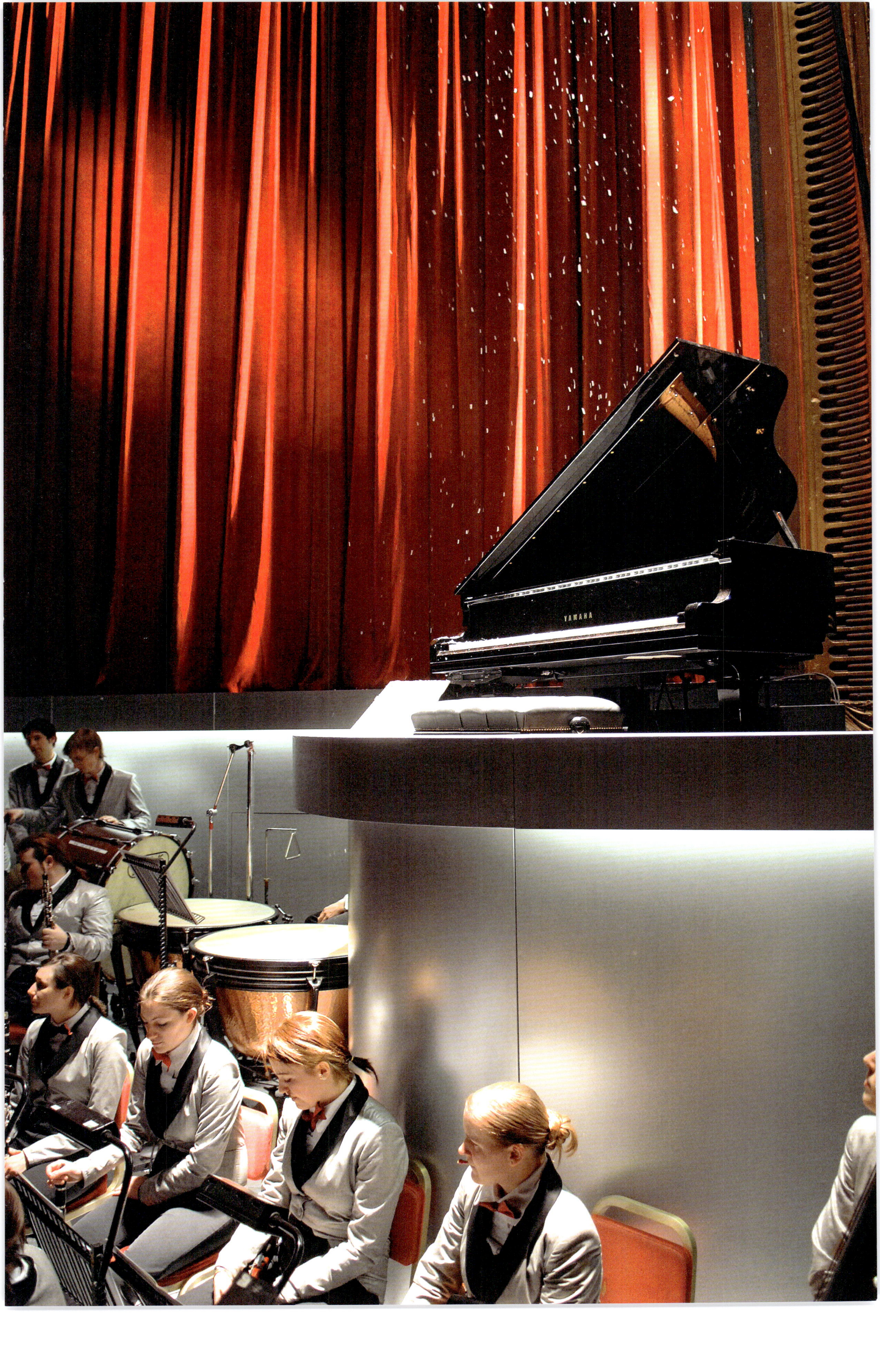
YAMAHA

Vincente, Grenada, Spain || 5 editions § Courtesy Pilar Corrias Inc., London **This work was made at Federico Garcia Lorca's country house, La Huerta de San Vincente, on the outskirts of Grenada, which has now become a museum dedicated to the memory of the dead poet. The acid engraving, which resembles a trace of condensation, is placed where García Lorca's breath would have condensed as he looked out of his window.**

Marquee, 2008 ✎ Translucid acrylic glass (10 mm thick), steel frame, 12 light bulbs (diam.: 8 cm) and 15 fluorescent tubes, electrical system; 230 × 100 × 20 cm approx.; (056) || 1 edition § Courtesy Air de Paris, Paris, and Esther Schipper, Berlin

Marquee, 2008 ✎ Translucid acrylic glass (10 mm thick), steel frame, 14 light bulbs (diam.: 8 cm) and 4 fluorescent tubes, electrical system; 230 × 96.5 × 62 cm approx.; (057) ‡ June 4–8, 2008, Esther Schipper Gallery booth, Art Basel, Basel, Switzerland || 1 edition ∫ Private collection, Cologne, Germany

The Ultrasonic Scream of the Squirrel, 2008 ✎ Performance with the ventriloquist Jay Johnson ‡ September 14, 2008, "The Yokohama Triennale: Time Crevasses," Yokohama, Japan; exhibition curators: Daniel Birnbaum, Hu Fang, Miyake Akiko, Hans Ulrich Obrist, Beatrix Ruf § Courtesy of the artist

Marquee, 2008 ✎ Translucid acrylic glass (10 mm thick), steel frame, 42 light bulbs (diam.: 8 cm), 4 fluorescent tubes, electrical system, glass chains; 213 × 100 × 50 cm approx.; (059) || 1 edition ∫ Private collection, Paris, France

Marquee, 2008 ✎ Red acrylic glass (10 mm thick), steel frame, 231 light bulbs (diam.: 8 cm), 3 groups of 6 fluorescent tubes, 2 acrylic glass chains; 200 × 150 × 20 cm approx.; (055) ‡ "Suicide in Vermillon Sands," October 10–November 15, 2008, Friedrich Petzel Gallery, New York, United States || 1 edition § Courtesy Friedrich Petzel, New York

Marquee, 2008 ✎ Translucid acrylic glass (10 mm thick), steel frame, 2 steel rods, 3 groups of 5 fluorescent tubes; 230 × 100 × 20 cm approx.; (058) ‡ "Suicide in Vermillon Sands," October 10–November 15, 2008, Friedrich Petzel Gallery, New York, United States || 1 edition § Courtesy Friedrich Petzel, New York **In an empty white room a ghostly white *Marquee* flashes continuously while a magician standing on a pedestal performs. The magician leaves after the performance, as the *Marquee* continues to flash.**

Sans titre (Socle du magicien) [Magician's pedestal], 2008 ✎ White painted wood; 17 × 107 × 121 cm ‡ "Suicide in Vermillon Sands," October 10–November 15, 2008, Friedrich Petzel

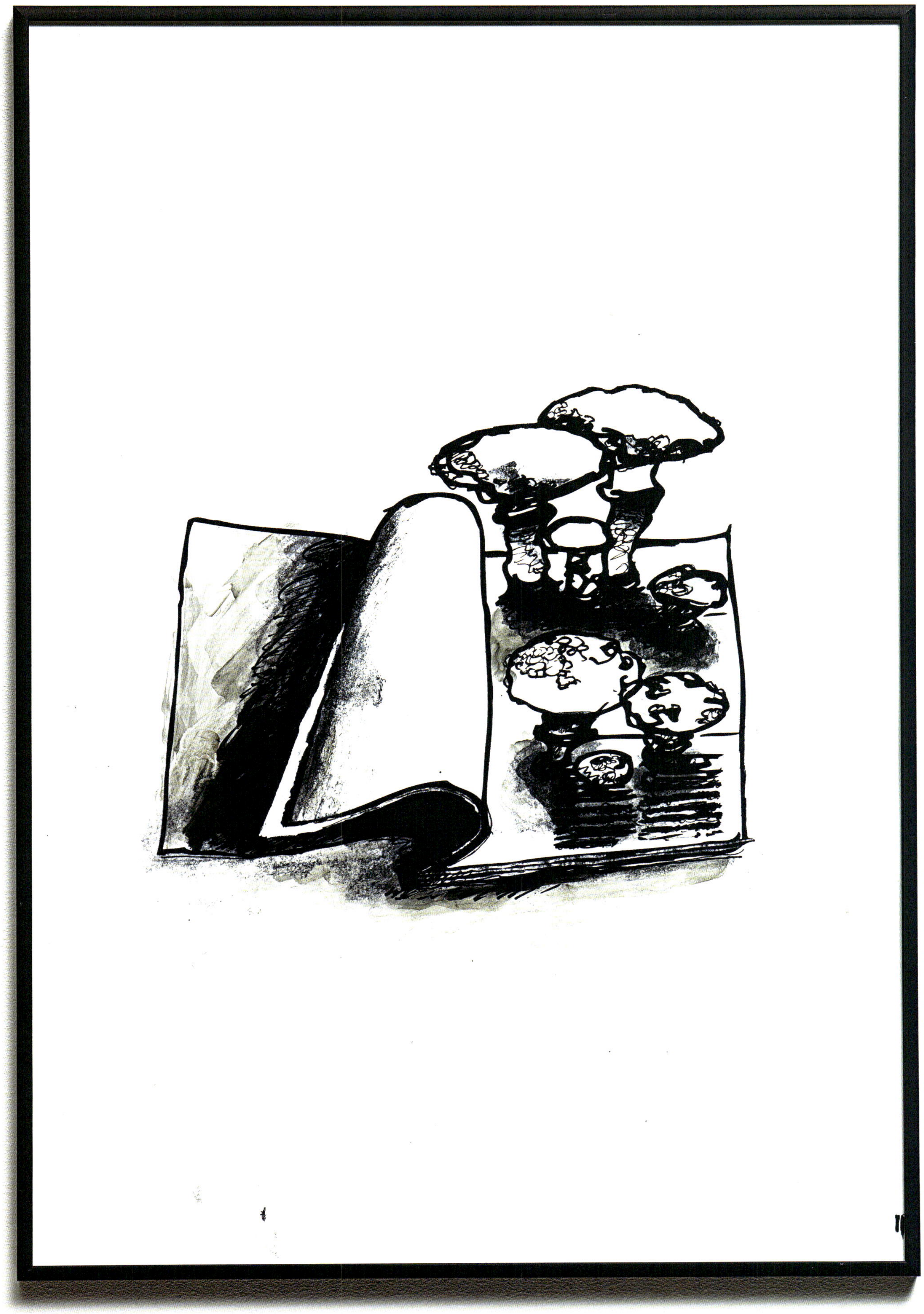

Are There Possibilities To Unify Dispersed Fragments In A Coherent Narrative Framework?, 2007

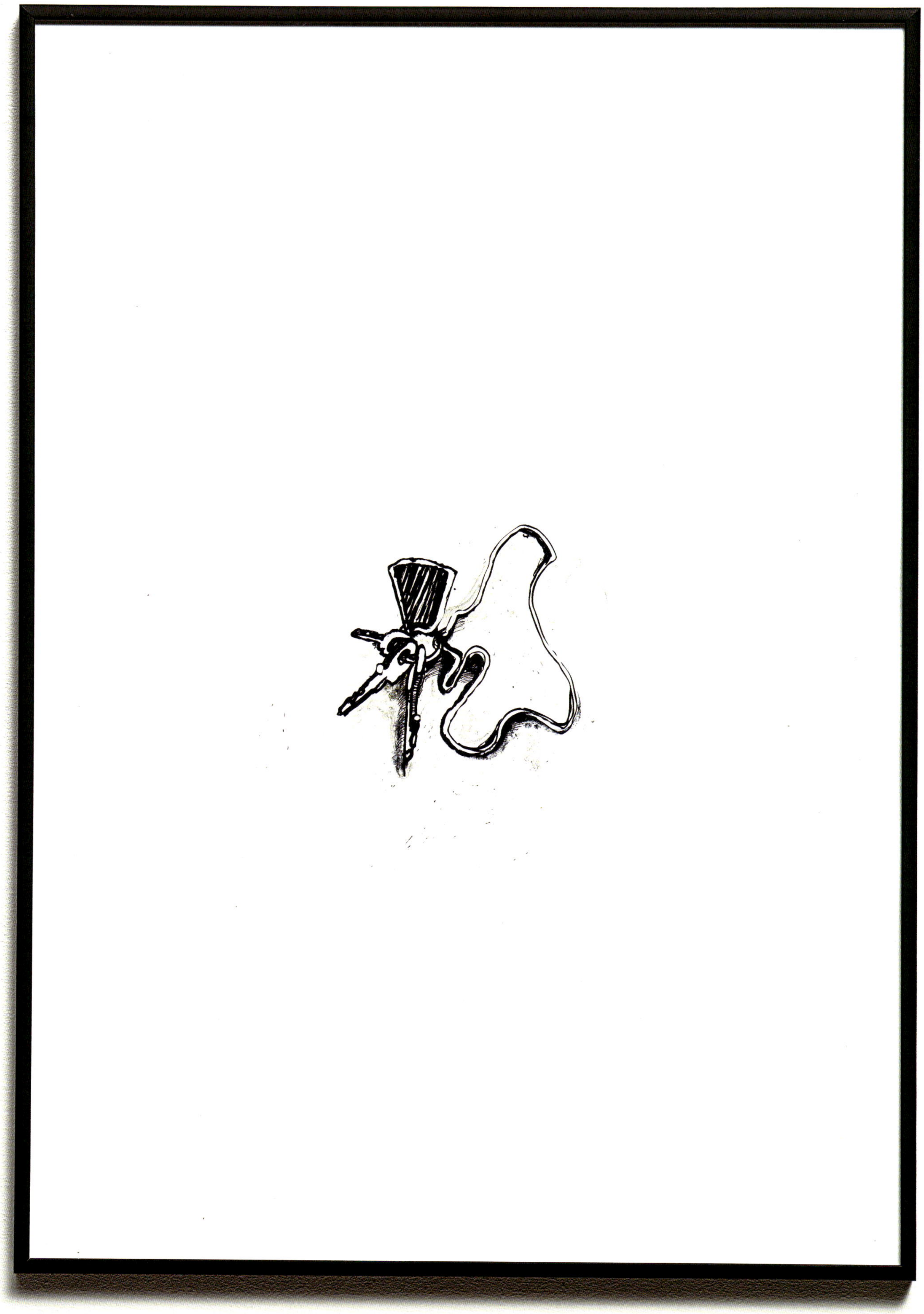

Are There Possibilities To Unify Dispersed Fragments In A Coherent Narrative Framework?, 2007

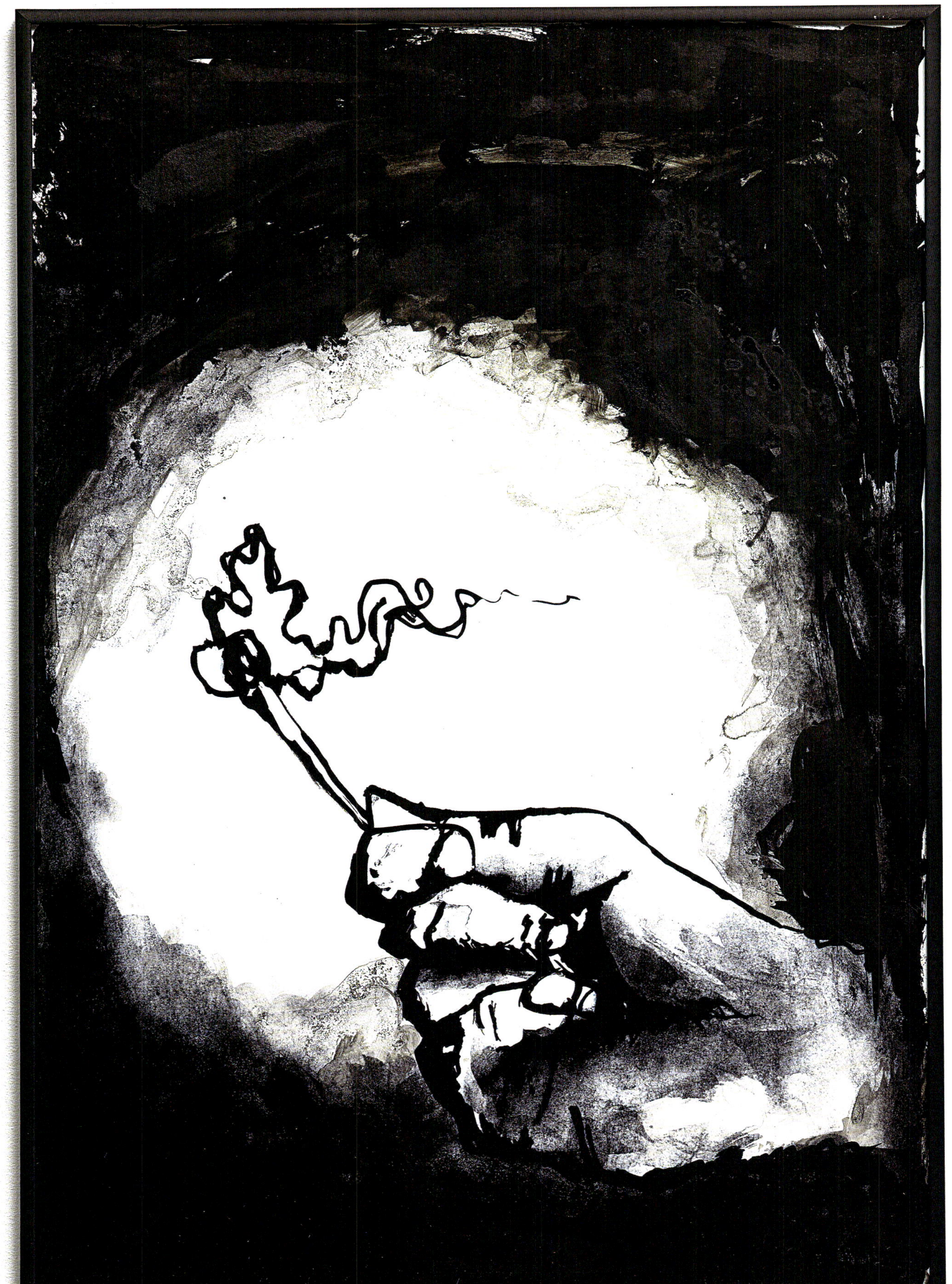

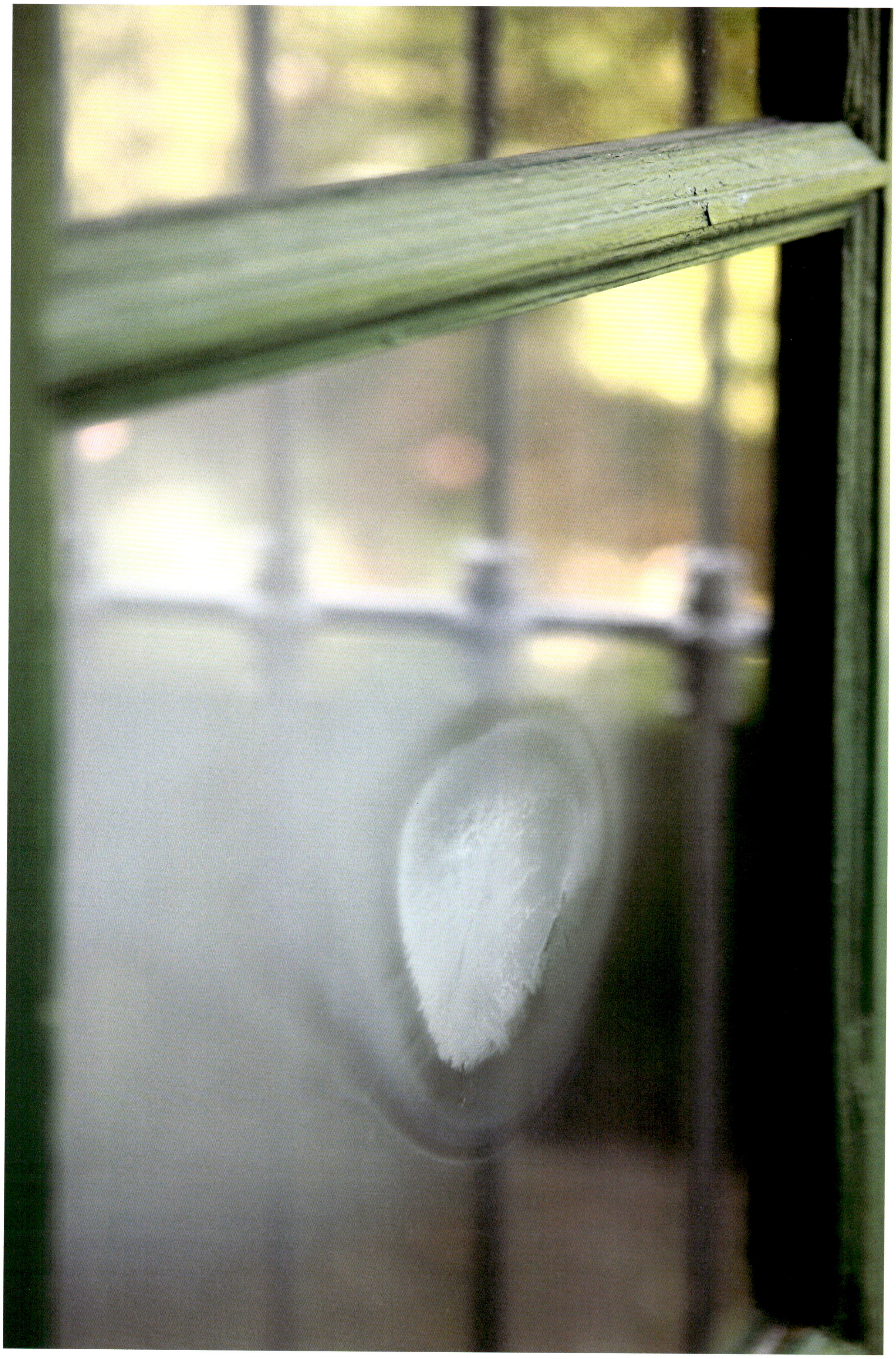

Federico, 2008, exhibition view “Everstill/Siempre Todavía”, La Huerta de San Vincente, Granada, 2008

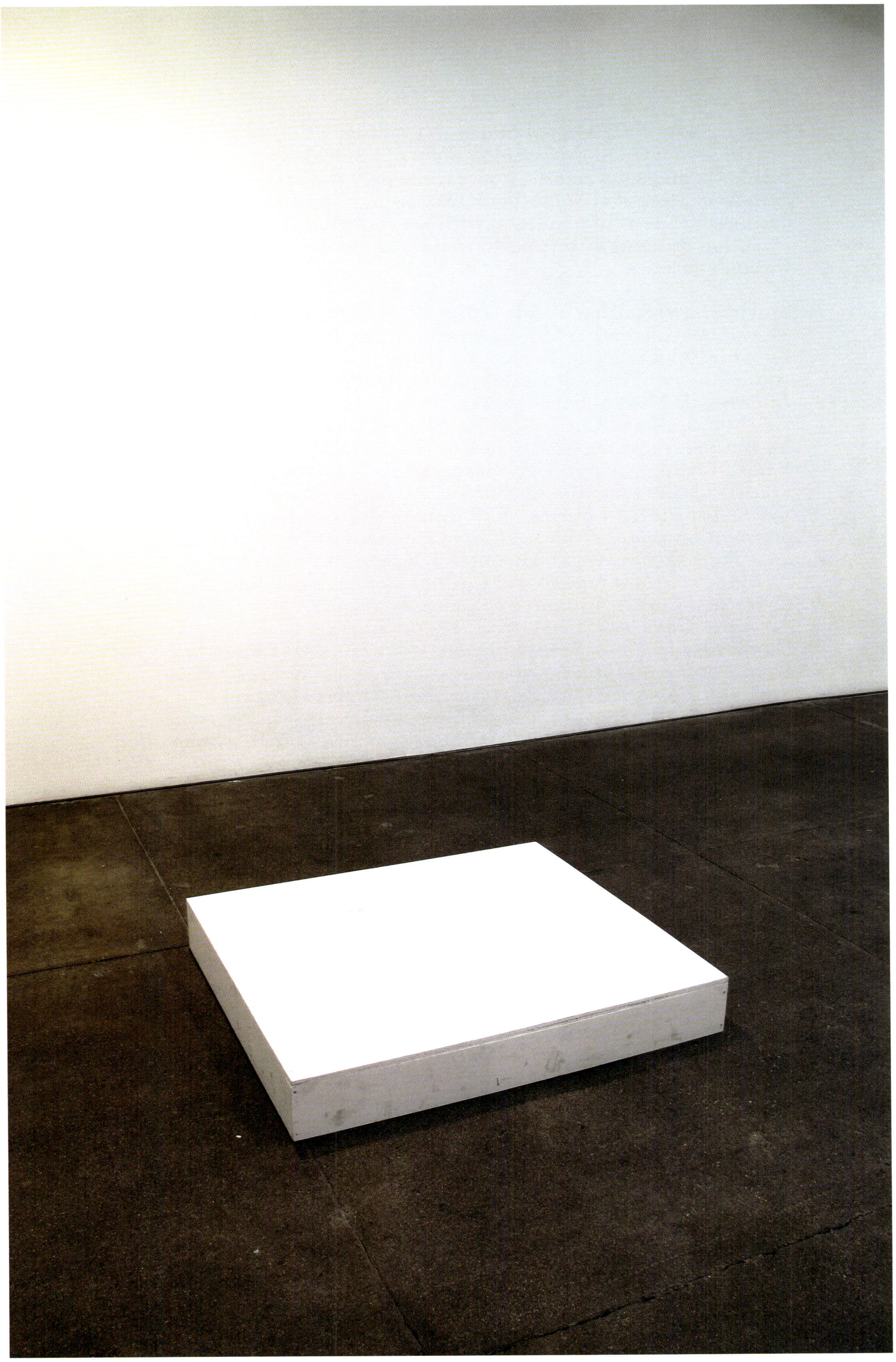

Untitled (Le socle du magicien), 2008, exhibition view "Suicide in Vermillon Sands", Friedrich Petzel Gallery, New York, 2008

Gallery, New York, United States || 1 edition § Courtesy Friedrich Petzel **On the opening night of "Suicide in Vermillon Sands," a magician standing on a white pedestal makes the *Suicide in Vermillon Sands* book of drawings appear and disappear. The white pedestal with the footprints of the magician is all that remains of this performance as a site of presence through absence.**

Suicide in Vermillon Sands, 2008 With Maxime Barbier, Marion Bayot, Esther Berelowitsch, Marc Borneo, Maxime Buechi, Roch Deniau, Stéphanie Dupont, Nicolas Gallet, Aline Girard, Thibault Gleize, James Goggin, Charlotte Jankowski, Masha Karpushina, Körner Union, Aude Lehmann, Urs Lehni, Marie Lusa, Gaël Le Maitre, Pierre Marie, Véronique Marques, Claire le Roy, Laurent Meszaros, Peter Maybury, Aurélie Morassut, Chris Neal, Andreas Och Fredrika, Clément Rodzielski, Tomoë Sugiura, Régis Tosetti, Sylvia Tournerie ◊ Series of 79 unique drawings, vermilion pigment on paper, 76.8 × 57.2 cm List of drawings: *First Page, Last Page* (2 drawings); Chapitre I, Scene Setting, A: *Infinite Urban landscape; Curious Echoes Stir; A Light Hysterical Laugh;* Chapitre I, Scene Setting, B: *Skies Are Larger; Air More Generous;* Chapitre I, Scene Setting, C: *A New Dimension in Living; Psychotropic Houses; Clear Concrete; Liquid Stone Sodium Lights; Non-Aural Music & Erotic Food; Idyll and Romance; Shy Objects; Sonic Jewels Glinting;* Chapitre II, Background: *Imperceptible Transition Between the Real and the Superreal; 3D Snapshots; Computers Controlled with your Tongue; Psychoacoustic Fictional Spaces of Interludes and Intros; The World is Made of Nows; Transparent Block of Condensed Time; No More Reality; Stay Tuned to the Real;* Chapitre III, Introducing Characters, A: *I Introduce Myself as a Mistake;* Chapitre III, Introducing Characters, B: *Born From the Living Dead; The Underground Man; No City Wants Me; Inhabiting Someone Else's Brain; Never Show any Emotion or Response; Ice Face;* Chapitre IV, Develop Character in Context: *Anguished Squid; I Don't Sweat Anymore; Self-Destructive Cells; Keep your Secret Secretly; It Doesn't Do any Good to Talk; Darling, you're Getting Over-Intuitive Again;* Chapitre V, Intro Problem/Tension, A: *Dreaming the Real; Phonoglutamate; A Red Signal/Underlying Neural Activity; Does It Burn or Tingle?; Concatenated Reentrant Loops. Semiophysis; Fall into the Dimensions of the Pictogram;* Chapitre V, Intro Problem/Tension, B: *Darkened Mirrors; Your Processed Life; Music is a Soundtrack; Clothing is a Costume; Conversations Are Dialogues; The World Is a Standing Stock of Material; Beside Yourself, Dileneated; Lack of Finality; Pay Attention; Take Notes;* Chapitre VI, Develop Problem: *Night Fell Quickly; Everything Turned Blue; Running my Hands Over the Smooth Plastex Walls; See the Chemistry Operating; There's no Way to Stop me; The Upcoming*

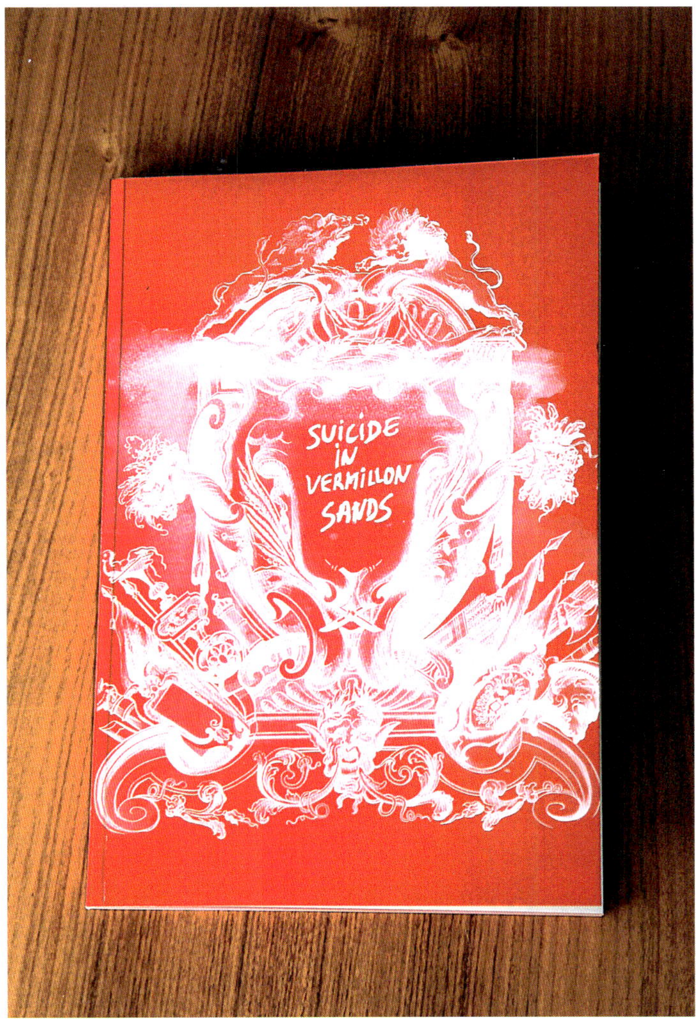

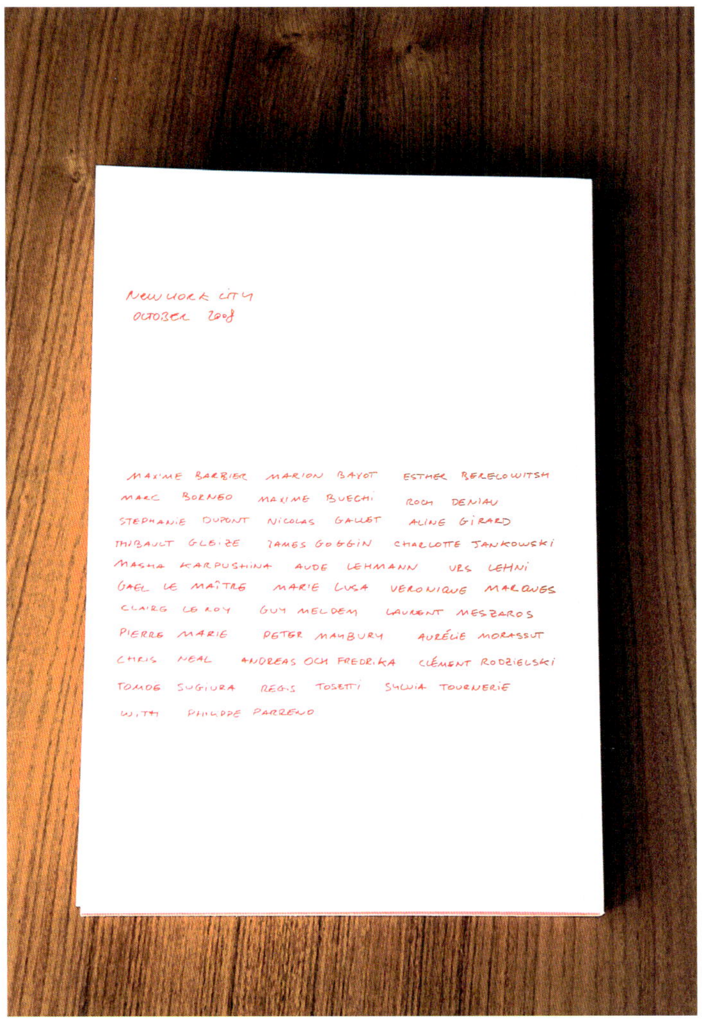

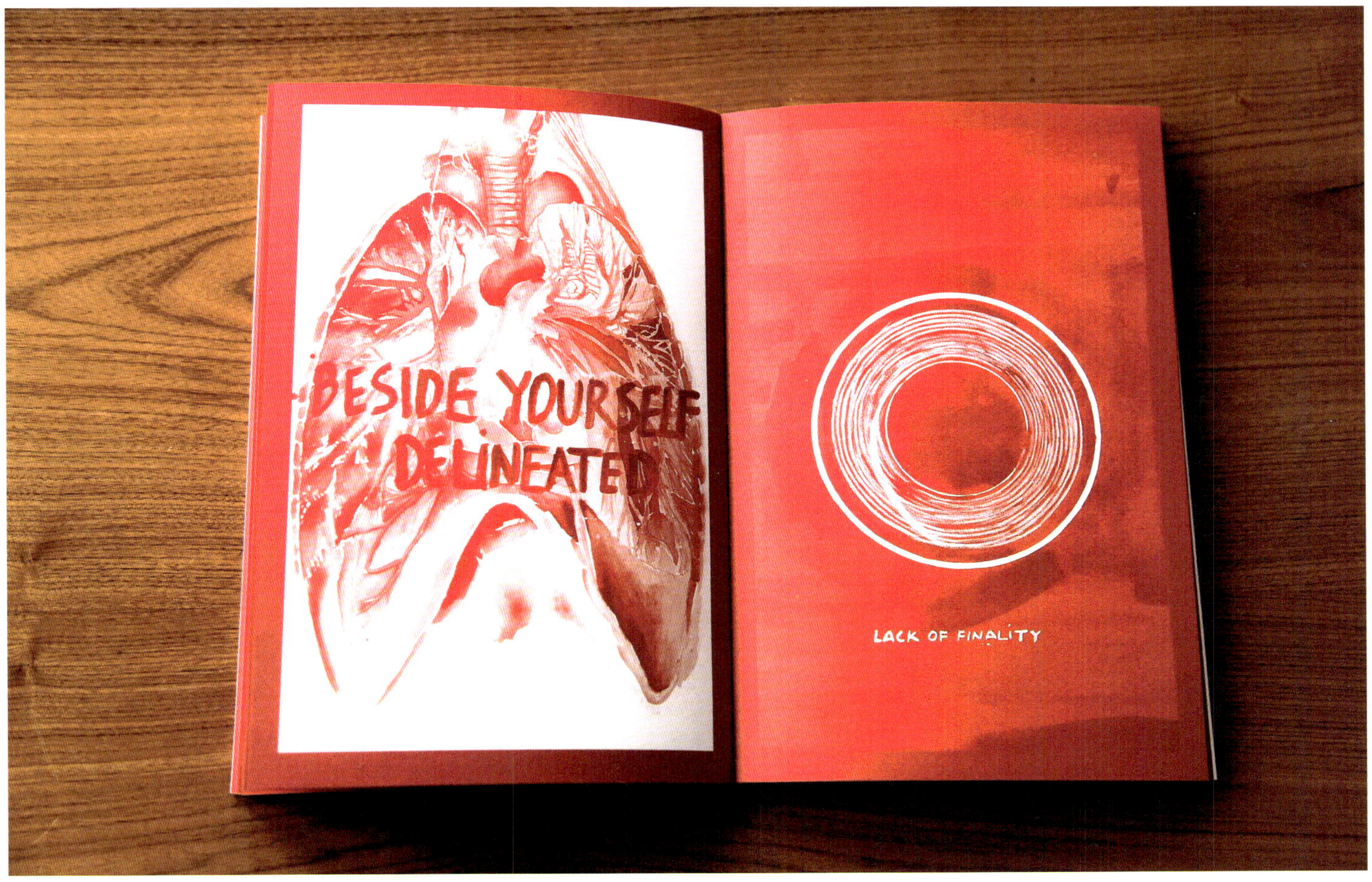

Suicide in Vermillon Sands, 2008

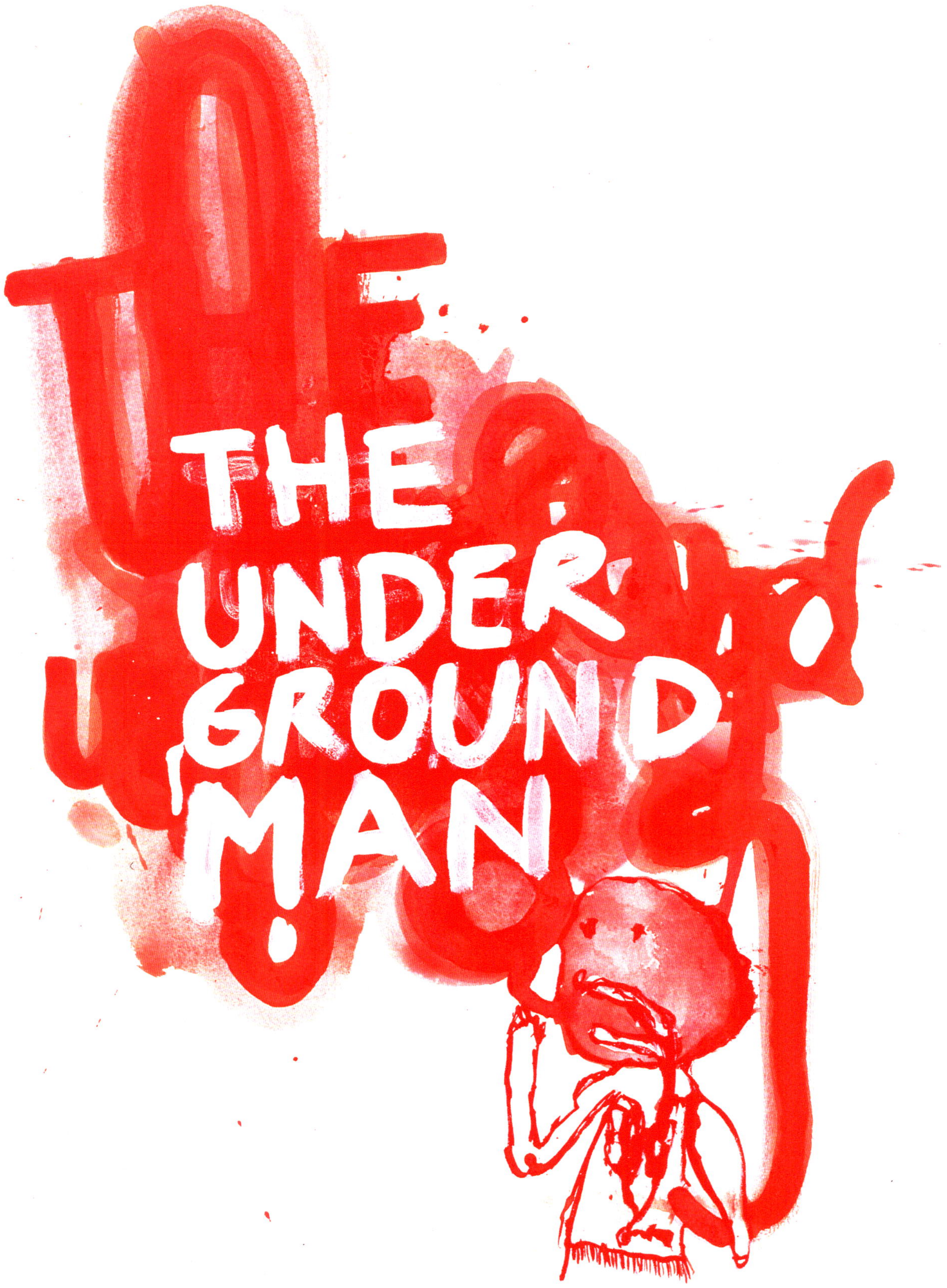

Suicide in Vermillon Sands, 2008, *The Underground Man*, with Claire Leroy

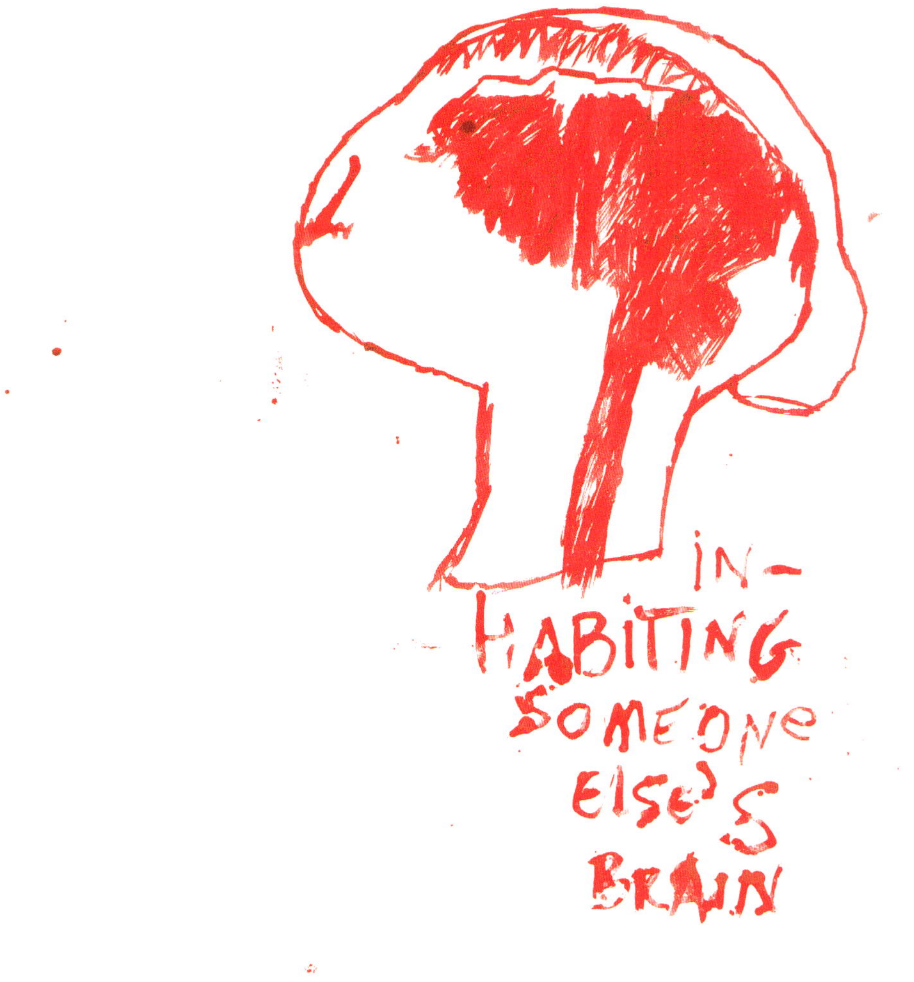

Suicide in Vermillon Sands, 2008, *Inhabiting Someone Else's Brain*, with Gaël Le Maitre

Tragedy; Chapitre VII, Explode Problem (Climax), A: *I'll Take your Brain into Another Dimension; Feel the Fever Rising; Where Are You Going?; Say Goodbye to the Wind; Everything is Dead in Here;* Chapitre VII, Explode Problem (Climax), B: *Everything Fall Into Place; Release the Repressed Material;* Chapitre VII, Explode Problem (Climax), C: *Acute Urgency; Ultrasonic Squirrel Screams; Crushing Skulls and Bones; Violence Is Unique; Suicide Party; Your Own Self-Requiem;* Chapitre VIII, Troubled Ending: *Severe Sonic Trauma; Literally Black; You Are Weightless...;* Épilogue: *After Affects; The Whole World Is Singing; The Tailor Killed By his Own Cloth; I Can Hear them Laughing;* Very Last Word: *I-Go* ‡ "Suicide in Vermillon Sands," October 10–November 15, 2008, Friedrich Petzel Gallery, New York, United States § Courtesy Air de Paris, Paris; Esther Schipper, Berlin; Friedrich Petzel Gallery, New York; Pilar Corrias Inc., London

Suicide in Vermillon Sands, 2008 With Maxime Barbier, Marion Bayot, Esther Berelowitsch, Marc Borneo, Maxime Buechi, Roch Deniau, Stéphanie Dupont, Nicolas Gallet, Aline Girard, Thibault Gleize, James Goggin, Charlotte Jankowski, Masha Karpushina, Körner Union, Aude Lehmann, Urs Lehni, Marie Lusa, Gaël Le Maitre, Pierre Marie, Véronique Marques, Claire le Roy, Laurent Meszaros, Peter Maybury, Aurélie Morassut, Chris Neal, Andreas Och Fredrika, Clément Rodzielski, Tomoë Sugiura, Régis Tosetti, Sylvia Tournerie ◁ Book: 106 pages, color, 17 × 22 cm ‡ "Suicide in Vermillon Sands," October 15–November 15, 2008, Friedrich Petzel Gallery, New York, United States || 500 numbered and signed copies § Courtesy Friedrich Petzel, New York **Parreno wrote a story composed of 78 captions or headers and sent it to 31 graphic designers. He then made 78 vermilion red drawings from the designs he received from the designers. The work's polyphony was inspired by Mikhail Bakhtin's analysis of Dostoevsky. The following sentence by the Russian theorist inspired the exhibition: "What unfolds is not a multitude of characters and fates in a single objective world, illuminated by a single authorial consciousness; rather a plurality of consciousnesses, with equal rights and each with its own world, combine but (are) not merged in the unity of the event."[61] A book of the same name, printed in 500 copies, was published of this group of drawings.**

61. Mikhail Bakhtin, *Problems of Dostoevsky's Poetics*, Minneapolis, University of Minnesota Press, "Theory and History of Literature" collection, vol.8, 1989.

The Sorcerer's Apprentice (White Fireworks in Daytime, Launching a Sigil in the Sky), 2008 ◁ Screen print: phosphorescent ink on black velvet, 150 × 110 cm ‡ 4–8 June 2008, Beyeler Foundation booth, Art Basel, Switzerland || 8 editions and 4 artist editions ∫ First private collection: Private collection, Paris, France (1/8) § Courtesy Air de Paris, Paris; Friedrich Petzel,

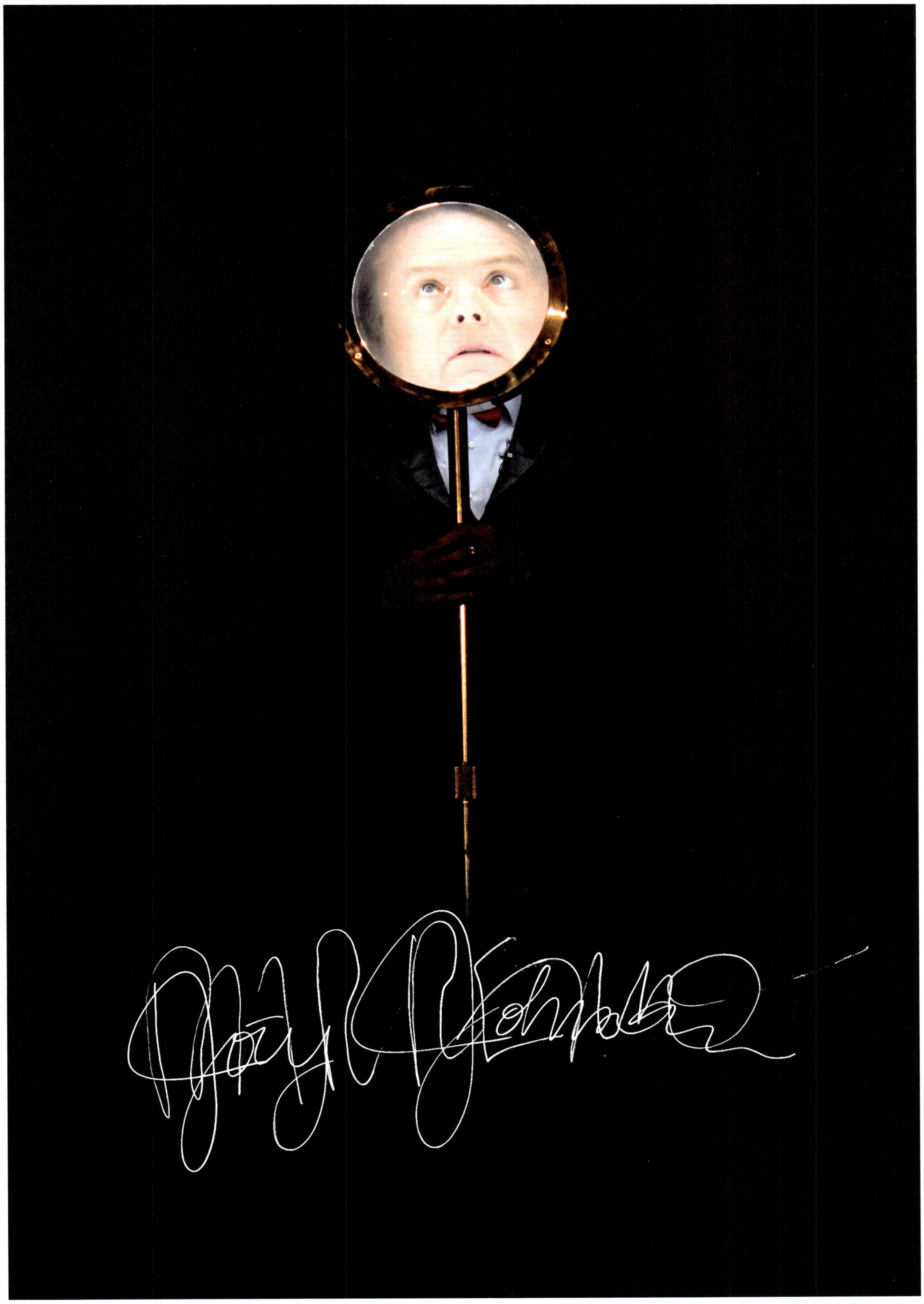

Postman Time, 2007
Following pages: The Sorcerer's Apprentice (White Fireworks in Daytime, Launching a Sigil in the Sky), 2008, Mas Thibert, France,

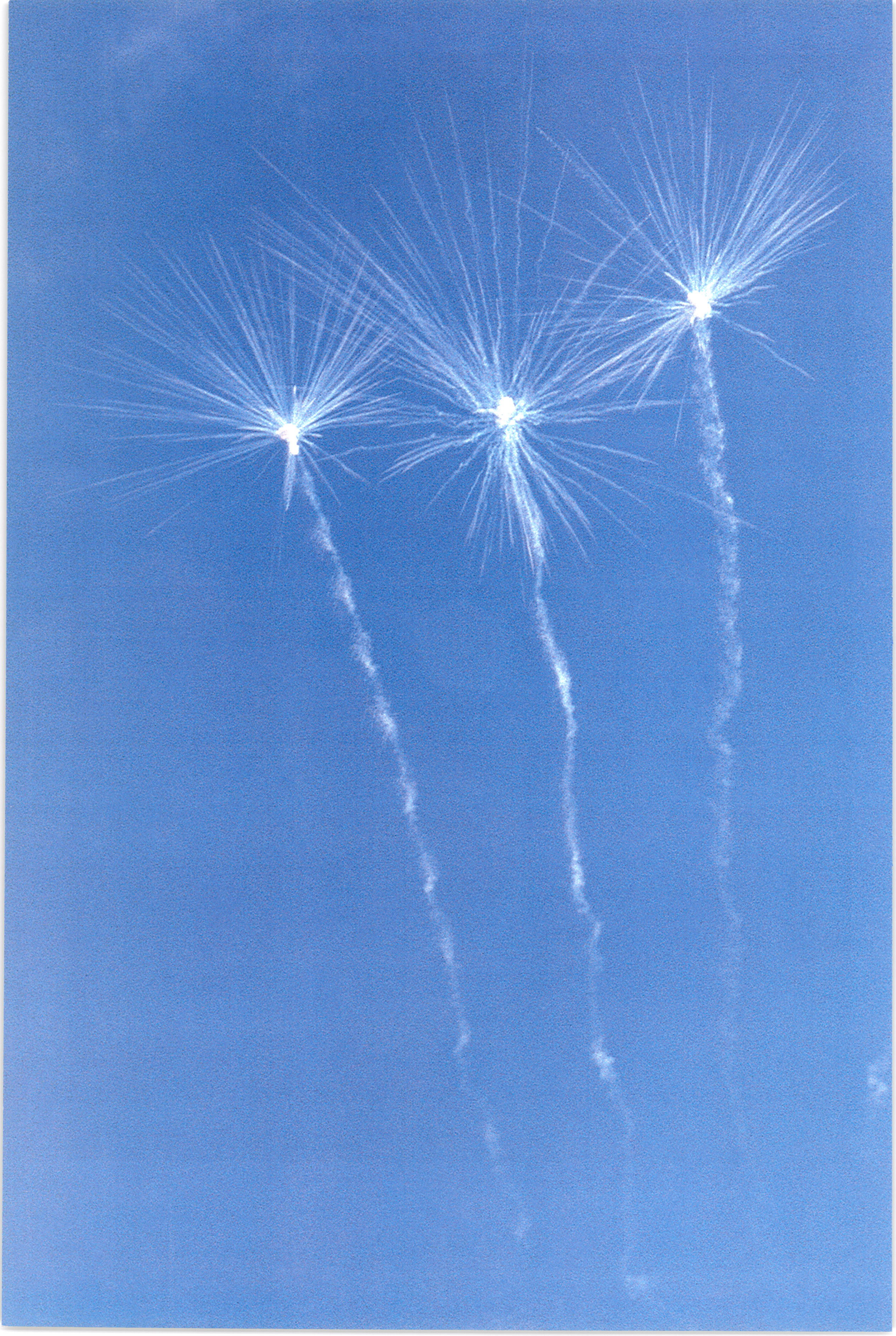

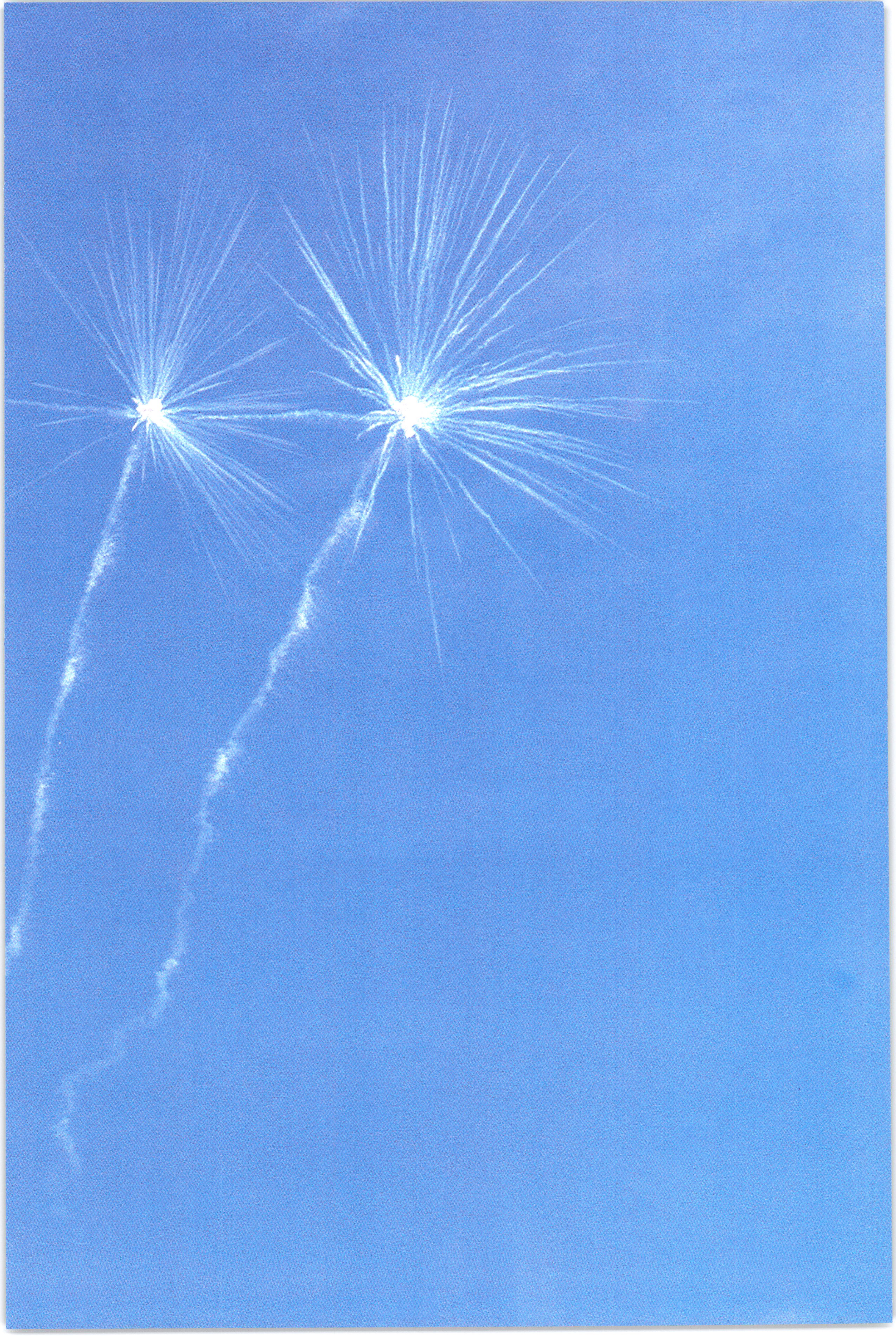

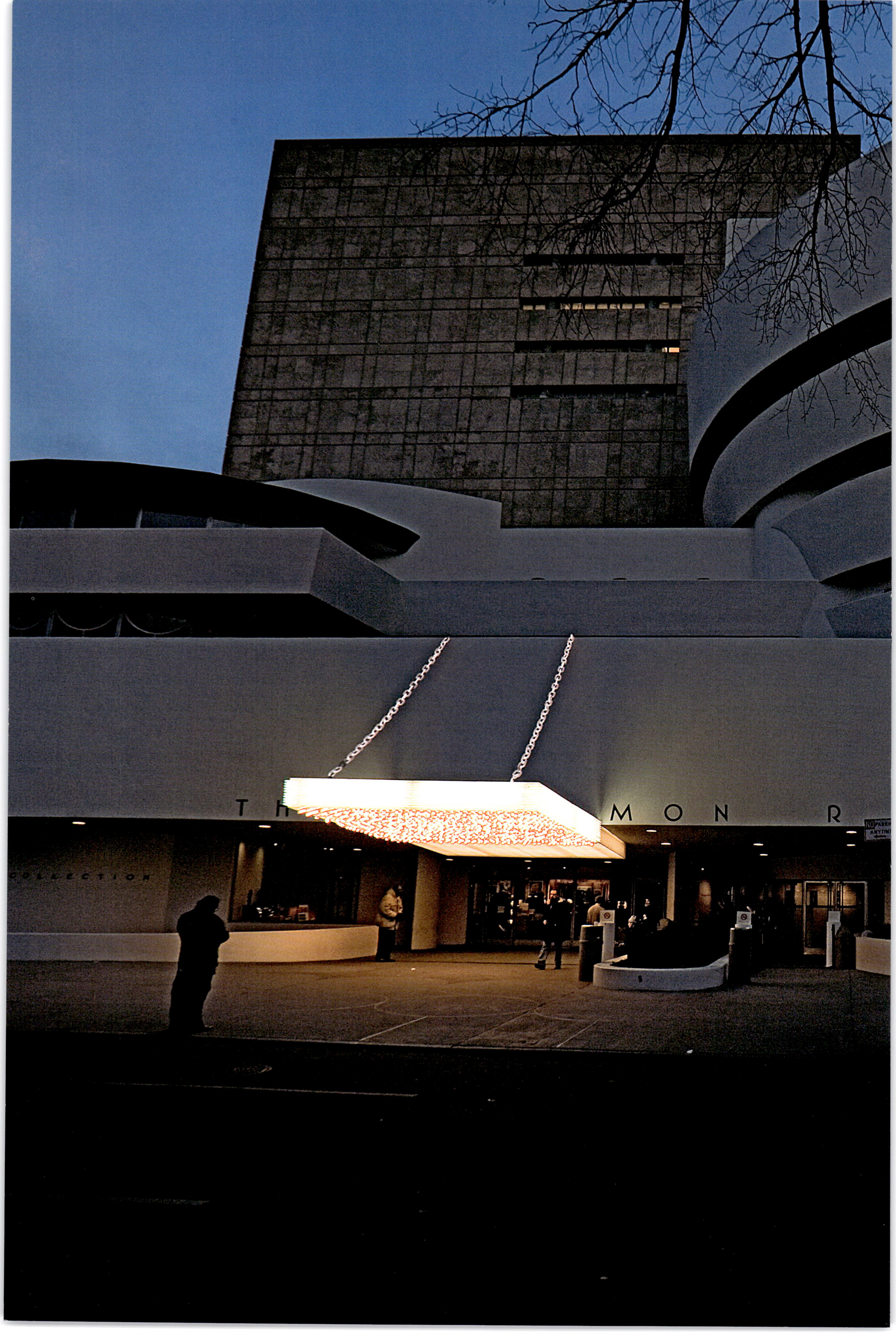

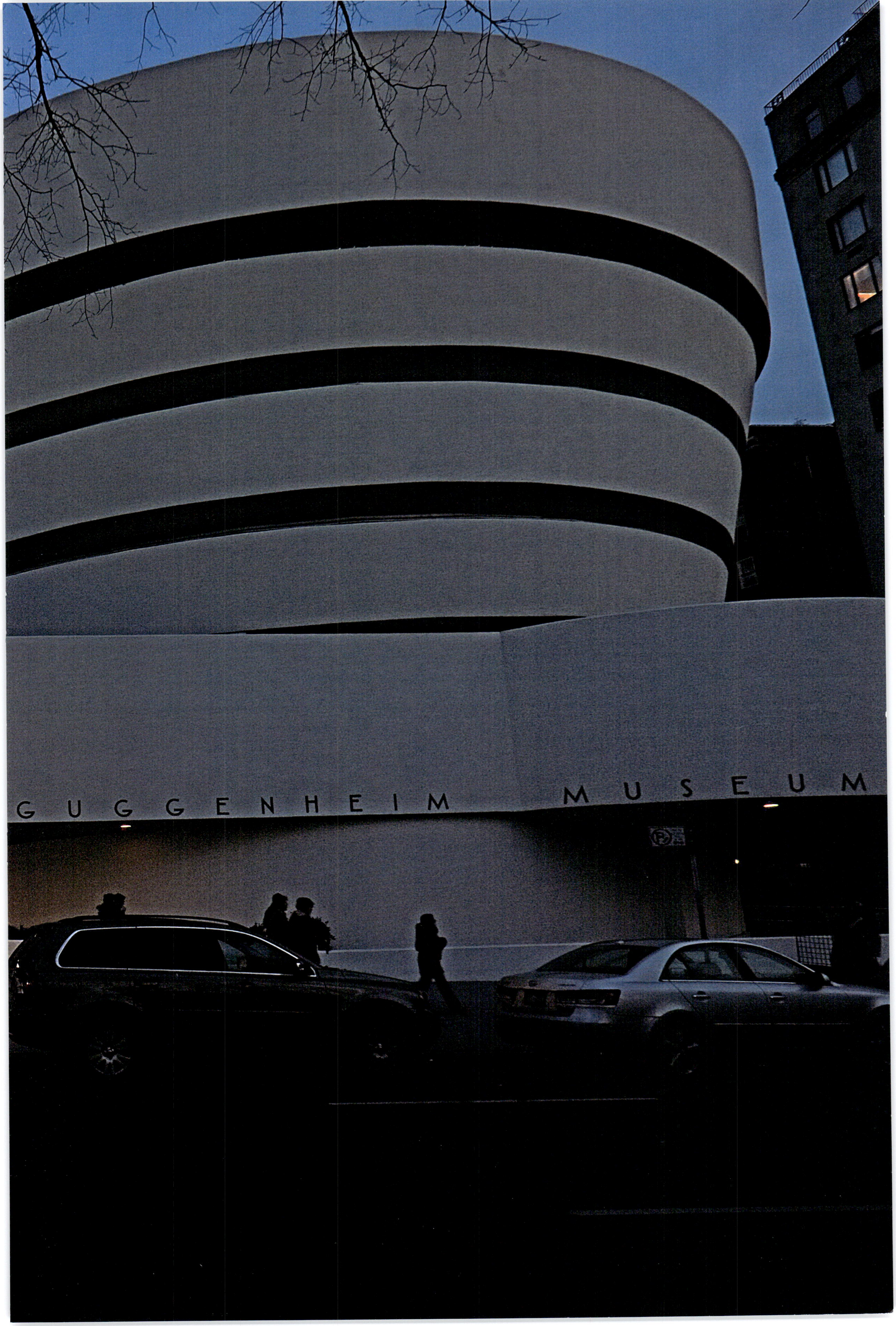
GUGGENHEIM MUSEUM

New York; Esther Schipper, Berlin, Pilar Corrias Inc., London This image is the product of a performance done in the Camargue. In an attempt to cast a spell, Parreno made a firework where each rocket carries a sigil—a magical symbol drawn on a piece of paper and burned into the sky.

Marquee, 2008 ◁ Translucid acrylic glass, steel frame, fluorescent tubes, 800 incandescent light bulbs, 30 neon lights (L.: 250 cm), 2 translucid acrylic glass chains; 80 × 500 × 500 cm approx.; (062) ‡ "Theanyspacewhatever," October 24, 2008–January 7, 2009, Solomon R. Guggenheim Museum, New York, United States (exhib. cat.); exhibition curator: Nancy Spector || 1 edition § Courtesy Esther Schipper, Berlin, and Friedrich Petzel, New York Inspired by the marquees at the entrances of American movie theaters, Parreno affixed a gigantic *Marquee* to the Frank Lloyd Wright Guggenheim Museum. It was suspended by luminous chains referencing a drawbridge and had computer-controlled flickering light bulbs alluding to the effect of the light of a fire. This luminous sculpture was made specifically for the group exhibition organized by Nancy Spector on the collective practices of artists from the 1990s, including Pierre Huyghe, Dominique Gonzalez-Foerster, Liam Gillick, Rirkrit Tiravanija, Douglas Gordon, Jorge Pardo, Angela Bulloch, Carsten Höller and Maurizio Cattelan. Suggesting the entrance into a collective film showing, into a story that has already happened, the work transformed the iconic New York building into an abandoned movie theater, a place where blockbusters were once screened.

Audioguide 11, Guggenheim, NY, 2008 ◁ Installation: ¬ headphones • MP3 players • soundtrack (English, 32') ‡ "Theanyspacewhatever," October 24, 2008–January 7, 2009, Solomon R. Guggenheim Museum, New York, United States (exhib. cat.); exhibition curator: Nancy Spector || 1 edition § Courtesy Friedrich Petzel, New York; Air de Paris, Paris; Esther Schipper, Berlin; Pilar Corrias Inc., London This audio guide available for visitors to the exhibition, is a redux of the audio guides the artist made at the beginning of the 1990s. The world's word memory champion, Boris Konrad, recites from memory an eight-page text written by Parreno about the shared story of the artists in the exhibition. Central to this work is the gap between the facts and the way they are remembered by the memorist. As he speaks, Konrad hesitates and forgets.

Fraught Times: For Eleven Months of the Year It's an Artwork and in December It's Christmas (October), 2008 ◁ Christmas tree in cast aluminum, paint (272 × 205 cm), musical score by Monroe Transfer ‡ "Philippe Parreno," October 16–November 19, 2008, Pilar Corrias Ltd, London, United Kingdom || 1 edition ∫ Private collection, Zurich, Switzerland

Previous pages: **Marquee, 2008,** exhibition view "Theanyspacewhatever", Solomon R. Guggenheim Museum, New York, 2008

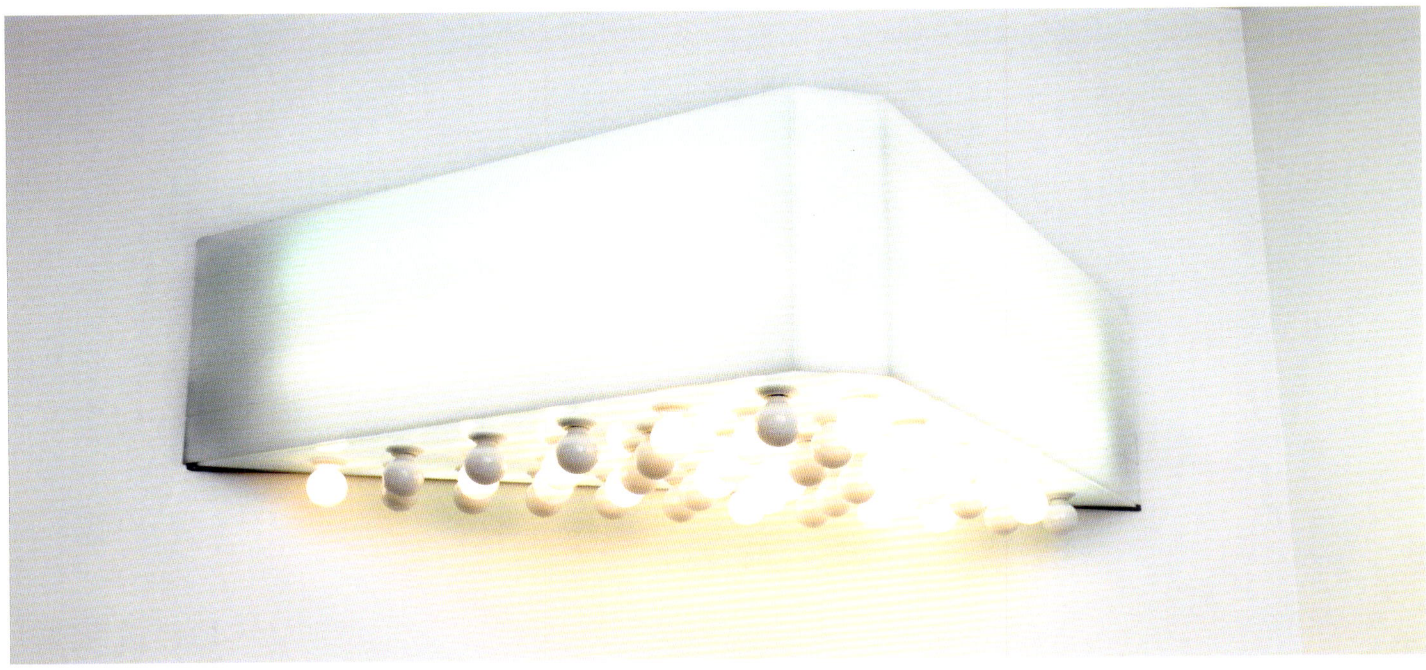

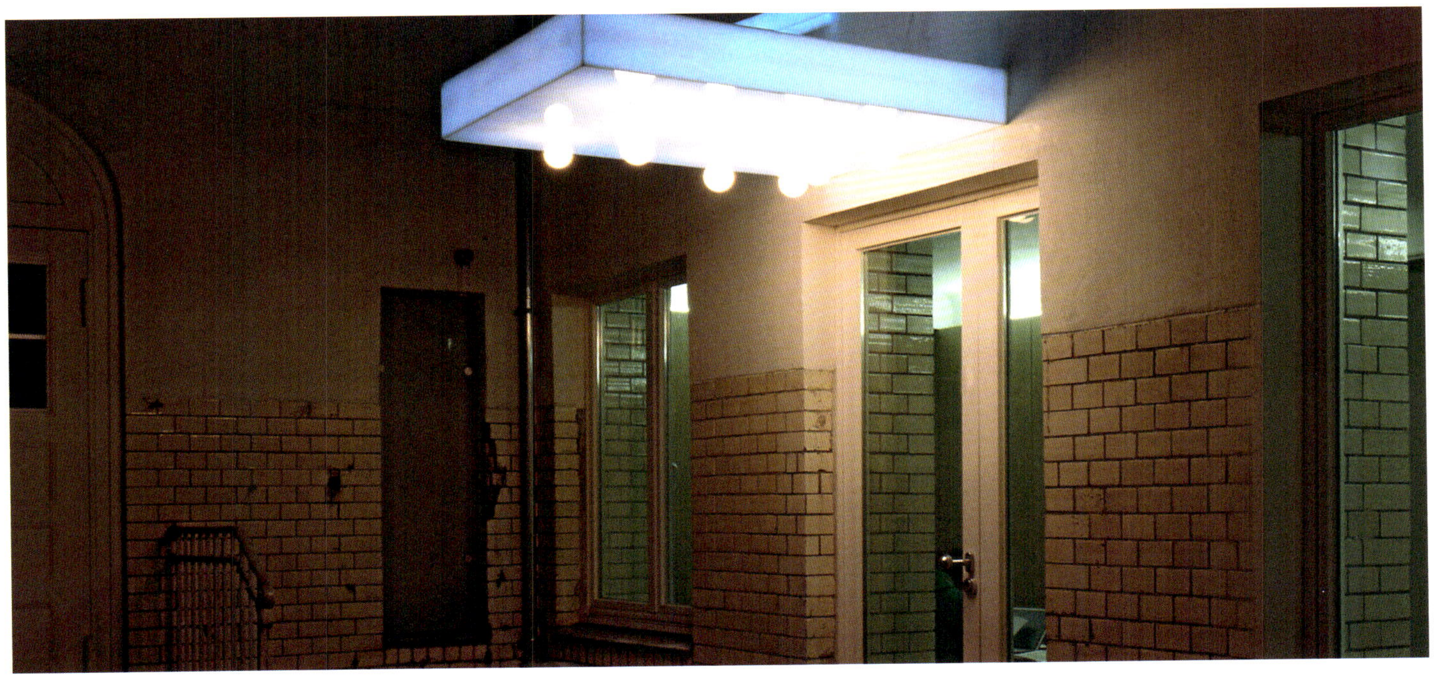

Marquee, 2008 ; Marquee, 2008
Marquee, 2007, exhibition view "Interior Cartoons", Esther Schipper, Berlin, 2007

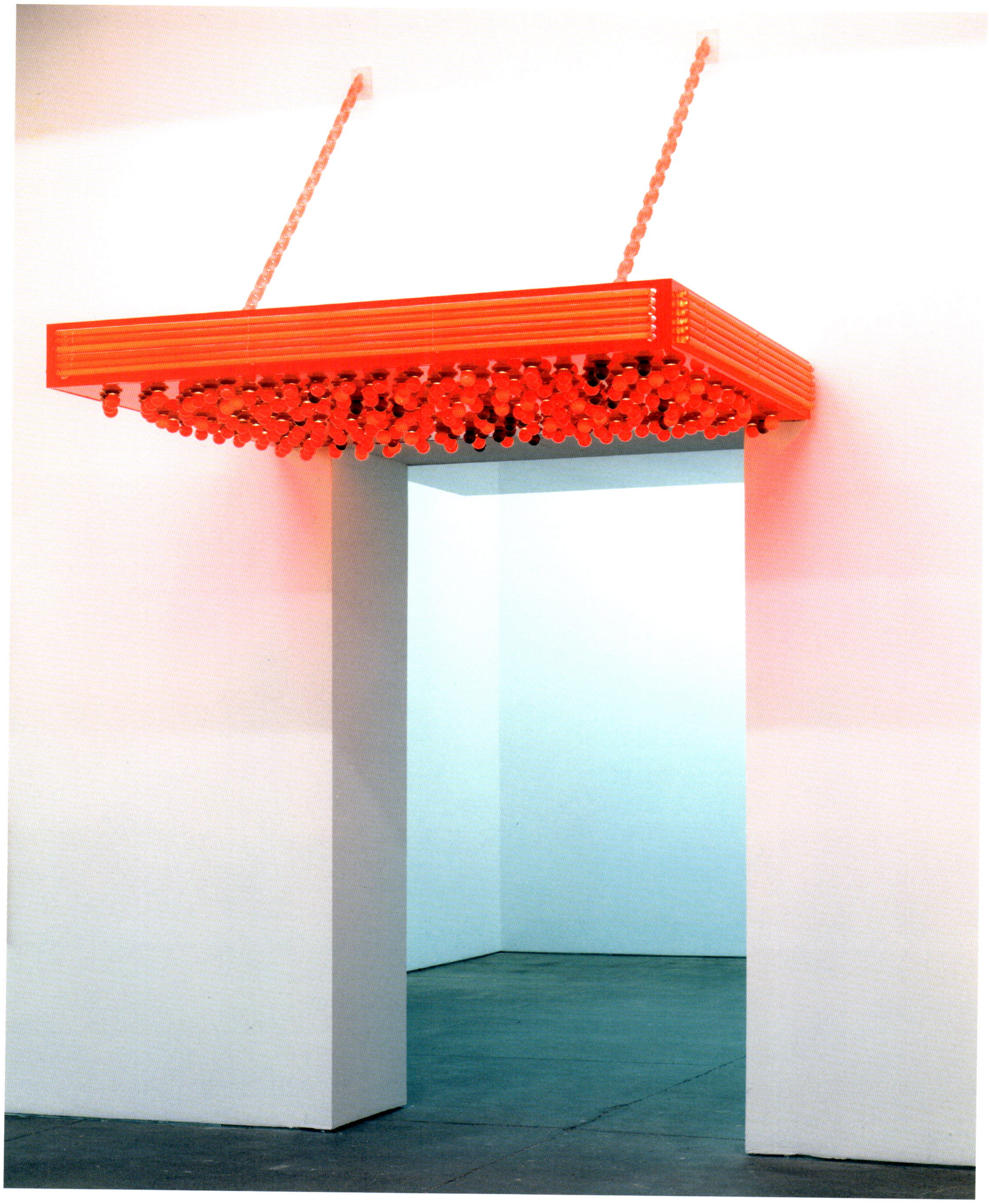

Marquee, 2008, exhibition view "Suicide in Vermillon Sands", Friedrich Petzel Gallery, New York, 2008

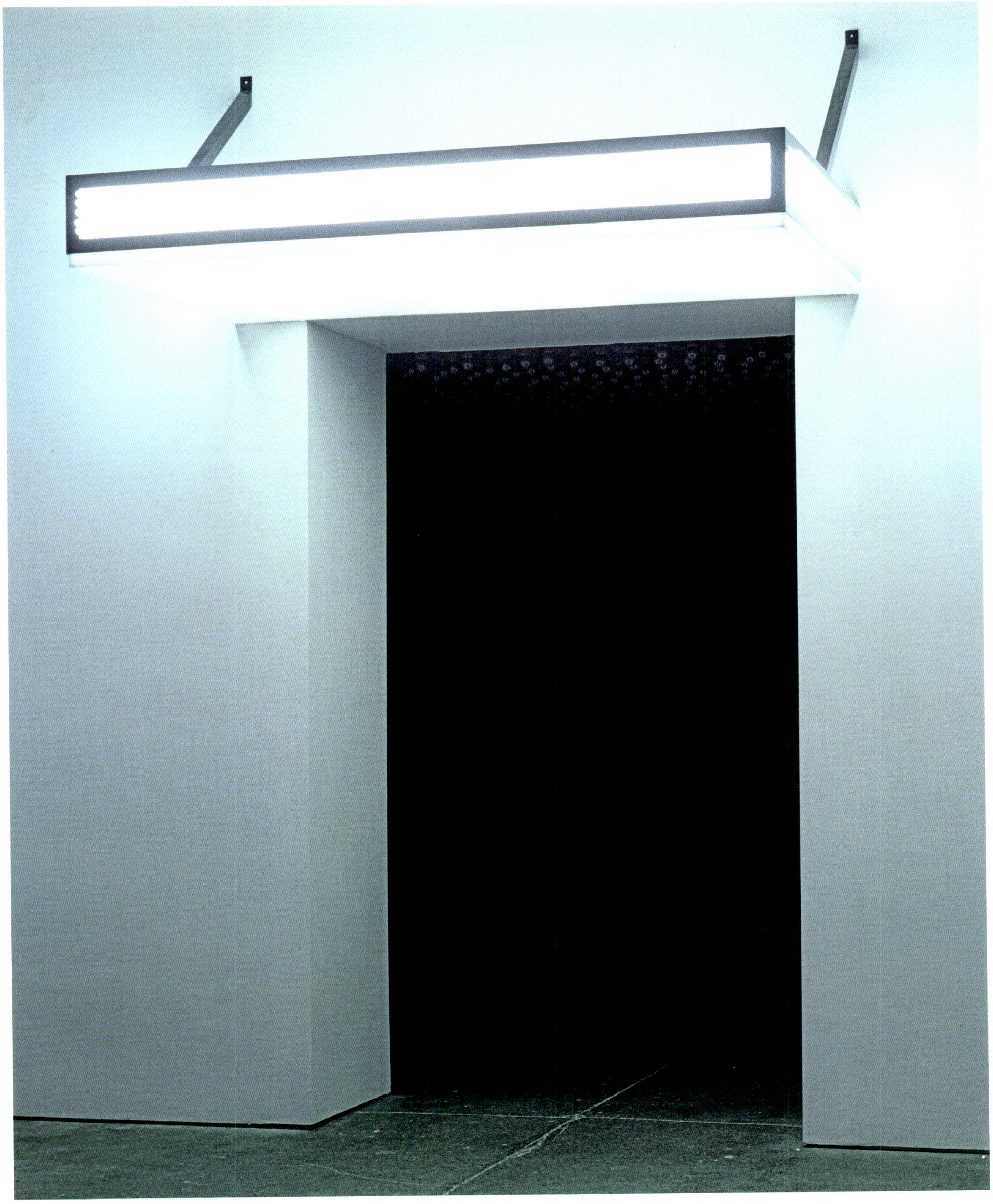

Marquee, 2008, exhibition view "Suicide in Vermillon Sands", Friedrich Petzel Gallery, New York, 2008

62. Parreno, text for the exhibition, Paris December 3, 2007.

This cast aluminum sculpture, a painted Christmas tree, is both a decorative object and a cultural marker of time. This "monument of time"[62] exists as an art object for eleven months of the year, but is only functional during the month of December. In a Postmodern era, *Fraught Times* abandons time-based media, offering a new way of understanding the temporal-element of the artwork through the mutability of a familiar cultural object. ◊ This project celebrates the opening of a new London gallery space, Pilar Corrias Gallery. A musical score written by Monroe Transfer, a London-based band, is hung next to the tree. The purchaser of the work has the option of organizing a performance around the tree with children who can play sad and romantic music originally composed for guitar, violin and percussion, with instruments of their choice. It is left to the collector to determine whether to carry out the protocol which accompanies *Fraught Times*.

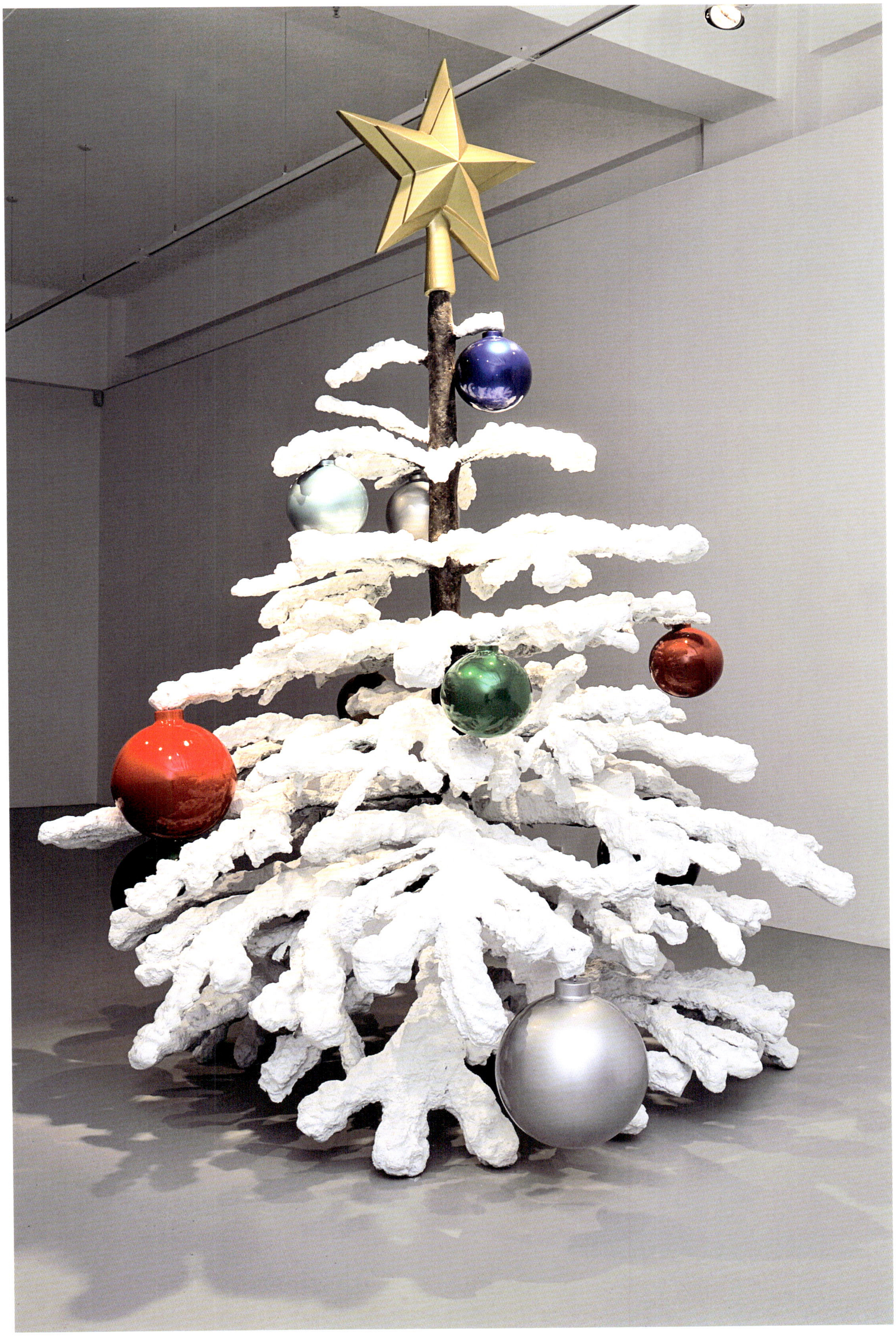

Fraught Times: For Eleven Months of the Year it's an Artwork and in December it's Christmas (October), 2008, exhibition view "October", Pilar Corrias ltd, London, 2008

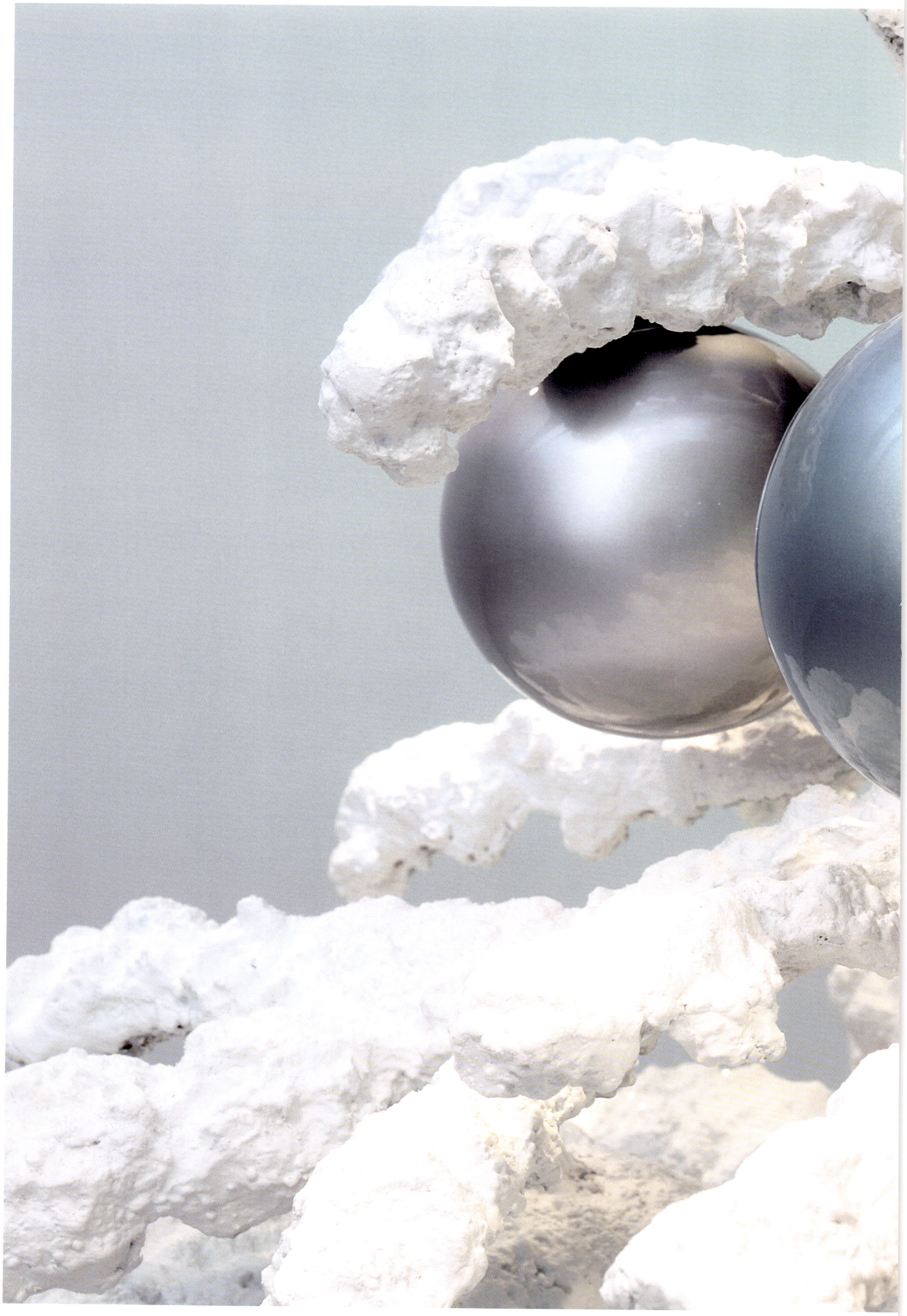

Fraught Times: For Eleven Months of the Year It's an Artwork and in December It's Christmas (October), 2008

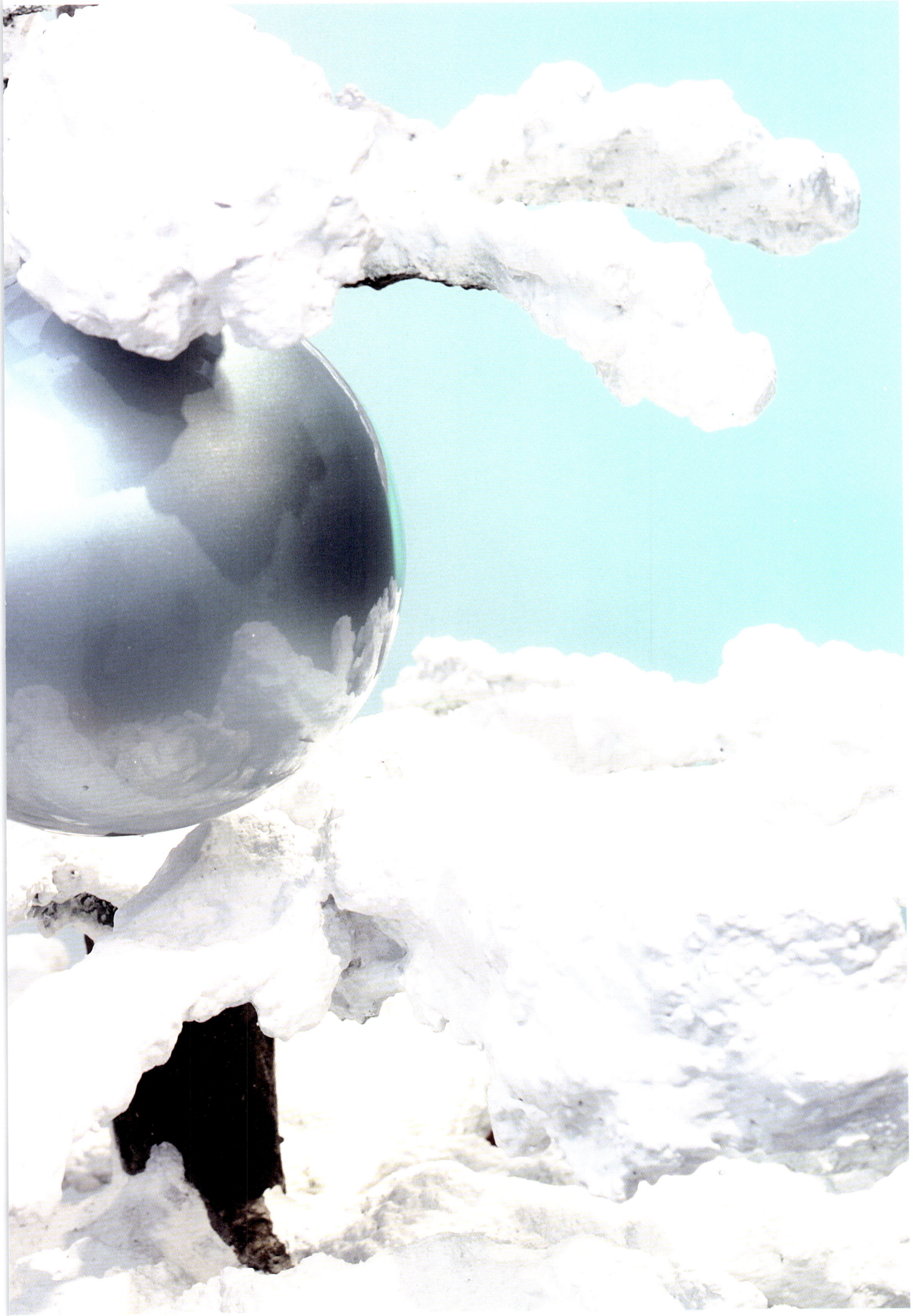

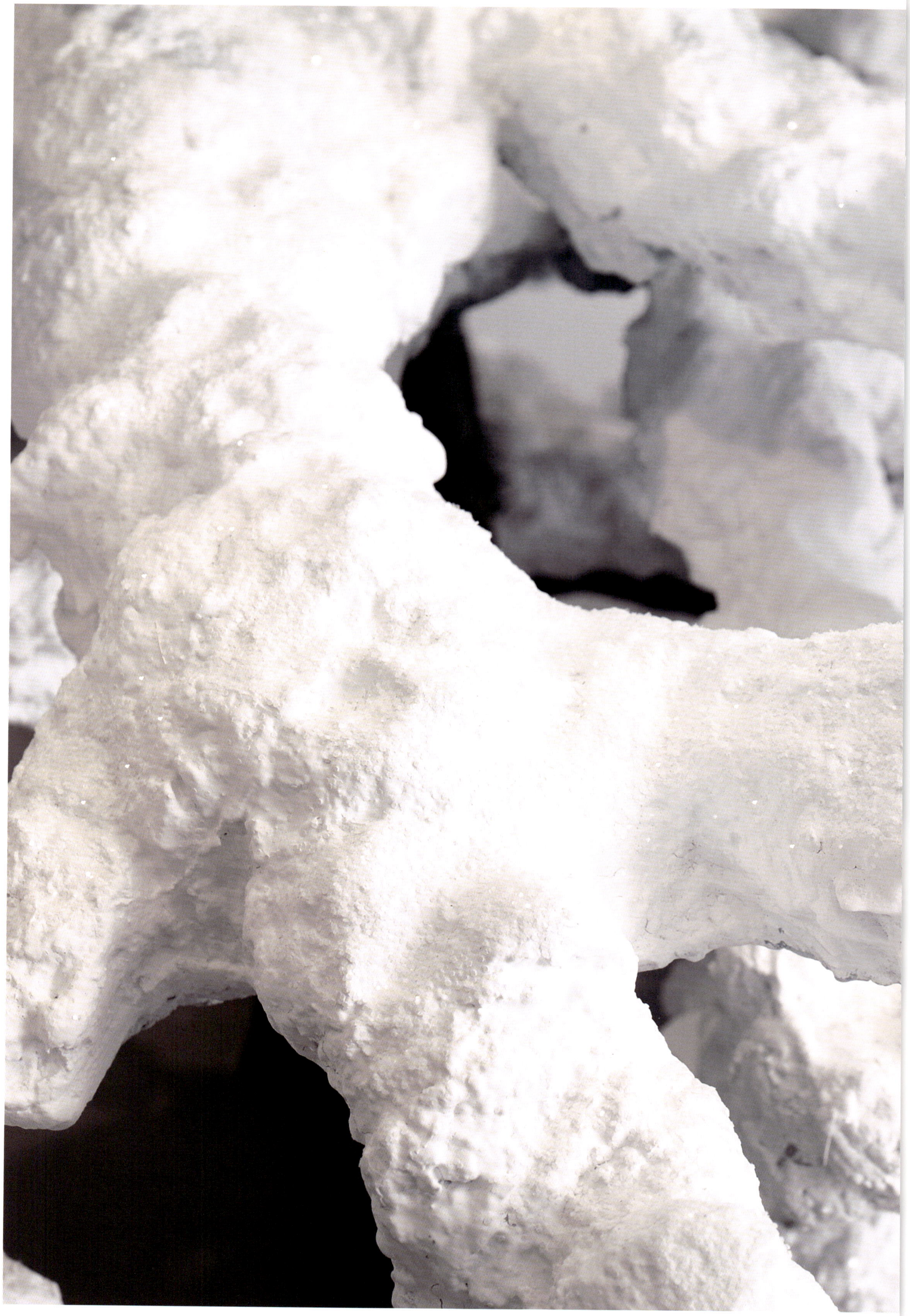

Fraught Times: For Eleven Months of the Year It's an Artwork and in December It's Christmas (October), 2008

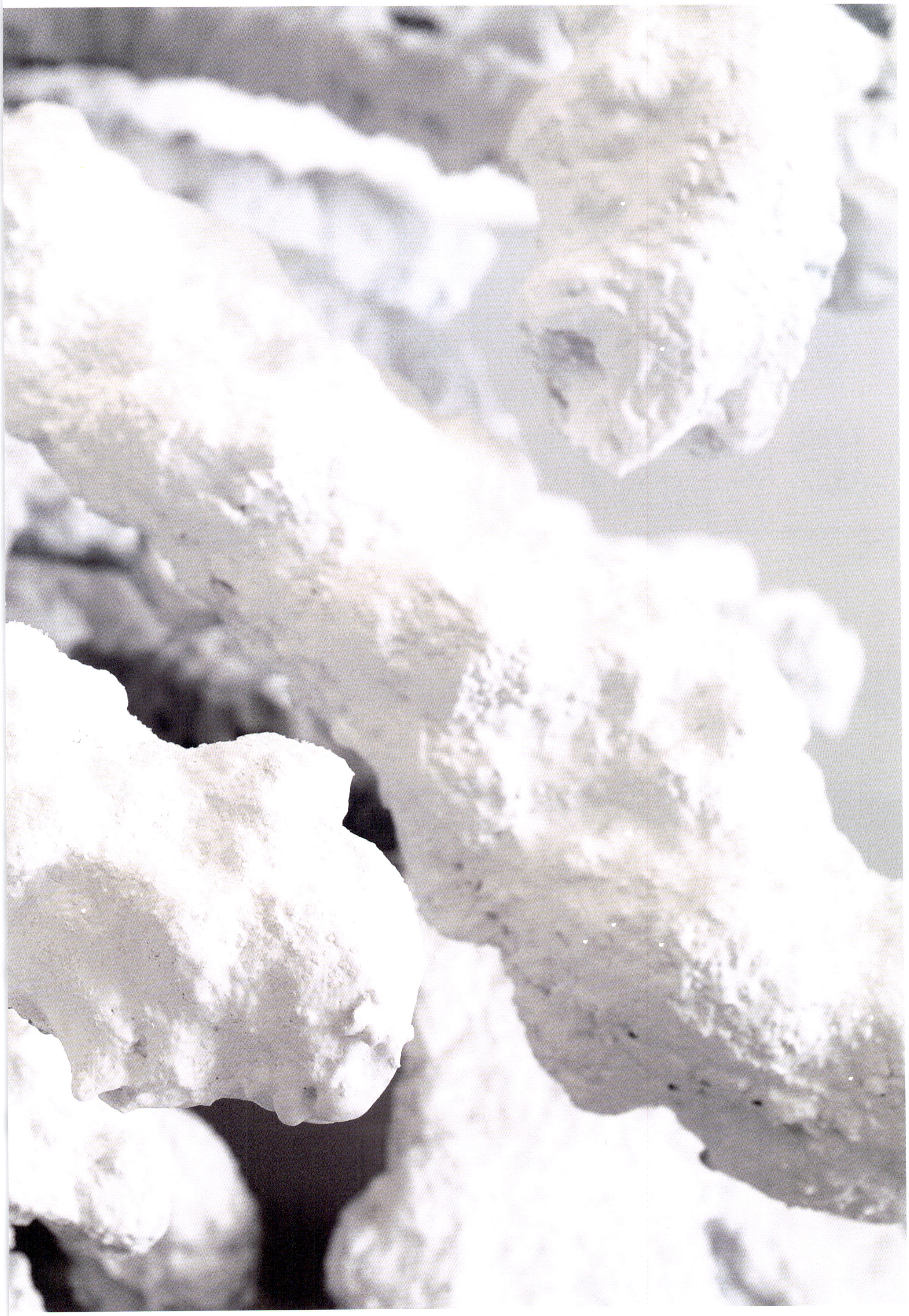

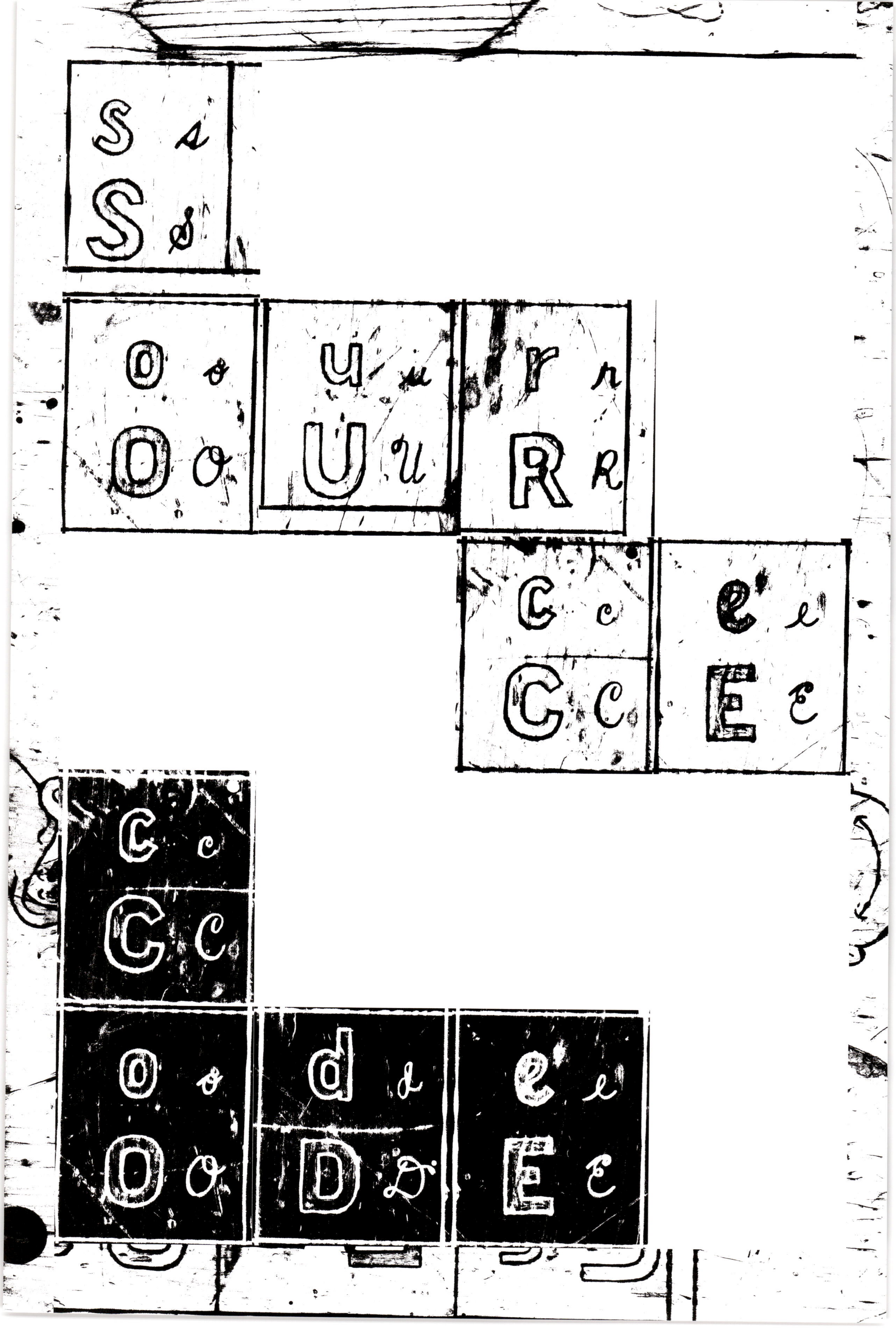
S s S s
O o O o
U u U u
R r R r
C c C c
E e E e
C c C c
O o O o
D d D d
E e E e

Source Code ◊ Notes and captions on an invisible text

Charles Arsène-Henry

"*You are like a rich man entering heaven*
Through the ear of a raindrop." Seamus Heaney, *The Rain Stick*

In the first days of January, I interviewed Philippe Parreno several times in his studio. He was working on this exhibition and I was working on a project /*White Box Black Box*/ which triggered the idea of collecting the principles of an event rather than recording the event itself. Instead of describing Philippe's work for the catalogue, I decided to unfold his references through footnotes and captions, thus revealing the subtext of our conversations and of the surface of his work.

Michelangelo Antonioni, *La Notte*: Jeanne Moreau wandering the streets of the modern new town. Semi-deserted, semi-populated landscape. Ordinary people observing the beginning whose end will be witnessed by the child, Philippe Parreno.

1. See Édouard Dujardin, *The Bays are Sere*, London, Libris, 1991, p.1: "For from the chaos of appearances, amid periods and sites, in the illusion of things being begotten and born, one among the others, distinct from the others, yet similar to the others, one the same and yet another, from the infinity of possible existences, I appear; and this is time and space being defined; it is the Now, it is the Here; the clock striking; and around me, life; the time, the place, an April evening. Paris, on a bright evening of setting sun, the monotonous noises, the pale houses, the foliage of shadows; a milder evening; and the joy of being someone, of walking; the streets and multitudes, and, stretching far in the air, the sky; all around, Paris sings, and, in the haze of shapes perceived, softly it frames the idea."

2. Triggered by the appearance of the first Walkman in 1979, the TPS-L2, he referred to the ability to walk through the streets of a city enveloped in a halo of sound as *pure epiphany*.

3. *Sandanista!* was the fourth album by The Clash. Released in 1980, it featured three discs, each containing six songs, a total of 36 tracks. The band members sacrificed a substantial percentage of their royalties to enable the three vinyl records to be sold for the price of one. "To buy the album, walk along carrying the boxed set in my hands, open it as soon as I was in my bedroom and discover the *three* white sleeves, *three* discs, was just incredible. I discovered that one could actually transmit an idea *physically*, it was as though they were whispering in my ear, as though they had placed those hours of music right into my hands, it felt as if the whole thing was directly addressed to me," he recalled.

4. See Serge Daney, *Persévérance*, Paris, P.O.L., 1994, pp.78-79: "The cinema [...] is an *art of showing*. And showing is a gesture, a gesture that forces you to see, to look. Without this gesture, there is only imagery. But once something has been shown, somebody *has to* acknowledge it."

5. See Douglas Coupland, *Girlfriend in a Coma*, Harper Perennial, 1997: "She unzipped her overalls on a steep, breast-shaped mogul, then hauled me into the woods, where she yanked me down into the scraping snow, a snow too icy for snow angels. I felt so young, and she looked so mature. She pulled me with unfamiliar urgency, as though an invasion were about to occur that would send us off to war. And so there we lay, pumping like lions, the insides of our heads like hot slot machines clanging out silver dollars, rubies, and sugar candies."

6. Joy Division, *Love Will Tear Us Apart*: "*You cry out in your sleep / All my failings exposed? / And there's a taste in my mouth / As desperation takes hold / Just that something so good / Just can't function no more / When love, love will tear us apart again*"

7. He has never perceived any difference between the everyday experience of the real, the books he was reading, the images he sees or the music he was listening to. He has always wondered whether his childhood memories correspond to his recorded memories of past events or to the images his father showed him. Kissing a girl in a corridor, reading a book describing a love affair or hearing one of his favorite songs sparked similar emotions in him. Mediated and immediate experiences overlaped.

8. See Serge Daney, *Persévérance, op. cit.*, pp. 54-55: "[...] I [made] the films talk as though they were beings with whom one could have a relationship of *filiation*. To satisfy maternal aspirations, the editing could only be over the top: I was cinephilial, cinefilial, a child of the cinema, born mythologically in such and such a film, several times over, because it was in that world, in the *limbo* of the cinema, that my father's body, neither dead nor alive, probably wandered like a ghost to whom no one had attributed a grave, as in Greek tragedy."

9. See Jean-François Lyotard, *Lectures d'enfance*, Paris, Galilée, 1991, p.9: "Childhood is not a stage of life and does not fade. It haunts discourse, which ceaselessly sets it aside, this is its separation. And yet precisely thus, the latter is determined to rebuild it, as though it were lost. It envelops it, unaware. Perpetuating it. If childhood remains, it is not despite but because it is lodged within the adult. Blanchot wrote: "*Noli me legere*, thou shalt not read me. That which does not allow itself to be written, in the written form, calls perhaps for a reader who can no longer or not yet read."

Jean-Luc Godard, *Le Mépris*: as she goes down the steps of the Villa Malaparte, Camille tells Paul that she despises him.
Poster of Paraguay.
Televised image of as Saint-Étienne's defeat against Bayern Munich in the Champions Clubs Cup.

10. It was in Grenoble's School of Fine Arts that reading first became an intense and regular activity for him. The school librarian, Jean-Claude Noué, played a vital matchmaking role, directing him toward books that would shed light on his research and ordering all the texts from *The Face* to *American Scientist* that he wanted: philosophy, literature, history, mathematics, essays, reviews and magazines. The library was a bottomless textual pit, from which he would pluck themed carrots, as he began to freely associate between ideas, forging parallel paths across the disciplines.

11. "What is Time, but a variety of one thing?" Austin Osman Spare, *Focus of Life*, London, The Morland Press, 1921, p. 25.

12. He holds science-fiction to be the ultimate expression of the power of the novel, the spectacular figure of literature: black signs on white rectangles capable of creating galaxies. It is also a form of literature that is consumed differently: reading becomes a *trip*, static yet a real journey.

13. He has described collaboration several times as a *holographic figure*: a number of viewpoints on a single object produce a new common object. Each person can lay claim to his own point of view but the convergence of aims generates an object that belongs to no one in particular and to all in general.

14. He sees in Stephen Donaldson's epic cycle *The Gap Sequence*, a face-to-face encounter between the captains of three interstellar vessels who confront and use one another to the utmost, the outstanding figure of a collaboration which, whatever the outcome, has been pushed to its maximum. The image of a narrowed-down community which decides to produce a story by laying itself entirely at its disposal: "The story is all. The three protagonists are destroying one another but at the same time, they are creating the most sublime pages."

15. See Serge Daney, "Borg-McEnroe ou les beautés de la raison pure", in *L'Amateur de tennis*, Paris, P.O.L., 1994, p. 39: "Perhaps surprising themselves with the success of their shots, one gets the feeling, in this top-ranked duel, that they too are succumbing to the dizzying effects of symmetry, *wanting yet not wanting* to come down on one side or the other."

16. Plato, *The Laws*, in *Complete Works*, 797 (a), Indianapolis, Hackett, 1997, p.1465: "ATHENIAN: I maintain that no one in any state has really grasped that children's games affect legislation so crucially as to determine whether the laws that are passed will survive or not."

17. A theory of *otium*, a necessity not merely in the work-vs-leisure context, can be found in Jean-Claude Milner, *Le Salaire de l'idéal*, Paris, Seuil, 1997.

18. *Dune*, by David Lynch, is the film he has seen most often. "*Dune* is constantly starting over, it's a series of *trailers*, which carry the promise of a story. It affects me in the same way as a mantra: the more I recite it, the deeper is the ecstasy."

19. He stresses the schism that has taken place within science-fiction: "Cyberpunk isn't an epic or sidereal form of literature, it focuses the drama on assemblage, the accumulation of the details that make up a world. A whole novel can be triggered by a fault in an IT exploitation system. There is no master-plan, no great lyrical flights of fancy relating to imaginary or parallel universes, but the demonstration of a future reliant on ordinary reality, on daily life. Obliques and paradoxes are always ignited from a world that already exists. This *exhibition literature* left its mark on me: it is by picking up on or provoking minor flaws that I can alter a situation, because it doesn't take much for reality to create fiction. The exhibition at Beaubourg is an example of this: the space is simply a large platform and I have no intention of building a wall of any kind, I just want to see how I can function with this bare platform. Not going against things but flowing with them."

20. To find out more about the notion of assemblage, see Neal Stephenson, *Snow Crash*, Bantam Spectra Books, 1992.

21. See Gilles Deleuze and Félix Guattari, *Mille Plateaux*, Paris, Les Editions de Minuit, 1980, pp. 643-645.

John Badham, *War Games* (final scene): Stephen Falken, a young programmer, and Joshua, the computer, are playing tick-tack-toe. The young man beats the machine and trains it to play endless matches against itself, all of them draws. In doing so, it exhausts every possible scenario of global nuclear war and understands that the game can never be won. The challenge has gone and all that remains is the pleasure of playing: *Joshua: "A strange game. The only move is not to play. How about a nice game of chess?"*
Tim Burton, *Edward Scissorhands*: a filmmaker with whom he felt he shared a *common* imaginary, as though the visual content of his brain was projected before his eyes. He still considers Burton to be the inventor of the modern-day tale.

22. In common with other artists of his generation, he detected in cyberpunk literature the signs of a new strategic positioning, essential in his eyes: from now on one needs to become part of the system in order to manipulate or pervert it. The role of outsider has disappeared, thus it is impossible to escape the world in which one acts. By following the thread of the cyberpunk novels, one of the most prevalent misinterpretations found in texts devoted to his work can be avoided: the idea was never to abandon or eliminate the object but actually to modify and redefine it.

23. Again this is a reference to the ambiguous link between the image and the real. The idea was to extract a cinematographic image from a movie and produce it in 3-D: what happens when an image penetrates reality?

24. Jacques Lacan, The Seminar of Jacques Lacan, *Freud's papers on technique 1953-1954*, Cambridge University Press, 1988, Book I, p.178: "Think for a moment in the real. It is owing to the fact that the word elephant exists in their deliberations, that men have been capable of taking, in relation to elephants, even before touching them, decisions which are more far-reaching for these pachyderms than anything else that has happened to them throughout their history - the crossing of a river or the natural decimation of a forest. With nothing more than the word elephant and the way in which men use it, propitious or unpropitious things, auspicious or inauspicious things, in any event catastrophic things, have happened to elephants long before anyone raised a bow or a gun to them."

25. Austin Osman Spare, *The Book of Pleasure*, Thames, I-H-O Books, 2005, p. 50: "By Sigils I have endowed fools with wisdom, made the wise fools, giving health to the sick and weak, disease to the strong, etc. Now, if for some purpose, you wanted the strength of a tiger—you should make a sentence such as: 'This is my wish, to obtain the strength of a tiger.'"

26. Jaron Lanier came up with an alternative to the software/hardware system by viewing the way a computer works in terms of a musical instrument. A violin does not contain a program, only when it comes into contact with a violinist does it realize its full potential. Just as a stone is only aware of gravity when it comes into contact with the ground, so can a computer learn by being handled and be configured as a result of individual practice.

27. Cedric Price, *CP 1965*, reproduced in *Re: CP*, Bâle/Boston, Birkhäuser, 2003, p. 57: "Since the social concept of the Fun Palace is primarily a people's workshop or university of the streets, the self-participatory element of the activities must extend to a degree of control by the users of their physical environment. Inbuilt flexibility, or planned obsolescence, can be achieved only if the time factor is included as an absolute design factor in the total design process."

28. On the performative aspect of image creation, see Jacques Rivette, "De l'abjection", *Cahiers du cinéma*, 120 (June 1961), pp.54-55; reproduced in the special issue of *Cahiers du cinéma*, "Le Siècle du cinéma" (November 2000), p. 67. Translated by David Phelps, with the assistance of Jeremi Szaniawski: "Look, however, in *Kapo*, at the shot where Riva kills herself by throwing herself on an electric barbed-wire fence; the man who decides, at that moment, to have a dolly in to tilt the body, while taking care to precisely note the hand raised in the angle of its final framing - this man deserves nothing but the most profound contempt."

29. Cephalopods embody the possibility of "post-symbolic communication," a method of expression in which the word is also the object: these creatures *become what they name*. But even if the sheer power of their brain is greater than that of humans, these animals have not produced any form of culture. For culture can be defined precisely as the coalescence of the desire to be *something* and the *impossibility* of such a desire.

30. See Steven Spielberg, *Close Encounters of the Third Kind*.

John Carpenter, *They Live*: two men are fighting with their fists, heads, knees and wooden planks for minutes at a time. One of them, by means of his magic glasses, sees the world as it really is and is determined to persuade the other to reach this level of reality. The latter refuses. They fight.

31. He made a similar remark on another occasion: "I was insatiable about signs. What appealed to me in the *Cahiers du cinéma* and Daney in particular was the way they developed a language that was capable of talking about images. When Daney started writing for *Libération*, he opened up an even wider spectrum: without any kind of hierarchical value judgment, he observed every type of image. He would pick two elements, the Benetton campaign and *Palombella Rossa* for instance, and make something else of them. The commentary became in turn a generator of forms. That was important to me, the idea that the commentary could be as interesting as the object to which it was referring. And yet a dimension was lost in the move to the written word. The exhibition format, on the other hand, allowed me to lay myself open to an avalanche of signs and retaliate with signs of the same type. I began to return signs in the same way as I received them."

32. For a long time, Kenji Mizoguchi was his favorite film-maker.

33. See Pier Paolo Pasolini, *Scritti corsiri*. Translated by Cédric Moullier: "The Christian Democrat regime went through two completely distinctive phases, two phases that not only cannot be compared to one another because this would imply a form of continuity between them, but two phases which have become utterly irreconcilable from an historic point of view. The first phase of this regime (as the Radicals always justifiably insisted on calling it) begins with the end of the war and lasts until the fireflies have vanished, and the second spans the disappearance of the fireflies to the present time."

34. Phosphorescence is one example of this indexation of art based on temporality, its analysis, an antidote to a second recurrent misinterpretation, the notion that he produces *ephemeral* objects: "One of the fundamental tenets was that without an exhibition there is no object, and that at a given moment the object is liable to merge into the exhibition entirely. That does not make it an ephemeral work but a *stochastic* entity, that which appears in order to disappear. Without an exhibition there is no object, because it is the exhibition that becomes the object."

35. Following from these reflections on the event as a collective image, Wolfgang Tillmans' photographs published in *i-D* showed that the *fact* of merely being there could create an image. An image *negotiated* between its protagonists, an image manufactured at the instigation of a social moment.

36. He spent a great deal of time talking to me about Kazuo Shinohara, one of his heroes who was the first architect to create buildings in accordance with the city's *black flows*: pollution, industrial secretions, accidents, resistance. His buildings, whose forms arise from this sombre context and are essentially made out of concrete, are camouflaged within the city, merging into it. The structures are so heavy that the architecture needs to be colonized, to find its place and curl up into it: the antithesis of design. Observing the images of *House under High Voltage Lines* and *House with Earthen Floor*, he said "It's so beautiful you would think it was a film."

37. In the 1990s he would listen endlessly to soundtracks of Japanese mangas, as though drawn into an abyss. He saw in them the ultimate version of a type of music that had succeeded in breaking free of Man, having nothing left to say to him, and was now a monstrous organism.

38. See Louis Althusser, *L'Avenir dure longtemps*, Paris, Stock/IMEC, 1992 [*The Future Lasts a Long Time*, Vintage, 1994, translated by Richard Veasey].

39. In the course of our interview, on January 10, 2009, I noticed two microphones stuck to one of the windows of his studio and connected to the loudspeakers of his computer. "The microphones pick up the vibrations of the street," he explained, "so that you're actually capturing the *radio of the city*. I'm incredibly drawn to the concept of radio, I've always been fascinated by pirate radio stations and if I hadn't opted for art, I would have worked in radio." He went on to maintain that this was the only form of expression that would survive the disappearance of Man, with the radio waves infinitely scanning interstellar space.

40. *In the Beginning… Was the Command Line.*

James Cameron, *The Abyss*: a liquid corridor visiting an underwater oil platform.
James Cameron, *Terminator 2*: T 1000, the polymorphic droid, in liquid metal.
Shuji Terayama, *Emperor Tomato Ketchup*: at the end of the film, a pirate-child comes towards the camera, a bottle of Coca-Cola in his hand. Inside it is a lizard, bent double, trapped, too big to fit into the container, probably on the verge of asphyxiation. The child, facing the camera, brandishes the bottle and cries: "That's Japan!"

Biographical notes / List of exhibitions

Born in 1964 in Oran (Algeria)

Lives and works in Paris (France)

Education

1981–1983 First/second year advanced maths class preparing for the *Grandes Écoles*, Grenoble, France

1983–1988 École des beaux-arts de Grenoble, France

1988–1989 Institut des hautes études en arts plastiques (first session), Palais de Tokyo, Paris, France

Solo Exhibitions
* With publication

2010

Center for Curatorial Studies and Art in Contemporary Culture, Bard College, Annandale-on-Hudson, NY, United States*

2009

Kunsthalle Zürich, Zürich, Switzerland*

Centre Pompidou, Musée national d'art moderne (Mnam), Paris, France*

Irish Museum of Modern Art (IMMA), Dublin, Ireland*

2008

"Suicide in Vermillon Sands," Friedrich Petzel Gallery, New York, United States*

"October," Pilar Corrias Inc., London, United Kingdom

2007

"Interior Cartoons" Esther Schipper, Berlin, Germany

"Stories Are Propaganda," Friedrich Petzel Gallery, New York, United States

"What Do You Believe, Your Eyes or My Words?," Haunch of Venison, London, United Kingdom

"Le Cri ultrasonic de l'écureuil," Air de Paris, Paris, France

"Il Tempo Del Postino: A Group Show" (with Hans Ulrich Obrist), Opera House, Manchester, United Kingdom*

2006

"Interior Cartoons," Esther Schipper, Berlin, Germany

" Le Cri ultrasonic de l'écureuil" (with Ronn Lucas), Studio 28, Paris, France

"The Boy From Mars," Center for Contemporary Art Kitakyushu (CCA), Kitakyushu, Japan

". all hawaii eNtrées / LuNar reGGae" (with Rachael Thomas), Irish Museum of Modern Art (IMMA), Dublin, Ireland*

2005

"The Boy From Mars," Friedrich Petzel Gallery, New York, United States

"Atlas of Clouds," 1301PE, Los Angeles, United States

" Philippe Parreno," Air de Paris, Paris, France

2004

"Fade Away," Kunstverein München, Munich, Germany

"Anna Sanders Films," World Wide Video Festival, Filmmuseum, Amsterdam, Netherlands

2003

"Alien Seasons," Friedrich Petzel Gallery, New York, United States

"TV Channel," Galerie Yvon Lambert, Paris, France

"Sky of the Seven Colors," Center for Contemporary Art Kitakyushu (CCA), Kitakyushu, Japan

"No Ghost Just a Shell" (with Pierre Huyghe), Van Abbemuseum, Eindhoven, Netherlands*

"No Ghost Just a Shell" (with Pierre Huyghe), Rosa de la Cruz Collection, Miami, United States*

2002

"Alien Seasons," Arc/musée d'Art moderne de la Ville de Paris, Paris, France*

"El sueño de una cosa," Portikus, Frankfurt, Germany

"Anywhere Out of the World," Kunstverein München, Munich, Germany

"No Ghost Just a Shell" (with Pierre Huyghe), Kunsthalle Zürich, Zürich, Switzerland*

"No Ghost Just a Shell" (with Pierre Huyghe), Institute of Visual Culture, Fitzwilliam Museum, Cambridge, United Kingdom*

"No Ghost Just a Shell" (with Pierre Huyghe), San Francisco Museum of Modern Art (SFMoMA), San Francisco, United States*

2001

"Mont Analogue," Air de Paris, Paris, France; Friedrich Petzel Gallery, New York, United States; Rirkrit Tiravanija's Studio, Bangkok, Thailand

"MMP : Philippe Parreno," Moderna Museet, Stockholm, Sweden

"One Thousand Pictures Falling From One Thousand Walls," Friedrich Petzel Gallery, New York, United States

"No Ghost Just a Shell in Exploding Cinema–Cinema Without Walls" (with Pierre Huyghe), Museum Boijmans Van Beuningen, Rotterdam, Netherlands

2000

"No Ghost Just a Shell: Anywhere Out of the World," Air de Paris, Paris, France; Schipper & Krome, Berlin, Germany

"One Thousand Pictures Falling From One Thousand Walls, 1997-2000," musée d'Art moderne et contemporain (Mamco), Geneva, Switzerland

1998

"Blue Almost Transparent," Kunstverein Ludwigsburg, Ludwigsburg, Germany

"Dominique Gonzalez-Foerster, Philippe Parreno, Pierre Huyghe," Arc/musée d'Art moderne de la Ville de Paris, Paris, France*

Institute of Visual Arts (Inova), University of Wisconsin, Milwaukee, United States

"Listen to the Picture," Schipper & Krome, Berlin, Germany

"Le Procès de Pol Pot" (with Liam Gillick), Le Magasin–Centre national d'art contemporain (Cnac), Grenoble, France

1997

"Postman Time, On art and its places open to 21 C," Kunsthalle Nürnberg, Nürnberg, Germany

"Philippe Parreno," Air de Paris, Paris, France

"Vitrines des artistes," Nina Ricci, Paris, France

"Speech Bubbles," galerie Sous-sol, Geneva, Switzerland

1996

"Ou," Air de Paris, Paris, France

"While, Snow Dancing, or the Merlin Disease, A Birthday Tree," Robert Prime Gallery, London, United Kingdom

"Happy Ending Sweden," Ynglagaten, Stockholm, Sweden

1995

"Snow Dancing," Le Consortium, Dijon, France

"Possessions," NZET Projekt, Ghent, Belgium

"While...," Kunstverein in Hamburg, Hamburg, Germany

"Le 1er Mai 1995," Schipper & Krome, Cologne, Germany

"Le Labyrinthe moral" (with Liam Gillick), Le Consortium, Dijon, France

1994

"Performance#1 (L'ordre du discours)" (with Yves Lecoq), musée d'Art contemporain (MAC), Marseilles, France

"Performance#2" (with Yves Lecoq), Fonds régional d'art contemporain (Frac) Burgundy, Dijon, France

"Cette Culture qui nous vient de la rue...," Galerie municipale, Vitry-sur-Seine, France

"La Nuit des héros," salle Garance, Centre Pompidou, Musée national d'art moderne (Mnam), Paris, France; Fonds régional d'art contemporain (Frac) Poitou-Charentes, Angoulême, France

1993

"Gegenüber von Buchholz & Buchholz," galerie Daniel Buchholz, Cologne, Germany

"Plädoyer," Esther Schipper, Cologne, Germany

"L'Imitateur," MAgalerie [galerie Emmanuel Perrotin], Paris, France

1992

"Philippe Parreno," galerie Claudine Papillon, Paris, France

1988

"Fleurs," Canal +, France

Collaborative Exhibitions
* With publication

2008

"Zidane: A 21st Century Portrait" (with Douglas Gordon), Magasin 3, Stockholm Konsthall, Stockholm, Sweden

"Douglas Gordon," doART, Gallery Hyunday Company, Beijing, China

"Zidane: A 21st Century Portrait" (with Douglas Gordon), DAAD Galerie, Berlin, Germany

2007

"Zidane: A 21st Century Portrait" (with Douglas Gordon), National Gallery of Canada, Ottawa, Canada

"Zidane: A 21st Century Portrait" (with Douglas Gordon), Institute of Modern Art (IMA), Brisbane, Australia

2006

"Philippe Parreno & Rirkrit Tiravanija," Friedrich Petzel Gallery, New York, United States

"Briannnnnn & Ferryyyyyy/ Law Creativity" (with Liam Gillick), Kunsthalle Zürich, Zürich, Switzerland; Konsthall Malmö, Malmö, Sweden; Vamiali's, Athens, Greece

"06.00 pm" (with Pierre Huyghe), San Francisco Art Institute, San Francisco, United States

2005

"Rirkrit Tiravanija: Une rétrospective (Tomorrow is Another Fine Day)" (with Rirkrit Tiravanija and Bruce Sterling), Couvent des Cordeliers, Paris, France*

"Briannnnnn & Ferryyyyyy/ Law and Creativity" (with Liam Gillick), Konsthall Malmö, Malmö, Sweden

"You and Me, Me and You" (with Douglas Gordon), Fondazione Davide Halevim, Milan, Italy

2004

"Rirkrit Tiravanija: No Vitrines, No Museums, No Artists, just a lot of People" (with Rirkrit Tiravanija, Pierre Huyghe and Maurizio Nannucci), Telecom Italia Future Center, Venice, Italy

"Law & Creativity" (with Liam Gillick), Lunds Konsthall, Lund, Sweden

2003

"Sodium Dreams" (with Dominique Gonzalez-Foerster and Pierre Huyghe), Center for Curatorial Studies and Art in Contemporary Culture, Bard College, Annandale-on-Hudson, NY, United States

"Annlee," Les Abattoirs, Toulouse, France

"Pardo/Parreno," Air de Paris, Paris, France

"25th International Graphic Biennal" (with Pierre Huyghe), Ljubljana, Slovenia

2002

"A Smile Without a Cat" (with Pierre Huyghe), Art Basel Miami, Miami, United States

"Jorge Pardo, Philippe Parreno," 1301PE Gallery, Los Angeles, United States

"Canal Bourgogne" (with François Roche), Pouilly-en-Auxois, France

"In Many Ways the Exhibition Already Happened" (with Pierre Huyghe, M/M (Paris), R&Sie), Institute of Contemporary Arts (ICA), London, United Kingdom

2001

"Animations," P.S.1 Contemporary Art Center, Long Island City, New York, United States

"Café Étienne Marcel" (with Pierre Huyghe and M/M (Paris)), Paris, France

"About" (with Dominique Gonzalez-Foerster and Pierre Huyghe), Contemporary Arts Center, Cincinnati, United States

2000

"Dominique Gonzalez-Foerster, Philippe Parreno, Pierre Huyghe," Kunstverein in Hamburg, Hamburg, Germany*

"AnnLee in Anzen Zone" (film by Dominique Gonzalez-Foerster presented by Pierre Huyghe and Philippe Parreno), galerie Jennifer Flay, Paris, France

"06.00 pm" (with Pierre Huyghe), San Francisco Art Institute, San Francisco, United States

1999

"D'Apertutto" (with Dominique Gonzalez-Foerster and Pierre Huyghe), 47th Venice Biennale, Venice, Italy*

"Le Pont du trieur" (with Charles de Meaux), cinéma 7 Parnassiens, Paris, France

1996

"Vicinato" (with Carsten Höller and Rirkrit Tiravanija), Raum Aktueller Kunst [Martin Janda Gallery], Vienna, Austria

"Temporary School" (with Dominique Gonzalez-Foerster and Pierre Huyghe), travelling project

1995

"Vicinato" (with Carsten Höller, Rirkrit Tiravanija), Guenzani Studio, Milan, Italy

"Volatile Colonies" (with Rirkrit Tiravanija), Johannesburg Biennale, Johannesburg, South Africa*

1994

"No More Reality versus Zukunft" (with Carsten Höller), Galleri Nicolai Wallner, Copenhagen, Denmark*

"Innocent et emprisonné : mais ce que vous avez contre moi, c'est que j'ai abandonné mon premier amour" (with Carsten Höller), Air de Paris, Paris, France

1992

"I, Myself and the Others" (with Dominique Gonzalez-Foerster, Pierre Joseph, Philippe Perrin), Le Magasin-Centre national d'art contemporain (Cnac), Grenoble, France*

1991

"La Vérité" (with Pierre Joseph, Dominique Gonzalez-Foerster and Bernard Joisten), Lyons Biennale of Contemporary Art, Lyons, France*

"Try Snaking" (with Pierre Joseph), Air de Paris, Nice, France; Giò Marconi Gallery, Milan, Italy*; Yaki Kornblit Gallery, Amsterdam, Netherlands; Fonds régional d'art contemporain (Frac) Poitou-Charentes, Angoulême, France; Tiefgarage, Cologne, Germany*

1990

"Les Ateliers du Paradise" (with Pierre Joseph and Philippe Perrin), Air de Paris, Nice, France

"Once Upon a Time… in City Bild" (with Pierre Joseph), Esther Schipper, Cologne, Germany

"How We Gonna Behave" (with Bernard Joisten and Pierre Joseph), Galerie Max Hetzler, Cologne, Germany*

"Galerie intelligente II" (with Pierre Joseph), Galerie des Archives, Paris, France

"Courts-métrages immobiles" (with Bernard Joisten and Pierre Joseph), the 44th Venice Biennale, Venice, Italy*

1989

"Ozone" (with Dominique Gonzalez-Foerster, Bernard Joisten and Pierre Joseph), Association pour l'art contemporain (Apac), Nevers, France

"Ozone" (with Dominique Gonzalez-Foerster, Bernard Joisten and Pierre Joseph), Esther Schipper booth, Art Cologne, Cologne, Germany

"Galerie intelligente" (with Pierre Joseph), Galerie des Archives, Paris, France

"Vidéo Ozone" (with Dominique Gonzalez-Foerster, Bernard Joisten and Pierre Joseph), "De l'instabilité," Centre national des arts plastiques (Cnap), Paris, France*

1988

"Hyper Hyper" (with Dominique Gonzalez-Foerster, Bernard Joisten and Pierre Joseph), Salon de la jeune sculpture, quai d'Austerlitz, Paris, France

"Composit" (with Bernard Joisten and Pierre Joseph) "Situation" Centre d'art contemporain d'Ivry-sur-Seine (Credac), Ivry-sur-Seine, France*

"Siberia" (with Bernard Joisten and Pierre Joseph), Le Magasin-Centre national d'art contemporain (Cnac) Grenoble, France

Public Collections and Foundations

21st Century Museum of Contemporary Art, Kanazawa, Japan

Banca Svizzera Internationale (BSI) Art Collection, Lugano, Switzerland

Bunbury Management Corp., Geneva, Switzerland

CCA Kitakyushu, Kitakyushu, Japan

Le Centre international de recherche sur le verre et les arts plastiques (Cirva), Marseilles, France

Collector's Circle, New York, United States

Daimler Art Collection, Stuttgart and Berlin, Germany

Fondation Louis Vuitton pour la création, Paris, France

Foundation 20.21, New York, United States

Fondazione Sandretto Re Rebaudengo, Turin, Italy

Fonds national d'art contemporain (Fnac), Puteaux, France

Fonds régional d'art contemporain (Frac) Burgundy, Dijon, France

Fonds régional d'art contemporain (Frac) Corsica, Corte, France

Fonds régional d'art contemporain (Frac) Languedoc-Roussillon, Montpellier, France

Fonds régional d'art contemporain (Frac) Lorraine, Metz, France

Fonds régional d'art contemporain (Frac) Nord-Pas-de-Calais, Dunkirk, France

Fonds régional d'art contemporain (Frac) Poitou-Charentes, Angoulême, France

Fonds régional d'art contemporain (Frac) Provence-Alpes-Côte d'Azur, Marseilles, France

Fonds régional d'art contemporain (Frac) Rhône-Alpes, Villeurbanne, France

Solomon R. Guggenheim Museum, New York, United States

Irish Museum of Modern Art, Dublin, Ireland

Jones Day, Reavis & Pogue, New York, United States

The Judith Rothschild Foundation, New York, United States

Landesbank Baden-Württemberg, Stuttgart, Germany

Musée d'Art moderne Grand-Duc Jean (Mudam), Luxemburg

Musée d'Art moderne de la Ville de Paris, Paris, France

Musée d'Art contemporain, Lyons, France

Centre Pompidou, Musée national d'art moderne (Mnam), Paris, France

Museum of Contemporary Art North Miami, Miami, United States

Museum of Modern Art (MoMA), New York, United States

Peconic Fine Arts LLC, New York, United States

Pinchuk Art Center, Kiev, Ukraine

Sammlung Energieversorgung Niederösterreich (EVN AG), Vienna, Austria

Sommer Contemporary Art, Tel Aviv, Israel

Südwest LB, Stuttgart, Germany

Tate Modern, London, United Kingdom

Thyssen-Bornemisza Contemporary Art, Vienna, Austria

Van Abbemuseum, Eindhoven, Netherlands

Walker Art Center, Minneapolis, United States

Watari-UM, the Watari Museum of Contemporary Art, Tokyo, Japan

Bibliography

Writings by the artist and monographs

2008

Obrist Hans Ulrich, *Philippe Parreno. The Conversation Series 14*, Cologne, Walther König, 2008, 154 pages

Parreno Philippe, "Audio Commentary," Arsène-Henry Charles (ed.), *Live Recorded Delay – An Archive of 'Il Tempo del Postino'*," Berlin / New York, Sternberg Press, 2008, p.5-14

Parreno Philippe (preface), in Obrist Hans Ulrich, *Conversations. Volume I*, Paris, Manuella Editions, 2008, p.11-12

Parreno Philippe, Obrist Hans Ulrich, "Pierre Boulez," *Conversations. Volume I*, Paris, Manuella Editions, 2008, p.71-82

Parreno Philippe, Obrist Hans Ulrich, "Melvil Poupaud," *Conversations. Volume I*, Paris, Manuella Editions, 2008, p.689-697

Parreno Philippe, "The Invisible Ape Boy," Morgan Jessica (ed.), *TH 2058: Dominique Gonzalez-Foerster*, London, Tate Publishing, 2008, p.77-95 (exh. cat.; Tate Modern, London, 14th October, 2008-13th April, 2009)

Parreno Philippe (ed.), *Suicide in Vermillon Sands*, New York, Friedrich Petzel, 2008, 106 pages (exh. cat.; Friedrich Petzel Gallery, New York, 10th October-15th November, 2008)

2007

Obrist Hans Ulrich, Parreno Philippe, Robinson Tim, "La Musique des événements" [interview], *Maps and Legends*, Geneva / Lausanne, JRP-Ringier and BSI Art Collection, 2007, p.192-223 [bilingual French / English]

Parreno Philippe, "Are There Possibilities To Unify Dispersed Fragments In a Coherent Narrative Framework?," *Parkett*, no.80, 2007, p.88-92

Parreno Philippe, "Undergroundman," *Playboy*, no.83, October 2007, p.30

2006

Parreno Philippe, Thomas Rachael (eds.), *All Hawaii Entrées / Lunar Reggae*, Dublin / Milan, Irish Museum of Modern Art / Editions Charta, 2006, 224 pages (exh. cat.; Irish Museum of Modern Art, Dublin, 30th November, 2006-18th February, 2007)

Dupuis Dorothée, "Les plus belles images sont celles que je me suis projetées dans la tête. Entretien avec Philippe Parreno," *Les Cahiers du Mnam*, no.97, fall 2006, p.84-93

Parreno Philippe, "After Affects #6: The Doppler Effect," *Again for Tomorrow*, London, Royal College of Art, p.146-147 (exh. cat.; Royal College of Art, London, 17th March-9th April, 2006)

Parreno Philippe, "After Affects #3," *Again for Tomorrow*, London, Royal College of Art, p.51-53 (exh. cat.; Royal College of Art, London, 17th March-9th April, 2006)

2005

Parreno Philippe (ed.), *Fade to Black*, Brussels, Mfc-Michèle Didier, 2005, 32 pages [600 copies, 60 of which numbered and signed and 20 artist's proofs]

Parreno Philippe, "*Fantôme de sitcom*," *Rirkrit Tiravanija: Une rétrospective (Tomorrow is Another Day)*, Paris, Paris-Musées, 2005, p.41-43 (exh. cat.; Couvent des Cordeliers, Paris, 10th February-20th March, 2005)

2004

Parreno Philippe (ed.), *The Boy From mars*, Kitakyushu, CCA Kitakyushu, 2004, n.p. [*ca* 164 pages]

Parreno Philippe, "Sitcom Ghost," *Rirkrit Tiravanija: A Retrospective (Tomorrow is Another Day)*, Rotterdam, Museum Boijmans Van Beuningen, 2004, p.97-116 [bilingual English / Dutch] (exh. cat.; Museum Boijmans van Beuningen, Rotterdam, 4th December, 2004-6 February, 2005)

Parreno Philippe, "Fonoglutammato / Phonoglutamate," *Domus*, no.875, November 2004, p.70-72 [bilingual Italian / English]

Parreno Philippe, "Replay," *Flash Art International*, no.238, October 2004, p.136

Parreno Philippe, "L'Effetto Doppler / The Doppler Effect," *Domus*, no.873, September 2004, p.246-247 [bilingual Italian / English]

Parreno Philippe, "La nuova dimensione del vivere / A new dimension in living," *Domus*, no.871, June 2004, p.162-163 [bilingual Italian / English]

Parreno Philippe, "After Affect #4," *Domus*, no.869, p.192-193, April 2004, p.76-77 [bilingual Italian / English]

Parreno Philippe, "After Affect: A Journey Through an Infinite Urban Landscape," *Domus*, no.868, March 2004, p.76-77 [bilingual Italian / English]

Parreno Philippe, "The Underground Man," *Domus*, no.867, February 2004, p.72-74 [bilingual Italian / English]

Parreno Philippe, "After Effect," *Domus*, no.866, January 2004, p.86-87 [bilingual Italian / English]

Point d'ironie, no.33, Paris, 2004

2003

Parreno Philippe, "The Taste of Pink Flamingoes," *Spoiled Climate*, Ruby Andreas, Durantin Benoît (eds.), Paris / Basel, Ante Prima / Birkhaüser, 2003, p.60-62

Parreno Philippe, Huyghe Pierre (eds.), *No Ghost Just a Shell*, Cologne, Walther König, 2003, 336 pages (exh. cat.; Kunsthalle Zürich, Zürich, 24th August-27th October, 2002; Institute of Visual Culture, Cambridge, 8th December, 2002-26th January, 2003; SFMoMA, San Francisco, 14th December, 2002-16th March, 2003; Van Abbemuseum, Eindhoven, 19th January-August, 2003; Rosa et Carlos de la Cruz, Miami, November 2003-October 2005)

2002

Parreno Philippe, "Also sprach Rirkrit Tiravanija zu Philippe Parreno," *Rirkrit Tiravanija : Secession*, Cologne, Walther König, 2003, p.6-9 [English version: "As said by Rirkrit Tiravanija to Philippe Parreno," p. 12-15] (exh. cat.; Secession, Vienna, 5th July-1st September, 2002)

Parreno Philippe (ed.), *Alien Affection*, Paris / Dijon, Arc/musée d'Art moderne de la Ville de Paris and Les presses du réel, 2002, n.p., [*ca* 392 p.] (exh. cat.; Arc/musée d'Art moderne de la Ville de Paris, Paris, 31st May-15th September, 2002)

2001

Parreno Philippe, *Speech Bubbles*, Dijon, Les presses du réel, 2001, 128 pages [compilation of texts by the artist]

Lind Maria (ed.), *Moderna Museet Project. Philippe Parreno*, Stockholm, Moderna Museet Project, 2002, 32 pages (exh. cat.; Moderna Museet, Stockholm, 7th September -4th October, 2001)

2000

Parreno Philippe, "It's me and the system…," *Jorge Pardo: What Does This Object Do?*, Ostfildern-Ruit, Hatje Cantz Verlag, 2000, p.64-79 [bilingual English / German]

Parreno Philippe, "La séquence du spectateur," *Art Press*, no.255, March 2000, p.32 [bilingual French / English]

1999

Parreno, Philippe, "My days are shorter than your T-shirt," *German Open 1999: Gegenwartskunst in Deutschland*, Wolfsburg, Kunstmuseum Wolfsburg, 1999, n.p. [in chapter "Olafur Eliasson"; exh. cat., bilingual German / English]

Parreno Philippe, "Evidences to be submitted to the free time litigation," *Pierre Huyghe. The Trial*, Munich, Kunstverein München / Zürich, Kunsthalle Zürich / Vienna, Secession / Dijon, Le Consortium, 1999, p.5-9 [exh. cat., bilingual German / English]

1998

Parreno Philippe, "Notes pour Snow Dancing," *Compilation : Une expérience de l'exposition*, Douroux Xavier, Gautherot Franck, Troncy Eric (eds.), Dijon, Les presses du réel, 1998, p.546-557 [bilingual French / English] (exh. cat.; Centre Pompidou, Paris, 4th November-4th December, 1998)

Parreno Philippe, "1998 – Bleu transparent," *Purple*, no.2, winter 1998-1999, p.266-267

Parreno Philippe, "The Imitator," *Mai 98*, Oetker Brigitte, Schneider Christiane (eds.), Cologne, Oktagon Verlag, 1998, p.136 [in German] (exh. cat.; Kunsthalle Köln, Cologne, 21th May-19th July, 1998)

1997

Parreno Philippe et Huyghe Pierre (eds.), *Anna Sanders. L'histoire d'un sentiment*, no.1, Paris, AFAA, 1997, 60 pages

Parreno Philippe, "The Audience is Listening," *1 Minute Scénario : Le Printemps de Cahors*, Arles, Actes Sud, 1997, p.64-65 (exh. cat.; Le Printemps de Cahors, 6th-22nd June, 1997)

1996

Höller Carsten, Tiravanija Rirkrit, Parreno Philippe, *Vicinato*, London, G-W Press Ltd., 1996, 56 pages

1995

Parreno Philippe, "Une exposition serait-elle un cinéma sans caméra ?," *Libération*, 27-28 mai 1995, p.29

Bourriaud Nicolas, Parreno Philippe, "Korrespondens: Nicolas Bourriaud, Philippe Parreno / Correspondence: Nicolas Bourriaud, Philippe Parreno," *Paletten*, no.223, April 1995, p.26-36 [bilingual Swedish / English]

Parreno Philippe, "Dominique Gonzalez-Foerster: I'm Not a Customer, I'm a Passenger," *Documents sur l'art*, no.7, spring 1995, p.20-25 [bilingual French / English]

Parreno Philippe, "L'Imitateur," *Is it nice?*, Neuchâtel, Centre d'art Neuchâtel (CAN), 1995, p.14-15 (exh. cat.; Centre d'art Neuchâtel (CAN), Neuchâtel, Switzerland, 11th March-14th May, 1995)

Parreno Philippe, *Snow Dancing*, London, GW Press Ltd., 1995, 53 pages (exh. cat.; Le Consortium, Dijon, 20th January-8th March, 1995)

1994

Parreno Philippe, "Facteur temps / Time Factor," *Documents sur l'art*, no.6, October 1994, p.22-23 [bilingual French / English]

1993

Parreno Philippe, "Z.A.C.," *L'Endroit idéal (Ideal Place)*, Troncy, Eric (ed.), Val-de-Reuil, Centre d'art et jardin, 1993, p.138-140

Parreno Philippe, "General Idea," *Documents sur l'art*, no.4, October 1993, p.21-26 [bilingual French / English]

Parreno Philippe, "The Imitator," *Backstage : Topologie zeitgenössischer Kunst*, Schmidt-Wulffen Stefan, Steiner Barbara (eds.), Hamburg / Lucerne, Kunstverein in Hamburg / Kunstmuseum Luzern, 1993, p.42-45 (exh. cat.; Kunstverein in Hamburg, Hamburg, 10th September -24th October, 1993; Kunstmuseum Luzern, Lucerne, 5th February-4th April, 1994)

1992

Parreno Philippe, "The Imitator," Rubinstein Raphael (ed.), *Postcards From Alphaville, Jean-Luc Godard in Contemporary Art, 1963-1992*, New York, The Institute for Contemporary Art, p.16-17 (exh. cat.; The Institute for Contemporary Art, P.S.1 Museum, New York, 8th November, 1992-10th January, 1993)

Parreno Philippe, "La Peur des anges / Fear of Angels," *Documents sur l'art*, no.1, October 1992, p.56 [bilingual French / English]

Parreno Philippe, "On ne peut plus s'installer devant une image comme au temps du 1er degré," *Documents sur l'art*, no.0, March 1992, p.26-27 [bilingual French / English]

Parreno Philippe, [Untitled], *Il faut construire l'Hacienda*, Bourriaud Nicolas, Julien-Laferrière Alain, Troncy Eric (eds.), Tours, CCC, 1992, p.36-37 (exh. cat.; CCC, Tours, 18th January- 8th March, 1992)

1991

Parreno Philippe, "Entretien par fax avec Alain Merlet du 23 juin au 26 juin 1991," *No Man's Time*, Nice, Villa Arson, 1991, p.124-125, 193-195 (exh. cat.; Villa Arson, Nice, 6th July-30th September, 1991)

Other publications

2008

Heiser Jörg, *All of a Sudden, Things That Matter in Contemporary Art*, Berlin / New York, Sternberg Press, 2008, p.180-201

Macel Christine, "Philippe Parreno: Juste un sourire dans la coquille," *Le Temps pris*, Paris, Monografik Éditions / Centre Pompidou, 2008, p.42-55

Obrist Hans Ulrich, "Douglas Gordon et Philippe Parreno," *Conversations. Volume II*, Paris, Manuella Éditions, 2008, p.329-336

Richard Lionel, *Art et énergies*, Paris, Cercle d'art, 2008

Spector Nancy (ed.), *Theanyspacewhatever*, New York, Solomon R. Guggenheim Museum, 2008, p.9, 13-27, 98-104, 116-122, 129-135, 142-148, 167-186, 197-192, 204-218, 223-247, 251 (exh. cat.; Solomon R. Guggenheim Museum, New York, 24th October, 2008-16th January, 2009)

Gunti Claus, "La Réalité remise en question : le statut de l'image dans l'œuvre de Philippe Parreno," *Décadrages*, no.13, fall 2008, p.31-40

Launay Aude, "Le Cercle hors de Vienne," *Zéroquatre*, no.3, fall 2008, p.8-9

Aguirre Peio, "Cinema Models," *Art & Co.*, no.3, summer 2008, p.115-116

Doyle Jennifer, "Fever Pitch," *Frieze*, no.116, June-July-August 2008, p.29-30

Thompson Nato, "The Puppet Show," *Frieze*, no.116, June-August 2008, p.251

Lebovici Élisabeth, "Autant en emporte le temps," *Art Press*, no.342, February 2008, p.57-60 [bilingual French / English]

Morgan Jessica, "Il Tempo del Postino, Festival international de Manchester," *Frog*, no.6, January-June 2008, p.60-64

2007

Achour Boris, Désanges Guillaume, Renard Émilie (eds.), *Prédictions : une exposition conçue par Trouble*, Paris, Trouble, 2007, p.63

Blom Ina, *On the Style Site. Art, Sociality, and Media Culture*, Berlin / New York, Sternberg Press, 2007, p.58, 153, 172, 174, 200-211, 220, 224-225

Bourgeois Caroline, *Passage du temps. Une sélection d'œuvres autour de l'image. Collection François Pinault Foundation*, Milan, Skira, 2007, p.104-107

Caioli Luca, "Le miroir" [interview with Philippe Parreno], *Zidane. Cent-dix minutes pour partir*, Issy-les-Moulineaux, Éditions Prolongations, 2007, p.147-149

Cassagnau Pascale, *Future Amnesia, enquêtes sur un troisième cinéma*, Paris, Isthme Éditions, 2007, p.87-92, 326-329

Charbau Gaël (dir.), *AF21.1 Art France 1990-2007*, Paris, Cornette de Saint Cyr / Particules, 2007, p.154

Duplaix Sophie (dir.), *Collection Art contemporain*, Paris, Centre Pompidou, 2007, p.351

Guichon Françoise, Barral Xavier (eds.), *L'Artiste, l'atelier, le verre*, Marseilles / Paris, Cirva / Xavier Barral, 2007, p.138-139, 196-197

Richardson Phyllis, *XS Green: Big Ideas Small Buildings*, London, Thames & Hudson, 2007, p.162-165

Van Assche Christine (dir.), *Collection Nouveaux Médias. Installations*, Paris, Centre Pompidou, 2007, p.238

Birnbaum Daniel, Herbert Martin, "The Postman Rings Twice," *Artforum International*, vol.46, no.4, September 2007, p.97-101

Dahan Alexis, Zahm Olivier, "Philippe Parreno," *Purple Fashion*, no.8, fall-winter 2007-2008, p.120-133

Griffin Jonathan, "Reviews: Il Tempo del Postino," *Frieze*, no.109, September 2007, p.176-177

Rappolt Mark, "Il Tempo del Postino: Playing for Time," *Art Review*, no.14, September 2007, p.52-61

Birnbaum Daniel, Macel Christine (eds.), *Airs de Paris*, Paris, Centre Pompidou, 2007, p.26-27, 106-107 (exh. cat.; Centre Pompidou, Paris, 25th April-16th August, 2007)

Buren Daniel (ed.), *L'Emprise du lieu. Expérience Pommery #4*, Paris / Reims, TTM Éditions / Vranken Pommery Monopole, p.74, 84, 87 (exh. cat.; Domaine Pommery, Reims, 28th March-15th November, 2007)

Marcoci Roxana (ed.), *Comic Abstraction: Image-Breaking, Image-Making*, New York, The Museum of Modern Art (MoMA), 2007, p.24-25, 102-108 [interview with Philippe Parreno] (exh. cat.; MoMA, New York, 4th March-11th June, 2007)

Funcke Bettina, "Displaced Struggles," *Artforum International*, vol.45, no.7, March 2007, p.282-286

von Fürstenberg Adelina (ed.), *Collateral. When Art Looks at Cinema*, Milan, Charta, 2007, p.64-67, 140-141 (exh. cat.; Hangar Bicocca, Milan, 2nd February-15th March, 2007)

Slyce John, "all hawaii eNtrées / LuNar reGGae," *Art Monthly*, February 2007, p.26-28

Obrist Hans Ulrich, "Portrait of the Artist as a Blogger," *Janus*, no.21, January 2007, p.16-21

2006

Alizart Mark, Kihm Christophe (eds.), *Fresh Théorie II*, Paris, Léo Scheer, 2006

Gillick Liam, "Ice Sculpture / Important Postmen," *Proxemics: Selected Writings (1988-2006)*, Zürich / Dijon, JRP-Ringier / Les presses du réel, 2006, p.248-255

Moulène Claire, *Art contemporain et lien social*, Paris, Cercle d'art, 2007

Obrist Hans Ulrich, "Philippe Parreno : la chaîne est belle," *...dontstopdontstop dontstop*, Berlin / New York, Sternberg Press, 2006, p.55-62

Obrist Hans Ulrich, "How Annlee Changed Its Spots," *...dontstopdontstop dontstop*, Berlin / New York, Sternberg Press, 2006, p.62-75

Troncy Éric, "Philippe Parreno," *Qu'est-ce que l'art contemporain en France ? 100 Artistes*, Paris, Beaux Arts Magazine [special issue], June 2006, p.142-143

Blom Ina, "Lamps, Televisuality and Biopolitics: Introductory Comments to Another History of Video Art," *Verksted*, no.8, 2006, p.167-183

Föll Heike, "L'Odeur de cinéma," *Texte zur Kunst*, no.64, December 2006 p. 117

Iles Chrissie, "Best of 2006," *Artforum International*, vol.45, no.4, December 2006, p.272-273

Derieux Florence, "Parreno's puppet," *Flash Art International*, no.251, November-December 2006, p.46

Moisdon Stéphanie, "Eden Roc," *Frog*, no.4, fall-winter 2006, p.200-201

Obrist Hans Ulrich, "Interview," *MAP*, no.7, fall 2006, p.28-33

Bourriaud Nicolas, Solovyov Oleksander (eds.), *New Space*, Kiev, Pinchuk Art Centre, 2006 (exh. cat.; Pinchuk Art Centre, Kiev, 16th September-16th December, 2006)

Fried Michael, "*Absorbed in the Action*," *Artforum International*, vol.45, no.1, September 2006, p.332-335, 398

Farquharson Alex, "Bureaux de change," *Frieze*, no.101, September 2006, p.156-159

Griffin Tim, "The Job Changes You," *Artforum International*, vol.45, no.1, September 2006, p.336-339

Huitorel Jean-Marc, "Philippe Parreno et Douglas Gordon : Zidane, un portrait du XXIe siècle," *Art Press*, no.326, September 2006, p.90-91 [bilingual French / English]

de Brugerolle Marie, "'Zidane' by Douglas Gordon and Philippe Parreno," *Flash Art International*, no.249, July-September 2006, p.114

Romney Jonathan, "Cannes Uncanned," *Modern Painters*, July-August 2006, p.40-43

Pluot Sébastien, "Mind Control(ed)," *Trouble*, no.6, summer 2006, p.66-96

Obrist Hans Ulrich, "21st Century Portrait," *Spike*, no.8, summer 2006, p.52-59

Delorme Stéphane, "Le Roi tauto," *Cahiers du cinéma*, no.613, June 2006, p.19

Neyrat Cyril, "Rêverie d'un solitaire," *Cahiers du cinéma*, no.613, June 2006, p.29-30

Molon Dominic, "Reality Football," *Art Review*, May 2006, p.106-109

Tarsia Andrea (ed.), *A Short History of Performance Part IV*, London, Whitechapel Gallery, p.48-49 (exh. cat.; Whitechapel Gallery, London, 1st-14th April, 2006)

Chapon Frédéric, "Philippe Parreno," *Frog*, no.3, spring-summer 2006, p.118-119

Colard Jean-Max, "Peut-on exister sans produire de récit ?" [interview], *Zérodeux*, no.37, spring 2006, p.16-17

Gleadowe Teresa, Key Fiona (eds.), *Again for Tomorrow*, London, Royal College of Art, p.40-41, 51-53, 146-147 (exh. cat.; Royal College of Art, London, 17th March-9th April, 2006)

Eleey Peter, "Looking Forward," *Frieze*, no.96, January-February 2006, p.124

2005

Aupetitallot Yves, *Magasin 1986-2006*, Grenoble / Zürich, Le Magasin / JRP-Ringier, 2005 [bilingual French / English]

Birnbaum Daniel, "Future Arrivals," *Chronology*, Berlin / New York, Sternberg Press, 2005, p.89-103

Douroux Xavier, *Nouveaux Commanditaires en Bourgogne*, Dijon, Les presses du réel, 2005, p.29, 42-43

Huitorel Jean-Marc, *La Beauté du geste : l'art contemporain et le sport*, Paris, Éditions du Regard, 2005, p.181

Piron François, "Philippe Parreno," Mangion Éric (ed.), *Prêts à prêter : acquisitions et rapport d'activités 2000-2004*, Paris / Marseilles, Isthme éditions/frac Provence-Alpes-Côte d'Azur, 2005, p.345

Birnbaum Daniel, "The lay of the land," *Artforum International*, XLIII, no.10, summer 2005, p.270-274

Moisdon Stéphanie, "Philippe Parreno: Portikus Francfort," *Frog*, no.1, spring-summer 2005, p.56-58

Allen Jennifer, "1000 words: Liam Gillick and Philippe Parreno talk about 'Briannnnnn and Ferryyyyyy'," *Artforum International*, vol.43, no.6, February 2005, p.144-147

Midal Alexandra, "Design et art: à la conquête de l'Ouest," *Parachute*, no.117, January 2005, p.12-27

2004

Couturier Élisabeth, *L'Art contemporain mode d'emploi*, Paris, Filipacchi, 2004

Mattick Paul, Siegel Katy, *Money*, London, Thames & Hudson, 2004, p.84-85, 158-159

Volz Jochen (ed.), *Turbulenz. Portikus Projekte 2001-2004*, Frankfurt, Portikus, 2004 [bilingual German / English]

Tschida Anne, "Living the Moment," *Loft: The Art Issue*, December 2004, p.32-33

Obrist Hans Ulrich, "Utopie en herbe," *Mixte*, October-December 2004, p.92-99

Rosset Clément, "Hans Ulrich Obrist and Philippe Parreno" [interview], *Flash Art International*, vol.37, no.238, October 2004, p.73-74

Obrist Hans Ulrich, "Philippe Parreno, Post-Apocalyptic Now," *Flash Art International*, vol.37, no.238, October 2004, p.110-112

Troncy Éric, "Disengagement," *Art Monthly*, no.174, October 2004, p.15

Hollein Max, Obrist Hans Ulrich, Weinhart Martina (eds.), *3'*, Cologne, DuMont Literatur und Kunst Verlag, 2004, p.134-146 [bilingual German / English] (exh. cat.; Kunsthalle Frankfurt, Frankfurt, 30th September, 2004-January, 2005)

Bishop Claire, "Antagonism and Relational Aesthetics," *October*, no.110, fall 2004, p.51-79

Mytkowska Joanna, Przywara Andrzej, Cichocki Sebastian (eds.), *Akcja równloegła / The Parallel Action*, Warsaw, Foksal Gallery Foundation, 2004, p.6-8 [bilingual Polish / English] (exh. cat.; Ciesyn, Poland, 22nd July-1st August, 2004)

Troncy Éric, "Comment l'art contemporain a inventé la TV-réalité," *Beaux-Arts Magazine*, no.242, July 2004, p.44-49

Obrist Hans Ulrich, "The Museum of the Future: Art, Architecture, Science and Technology," *Yishu Journal of Contemporary Art*, summer issue, June 2004 p.67-72

Sterling Bruce, "Thailand Hybrid Muscle," *Domus*, no.870, May 2004, p.42-47

Sterling Bruce, "The Boy From Paris," *Domus*, no.870, May 2004, p.48

Hauffen Michael, "Philippe Parreno: Fade Away," *Springerin*, vol.10, no.1, Spring 2004, p.66-67

Lind Maria, "Fade Away," *Drucksache Kunstverein München*, Spring 2004, p.2-8

Morton Tom, "Tom Morton Talks to Philippe Parreno: Team Spirit" [interview], *Frieze*, no.81, March 2004, p.80-85

Roche François, "Une batterie organique pour le Land de Rirkrit Tiravanija, Thaïlande," *Archistorm*, no.7, February 2004, p.10-11

Troncy Éric, Moisdon-Trembley Stéphanie, Bousteau Fabrice, "Numéro Scope : Les 30 artistes vivants les plus importants au monde," *Beaux-Arts Magazine*, no.236, January 2004, p.64-75

2003

Bourriaud Nicolas, *Postproduction*, Dijon, Les presses du réel, 2003

Copeland Mathieu (ed.), *The In-Between – Anna Sanders Films*, London / Dijon, Forma / Les Presses du réel, 2003, p.68-81, 91-104

Williams Gilda, *Cream 3. Contemporary Art in Culture: 10 Curators, 100 Contemporary Artists, 10 Source Artists*, London, Phaidon, 2003, p.272-275

Raspail Thierry (ed.), *AVANT : 7e Biennale d'art contemporain de Lyon*, Dijon / Lyons, Les presses du réel / Éditions Fage, 2003, p.146-149 (exh. cat.; 7th Lyons Biennale of Contemporary Art, Lyons, 18th September, 2003-4th January, 2004)

Weil Benjamin, "Souvenirs des immatériaux," *Purple Prose*, no.3, summer 1993, p.66-68

Troncy Éric, *Coollustre - Weather Everything - Dramatically Different*, Dijon, Les presses du réel, 2003 (exh. cat.; Collection Lambert, Avignon, 24th May-28th September, 2003)

Torres David G., *Falsa innocència / Falsa inocencia / False Innocence*, Barcelona, Fundazió Juan Miró, 2003 (exh. cat.; Fundazió Juan Miró, Barcelona, 21st March-1st June, 2003)

Menin Samuel, Sansone Valentina, "Focus Video and Film," *Flash Art International*, no.229, March-April 2003, p.96

Obrist Hans Ulrich, "Philippe Parreno," *Boiler*, no.1, January-March 2003, p.16-23

van den Boogert Kate, "Alien, Philippe Parreno," *Tate International Arts and Culture*, no.3, January-February 2003, p.48-53

Nobel Philip, "Sign of the Time," *Artforum International*, vol.41, no.5, January 2003, p.104-111

2002

Bourriaud Nicolas, *Postproduction*, Berlin / New York, Sternberg Press, 2002

Bourriaud Nicolas, *Relational Aesthetics*, Dijon, Les presses du réel, 2001

Riemschneider Burkhard, Grosenick Uta (eds.), *Art Now*, Cologne, Taschen, 2002, p.376-379

Obrist Hans Ulrich, "The Tale of the One Thousand Signs," *Parkett*, no.66, 2002, p.141-155

Wetterwald Élisabeth, "Annlee, signe en expansion," *Zérodeux*, no.22, 3rd term 2002, p.8-9

Bourriaud Nicolas, "Pliage d'œuvres," *Beaux-Arts Magazine*, no.220, September 2002, p.35

Troncy Éric, "Philippe Parreno," *Art Press*, no.282, September 2002 p.79-80 [bilingual French / English]

Fiers Els, "Philippe Parreno, *Alien Seasons*," *Metropolis M*, no.4, August-September 2002, p.48-53

Obrist Hans Ulrich, "Pierre Huyghe," *Flash Art International*, vol.34, no.225, July-September 2002, p.76-81

Curtis Penelope (ed.), *The Object Sculpture*, Leeds, Henry Moore Institute, 2002, p.75 (exh. cat.; Henry Moore Institute, Leeds, 1st June-1st September, 2002)

Demir Anaïd, "Philippe Parreno : portrait d'artiste," *L'Œil*, no.537, June 2002, p.26-27

Rongier Sébastien, "Ann Lee. Image rebelle," *Art présence*, no.42, April-May-June 2002, p.16-25

Rongier Sébastien, "Small Talk: Philippe Parreno," *Frame: the State of Art*, no.11, April-May 2002, p.146

Nabakowski Gislind, "Fréquences espaces audiovisuels," *Art Press*, no.278, April 2002, p.72 [bilingual French / English]

McFarland Dale, "In Many Ways the Exhibition Already Happened," *Frieze*, no.65, March 2002, p.90-91

McFarland Dale, "Ann Lee," *Diatxt.*, vol.6, March 2002, p.57-64

Eshun Ekow, "In Many Ways the Exhibition Has Already Happened," *Contemporary*, February 2002, p.92-93

2001

Mangion Éric, "L'Effet bande-annonce," *Art Press*, special issue, no.22, 2001, p.34-38

Buchloh H.D. Benjamin, "Control, by Design," *Artforum International*, vol.40, no.2, September 2001, p.162-163

Breitwieser Sabine (ed.), *Double Life: Identity and Transformation in Contemporary Art*, Vienna / Cologne, Generali Foundation / Walther König, 2001, p.196-197, 236 (exh. cat.; Generali Foundation, Vienna, 11th May-12th August, 2001)

Troncy Éric, "Philippe Parreno," *49/3*, no.1, May 2001, n.p.

Poitevin Michel (ed.), *Histoire de cœur, collection Michel Poitevin*, Les Mesnuls, Fondation d'art contemporain Daniel et Florence Guerlain, 2001, p.42-45, 55 (exh. cat.; Fondation d'art contemporain Daniel et Florence Guerlain, Les Mesnuls, France, 4th March-8th May, 2001)

Mahoney Élisabeth, "Vivre sa vie," *Art Monthly*, no.243, February 2001, p.31-33

Vaillant Alexis, "Morceaux de temps estampillés," *Kunst-Bulletin*, 1/2, January-February 2001, p.34-35

Vergne Philippe, "Philippe Parreno, la représentation en question : 'Speech Bubbles'," *Art Press*, no.264, January 2001, p.22-28 [bilingual French / English]

2000

Bony Anne (ed.), *Les Années 90*, Paris, Éditions du Regard, 2000

Beauvais Yann, Bouhours Jean-Michel (dir.), *Monter / Sampler. L'Échantillonnage généralisé*, Paris, Centre Pompidou / Scratch Projection, 2000, p.128, 130 (exh. cat.; Centre Pompidou, Paris, 15th November-21st December, 2000)

Troncy Éric, "No Ghost, Just a Shell," *Art Press*, no.260, September 2000, p.82-83 [bilingual French / English]

Wetterwald Élisabeth, "Philippe Parreno. L'exposition comme pratique de liberté," *Parachute*, no.102, April-May-June 2000, p.32-43

Païni Dominique, "Le retour du flâneur / The Return of the Flâneur," *Art Press*, no.255, March 2000, p.33-41 [bilingual French / English]

Inkster Dean, "Défense de la lecture: *Le Procès de Pol Pot*," *Art Press*, special issue, no.21, March 2000, p.64-69

Vaillant Alexis, "Customiser l'exposition. Remake et sur mesure," *Art Press*, special issue, no.21, March 2000, p.33-41

Stepken Angelika, *EDIT*, Karlsruhe, Badischer Kunstverein Karlsruhe, 2000, p.28-29 (exh. cat.; Badischer Kunstverein Karlsruhe, 13th January-5th March, 2000)

Restany Pierre, "Art now: in the hour of the internet, aesthetics gives way to industrial anthropology," *Domus*, no.822, January 2000, p.80-86

1999

Riemschneider Burkhard, Grosenick Uta (eds.), *Art at the Turn of the Millenium*, Cologne, Taschen, 1999, p.378-381

Troncy Éric, "La Fabrique du réel," *Qu'est-ce que l'art (aujourd'hui)? / What is art (today)?*, Paris, *Beaux-Arts Magazine* [special issue], December 1999, p.182-185

Gagnon Paulette, Grant Marchand Sandra (eds.), *Culbutes: Œuvre d'impertinence*, Montreal, musée d'Art contemporain de Montréal, p.40-41 (exh. cat., musée d'Art contemporain de Montréal, 18th November, 1999-23rd April, 2000)

Ardenne Paul, "*Le Procès de Pol Pot* selon Gillick et Parreno : Vademecum de la non-esthétisation de l'horreur," no.7/8, *Visuel(s) Revue d'arts*, fall-winter 1999, p.11-15

Prévost Jean-Marc (ed.), *France : une nouvelle génération*, Paris, ADIAF, 1999, p.54-59 (exh. cat.; Circula de Bellas Artes, Madrid, 12th February-7th March, 1999; Sintra Museu de Arte Moderna, Sintra, Portugal, 15th May-29th August, 1999)

1998

Bourriaud Nicolas, *Esthétique relationnelle*, Dijon, Les presses du réel, 1998

Troncy Éric, *Le Colonel Moutarde dans la bibliothèque avec le chandelier (textes 1988-1998)*, Dijon, Les presses du réel, 1998

Douroux Xavier, Gautherot Franck, Troncy Éric (eds.), *Compilation. Une expérience de l'exposition*, Dijon, Les presses du réel, 1998, p.546-557, 563-568 [bilingual French / English] (exh. cat.; Centre Pompidou, Paris, 4th November-4th December, 1998)

Troncy Éric, "Gonzalez-Foerster & Huyghe & Parreno," *Beaux-Arts Magazine*, no.174, November 1998, p.46-51

Bossé Laurence (ed.), *Dominique Gonzalez-Foerster / Pierre Huyghe / Philippe Parreno*, Paris, Arc/ musée d'Art moderne de la Ville de Paris, 1998, p.62-119, 177-191 [bilingual French / English] (exh. cat.; Arc/musée d'Art moderne de la Ville de Paris, 30th October, 1998-10th January, 1999)

Wulffen Thomas, "Philippe Parreno. Listen to the Picture," *Kunstforum International*, no.141, July 1998, p.348

Oetker Brigitte, Schneider Christiane (eds.), *Mai 98*, Cologne, Oktagon Verlag, 1998, p.20-21, 42, 136, 145-146 (exh. cat.; Kunsthalle Köln, Cologne, 21st May-19th July, 1998)

1997

Gonzalez-Foerster Dominique (ed.), *Moment Ginza: a City Guide*, Grenoble / Stockholm, Le Magasin / Färgfabriken, 1997, p.46-49 (exh. cat.; Le Magasin, Grenoble, 5th April-7th September, 1997; Färgfabriken, Stockholm, 10th October-7th December, 1997)

Bonami Francesco, *Campo 06: The Spiral Village*, Turin, Fondazione Sandretto Re Rebaudengo per l'Arte, 1997, p.155 (exh. cat.; Galleria Civica d'Arte Moderna e Contemporanea di Torino, Turin, 28th September, 1996-25th May, 1997; Bonnefanten Museum, Maastricht, 26th January-25th May, 1979)

Joon-Eui Noh (ed.), *Projet 8*, Seoul, Total Museum of Contemporary Art, 1997, p.46-49 (exh. cat.; Total Museum of Contemporary Art, Seoul, 3rd September-12th October, 1997)

Troncy Éric, "Participation and Accident," *Art Press*, no.226, July-August 1997, p.43-47 [bilingual French / English]

Steiner Barbara, "Interview mit Philippe Parreno," *Enter: Audience, Artist, Institution*, Lucerne, Kunstmuseum Luzern, 1998, p.32-35 (exh. cat.; Kunstmuseum Luzern, Lucerne, 12th April-25th May, 1997)

Weil Benjamin, "Le réalisme opératoire. Entretien avec Nicolas Bourriaud," *Parachute*, no.85, January-March 1997, p.8-11

1996

Schmidt-Wulffen Stephan, "Kunst ohne Publikum," *Zeitgenössische Kunst und ihre Betrachter, Jahresring 43, Jahrbuch für moderne Kunst*, Cologne, Oktagon Verlag, 1996, p.185-195

Restany Pierre, "New Orientations in Art," *Domus*, no.788, December 1996, p.88-92

Larsen Lars Bang, "Traffic," *Flash Art International*, no.189, summer 1996, p.126-127

Perreau David, Rouart Julie, "Les Ateliers du Paradise," *Documents sur l'art*, no.8, spring 1996, p.106-115 [bilingual French / English]

Bourriaud Nicolas (ed.), *Traffic*, Bordeaux, CAPC, 1996, p.15 (exh. cat.; CAPC, Bordeaux, 26th January-24th March, 1996)

Steiner Barbara, "Film as a Method of Thinking and Working," *Paletten*, no.224, January 1996, p.53-55

1995

Bourriaud Nicolas, "Philippe Parreno: Real Virtuality," *Art Press*, no.208, December 1995, p.41-44 [bilingual French / English]

Verzotti Giorgio, "Philippe Parreno / Schipper & Krome," *Artforum International*, vol.34, no.3, November 1995, p.100-101

Jouannais Jean-Yves, *Infamie*, Paris, Hazan, 1995, p.64-67 (exh. cat.; "Histoire de l'infamie," Venice Biennale, Cercle de l'Arsenal, 7th June-31st July, 1995; "Autres victoires," château de la Louvière, Montluçon, 7th July-1st October, 1995)

Chupin Olivier (ed.), *Collection, fin 20e: 1983-1995, douze ans d'acquisition d'art contemporain en Poitou-Charentes*, Poitiers, Fonds régional d'art contemporain Poitou-Charentes, 1995 (exh. cat.; musée Sainte-Croix, Poitiers, 9th May-17th September, 1995)

Schiff Hajo, "Traum von Kunst. Philippe Parreno über das Modell Ausstellung," *Taz*, 4th May, 1995, p.23

Troncy Éric, "Philippe Parreno : Le Consortium / NZET Project," *Art Press*, no.201, April 1995, p.77 [bilingual French / English]

Wahler Marc-Olivier, *Is it Nice*, Neuchâtel, Centre d'art Neuchâtel (CAN), 1995, p.14-15 (exh. cat.; CAN, 11th March-14th May, 1995)

Bourriaud Nicolas, "Relational Aesthetic (Part 2)," *Documents sur l'art*, no.8, spring 1995, p.40-47 [bilingual French / English]

Roche François, "Philippe Parreno," *Documents sur l'art*, no.7, spring 1995, p.10-11 [bilingual French / English]

Jarton Cyril, "Philippe Parreno, éduquer et subvertir," Beaux-Arts Magazine, no.131, February 1995, p.102

Troncy Éric (ed.), *Surface de réparations*, Dijon, Frac Bourgogne, 1995 (exh. cat.; "Surface de réparations 1," Frac Bourgogne, Dijon, 28th January-12th March, 1994; "Surface de réparations 2," Frac Bourgogne, Dijon, 29 October 1994-14 January 1995)

1994

Steiner Barbara (ed.), *Lost Paradise*, Munich / Stuttgart, Oktagon Verlag, 1995 (exh. cat.; Kunstraum Wien, Vienna, 21st October-11th December, 1994)

Troncy Éric, "Inter-activity," *Documents sur l'art*, no.6, fall 1994, p.24 [bilingual French / English]

Troncy Éric, "Carsten Höller / Philippe Parreno / Air de Paris," *Flash Art International*, XXVII, no.178, fall 1994, p.104

Verzotti Giorgio, Pasini Francesca (eds.), *Soggetto Soggetto. Una nuova relazione nell'arte di oggi*, Milan, Charta, 1994 (exh. cat.; Castello di Rivoli, Turin, 23rd June-5th September, 1994)

Troncy Éric, "It is Alive! Live wires in art's body eclectic," *Flash Art International*, no.177, summer 1994, p.105-108

Magda Pierre, "La Nuit des héros," *Art Press*, no.191, May 1994, p.75 [bilingual French / English]

1993

Joseph Pierre, "Philippe Parreno," *Flash Art International, Aperto '93*, special issue, 1993, p.364-365

Müller Silke, "Backstage. Eine Topologie zeitgenössischer Kunst," *Kunstforum International*, no.124, November-December 1993, p.389-391

Troncy Éric, "Project Unité," *Flash Art International*, vol.26, no.172, October 1993, p.117

Zahm Olivier, "Dante et Godard," *Purple Prose*, no.4, fall 1993, p.54-59

Schmidt-Wulffen Stefan, Steiner Barbara (eds.), *Backstage: Topologie zeitgenössischer Kunst*, Hamburg / Lucerne, Kunstverein in Hamburg / Kunstmuseum Luzern, 1993, p.42-45 (exh. cat.; Kunstverein in Hamburg, 10th September-24th October, 1993; Kunstmuseum Luzern, Lucerne, 5th February-4th April, 1994)

Bernard Christian (ed.), *Le Principe de réalité 9: Album*, Nice, Villa Arson, 1993, p.21-23, 33-34 (exh. cat.; Villa Arson, Nice, 3rd July-3rd October, 1993)

Blase Christoph, "Die grossen Wanderungen mit ungewissem Ziel," *Kunst-Bulletin*, no.7/8, July - August 1993, p.18-25

Jouannais Jean-Yves, "Unité," *Art Press*, no.182, July-August 1993, p.80 [bilingual French / English]

Gonzalez-Foerster Dominique, Joisten Bernard, "It's more like Post-Art," *Purple Prose*, no.3, summer 1993, p.24

Bourriaud Nicolas, "Michel Foucault et l'expérience artistique," *Documents sur l'art*, no.2, February 1993, p.47-51 [bilingual French / English]

1992

Rubinstein Raphael (ed.), *Postcards From Alphaville, Jean-Luc Godard in Contemporary Art, 1963-1992*, New York, The Institute for Contemporary Art, p.16-17 (exh. cat.; The Institute for Contemporary Art, P.S.1 Museum, New York, 8th November, 1992-10th January, 1993)

Bourriaud Nicolas, "The Work of Art in the Age of Ecological Recycling," *Flash Art International*, vol.25, no.167, November-December 1992, p.60-63

Jouannais Jean-Yves, "Philippe Parreno - Galerie Claudine Papillon," *Art Press*, no.168, April 1992, p.94-95 [bilingual French / English]

Verzotti Giorgio (ed.), *Le Dimanche de la vie: nuova arte francese*, Milan, Giò Marconi Gallery, 1992 (exh. cat.; Giò Marconi Gallery, Milan, March 1992)

Bourriaud Nicolas, "Première: Philippe Parreno," *Galeries Magazine*, no.47, February-March 1992, p.68-69

Bourriaud Nicolas, Julien-Laferrière Alain, Troncy Éric (eds.), *Il faut construire l'Hacienda*, Tours, CCC, 1992, p.36-37 (exh. cat.; CCC, Tours, 18th January-8th March, 1992)

1991

Troncy Éric, "No Man's Time," *Flash Art International*, no.161, November-December 1991, p.119-122

Eiblmayr Silvia (ed.), *Topographie II : Untergrund. Videoinstallationen in der Wiener U-Bahn*, Vienna, Wiener Festwochen, 1991, p.78-81 (exh. cat.; Wiener Festwochen, Vienna, 27th September-3rd November, 1991)

Raspail Thierry, Prat Thierry (eds.), *L'Amour de l'art*, Lyons, Lyons Biennale of Contemporary Art, 1991, p.301-302 (exh. cat.; Lyons Biennale of Contemporary Art, 3rd September-13th October, 1991)

Blase Christoph, "Mit der Schlange unterwegs," *Kunst-Bulletin*, no.9, September 1991, p.18

Bernard Christian, Troncy Éric (eds.), *No Man's Time*, Nice, Villa Arson, 1991, p.124-128, 193-195, 210 (exh. cat.; Villa Arson, Nice, 6th July-30th September, 1991)

1990

Gillick Liam, "Philippe Perrin / Philippe Parreno / Pierre Joseph," *Artscribe International*, no.84, November-December 1990, p.95-96

Troncy Éric, "French Models," *Artscribe International*, no.83, September-October 1990, p.10-11

Foray Jean-Michel, "Du collage et de ses extensions," *Art Press*, no.150, September 1990, p.28-31 [bilingual French / English]

Troncy Éric, " The Köln Show," *Art Press*, no.149, July-August 1990, p.88 [bilingual French / English]

Sourbier-Pinter Line (ed.), *Grenoble in Innsbruck*, Innsbruck, Innsbruck French Institute, 1990 [bilingual French / German] (exh. cat.; Galerie im Taxipalais, Innsbruck, 27th May-30th September, 1990)

Troncy Éric, "Air de Paris, galerie modèle," *Halle Sud*, no.26, 1st term 1990, p.4-7 [bilingual French / German]

Troncy Éric (ed.), *French Kiss*, Geneva, Halle Sud, 1990 (exh. cat.; Halle Sud, Geneva, 3rd May-17th June, 1990)

Bourriaud Nicolas, "Nouvelle Vague," *Beaux-Arts Magazine*, no.78, April 1990, p.106-113

Bourriaud Nicolas, "Reviews: Pierre Joseph, Philippe Parreno," *Flash Art International*, no.151, March-April 1990, p.152-153

Bourriaud Nicolas (ed.), *Courts-métrages immobiles*, Paris, AFAA, 1990 (exh. cat.; 44th Venice Biennale, 27th May-30th September, 1990)

Bourriaud Nicolas, "Ozone," *Art Press*, no.143, January 1990, p.76-77 [bilingual French / English]

1989

Foray Jean-Michel (ed.), *De l'instabilité*, Paris, Centre national des arts plastiques (Cnap), 1989, p.22-23, 39 (exh. cat.; Cnap, Paris, 16 November-10 December 1989)

Bourriaud Nicolas, "The Trailer Effect," *Flash Art International*, no.149, November-December 1989, p.112-115

Troncy Éric, "Ozone : Vers une écologie du regard," *Halle Sud*, no.22, 4th term 1989, p.14-17

Photo Credits

© Philippe Parreno, p.29, 47, 48-49, 95, 97, 107, 125, 127, 130-131, 133, 136-137, 151 top, 152-153, 154-155, 171 bottom, 173 bottom, 178-179, 183 bottom, 185, 205, 207, 208-209, 211 top, 225, 229, 230-231
© Jason Schmidt, p.75
© André Morin / LE MAGASIN, p.78-79
© Guy Braeckman (AD/ART bvba), p.118 top
Digital Image, © 2009, The Museum of Modern Art/Photo SCALA, Florence p. 118 bas p.118 bottom
© Fondazione Davide Halevim, Milan, p.119 top
© Musée d'Art moderne de la Ville de Paris, p.119 bottom, 129, 131, 135, 140-141, 142-143, 145
© Ruth Clark, p.121
© David de Armas, p.122-123
© Moderna Museet, Stockholm, p.139
© Fredrik Nilsen, p.147 top
© Marc Domage, p.147 bottom
© Angel Art Ltd, p.148-149
© R&Sie, p.151 bottom
© Wilfried Petzi/Adagp, p.168
© Air de Paris, p.77, 169 top, p.198-199
© FBM Studio / Kunsthaus Zürich, Zurich, p.169 bottom
© Terje Ostling/Lunds Konsthall, Lund, p.171 top
© Friedrich Petzel Gallery, New York, p.173 top, 174-175, 223, 236-237
© 1301PE Gallery [photo: Fredrik Nilsen], Los Angeles, p.177
© Philippe Parreno, Rirkrit Tiravanija, p.181
© Blaise Adilon, p.183 top
© Philippe Parreno, Douglas Gordon, p.186-187, 188, 189 bottom
© Fondazione Sandretto Re Rebaudengo, Turin, p.189 top
© Esther Schipper Gallery, Berlin, p.201, 202-203 [photo: Tony Izaaks], 235 center, 235 bottom [photo: Carsten Eisfeld, Berlin]
© Rodney Todd-White & Son 2009 – All Rights Reserved, p.211 bottom
© Giorgio Zucchiatti, p.213
© Julie Delaittre-Vichnievsky, p.214-215
© Howard Barlow, p.217
© Dave Morgan, p.219-221
© Luis Asìn, p.222
© Centre Pompidou [photo : Jean-Claude Planchet], p.226-227, 235 top
© Kristopher McKay / Solomon R. Guggenheim Foundation, New York, p.232-233
© Thierry Bal, p.239-243

JRP|Ringier books

are available internationally at selected bookstores and from the following distribution partners:

Switzerland:
Buch 2000, AVA Verlagsauslieferung AG, Centralweg 16, CH-8910 Affoltern a.A, buch2000@ava.ch, www.ava.ch

France:
Les presses du réel, 35 rue Colson, F-21000 Dijon, info@lespressesdureel.com www.lespressesdureel.com

Germany and Austria:
Vice Versa Vertrieb, Immanuelkirchstrasse 12, D-10405 Berlin, info@ vice-versa-vertrieb.de www. vice-versa-vertrieb.de

UK and other European countries:
Cornerhouse Publications, 70 Oxford Street, UK-Manchester M1 5NH, publications@ cornerhouse.org, www.cornerhouse.org/ books

USA, Canada, Asia and Australia:
D.A.P./Distributed Art Publishers, 155 Sixth Avenue, 2nd Floor, USA-New York, NY 10013, dap@dapinc.com, www.artbook.com

Photoengraving by IGS, Angoulême, France

Printed by Musumeci, S.p.A, Quart (Aosta) in April 2009.
Printed in Italy